Lecture Notes in Computer Science 13022

Founding Editors

Gerhard Goos
Karlsruhe Institute of Technology, Karlsruhe, Germany

Juris Hartmanis
Cornell University, Ithaca, NY, USA

Editorial Board Members

Elisa Bertino
Purdue University, West Lafayette, IN, USA

Wen Gao
Peking University, Beijing, China

Bernhard Steffen
TU Dortmund University, Dortmund, Germany

Gerhard Woeginger
RWTH Aachen, Aachen, Germany

Moti Yung
Columbia University, New York, NY, USA

More information about this subseries at http://www.springer.com/series/7412

Huimin Ma · Liang Wang · Changshui Zhang ·
Fei Wu · Tieniu Tan · Yaonan Wang ·
Jianhuang Lai · Yao Zhao (Eds.)

Pattern Recognition and Computer Vision

4th Chinese Conference, PRCV 2021
Beijing, China, October 29 – November 1, 2021
Proceedings, Part IV

Editors
Huimin Ma
University of Science and Technology Beijing
Beijing, China

Liang Wang
Chinese Academy of Sciences
Beijing, China

Changshui Zhang
Tsinghua University
Beijing, China

Fei Wu
Zhejiang University
Hangzhou, China

Tieniu Tan
Chinese Academy of Sciences
Beijing, China

Yaonan Wang
Hunan University
Changsha, China

Jianhuang Lai
Sun Yat-Sen University
Guangzhou, Guangdong, China

Yao Zhao
Beijing Jiaotong University
Beijing, China

ISSN 0302-9743 ISSN 1611-3349 (electronic)
Lecture Notes in Computer Science
ISBN 978-3-030-88012-5 ISBN 978-3-030-88013-2 (eBook)
https://doi.org/10.1007/978-3-030-88013-2

LNCS Sublibrary: SL6 – Image Processing, Computer Vision, Pattern Recognition, and Graphics

© Springer Nature Switzerland AG 2021
This work is subject to copyright. All rights are reserved by the Publisher, whether the whole or part of the material is concerned, specifically the rights of translation, reprinting, reuse of illustrations, recitation, broadcasting, reproduction on microfilms or in any other physical way, and transmission or information storage and retrieval, electronic adaptation, computer software, or by similar or dissimilar methodology now known or hereafter developed.
The use of general descriptive names, registered names, trademarks, service marks, etc. in this publication does not imply, even in the absence of a specific statement, that such names are exempt from the relevant protective laws and regulations and therefore free for general use.
The publisher, the authors and the editors are safe to assume that the advice and information in this book are believed to be true and accurate at the date of publication. Neither the publisher nor the authors or the editors give a warranty, expressed or implied, with respect to the material contained herein or for any errors or omissions that may have been made. The publisher remains neutral with regard to jurisdictional claims in published maps and institutional affiliations.

This Springer imprint is published by the registered company Springer Nature Switzerland AG
The registered company address is: Gewerbestrasse 11, 6330 Cham, Switzerland

Preface

Welcome to the proceedings of the 4th Chinese Conference on Pattern Recognition and Computer Vision (PRCV 2021) held in Beijing, China!

PRCV was established to further boost the impact of the Chinese community in pattern recognition and computer vision, which are two core areas of artificial intelligence, and further improve the quality of academic communication. Accordingly, PRCV is co-sponsored by four major academic societies of China: the China Society of Image and Graphics (CSIG), the Chinese Association for Artificial Intelligence (CAAI), the China Computer Federation (CCF), and the Chinese Association of Automation (CAA).

PRCV aims at providing an interactive communication platform for researchers from academia and from industry. It promotes not only academic exchange but also communication between academia and industry. In order to keep track of the frontier of academic trends and share the latest research achievements, innovative ideas, and scientific methods, international and local leading experts and professors are invited to deliver keynote speeches, introducing the latest advances in theories and methods in the fields of pattern recognition and computer vision.

PRCV 2021 was hosted by University of Science and Technology Beijing, Beijing Jiaotong University, and the Beijing University of Posts and Telecommunications. We received 513 full submissions. Each submission was reviewed by at least three reviewers selected from the Program Committee and other qualified researchers. Based on the reviewers' reports, 201 papers were finally accepted for presentation at the conference, including 30 oral and 171 posters. The acceptance rate was 39.2%. PRCV took place during October 29 to November 1, 2021, and the proceedings are published in this volume in Springer's Lecture Notes in Computer Science (LNCS) series.

We are grateful to the keynote speakers, Larry Davis from the University of Maryland, USA, Yoichi Sato from the University of Tokyo, Japan, Michael Black from the Max Planck Institute for Intelligent Systems, Germany, Songchun Zhu from Peking University and Tsinghua University, China, and Bo Xu from the Institute of Automation, Chinese Academy of Sciences, China.

We give sincere thanks to the authors of all submitted papers, the Program Committee members and the reviewers, and the Organizing Committee. Without their contributions, this conference would not have been possible. Special thanks also go to all of the sponsors and the organizers of the special forums; their support helped to make the conference a success. We are also grateful to Springer for publishing the proceedings.

October 2021

Tieniu Tan
Yaonan Wang
Jianhuang Lai
Yao Zhao
Huimin Ma
Liang Wang
Changshui Zhang
Fei Wu

Organization

Steering Committee Chair

Tieniu Tan	Institute of Automation, Chinese Academy of Sciences, China

Steering Committee

Xilin Chen	Institute of Computing Technology, Chinese Academy of Sciences, China
Chenglin Liu	Institute of Automation, Chinese Academy of Sciences, China
Yong Rui	Lenovo, China
Hongbing Zha	Peking University, China
Nanning Zheng	Xi'an Jiaotong University, China
Jie Zhou	Tsinghua University, China

Steering Committee Secretariat

Liang Wang	Institute of Automation, Chinese Academy of Sciences, China

General Chairs

Tieniu Tan	Institute of Automation, Chinese Academy of Sciences, China
Yaonan Wang	Hunan University, China
Jianhuang Lai	Sun Yat-sen University, China
Yao Zhao	Beijing Jiaotong University, China

Program Chairs

Huimin Ma	University of Science and Technology Beijing, China
Liang Wang	Institute of Automation, Chinese Academy of Sciences, China
Changshui Zhang	Tsinghua University, China
Fei Wu	Zhejiang University, China

Organizing Committee Chairs

Xucheng Yin	University of Science and Technology Beijing, China
Zhanyu Ma	Beijing University of Posts and Telecommunications, China
Zhenfeng Zhu	Beijing Jiaotong University, China
Ruiping Wang	Institute of Computing Technology, Chinese Academy of Sciences, China

Sponsorship Chairs

Nenghai Yu	University of Science and Technology of China, China
Xiang Bai	Huazhong University of Science and Technology, China
Yue Liu	Beijing Institute of Technology, China
Jinfeng Yang	Shenzhen Polytechnic, China

Publicity Chairs

Xiangwei Kong	Zhejiang University, China
Tao Mei	JD.com, China
Jiaying Liu	Peking University, China
Dan Zeng	Shanghai University, China

International Liaison Chairs

Jingyi Yu	ShanghaiTech University, China
Xuelong Li	Northwestern Polytechnical University, China
Bangzhi Ruan	Hong Kong Baptist University, China

Tutorial Chairs

Weishi Zheng	Sun Yat-sen University, China
Mingming Cheng	Nankai University, China
Shikui Wei	Beijing Jiaotong University, China

Symposium Chairs

Hua Huang	Beijing Normal University, China
Yuxin Peng	Peking University, China
Nannan Wang	Xidian University, China

Doctoral Forum Chairs

Xi Peng	Sichuan University, China
Hang Su	Tsinghua University, China
Huihui Bai	Beijing Jiaotong University, China

Competition Chairs

Nong Sang	Huazhong University of Science and Technology, China
Wangmeng Zuo	Harbin Institute of Technology, China
Xiaohua Xie	Sun Yat-sen University, China

Special Issue Chairs

Jiwen Lu	Tsinghua University, China
Shiming Xiang	Institute of Automation, Chinese Academy of Sciences, China
Jianxin Wu	Nanjing University, China

Publication Chairs

Zhouchen Lin	Peking University, China
Chunyu Lin	Beijing Jiaotong University, China
Huawei Tian	People's Public Security University of China, China

Registration Chairs

Junjun Yin	University of Science and Technology Beijing, China
Yue Ming	Beijing University of Posts and Telecommunications, China
Jimin Xiao	Xi'an Jiaotong-Liverpool University, China

Demo Chairs

Xiaokang Yang	Shanghai Jiaotong University, China
Xiaobin Zhu	University of Science and Technology Beijing, China
Chunjie Zhang	Beijing Jiaotong University, China

Website Chairs

Chao Zhu	University of Science and Technology Beijing, China
Zhaofeng He	Beijing University of Posts and Telecommunications, China
Runmin Cong	Beijing Jiaotong University, China

Finance Chairs

Weiping Wang	University of Science and Technology Beijing, China
Lifang Wu	Beijing University of Technology, China
Meiqin Liu	Beijing Jiaotong University, China

Program Committee

Jing Dong	Chinese Academy of Sciences, China
Ran He	Institute of Automation, Chinese Academy of Sciences, China
Xi Li	Zhejiang University, China
Si Liu	Beihang University, China
Xi Peng	Sichuan University, China
Yu Qiao	Chinese Academy of Sciences, China
Jian Sun	Xi'an Jiaotong University, China
Rongrong Ji	Xiamen University, China
Xiang Bai	Huazhong University of Science and Technology, China
Jian Cheng	Institute of Automation, Chinese Academy of Sciences, China
Mingming Cheng	Nankai University, China
Junyu Dong	Ocean University of China, China
Weisheng Dong	Xidian University, China
Yuming Fang	Jiangxi University of Finance and Economics, China
Jianjiang Feng	Tsinghua University, China
Shenghua Gao	ShanghaiTech University, China
Maoguo Gong	Xidian University, China
Yahong Han	Tianjin University, China
Huiguang He	Institute of Automation, Chinese Academy of Sciences, China
Shuqiang Jiang	Institute of Computing Technology, China Academy of Science, China
Lianwen Jin	South China University of Technology, China
Xiaoyuan Jing	Wuhan University, China
Haojie Li	Dalian University of Technology, China
Jianguo Li	Ant Group, China
Peihua Li	Dalian University of Technology, China
Liang Lin	Sun Yat-sen University, China
Zhouchen Lin	Peking University, China
Jiwen Lu	Tsinghua University, China
Siwei Ma	Peking University, China
Deyu Meng	Xi'an Jiaotong University, China
Qiguang Miao	Xidian University, China
Liqiang Nie	Shandong University, China
Wanli Ouyang	The University of Sydney, Australia
Jinshan Pan	Nanjing University of Science and Technology, China
Nong Sang	Huazhong University of Science and Technology, China
Shiguang Shan	Institute of Computing Technology, Chinese Academy of Sciences, China
Hongbin Shen	Shanghai Jiao Tong University, China
Linlin Shen	Shenzhen University, China
Mingli Song	Zhejiang University, China
Hanli Wang	Tongji University, China
Hanzi Wang	Xiamen University, China
Jingdong Wang	Microsoft, China

Nannan Wang	Xidian University, China
Jianxin Wu	Nanjing University, China
Jinjian Wu	Xidian University, China
Yihong Wu	Institute of Automation, Chinese Academy of Sciences, China
Guisong Xia	Wuhan University, China
Yong Xia	Northwestern Polytechnical University, China
Shiming Xiang	Chinese Academy of Sciences, China
Xiaohua Xie	Sun Yat-sen University, China
Jufeng Yang	Nankai University, China
Wankou Yang	Southeast University, China
Yang Yang	University of Electronic Science and Technology of China, China
Yilong Yin	Shandong University, China
Xiaotong Yuan	Nanjing University of Information Science and Technology, China
Zhengjun Zha	University of Science and Technology of China, China
Daoqiang Zhang	Nanjing University of Aeronautics and Astronautics, China
Zhaoxiang Zhang	Institute of Automation, Chinese Academy of Sciences, China
Weishi Zheng	Sun Yat-sen University, China
Wangmeng Zuo	Harbin Institute of Technology, China

Reviewers

Bai Xiang
Bai Xiao
Cai Shen
Cai Yinghao
Chen Zailiang
Chen Weixiang
Chen Jinyu
Chen Yifan
Cheng Gong
Chu Jun
Cui Chaoran
Cui Hengfei
Cui Zhe
Deng Hongxia
Deng Cheng
Ding Zihan
Dong Qiulei
Dong Yu
Dong Xue
Duan Lijuan
Fan Bin
Fan Yongxian
Fan Bohao
Fang Yuchun
Feng Jiachang
Feng Jiawei
Fu Bin
Fu Ying
Gao Hongxia
Gao Shang-Hua
Gao Changxin
Gao Guangwei
Gao Yi
Ge Shiming
Ge Yongxin
Geng Xin
Gong Chen
Gong Xun
Gu Guanghua
Gu Yu-Chao
Guo Chunle
Guo Jianwei
Guo Zhenhua
Han Qi
Han Linghao
He Hong
He Mingjie
He Zhaofeng
He Hongliang
Hong Jincheng
Hu Shishuai
Hu Jie
Hu Yang
Hu Fuyuan
Hu Ruyun
Hu Yangwen
Huang Lei
Huang Sheng
Huang Dong
Huang Huaibo
Huang Jiangtao
Huang Xiaoming
Ji Fanfan
Ji Jiayi
Ji Zhong
Jia Chuanmin
Jia Wei
Jia Xibin
Jiang Bo
Jiang Peng-Tao
Kan Meina
Kang Wenxiong

Lei Na
Lei Zhen
Leng Lu
Li Chenglong
Li Chunlei
Li Hongjun
Li Shuyan
Li Xia
Li Zhiyong
Li Guanbin
Li Peng
Li Ruirui
Li Zechao
Li Zhen
Li Ce
Li Changzhou
Li Jia
Li Jian
Li Shiying
Li Wanhua
Li Yongjie
Li Yunfan
Liang Jian
Liang Yanjie
Liao Zehui
Lin Zihang
Lin Chunyu
Lin Guangfeng
Liu Heng
Liu Li
Liu Wu
Liu Yiguang
Liu Zhiang
Liu Chongyu
Liu Li
Liu Qingshan
Liu Yun
Liu Cheng-Lin
Liu Min
Liu Risheng
Liu Tiange
Liu Weifeng
Liu Xiaolong
Liu Yang
Liu Zhi
Liu Zhou
Lu Shaoping
Lu Haopeng
Luo Bin
Luo Gen
Ma Chao
Ma Wenchao
Ma Cheng
Ma Wei
Mei Jie
Miao Yongwei
Nie Liqiang
Nie Xiushan
Niu Xuesong
Niu Yuzhen
Ouyang Jianquan
Pan Chunyan
Pan Zhiyu
Pan Jinshan
Peng Yixing
Peng Jun
Qian Wenhua
Qin Binjie
Qu Yanyun
Rao Yongming
Ren Wenqi
Rui Song
Shen Chao
Shen Haifeng
Shen Shuhan
Shen Tiancheng
Sheng Lijun
Shi Caijuan
Shi Wu
Shi Zhiping
Shi Hailin
Shi Lukui
Song Chunfeng
Su Hang
Sun Xiaoshuai
Sun Jinqiu
Sun Zhanli
Sun Jun
Sun Xian
Sun Zhenan
Tan Chaolei
Tan Xiaoyang
Tang Jin
Tu Zhengzheng
Wang Fudong
Wang Hao
Wang Limin
Wang Qinfen
Wang Xingce
Wang Xinnian
Wang Zitian
Wang Hongxing
Wang Jiapeng
Wang Luting
Wang Shanshan
Wang Shengke
Wang Yude
Wang Zilei
Wang Dong
Wang Hanzi
Wang Jinjia
Wang Long
Wang Qiufeng
Wang Shuqiang
Wang Xingzheng
Wei Xiu-Shen
Wei Wei
Wen Jie
Wu Yadong
Wu Hong
Wu Shixiang
Wu Xia
Wu Yongxian
Wu Yuwei
Wu Xinxiao
Wu Yihong
Xia Daoxun
Xiang Shiming
Xiao Jinsheng
Xiao Liang
Xiao Jun
Xie Xingyu
Xu Gang
Xu Shugong
Xu Xun

Xu Zhenghua
Xu Lixiang
Xu Xin-Shun
Xu Mingye
Xu Yong
Xue Nan
Yan Bo
Yan Dongming
Yan Junchi
Yang Dong
Yang Guan
Yang Peipei
Yang Wenming
Yang Yibo
Yang Lu
Yang Jinfu
Yang Wen
Yao Tao
Ye Mao
Yin Ming
Yin Fei
You Gexin
Yu Ye
Yu Qian
Yu Zhe
Zeng Lingan
Zeng Hui
Zhai Yongjie
Zhang Aiwu
Zhang Chi
Zhang Jie
Zhang Shu
Zhang Wenqiang
Zhang Yunfeng
Zhang Zhao
Zhang Hui
Zhang Lei
Zhang Xuyao
Zhang Yongfei
Zhang Dingwen
Zhang Honggang
Zhang Lin
Zhang Mingjin
Zhang Shanshan
Zhang Xiao-Yu
Zhang Yanming
Zhang Yuefeng
Zhao Cairong
Zhao Yang
Zhao Yuqian
Zhen Peng
Zheng Wenming
Zheng Feng
Zhong Dexing
Zhong Guoqiang
Zhou Xiaolong
Zhou Xue
Zhou Quan
Zhou Xiaowei
Zhu Chaoyang
Zhu Xiangping
Zou Yuexian
Zuo Wangmeng

Contents - Part IV

Machine Learning, Neural Network and Deep Learning

Special Session: New Advances in Visual Perception and Understanding

Machine Learning, Neural Network and Deep Learning

Edge-Wise One-Level Global Pruning on NAS Generated Networks

Qiantai Feng[1,2], Ke Xu[1,2], Yuhai Li[3], Yuxin Sun[4], and Dong Wang[1,2(✉)]

[1] Institute of Information Science, Beijing Jiaotong University, Beijing 100044, China
[2] Beijing Key Laboratory of Advanced Information Science and Network Technology, Beijing 100044, China
wangdong@bjtu.edu.cn
[3] Science and Technology on Electro-Optical Information Security Control Laboratory, Tianjin 300308, China
[4] Tianjin University, Tianjin 300072, China

Abstract. In recent years, there has been a lot of studies in neural architecture search (NAS) in the field of deep learning. Among them, the cell-based search method, such as [23,27,32,36], is one of the most popular and widely discussed topics, which usually stacks less cells in search process and more in evaluation. Although this method can reduce the resource consumption in the process of search, the difference in the number of cells may inevitably cause a certain degree of redundancy in network evaluation. In order to mitigate the computational cost, we propose a novel algorithm called Edge-Wise One-Level Global Pruning (EOG-Pruning). The proposed approach can prune out weak edges from the cell-based network generated by NAS globally, by introducing an edge factor to represent the importance of each edge, which can not only greatly improve the inference speed of the model with reducing the number of edges, but also promote the model accuracy. Experimental results show that networks pruned by EOG-Pruning achieve significant improvement in accuracy and speedup rate on CPU in common with 50% pruning rate on CIFAR. Specifically, we reduced the test error rate by 1.58% and 1.34% on CIFAR-100 for DARTS (2nd-order) and PC-DARTS.

Keywords: Neural architecture search · Network pruning

1 Introduction

In the field of machine learning, research based on deep learning has gradually become the mainstream. As the networks go deeper and larger, how to design

Supported by Beijing Natural Science Foundation (4202063), Fundamental Research Funds for the Central Universities (2020JBM020), Research Founding of Electro-Optical Information Security Control Laboratory, National Key Research and Development Program of China under Grant 2019YFB2204200, BJTU-Kuaishou Research Grant.

© Springer Nature Switzerland AG 2021
H. Ma et al. (Eds.): PRCV 2021, LNCS 13022, pp. 3–15, 2021.
https://doi.org/10.1007/978-3-030-88013-2_1

high-performance network structure for a certain task under certain constraints has become a topic of interest to researchers. Neural network architecture search (NAS) is one of the methods to reduce the reliance on human expertise and artificial priors, and obtain the optimal model by exploring the model architecture in a large search space by specific search algorithms. At the beginning, most of the work focuses on how to get a complete network [1,29]. A large number of models are sampled in the search space and these models are individually trained and evaluated.

Inspired by the success of stacking the same cell or block [13,15] in images classification task, more attention has been paid to finding the well behaved and robust cell. Some heuristic methods are usually used, such as reinforcement learning [36], evolutionary learning [27,32], etc. However, they take a lot of computational cost, *e.g.*, thousands of GPU-days, so these methods are difficult to use widely. In order to reduce the amount of computation overhead, a series of gradient-based methods have been proposed [23,28]. So as to avoid the problem of excessive memory cost during search process, the approach such as DARTS [23], which becomes the most popular gradient-based method recently, uses less cells for search and more cells for evaluation.

However, there are some problems for us with this cell-based NAS strategy. The first is the deeper network in evaluation is not necessarily compact and may has a great redundancy, because all cells are the same, and the number of stacking cells and some configuration are artificially set, without adapting to the actual task. For instance, in DARTS [23], there are 20 cells with 2 predecessor inputs stacking together on CIFAR, following NASNet [36], AmoebaNet [27], PNAS [6], etc. Although manual design configuration can narrow the search space for lower computational cost and keep the stability of networks, it causes the over-parameterized and redundancy. The second is the *depth gap* mentioned in PDARTS [6]. An optimal narrow network in search processs cannot guarantee the optimality of deeper network in evaluation. So it is necessary to optimize the structure of the model.

The weakness of cell-based network mentioned above leads us naturally to try a further structure search and compression. The traditional compression methods, like unstructured or structured pruning, can indeed compress the model, but they cannot verify the redundancy of the searched network and cannot find a better substructure.

In this work, We propose Edge-Wise One-Level Global Pruning on Architecture Search (EOG-Pruning), a novel algorithm to prune the cell-based network of NAS. We allocate a weight for each edge in a cell-based network. After compression through edge-wise structured pruning, some of the less important ones are removed by the weight size, so that the size of the model will be cut down and the inference performance will be accelerated. Furthermore, the obvious improvement of accuracy has been widely found in our solid experiments.

We conduct experiments on popular image classification benchmark, *i.e.*, CIFAR-10, CIFAR-100 [16], ImageNet [8], with mainstream networks based on DARTS, like DARTS [23], P-DARTS [6], PC-DARTS [33]. Through a series of validation and contrast tests, we can verify the our algorithm is feasible and effective. Specifically, we reduce the test error rate by 1.58% and 1.34% on CIFAR-100 for DARTS (2nd-order) and PC-DARTS. Moreover, the performance of EOG-Pruning under different pruning rates is verified, and the accuracy of pruning rate below 50% is often higher than that of the original.

2 Related Work

2.1 Neural Architecture Search

Neural network architecture search technology hopes to replace human experts with prior knowledge of artificial experience by finding an optimal model that meets the needs through specific algorithms in a design search space. The current method has achieved competitive performance in tasks, in the fields of image classification [36], object detection [10,34] and so on. The NAS approach designs a search space containing the model architecture, and looks for the optimal architecture or hyperparameters through a specific search algorithm, *e.g.*, random search [21], meta learning [20], Bayesian optimization [2], evolutionary algorithms [32], reinforcement learning [1], gradient-based algorithms [23]. In architecture search, the pioneering work comes from Google Brain, using reinforcement learning [35] to search in 2016. Later, more and more companies and research institutes are beginning to join the research, with various search approach to explore different designed search space. Unlike the previous work [1,29], most of resent works focus on finding an optimal cell or block structure [13,15], and some search methods achieve great performance, such as reinforcement learning [36], evolutionary learning [27,32]. Following works aim at solving the calculation consumption in search process, *e.g.*, PNASNet [22], ENAS [26], ProxylessNAS [5], DARTS [23].

DARTS is a gradient-based one-shot neural network search algorithm. By combining the network weight and the architecture parameter for bi-level optimization, an optimal model can be searched out, which can be applied to convolutional and recurrent neural networks. The performance on some tasks is even better than some non-differentiable search techniques. The models searched on the small data set (CIFAR-10) can be migrated to ImageNet for search. DARTS will search the architecture in a narrow network while evaluating in a larger one with more cells stacking together, *e.g.*, 20 cells in CIFAR evaluation, bringing on redundancy inevitably.

2.2 Network Pruning

The network pruning technology reduces the model by removing some redundant parameters or structures, and realizes the acceleration of the model. Deep neural networks have been widely used, and even replaced many traditional machine learning methods. It is also widely used in some mobile devices or some embedded devices. Although deep learning has better performance, it still has problems such as high computational cost and slow inference speeds, so that it is not easy to deploy on lightweight devices. In order to solve this problem, methods such as pruning and quantification of neural networks have been proposed, which can reduce the size of the network, accelerate the speed of inference.

Pruning is classified according to the granularity of pruning from fine to coarse, which can be roughly divided into unstructured pruning and structured pruning. Unstructured pruning [12,18] mainly constructs a sparse weight matrix by setting independent weight parameters to 0. However, this method is currently not well supported on general hardware computing devices, but the sparse weight cannot achieve the acceleration of the target. So research began to lean towards structured pruning [14,19,24,25]. Through pruning on the channel or on the layer, the calculation amount and parameter amount of the model can be reduced. This method does not destroy the basic structure, such as channel pruning does not destroy the structure of the convolution layer, and it is easily supported by various computing devices and acceleration libraries.

3 Edge-Wise One-Level Global Pruning on DARTS-Based Network

Nowadays, there are many cell-based networks with different methods, and DARTS is one of the popular methods among them. So our approach focus on the DARTS-based networks [6,23,33] with the same search space, to make our approach more practical and convincing.

DARTS-based networks regard as our baseline framework, from which we work on extracting more concise one by remove weak edges. There are L cells in a network, and each cell is represented as a directed acyclic graph (DAG) with N nodes. The predefined space of operations denoted by $\mathcal{O}$, including all possibilities of edges.

After search procedure, one operation has been chosen from $\mathcal{O}$ to connect each pair of nodes (i, j). Each node j keeps only two strong predecessors $i \leq j$, where $0 \leq i \leq j \leq N-1$, so there are $2NL$ edges in a network.

3.1 Edge Weight Assignment

As shown in Fig. 1, we introduce a factor α for every edges, indicating the importance of the edge. After training process, the edge with small edge weight α will be pruned. In order to get close to the final pruned network, α is initialized to a number in $[0,1]$, *e.g.*, α is set to 1-pruning rate in our experiments. Then we want to keep alpha in a reasonable range, so we simply crop the α value to $[0,1]$ in the training procedure, and it is formulated as:

$$\alpha^* = \begin{cases} 1 & 1 \leq \alpha \\ \alpha & 0 \leq \alpha < 1 \\ 0 & \alpha \leq 0 \end{cases} \tag{1}$$

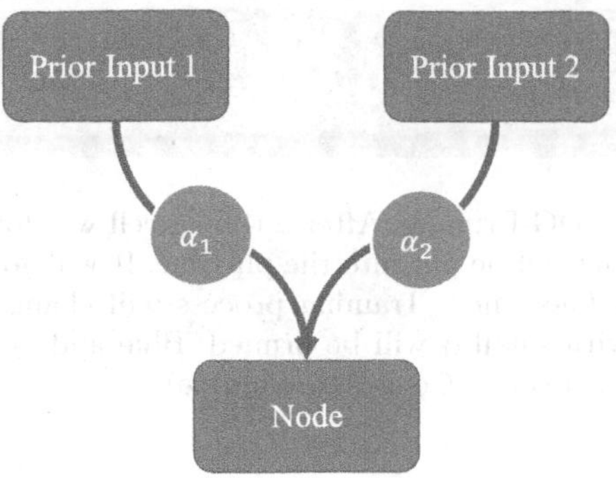

Fig. 1. Method of adding weight to two predecessors. Orange and blue mean weights and nodes, respectively. (Color figure online)

Then we multiply α^* with the output of that edge$f^{(i,j)}(x^{(i)})$:

$$x^{(j)} = \sum_{i<j} \alpha^{*(i,j)} f^{(i,j)}(x^{(i)}) \tag{2}$$

With one exception, we don't want to affect operation *skip-connection*, because it has a significant impact on recognition accuracy at the evaluation stage [6]. What's more, as an operation without parameters, skip-connection won't affect the model inference speed too much. Assuming that the number of skip-connection is s and pruning rate is p, there are $[p(NL-s)]$ edges left in a network after the pruning procedure.

3.2 One-Level Structure Learning

In structure learning procedure, EOG-Pruning aims to optimize the training loss, by learning the edge weights α and the network weights w.

As we introduce edge weight α, the goal of structure learning is to solve following objective function, which seems like the goal of DARTS:

$$\min_{\alpha} \mathcal{L}_{train}\Big(\omega^*(\alpha), \alpha\Big) \tag{3}$$

$$\text{s.t. } \omega^*(\alpha) = \text{argmin}_{\omega} \mathcal{L}_{train}(\omega, \alpha) \tag{4}$$

In the actual training process, the quantity gap between α and w is obvious, so DARTS proposed bi-level optimization to alleviate the problem. As pointed out in the [3], bi-level optimization takes more computational overhead, leading to critical weakness known as considerable inaccuracy of gradient estimation and instability. So we follow the one-level optimization method just like [4], which adds some regularization (*e.g.*, Cutout [9], AutoAugment [7], etc.) to a small data set. One-level optimization involves updating α and w simultaneously in each step:

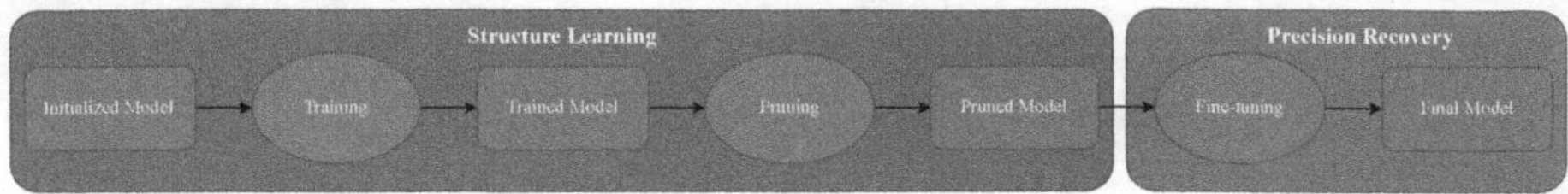

Fig. 2. The pipeline of EOG-Pruning. After a robust cell was found in search process, a network of stacked cells will be put into the pipeline. It will go through three stages: initialized, pruned and fine-tuned. Training process will change distribution of edge weight, and the edge with small α will be pruned. Blue and green indicate the stage and the treatment of a network. (Color figure online)

$$\omega_{t+1} \leftarrow \omega_t - \xi_w \cdot \nabla_\omega \mathcal{L}_{train}\Big(\omega_t, \alpha_t\Big) \tag{5}$$

$$\alpha_{t+1} \leftarrow \alpha_t - \xi_\alpha \cdot \nabla_\alpha \mathcal{L}_{train}\Big(\omega_t, \alpha_t\Big) \tag{6}$$

It balances the optimization process between α and w, while alleviating overfitting phenomenon. What's more, the learning rates ξ_α and ξ_w of α and w correspondingly need to be set to different sizes to fix the issue above.

3.3 Procedure of EOG-Pruning

As shown in Fig. 2, the process of EOG-Pruning can be summarized as three steps: training, pruning and fine-tuning. The network learns structure through one-level optimization training, and restores accuracy through fine-tuning. There are two mainstream strategies to restore the recovery precision. One way is to prune once and retrain the network until restore the accuracy of the baseline, and the other way is to prune and retrain the model iteratively [19]. For simplicity and effectiveness, We just adopt the first method.

3.4 Comparison with Previous Work

Network Slimming [24] associates a scaling factor γ which is reused from a batch normalization layer with each channel in convolutional layers, and the channels with tiny scaling factor values will be removed. EOG-Pruning is more coarse-grained pruning paradigm, suitable for networks composed of cells and edges, without L1 regularization on α. PC-DARTS [33] also associates a factor with each edge for training stability, so the purpose is different from us.

4 Experiments

4.1 Datasets

We demonstrate the effectiveness of EOG-Pruning on several datasets, including CIFAR-10, CIFAR-100 [16] and ImageNet [8]. Each of CIFAR-10 and CIFAR-100 datasets consists of 50K/10K training/testing 32 $\times$ 32 natural colour images, with 6K/0.6K images per class. ImageNet dataset contains 1.2 million training images and 50K validation images of 1K classes. Following the mobile setting in DARTS [23], the input image size is fixed to be 224 × 224 and the number of multi-add operations does not exceed 600M in the testing stage.

Table 1. Results for EOG-Pruning on CIFAR-10, CIFAR-100 and ImageNet

Dataset	Model	Test error (%)	Params (M)	FLOPs (M)	Latency (s)	Edge#	Conv#	Pool#
CIFAR10	DARTS (1st-order)(Baseline)	3	3.3	511	12.89	100	403	10
	DARTS (1st-order)(50% Pruned)	2.54(−0.46)	2.4(27.3%)	371(27.4%)	7.35(1.8×)	50	227	4
	DARTS (2nd-order)(Baseline)	2.76	3.3	539	13.69	118	439	10
	DARTS (2nd-order)(50% Pruned)	2.53(−0.23)	2.4(27.3%)	380(29.5%)	7.56(1.8×)	59	237	6
	PDARTS (Baseline)	2.50	3.4	542	13.23	124	435	4
	PDARTS (50% Pruned)	2.42(−0.08)	2.3(32.4%)	385(29.0%)	7.71 (1.7×)	62	239	4
	PC-DARTS (Baseline)	2.57	3.6	567	13.85	142	459	20
	PC-DARTS (50% Pruned)	2.34(−0.23)	2.5(30.6%)	393(30.7%)	7.57(1.8×)	71	255	8
	GOLD-NAS-H	2.70	2.5	402	–	–	–	–
CIFAR100	DARTS (1st-order)(Baseline)	17.76	3.3	511	12.89	100	403	10
	DARTS (1st-order)(50% Pruned)	17.19(−0.57)	2.4(27.3%)	371 (27.4%)	7.35(1.8×)	50	227	4
	DARTS (2nd-order)(Baseline)	17.54	3.3	539	13.69	118	439	10
	DARTS (2nd-order)(50% Pruned)	15.96(−1.58)	2.4(27.3%)	384(28.8%)	7.96(1.7×)	59	243	6
	PDARTS (Baseline)	16.55	3.4	542	13.23	124	435	4
	PDARTS (50% Pruned)	16.76(+0.21)	2.4(29.4%)	386(28.8%)	7.98(1.7×)	62	241	4
	PC-DARTS (Baseline)	17.01†	3.6	567	13.85	142	459	20
	PC-DARTS (50% Pruned)	15.67(−1.34)	2.5(30.6%)	393(30.7%)	7.57(1.8×)	71	245	11
ImageNet	DARTS (Baseline)	26.7	4.7	574	6.93	82	298	10
	DARTS (30% Pruned)	26.05(−0.65)	4.4(6.4%)	460(19.9%)	5.66(1.2×)	57	224	6
	DARTS (50% Pruned)	27.64(+0.97)	3.9(17.0%)	393(31.5%)	4.18(1.7×)	41	160	6

4.2 EOG-Pruning on CIFAR-10 and CIFAR-100

Compare with the evaluation process of DARTS [23], we just add an extra joint training procedures of α and w training before the normal evaluation training. The training process is equivalent to modifying the learning rates ξ_α and ξ_w,

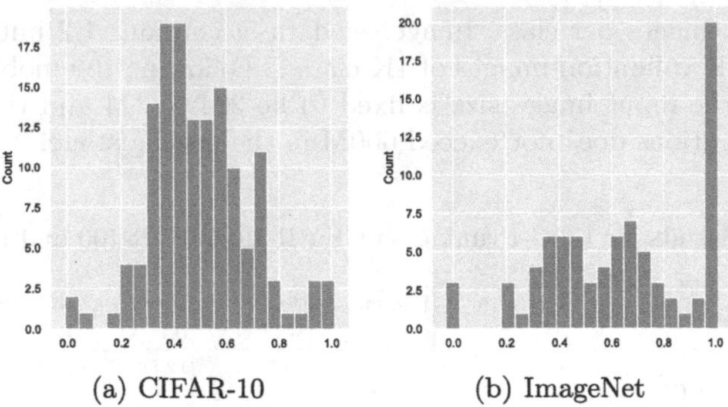

Fig. 3. Distribution of α in DARTS on CIFAR-10 and ImageNet separately after training.

while adding AutoAugment [7] strategy to train on the basis of all configurations in DARTS. We initialize the network randomly, and simply set α to $1 - p$. α and w in the network of 20 cells is trained jointly for 50 epochs by one-level optimization with batch size 128. The initial learning rates for α and w are 0.025 and 0.01, accordingly, using *Cosine Annealing*. Cutout regularization [9] of length 16, drop-path [17] of probability 0.3 and auxiliary towers [30] of weight 0.4 are applied. When the joint training process is over, the model will be pruned by manual pruning percentage p. Then we fine-tune the pruned model for 600 epochs with the previous configuration, and set the learning rate of w to 0.025.

The results of EOG-Pruning on CIFAR-10 and CIFAR-100 are summarized in Table 1. The pruning rate is set to 50%. We also test the model inference speed. We define that latency is the average 10 rounds of time required for inference once when batch size is equal to 1, and the speedup rate means the speed of baseline model divided by the speed of pruned model. The speed test is performed on the Intel(R) Xeon(R) CPU E5-2609.

As demonstrated in Table 1, the networks pruned by EOG-Pruning surpass the baselines in speed and accuracy generally, with 50% pruning rate, achieving 0.23% improvement of accuracy on CIFAR-10 basically and 1.8 speedup rate in common. Specially, the accuracy of DARTS (2nd-order) and PC-DARTS on CIFAR100 is 1.58% and 1.34% higher than the original respectively. Only the PDARTS on CIFAR-100 has a slightly decrease in accuracy. We also compare our result to GOLD-NAS on CIFAR-10, which adopts a progressive pruning strategy in search process. Under similar parameters scale, EOG-Pruning performs better. The distribution of α in DARTS is shown in Fig. 3 (a). Most of α are chiefly distribute between 0.4 and 0.6. It shows that the training procedure makes a certain degree of discrimination conductive to pruning.

4.3 EOG-Pruning on ImageNet

We embrace the same pruning framework of CIFAR to ImageNet. In training process, we optimize α and w jointly for 10 epochs, and fine-tuning for 250

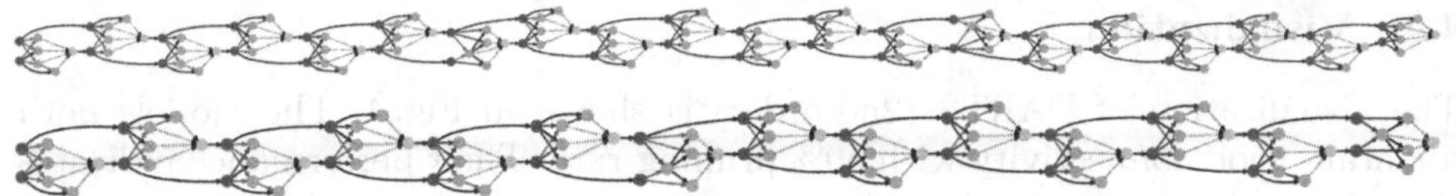

Fig. 4. The structure of 50% pruned percentage of DARTS (2nd-order) on CIFAR-10 and ImageNet, separately, containing 20/14 cells in the network. The red, blue, black, dotted lines indicate the pruned edges, preserved edges, concatenation, skip-connection, respectively. The orange, purple, pink circles mean the nodes in cell, the predecessors and output of each cell, respectively. (Color figure online)

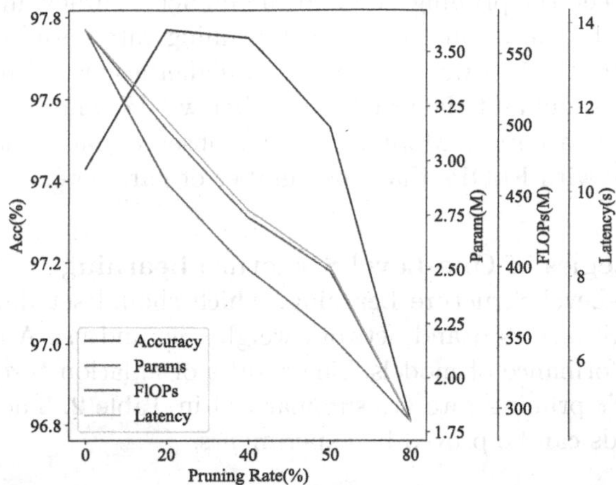

Fig. 5. Effectiveness of different pruning rates based on PC-DARTS. The learning rates ξ_α and ξ_w are all set to 0.025 for brevity.

epochs after pruning. The network configuration of DARTS is adopted in our training and fine-tuning procedure, except that we don't employ the learning rate warmup [11] at the beginning empirically. The network of 14 cells is trained with batch size 128. The learning rates ξ_α and ξ_w are 0.025 and 0.01 in training, and in fine-tuning, learning rate of w is set to 0.5. Both of α and w are optimized by SGD with the momentum of 0.9 and the weight decay of 3×10^{-5}. Additional enhancements including label smoothing [31] and auxiliary loss tower [30] are applied during training.

The results of EOG-Pruning on ImageNet are summarized in Table 1. We can observe that our method outperforms the baseline with different pruning rate. The distribution of α is shown in Fig. 3 (b), and it's easy to distinguish the relatively unimportant edges. We can see that the pruned edges are mainly distributed in the front of the network.

4.4 Visualization

The visualization of DARTS (2nd-order) is shown in Fig. 4. The models both maintain good connectivity with 50% pruning rate. Their performance indicates that some edges are redundant.

4.5 Ablation Study

Effectiveness of Pruned Percentage. In EOG-Pruning, we should set the pruning rate before the pruning process. So it is necessary for us to figure out the relationship between the pruning rate and the model accuracy, in order to make a desired trade-off. The results of different pruning rate based on PC-DARTS are summarized in Fig. 5. If we want to obtain higher accuracy than the original on CIFAR-10, we should set the pruning rate below 50%, and large pruning rate may result in loss of accuracy. Moreover, we can observe that the latency changes more consistently with FLOPs than the number of parameters.

Different Strategies of One-Level Structure Learning. In EOG-Pruning, we suppose One-Level Structure Learning, which should set different learning rates for structure factors α and network weights w, and use AutoAugment [7] to boost the performance of models. The results of ablation test based on PC-DARTS with 50% pruning rate are summarized in Table 2. The advantages of these two methods can be proved by experiments.

Table 2. Different strategies of one-level optimization on PC-DARTS with 50% pruning rate.

Model	Acc. (%)	Diff. lr (M)	AutoAug. (M)
PC-DARTS (Baseline)	97.43	–	–
PC-DARTS (50% Pruned)	**97.66**	✓	✓
PC-DARTS (50% Pruned)	97.53	✗	✓
PC-DARTS (50% Pruned)	97.15	✓	✗
PC-DARTS (50% Pruned)	97.31	✗	✗

5 Conclusion

We propose a pioneering pruning approach called EOG-Pruning (Edge-Wise, One-Level, Global) for the cell-based NAS networks to reduce the redundancy caused by model stacking. It imposes some factors to indicate the importance of edges in the network. The factors will be sorted after the training process, and the edges with the factors lower than the manual threshold will be pruned. Our approach not only reduces the model size and achieves speedup, but also further improves the accuracy proved by our experiments on various datasets.

References

1. Baker, B., Gupta, O., Naik, N., Raskar, R.: Designing neural network architectures using reinforcement learning. In: Submitted to International Conference on Learning Representations (2016)
2. Bergstra, J., Bardenet, R., Bengio, Y., Kégl, B.: Algorithms for Hyper-parameter optimization. In: Proceedings of the 24th International Conference on Neural Information Processing Systems, pp. 2546–2554. NIPS 2011, Curran Associates Inc., Red Hook, NY, USA (2011), event-place: Granada, Spain
3. Bi, K., Hu, C., Xie, L., Chen, X., Wei, L., Tian, Q.: Stabilizing DARTS with Amended Gradient Estimation on Architectural Parameters. arXiv e-prints arXiv:1910.11831 (2019)
4. Bi, K., Xie, L., Chen, X., Wei, L., Tian, Q.: GOLD-NAS: Gradual, One-Level, Differentiable. arXiv e-prints arXiv:2007.03331 (2020)
5. Cai, H., Zhu, L., Han, S.: ProxylessNAS: Direct Neural Architecture Search on Target Task and Hardware. arXiv e-prints arXiv:1812.00332
6. Chen, X., Xie, L., Wu, J., Tian, Q.: Progressive Differentiable Architecture Search: Bridging the Depth Gap between Search and Evaluation. arXiv e-prints arXiv:1904.12760 (2019)
7. Cubuk, E.D., Zoph, B., Mane, D., Vasudevan, V., Le, Q.V.: AutoAugment: learning augmentation strategies from data. In: 2019 IEEE/CVF Conference on Computer Vision and Pattern Recognition (CVPR), pp. 113–123. IEEE, Long Beach, CA, USA, June 2019. https://doi.org/10.1109/CVPR.2019.00020, https://ieeexplore.ieee.org/document/8953317/
8. Deng, J., Dong, W., Socher, R., Li, L., Li, K., Fei-Fei, L.: ImageNet: a large-scale hierarchical image database. In: 2009 IEEE Conference on Computer Vision and Pattern Recognition, pp. 248–255 (2009). https://doi.org/10.1109/CVPR.2009.5206848
9. DeVries, T., Taylor, G.W.: Improved Regularization of Convolutional Neural Networks with Cutout. arXiv e-prints arXiv:1708.04552 (2017)
10. Ghiasi, G., Lin, T.Y., Pang, R., Le, Q.V.: NAS-FPN: Learning Scalable Feature Pyramid Architecture for Object Detection. arXiv e-prints arXiv:1904.07392, April 2019
11. Goyal, P., et al.: Accurate, Large Minibatch SGD: Training ImageNet in 1 Hour. arXiv e-prints arXiv:1706.02677 (2017)
12. Han, S., Mao, H., Dally, W.J.: Deep compression: compressing deep neural networks with pruning. ICLR, trained quantization and huffman coding (2016)
13. He, K., Zhang, X., Ren, S., Sun, J.: Deep residual learning for image recognition. In: 2016 IEEE Conference on Computer Vision and Pattern Recognition (CVPR), pp. 770–778 (2016). https://doi.org/10.1109/CVPR.2016.90
14. He, Y., Zhang, X., Sun, J.: Channel pruning for accelerating very deep neural networks. In: 2017 IEEE International Conference on Computer Vision (ICCV), pp. 1398–1406 (2017). https://doi.org/10.1109/ICCV.2017.155

15. Huang, G., Liu, Z., Maaten, L.V.D., Weinberger, K.Q.: Densely connected convolutional networks. In: 2017 IEEE Conference on Computer Vision and Pattern Recognition (CVPR), pp. 2261–2269 (2017). https://doi.org/10.1109/CVPR.2017.243
16. Krizhevsky, A., Hinton, G.: Learning multiple layers of features from tiny images. Handb. Syst. Autoimmune Dis. **1**(4) (2009)
17. Larsson, G., Maire, M., Shakhnarovich, G.: Fractalnet: Ultra-deep neural networks without residuals. In: ICLR (2017)
18. LeCun, Y., Denker, J.S., Solla, S.A.: Optimal brain damage. In: Touretzky, D.S. (ed.) Advances in Neural Information Processing Systems 2, pp. 598–605. Morgan-Kaufmann (1990). http://papers.nips.cc/paper/250-optimal-brain-damage.pdf
19. Li, H., Kadav, A., Durdanovic, I., Samet, H., Graf, H.P.: Pruning filters for efficient ConvNets. In: International Conference on Learning Representations (ICLR) (2016)
20. Li, K., Malik, J.: Learning to Optimize. arXiv e-prints arXiv:1606.01885 (2016)
21. Li, L., Talwalkar, A.: Random Search and Reproducibility for Neural Architecture Search. arXiv e-prints arXiv:1902.07638 (2019)
22. Liu, C., et al.: Progressive Neural Architecture Search. arXiv e-prints arXiv:1712.00559 (2017)
23. Liu, H., Simonyan, K., Yang, Y.: DARTS: Differentiable Architecture Search. arXiv e-prints arXiv:1806.09055 (2018)
24. Liu, Z., Li, J., Shen, Z., Huang, G., Yan, S., Zhang, C.: Learning efficient convolutional networks through network slimming. In: Proceedings of the IEEE International Conference on Computer Vision (ICCV) (2017)
25. Luo, J.H., Wu, J., Lin, W.: ThiNet: a filter level pruning method for deep neural network compression. In: ICCV, pp. 5068–5076 (2017). https://doi.org/10.1109/ICCV.2017.541
26. Pham, H., Guan, M.Y., Zoph, B., Le, Q.V., Dean, J.: Efficient neural architecture search via parameter sharing. In: ICML, pp. 4092–4101 (2018). http://proceedings.mlr.press/v80/pham18a.html
27. Real, E., Aggarwal, A., Huang, Y., Le, Q.V.: Regularized evolution for image classifier architecture search. In: AAAI, pp. 4780–4789 (2019). https://doi.org/10.1609/aaai.v33i01.33014780
28. Shin*, R., Packer*, C., Song, D.: Differentiable neural network architecture search. In: In International Conference on Learning Representationss-Workshops (2018). https://openreview.net/forum?id=BJ-MRKkwG
29. Suganuma, M., Shirakawa, S., Nagao, T.: A genetic programming approach to designing convolutional neural network architectures. In: IJCAI, pp. 5369–5373 (2018). https://doi.org/10.24963/ijcai.2018/755
30. Szegedy, C., et al.: Going deeper with convolutions. In: 2015 IEEE Conference on Computer Vision and Pattern Recognition (CVPR), pp. 1–9 (2015). https://doi.org/10.1109/CVPR.2015.7298594
31. Szegedy, C., Vanhoucke, V., Ioffe, S., Shlens, J., Wojna, Z.: Rethinking the inception architecture for computer vision. In: CVPR, pp. 2818–2826 (2016). https://doi.org/10.1109/CVPR.2016.308
32. Xie, L., Yuille, A.: Genetic CNN. In: 2017 IEEE International Conference on Computer Vision (ICCV), pp. 1388–1397 (2017). https://doi.org/10.1109/ICCV.2017.154
33. Xu, Y., et al.: PC-DARTS: partial channel connections for memory-efficient architecture search. In: Submitted to International Conference on Learning Representations (2020). https://openreview.net/forum?id=BJlS634tPr

34. Yao, L., Xu, H., Zhang, W., Liang, X., Li, Z.: SM-NAS: Structural-to-Modular Neural Architecture Search for Object Detection. arXiv e-prints arXiv:1911.09929 (2019)
35. Zoph, B., Le, Q.V.: Neural Architecture Search with Reinforcement Learning. arXiv e-prints arXiv:1611.01578 (2016)
36. Zoph, B., Vasudevan, V., Shlens, J., Le, Q.V.: Learning transferable architectures for scalable image recognition. In: Proceedings of the IEEE Conference on Computer Vision and Pattern Recognition (CVPR), June 2018

Convolution Tells Where to Look

Fan Xu[1,2], Lijuan Duan[1,3,4(✉)], Yuanhua Qiao[5], and Ji Chen[2]

[1] Faculty of Information Technology, Beijing University of Technology, Beijing, China
ljduan@bjut.edu.cn
[2] Peng Cheng Laboratory, Shenzhen, China
[3] Beijing Key Laboratory of Trusted Computing, Beijing, China
[4] National Engineering Laboratory for Key Technologies of Information Security Level Protection, Beijing, China
[5] College of Mathematics and Physics, Beijing University of Technology, Beijing, China

Abstract. Many attention models have been introduced to boost the representational power of convolutional neural networks (CNNs). Most of them are self-attention models which generate an attention mask based on current features, like spatial attention and channel attention model. However, these attention models may not achieve good results when the current features are the low-level features of CNNs. In this work, we propose a new lightweight attention unit, feature difference (FD) model, which utilizes the difference between two feature maps to generate the attention mask. The FD module can be integrated into most of the state-of-the-art CNNs like ResNets and VGG just by adding some shortcut connections, which does not introduce any additional parameters and layers. Extensive experiments show that the FD model can help improve the performance of the baseline on four benchmarks, including CIFAR10, CIFAR100, ImageNet-1K, and VOC PASCAL. Note that ResNet44 (6.10% error) with FD model achieves better results than ResNet56 (6.24% error), while the former has fewer parameters than the latter one by 29%.

Keywords: Feature representation · Attention model · Image classification

1 Introduction

Convolutional neural networks (CNNs) have become one of the most effective methods in the field of image processing. Because of their powerful feature extraction capabilities [6,9,14,16,22,23]. Recently, some researchers introduce the attention mechanism to tell the convolutional neural network where to look, which significantly improve the feature extraction power of CNNs [4,24,25,28], like channel attention [4] and spatial attention [28].

From Fig. 1(e), we can observe that the attention values applied to the different channels of the low-level feature do not reflect the prominent differences between the different classes. From Fig. 1(b), we see that the spatial attention

© Springer Nature Switzerland AG 2021
H. Ma et al. (Eds.): PRCV 2021, LNCS 13022, pp. 16–28, 2021.
https://doi.org/10.1007/978-3-030-88013-2_2

Fig. 1. The results of (b), (c), (d) and (e) are based on ResNet50. (a) An image from the validation set of ImageNet-1K. (b) The grad-CAM [19] visualization of the 5th convolutional outputs (conv1). (c) The grad-CAM visualization of the 6th convolutional outputs (conv2). (d) The grad-CAM visualization of $|conv1 - conv2|$.

mask based on the low-level feature can not tell the position of the object well. Both of the two attention model generate attention mask based on current features. However, the low-level features of CNNs are general for all objects which do not reflect differences between different categories well [29]. So it is not easy to obtain the excellent attention mask when these two attention models are applied for the low-level features and the input image has a very complicated background. What is more, Fig. 1(c) is obtained after a convolutional operation is applied to the feature of Fig. 1(b). If we subtract the Fig. 1(b) from the Fig. 1(c), we can get the Fig. 1(d). We observed that the Fig. 1(d) could show the position of the object than Fig. 1(b) or the Fig. 1(c) better. Base on that, in this paper, we propose a novel attention model that can locate the object quickly based on low-level features of CNNs, which we term the *"Feature Difference"* (FD) module. The FD module can tell the network which areas in a feature map should be enhanced and which ones should be suppressed based on the difference between two features, especially for low-level features. The structure of the FD module we proposed is shown in Fig. 2. Given an input feature $\mathbf{X}$, we get the output feature $\mathbf{F}$ after a convolutional operation is applied. So, there should be a difference between the output $\mathbf{F}$ and input $\mathbf{X}$ because of the convolutional operation. The difference can reflect the effect of the convolutional operation on the input $\mathbf{X}$ and the response of input $\mathbf{X}$ to it. The areas with the high response

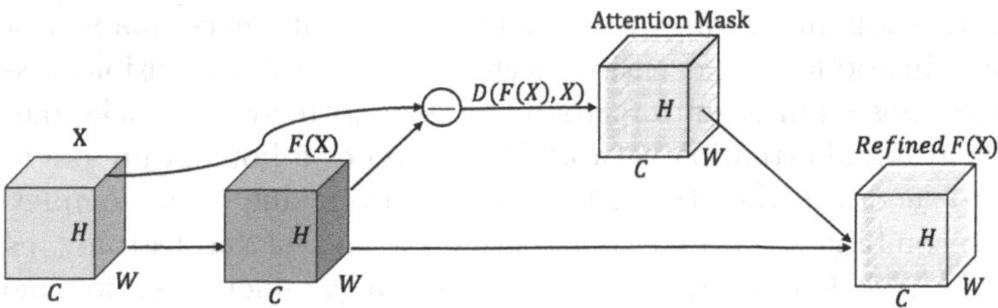

Fig. 2. The architecture of a feature difference module. It infers attention mask along both of channel and spatial dimensions.

should be enhanced, while the area with the low response should be suppressed. Therefore, we can let the convolutional layer itself tell the network where to look by mapping the response to an attention mask and using it to refine the output feature.

In order to validate the effects of the proposed FD module, we embed it into some very popular CNNs to build the FDNets and test the performance of FDNets on four benchmark datasets (CIFAR-10 [5], CIFAR-100 [5], ImageNet-1K [1], and VOC PASCAL). We find that FDNets achieve good performance on those datasets, which demonstrates that the FD module can help improve the performance of CNNs without additional parameters. In summary, our work makes the following contributions:

1. The proposed FD model is tiny and can be embedded into most of the popular CNNs easily, such as ResNets and VGG, with no additional parameters.
2. We verify the performance of the FD model on four benchmark datasets, including CIFAR10, CIFAR100, ImageNet-1K, and VOC PASCAL.

2 Related Work

Convolutional Neural Network. VGGNets [20] generate a larger receptive field by stacking multiple small filter kernels, which significantly reduce thes training parameters of CNNs. VGGNets reach a depth of 16 or 19 layers, but deeper networks cause the problem of vanishing/exploding gradients, which makes the networks difficult to train and optimize. Inspired by the idea of control gates in long short-term memory networks, ResNets [3] add the input of one layer to the output with a shortcut connection, which makes information of the low layer transmitted to the higher one completely. And it also solves the problem that the deep neural network is difficult to train and achieve better performance than HighWay [21]. ResNeXt [26] adopt grouped convolution instead to reduce the parameters of the convolutional layer so that larger feature dimensions can be used for better results. SKNet [8] employs the channel attention model to select the convolution kernel, which makes the network use convolutional kernels with different receptive field sizes based on input feature adaptively.

Attention Mechanism. The visual attention mechanism plays a significant role in human vision, which greatly improves the efficiency and accuracy of visual information processing [2,11,13,18]. In recent years, many researchers have tried to introduce the attention mechanism to computer vision tasks to find and enhance those significant foreground while ignoring those background [7,10,15,27]. The residual attention network [24] proposes a bottom-up and top-down structure to generates the attention mask. However, due to its complexity, it is not easy to combine it with CNNs that contain no residual learning, especially when CNNs have few layers. Hu [4] proposes a channel attention module to recalibrate the feature adaptively with the squeeze-and-excitation block. On that work, Sanghyun [25] proposes the convolutional block attention module (CBAM) which infers attention maps both along the channel and spatial dimensions.

3 Feature Difference Module

In a convolutional layer of CNNs, given an input feature **X**, we get the output **F** after a convolutional operator:

$$\mathbf{F} = f\{\mathbf{X}, \mathbf{W}\}, \tag{1}$$

where **X** and **F** are the input and output features of a convolutional layer and $f(\cdot)$ represents the convolutional operator; **W**denotes the trainable parameters of a set of convolutional kernels (for simplicity, we omit the biases). When a convolutional operator is applied to input **X**, it changes the input **X** and causes a difference between output **F** and input **X**. Therefore, we consider that the difference between output **F** and input **X** reflects the effect of the convolutional operator on the input **X** and also represents the response of input **X** to the convolutional operator. Because of the backpropagation algorithm, the value of the response is related to the label. So, those areas that are highly responsive to the convolutional operator should be enhanced, while others that are low responsive to the convolutional operator should be suppressed. Based on that, we design the feature difference (FD) module to measures the response of input **X** to the convolutional operator by calculating the difference between input **X** and output **F**. And then an attention mask is generated to refine the output feature maps **F** based on those response. The structure of the FD module is shown in Fig. 2.

3.1 Feature Difference

In order to measure the difference between two feature maps conveniently, we assume that the pixel value of any position in input $\mathbf{X} \in \mathbb{R}^{H \times W \times C}$ can be denoted as $p_{i,j,k}$, where $i \in [0, W)$, $j \in [0, H)$, $k \in [0, C)$. After applying the convolutional operator to the input **X**, we obtain the output feature maps $\mathbf{F} \in \mathbb{R}^{H \times W \times C}$ (specify that the convolutional operator does not change the size of input **X**). The pixel value of any position in F is denoted as $p'_{i,j,k}$. If the pixel values in some positions do not change after the convolutional operator, that is $p'_{i,j,k} = p_{i,j,k}$, we can assume the convolutional operator has no effect to those pixels. If the pixel values in some positions changed, that is $p'_{i,j,k} \neq p_{i,j,k}$, we think that the convolutional operator has effect on this pixel. The changes of pixel values in input **X** reflects the response of the input **X** to the convolutional operator. Inspired by smooth L_1 loss, we measure the effect of the convolutional operator on input **X** by the following equation:

$$\mathbf{D}(\mathbf{X}) = smooth(\mathbf{F} - \mathbf{X}), \tag{2}$$

in which

$$smooth(x) = \begin{cases} \frac{0.5}{\beta} x^2 & if\,|x| < 1 \\ |x| - 0.5\beta & otherwise \end{cases} \tag{3}$$

where β is a hyperparameter and it is set to 1 in this work.

When $\mathbf{D}_{i,j,k}(x)$ is large, it indicates that the convolutional operator has more effect on this pixel and when $\mathbf{D}_{i,j,k}(x)$ is small, it indicates that the convolutional operator has less effect on that one. In particular, when $\mathbf{D}_{i,j,k}(x)$ equals to 0, it indicates that the convolutional operator has no effect on it.

$\mathbf{D}$ tells CNNs that in the current feature maps, which areas should be focused on and enhanced, and which areas should be suppressed. So, we have the following way to refine the output feature maps $\mathbf{F}$:

$$\mathbf{M}(\mathbf{X}) = \sigma(\mathbf{D}(\mathbf{X})), \tag{4}$$

$$\tilde{\mathbf{F}} = \mathbf{M}(\mathbf{X}) \otimes \mathbf{F}, \tag{5}$$

where $\otimes$ denotes element-wise multiplication. σ is an activation function and we will discuss it in the next section. $\tilde{\mathbf{F}}$ is refined feature maps by attention mask $\mathbf{M}$. $\mathbf{F}$, $\mathbf{M}$ and $\tilde{\mathbf{F}}$ have the same size.

3.2 FD Networks

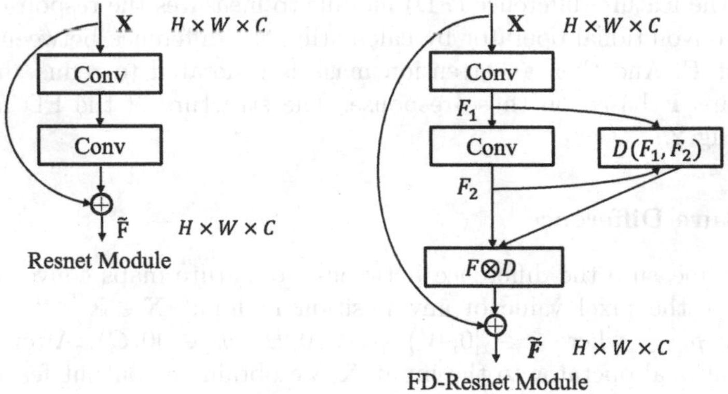

Fig. 3. The original residual module (left) and the FD-residual module (right).

The proposed FD module is very tiny and easy to implement, so we can embed FD module into some popular CNNs easily to build FDNets. To illustrate that, we describe how to embed the FD module into ResNets [3] and VGG to build FDNets in this section.

The FD-residual block structure that makes up FD-ResNets is shown in Fig. 3 and the FD-VGG block structure that makes up FD-VGG is shown in Fig. 4. Since we use Eq. 2 to calculate the difference between two feature maps, we need to ensure that they have the same size. Therefore, when the convolutional operator does not change the size of the input feature, we use the FD module to refine the output feature. Note that we just introduced some new short connections and operations on the original module to build the FD model, so it is no additional parameters.

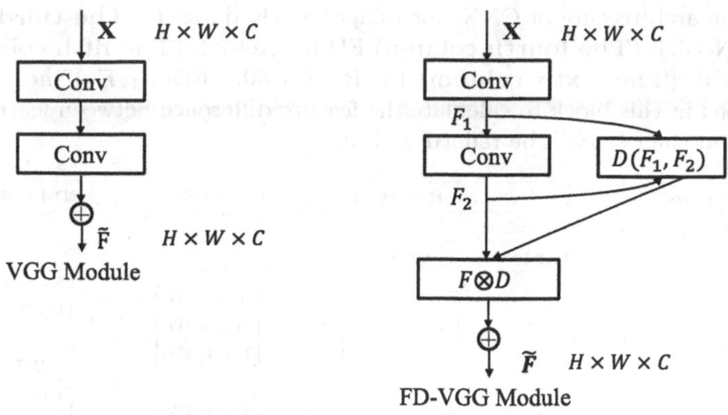

Fig. 4. The original VGG module (left) and the FD-VGG module (right).

4 Experiments

In this section, we embed the FD module into some benchmark CNNs to build FDNets and evaluate the performance of FDNets on four datasets (CIFAR-10 [5], (CIFAR-100 [5], VOC 2012), and ImageNet-1K [1]). In order to perform an apple-to-apple comparison, all results are reproduced in the PyTorch framework. Firstly, we conduct a simple ablation analysis to determine the final structure of FDNets, which mainly includes the position of the FD module. Then we compare the performance of FDNets with original ones on CIFAR-10 and CIFAR-100 and ImageNet-1K datasets, and we also compare FDNets with other state-of-the-art models, including some other attention models. In addition, an experiment is done on VOC PASCAL object detection data to verify the generalization of the FD model.

Table 1. Test error (%) on CIFAR-10 and CIFAR-100 and all results are reproduced in the PyTorch framework. Note that ResNets have same parameters with ResNets-FD

Description	CIFAR-10	CIFAR100
ResNet-32 [3]	7.16	29.13
ResNet-32 + FD	6.77	28.75
ResNet-44	6.55	28.16
ResNet-44 + FD	6.10	27.83
ResNet-56	6.24	27.30
ResNet-56 + FD	5.82	27.11
ResNet-110	5.82	26.26
ResNet-110 + FD	5.60	25.99

Table 2. The architecture of CNNs for ImageNet-1K dataset. (**The third column**) original ResNet-34. (**The fourth column**) FD-ResNet-34. (**The fifth column**) original ResNet-50. (**The sixth column**) FD-ResNet-50. "FD($\mathbf{F_1}, \mathbf{F_2}$)"means that FD module is used in this block to calculate the feature difference between feature $\mathbf{F_1}$ and feature $\mathbf{F_2}$ and then $\mathbf{F_2}$ will be refined with it.

Layer	Output size	ResNet-34	FD-ResNet-34	ResNet-50	FD-ResNet-50
conv1	112 × 112	7 × 7, 16, stride 2			
		3 × 3 max pooling, 16, stride 2			
conv2_x	56 × 56	$\begin{bmatrix}3\times3,64\\3\times3,64\end{bmatrix}\times3$	$\begin{bmatrix}\mathbf{F_1},3\times3,64\\\mathbf{F_2},3\times3,64\\FD(\mathbf{F_1},\mathbf{F_2})\end{bmatrix}\times3$	$\begin{bmatrix}1\times1,64\\3\times3,64\\1\times1,256\end{bmatrix}\times3$	$\begin{bmatrix}\mathbf{F_1},1\times1,64\\\mathbf{F_2},3\times3,64\\1\times1,256\\FD(\mathbf{F_1},\mathbf{F_2})\end{bmatrix}\times3$
conv3_x	28 × 28	$\begin{bmatrix}3\times3,128\\3\times3,128\end{bmatrix}\times4$	$\begin{bmatrix}\mathbf{F_1},3\times3,128\\\mathbf{F_2},3\times3,128\\FD(\mathbf{F_1},\mathbf{F_2})\end{bmatrix}\times4$	$\begin{bmatrix}1\times1,128\\3\times3,128\\1\times1,512\end{bmatrix}\times4$	$\begin{bmatrix}\mathbf{F_1},1\times1,128\\\mathbf{F_2},3\times3,128\\1\times1,512\\FD(\mathbf{F_1},\mathbf{F_2})\end{bmatrix}\times4$
conv4_x	14 × 14	$\begin{bmatrix}3\times3,256\\3\times3,256\end{bmatrix}\times6$	$\begin{bmatrix}\mathbf{F_1},3\times3,256\\\mathbf{F_2},3\times3,256\\FD(\mathbf{F_1},\mathbf{F_2})\end{bmatrix}\times6$	$\begin{bmatrix}1\times1,256\\3\times3,256\\1\times1,1024\end{bmatrix}\times6$	$\begin{bmatrix}\mathbf{F_1},1\times1,256\\\mathbf{F_2},3\times3,256\\1\times1,1024\\FD(\mathbf{F_1},\mathbf{F_2})\end{bmatrix}\times6$
conv5_x	7 × 7	$\begin{bmatrix}3\times3,512\\3\times3,512\end{bmatrix}\times3$	$\begin{bmatrix}\mathbf{F_1},3\times3,512\\\mathbf{F_2},3\times3,512\\FD(\mathbf{F_1},\mathbf{F_2})\end{bmatrix}\times3$	$\begin{bmatrix}1\times1,512\\3\times3,512\\1\times1,2048\end{bmatrix}\times3$	$\begin{bmatrix}\mathbf{F_1},1\times1,512\\\mathbf{F_2},3\times3,512\\1\times1,2048\\FD(\mathbf{F_1},\mathbf{F_2})\end{bmatrix}\times3$
	1 × 1	Global average pool, 1000-d fc, softmax			
	Param.	11.69M		25.56M	

4.1 Results on CIFAR-10 and CIFAR-100

Implementation. The CIFAR-10 dataset contains 60,000, 32 × 32 color images of 10 classes. We use ResNets [3] as our plain network to build FD-ResNets. In order to perform apple-to-apple comparison, we keep most of the training methods same as ResNets [3] when training the FD-ResNets.

In this section, we embed FD module into ResNet-32, ResNet-44, ResNet-56, and ResNet-110 to build FD-ResNets and compare the performance of FD-ResNets with original ResNets on CIFAR-10 and CIFAR-100 datasets. We keep the same training strategy on CIFAR-100 as CIFAR-10. The experimental results are shown in Table 1. We find that FD-ResNets achieve better results than the original ResNets both on CIFAR-10 as CIFAR-100 dataset. What is more, FD-ResNet-44 (6.10% error) even achieves better results than ResNet-56 (6.24% error) by 0.14%. FD-ResNet-44 and ResNet-44 have the same number of parameters. ResNet-56 has more parameters than FD-ResNet-44 by ~28.7%, which means that the FD model helps the network achieve better results with fewer parameters.

4.2 ImageNet Classification

Implementation. The ImageNet-1K contains 1.2 million training, 50,000 validation and 100,000 test images of 1000 classes. We use ResNets [3] as the base

Table 3. Comparisons of single-crop validation error rates (%) on ImageNet-1K dataset. The VGG and FD-VGG are trained with batch normalization for 100 epochs

Description	top-1	top-5
ResNet-34 [3]	26.69	8.60
ResNet-34 + FD	26.41	8.49
ResNet-50 [3]	24.56	7.50
ResNet-50 + FD	24.15	7.29
ResNet-101 [3]	23.38	6.88
ResNet-101 + FD	22.73	6.48
ResNext-50 [26]	22.85	6.48
ResNext-50+ FD	22.49	6.34
Vgg16 [20]	25.93	8.02
Vgg16 + FD	25.48	7.81

Table 4. Classification results (error (%)) on ImageNet-1K using the light-weight network.

Description	top-1	top-5
MobileNet [17]	34.85	13.6
MobileNet + FD	34.32	13.15

network to build FD-ResNets and evaluate the performance of FD-ResNets on the ImageNet-1K dataset [1]. The structures of networks are shown in Table 2. We evaluate the networks on the validation dataset like others [3,4,25]. To ensure a fair comparison, we use the same training strategy as ResNet [3], including the same data augmentation scheme. A 224×224 crop is randomly sampled from an augment image or its horizontal flip during the training and a single crop with a size of 224×224 from the center of original images is sampled for testing. The per-pixel value of images is scaled to [0, 1], following the mean value subtracted and standard variance divided both for training and testing. We use SGD with a momentum of 0.9 to train the networks with the mini-batch size of 256 in 4 GPUs. We set the initial learning rate to 0.1, and then it is divided by 10 at 30, 60, 90 epochs. The total training epochs are 90 if there is no special statement.

Results on ImageNet-1K. We compare the performance of FD module based on ResNets. The experimental results are shown in Table 3. Note that the FD module we proposed does no bring additional parameters. From the results, we have the those following observations: Firstly, FD-ResNets perform better than the original ResNets, including, ResNet34, ResNet50, and ResNet101. As the depth of the network increases, the improvement brought by the FD model becomes more obvious. For example, the FD model results in only 0.28% (Top1 error) on ResNet34, while it is 0.65% for ResNet101. It suggests that multiple

Table 5. Comparisons of single-crop validation error rates (%) and complexity on ImageNet-1K dataset and the best result are shown in bold

Description	top-1 error (%)	top-5 error (%)	Param	GFLOPs
ResNeXt-50 [26]	22.85	6.48	25.03M	3.768
ResNeXt-50 + BAM [12]	22.56	6.40	25.39M	3.85
ResNeXt-50 + CBAM [25]	21.92	**5.91**	27.56M	3.774
SENet [4]	**21.91**	6.04	27.56M	3.771
FDNet (ours)	22.49	6.34	25.03M	3.768
ResNet-50 [3]	24.56	7.50	25.56	3.858
SENet [4]	23.14	6.70	28.09M	3.860
FDNet (ours)	24.15	7.29	25.56M	3.858
SENet + FD (ours)	**22.84**	**6.43**	28.09M	3.860

uses of the FD model lead to better performance, which is consistent with the conclusion of the ablation study.

Secondly, The FD model also achieves good results on networks with grouped convolutional layers like ResNeXt [26].

Thirdly, not only do we test the performance of the FD model on CNNs with residual connections, but we also do it on networks without residual connections. On the VGG16, the FD model achieve a boost of 0.45% (Top 1 error).

In addition, since the FD model is an extremely lightweight model and it brings almost no additional parameters and very little computation, embedding it into some lightweight models is a natural choice like MobileNetv2 [17]. We only embed the FD model into the depthwise convolutional layers. Experimental results are shown in Table 4. FD-MobileNet achieves better results than the original one, which fully demonstrates the potential of the FD model in low-end devices like mobile phones, etc.

Comparision with Other Attention Models In this section, we compare the performance of the FD model with other state-of-the-art attention models, including BAM [12], CBAM [25], and SE [4] attention models, and all three attention models include channel attention block. What is more, the BAM and CBAM are based on the SE model, and the FD model is the only one in all four attention models that bring no additional parameters. The experimental results are shown in Table 5. Firstly, like other attention models, the FD model help to improve the performance of the baseline, and it achieves better results than BAM with fewer parameters. Secondly, Although the FD model does not achieve better results than CBAM or SE, it is different from other attention models. So, it is a natural choice to combine the FD model with other attention models without additional parameters. We embed the FD model into SENet and achieve a better results. These experiments indicate that the FD-model can not only be embedded into a backbone network but also work with other attention models to further improve the performance of CNNs.

4.3 VOC 2012 Object Detection

Table 6. Object detection mAP(%) on the VOC 2012 test set.

Detector	Backbone	mAP@.5
Faster-RCNN	ResNet101	73.6
Faster-RCNN	ResNet101 + FD	74.2

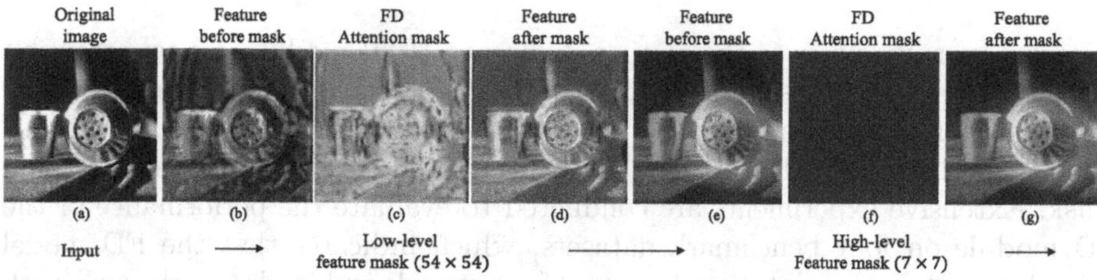

Fig. 5. Example images illustrating how the FD model works. The low-level feature is from the first residual block of FD-ResNet101 and the high-level feature is from the last residual block.

We also conduct experiments on the detection task to prove the generalization of the FD model. In this section, the performance of the FD model is evaluated on VOC PASCAL dataset. We use the Faster RCNN [14] as the detector to compare the effects of different backbone networks. All methods are trained on VOC 2007 and VOC 2012 trainval sets plus VOC 2007 test set and tested on VOC 2012 test set For an apple-to-apple comparison, the same experimental strategy is employed as the faster RCNN [14], and we reproduced all the results on the PyTorch platform. The experimental results are summarized in Table 6. We can see that compared to ResNet101 as the backbone network, the FD-ResNet101 achieves better results. Note that ResNet101 and FD-ResNet101 have the same parameters, which means the FD model can help improve the performance of the faster RCNN detector with little additional computation. That is extremely important when the speed of a detector can affect its application.

5 Analysis and Interpretation

To understand how the FD model works, we visualize the attention mask generated by the FD model, as shown in Fig. 1. We observer the following findings:

Firstly, the FD model can locate the object well base on the low-level features while most of the self-attention models can not do it because they generate an attention mask just based on the feature (b).

Secondly, for the high-level feature, the difference between two features is minimal, which leads to that most of the value in the attention mask is close to 0.5. At this time, the FD model cannot locate the object. However, we can see from (e) that the current feature can locate the object itself. Therefore, for the high-level feature, no additional attention model is needed to find the object when the low-level feature already does it well. Besides, the output of the FD model closing to zero indicates that the current convolutional operation does not change the value of the feature. It means that this convolutional layer do not learn new features, so it can be removed from the network.

6 Conclusion

In this paper, we propose the feature difference (FD) module, a new attention block to boost the representation power of CNNs, which is different from the previous works like SE [4] and CBAM [25]. It uses the difference between the input feature and the output feature of a convolutional layer to generate the attention mask. Extensive experiments are conducted to evaluate the performance of the FD module on four benchmark datasets, which indicates that the FD model helps boost the representational power of a network and it also works well with other attention models, like channel attention model, to further improve the classification accuracy of a network. Besides, we find that the FD model has different effects between low-level features and high-level features, which suggests that we can use a small number of attention blocks to locate objects quickly. We hope that this discovery will inspire the future design of the attention model. Finally, the FD model can be used to evaluate the effect of the convolutional operation on features, which could help to find those convolutional layers that have little effect on the accuracy of recognition for the network pruning.

Acknowledgements. This research is partially sponsored by Key Project of Beijing Municipal Education Commission (No. KZ201910005008).

References

1. Deng, J., Dong, W., Socher, R., Li, L.J., Li, K., Fei-Fei, L.: Imagenet: a large-scale hierarchical image database. In: IEEE Conference on Computer Vision and Pattern Recognition, 2009. CVPR 2009, pp. 248–255. IEEE (2009)
2. Fox, M.D., Corbetta, M., Snyder, A.Z., Vincent, J.L., Raichle, M.E.: Spontaneous neuronal activity distinguishes human dorsal and ventral attention systems. Proc. Natl. Acad. Sci. **103**(26), 10046–10051 (2006)
3. He, K., Zhang, X., Ren, S., Sun, J.: Deep residual learning for image recognition. In: Proceedings of the IEEE Conference on Computer Vision and Pattern Recognition, pp. 770–778 (2016)

4. Hu, J., Shen, L., Sun, G.: Squeeze-and-excitation networks. In: Proceedings of the IEEE Conference on Computer Vision and Pattern Recognition, pp. 7132–7141 (2018)
5. Krizhevsky, A., Hinton, G.: Learning multiple layers of features from tiny images. Tech. rep, Citeseer (2009)
6. Krizhevsky, A., Sutskever, I., Hinton, G.E.: Imagenet classification with deep convolutional neural networks. In: International Conference on Neural Information Processing Systems, pp. 1097–1105 (2012)
7. Larochelle, H., Hinton, G.E.: Learning to combine foveal glimpses with a third-order Boltzmann machine. In: Advances in Neural Information Processing Systems, pp. 1243–1251 (2010)
8. Li, X., Wang, W., Hu, X., Yang, J.: Selective kernel networks. In: Proceedings of the IEEE Conference on Computer Vision and Pattern Recognition, pp. 510–519 (2019)
9. Liu, N., Han, J.: Dhsnet: deep hierarchical saliency network for salient object detection. In: Computer Vision and Pattern Recognition, pp. 678–686 (2016)
10. Nuechterlein, K.H., Parasuraman, R., Jiang, Q.: Visual sustained attention: image degradation produces rapid sensitivity decrement over time. Science **220**(4594), 327–329 (1983)
11. Pardo, J.V., Fox, P.T., Raichle, M.E.: Localization of a human system for sustained attention by positron emission tomography. Nature **349**(6304), 61 (1991)
12. Park, J., Woo, S., Lee, J., Kweon, I.S.: BAM: bottleneck attention module. In: British Machine Vision Conference 2018, BMVC 2018, Newcastle, UK, 3–6 September 2018, p. 147. BMVA Press (2018). http://bmvc2018.org/contents/papers/0092.pdf
13. Petersen, S.E., Posner, M.I.: The attention system of the human brain: 20 years after. Ann. Rev. Neurosci. **35**, 73–89 (2012)
14. Ren, S., He, K., Girshick, R., Sun, J.: Faster r-CNN: towards real-time object detection with region proposal networks. In: International Conference on Neural Information Processing Systems, pp. 91–99 (2015)
15. Rensink, R.A., O'Regan, J.K., Clark, J.J.: To see or not to see: the need for attention to perceive changes in scenes. Psychol. Sci. **8**(5), 368–373 (1997)
16. Ronneberger, O., Fischer, P., Brox, T.: U-Net: convolutional networks for biomedical image segmentation. In: Navab, N., Hornegger, J., Wells, W.M., Frangi, A.F. (eds.) MICCAI 2015. LNCS, vol. 9351, pp. 234–241. Springer, Cham (2015). https://doi.org/10.1007/978-3-319-24574-4_28
17. Sandler, M., Howard, A., Zhu, M., Zhmoginov, A., Chen, L.C.: Mobilenetv 2: inverted residuals and linear bottlenecks. In: Proceedings of the IEEE Conference on Computer Vision and Pattern Recognition, pp. 4510–4520 (2018)
18. Schneider, W., Shiffrin, R.M.: Controlled and automatic human information processing: I. detection, search, and attention. Psychol. Rev. **84**(1), 1 (1977)
19. Selvaraju, R.R., Cogswell, M., Das, A., Vedantam, R., Parikh, D., Batra, D.: Grad-cam: Visual explanations from deep networks via gradient-based localization. In: Proceedings of the IEEE International Conference on Computer Vision, pp. 618–626 (2017)
20. Simonyan, K., Zisserman, A.: Very deep convolutional networks for large-scale image recognition. In: Bengio, Y., LeCun, Y. (eds.) 3rd International Conference on Learning Representations, ICLR 2015, San Diego, CA, USA, 7–9 May 2015, Conference Track Proceedings (2015). http://arxiv.org/abs/1409.1556
21. Srivastava, R.K., Greff, K., Schmidhuber, J.: Highway networks. arXiv preprint arXiv:1505.00387 (2015)

22. Tan, M., et al.: Mnasnet: platform-aware neural architecture search for mobile. In: Proceedings of the IEEE Conference on Computer Vision and Pattern Recognition, pp. 2820–2828 (2019)
23. Tan, M., Le, Q.V.: Efficientnet: rethinking model scaling for convolutional neural networks. In: Chaudhuri, K., Salakhutdinov, R. (eds.) Proceedings of the 36th International Conference on Machine Learning, ICML 2019, 9–15 June 2019, Long Beach, California, USA. Proceedings of Machine Learning Research, vol. 97, pp. 6105–6114. PMLR (2019). http://proceedings.mlr.press/v97/tan19a.html
24. Wang, F., et al.: Residual attention network for image classification. In: Proceedings of the IEEE Conference on Computer Vision and Pattern Recognition, pp. 3156–3164 (2017)
25. Woo, S., Park, J., Lee, J.Y., Kweon, I.S.: Cbam: Convolutional block attention module. In: Proceedings of the European Conference on Computer Vision (ECCV) (2018)
26. Xie, S., Girshick, R., Dollár, P., Tu, Z., He, K.: Aggregated residual transformations for deep neural networks. In: Proceedings of the IEEE Conference on Computer Vision and Pattern Recognition, pp. 1492–1500 (2017)
27. Xu, K., et al.: Show, attend and tell: Neural image caption generation with visual attention. In: International Conference on Machine Learning, pp. 2048–2057 (2015)
28. Zagoruyko, S., Komodakis, N.: Paying more attention to attention: improving the performance of convolutional neural networks via attention transfer. In: 5th International Conference on Learning Representations, ICLR 2017, Toulon, France, 24–26 April 2017, Conference Track Proceedings. OpenReview.net (2017). https://openreview.net/forum?id=Sks9_ajex
29. Zeiler, M.D., Fergus, R.: Visualizing and understanding convolutional networks. In: Fleet, D., Pajdla, T., Schiele, B., Tuytelaars, T. (eds.) ECCV 2014. LNCS, vol. 8689, pp. 818–833. Springer, Cham (2014). https://doi.org/10.1007/978-3-319-10590-1_53

Robust Single-Step Adversarial Training with Regularizer

Lehui Xie[1,2], Yaopeng Wang[1,2], Jia-Li Yin[1,2], and Ximeng Liu[1,2](✉)

[1] College of Mathematics and Computer Science, Fuzhou University, Fuzhou 350108, China

[2] Fujian Provincial Key Laboratory of Information Security of Network Systems, Fuzhou University, Fuzhou 350108, China

Abstract. High cost of training time caused by multi-step adversarial example generation is a major challenge in adversarial training. Previous methods try to reduce the computational burden of adversarial training using single-step adversarial example generation schemes, which can effectively improve the efficiency but also introduce the problem of "catastrophic overfitting", where the robust accuracy against Fast Gradient Sign Method (FGSM) can achieve nearby 100% whereas the robust accuracy against Projected Gradient Descent (PGD) suddenly drops to 0% over a single epoch. To address this issue, we focus on single-step adversarial training scheme in this paper and propose a novel Fast Gradient Sign Method with PGD Regularization (FGSMPR) to boost the efficiency of adversarial training without catastrophic overfitting. Our core observation is that single-step adversarial training can not simultaneously learn robust internal representations of FGSM and PGD adversarial examples. Therefore, we design a PGD regularization term to encourage similar embeddings of FGSM and PGD adversarial examples. The experiments demonstrate that our proposed method can train a robust deep network for L_∞-perturbations with FGSM adversarial training and reduce the gap to multi-step adversarial training.

Keywords: Deep learning · Adversarial training · Adversarial defense

1 Introduction

Deep learning has shown outstanding success in near all machine learning fields. However, it has been proved that deep neural networks are vulnerable to adversarial examples, i.e., small disturbances to the input signal, which are usually invisible to the human eyes, are enough to induce large changes in model output [17]. This phenomenon has aroused people's concerns about the safety of deep learning in the adversarial environment, where malicious attackers may significantly degrade the robustness of deep learning based applications. To mitigate the harm caused by the adversarial examples, numerous defensive methods

The first author is a student.

© Springer Nature Switzerland AG 2021
H. Ma et al. (Eds.): PRCV 2021, LNCS 13022, pp. 29–41, 2021.
https://doi.org/10.1007/978-3-030-88013-2_3

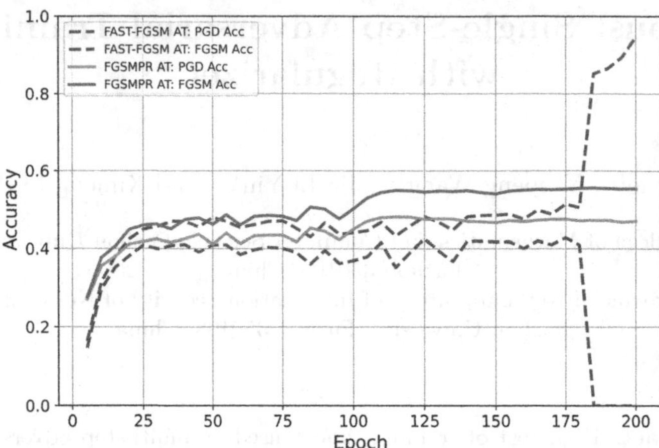

Fig. 1. (CIFAR-10) Visualization of the FGSM and PGD robustness of the model trained with FAST-FGSM AT (dashed), FGSMPR AT (solid). All statistics are evaluated against FGSM attacks and 50 steps PGD attacks with 10 random restarts on the test dataset. FAST-FGSM AT occurs catastrophic overfitting at 180 epochs, characterized by a sudden drop of PGD robustness and a rapid increase of FGSM robustness. FGSMPR AT (ours) does not suffer from catastrophic overfitting and maintains stable robustness during the whole training process.

including pre-processing based [6], modified networks based [3] and detection based [13] have been proposed. Among these methods, adversarial training [12] is one of the most powerful approaches for robust defense against adversarial attacks since [2] a set of purportedly robust defenses by the adaptive attack.

Adversarial Training (AT) aims to augment each small batch of training data with adversarial examples for learning a robust model. It is generally considered to be more expensive than traditional training because it is necessary to construct adversarial examples through first-order methods such as projection gradient descent (PGD). To combat the increased computational overhead of PGD AT, a recent line of work focused on improving the efficiency of AT. [20] proposed to perform multi-step PGD adversarial attacks by chopping off redundant computations during backpropagation when computing adversarial examples to obtain additional speedup. [15] proposed a variant of K steps PGD AT with a single-step Fast Gradient Sign Method (FGSM) AT overhead, called "FREE AT", which can update model weights as well as input perturbations simultaneously by using a single backpropagation in a way that is less expensive than PGD AT overheads. Inspired by [15,19] found that previously non-robustness FGSM AT, with a random initialization, could reach similar robustness to PGD AT, called "FAST-FGSM AT". However, FGSM-based AT suffers from catastrophic overfitting where the robustness against PGD attacks increases in the early stage of training, but suddenly drops to 0 over a single epoch, as shown in Fig. 1. Several methods have been proposed to prevent the overfitting of AT

[1,11,18,19]. However, these methods are either computationally inefficient or decrease the robustness accuracy.

In this paper, we first analyze the reason why FGSM AT suffers catastrophic overfitting in the training process. We observe that FGSM AT is prone to learn spurious functions that excessively fit the FGSM adversarial data distribution but have undefined behavior off the FGSM adversarial data manifold. Then we discuss the difference behind the logits output between the FGSM and PGD adversarial examples in the model trained with FGSM AT and PGD AT, where we show that the logits become significantly different when the FGSM AT trained model suffers from overfitting, while the robust model trained with PGD AT remains stable. We additionally provide for this case an experimental analysis that helps to explain why the FGSM AT trained model generates vastly different logit outputs for single-step and multi-step adversarial examples when catastrophic overfitting occurs. Finally, we propose a novel Fast Gradient Sign Method with PGD regularization (FGSMPR), in which a PGD regularization item is utilized to prompt the model to learn logits that are a function of the truly robust features in the image and ignore the spurious features, thus preventing catastrophic overfitting, as shown in Fig. 1.

The contribution of this paper is summarized as follows:

- We analyze the reason why FGSM AT suffers from catastrophic overfitting and demonstrate that the logit distribution of the FGSM AT trained model evaluated against FGSM and PGD adversarial examples have significant difference when suffering from catastrophic overfitting.
- We propose a Fast Gradient Sign Method with PGD regularization (FGSMPR), which can effectively prevent FGSM AT from catastrophic overfitting by explicitly minimizing the difference in the logit of the model against FGSM and PGD adversarial examples.
- The extensive experiments show that the FGSMPR can learn a robust model comparable to PGD AT with low computational overhead while in relief of catastrophic overfitting. Specially, the FGSMPR takes only 30 min to train a CIFAR-10 model with 46% robustness against 50 steps PGD attacks.

2 Related Work

2.1 Adversarial Training

Previous work [12] formalized the training of adversarial robust model into the following non-convex non-concave min-max robust optimization problem:

$$\min_{\theta} \mathbb{E}_{(x,y)\sim\mathcal{D}}[\max_{\delta\in\mathcal{S}} \mathcal{L}(\theta, x+\delta, y)]. \tag{1}$$

The parameter θ of the network is learned by Eq. 1 on the example $(x, y) \sim \mathcal{D}$, where $\mathcal{D}$ is the data generating distribution. $\mathcal{S}$ denotes the region within the

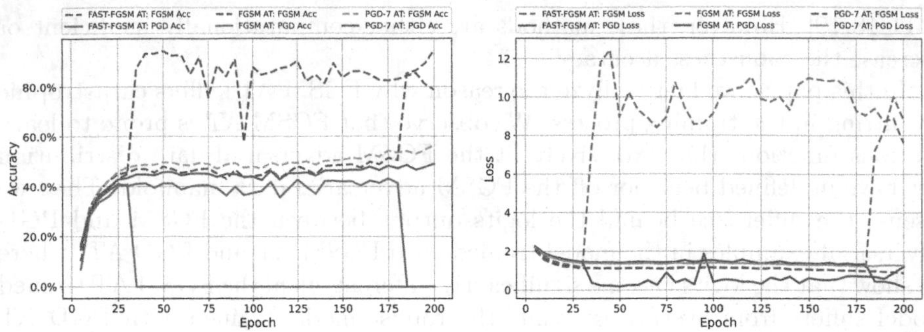

Fig. 2. (CIFAR-10) Visualization of the FGSM and PGD accuracy/loss of the model trained with FGSM AT, FAST-FGSM AT, PGD-7 AT and tested against FGSM adversarial attacks and 50 steps PGD attack with 10 random restarts during the training process. All results are averaged over three independent runs. FGSM AT and FAST-FGSM AT occurs catastrophic overfitting around 30 and 180 epochs, respectively, characterized by a sudden drop in PGD accuracy and FGSM loss and a rapid increase in PGD loss and FGSM accuracy.

ϵ perturbation range under the ℓ_∞ threat model for each example, i.e., $\mathcal{S} = \{\delta : \|\delta\|_\infty \le \epsilon\}$, which is usually chosen so that it contains only visually imperceptible perturbations. The procedure for AT is to use adversarial attacks to approximate the internal maximization over $\mathcal{S}$.

FGSM AT. One of the earliest versions of AT used the FGSM attack to find adversarial examples x' to approximate the internal maximization, formalized as follows [5]:

$$x' = x + \epsilon \cdot \mathrm{sign}(\nabla_x \mathcal{L}(\theta, x, y)). \tag{2}$$

FGSM AT is cheap since it only relies on computing the gradient once. However, the FGSM AT is easily defeated by multi-step adversarial attacks.

PGD AT. PGD attacks [12] used multi-step gradient projection descent to approximate the inner maximization, which is more accurate than FGSM but computationally expensive, formalized as follows:

$$x^{t+1} = \Pi_{x+\mathcal{S}}\left(x^t + \alpha\, \mathrm{sign}\left(\nabla_x \mathcal{L}(\theta, x, y)\right)\right), \tag{3}$$

where x^0 initialized as the clean input x, Π refers to the projection operator, which ensures projecting the adversarial examples back to the ball within the radius ϵ of the clean data point. The number of iterations K in the PGD attacks (PGD-K) determines the strength of the attack and the computational cost. Further, N random restarts are usually employed to verify robustness under strong attacks (PGD-K-N).

2.2 Single-Step Adversarial Training

FREE AT [15], a single-step training method that generates adversarial examples while updating network weights, is quite similar to FGSM AT. By deeply analyzing the differences between FREE AT and FGSM AT, [19] found that an important property of FREE AT is that the perturbation of the previous sign of gradient is used as the initial perturbation of the next iteration. Based on this observation, [19] proposed a FAST-FGSM AT with almost the same robustness as the PGD AT, but the spent time close to the normal training by adding non-zero initialization perturbations to FGSM AT and further combining some standard techniques [14,16] to accelerate the training. However, FAST-FGSM AT suffers from catastrophic overfitting, where the robustness for PGD adversarial examples suddenly drop to 0% over a single epoch.

A recent line of work foucs on addressing the catastrophic overfitting problem in single-step AT. [19] used the early stopping method to stop training the model when the model robustness decreases beyond a threshold. [18] introduced dropout layers after each non-linear layer of the model and further decay its dropout probability as the training progresses. [11] monitored the FGSM AT process and performed PGD AT with a few batches to help the FGSM model recover its robustness when the robustness decreases beyond a threshold. [1] proposed the Gradient Alignment (GradAlign) regularization item that maximizes the gradient alignment based on the connection between FAST-FGSM AT overfitting and local linearization of the model as a way to prevent the occurrence of catastrophic overfitting. Although these methods provide a better understanding of catastrophic overfitting prevention, but still cannot essentially explain the problem of catastrophic overfitting. Moreover, these methods can improve the robustness of single-step AT models to some extent, but sacrifice a large amount of computational overhead and lose the efficient advantage of single-step AT, even up to the training time of multi-step AT.

3 Proposed Approach

3.1 Observation

To investigate catastrophic overfitting, we begin by recording the robust accuracy of FGSM AT on CIFAR-10 [9]. We evaluate the robust accuracy of the model against 50 steps PGD attacks with 10 random restarts (PGD-50-10) for step size $\alpha = 2/255$ and maximum perturbation $\epsilon = 8/255$. Figure 2 visualizes the accuracy and loss of the FGSM AT trained, FAST-FGSM AT trained, and PGD-7 AT trained model and evaluated against FGSM and PGD-50-10 attack during the training phase. As we can see, when FGSM AT and FAST-FGSM AT occur catastrophic overfitting around 30 and 180 epochs respectively, the robustness against PGD-50-10 attack of the model trained with FGSM AT and FAST-FGSM AT begin to drop suddenly, whereas the accuracy against FGSM increases rapidly. However, for the robust PGD-7 AT, the accuracy and loss of the model tend to stabilize after a certain number of epochs.

We maintain that the reason the models trained using FGSM AT suffer from catastrophic overfitting is that it is prone to learn spurious functions that fit the FGSM data distribution but have undefined behavior off the FGSM data manifold. Therefore, the FGSM AT is highly susceptible to overfitting due to a single-step adversarial perturbation, resulting in a sudden drop in the PGD robustness of the model, while the FGSM accuracy increases instantaneously. To study the differences in the performance of the models trained with FGSM AT and PGD-7 AT for evaluating at the FGSM and PGD adversarial examples, we utilize a distance function $\mathcal{L}$ to measure the difference between the output of the model evaluated at single-step and multi-step adversarial attacks. For a model that take inputs x and output logits $f(x)$, we have:

$$\mathcal{L}(f(x^{fgsm}), f(x^{pgd})), \tag{4}$$

where x^{fgsm} and x^{pgd} are adversarial examples crafted by FGSM and PGD-7, respectively. Here, we choose L_2 for $\mathcal{L}$. For a well-generalized and robustness model, we assume that the logit $f(x^{fgsm})$ and $f(x^{pgd})$ of the model evaluated at FGSM and PGD adversarial examples should be as similar as possible, i.e., $||f(x^{fgsm}) - f(x^{pgd})||_2$ should be very small.

To demonstrate our intuition, we firstly train several CIFAR-10 models using FGSM AT and PGD-7 for 200 epochs. For each model, we compute the difference between the output of the model evaluated at FGSM and PGD-7 adversarial examples by using Eq. 4, and performed data processing using a logarithmic function to visualize the differences more clearly, as shown in Fig. 3. In Fig. 3 (b), it can be observed that there is no significant difference in the logits from FGSM and PGD adversarial examples during the early phase of training, which matches our intuition. Once catastrophic overfitting occurs, the gap between the logit of the model evaluated at single-step and multi-step adversarial attacks are increasing rapidly around 30 and 180 epochs respectively, which is consistent with PGD loss. In contrast, the PGD-7 AT does not suffer catastrophic overfitting and the difference of the logit of the model is keeping stable. This phenomenon will also appear on the simple MNIST dataset [10], but it is not as clear as CIFAR-10, as shown in Fig. 3(a).

3.2 PGD Regularization

Based on the analysis in Sect. 3.1, the only FGSM adversarial loss is not enough for the model to learn the robust features of both single-step and multi-step adversarial examples. To solve this problem, inspired by [8], we use the logit pairing to encourage the model to learn robust internal representation of FGSM and PGD adversarial examples so that the logit outputs $f(x^{fgsm})$ and $f(x^{pgd})$ of the model for FGSM and PGD adversarial examples to be as similar as possible:

$$\lambda \frac{1}{m} \sum_{i=1}^{m} \mathcal{L}(f(x_i^{fgsm}; \theta), f(x_i^{pgd}; \theta)), \tag{5}$$

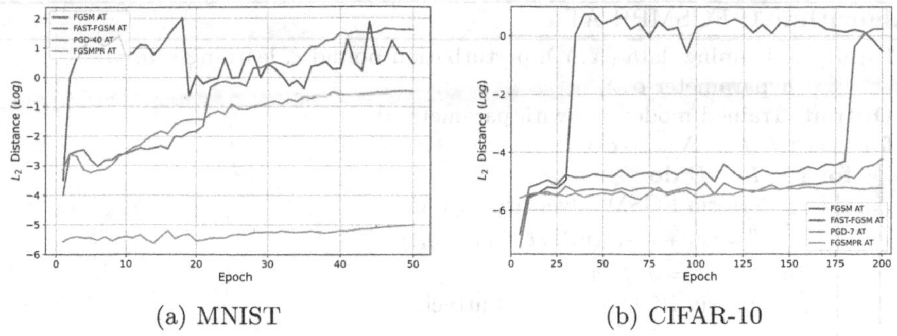

(a) MNIST (b) CIFAR-10

Fig. 3. Visualization of the $\mathcal{L}_2$ distance of logit of the FGSM AT trained, FAST-FGSM AT trained, PGD-7 AT trained model and evaluated against FGSM and PGD adversarial attack. (a) In MNIST, when the model is not robust, the difference in $\mathcal{L}_2$ distance starts to fluctuate, while PGD AT is relatively smooth. (b) In CIFAR10, FGSM AT and FAST-FGSM AT occurs catastrophic overfitting around 30 and 180 epochs, respectively, and is characterized by a rapid increase of L_2 distance.

where $\mathcal{L}$ is L_2 norm; x_i^{fgsm} and x_i^{pgd} are adversarial examples crafted by FGSM and PGD attacks, respectively; λ is a hyparameter to balance FGSM loss and PGD regularization item. Combining with the proposed regularization, the FGSM AT can learn a robustness model comparable with PGD-7 AT, as validated in Sect. 4.

We hold that PGD regularization works well because it provides an additional prior that regularizes the model toward a more accurate understanding of adversarial examples. If we train the model with only the single-step FGSM adversarial loss, it is prone to learn spurious functions that excessively fit the FGSM adversarial data distribution but have undefined behavior off the FGSM data manifold (e.g., multi-step adversarial examples). PGD regularization forces the explanations of the FGSM adversarial example and multi-step adversarial example to be similar. This is essentially a prior encouraging the model to learn logits that are a function of the truly significant features in the image and ignore the spurious features.

3.3 Training Route

The overall training procedure of the FGSMPR AT is summarized in Algorithm 1. We first perform FGSM adversarial attack to generate FGSM adversarial examples x_i^{fgsm} and compute FGSM AT loss $fgsm\_loss$ using cross-entropy. Then, we perform PGD adversarial attack for m examples, from a batch of natural examples, to generate m PGD adversarial examples. After generating FGSM and PGD adversarial examples, the regularization loss reg_loss of m FGSM and PGD adversarial examples are calculated using Eq. 5 and used as part of the total loss $total\_loss$. Finally, the parameter θ of the model is updated using a proper optimizer (e.g., stochastic gradient descent). The hyperparameter

Algorithm 1: FGSMPR AT

Input : Training data (X, Y), perturbation bound ϵ, learning rate γ, hyparameter α, λ.

Output: Trained model $f(\cdot)$ with parameter θ

for *epoch* $= 1 \ldots N_{epoch}$ **do**
  for $i = 1 \ldots B$ **do**
    // Perform FGSM adversarial attack
    $x_i^{fgsm} = x_i + \alpha \cdot \text{sign}(\nabla_\delta \ell(f_\theta(x_i), y_i))$
    $fgsm\_loss = J(f_\theta, x_i^{fgsm}, y_i)$
    // Perform PGD adversarial attack
    for $k = 1 \ldots K$ **do**
      $\delta = \delta + \alpha \cdot \text{sign}(\nabla_\delta \ell(f_\theta(x_i + \delta), y_i))$
      $\delta = \max(\min(\delta, \epsilon), -\epsilon))$
    end for
    $x_i^{pgd} = x_i + \delta$
    $reg\_loss = \lambda \frac{1}{m} \sum_{j=1}^{m} \mathcal{L}(f(x_{i,j}^{fgsm}; \theta), f(x_{i,j}^{pgd}; \theta))$
    $total\_loss = fgsm\_loss + reg\_loss$
    Update model parameter θ based on *total_loss*
  end for
end for
return $f(\cdot)$.

λ shall be properly chosen to balance FGSM loss $fgsm\_loss$ and PGD regularization reg_loss item. In practice, we take $\alpha = \epsilon/K$, $K = 3$ and $m = 1$. In other words, we only pick a single example from a batch for generating a PGD-3 adversarial example, which is then used for regularization to encourage the model to learn similar logit output. The experiments show that a single PGD adversarial example for regularization is enough to learn a robustness model.

4 Experiments

In this section, we demonstrate that the proposed FGSMPR is robust against strong PGD attacks. All experiments are run on a single RTX 2070, in which we use half-precision computation recommended in [19] to speed up the training of CIFAR-10 model, which was incorporated with the Apes amp package at the O1 optimization level for all CIFAR-10 experiments.

Attacks: We attack all models using PGD attacks with K iterations and 10 random restarts on both cross-entropy loss (PGD-K-10) and the Carlini-Wagner loss (CW-K-10) [4]. All PGD attacks used at evaluation for MNIST [10] are run with 10 random restarts for 20/40 iterations. All PGD attacks used at evaluation for CIFAR-10 [9] are run with 10 random restarts for 20/50 steps.

Perturbation: For MNIST, we set the maximum perturbation ϵ to 0.3 and the PGD step size α to 0.1. For CIFAR-10, we set the maximum perturbation ϵ to 8/255 and the PGD step size α to 2/255.

Table 1. Validation accuracy (%) and robustness of MNIST models trained with FGSM AT, FAST-FGSM AT, GradAlign AT, FREE AT, PGD-40 AT, FGSMPR AT without early stopping and the corresponding training time. All statistics are evaluated against PGD/CW attacks with 20/40 iterations and 10 random restarts for $\alpha = 0.1$, $\epsilon = 0.3$ over three independent runs. The bold indicates the best performance except for PGD-40 AT.

Method	Standard accuracy	PGD-20-10	PGD-40-10	CW-20-10	CW-40-10	Training time (s)
FGSM AT	97.53 ± 0.39	39.31 ± 20.68	12.45 ± 12.15	40.14 ± 20.64	13.46 ± 12.89	481.03 ± 0.81
FAST-FGSM AT	98.52 ± 0.34	42.60 ± 12.47	11.19 ± 6.52	43.41 ± 12.55	11.85 ± 7.26	491.24 ± 1.71
GradAlign AT	**99.05 ± 0.03**	91.42 ± 0.57	75.94 ± 3.23	91.23 ± 0.51	75.86 ± 3.16	633.96 ± 3.55
FREE AT	98.49 ± 0.05	92.90 ± 0.20	90.06 ± 0.36	92.70 ± 0.15	89.85 ± 0.32	**175.45 ± 1.99**
PGD-40 AT	99.16 ± 0.03	94.72 ± 0.08	92.52 ± 0.14	94.75 ± 0.03	92.65 ± 0.10	3652.39 ± 1.00
FGSMPR AT (ours)	98.35 ± 0.09	**93.77 ± 0.32**	**90.83 ± 0.49**	**93.65 ± 0.26**	**90.56 ± 0.55**	626.57 ± 1.68

Table 2. Validation accuracy (%) and robustness of CIFAR-10 models trained with FGSM AT, FAST-FGSM AT, GradAlign AT, FREE AT, PGD-7 AT, FGSMPR AT without early stopping and the corresponding training time. All statistics are evaluated against PGD/CW attacks with 20/50 iterations and 10 random restarts for $\alpha = 2/255$, $\epsilon = 8/255$ over three independent runs. The bold indicates the best performance except for PGD-7 AT.

Method	Standard accuracy	PGD-20-10	PGD-50-10	CW-20-10	CW-50-10	Training time (m)
FGSM AT	88.51 ± 1.27	0.01 ± 0.17	0.00 ± 0.00	0.01 ± 0.11	0.00 ± 0.00	119.04 ± 0.41
FAST-FGSM AT	**90.33 ± 0.42**	0.92 ± 0.49	0.32 ± 0.25	0.52 ± 0.30	00.17 ± 0.08	123.81 ± 0.18
GradAlign AT	82.82 ± 0.13	32.94 ± 0.83	32.50 ± 0.80	32.94 ± 0.83	32.52 ± 0.81	486.20 ± 0.67
FREE AT	82.32 ± 0.12	46.97 ± 0.05	46.07 ± 0.82	45.77 ± 0.23	45.64 ± 0.24	**61.94 ± 0.15**
PGD-7 AT	84.75 ± 0.87	48.33 ± 0.62	47.99 ± 0.66	47.80 ± 0.31	47.59 ± 0.38	493.41 ± 0.04
FGSMPR AT (ours)	83.31 ± 0.40	**47.59 ± 0.51**	**47.19 ± 0.42**	**46.98 ± 0.18**	**46.79 ± 0.20**	211.65 ± 0.61

Comparisions: We compare the performance of our proposed method (FGSMPR) with FGSM: standard FGSM AT [5]; FAST-FGSM AT: FGSM AT with a random initialization [19]; FREE AT: recently proposed single-step AT method [15]; GradAlign AT: recently proposed method solving catastrophic overfitting [1]; PGD-K AT: AT with a K iterations PGD attack [12].

Evaluation: We demonstrate that the performance of models against PGD-K-10/CW-K-10 adversarial attacks under white-box settings. For all experiments, the mean and standard deviation over three independent runs are reported.

4.1 Results on MNIST

First, we conduct a study to demonstrate that our proposed approach is highly working in MNIST benchmark dataset [10]. We train models for MNIST dataset with the same architecture used by [19], using FGSM AT, FAST-FGSM AT,

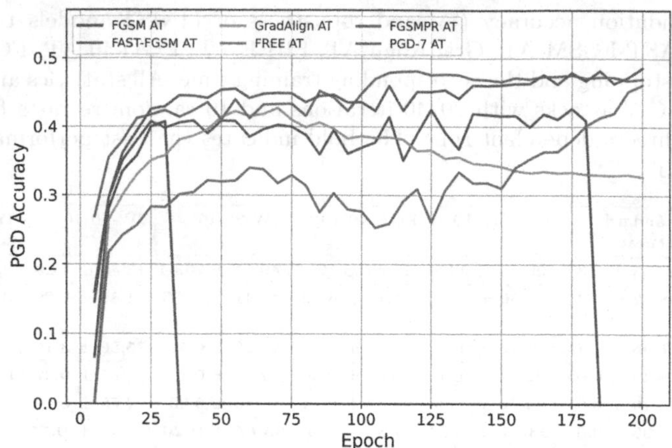

Fig. 4. Visualization of the accuracy of the CIFAR-10 model trained for FGSM AT, FAST-FGSM AT, GradAlign AT, FREE AT, PGD-7 AT, and FGSMPR AT. All the statistics are tested against 50 steps PGD attacks with 10 random restarts for $\alpha = 2/255$, $\epsilon = 8/255$. Catastrophic overfitting for the FGSM and FAST-FGSM AT occur around 30 and 180 epochs, respectively, and is characterized by a sudden drop in the PGD accuracy.

FREE AT, PGD-40 AT, FGSMPR AT. Except that the AT free replays each batch of $m = 8$ for a total of 7 epochs, all other models are trained for 50 epochs. For the proposed method, we set the hyparameter λ, K and m to $(0.1, 3, 1)$. The experimental results are provided in Table 1. It can be observed that our proposed FGSMPR AT is more robust against both PGD and CW attacks on the MNIST dataset than the GradAlign AT and FREE AT, and is second only to the PGD AT model with a small difference. In the course of testing the robustness of FAST-FGSM AT on the MNIST dataset, we found an interesting problem where increasing the number of MNIST training epochs to 50 also resulted in catastrophic overfitting, although this phenomenon was previously found only in CIFAR-10. Besides, the GradAlign AT [1] can keep the model from suffering catastrophic overfitting to some extent, but it is far inferior to other comparison methods in defending against the higher iteration adversarial attacks.

4.2 Results on CIFAR-10

To verify whether AT scheme suffers from catastrophic overfitting, we train 200 epoch for all CIFAR-10 models using the Preact ResNet-18 [7] architecture without early stopping, especially the FREE AT replays each batch $m = 8$ times for a total of 25 epochs as recommend in [15]. For the FGSMPR, we set the hyparameter λ, K and m to $(0.5, 3, 1)$. The experimental results are provided in Table 2. It can be observed that FGSMPR AT is quite similar to PGD-7 AT while our training time is half of PGD-7 AT. To demonstrate that the proposed FGSMPR does not suffer from catastrophic overfitting, we takes 211 min to

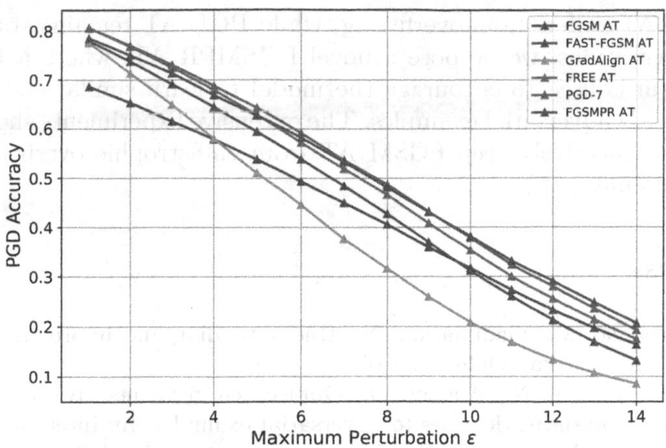

Fig. 5. Accuracy of the model trained for FGSM AT, FAST-FGSM AT, GradAlign AT, FREE AT, PGD-7 AT and FGSMPR AT with early stopping. All the statistics are evaluated against 50 steps PGD attacks with 10 random restarts for different l_∞-perturbation ϵ.

train a CIFAR-10 model for 200 epochs, which is longer than time for FREE AT. However, our method was able to achieve 46% robustness by training 30 epochs in only 30 min, which is half less than FREE AT. Further, we visualize the robustness of the training process of different AT method and tested against a 10 random restart PGD-50 attack, as shown in Fig. 4. It can be observed that the robustness of the FGSMPR against PGD has steadily increased, which is only 0.8% behind PGD-7 AT and does not suffer from catastrophic overfitting even when trained to 200 epochs. Instead, FAST-FGSM AT started to have a trend similar to PGD AT, but there is a sharp drop in robustness around 180 epochs when occuring catastrophic overfitting. The GradAlign AT was proposed to prevent the FGSM AT from catastrophic overfitting, but the accuracy still dropped by more than 10% and took more than two times longer compared to our FGSMPR AT. Besides, we also test the model's robustness under different l_∞ perturbation where all models are trained with early stopping. In the case of larger l_∞ perturbations, FGSMPR AT is essentially indistinguishable from PGD-7 AT, and even slightly better than PGD-7 AT, as shown in Fig. 5.

5 Conclusion

In this paper, we analyze and address the catastrophic overfitting in FGSM AT. We empirically show that FGSM AT is prone to learn spurious functions that fit the FGSM adversarial data distribution but have undefined behavior off the FGSM data manifold. We therefore exploit the difference behind the logits between the FGSM and PGD adversarial examples in the model trained with FGSM AT and PGD AT, where the logit becomes significantly different when FGSM AT suffers from overfitting, while PGD AT remains stable. Based on these observations, we propose a novel FGSMPR AT, where a PGD regularization term is used to encourage the model to learn similar embeddings of FGSM and PGD adversarial examples. The extensive experiments show that the FGSMPR can effectively keep FGSM AT from catastrophic overfitting with a low computational cost.

References

1. Andriushchenko, M., Flammarion, N.: Understanding and improving fast adversarial training. Virtual, Online (2020)
2. Athalye, A., Carlini, N., Wagner, D.: Obfuscated gradients give a false sense of security: circumventing defenses to adversarial examples. In: International conference on machine learning, pp. 274–283. Stockholm, Sweden (2018)
3. Buckman, J., Roy, A., Raffel, C., Goodfellow, I.: Thermometer encoding: one hot way to resist adversarial examples. In: International Conference on Learning Representations. Vancouver, BC, Canada (2018)
4. Carlini, N., Wagner, D.: Towards evaluating the robustness of neural networks. In: 2017 IEEE Symposium on Security and Privacy (sp), pp. 39–57. IEEE (2017)
5. Goodfellow, I.J., Shlens, J., Szegedy, C.: Explaining and harnessing adversarial examples. San Diego, CA, United states (2015)
6. Guo, C., Rana, M., Cisse, M., Van Der Maaten, L.: Countering adversarial images using input transformations. Vancouver, BC, Canada (2018)
7. He, K., Zhang, X., Ren, S., Sun, J.: Identity mappings in deep residual networks. In: Leibe, B., Matas, J., Sebe, N., Welling, M. (eds.) ECCV 2016. LNCS, vol. 9908, pp. 630–645. Springer, Cham (2016). https://doi.org/10.1007/978-3-319-46493-0_38
8. Kannan, H., Kurakin, A., Goodfellow, I.: Adversarial logit pairing (2018)
9. Krizhevsky, A., Hinton, G., et al.: Learning multiple layers of features from tiny images. https://www.cs.toronto.edu/ kriz/learning-features-2009-TR.pdf (2009)
10. LeCun, Y., Bottou, L., Bengio, Y., Haffner, P.: Gradient-based learning applied to document recognition. Proc. IEEE **86**(11), 2278–2324 (1998)
11. Li, B., Wang, S., Jana, S., Carin, L.: Towards understanding fast adversarial training. arXiv preprint arXiv:2006.03089 (2020)
12. Madry, A., Makelov, A., Schmidt, L., Tsipras, D., Vladu, A.: Towards deep learning models resistant to adversarial attacks (2018)
13. Metzen, J.H., Genewein, T., Fischer, V., Bischoff, B.: On detecting adversarial perturbations. Toulon, France (2017)
14. Narang, S., et al.: Mixed precision training. Vancouver, BC, Canada (2018)
15. Shafahi, A., et al.: Adversarial training for free! In: Advances in Neural Information Processing Systems, pp. 3358–3369 (2019)
16. Smith, L.N.: Cyclical learning rates for training neural networks. In: 2017 IEEE Winter Conference on Applications of Computer Vision (WACV), pp. 464–472. IEEE (2017)
17. Szegedy, C., et al.: Intriguing properties of neural networks. Banff, AB, Canada (2014)
18. Vivek, B., Babu, R.V.: Single-step adversarial training with dropout scheduling. In: 2020 IEEE/CVF Conference on Computer Vision and Pattern Recognition (CVPR), pp. 947–956. IEEE (2020)

19. Wong, E., Rice, L., Kolter, J.Z.: Fast is better than free: Revisiting adversarial training. Addis Ababa, Ethiopia (2020)
20. Zhang, D., Zhang, T., Lu, Y., Zhu, Z., Dong, B.: You only propagate once: accelerating adversarial training via maximal principle. In: Advances in Neural Information Processing Systems, pp. 227–238 (2019)

Texture-Guided U-Net for OCT-to-OCTA Generation

Ziyue Zhang[1], Zexuan Ji[1(✉)], Qiang Chen[1], Songtao Yuan[2], and Wen Fan[2]

[1] School of Computer Science and Engineering, Nanjing University of Science and Technology, Nanjing 210094, China
jizexuan@njust.edu.cn

[2] Department of Ophthalmology, The First Affiliated Hospital with Nanjing Medical University, Nanjing 210029, China

Abstract. As a new imaging modality, optical coherence tomography angiography (OCTA) can fully explore the characteristics of retinal blood flow. Considering the inconvenience of acquiring OCTA images and inevitable mechanical artifacts, we introduce deep learning to generate OCTA from OCT. In this paper, we propose a texture-guided down- and up-sampling model based on U-Net for OCT-to-OCTA generation. A novel texture-guided sampling block is proposed by combining the extracted texture features and content-adaptive convolutions. The corresponding down-sampling and up-sampling operations would preserve more textural details during the convolutions and deconvolutions, respectively. Then a deeply-supervised texture-guided U-Net is constructed by substituting the traditional convolution with the texture-guided sampling blocks. Moreover, the image Euclidean distance is utilized to construct the loss function, which is more robust to noise and could explore more useful similarities involved in OCT and OCTA images. The dataset containing paired OCT and OCTA images from 489 eyes diagnosed with various retinal diseases is used to evaluate the performance of the proposed network. The results based on cross validation experiments demonstrate the stability and superior performances of the proposed model comparing with state-of-the-art semantic segmentation models and GANs.

Keywords: Optical coherence tomography angiography · Generation · Deep learning

1 Introduction

As an important imaging modality, Optical coherence tomography (OCT) has become more and more popular in the evaluation and diagnosis of retinal dis-

The authors declare no conflicts of interest. This work was supported in part by National Science Foundation of China under Grants No. 62072241, in part by Natural Science Foundation of Jiangsu Province under Grant No. BK20180069, in part by Six talent peaks project in Jiangsu Province under Grant No. SWYY-056, and in part by National Institutes of Health Grant No. P30-EY026877.

© Springer Nature Switzerland AG 2021
H. Ma et al. (Eds.): PRCV 2021, LNCS 13022, pp. 42–52, 2021.
https://doi.org/10.1007/978-3-030-88013-2_4

ease. The technology of OCT is not only noninvasive but also can help imaging intra-ocular structures, which makes it rather valuable in practice. Thanks to OCT, optical coherence tomography angiography (OCTA) takes a step forward for diagnosing retinal disease. With the help of OCTA, a map of blood flow can be obtained by comparing the decorrelation signal between serial OCT B-scans, which are taken at the same location [1]. Therefore, comparing with fluorescein angiography imaging, OCTA is able to noninvasively visualize both superficial capillary and deep capillary of retina, which enables better diagnosis and detection of retinal disease free from side effects [2]. Theoretically, the OCT hardware is able to obtain the corresponding OCTA data. However, some hardware and software modifications on the existing OCT machines are needed to acquire the OCTA data [3]. Some OCTA scanning protocols easily introduce background noise and thus degrade OCTA image quality [4,5]. In addition, OCTA technology need to perform the acquisition multiply, which leads to motion artifacts and degradation in image quality [6]. Moreover, due to the time difference in the development of OCT and OCTA modalities, there are a large number of OCT images in the hospital lacking corresponding OCTA data. It is of great significance to explore the relationship between OCT and their corresponding OCTA images, thereby handily acquiring OCTA image from its counterpart.

Various OCTA algorithms have been proposed to measure OCT signal changes. However, traditional OCTA algorithms have a limited ability to make good use of the OCT signal variation [7]. Nowadays, deep learning shows strong capability in ophthalmology and achieves robust performances in detection of diabetic retinopathy, optic disc with glaucoma, macular oedema and age-related macular degeneration [8]. Although it is inconvenient to obtain OCTA images, the similar structure can explore the relationship between OCTA and OCT images. This inspires researchers to explore the potential of deep learning to generate OCTA images from the corresponding OCT images. Liu et al. [9] employed a deep learning based method for OCTA predicting on the datasets, which are generated by a conventional method. And the results demonstrated that deep learning has the ability to surpass traditional methods. According to our experience, there are two main methods for cross-modal image-to-image translation, which are Generative adversarial networks (GANs) based methods and segmentation based method. Generative adversarial networks [10–15] (GANs) are widely used for image generation and image-to-image translation. Considering that OCT and OCTA images are spatially aligned, the GANs [7,16] has been designed for paired images to perform cross-modal translation. However, it has been proven that GAN-generated ones, share some common systematic flaws, which prevents GANs from achieving realistic image synthesis [17].

The other method for cross-modal translation is segmentation based method. U-Net [18] is a famous network with the structure of encoder-decoder and is widely used for medical images segmentation. Lee et al. [3] employed U-Net to generate blood flow from single OCT images, whose results are significantly superior than experts and clinicians. Yang et al. [19] utilized a fovea attention mechanism together with a residual neural network to visualize capillaries around the foveal avascular zone better. Down-sampling and up-sampling are inevitable for encoder-decoder based models to produce the output which have the same size with the input. However, sampling is the primary cause of lost details. Except for preserving details by simple concatenation like U-Net, some other methods focus on local spatial changes while sampling [20–23]. Considering that rich texture information in the input medical images will be missing during convolutions, we combine the extracted texture features and content-adaptive convolutions to guide U-Net to generate more detailed images.

Commonly used metrics for evaluating similarity between images are mean-square error (MSE), structural similarity (SSIM) and peak signal-to-noise ratio. These metrics evaluate pixel-to-pixel difference and are vulnerable to noise. Due to OCT and OCTA images are naturally highly noisy, it is inappropriate to employ these pixel-to-pixel metrics as loss function. Image Euclidean Distance (IMED) [24] measures the spatial relationships of pixels, which is more robust to small perturbations. IMED is reasonable and agrees with human vision perception for image evaluation. The loss function of U-Net is cross entropy loss, which is commonly used for image segmentation tasks. We replace it with IMED loss to guide U-Net to generate OCTA from OCT images.

Consequently, the main contributions of this study are summarized as follows:

- A novel texture-guided sampling block is proposed by combining the extracted texture features and content-adaptive convolutions, where the weights of convolution kernels are multiplied by learnable textural features extracted from input images. Therefore, the corresponding down-sampling and up-sampling operations would preserve more textural details during the convolutions and deconvolutions, respectively. Then a deeply-supervised texture-guided U-Net is constructed by substituting the traditional convolution with the texture-guided sampling blocks.
- The image Euclidean distance (IMED) is utilized to construct the loss function, which is more robust to noise and could explore more useful similarities involved in OCT and OCTA images.
- We evaluate the performance of our method on a large dataset collected from Nanjing Provincial People's Hospital between March 2018 and September 2019. A 3-fold cross validation is performed. The results based on cross validation experiments demonstrate the stability and superior performances of the proposed model compared with state-of-the-art semantic segmentation models and GANs.

2 Method

CNNs are made up of convolutions of which the weights are spatially shared. [22] proposed a pixel-adaptive convolution (PAC), which simply and effectively introduced pixel-level features to standard convolutions. The filter weights in PAC are multiplied with a kernel, which are spatially varying and obtained from local pixel features. Mostayed et al. [23] introduced an economical solution, which is eliminating the concatenation operations in U-Net and using the

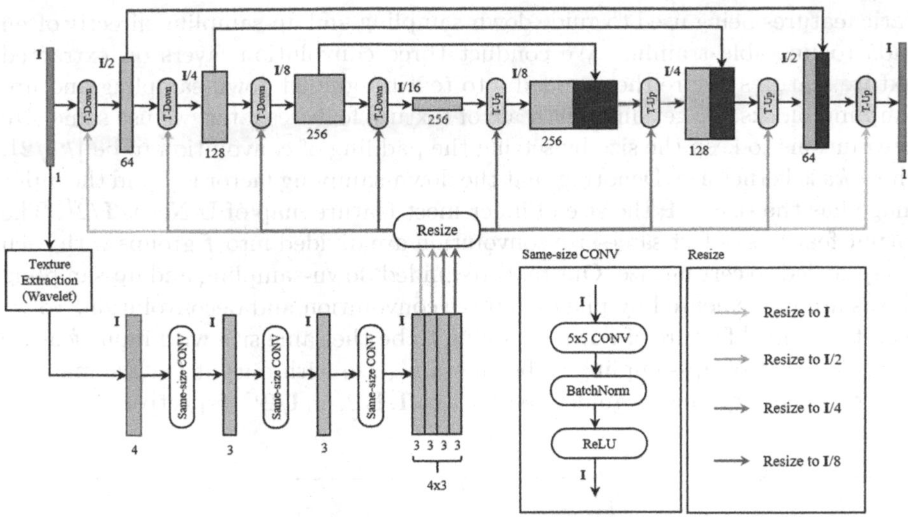

Fig. 1. The workflow of texture-guided down-sampling and up-sampling based on U-Net. The architecture consists of two parts, which is preprocessing of textural features (below) and modified U-Net (above). For convenience, we set down-sampling factor f to be 4. In the modified U-Net, we replace the standard convolution and deconvolution layers with texture-guided down-sampling (T-Down block) and up-sampling (T-Up block).

encoder features as guiding features. However, this architecture is efficient with limited input image size and cannot make good use of medical images with high resolution. In medical images, texture analysis is regarded as a useful tool to distinguish between different pathological areas, and texture information is proven to be more valuable and effective than human vision [25]. Thus we combine the texture feature and pixel-adaptive convolution to guide U-Net to generate more detailed images. We propose a deeply-supervised U-Net substituting the traditional convolution for a pixel-adaptive convolution, where the weights of convolution kernels are multiplied by learnable textural features extracted from input images. Figure 1 depicts the workflow of our texture-guided U-Net. The framework includes the preprocessing of textural features and U-Net with pixel-adaptive convolution and deconvolution.

We first conduct texture feature extraction on the input images, which aims at guiding the process of both down-sampling and up-sampling with more detailed and latent feature. In this paper, we utilize discrete wavelet transform, which has the advantage of capturing localized frequency and spatial information [26]. Notably, our texture-guided method is a rather generic framework, so any particular pixel-based texture extraction method, even edge, color and line features, can be applied to preserve detail information while generation.

The results of texture extraction are reasonable to visual perception, like low- and high-frequency components obtained from wavelet transform. However, static features being used to guide down-sampling and up-sampling directly often leads to unstable training. We conduct three convolution layers on extracted texture features before they are fed into texture-guided down-sampling and up-sampling blocks. To get different scale of texture features later, we use same-size convolutions to keep the size by setting the padding of convolution to be $\lfloor ks/2 \rfloor$, where ks is kernel size. Denoting that the down-sampling factor is f and the input image has the size of $\mathbf{I}$, the size of inner-most feature map of U-Net is $\mathbf{I}/2^f$. The output features of last same-size convolution are divided into f groups with each group scaled to certain size. Our texture-guided down-sampling and up-sampling blocks are implemented by pixel-adaptive convolution and deconvolution. So we need the guided feature of down-sampling to be the same size with input feature map, and that of up-sampling to be the same size with output feature map. So we resize the f groups of guided features to $\mathbf{I}, \mathbf{I}/2, ..., \mathbf{I}/2^f$ respectively.

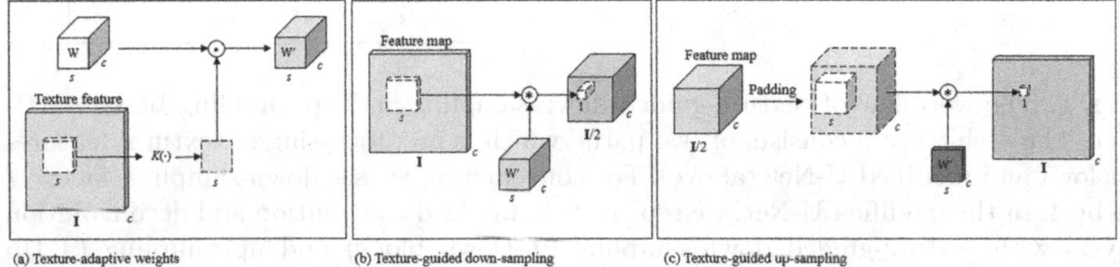

Fig. 2. The texture-adaptive weights (a) and texture-guided down-sampling (b) and up-sampling (c) blocks. The blue cube denotes extracted texture feature with size $\mathbf{I}$ and channel c. Each $s \times s$ window is compressed to single channel by kernel function, like Gaussian. With each channel in weights multiplied by single channel guidance (gray dashed square), weights vary from window to window. For texture-guided down-sampling (b) and up-sampling (c) blocks, we take the down-sampling from $\mathbf{I}$ to $\mathbf{I}/2$ and the inverse up-sampling for examples. This is accomplished by standard convolution and deconvolution with texture-guided weights (red and yellow cubes) which are derived from blocks in (a) (Color figure online).

The preprocessing of textural features outputs learnable texture features which are then fed into pixel-adaptive convolution and deconvolution.

The standard spatial convolution with image features $\mathbf{v} = (\mathbf{v}_1, ..., \mathbf{v}_n), \mathbf{v}_i \in \mathbb{R}^c$ and weights $\mathbf{W} \in \mathbb{R}^{c' \times c \times s \times s}$ can be defined as

$$\mathbf{v}'_i = \sum_{j \in \Omega(i)} \mathbf{W}[\mathbf{p}_i - \mathbf{p}_j]\mathbf{v}_j + \mathbf{b} \tag{1}$$

where $\mathbf{p}_i = (x, y)^T$ denotes pixel coordinates, $\Omega(\cdot)$ denotes an $s \times s$ convolution window, as shown in Fig. 2 with the dashed box. And $\mathbf{b} \in \mathbb{R}^{c'}$ denotes biases. Following [22], $[\mathbf{p}_i - \mathbf{p}_j]$ indexes the spatial dimension of an array with a two-dimensional spatial offset. Considering that standard convolution uses spatially shared weights which ignore adaptation of each pixel, we use extracted texture features as guidance to make proper adjustment to the weights. Each $s \times s$ window in the extracted texture features is compressed to single channel by kernel function, like Gaussian. With each channel in weights multiplied by single channel guidance, weights vary from window to window. When the texture-adaptive weights are utilized in standard convolution and deconvolution, we get the texture-guided down- and up-sampling blocks, as shown in Fig. 2. Since the spatially varying kernel function $K \in \mathbb{R}^{c' \times c \times s \times s}$ is utilized to modify the invariant convolution, the convolution with kernel obtained from pixel features can be written as [22]

$$\mathbf{v}'_i = \sum_{j \in \Omega(i)} K(\mathbf{f}_i, \mathbf{f}_j)\mathbf{W}[\mathbf{p}_i - \mathbf{p}_j]\mathbf{v}_j + \mathbf{b} \tag{2}$$

where K is a Gaussian kernel function.

Since U-Net [18] is a widely-used and acknowledged image segmentation network, which contains couples of down-sampling and up-sampling operations, we use U-Net as our backbone. Similar with any other convolution-based networks, U-Net makes adjustment to channels in the purpose of preserving details. Our texture-guided sampling focuses on pixels, thereby introducing extracted texture features or manual features at each pixel. Compared to PacNet [22], we make use of the original image to get guided texture features by themselves instead of depending on paired extra modal. It should be noted that self-extracted features not only bring in latent information of original images, but also meet the requirement of pixel pairing at the same time.

While Euclidean distance is known as the most popular image metrics, traditional Euclidean distance and most of its variants are inappropriate for evaluating image distance. Image Euclidean Distance (IMED) [24] measures the spatial relationships of pixels, which is more robust to small perturbations. IMED is reasonable and agrees with human vision perception for image evaluation.

Let x, y be two $M \times N$ images, the Euclidean distance with metric coefficients $d_E^2(x, y)$ is written by

$$d_E^2(x, y) = (x - y)^T G(x - y) \tag{3}$$

where $G = (g_{ij})_{MN \times MN}$ denotes metric matrix. When G is a identity matrix, Eq. (3) denotes the traditional Euclidean distance. Similarly, it becomes the weighted Euclidean distance if G is a diagonal matrix. Following [24], we also utilize the Gaussian function to construct the metric coefficients. The IMED metric is able to provide intuitively reasonable results, and we use this metric as loss function.

3 Experiments

3.1 Dataset and Metrics

In this paper, a large dataset collected from Nanjing Provincial People's Hospital between March 2018 and September 2019 was used to evaluate the performance of the proposed network. The dataset contains 489 projects with 6 mm × 6 mm FOV. The data were collected using a commercial 70 kHz spectral-domain OCT system with a center wavelength of 840 nm (RTVue-XR, Optovue, CA). The dataset contains paired OCT and OCTA images from 489 eyes and can be categorized into NORMAL, OTHERS and various retinal diseases, including Age-related Macular Degeneration (AMD), Choroidal Neovascularization (CNV), Central Serous Chorioretinopathy (CSC), Diabetic Retinopathy (DR) and Retinal Vein Occlusion (RVO). Since 400 B-scans are collected for each eye, the dataset includes 195600 OCT and OCTA images each. We performed a 3-fold cross validation based on eyes, thus each train set and test set contain 326 and 163 eyes respectively.

We utilized U-Net as the backbone of the generator and wavelet transform as texture extraction method. The input of U-Net is OCT images with the original size 640 × 400 and the feature map will be down-sampled to 40 × 25 at bottleneck with f set to 4. We utilized Adam solver [27] to optimize the proposed texture-guided U-net and IMED [24] as loss function. We set the batch size to 1 and initialized the learning rate as 0.0002.

The evaluation metrics include mean-square error (MSE), structural similarity (SSIM) [28] and feature similarity (FSIM) [29]. All the metrics are evaluated with the ground truth (GT), averaged over all test B-scans. While MSE focuses on average difference of two images, SSIM focuses on the structural information between two images. Because luminance and contrast vary a lot, SSIM utilizes the local metrics to evaluate. FSIM [29] employs two complementary metrics, phase congruency and gradient magnitude, to compute the local similarity map.

3.2 Results

The intensity of each B-scan ranges from 0 to 255. Mean MSE of generated scans on three folds are 6.858, 6.950 and 7.001, respectively, which reveals that our model performed stably.

The intensity of each B-scan ranges from 0 to 255. Mean MSE of generated scans on three folds are 6.858, 6.950 and 7.001, respectively, which reveals that our model performed stably. Compared with other methods of segmentation and GANs, our method achieved minimum mean and var of MSE and maximum SSIM and FSIM, as shown in Table 1. Note that U-Net is specially designed for segmenting detailed medical images and other methods, like RefineNet [30], DeepLabv3+ [31] and FCN [32], are for general segmentation tasks. Though the overall performance of U-Net is comparable, the corresponding MSE fluctuates a lot. The variance of U-Net is 2.885, and ours keep it low at 1.714, which proves our model to be stable and reliable.

Figure 3 presents comparisons on several methods of segmentation and GAN. We present OCT, GT OCTA and generated OCTA projections of one case for each category. The generated results are from test datasets and are projected by sum. While generation results of segmentation methods share similar structures with the ground-truth, there still exist the situation of lost details. RefineNet [30], for example, exploits various levels of detail from the scale of 1/32 to 1/4.

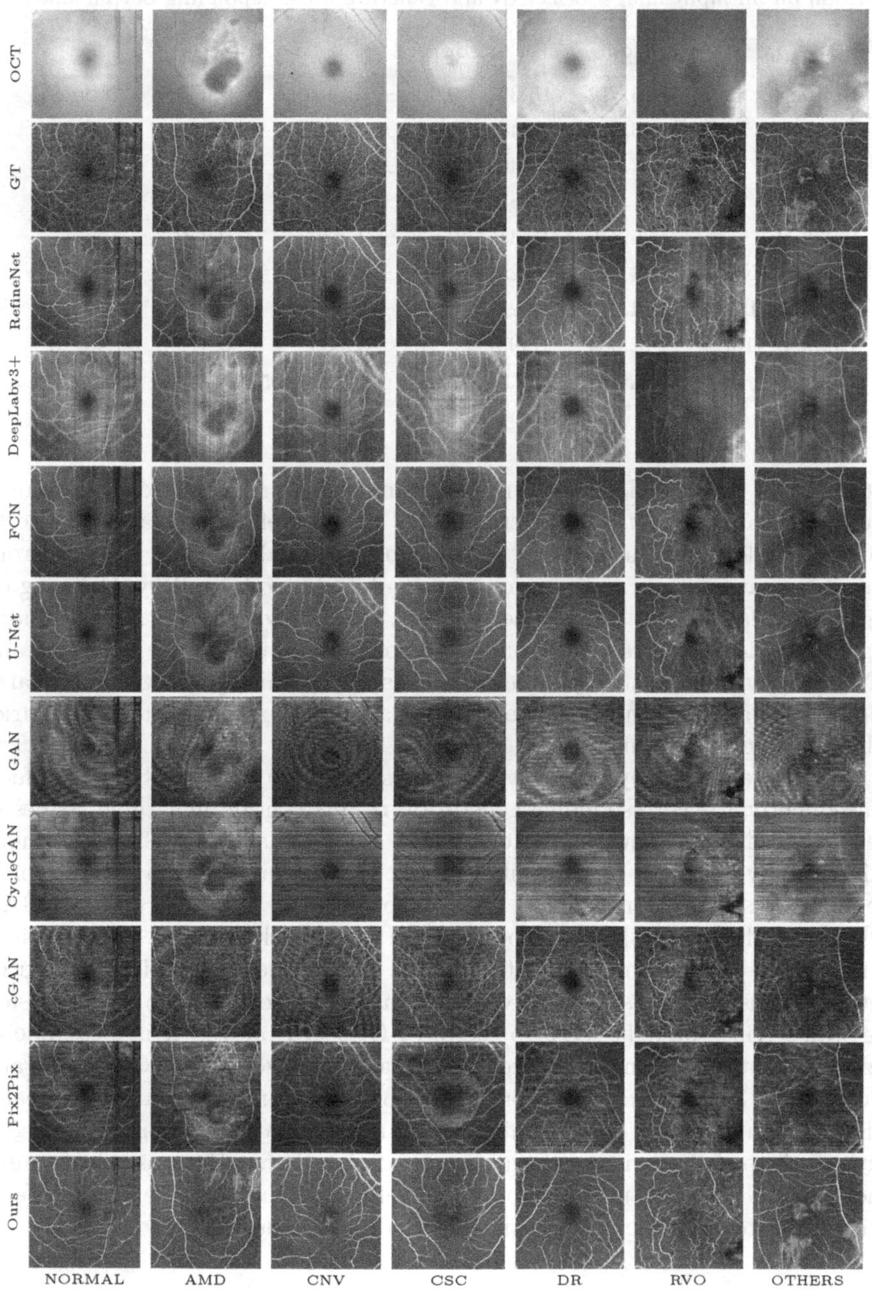

Fig. 3. Comparisons on several methods of segmentation and GAN. We present OCT, GT OCTA and generated OCTA projections of one case for each category.

Table 1. Comparison on other methods of segmentation and GAN. Following [15], we condition on an input image for cGAN and generate a corresponding output image.

Methods	MSE	SSIM	FSIM
RefineNet [30]	15.612 ± 15.377	0.908 ± 3.667e–4	0.963 ± 1.100e–3
DeepLabv3+ [31]	8.911 ± 2.344	0.929 ± 4.947e–5	0.944 ± 1.700e–3
FCN [32]	7.896 ± 2.740	0.938 ± 6.958e–5	0.976 ± 2.587e–5
U-Net [3]	7.925 ± 2.885	0.941 ± 6.501e–5	0.977 ± 2.315e–5
GAN [10]	26.750 ± 19.317	0.870 ± 1.839e–2	0.959 ± 6.593e–5
CycleGAN [13]	21.999 ± 12.292	0.894 ± 1.032e–4	0.957 ± 8.469e–5
cGAN [14]	14.252 ± 4.622	0.912 ± 9.435e–5	0.972 ± 2.509e–5
Pix2Pix [15]	12.054 ± 10.957	0.922 ± 1.689e–4	0.972 ± 3.865e–5
Ours	**6.858 ± 1.714**	**0.947 ± 4.496e–5**	**0.978 ± 2.496e–5**

Details could be spoiled when fusing both small and large scales of feature map to obtain a high-resolution prediction. This makes RefineNet inappropriate to fulfill the task of natural textures generations. DeepLabv3+ [31] applies atrous convolution at multiple scales which leads to fuzzy blood capillary. Focusing on object boundaries from a macro perspective, DeepLabv3+ [31] is also incapable to generate rich textures. Traditional segmentation networks, like FCN [32] and U-Net [18], achieve relatively detailed results. They fail to manage blurry large blood vessels and broken small blood vessels, and our model keeps the boundaries of blood vessels sharp and clear.

B-scans generated by GAN based models suffer from checkerboard artifact. Consequently, the corresponding generation results contain inevitable stripes in the projected blood flow maps. It is worth noting that some GANs methods which heavily depend on the distribution of the data tend to reverse the color of the blood vessels in the flow maps. For example, the flow maps obtained by GAN [10] and CycleGAN [13] mark blood vessels with black (see Fig. 3), yet others including the ground-truth mark them with white. These kind of unsupervised methods focus on the distribution which is an advantage for image style transfer, like transferring the light OCT to the dark OCTA. However, it is incapable to seize the subtle differences between the images. Consequently, GAN [10] and CycleGAN [13] suffer from inferior generation quality most. cGAN [14] greatly reduces the artifacts by conditioning on extra information, as shown in Fig. 3. With the help of supervision information, pix2pix achieves the most ideal results among four GAN based models. Comparatively, our results are free from artifacts which indicates that our model can achieve desirable performance.

4 Conclusion

In this paper, we presented a texture-guided U-Net architecture which is able to generate more detailed images by texture-guided down- and up-sampling and achieves very good performance on generation of retinal flow maps. Visual results of generated OCTA images demonstrate that the proposed model can accurately explore the unseen features of OCT and translate them into blood flow signals. While our main counterpart [3] costs 6 days of training time, our texture-guided U-Net only takes a very prominent training time of 4 h each fold to achieve comparable and stable results. What's more, the efficient space consumption of 2.290M makes our texture-guided U-Net superior to embed in commercial medical systems. The architecture provides an efficient way to generate inaccessible and paired images, which will be investigated as our future work.

References

1. de Carlo, T.E., Romano, A., Waheed, N.K., Duker, J.S.: A review of optical coherence tomography angiography (octa). Int. J. Retina Vitreous **1**(1), 5 (2015). https://doi.org/10.1186/s40942-015-0005-8
2. Dsw, T., Gsw, T., Agrawal, R., et al.: Optical coherence tomographic angiography in type 2 diabetes and diabetic retinopathy, JAMA Ophthalmol. **135**(4), 306–312 (2017). https://doi.org/10.1001/jamaophthalmol.2016.5877
3. Lee, C.S., et al.: Generating retinal flow maps from structural optical coherence tomography with artificial intelligence, CoRR abs/1802.08925 (2018). arXiv:1802.08925
4. Rabiolo, A., et al.: Macular perfusion parameters in different angiocube sizes: does the size matter in quantitative optical coherence tomography angiography? Invest. Opthalmol. Vis. Sci. **59**, 231 (2018). https://doi.org/10.1167/iovs.17-22359
5. Kadomoto, S., Uji, A., Muraoka, Y., Akagi, T., Tsujikawa, A.: Enhanced visualization of retinal microvasculature in optical coherence tomography angiography imaging via deep learning. J. Clin. Med. **9**, 1322 (2020). https://doi.org/10.3390/jcm9051322
6. Zhang, Q., et al.: Wide-field optical coherence tomography based microangiography for retinal imaging. Sci. Rep. **6**, 22017 (2016). https://doi.org/10.1038/srep22017
7. Jiang, Z., et al.: Comparative study of deep learning models for optical coherence tomography angiography. Biomed. Opt. Express **11**(3), 1580–1597 (2020). https://doi.org/10.1364/BOE.387807
8. Ting, D.: Artificial intelligence and deep learning in ophthalmology, Br. J. Ophthalmol. **103** (2018) bjophthalmol-2018. https://doi.org/10.1136/bjophthalmol-2018-313173
9. Xi, L.: A deep learning based pipeline for optical coherence tomography angiography. J. Biophotonics **12** (2019). https://doi.org/10.1002/jbio.201900008
10. Goodfellow, I.J.: Generative adversarial networks (2014). arXiv:1406.2661
11. Arjovsky, M., Chintala, S., Bottou, L.: Wasserstein GAN (2017). arXiv:1701.07875
12. Radford, M., Metz, L., Chintala, S.: Unsupervised representation learning with deep convolutional generative adversarial networks (2015). arXiv:1511.06434
13. Zhu, J.-Y., Park, T., Isola, P., Efros, A.A.: Unpaired image-to-image translation using cycle-consistent adversarial networks (2017). arXiv:1703.10593
14. Zhu, J.-Y., Park, T., Isola, P., Efros, A.A.: Unpaired image-to-image translation using cycle-consistent adversarial networks (2017). arXiv:1703.10593
15. Isola, P., Zhu, J.-Y., Zhou, T., Efros, A.A.: Image-to-image translation with conditional adversarial networks (2016). arXiv:1611.07004

16. Li, P.L., et al.: Deep learning algorithm for generating optical coherence tomography angiography (OCTA) maps of the retinal vasculature. In: Zelinski, M.E., Taha, T.M., Howe, J., Awwal, A.A.S., Iftekharuddin, K.M. (eds.), Applications of Machine Learning 2020, vol. 11511, International Society for Optics and Photonics, SPIE, 2020, pp. 39–49. https://doi.org/10.1117/12.2568629
17. Wang, S.-Y., Wang, O., Zhang, R., Owens, A., Efros, A.A.: CNN-generated images are surprisingly easy to spot... for now (2019). arXiv:1912.11035
18. Ronneberger, O., Fischer, P., Brox, T.: U-net: Convolutional networks for biomedical image segmentation, CoRR abs/1505.04597 (2015). arXiv:1505.04597
19. Yang, J., Liu, P., Duan, L., Hu, Y., Liu, J.: Deep learning enables extraction of capillary-level angiograms from single oct volume (2019). arXiv:1906.07091
20. Saeedan, F., Weber, N., Goesele, M., Roth, S.: Detail-preserving pooling in deep networks, CoRR abs/1804.04076 (2018). arXiv:1804.04076
21. Weber, N., Waechter, M., Amend, S.C., Guthe, S., Goesele, M.: Rapid, detail-preserving image downscaling, ACM Trans. Graph. **35** (6) (2016). https://doi.org/10.1145/2980179.2980239
22. Su, H., Jampani, V., Sun, D., Gallo, O., Learned-Miller, E.G., Kautz, J.: Pixel-adaptive convolutional neural networks, CoRR abs/1904.05373 (2019). arXiv:1904.05373
23. Mostayed, A., Wee, W., Zhou, X.: Content-adaptive u-net architecture for medical image segmentation. In: International Conference on Computational Science and Computational Intelligence (CSCI), pp. 698–702 (2019)
24. Wang, L., Zhang, Y., Feng, J.: On the Euclidean distance of images. IEEE Trans. Pattern Anal. Mach. Intell. **27**(8), 1334–1339 (2005)
25. Nailon, W.H.: Texture analysis methods for medical image characterisation. Biomed. Imaging **75**, 100 (2010)
26. Humeau-Heurtier, A.: Texture feature extraction methods: a survey. IEEE Access **7**, 8975–9000 (2019)
27. Kingma, D.P., Ba, J.: Adam: A method for stochastic optimization (2014). arXiv:1412.6980
28. Wang, Z., Bovik, A.C., Sheikh, H.R., Simoncelli, E.P.: Image quality assessment: from error visibility to structural similarity. IEEE Trans. Image Process. **13**(4), 600–612 (2004)
29. Zhang, L., Zhang, L., Mou, X., Zhang, D.: FSIM: a feature similarity index for image quality assessment. IEEE Trans. Image Process. **20**(8), 2378–2386 (2011)
30. Lin, G., Milan, A., Shen, C., Reid, I.: Refinenet: Multi-path refinement networks for high-resolution semantic segmentation (2016). arXiv:1611.06612
31. Chen, L.-C., Zhu, Y., Papandreou, G., Schroff, F., Adam, H.: Encoder-decoder with atrous separable convolution for semantic image segmentation (2018). arXiv:1802.02611
32. Long, J., Shelhamer, E., Darrell, T.: Fully convolutional networks for semantic segmentation (2014). arXiv:1411.4038

Learning Key Actors and Their Interactions for Group Activity Recognition

Yutai Duan and Jianming Wang(✉)

TianGong University, Tianjin 300387, China
wangjianming@tiangong.edu.cn

Abstract. Group activity recognition is a challenging task. Group activities usually involves many actors, while only some key actors play a decisive role in group activity recognition. Therefore, extraction of key actors and their interactions is an important problem in group activity recognition. To tackle this problem, we propose a new method based on graph convolutional layers and self-attention mechanisms to extract the Subgraphs of the Actor Relation Graph (SARG). SARG is a scene representation that only contains key actors and their interactions, which is used to enhance the importance of key actors in each group activity. First, the actor relation graph was generated via the appearance and location information of the actors; it was further analyzed by using a graph convolutional layer. Second, we use the graph convolutional layer to generate the self-attention features for each participant and extract the actor relation subgraphs that can ascertain group activities. Finally, we fuse actor relation subgraphs, actor relation graphs and original features to recognize group activities. We evaluate our model over two datasets: the collective activity dataset and the volleyball dataset. SARG has an average improvement of 4%, compared to 8 benchmarks.

Keywords: Group activity recognition · Graph convolution · Subgraph extraction

1 Introduction

Group activity recognition is an important task, often with many people active in the scene but only a small subset contributing to an actual event [1]. Therefore, extracting key actors is a crucial and challenging problem in group activity recognition [2,3]. In sports video analysis and video surveillance, the model should always focus on the key actors. For example, in Fig. 1(a), group activity is only defined by looking at the actions of actors 1,2 and 3. However, other actors in the same frame, such as actors 4,5 and 6 in Fig. 1(a), often have the same action labels, such as standing or waiting, but are not as important. It is crucial for group activity recognition that modeling extracts key actors and their interactions, which is shown in Figs. 1(b) and 1(c). However, the dataset does

© Springer Nature Switzerland AG 2021
H. Ma et al. (Eds.): PRCV 2021, LNCS 13022, pp. 53–65, 2021.
https://doi.org/10.1007/978-3-030-88013-2_5

not supply the model with any information about the importance of individual actors. Therefore, designing a method that can extract information about key actors is a challenging problem.

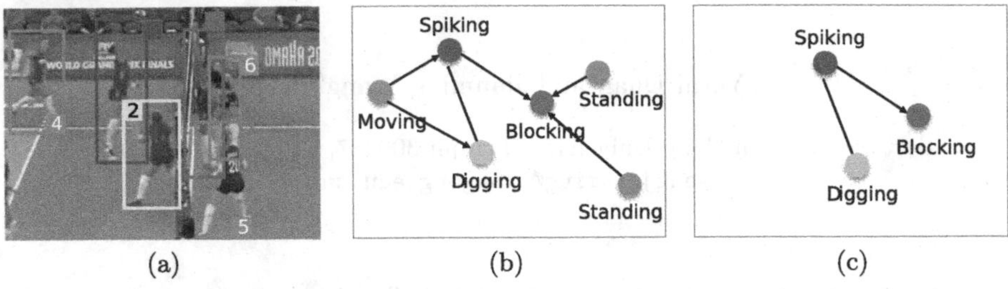

(a) (b) (c)

Fig. 1. Group activities are often determined by a part of key actors and their interactions. Our model performs group activity reasoning by extracting actor relationship subgraph and filtering irrelevant actors.

To tackle this problem, we propose a new method to extract the actor relation subgraph, creating a scene representation that only contains the key actors and their interactions. Our method is inspired by [4,5], which extracts hierarchical structure in graph classification tasks. Specifically, based on the method of [4], we first construct an actor relation graph (ARG), which reflects the relationship of various positions and appearance among actors. ARG is supplemented with a graph convolutional layer (GCN) to generate whole scene representation. In the second step, we generate action representation vectors for each actor. Next, a graph convolution layer is added to generate the self-attention score of each actor. Furthermore, we extract the subgraph of the actor graph according to the self-attention score, to capture the key actors and their interactions. Finally, actor relation subgraphs, actor relation graphs and original features are combined for group activity recognition.

In summary, the contributions of this paper can be summarized as: (1) We propose a novel actor relation subgraph extracting framework for group activity recognition, by abstracting group activity recognition as a graph classification task. (2) We designed multiple model variants and provided ablation studies, demonstrating that Subgraphs of the Actor Relation Graph (SARG) can improve the performance of the model and offer additional information. (3) We evaluate our model using two datasets: the collective activity dataset and the volleyball dataset. SARG has an average improvement of 4%, compared to 8 benchmarks.

2 Related Work

2.1 Group Activity Recognition

Group activity recognition is an important topic in video understanding [2,3], which has received more and more attention in recent years. Group activity recognition has many applications, such as video surveillance and sports video analysis. Different from the action recognition of individuals, group activity recognition is based on the comprehension of individual actions while concurrently inferring the spatiotemporal connections between actors to complete the recognition of group activities [6–8].

Group activity recognition uses an image as holistic input and uses a deep model to extract information for classification. The application of deep learning technology [9] has effectively improved the model performance of group activity recognition. In recent years, some approaches have demonstrated the positive influence of interaction networks on actors in group activity recognition [8]; however, many of the methods are not flexible because a manual construction is required in advance. Other methods use LSTM, RNN, or complex message propagation methods [10,11], resulting in a large amount of computational cost.

2.2 Graph Neural Networks

In recent years, because most conventional convolution methods cannot process data in non-Euclidean spaces, generalizing a convolution operator to graph data has become an interesting topic.

[12,13] proposes to use GCN for semi-supervised node classification. For graph-level problems, the graph pooling layer [5,14] provides sampling strategies and introduces new parameters to fit the data. Meanwhile, pooling layers are also considered to be effective in extracting hierarchical structures. In this work, we use a graph convolution layer to generate the high-level representation for graph, and then use graph pooling layers to extract subgraphs.

3 Approach and Framework

3.1 Preliminaries

Our goal is to identify group activities by explicitly exploiting the information of key actors and their interactions. Therefore, we generate scene representations by extracting the SARG. We begin by extracting image features, generating features and extracting the bounding box vector for each actor. Then, we construct the ARG and supplement it with GCN layers. We follow the strategy of ARG construction used in [4]. The next step is to use the method we designed, namely, to extract the SARG. Finally, we design a series of feature fusing methods to fuse the original information, ARG, and SARG to complete the group activity recognition process. We just described a brief introduction to the feature extraction method, the ARG construction strategy and using GCN to learn ARG. In Sects. 3.2 and 3.3, we will focus on how to extract subgraphs and fuse multi-scale features.

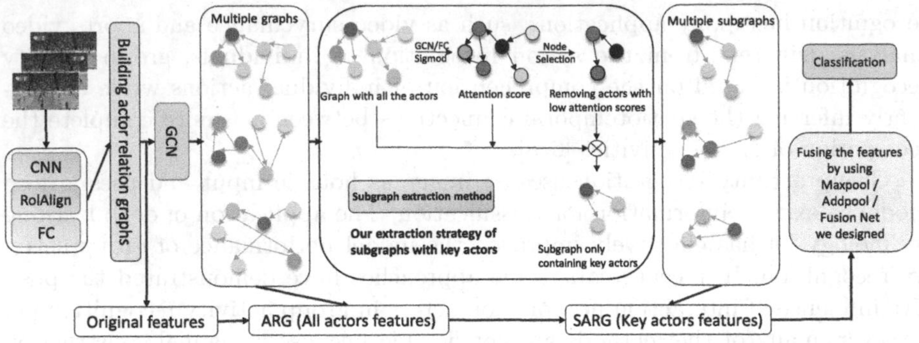

Fig. 2. An overview of our network framework for group activity recognition.

Feature Extraction. We first sample a fixed set of K frames from a given video sequence clip and generate the actor's feature vector. We use VGG [15] or Inception-v3 [16] to extract a multi-scale feature map for each frame. Roialign [17] is used to extract the bounding box for each actor. To align the feature dimension, we use a full connection layer to obtain d-dimensional features for each actor. The total number of actors appearing in K frames is N, and the feature vector of N actors are concatenated to obtain the feature matrix $\mathbf{X} \in \mathbb{R}^{N\times f}$ of the actor.

ARG Construction Strategy. We follow the ARG construction strategy $\mathbf{G}(\mathbf{A}, \mathbf{X})$ in [4]. Each node in the actor graph represents an actor; its adjacency matrix is represented by $\mathbf{A}$ and the edge weight is determined by the appearance information and position information between actors. The calculation equation of edge weight is as follows:

$$\mathbf{A}_{ij} = \frac{f_s\left(\mathbf{x}_i^s, \mathbf{x}_j^s\right) \exp\left(f_a\left(\mathbf{x}_i^a, \mathbf{x}_j^a\right)\right)}{\sum_{j=1}^{N} f_s\left(\mathbf{x}_i^s, \mathbf{x}_j^s\right) \exp\left(f_a\left(\mathbf{x}_i^a, \mathbf{x}_j^a\right)\right)} \tag{1}$$

where $f_a\left(\mathbf{x}_i^a, \mathbf{x}_j^a\right)$ represents the appearance relation value between two actors, and the position relation is performed by $f_s\left(\mathbf{x}_i^s, \mathbf{x}_j^s\right)$. The appearance relation values and position relation values are calculated as follows:

$$f_a\left(\mathbf{x}_i^a, \mathbf{x}_j^a\right) = \frac{\left(\mathbf{x}_i^a\right)^{\mathrm{T}} \mathbf{x}_j^a}{\sqrt{d}}, f_s\left(\mathbf{x}_i^s, \mathbf{x}_j^s\right) = \mathbb{I}\left(d\left(\mathbf{x}_i^s, \mathbf{x}_j^s\right) \leq \mu\right) \tag{2}$$

where $\sqrt{d}$ acts as a normalization factor. We get the adjacency matrices $\mathbf{A}$ and $\mathbf{X}$, which will go through the graph convolution layer to learn the relation representation $\mathbf{H}^{(1)}$ between the actors.

Learning Relation Representation by Graph Convolutional Layers. After obtaining the actor relation adjacency matrix $\mathbf{A}$ and the actor feature matrix $\mathbf{X}$, we perform relational reasoning on them. We use the graph convolution layer [12,13,18]. A graph convolution layer is a kind of message passing model that takes an adjacency matrix and a feature matrix as input to obtain the output of new feature matrix. Formally, we can write the process as:

$$\mathbf{H}^{(l+1)} = \sigma\left(\mathbf{A}\mathbf{H}^{(l)}\mathbf{W}^{(l)}\right) \tag{3}$$

where $\mathbf{A} \in \mathbb{R}^{N\times N}$ is the matrix representation of graph with a structural relationship. $\mathbf{H}^{(l)} \in \mathbb{R}^{N\times f}$ is the feature matrix of nodes, which is the output of the lth layer, and $\mathbf{H}^{(0)} = \mathbf{X}$. $\mathbf{W} \in \mathbb{R}^{f\times d}$ are the learnable parameters for which dimension d can be adjusted. In this work we adjust d equal to f. $\sigma(\cdot)$ is an activation function, and we adopt RELU in this work. In [4], multiple graphs $\mathcal{G} = \left(\mathbf{G}^1, \mathbf{G}^2, \cdots, \mathbf{G}^{N_g}\right)$ are constructed as:

$$\mathbf{H}^{(l+1,N_g)} = \sigma\left(\mathbf{A}^i\mathbf{H}^{(l,N_g)}\mathbf{W}^{(l,N_g)}\right), \tag{4}$$

where N_g is a hyper-parameter. We extend the work by extracting multiple subgraphs $\mathcal{G}_f = \left(\mathbf{G}_s^1, \mathbf{G}_s^2, \cdots, \mathbf{G}_s^{N_g}\right)$. Every actor relation subgraph is constructed in the same way according to Sect. 3.2, but with unshared weights. We use the same temporal modeling as [4] to extract 3 frames from a group of videos.

3.2 Extracting the SARG

In the field of Graph Neural Networks, extracting the hierarchical structure of graphs via a pooling layer is an effective method for graph classification [5, 19]. When the ARG is established, the group activity recognition problem is essentially abstracted into the graph classification problem. In this work, we introduce a method of subgraph extraction to obtain a scene representation only containing key actors.

Action Feature. After reasoning by a graph convolutional layer, we find that $\mathbf{H}^{(1)}$ contains a relational representation. We extract the SARG based on this analysis, which contains key actors and their interactions. Subgraph extraction is based on the self-attention scores of each actor about individual actions. Current models [4,7] for individual action classification use a full connection layer classification. This process transforms the features extracted from the network into action features. We simulate this process by passing the feature matrix $\mathbf{H}^{(1)}$ through a full connection layer to generate a behavior vector for each actor. The output dimension of the full connection layer will remain d.

Self-attention Mask. An attention mechanism is a widely used new method in the field of deep learning [20,21]. This mechanism allows the model to focus more on important features and less on unimportant ones. In particular, the self-attention mechanism allows input features to generate attention according to their own criteria. We generate the action self-attention score of each actor based on the action feature matrix. Specifically, we investigate two methods we designed to calculate the action self-attention score $\mathbf{S} \in \mathbb{R}^{N\times 1}$ of each actor. Each scalar S_i in $\mathbf{S} \in \mathbb{R}^{N\times 1}$ represents the action self-attention score of the ith actor.

(1) GCN Attention Encoder: Generally, predicting individual actions in a group activity requires reference to the local entities. Based on these observations, we use a graph convolutional network to calculate the actor's action self-attention score $\mathbf{S} \in \mathbb{R}^{N\times 1}$, which can propagate the signals from local entities to target entities. The calculation equation is as follows:

$$S = sigmod\left(\hat{\mathbf{A}}\mathbf{H}\mathbf{\Theta}_{att}\right) \tag{5}$$

where $\hat{\mathbf{A}} = \mathbf{A} + \mathbf{I}$, which makes the node emphasize its own features more when calculating action self-attention. Additionally, $\mathbf{\Theta} \in \mathbb{R}^{N\times 1}$ is a trainable parameter. Self-attention is obtained by using a graph convolution based on graph features and topology.

(2) FC Attention Encoder: We can generate action self-attention for each actor via a full connection neural network. We choose a two-layer full connected neural network to compute the action self-attention.

$$S = F_{attn}\left(\mathbf{H}\right) \tag{6}$$

where $F_{attn}\left(\cdot\right)$ is a two-layer full connected neural network, with an input of $\mathbf{H} \in \mathbb{R}^{N\times d}$ and an output of $S \in \mathbb{R}^{N\times 1}$. The number of neurons in the first layer is $1/2d$, and the number of neurons in the second layer should be 1. Generated from attention mechanisms using a full connection neural network, the result is only based on the action vectors of each actor.

Extracting Subgraph. For subgraph extraction, we follow the rules of node selection, which retains a portion of nodes of the input graph even when graphs of varying sizes and structures are inputted [22]. We first ranked the self-attention score S that we obtained from the largest to the smallest. The ranked scores yield a fixed ratio of nodes. The ratio $k \in (0, 1]$ is a hyper-parameter that determines the number of nodes to keep. In this work, we set $K = 0.5$. The top $\lceil kN \rceil$ nodes are selected based on S.

$$\mathrm{idx} = \textit{top-rank}(S, \lceil kN \rceil), \quad S_{\mathrm{mask}} = S_{\mathrm{idx}} \tag{7}$$

where *top-rank*$(\cdot,\cdot)$ is the function that returns indices of the top $\lceil kN \rceil$ values. The $\cdot_{idx}$ is an indexing operation. S_{mask} is the feature attention mask. The subgraph is extracted in the following ways (shown in Fig. 2):

$$\mathbf{H}_s = \mathbf{H}_{\text{idx},:}, \mathbf{A}_{out} = \mathbf{A}_{\text{idx},\text{idx}} \tag{8}$$

where $X_{\text{idx},:}$ is the row-wise indexed feature matrix and $A_{\text{idx},\text{idx}}$ is the row-wise and column-wise indexed adjacency matrix. The $\odot$ is the broadcasted element-wise product. Furthermore, according to the method in [5], the feature matrix of the subgraph can be multiplied by the attention mechanism and used to expand and contract the matrix.

$$\mathbf{H_s} = \mathbf{H}_s \odot S_{mask} \tag{9}$$

So far, we have completed the extraction of the subgraph, which contains a new feature matrix and a new actor relation adjacency matrix. We set the extraction ratio $\mathbf{K} = 0.5$, which means that every time the actor relation subgraph is extracted, half of the irrelevant actors/nodes will be filtered.

3.3 Feature Fusion

The overall network framework is shown in Fig. 2. The original feature matrix $\mathbf{H}^{(0)} \in \mathbb{R}^{N \times f}$, containing all actor features, is extracted by a backbone and RoIAlign [17]. The relation representation of data is learned by using a graph convolutional layer, the feature matrix $\mathbf{H}^{(1)} \in \mathbb{R}^{N \times d}$ with a relation representation is obtained. Finally, after the subgraph extraction module, the feature matrix $\mathbf{H_s^{(1)}} \in \mathbb{R}^{\lceil kN \rceil \times d}$ of the actor relation subgraph is obtained. We fuse $\mathbf{H}^{(0)}$, $\mathbf{H}^{(1)}$ and $\mathbf{H_s^{(1)}}$ in different ways to describe scene-level representation. In this paper, we investigate three feature fusion methods we designed.

Maxpool Fusing. The first method uses the unified maxpool method, which is used in [4]. Maxpool is a graph representation method commonly used in the graph classification task, which is regarded as an approach that represents outstanding features. To use the maxpool method, we need to set the dimension of $\mathbf{H_s^{(1)}}$ equal to $\mathbf{H}^{(1)}$ to make the matrices additive. To this end, we generate a zero matrix $\mathbf{0_{N \times d}} \in \mathbb{R}^{N \times d}$ and construct a new subgraph feature matrix $\mathbf{H}_s^{(1)\prime}$ as follows:

$$\mathbf{H}_s^{(1)\prime} = distribute\left(\mathbf{0}_{N \times d}, \mathbf{H}_s^{(1)}, \text{idx}\right) \tag{10}$$

where $distribute\left(\mathbf{0}_{N \times d}, \mathbf{H}_s^{(1)}, \text{idx}\right)$ is the operation that distributes row vectors in $\mathbf{H}_s^{(1)}$ into $\mathbf{0}_{N \times d}$ feature matrix according to their corresponding indices stored in idx. Each row in the feature matrix represents an actor. According to Eq. 10, we can find that if actors are filtered during subgraph extraction, the feature vector corresponding to actors is $\mathbf{0}$. If retained, the feature is retained. The scene-level representation is generated as follows:

$$\mathbf{Z} = \mathbf{X} + \sum_{i=1}^{N_g} (\mathbf{H}^{(1,i)} + \mathbf{H}_s^{(1,i)\prime}), \mathbf{Z}' = \max_{i=1}^{N} \mathbf{z}_i \tag{11}$$

where $\max_{i=1}^{N}$ is the function that returns max value of column dimension.

Addpool Fusing. For the graph classification problem, [23] proves that addpool is more capable than maxpool for distinguishable non-isomorphic graphs. The actor representations are added together to generate scene-level representation as follows:

$$\mathbf{Z} = \mathbf{X} + \sum_{i=1}^{N}(\mathbf{H}^{(1,i)} + \mathbf{H}_s^{(1,i)\prime}), \mathbf{Z}' = \sum_{i=1}^{N}\mathbf{Z}_i \tag{12}$$

Graph Feature Fusion Network. We also evaluate the learnable approach, which is inspired by [18]. It can be written as:

$$\mathbf{Z} = \sum_{i=1}^{N_g}(relu\left(\left[\mathbf{X}, \mathbf{H}^{(1,i)}, \mathbf{H}_s^{(1,i)\prime}\right]\mathbf{W}^{p,i} + \mathbf{b}^{p,i}\right))_i, \mathbf{Z}' = \sum_{i=1}^{N}\mathbf{Z}_i \tag{13}$$

where $[\cdot,\cdot]$ is the concatenation operation and $\mathbf{W}^{p,i}$ and $\mathbf{b}^{p,i}$ are learnable parameters that project the concatenated vector to the same dimension as $\mathbf{Z} \in \mathbb{R}^{N\times d}$, followed by a RELU non-linearity.

3.4 Training Loss

The final scene-level representation, $\mathbf{Z} \in \mathbb{R}^{N\times d}$ and $\mathbf{Z}' \in \mathbb{R}^{1\times d}$, are fed to two classifiers consisting of a full connection layer to generate individual actions and group activity predictions. The whole process can be trained in a single end-to-end model, combined with cross-entropy loss commonly used in classification problems. The final loss is the sum of an individual action prediction and activity prediction loss:

$$\mathcal{L} = \mathcal{L}_1\left(y^G, \hat{y}^G\right) + \lambda\mathcal{L}_2\left(y^I, \hat{y}^I\right) \tag{14}$$

where $\mathcal{L}_1$ and $\mathcal{L}_2$ are the cross-entropy elements, $\hat{y}^G$ and $\hat{y}^I$ represent the predictions of group activity and individual action, y^G and y^I represent the labels of group activity and individual action. The weight λ is a hyper-parameter that is used to balance the loss of activity and action.

4 Experiments

In this section, we evaluate the performance of our proposed model and its variants; then we compare our model to several benchmarks. We conduct experiments on two widely adopted datasets, the Volleyball dataset [6] and the Collective Activity dataset [24]. We use the ADMA optimizer and follow the hyper-parameter settings in [4]. Additionally, we set $d = 1024$, $f = 1024$ and $K = 0.5$.

Table 1. Ablation studies about different types of self-attention calculation methods.

Method	Accuracy (%)
No subgraph extraction	89.1
GCN attention encoder	**89.8**
FC attention encoder	89.5

Table 2. Ablation studies about different types of feature fusion methods.

Method	Accuracy (%)
Base model (with GCN attention encoder)	89.8
Base model + Addpool	**90.1**
Base model + Fusion Net	90.1

4.1 Ablation Studies

To understand the contribution of proposed model components to model performance, we conduct detailed ablation experiments on the collective dataset. In this experiment, we take recognition accuracy as an evaluation metric.

Action Self-attention Computation. Firstly, we investigate the influence of different ways of calculating the attention value on performance. To eliminate other influences, our baseline is based on a single frame, $N_g = 1$, without using temporal modeling. The base model is only reasoned by a GCN layer but with no subgraph extraction. We choose VGG-16 as the backbone network. In this section, we use maxpool feature fusion.

The results are shown in Table 1. We can observe that, compared with the baseline, extracting subgraphs can bring significant performance improvement. The performance improvements illustrate that offering the scene representation of key actors can bring identifiable information. Compared with the relation graph between all actors, the subgraph only containing key actors also provides additional information for group activity recognition. Moreover, the attention values calculated using GCN are better than using the full connection layer. We conjecture those individual actions in group activities require the reference of surrounding entities, thus generating more representative attention. In the following experiments, we use GCN attention encoder to compute the appearance relation value.

Feature Fusion Methods. In this section, we investigated the influence of different feature fusion methods based on model performance. We set the base model with the GCN attention encoder as the base model. The results are shown in Table 2. We can observe that the *Addpool* and *Fusion Net* we designed have good performance. We conjecture that the three fusion methods we designed potentially highlight the expressiveness of key actors. Moreover, *Addpool* and *Fusion Net* have better performance, which compute the representation by sum the features of all nodes/actors. [23] proved that the add aggregator is more effective than the max/mean aggregator. In the following experiments, we use *Fusion Net* to fuse features.

Table 3. Ablation study of number of graphs and subgraphs.

ARG [4]	The number of graph	1	4	8	16	32
	Accuracy (%)	89.1	89.4	89.5	**89.8**	89.3
OURS	The number of graph	1	4	8	16	32
	Accuracy (%)	90.1	90.4	**90.7**	90.5	90.2

Multiple Graphs and Subgraphs. We also investigate the effect of the number of graphs on model performance. The number of graphs is equal to the number of subgraphs. The results are shown in Table 3, where we compare with ARG, we conduct experiments using the published ARG code and following the author's hyper-parameter settings. Subgraph extraction brings significant improvement. As we increase the number of graphs, the accuracy of ARG and our model improve. Compared with ARG, our model achieves optimal performance with only half the number of graphs in the ARG. Our best performance is 1% higher than that of ARG. The results demonstrate that the addition of subgraph of key actors brings additional information to group activity recognition.

4.2 Compared with SOTA

In this section, we compare our best model (with $K = 3$ and *Temporal modeling*) with existing SOTA methods. We performed experiments on different backbone networks, including Inception-v3 and VGG. The results are shown in Table 4, and our model shows encouraging results.

The results show that our results surpass all existing methods, thus establishing a new state-of-the-art, including all backbone. This indicates that our method is generalizable. Our method extracts the key actors of group activities and their interactions, which are identifiable information in group activity recognition; thus, our method is better than the ARG method [4]. Our method is also superior to the hierarchical relational network and the method using RNN [6], mainly because we can extract key actor's action information.

Table 4. Comparison with SOTA on the volleyball dataset and collective dataset.

Volleyball dataset			Collective dataset		
Method	Backbone	Accuracy (%)	Method	Backbone	Accuracy (%)
CERN [25]	VGG16	83.3	HDTM [6]	AlexNet	81.9
StageNet [8]	VGG16	89.3	SIM [26]	VGG16	83.3
HRN [7]	VGG16	87.6	SBGAR [27]	VGG16	89.3
SSU [28]	Inception-v3	90.6	CERN [25]	VGG16	87.6
ARG [4]	VGG16	91.9	StageNet [8]	Inception-v3	90.6
ARG [4]	Inception-v3	92.5	ARG [4]	Inception-v3	91.0
PRL [29]	VGG16	91.4	ARG [4]	VGG16	90.1
OURS	Inception-v3	**92.8**	OURS	Inception-v3	**91.3**
OURS	VGG16	**92.4**	OURS	VGG16	**91.1**
OURS	VGG19	**92.5**	OURS	VGG19	**91.0**

In general, instead of explicitly giving key actors more attention, our approach increases the importance of key actors. Our method provides a more recognizable representation of the scene only containing key actors for the network, which distinguishes (characterizes) the different activities. Compared with ARG [4], our approach improves the VGG network more than it improves the Inception-v3 network, which we conjecture is due to the strong fitting capability of the Inception-v3 network. The improvement on VGG validates the effectiveness of our approach, demonstrating that SARG can bring additional useful information.

5 Conclusion

We proposed a novel end-to-end deep learning architecture and designed a subgraph extraction method to learn key actors and their interactions in group activity recognition. Based on the actor action self-attention method, the subgraph is extracted from the actor relationship graph to obtain a new scene representation that only contains the key actors and their interactions. Our method provides additional information for group activity recognition and distinguishes different group activities. In addition, we design a variation of attention calculation and three methods for information fusion. Additional ablation experiments demonstrated that: (1)Our method can learn and extract information about key actors and their interactions. (2) The subgraph of key actors brings additional information to group activity recognition. We evaluate our model over two datasets: the collective activity dataset and the volleyball dataset. SARG has an average improvement of 4%, compared to 8 benchmarks.

References

1. Ramanathan, V., et al.: Detecting events and key actors in multi-person videos. In: Proceedings of the IEEE Conference on Computer Vision and Pattern Recognition (CVPR), June 2016
2. Tran, D., Bourdev, L., Fergus, R., Torresani, L., Paluri, M.: Learning spatiotemporal features with 3d convolutional networks. IEEE (2015)
3. Wang, L., Li, W., Li, W., Van Gool, L.: Appearance-and-relation networks for video classification. In: 2018 IEEE/CVF Conference on Computer Vision and Pattern Recognition (2017)
4. Wu, J., Wang, L., Wang, L., Guo, J., Wu, G.: Learning actor relation graphs for group activity recognition. In: CVPR (2019)
5. Lee, J., Lee, I., Kang, J.: Self-attention graph pooling. In: 36th International Conference on Machine Learning (2019)
6. Ibrahim, M., Muralidharan, S., Deng, Z., Vahdat, A., Mori, G.: A hierarchical deep temporal model for group activity recognition. In: 2016 IEEE Conference on Computer Vision and Pattern Recognition (CVPR) (2016)
7. Ibrahim, M.S., Mori, G.: Hierarchical relational networks for group activity recognition and retrieval. In: Ferrari, V., Hebert, M., Sminchisescu, C., Weiss, Y. (eds.) ECCV 2018. LNCS, vol. 11207, pp. 742–758. Springer, Cham (2018). https://doi.org/10.1007/978-3-030-01219-9_44
8. Qi, M., Jie, Q., Li, A., Wang, Y., Luo, J., Gool, L.V.: Stagnet: an attentive semantic RNN for group activity recognition. In: European Conference on Computer Vision (2018)
9. Lecun, Y., Bengio, Y., Hinton, G.: Deep learning. Nature **521**(7553), 436 (2015)
10. Liu, J., Shahroudy, A., Xu, D., Wang, G.: Spatio-temporal LSTM with trust gates for 3d human action recognition. In: ECCV (2016)
11. Si, C., Chen, W., Wang, W., Wang, L., Tan, T.: An attention enhanced graph convolutional LSTM network for skeleton-based action recognition. In: 2019 IEEE/CVF Conference on Computer Vision and Pattern Recognition (CVPR) (2019)
12. Hamilton, W.L., Ying, R., Leskovec, J.: Inductive representation learning on large graphs. In: NIPS (2017)
13. Kipf, T.N.: Max Welling. Semi-supervised classification with graph convolutional networks (2016). arXiv preprint: arXiv:1609.02907
14. Ying, R., You, J., Morris, C., Ren, X., Hamilton, W.L., Leskovec, J.: Hierarchical graph representation learning with differentiable pooling. In: 32th Conference on Neural Information Processing Systems (2018)
15. Simonyan, K., Zisserman, A.: Very deep convolutional networks for large-scale image recognition. arXiv (2014)
16. Szegedy, C., Vanhoucke, V., Ioffe, S., Shlens, J., Wojna, Z.: Rethinking the inception architecture for computer vision. In: IEEE, pp. 2818–2826 (2016)
17. He, K., Gkioxari, G., Dollár, P., Girshick, R.: Mask R-CNN. IEEE (2017)
18. Veličković, P., Cucurull, G., Casanova, A., Romero, A., Liò, P., Bengio, Y.: Graph attention networks. Int. Conf. Learn. Represent. (2018) (accepted as poster)
19. Cheung, M., Shi, J., Jiang, L.Y., Wright, O., Moura, J.: Pooling in Graph Convolutional Neural Networks. IEEE (2020)
20. Parikh, A.P., Täckström, O., Das, D., Uszkoreit, J.: A decomposable attention model for natural language inference (2016). arXiv preprint: arXiv:1606.01933

21. Zhang, H., Goodfellow, I., Metaxas, D., Odena, A.: Self-attention generative adversarial networks. In: International Conference on Machine Learning, pp. 7354–7363. PMLR (2019)
22. Gao, H., Ji, S.: Graph u-nets. In: 36th International Conference on Machine Learning (2019)
23. Xu, K., Hu, W. Leskovec, J., Jegelka., S.: How powerful are graph neural networks? In: International Conference on Learning Representations (2019)
24. Choi, W., Shahid, K., Savarese, S.: What are they doing?: collective activity classification using spatio-temporal relationship among people. In: IEEE International Conference on Computer Vision Workshops (2009)
25. Shu, T., Todorovic, S. Zhu, S.C.: CERN: confidence-energy recurrent network for group activity recognition. In: 2017 IEEE Conference on Computer Vision and Pattern Recognition (CVPR) (2017)
26. Deng, Z., Vahdat, A., Hu, H., Mori, G.: Structure Inference Machines: Recurrent Neural Networks For Analyzing Relations In Group Activity Recognition. IEEE (2016)
27. Xin, L., Chuah, M.C.: SBGAR: semantics based group activity recognition. In: IEEE International Conference on Computer Vision (2017)
28. Bagautdinov, T., Alahi, A., Fleuret, F., Fua, P., Savarese, S.: Social scene understanding: end-to-end multi-person action localization and collective activity recognition. IEEE (2016)
29. Hu, G., Cui, B., He, Y., Yu, S.: Progressive relation learning for group activity recognin. In: 2020 IEEE/CVF Conference on Computer Vision and Pattern Recognition (CVPR) (2020)

Attributed Non-negative Matrix Multi-factorization for Data Representation

Jie Wang, Yanfeng Sun(✉), Jipeng Guo, Yongli Hu, and Baocai Yin

Beijing Key Laboratory of Multimedia and Intelligent Software Technology, Beijing Institute of Artificial Intelligence, Faculty of Information Technology, Beijing University of Technology, Beijing, China
{wangjie,guojipeng}@emails.bjut.edu.cn, {yfsun,huyongli,ybc}@bjut.edu.cn

Abstract. Non-negative matrix factorization (NMF) is an important method of latent data representation learning. Most of the existing NMF methods focus only on one single factorization and obtain one clustering solution. However, real data are usually complex and can be described from multiple attributes or sub-features. For example, face image consists of genders attribute and expressions attribute. And, the various attributes provide complementary information of data. Failing to explore multi-attribute representation and exploit the complementary information, it may be difficult to learn discriminative representation. In order to solve the above issue and obtain richer low-dimensional representations, we propose the Attributed Non-negative Matrix Multi-Factorization for Data Representation (ANMMF) model which simultaneously learns multiple low-dimensional representations from original data. By utilizing Hilbert Schmidt Independence Criterion (HSIC) to constrain the pairwise attributes, ANMMF enforces that each low-dimensional attribute representation is independent, which effectively mines complementary multi-attribute information embed in the original data. Further, graph Laplacian regularization is constrained to maintain the local geometrical structure. The low dimensional multi-attribute representation information embedded in the original data is fused to improve the clustering results. Finally, we develop the iterative updating schemes for the ANMMF model optimization, and extensive experiments on real-world databases demonstrate that our method has the most advanced performance compared with other related algorithms.

Keywords: Non-negative matrix factorization · Multi-attribute representation · Hilbert Schmidt Independence Criterion · Graph Laplacian constraint

The first author is a student.

Electronic supplementary material The online version of this chapter (https://doi.org/10.1007/978-3-030-88013-2_6) contains supplementary material, which is available to authorized users.

© Springer Nature Switzerland AG 2021
H. Ma et al. (Eds.): PRCV 2021, LNCS 13022, pp. 66–77, 2021.
https://doi.org/10.1007/978-3-030-88013-2_6

1 Introduction

High-dimensional data are becoming increasingly common in many fields, such as biomedical engineering, pattern recognition, computer vision and image engineering [4,7,18]. Thus, learning effective low-dimensional representation of original data is necessary. Some dimension reduction methods have achieved great successes, such as Principal Component Analysis (PCA) [1], Linear Discriminant Analysis (LDA) [13], and Locality Preserving Projection (LPP) [10]. However, they are difficult to provide a straightforward physical meaning. Non-negative matrix factorization (NMF) [12] gradually became the most popular dimension reduction tools owing to its straightforward interpretability of non-negative factorization results. The main idea of NMF algorithm can be simply described as follows: for any non-negative data matrix $\mathbf{X}$, NMF algorithm seeks to find two non-negative matrices $\mathbf{U}$ and $\mathbf{V}$, so that $\mathbf{X} \approx \mathbf{U}\mathbf{V}^T$ is satisfied. Thus, the NMF allows only non-subtractive combinations of non-negative components. This non-negativity constraints result in the parts-based representation of NMF.

Due to the good properties of NMF, various methods [11,16] are proposed to extend the standard NMF by adding additional constraints. Sparse NMF (SNMF) [6] introduces a penalty constraint to encode sparsity in the factor matrices, leading to a local-based representation. Orthogonal NMF [5] reduces the redundant information of data representation by inducing the orthogonality constraints on the factor matrices. The geometrical structure of data is of great importance for learning effective representation for unsupervised tasks. Thus, graph regularized NMF (GNMF) [2] preserves the local geometrical structure in the low-dimensional representation by the graph Laplacian regularization.

Although NMF and GNMF made the great successes in many applications, both tend to intuitively utilize the features of original data as a whole and they only obtain one pair of factorization factors from original data. However, real data is complex and can be described from multiple attributes and aspects. Concretely, one data representation can be regarded as a description of original data from one aspect. For example, face images include facial expressions, races, skin colors, facial features, decorations and other features. Because each attribute contains specific information, it is crucial to explore the diverse and complementary information among multiple attributes to learn a more discriminative low-dimensional representation.

To address the aforementioned issues, we propose an Attributed Non-negative Matrix Multi-Factorization (ANMMF) model for data representation, which describes data from different attributes and fuses the low-dimensional representations of these attributes to improve the clustering results. Specifically, a non-negative matrix $\mathbf{X}$ is decomposed into multiple pairs of factors, thus obtaining multiple low-dimensional representations. Then, Hilbert Schmidt Independence Criterion (HSIC) [9] is used to increase the diversity between different representations, which explores more complementary information. Each low-dimensional representation is enforced to be independent and correspond to a particular attribute. Similar to GNMF, the multiple representations learned by ANMMF also preserve the local geometric structure by the graph Laplacian regularization.

2 Related Work

In this section, we briefly review the closely related works, i.e., Non-negative Matrix Factorization (NMF) [12] and Graph regularized NMF (GNMF) [2].

2.1 NMF

Given a non-negative data matrix $\mathbf{X} = [\mathbf{x}_1, \mathbf{x}_2, \cdots, \mathbf{x}_n] \in \mathbb{R}_+^{D\times n}$, each column of $\mathbf{X}$ is a observed sample vector. $\mathbf{U} \in \mathbb{R}_+^{D\times m}$ is regarded as the basis matrix, $\mathbf{V} \in \mathbb{R}_+^{n\times m}$ is regarded as the representation coefficient matrix. NMF model can be mathematically expressed by the following objective function:

$$\min_{\mathbf{U}\geq 0,\mathbf{V}\geq 0} \|\mathbf{X} - \mathbf{U}\mathbf{V}^T\|_F^2, \tag{1}$$

where $\|\cdot\|_F^2$ is Frobenius norm of a matrix. Owing to the non-negativity of factor matrices, NMF learns a parts-based data representation, which is easy to explain in many real applications.

2.2 GNMF

In fact, the geometrical structure of data is of great importance for significantly improving the learning performance of data representation. To incorporate the geometric structure into the NMF, Graph regularized NMF (GNMF) [2] was proposed, in which geometric information was encoded by an affinity graph and preserved by the graph Laplacian regularization. As shown in [2], the objective function of GNMF model is as follows:

$$\min_{\mathbf{U}\geq 0,\mathbf{V}\geq 0} \|\mathbf{X} - \mathbf{U}\mathbf{V}^T\|^2 + \lambda \mathrm{tr}(\mathbf{V}^T\mathbf{L}\mathbf{V}), \tag{2}$$

where λ is a non-negative regularization parameter and is employed to balance the reconstruction error and regularized term. $\mathbf{L} = \mathbf{D} - \mathbf{W}$ is the graph Laplacian matrix corresponding to the affinity matrix $\mathbf{W} \in \mathbb{R}^{n\times n}$, in which $\mathbf{D}$ is a diagonal matrix and $\mathbf{D}_{jj} = \sum_{i=1}^{n} \mathbf{W}_{ij}$.

3 The Proposed Method

In this section, we first present our novel clustering framework, Then, we design an optimization algorithm for our approach.

3.1 Motivation and Objective Function

Learning a informative data representation is a crucial prerequisite for subsequent tasks. Although NMF and GNMF are promising to learn effective data representation, they still have some limitations. For example, for complex face images, it is difficult for NMF and GNMF to learn the representation of multiple attributes due to the only one factorization and capture the diverse information among them. In fact, different representations describe samples from different attributes and aspects, which can provide rich information.

To understand and represent data thoroughly and in-depth, we propose a flexible and robust non-negative matrix factorization model to effectively solve the data multi-representation problem, which is named as Attributed Non-negative Matrix Multi-Factorization (ANMMF). This model learns multiple representations from original data, i.e., multi-attribute representation $\{\mathbf{V}_i\}_{i=1}^{V}$. Each $\mathbf{V}_i$ represents an aspect/attribute of the data, and the latent information of each attribute can be fully explored, i.e., $\mathbf{V}_i$ and $\mathbf{V}_j$, are enforced to be independent to each other. From the perspective of model optimization, we note that the loss function (1) and (2) are non-convex in both variables $\mathbf{U}$, $\mathbf{V}$. This indicates that the solution for NMF or GNMF is not unique, i.e., the non-negative matrix factorization of data $\mathbf{X}$ is not unique. To this end, we propose the following matrix factorization model:

$$\begin{aligned} &\sum_{i=1}^{V} \|\mathbf{X} - \mathbf{U}_i \mathbf{V}_i^T\|_F^2 + \lambda_1 \sum_{i \neq j}^{V} \mathrm{HSIC}(\mathbf{V}_i, \mathbf{V}_j), \\ &\text{s.t.} \quad \mathbf{U}_i \geq \mathbf{0}, \mathbf{V}_i \geq \mathbf{0}, \forall i \in \{1, 2, \cdots, V\}, \end{aligned} \tag{3}$$

where $\lambda_1 \geq 0$ is the trade-off parameter. The $\sum_{i \neq j}^{V} \mathrm{HSIC}(\mathbf{V}_i, \mathbf{V}_j)$ is co-regularizing term which ensures that the correlation of different representations is minimum. Thus, the co-regularizing term exploits complementary information from various aspects. Here, we enforce different representations $\{\mathbf{V}_i\}_{i=1}^{V}$ to be diverse by adopting the Hilbert-Schmidt Independence Criterion (HSIC) [9]. One empirical version of HSIC is defined as follows:

Definition 1. *Consider a series of n observations $\mathbf{A} \times \mathbf{B} = \{(\mathbf{a}_1, \mathbf{b}_1), (\mathbf{a}_2, \mathbf{b}_2), \cdots, (\mathbf{a}_n, \mathbf{b}_n)\}$, an estimator of* HSIC, *written as* $\mathrm{HSIC}(\mathbf{A}, \mathbf{B})$, *is given by:*

$$\mathrm{HSIC}(\mathbf{A}, \mathbf{B}) = (n-1)^{-2} tr(\mathbf{K}_A \mathbf{H} \mathbf{K}_B \mathbf{H}), \tag{4}$$

where $\mathbf{K}_A$ and $\mathbf{K}_B$ are the Gram matrices with $\mathbf{k}_{A,ij} = k_A(\mathbf{a}_i, \mathbf{a}_j)$, $\mathbf{k}_{B,ij} = k_B(\mathbf{b}_i, \mathbf{b}_j)$, in which k_A and k_B are the kernel functions. $\mathbf{h}_{ij} = \delta_{ij} - \frac{1}{n}$ centers the Gram matrix to have zero mean in the feature space.

For more details of HSIC, please refer to the related paper [9]. As in GNMF, we also explore the local graph structure, which explicitly enforces the representations to meet the geometrical structure. For the sake of simplicity, we assume that different representations obey the same geometrical structure. Thus, the final model of ANMMF is defined as:

$$\begin{aligned} &\mathcal{O} = \sum_{i=1}^{V} \|\mathbf{X} - \mathbf{U}_i \mathbf{V}_i^T\|_F^2 + \lambda_1 \sum_{i \neq j}^{V} \mathrm{HSIC}(\mathbf{V}_i, \mathbf{V}_j) + \lambda_2 \sum_{i=1}^{V} \mathrm{tr}(\mathbf{V}_i^T \mathbf{L} \mathbf{V}_i) \\ &\text{s.t.} \quad \mathbf{U}_i \geq \mathbf{0}, \mathbf{V}_i \geq \mathbf{0}, \forall i \in \{1, 2, \cdots, V\}, \end{aligned} \tag{5}$$

where $\lambda_1 \geq 0$ and $\lambda_2 \geq 0$ are the trade-off parameters to balance the diversity among low-dimensional representations and graph regularization term for all attributes. V is the number of different low dimensional representations.

Here, we analyze the relations between NMF, GNMF and proposed ANMMF. Recall the objective function of ANMMF in (5), if we set $V = 1$ and $\lambda_1 = 0$, the above formula degenerates into the GNMF. When λ_1, λ_2 are both 0 and $V = 1$, the above formula degenerates into the basic NMF. We also find when $\lambda_2 = 0$, the above model degenerates to MCNMF [17]. Thus, NMF, GNMF and MCNMF can be seen as special cases of the proposed ANMMF. Theoretically, the proposed method ANMMF will have a better performance.

3.2 Model Optimization

Obviously, the objective function in Eq. (5) is non-convex in both of $\mathbf{U}_i$ and $\mathbf{V}_i$ together, so the global minimum and closed-form solution cannot be obtained. Here, we provide an iterative strategy to optimize the objective function.

First of all, the objective function of (5) can be rewritten as follows:

$$
\begin{aligned}
\mathcal{O} &= \sum_{i=1}^{V} \|\mathbf{X} - \mathbf{U}_i\mathbf{V}_i^T\|_F^2 + \lambda_1 \sum_{i \neq j}^{V} \mathrm{HSIC}(\mathbf{V}_i, \mathbf{V}_j) + \lambda_2 \sum_{i=1}^{V} \mathrm{tr}(\mathbf{V}_i^T\mathbf{L}\mathbf{V}_i) \\
&= \sum_{i=1}^{V} \left(\mathrm{tr}(\mathbf{X}\mathbf{X}^T) - 2\mathrm{tr}(\mathbf{X}\mathbf{V}_i\mathbf{U}_i^T) + \mathrm{tr}(\mathbf{U}_i\mathbf{V}_i^T\mathbf{V}_i\mathbf{U}_i^T)\right) \\
&\quad + \lambda_1 \sum_{i \neq j}^{V} \mathrm{HSIC}(\mathbf{V}_i, \mathbf{V}_j) + \lambda_2 \sum_{i=1}^{V} \mathrm{tr}(\mathbf{V}_i^T\mathbf{L}\mathbf{V}_i),
\end{aligned} \tag{6}
$$

where the second equation holds because of the matrix computation properties $\mathrm{tr}(\mathbf{AB}) = \mathrm{tr}(\mathbf{BA})$ and $\mathrm{tr}(\mathbf{A}) = \mathrm{tr}(\mathbf{A}^T)$. let Φ_i and Ψ_i be the Lagrangian multipliers for non-negative constraints $\mathbf{U}_i \geq 0$ and $\mathbf{V}_i \geq 0$, respectively. Let ϕ_{cd} and ψ_{ld} be the lagrange multiplier for constraint $u_{cd} \geq 0$ and $v_{ld} \geq 0$, respectively, and $\Phi_i = [\phi_{cd}]$, $\Psi_i = [\psi_{ld}]$. Then the Lagrange function is given as follows:

$$
\begin{aligned}
\mathcal{L} = &\sum_{i=1}^{V} \left(\mathrm{tr}(\mathbf{X}\mathbf{X}^T) - 2\mathrm{tr}(\mathbf{X}\mathbf{V}_i\mathbf{U}_i^T) + \mathrm{tr}(\mathbf{U}_i\mathbf{V}_i^T\mathbf{V}_i\mathbf{U}_i^T)\right) + \lambda_2 \sum_{i=1}^{V} \mathrm{tr}(\mathbf{V}_i^T\mathbf{L}\mathbf{V}_i) \\
&+ \lambda_1 \sum_{j=1, j \neq i}^{V} \mathrm{HSIC}(\mathbf{V}_i, \mathbf{V}_j) + \sum_{i=1}^{V} \left(\mathrm{tr}(\Phi_i\mathbf{U}_i^T) + \mathrm{tr}(\Psi_i\mathbf{V}_i^T)\right),
\end{aligned} \tag{7}
$$

With the alternating optimization strategy, we can approximately optimize equation (7) in the manner of minimizing with respect to one pair of factorization factors $\{\mathbf{U}_i, \mathbf{V}_i\}$ once at a time while fixing the others. Specifically, with all but one $\{\mathbf{U}_i, \mathbf{V}_i\}$ fixed.

In this paper, we use the simple and effective inner product nucleus to represent HSIC, i.e., $\mathbf{K}_i = \mathbf{V}_i\mathbf{V}_i^T$. Since $(n-1)^{-2}$ is an independent constant from the coefficient matrix $\mathbf{V}_i$ we are seeking, it is ignored for the convenience of optimization. It can be further written as follows:

$$\sum_{j=1,j\neq i}^{V} \mathrm{HSIC}(\mathbf{V}_i, \mathbf{V}_j) = \sum_{j=1,j\neq i}^{V} \mathrm{tr}(\mathbf{HK}_i\mathbf{HK}_j) = \sum_{j=1,j\neq i}^{V} \mathrm{tr}(\mathbf{V}_i^T\mathbf{HK}_j\mathbf{HV}_i) \\ = \mathrm{tr}(\mathbf{V}_i^T\mathbf{KV}_i), \tag{8}$$

where $\mathbf{K} = \sum_{j=1,j\neq i}^{V} \mathrm{tr}(\mathbf{HK}_j\mathbf{H})$. The variables $\mathbf{U}_i$ and $\mathbf{V}_i$ can be solved alternately by alternating minimization strategy of $\mathcal{L}(\mathbf{U}_i, \mathbf{V}_i)$ while keeping all the others fixed. The detailed optimization strategy is presented as follows.

Update $\mathbf{U}_i$ with Fixing Others. The partial derivation of (7) with respect to $\mathbf{U}_i$ is:

$$\frac{\partial\mathcal{L}(\mathbf{U}_i, \mathbf{V}_i)}{\partial\mathbf{U}_i} = -2\mathbf{XV}_i + 2\mathbf{U}_i\mathbf{V}_i^T\mathbf{V}_i + \Phi_i. \tag{9}$$

Using the KKT condition $\phi_{cd}u_{cd} = 0$, we get the following equation:

$$-(\mathbf{XV}_i)_{cd}u_{cd} + (\mathbf{U}_i\mathbf{V}_i^T\mathbf{V}_i)_{cd}u_{cd} = 0 \tag{10}$$

Formula (10) is further simplified to obtain the following updating rule of $\mathbf{U}_i$:

$$u_{cd} \leftarrow u_{cd}\frac{(\mathbf{XV}_i)_{cd}}{(\mathbf{U}_i\mathbf{V}_i^T\mathbf{V}_i)_{cd}} \tag{11}$$

Update $\mathbf{V}_i$ with Fixing Others. According to formula (8), the partial derivation of (7) with respect to variable $\mathbf{V}_i$ is presented as follows:

$$\frac{\partial\mathcal{L}(\mathbf{U}_i, \mathbf{V}_i)}{\partial\mathbf{V}_i} = (-2\mathbf{X}^T\mathbf{U}_i + 2\mathbf{V}_i\mathbf{U}_i^T\mathbf{U}_i) + (2\lambda_1\mathbf{KV}_i) + (2\lambda_2\mathbf{LV}_i) + \Psi_i. \tag{12}$$

Using KKT condition $\psi_{ld}v_{ld} = 0$, so we get the following equation:

$$-(\mathbf{X}^T\mathbf{U}_i)_{ld}v_{ld} + (\mathbf{V}_i\mathbf{U}_i^T\mathbf{U}_i)_{ld}v_{ld} + \lambda_1(\mathbf{KV}_i)_{ld}v_{ld} + \lambda_2(\mathbf{LV}_i)_{ld}v_{ld} = 0. \tag{13}$$

Since $\mathbf{L} = \mathbf{D} - \mathbf{W}$ and $\mathbf{K} = \mathbf{K}_+ - \mathbf{K}_-$ (in which $\mathbf{K}_+ = \frac{1}{2}(|\mathbf{K}| + \mathbf{K})$, $\mathbf{K}_- = \frac{1}{2}(|\mathbf{K}| - \mathbf{K})$), Formula (13) is further simplified to obtain the following updating rule of $\mathbf{V}_i$:

$$v_{ld} \leftarrow v_{ld}\frac{\mathbf{X}^T\mathbf{U}_i + \lambda_1\mathbf{K}_-\mathbf{V}_i + \lambda_2\mathbf{WV}_i)_{ld}}{(\mathbf{V}_i\mathbf{U}_i^T\mathbf{U}_i + \lambda_1\mathbf{K}_+\mathbf{V}_i + \lambda_2\mathbf{DV}_i)_{ld}}. \tag{14}$$

The whole procedure of ANMMF is summarized in Algorithm 1.

3.3 Algorithm Analysis

Convergence Analysis. In the following, we will investigate the convergence of the updating rules of (11) and (14). And regarding these two updating rules, we have the following convergence theorem:

Algorithm 1. Optimization Algorithm for ANMMF

Input: Data matrix $X \in \mathbb{R}^{D \times n}$, the number of reduced dimension m $(m \leq D)$, the number of multiple attribute factorization V,and the parameter λ_1, λ_2.
Initialize: $\mathbf{V}_i \in \mathbb{R}^{n \times m}$ by standard NMF $(i = 1, \cdots, V)$, $\epsilon = 10^{-5}$.
Output: $\{\mathbf{U}_i, \mathbf{V}_i\}_{i=1}^{V}$.

```
while not converged do
    for i=1:V do
        Updating {U_i, V_i} when fixing the other pair of factorization factors {U_j, V_j}_{j≠i}, i.e.,
        Updating variable U_i according to (11).
        Updating variable V_i according to (14).
    end for
    Checking the convergence conditions:
        |O_{t+1} − O_t| < ϵ.
end while
```

Theorem 1. *For* $\mathbf{X}$, $\mathbf{U}_i$, $\mathbf{V}_i \geq \mathbf{0}$, *the objective function in Eq.* (5) *is non-increasing under the updating rules of* (11) *and* (14).

Please see the Appendix for the detailed proof for the convergence theorem. And, we know that the multiplicative updating rules of (11) and (14) are specific cases of gradient decent with an automatic step parameter selection. Thus, Theorem 1 guarantees that the iterative multiplicative updating rules converge to a local optimum.

Complexity Analysis. In this section, we discuss the additional computational cost of our proposed algorithm, which is usually denoted by the symbol O. The complexity of algorithm 1 mainly comes from the following aspects. For ANMMF, if the number of iteration is T, when the non-negative matrix $\mathbf{U}_i$ and $\mathbf{V}_i$ are updated based on the formula (11) and (14), the calculation cost is $O(Tm(nm + Dn + D))$ and $O(T(Dmn + n^2m + nm^2 + m^2D + mn))$. Because the goal of our model is dimension reduction, considering that typically $m \ll D$ and $m \ll n$, the total cost of ANMMF is $O(T(Dmn + n^2m))$.

4 Experiments

4.1 Experiment Settings

We conducted experiments on several benchmark databases to evaluate the performance of proposed ANMMF, including four databases, namely ORL, CMU PIE [15], Yale and Extended YaleB (EYaleB) [8] databases. The basic information of the used databases is summarized in Table 1.

Table 1. The description of the databases.

Database	ORL	PIE	Yale	EYaleB
Size (V)	400	2856	165	2414
Dim (D)	1024	1024	1024	1024
Clusters (c)	40	68	15	38

We compare the performances of proposed algorithm ANMMF against six existing state-of-art clustering methods or related algorithms, including K-means, PCA [1], Ncut [14], NMF [12], GNMF [2], and MCNMF [17]. All experiments use the K-means method in the final clustering stage, and the regularization parameters are set by searching the grid $\{10^{-4}, 10^{-3}, \cdots, 10^{3}\}$. In the experiments, some algorithms perform K-means after dimension reduction or are sensitive to the initialization. For all the methods, we repeat each algorithm 10 times with random initialization and then report their average results.

The proposed model learns the different representations for clustering. For convenience, the V is set as 3 for all the data sets. The regularization parameters λ_1 and λ_2 are also set by searching the grid $\{10^{-4}, 10^{-3}, \cdots, 10^{3}\}$. To compare the methods fairly, we select several parameter combinations for the experiments and then choose the best results for comparison. ANMMF learns multiple different representations $\{\mathbf{V}_i\}_{i=1}^{V}$. Then the multi-view K-Means clustering method [3] is adopted to integrate the low-dimensional representations from different aspects and make full use of the information from all attributes.

In all experiments, we set the number of clusters and nearest neighbor k equal to the true number of classes c for all the clustering algorithms, we use the heat kernel weighting scheme for constructing the k-nearest neighbor graph. In addition, the data are non-normalized. The three evaluation metrics are used to evaluate all the methods, i.e., normalized Mutual Information (NMI), Accuracy (ACC), and F-score. These evaluation metrics comprehensively measure the quality of clustering algorithms from different aspects. For all the evaluation indicators, the higher the value is, the better the clustering effect will be.

4.2 Experiment Results

Table 2 shows the clustering results of different algorithms on the ORL, Yale, PIE, and EYaleB databases. We use multiple evaluation indicators to evaluate the clustering results and mark the best results in bold. As can be seen from Table 2, the ANMMF algorithm is superior to other clustering results in most cases, which proves the effectiveness of exploring diverse information among different attributes, especially on ORL and PIE databases. This indicates that our proposed method can learn better parts-based representations of data. We also find that GNMF model is superior to the method of K-means clustering in most cases and ANMMF model is superior to the method of MCNMF, indicating that the geometric structure can maintain local structure in the learning

Table 2. Clustering results on different databases.

Method	Metrics	ORL	PIE	Yale	EYaleB
K-means	ACC	0.5050	0.1359	0.4485	0.0932
	NMI	0.7104	0.2897	0.5006	0.1044
	F-score	0.5152	0.1472	0.4583	0.1020
PCA [1]	ACC	0.6200	0.2052	0.4000	0.1118
	NMI	0.7745	0.4217	0.4217	0.1312
	F-score	0.6144	0.1813	0.4215	0.1017
Ncut [14]	ACC	0.2525	0.4093	0.2364	0.0953
	NMI	0.4214	0.5061	0.2896	0.1265
	F-score	0.2182	0.3055	0.2231	0.0824
NMF [12]	ACC	0.5850	0.4205	0.4000	0.1810
	NMI	0.7305	0.6392	0.4531	0.2569
	F-score	0.5836	0.3852	0.3978	0.1613
GNMF [2]	ACC	0.6075	0.3628	0.4606	0.1301
	NMI	0.7632	0.5990	0.4848	0.1806
	F-score	0.5926	0.3288	0.4562	0.1260
MCNMF [17]	ACC	0.6275	0.6068	0.4545	0.2336
	NMI	0.7866	0.7532	0.4914	0.3353
	F-score	0.6310	0.5525	0.4315	0.2057
ANMMF	ACC	**0.6375**	**0.6544**	**0.4848**	**0.2386**
	NMI	**0.7954**	**0.7775**	**0.5073**	**0.3457**
	F-score	**0.6358**	**0.5957**	**0.4679**	**0.2068**

representation data representation and improve the clustering performance. In addition, since the data we used are non-normalized data, it is more difficult to capture characteristic information. However, our method can still obtain overall better experimental results. The results show that the attributed non-negative matrix multi-factorization can be achieved, the local structure is preserved by graph regularization and the redundant features are reduced by HSIC regularizer. And, ANMMF learns more comprehensive information of data by exploring diverse information among multiple independent low-dimensional representation and integrates them together to improve the clustering performances.

Below, we use two examples to investigate the effectiveness of any learned parts-based representations $\mathbf{V}_i$. We conduct the K-means clustering method on the all representations $\mathbf{V}_i$, respectively. The related results are shown in Table 3. The GNMF is the special case of proposed ANMMF when $V = 1$ and $\lambda_1 = 0$. By considering the Table 3, the any learned parts-based representation $\mathbf{V}_i$ of ANMMF outperforms the GNMF which is showed the efficacy of ANMMF to learn the more discriminative representation. This is mainly due to the fact

Table 3. Clustering results on different databases.

Data	Metrics	GNMF	ANMMF		
			$\mathbf{V}_1$	$\mathbf{V}_2$	$\mathbf{V}_3$
ORL	ACC	0.6075	0.6700	0.6525	0.6575
	NMI	0.7632	0.7894	0.7884	0.7987
	F-score	0.5926	0.6677	0.6492	0.6614
PIE	ACC	0.3628	0.6334	0.6247	0.6138
	NMI	0.5990	0.7574	0.7605	0.7585
	F-score	0.6329	0.5795	0.5663	0.5621

that ANMMF learns multiple attribute representations which contain the rich information from the original features.

4.3 Parameter Analysis

In this subsection, we analyze the parameters influence for the proposed ANMMF. The objective function of ANMMF model contains two balance parameters, λ_1 and λ_2. Concretely, λ_1 controls the importance of co-regularizing term and λ_2 controls the geometrical manifold regularization term. The clustering performance of ANMMF varies in terms of parameters is shown in the Fig. 1. As we can find, ANMMF is robust to the parameters with wide range. Especially, ANMMF can consistently achieve stable and excellent clustering performance even for λ_1 varies from 10^{-4} to 10^3 when the λ_2 is fixed.

We also test the effect of the number of components V. Here we fixed parameter in the best combinations for the experiments and varied V from 1 to 5 with an increment of 1. Seen from Fig. 2, The best performance of the number of multiple attributes always at $V = 3$ on most databases. Specifically, the accuracy increases sharply when V is tuned from 1 to 3, which indicates the effectiveness of ANMMF by exploring multiple attributes. Then the accuracy fluctuates slightly when V increases from 3 to 5. The fluctuation could be due to a compromise between the amount of features for each representation and the diverse information among them. Thus, we empirically fix $V = 3$.

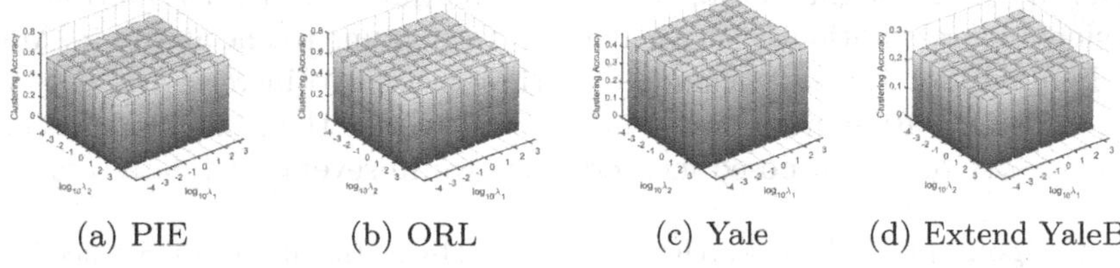

(a) PIE (b) ORL (c) Yale (d) Extend YaleB

Fig. 1. Clustering accuracy of ANMMF on four data sets with varying λ_1 and λ_2.

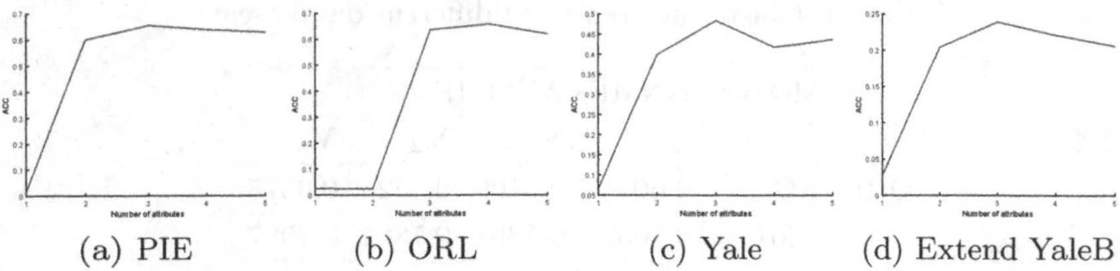

(a) PIE (b) ORL (c) Yale (d) Extend YaleB

Fig. 2. The effect of the number of components V.

4.4 Convergence Study

The updating rule of the minimized objective function of ANMMF is iterative in a natural way. In this section, we study the convergence behavior of the proposed algorithm from experimental aspect. The experimental convergence curve is shown in the Fig. 3, where y-axis is the value of the objective function and x-axis is the number of iterations. From the Fig. 3, we can clearly see that the optimization strategy monotonically decreases objective function and achieves a stable value in a few iterations, which indicates that the proposed ANMMF optimization method is very effective in practice.

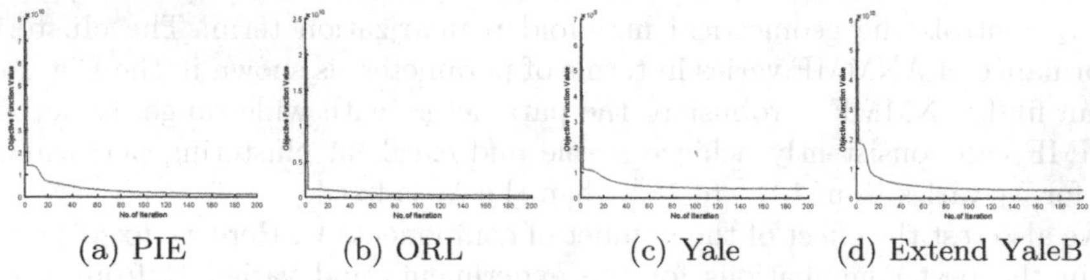

(a) PIE (b) ORL (c) Yale (d) Extend YaleB

Fig. 3. Convergence curves on the all data sets.

5 Conclusions

In this paper, we propose the Attributed Non-negative Matrix Multi-Factorization for Data Representation (ANMMF) approach which explores multi-attribute decomposition of data to understand data from various aspects. Different from NMF approaches that seek for a single low-dimensional representation based on original data, ANMMF simultaneously learns multiple low-dimensional representations with each one corresponding to one attribute. Moreover, Hilbert Independence Schmidt Criterion is used to increase the diversity between different attribute representations and reduce the redundant features. The superiority of the proposed method is shown in several real data sets.

Acknowledgements. This research was supported by National Natural Science Foundation of China under Grant No. 61772048, U19B2039, U1811463 and 61876012. It also was supported in part by Beijing Talents Project (2017A24).

References

1. Abdi, H., Williams, L.J.: Principal component analysis. Wiley Interdisc. Rev. Comput. Stats **2**(4), 433–459 (2010)
2. Cai, D., He, X., Han, J., Huang, T.S.: Graph regularized nonnegative matrix factorization for data representation. IEEE Trans. Pattern Anal. Mach. Intell. **338**, 1548–1560 (2011)
3. Cai, X., Nie, F., Huang, H.: Multi-view k-means clustering on big data. In: IJCAI (2013)
4. Dai, X., Zhang, K., Jiang, X., Zhang, X., Tu, Z., Zhang, N.: Weighted non-negative matrix factorization for image recovery and representation. In: 2020 10th ICIST, pp. 288–293. IEEE (2020)
5. Ding, C.H.Q., Li, T., Peng, W., Park, H.: Orthogonal nonnegative matrix trifactorizations for clustering. In: KDD 2006, pp. 20–23 (2006)
6. Eggert, J., Korner, E.: Sparse coding and NMF. In: IEEE IJCNN, vol. 4, pp. 2529–2533 (2004)
7. Ge, S., Luo, L., Li, H.: Orthogonal incremental non-negative matrix factorization algorithm and its application in image classification. Comput. Appl. Math. **39**(2), 1–16 (2020). https://doi.org/10.1007/s40314-020-1091-2
8. Georghiades, A.S., Belhumeur, P., Kriegman, D.: From few to many: illumination cone models for face recognition under variable lighting and pose. IEEE Trans. Pattern Anal. Mach. Intell. **23**, 643–660 (2001)
9. Gretton, A., Bousquet, O., Smola, A., Schölkopf, B.: Measuring statistical dependence with Hilbert-Schmidt norms. In: Jain, S., Simon, H.U., Tomita, E. (eds.) ALT 2005. LNCS (LNAI), vol. 3734, pp. 63–77. Springer, Heidelberg (2005). https://doi.org/10.1007/11564089_7
10. He, X., Niyogi, P.: Locality preserving projections. In: NIPS, vol. 16, no. 1, pp. 186–197 (2003)
11. Jia, Y., Kwong, S., Hou, J., Wu, W.: Semi-supervised non-negative matrix factorization with dissimilarity and similarity regularization. IEEE Trans. Neural Netw. Learn. Syst. **31**(7), 2510–2521 (2020)
12. Lee, D.D., Seung, H.S.: Learning the parts of objects by nonnegative matrix factorization. Nature **401**(7), 788–791 (1999)
13. Riffenburgh, R.H., Clunies-Ross, C.W.: Linear discriminant analysis. Pac. Sci. **3**(6), 27–33 (2013)
14. Shi, J., Malik, J.: Normalized cuts and image segmentation. IEEE Trans. Pattern Anal. Mach. Intell. **22**(8), 888–905 (2000)
15. Sim, T., Baker, S., Bsat, M.: The CMU pose, illumination, and expression database. IEEE Trans. Pattern Anal. Mach. Intell. **25**(12), 1615–1618 (2004)
16. Sun, J., Wang, Z., Sun, F., Li, H.: Sparse dual graph-regularized NMF for image co-clustering. Neurocomputing **316**(17), 156–165 (2018)
17. Wang, J., Tian, F., Wang, X., Yu, H., Liu, C.H., Yang, L.: Multi-component nonnegative matrix factorization. In: IJCAI (2017)
18. Yang, Z., Zhang, Y., Xiang, Y., Yan, W., Xie, S.: Non-negative matrix factorization with dual constraints for image clustering. IEEE Trans. Syst. Man Cybern. Syst. **50**, 2524–2533 (2020)

Improved Categorical Cross-Entropy Loss for Training Deep Neural Networks with Noisy Labels

Panle Li[1], Xiaohui He[2(✉)], Dingjun Song[1], Zihao Ding[3], Mengjia Qiao[1], Xijie Cheng[1], and Runchuan Li[1]

[1] School of Information Engineering, Zhengzhou University, Zhengzhou 450001, China

[2] School of Geoscience and Technology, Zhengzhou University, Zhengzhou 450001, China
hexh@zzu.edu.cn

[3] College of Communication Engineering, Xidian University, Xi'an 710000, China

Abstract. Deep neural networks (DNNs) have achieved impressive success in a variety of classification tasks. However, the presence of noisy labels in training dataset adversely affects the performance of DNNs. Recently, numerous noise-robust loss functions have been proposed to combat the noisy label problem. However, we find that these loss functions are either slow to learn the potential data pattern or not sufficiently robust against noisy labels. Here, we propose an improved categorical cross entropy (ICCE) to deal with this challenge. The ICCE can automatically adjust the weighting scheme based on the predicted probability distribution of DNNs by an exponential item, which makes it gain strong noise robustness and fast learning ability. A theoretical analysis of the ICCE is presented in the context of noisy labels. Experiments on datasets indicate that the ICCE can better improve the performance of DNNs even under high-level noise.

Keywords: DNNs · Noisy labels · Noise robustness

1 Introduction

Recently, deep neural networks (DNNs) have exhibited very impressive performance in many classification tasks [4,11,17]. However, in all such cases, very large and accurate training data are needed to achieve high-level performance. Although crowdsourcing platforms such as Amazon Mechanical Turk have made large-scale labeled data, noisy labels are often inevitable in the labeling process. The presence of noisy labels in the training dataset is known to impair the

---

Electronic supplementary material The online version of this chapter (https://doi.org/10.1007/978-3-030-88013-2_7) contains supplementary material, which is available to authorized users.

© Springer Nature Switzerland AG 2021
H. Ma et al. (Eds.): PRCV 2021, LNCS 13022, pp. 78–89, 2021.
https://doi.org/10.1007/978-3-030-88013-2_7

performance of DNNs [5,6,8,14]. Therefore, improving the robustness of DNNs with regard to noisy labels is of great importance, and it has attracted significant interest in recent years.

A promising method for handling noisy labels is to propose a noise-robust loss function [1,2,9,13,15]. [3] proposed a novel auxiliary image regularizer (AIR) for improving the loss function noise robustness. AIR aims to exploit the nonlinear manifold structure underlying images and encourage DNNs to select reliable images in the training process. [7] theoretically showed that the mean absolute error (MAE) can be robust against noisy labels under certain assumptions, while the categorical cross entropy (CCE) cannot. However, much researches show that the CCE has stronger learning ability than MAE [12], which can make DNNs obtain higher performance in a shorter training time. Therefore, [18] proposed a more generalized cross-entropy loss (GCE) for training DNNs under a noisy dataset. The GCE is a noise-robust loss function that combines the advantages of MAE and CCE. Following the works by [7] and [18], [16] proposed an improved MAE (IMAE) loss function to improve the learning speed of MAE. They transformed the gradients of MAE to nonlinear with an exponential function to enlarge the contribution of examples. However, as we demonstrate below, the IMAE is not sufficiently robust to noise since it places too much emphasis on noisy examples.

To deal with this challenge, we propose an improved categorical cross entropy (ICCE) for training DNNs under the noisy dataset. Based on the predicted probability distribution of DNNs, the ICCE can automatically adjust the weighting scheme of CCE by an exponential item. As a result, the ICCE gains strong noise robustness since it places a small weight on noisy samples. Meanwhile, by giving more weight to clean samples, the ICCE has a fast learning ability to learn the true label distribution hidden clean examples. The main contribution of this paper falls into two aspects. First, we develop a novel noise-robust loss function, ICCE, and present a theoretical analysis of the proposed loss functions in the context of noisy labels. Second, we report a thorough empirical evaluation of the proposed loss function using CIFAR-10 and CIFAR-100, which demonstrates significant improvement in terms of classification accuracy.

2 Improved Categorical Cross-Entropy Loss for Noise-Robust Classification

In this section, we start by analyzing the drawbacks of CCE and MAE as classification loss functions for DNNs on noisy datasets. Then, an improved categorical cross-entropy (ICCE) loss function is proposed to improve the noise robustness of DNNs. Finally, some novel analytical results about ICCE are presented to give a clear understanding.

2.1 Robustness Analysis of CCE and MAE

It is well known that the deep neural network f can be viewed as a black box, and the update of parameters θ is based on the backpropagation of the gradient.

$$\theta^{(l)} \leftarrow \theta^{(l)} + \tau \triangle \theta^{(l)} \tag{1}$$

where τ is the leaning rate. The $\triangle\theta^{(l)}$ is the update magnitude for each training sample, which is obtained through the gradient of the loss function. Therefore, an example's contribution can be measured by the gradient's magnitude of the loss function. This can be regarded as an example weighting that is a naturally built-in loss function. Let us look at the gradient of the CCE and MAE loss function respect to the output of the final layer z_j:

$$\frac{\partial L_{CCE}(f(\boldsymbol{x}), y)}{\partial z_j} = \begin{cases} p(y|\boldsymbol{x}) - 1 & j = y \\ p(j|\boldsymbol{x}) & j \neq y \end{cases} \tag{2}$$

$$\frac{\partial L_{MAE}(f(\boldsymbol{x}), y)}{\partial z_j} = \begin{cases} 2p(y|\boldsymbol{x})(1 - p(y|\boldsymbol{x})) & j = y \\ 2p(y|\boldsymbol{x})p(j|\boldsymbol{x}) & j \neq y \end{cases} \tag{3}$$

where y is the ground truth of example $\boldsymbol{x}$ and j is the predicted label. Let K is the total number class, $p(j|\boldsymbol{x})$ can be denoted

$$p(j|\boldsymbol{x}) = \frac{\exp(z_j)}{\sum_{i=1}^{K} \exp(z_i)}, j \in [K] \tag{4}$$

From the Eq. 2 and 3, we can see that CCE places more weight on the sample than MAE when the predicted probability $p(y|\boldsymbol{x})$ is smaller the 0.5. This is the reason why the CCE has a faster learning speed than MAE. However, this weighting scheme of CCE is desirable for training with clean data. When noisy examples are included in the training dataset, their predicted probability is usually lower than 0.5 at the beginning of training process [18] (See the Fig. 1). In this case, the CCE more easily overfits the noisy sample than MAE. Conversely, the MAE places small weights on the low prediction probability samples that are more likely to be noisy samples [16,18]. This trait makes it more robust to noisy labels, but it also slows the learning speed on the clean training examples and lead to a significantly longer training time before convergence. Furthermore, from the Eq. 2 and 3, the MAE tend to place more weight than CCE on examples in which the predicted probability is larger than 0.5. These samples are more likely to be clean at the later training stage. In this case, the training loss will fluctuate, and the classification accuracy can be affected.

2.2 Improved Categorical Cross Entropy

To exploit the benefits of both the noise robustness provided by MAE and the implicit weighting scheme of CCE, we propose an improved categorical cross-entropy (ICCE) loss function:

$$\begin{aligned} L_{ICCE}(f(\boldsymbol{x}), y) &= \sum_{j=1}^{K} \boldsymbol{y}_j \int_{p(j|\boldsymbol{x})}^{1} \frac{e^{T(p(j|\boldsymbol{x})-0.5)}}{p(j|\boldsymbol{x})} dp(j|\boldsymbol{x}) \\ &= \int_{p(y|\boldsymbol{x})}^{1} \frac{e^{T(p(y|\boldsymbol{x})-0.5)}}{p(y|\boldsymbol{x})} dp(y|\boldsymbol{x}) \end{aligned} \tag{5}$$

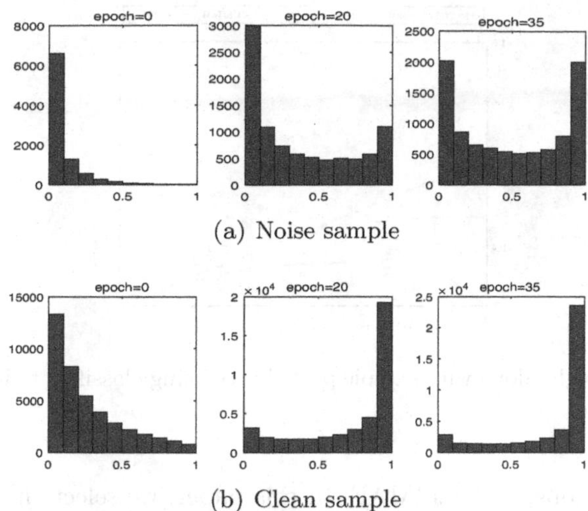

(a) Noise sample

(b) Clean sample

Fig. 1. The predicted probability distribution of ResNet56 on CIFAR-10 for clean and noisy samples ($\eta = 0.2$). The horizontal axis denotes the predicted probability and the vertical axis denotes the frequence.

where $\boldsymbol{y}$ is the one-hot encoded label of the sample $\boldsymbol{x}$ and $\boldsymbol{y}_j$ corresponds to the jth element of $\boldsymbol{y}$. T controls the exponential base. The ICCE loss combines the weighting advantages of CCE and MAE, which weights the samples with nonlinearly:

$$\frac{\partial L_{CCE}(f(\boldsymbol{x}), y)}{\partial z_j} = \begin{cases} e^{T(p(y|\boldsymbol{x})-0.5)}(p(y|\boldsymbol{x}) - 1) & j = y \\ e^{T(p(y|\boldsymbol{x})-0.5)}p(j|\boldsymbol{x}) & j \neq y \end{cases} \tag{6}$$

It is obvious that the proposed loss function is equivalent to CCE for $T = 0$. Hence, this loss is a generalization of CCE. The ICCE can achieve strong noise robustness and while has faster learning speed than other loss function. To make a clear understand, we provide a detail comparison with other popular loss functions for $j = y$ as following. For $j \neq y$, we can draw the same conclusion. The Fig. 2 shows the weight comparison of different loss functions for $j = y$. It can be shown that the weight of ICCE with T = 1 or 2 is less than the improved MAE (IMAE) [16] and larger than the generalized cross-entropy loss (GCE) [18] at $p(j|\boldsymbol{x}) < 0.5$. This means that the ICCE has more noise robustness than IMAE and more learning speed than GCE. Before $p(j|\boldsymbol{x}) < 0.5$, the weight change in MAE and CCE is similar to GCE and IMAE, respectively, which indicates that ICCE has an advantage in noise robustness over MAE and CCE. Moreover, the examples in which $p(j|\boldsymbol{x})$ is larger than 0.5 are more likely to be clean. In this case, the ICCE with $T < 1$ has a faster learning speed than GCE and CCE but a lower learning speed than IMAE and MAE. We can increase T to promote the learning speed of ICCE. However, too much T is more likely

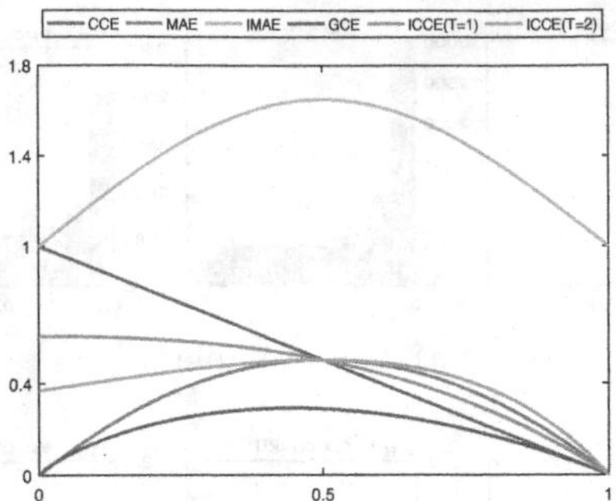

Fig. 2. Sample weight along with sample probability being classified to its labeled class.

to cause fluctuations, such as IMAE. In this paper, we select the optimal T by conducting several experiments.

2.3 Theoretical Analysis of ICCE

In this section, we present some novel analytical results about ICCE from the theory. First, the sum of ICCE with respect to all classes is proven to be bounded by Theorem 5 and Theorem 2. Then, Theorem 3 and Theorem 4 show the error bounds of the optimal classifier obtained by ICCE on uniform and class-dependent noise, respectively.

Theorem 1. *For any $p(y|\boldsymbol{x}) \in [\epsilon, 1]$ and $T \geq 1$, the L_{ICCE} loss is bounded by:*

$$0 \leq L_{ICCE}(f(\boldsymbol{x}), y) \leq B \tag{7}$$

where $B = (1-\epsilon)\max(\frac{e^{T(\epsilon-0.5)}}{\epsilon}, e^{0.5T})$ (The proof see Appendix).

Based on the Theorem 1, we will show the L_{ICCE} loss with respect to all classes is bounded under condition $p(y|\boldsymbol{x}) \in [\epsilon, 1]$ and $T \geq 1$.

Theorem 2. *For any $p(y|\boldsymbol{x}) \in [\epsilon, 1]$ and $T \geq 1$, the sum of L_{ICCE} loss with respect to all classes is bounded by:*

$$0 \leq \sum_{i=1}^{K} L_{ICCE}(f(\boldsymbol{x}), i) \leq A \tag{8}$$

where $A = KB$

Proof. Based on the Theorem 1, we can obtain:

$$\sum_{i=1}^{K} 0 \leq \sum_{i=1}^{K} L_{ICCE}(f(\boldsymbol{x}), i) \leq \sum_{i=1}^{K} B \Longrightarrow 0 \leq \sum_{i=1}^{K} L_{ICCE}(f(\boldsymbol{x}), i) \leq KB \tag{9}$$

□

Remark 1. Theorem 2 shows that the sum of L_{ICCE} with all class is bound under a weak condition, $p(y|\boldsymbol{x}) \in [\epsilon, 1]$ and $T \geq 1$. Since T is a constant that control the exponential base, it is easy to set $T \geq 1$. In addition, although $p(y|\boldsymbol{x}) \in [0, 1]$ in theory, but we observe that the $p(y|\boldsymbol{x})$ is not equal 0 since the output of softmax layer is large than 0. In a word, our restrictive condition is reasonable in real application.

Next, we will show that the optimal classifier obtained by L_{ICCE} through risk minimization has the error bound under the uniform noise and class dependent noise.

Theorem 3. *Using the bound in Theorem 2 and under uniform noise with* $\eta \leq 1 - \frac{1}{K}$*, we can show*

$$-\frac{\eta K B}{K-1} \leq R^{\eta}_{L_{ICCE}}(f^*_\eta) - R_{L_{ICCE}}(f^*) \leq B \tag{10}$$

where f^*_η *is the global optimal classifier on the* $\mathcal{D}_\eta$*, and* f^* *is the global optimal classifier on* $\mathcal{D}$*.* $R_{L_{ICCE}}(\cdot)$ *is the risk function of* L_{ICCE}*.*

Proof. Recall that for any classifier f, the risk of f is defined as

$$R_{L_{ICCE}}(f) = \mathbb{E}_{\mathcal{D}}[L_{ICCE}(f(\boldsymbol{x}), y)] = \mathbb{E}_{\boldsymbol{x},y}[L_{ICCE}(f(\boldsymbol{x}), y)]$$

where $\mathbb{E}$ denotes expectation. And since for uniform noise with noise rate η, we have

$$\begin{aligned}
R^{\eta}_{L_{ICCE}}(f) &= \mathbb{E}_{\mathcal{D}_\eta}[L_{ICCE}(f(\boldsymbol{x}), \hat{y})] = \mathbb{E}_{\boldsymbol{x},\hat{y}}[L_{ICCE}(f(\boldsymbol{x}), \hat{y})] \\
&= \mathbb{E}_{\boldsymbol{x}}\mathbb{E}_{y|\boldsymbol{x}}\mathbb{E}_{\hat{y}|y,\boldsymbol{x}}[L_{ICCE}(f(\boldsymbol{x}), \hat{y})] \\
&= \mathbb{E}_{\boldsymbol{x}}\mathbb{E}_{y|\boldsymbol{x}}[(1-\eta)L_{ICCE}(f(\boldsymbol{x}), y) + \frac{\eta}{K-1}\sum_{i \neq y} L_{ICCE}(f(\boldsymbol{x}), i)] \\
&= \mathbb{E}_{\boldsymbol{x}}\mathbb{E}_{y|\boldsymbol{x}}[(1-\eta)L_{ICCE}(f(\boldsymbol{x}), y) + \frac{\eta}{K-1}(\sum_{i=1}^{K} L_{ICCE}(f(\boldsymbol{x}), i) \\
&\qquad - L_{ICCE}(f(\boldsymbol{x}), y))] \\
&= (1-\eta)R_{L_{ICCE}}(f) - \frac{\eta}{K-1}R_{L_{ICCE}}(f) + \frac{\eta}{K-1}\mathbb{E}_{\boldsymbol{x}}\mathbb{E}_{y|\boldsymbol{x}}[\sum_{i=1}^{K} \\
&\qquad L_{ICCE}(f(\boldsymbol{x}), i)] \\
&= (1 - \frac{\eta K}{K-1})R_{L_{ICCE}}(f) + \frac{\eta}{K-1}\mathbb{E}_{\boldsymbol{x}}\mathbb{E}_{y|\boldsymbol{x}}[\sum_{i=1}^{K} L_{ICCE}(f(\boldsymbol{x}), i)]
\end{aligned}$$

Now, from Theorem 2, we have

$$\begin{aligned}
(1 - \frac{\eta K}{K-1})R_{L_{ICCE}}(f) \leq R^{\eta}_{L_{ICCE}}(f) \leq& \\
&(1 - \frac{\eta K}{K-1})R_{L_{ICCE}}(f) + \frac{\eta}{K-1}A
\end{aligned}$$

Thus, for f^*_η and f^* are the global optimal classifier on the $\mathcal{D}_\eta$ and $\mathcal{D}$, respectively.

$$\begin{aligned}
&R^{\eta}_{L_{ICCE}}(f^*_\eta) - R_{L_{ICCE}}(f^*) \leq \\
&(1 - \frac{\eta K}{K-1})R_{L_{ICCE}}(f^*_\eta) + \frac{\eta A}{K-1} - R_{L_{ICCE}}(f^*) \\
&\leq (1 - \frac{\eta K}{K-1})(R_{L_{ICCE}}(f^*_\eta) - R_{L_{ICCE}}(f^*)) + \frac{\eta A}{K-1} \\
&\leq B
\end{aligned}$$

because $\eta \leq 1 - \frac{1}{K}$ and $R_{L_{ICCE}}(f_\eta^*) - R_{L_{ICCE}}(f^*) < B$. This proves $R^\eta_{L_{ICCE}}(f_\eta^*) - R_{L_{ICCE}}(f^*)$ has the up-bound.

$$
\begin{aligned}
R^\eta_{L_{ICCE}}(f_\eta^*) - R_{L_{ICCE}}(\hat{f}) &\geq (1 - \frac{\eta K}{K-1}) R_{L_{ICCE}}(f_\eta^*) - R_{L_{ICCE}}(\hat{f}) \\
&= (1 - \frac{\eta K}{K-1})(R_{L_{ICCE}}(f_\eta^*) - R_{L_{ICCE}}(f^*)) - \frac{\eta K}{K-1} R_{L_{ICCE}}(f^*) \\
&\geq -\frac{\eta K B}{K-1}
\end{aligned}
$$

because $\eta \leq 1 - \frac{1}{K}$ and $R_{L_{ICCE}}(f_\eta^*) < B$. This proves $R^\eta_{L_{ICCE}}(f_\eta^*) - R_{L_{ICCE}}(f^*)$ has the bottom-bound. This completes the proof. □

Remark 2. Theorem 3 shows that the optimal classifier obtained by L_{ICCE} has the error bound when the uniform noise rate is small the $1 - \frac{1}{K}$. This does not depend on the data distribution. This theorem generalizes the existing results Theorem 1 in [7] and [18].

Theorem 4. *Using the bound in Theorem 3 and under class dependent noise with $\eta_{ij} \leq 1 - \eta_i$, $\forall j \neq i$, $\forall i, j \in [K]$, where $\eta_{ij} = p(\hat{y} = j | y = i), \forall j \neq i$, and $\eta_i = \sum_{j \neq i} \eta_{ij}$, then*

$$
\begin{aligned}
-A\mathbb{E}_{\mathcal{D}}(2 - \eta_y) - B \leq & R^\eta_{L_{ICCE}}(f_\eta^*) - R_{L_{ICCE}}(f^*) \\
& \leq A\mathbb{E}_{D}(1 - \eta_y) + (K-1)B
\end{aligned} \tag{11}
$$

where f_η^* is the global optimal classifier on the $\mathcal{D}_\eta$, and f^* is the global optimal classifier on $\mathcal{D}$.

Proof. From the Theorem 3, we have

$$
-\sum_{i \neq y}^{K} L_{ICCE}(f(\boldsymbol{x}), i) \leq L_{ICCE}(f(\boldsymbol{x}), y) \leq A - \sum_{i \neq y}^{K} L_{ICCE}(f(\boldsymbol{x}), i)
$$

Under class dependent noise, for any f

$$
\begin{aligned}
R^\eta_{L_{ICCE}}(f) &= \mathbb{E}_{\mathcal{D}}[(1 - \eta_y) L_{ICCE}(f(\boldsymbol{x}), y)] + \mathbb{E}_{\mathcal{D}}[\sum_{i \neq y}^{K} \eta_{y,i} L(f(\boldsymbol{x}), i)] \\
&\leq \mathbb{E}_{\mathcal{D}}[(1 - \eta_y)(A - \sum_{i \neq y}^{K} L(f(\boldsymbol{x}), i))] + \mathbb{E}_{\mathcal{D}}[\sum_{i \neq y}^{K} \eta_{y,i} L(f(\boldsymbol{x}), i)] \\
&= A\mathbb{E}_{\mathcal{D}}(1 - \eta_y) - \mathbb{E}_{\mathcal{D}}[\sum_{i \neq y}(1 - \eta_y - \eta_{y,i}) L(f(\boldsymbol{x}), i)]
\end{aligned}
$$

and

$$
\begin{aligned}
R^\eta_{L_{ICCE}}(f) &= \mathbb{E}_{\mathcal{D}}[(1 - \eta_y) L_{ICCE}(f(\boldsymbol{x}), y)] + \mathbb{E}_{\mathcal{D}}[\sum_{i \neq y}^{K} \eta_{y,i} L(f(\boldsymbol{x}), i)] \\
&\geq \mathbb{E}_{\mathcal{D}}[(1 - \eta_y)(-\sum_{i \neq y}^{K} L(f(\boldsymbol{x}), i))] + \mathbb{E}_{\mathcal{D}}[\sum_{i \neq y}^{K} \eta_{y,i} L(f(\boldsymbol{x}), i)] \\
&= -\mathbb{E}_{\mathcal{D}}[\sum_{i \neq y}^{K}(1 - \eta_y - \eta_{y,i}) L(f(\boldsymbol{x}), i)]
\end{aligned}
$$

Thus, for f_η^* and f^* are the global optimal classifier on the $\mathcal{D}_\eta$ and $\mathcal{D}$, respectively.

$$
\begin{aligned}
&R^\eta_{L_{ICCE}}(f_\eta^*) - R(f^*) \le \\
&A\mathbb{E}_\mathcal{D}(1-\eta_y) - \mathbb{E}_\mathcal{D}[\sum_{i\neq y}^{K}(1-\eta_y-\eta_{y,i})L(f_\eta^*(\boldsymbol{x}),i)] - \mathbb{E}_\mathcal{D}[L_{ICCE}(f^*(\boldsymbol{x}),y)] \\
&\le A\mathbb{E}_\mathcal{D}(1-\eta_y) - \mathbb{E}_\mathcal{D}[\sum_{i\neq y}^{K}(1-\eta_y-\eta_{y,i})L_{ICCE}(f_\eta^*(\boldsymbol{x}),i) \\
&\qquad + \sum_{i\neq y}^{K} L_{ICCE}(f^*(\boldsymbol{x}),i)] \le A\mathbb{E}_\mathcal{D}(1-\eta_y)
\end{aligned}
$$

because $\eta_{ij} \le 1-\eta_i$ and $L_{ICCE}(f) \ge 0$. This proves $R^\eta_{L_{ICCE}}(f_\eta^*) - R_{L_{ICCE}}(f^*)$ has the up-bound.

$$
\begin{aligned}
&R^\eta_{L_{ICCE}}(f_\eta^*) - R(f^*) \\
&\ge -\mathbb{E}_\mathcal{D}[\sum_{i\neq y}^{K}(1-\eta_y-\eta_{y,i})L_{ICCE}(f_\eta^*(\boldsymbol{x}),i) - \mathbb{E}_\mathcal{D}[L_{ICCE}(f^*(\boldsymbol{x}),y)] \\
&\ge -A - \mathbb{E}_\mathcal{D}[\sum_{i\neq y}^{K}(1-\eta_y-\eta_{y,i})L_{ICCE}(f_\eta^*(\boldsymbol{x}),i) - \sum_{i\neq y}^{K} L_{ICCE}(f^*(\boldsymbol{x}),i)] \\
&\ge -A - \mathbb{E}_\mathcal{D}[\sum_{i\neq y}^{K}(1-\eta_y-\eta_{y,i})(L_{ICCE}(f_\eta^*(\boldsymbol{x}),i) - L_{ICCE}(f^*(\boldsymbol{x}),i))] \\
&\ge -A - B\mathbb{E}_\mathcal{D}[\sum_{i\neq y}^{K}(1-\eta_y-\eta_{y,i})] \\
&= -A\mathbb{E}_\mathcal{D}(2-\eta_y) - B
\end{aligned}
$$

because $\eta_{ij} \le 1-\eta_i$ and $L_{ICCE}(f_\eta^*) - L_{ICCE}(f^*) < B$. This proves $R^\eta_{L_{ICCE}}(f_\eta^*) - R_{L_{ICCE}}(f^*)$ has the bottom-bound. □

Remark 3. Theorem 4 establishes an error bound of the optimal classifier trained on class dependent noise training dataset with L_{ICCE}. The condition only needs $\eta_{ij} \le 1-\eta_i$.

3 Experiment

3.1 Dataset and Model Architectures

The CIFAR-10 and CIFAR-100 [10] datasets are used in our experiments to verify the performance of ICCE. CIFAR-10 and CIFAR-100 [10] are two image classification image datasets that contain 10 and 100 classes, respectively. Both of them have approximately 50k images for training and 10k images for testing. The image size is 32×32.

In this paper, we use two DNN models, ResNet44 and ResNet56, which are given by the Keras office. All hyperparameter settings are kept fixed for all experiments using these datasets. Following previous works, we used stochastic gradient descent (SGD) with Ada and an initial learning rate of 0.0001. The learning rate divides 10 after 100 epochs for all datasets.

3.2 Label Noise

We synthesize noisy data from clean data by stochastically changing some of the labels. For uniform noise, the label of each image is replaced by one of the other class labels with a probability of η. Following [13,18], class-dependent noise is generated by flipping each class into the next circularly with probability η.

3.3 Evaluation of the CIFAR Dataset with Synthetic Noise

We validate our method through a series of experiments conducted on the CIFAR-10 and CIFAR-100 datasets. Two other state-of-the-art approaches are reimplemented in this paper. One is an improved mean absolute error (IMAE) [16], which exploits the potential performance of MAE. The other is the generalized cross-entropy loss (GCE) [18], which is an improvement of cross-entropy loss. We list all the experimental results in Table 1 and Table 2. The quantitative results on

Table 1. Average test accuracy on CIFAR-10. We report accuracies when the model achieves convergence. $T = 4$ is used for all experiments with ICCE loss. The best accuracy is boldfaced.

Network	Loss function	$\eta = 0.0$	Uniform noise			Class dependent noise		
			$\eta = 0.2$	$\eta = 0.3$	$\eta = 0.4$	$\eta = 0.2$	$\eta = 0.3$	$\eta = 0.4$
ResNet44	CCE	0.8635	0.6737	0.5823	0.5116	0.6835	0.6013	0.5068
	MAE	0.7604	0.7673	0.5963	0.5923	0.5587	0.5048	0.4320
	IMAE	0.8409	0.7615	0.6940	0.5791	0.7459	0.6084	0.5216
	GCE	0.8588	0.8066	0.7824	0.7366	0.7476	0.6381	0.5090
	ICCE	**0.8624**	**0.8213**	**0.7954**	**0.7543**	**0.7796**	**0.6634**	**0.5304**
ResNet56	CCE	0.8551	0.6697	0.5900	0.5830	0.6896	0.6027	0.5151
	MAE	0.7619	0.6688	0.4099	0.2470	0.4827	0.3784	0.3916
	IMAE	0.8529	0.7766	0.6869	0.6464	0.7542	0.6113	0.5169
	GCE	0.8530	0.8131	0.7848	0.7512	0.7454	0.6465	0.5105
	ICCE	**0.8616**	**0.8210**	**0.7919**	**0.7662**	**0.7737**	**0.6690**	**0.5217**

CIFAR-10 are summarized in Table 1. The T is set to 4 for ICCE in the following experiments. We have used uniform noise and class-dependent noise with $\eta = 0.0, 0.2, 0.3, 0.4$. We observe that ICCE is superior to the state-of-the-art (i.e., the bold values in Table 1). When $\eta = 0.0$, the ICCE only has a slight advantage over the other methods. When the noise rate increases from 0.0 to 0.4, the accuracy of all methods drops with the noise rate. However, in all cases, the decrease in accuracy with ICCE is much less than other methods, especially for MAE. This is because the MAE has a very slow learning speed and easily falls into the local optimal solution.

In Fig. 3, we show the test accuracies of ResNet56 with the number of training epochs on the CIFAR-10 dataset. We show the results for uniform noise and class-dependent noise under serious level. We can see that the ICCE loss is highly robust to uniform and class-dependent noise and the accuracy achieved with ICCE loss is higher than other methods. Specifically, as training goes, CCE always tries to fit the noisy training dataset, which shows that CCE learns considerable error information when severe noise exists. MAE has a very low learning speed, and the final accuracy is not compared with ICCE. In regard to the IMAE, we find that it has a fast learning speed. However, it is also easy to overfit the noisy example, which leads to a negative effect on model performance. The GCE shows better performance than other methods, but the best accuracy is smaller than that of ICCE regardless of the neural network and noise rate. Especially for $\eta = 0.4$, the gap between the ICCE and GCE is significantly larger than other noise rates. This demonstrates that the ICCE has strong noise robustness on the training dataset that suffered serious noise. Besides the higher test accuracies, we can find that ICCE is the earliest convergence compared with other methods in most cases.

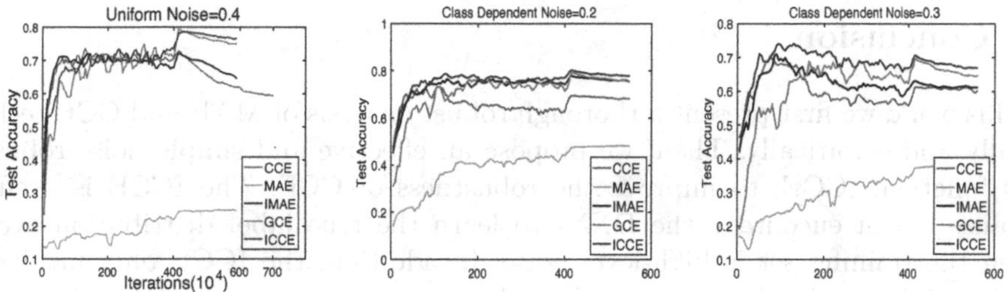

Fig. 3. The test accuracy of ResNet56 against training iterations on CIFAR-10 with noise.

The quantitative results on CIFAR-100 are summarized in Table 2. CIFAR-100 contains more class examples than CIFAR-10, and it is a more challenging dataset. Therefore, the overall test accuracies on CIFAR-100 are not compared with CIFAR-10. It is clear that the ICCE shows the best accuracy compared to the other methods. Although the MAE has strong noise robustness in theory, it shows worse performance in the challenge dataset. The IMAE and GCE indeed improve the noise robustness for DNNs. However, there are still some gaps between ICCE and IMAE and GCE, especially for larger noise level. These experimental results demonstrate that ICCE has the ability to obtain excellent noise robustness performance in the challenge classification dataset.

Table 2. Average test accuracy on CIFAR-100. We report accuracies when model achieves convergence. $T = 4$ was used for all experiments with ICCE. The best accuracy is boldfaced.

Network	Loss function	$\eta = 0.0$	Uniform noise			Class dependent noise		
			$\eta = 0.2$	$\eta = 0.3$	$\eta = 0.4$	$\eta = 0.2$	$\eta = 0.3$	$\eta = 0.4$
ResNet44	CCE	0.6891	0.6015	0.5433	0.4542	0.6226	0.5945	0.5529
	MAE	0.3086	0.2722	0.2521	0.2507	0.2446	0.2420	0.2417
	IMAE	0.6455	0.5876	0.5819	0.5337	0.6076	0.5427	0.4831
	GCE	0.6643	0.5731	0.5496	0.4349	0.5591	0.5552	0.5019
	ICCE	**0.6878**	**0.6177**	**0.6053**	**0.5540**	**0.6296**	**0.6093**	**0.5540**
ResNet56	CCE	0.6880	0.5677	0.5191	0.5026	0.6254	0.5857	0.5309
	MAE	0.2945	0.2830	0.3053	0.1831	0.2842	0.2351	0.2117
	IMAE	0.6631	0.6076	0.5924	0.5563	0.6137	0.5694	0.5012
	GCE	0.6646	0.5295	0.4938	0.4757	0.5539	0.5217	0.4918
	ICCE	**0.6913**	**0.6116**	**0.5947**	**0.5569**	**0.6323**	**0.5951**	**0.5438**

4 Conclusion

In this work, we first present a thorough robust analysis of MAE and CCE technically and empirically. Then, we propose an effective and simple noise-robust loss function, ICCE, to improve the robustness of CCE. The ICCE is useful because it can encourage the DNNs to learn the true label distribution even when the training set is high-level noise. In addition, the ICCE only involves minimal intervention to existing DNNs without any change in the network architecture. Furthermore, we present extensive theoretical analysis to illustrate the robustness of ICCE.

References

1. Algan, G., Ulusoy, I.: Image classification with deep learning in the presence of noisy labels: a survey. arXiv preprint arXiv:1912.05170 (2019)
2. Arpit, D., et al.: A closer look at memorization in deep networks. arXiv: Machine Learning (2017)
3. Azadi, S., Feng, J., Jegelka, S., Darrell, T.: Auxiliary image regularization for deep CNNs with noisy labels. arXiv: Computer Vision and Pattern Recognition (2015)
4. Ding, G., Guo, Y., Chen, K., Chu, C., Han, J., Dai, Q.: DECODE: deep confidence network for robust image classification. IEEE Trans. Image Process. **28**(8), 3752–3765 (2019)
5. Frenay, B., Verleysen, M.: Classification in the presence of label noise: a survey. IEEE Trans. Neural Networks **25**(5), 845–869 (2014)
6. Gevaert, C.M., Persello, C., Elberink, S.O., Vosselman, G., Sliuzas, R.: Context-based filtering of noisy labels for automatic basemap updating from UAV data. IEEE J. Sel. Topics Appl. Earth Observ. Remote Sens. **11**(8), 2731–2741 (2017)

7. Ghosh, A., Kumar, H., Sastry, P.: Robust loss functions under label noise for deep neural networks. In: Thirty-First AAAI Conference on Artificial Intelligence, pp. 1919–1925
8. Jiang, L., Zhou, Z., Leung, T., Li, L., Fei-Fei, L.M.: Regularizing very deep neural networks on corrupted labels. ICML (2018)
9. Karimi, D., Dou, H., Warfield, S.K., Gholipour, A.: Deep learning with noisy labels: exploring techniques and remedies in medical image analysis. Med. Image Anal. **65**, 101759 (2020)
10. Krizhevsky, A., Hinton, G., et al.: Learning multiple layers of features from tiny images (2009)
11. Krizhevsky, A., Sutskever, I., Hinton, G.E.: ImageNet classification with deep convolutional neural networks, pp. 1097–1105 (2012)
12. Manwani, N., Sastry, P.: Noise tolerance under risk minimization. IEEE Trans. Cybernet. **43**(3), 1146–1151 (2013)
13. Patrini, G., Rozza, A., Krishna Menon, A., Nock, R., Qu, L.: Making deep neural networks robust to label noise: a loss correction approach. In: Proceedings of the IEEE Conference on Computer Vision and Pattern Recognition, pp. 1944–1952 (2017)
14. Pelletier, C., Valero, S., Inglada, J., Dedieu, G., Champion, N.: Filtering mislabeled data for improving time series classification. In: 2017 9th International Workshop on the Analysis of Multitemporal Remote Sensing Images (MultiTemp), pp. 1–4. IEEE (2017)
15. Reed, S., Lee, H., Anguelov, D., Szegedy, C., Erhan, D., Rabinovich, A.: Training deep neural networks on noisy labels with bootstrapping. arXiv preprint arXiv:1412.6596 (2014)
16. Wang, X., Hua, Y., Kodirov, E., Robertson, N.M.: IMAE for noise-robust learning: mean absolute error does not treat examples equally and gradient magnitude's variance matters (2019)
17. Yuan, J.: Learning building extraction in aerial scenes with convolutional networks. IEEE Trans. Pattern Anal. Mach. Intell. **40**(11), 2793–2798 (2018)
18. Zhang, Z., Sabuncu, M.: Generalized cross entropy loss for training deep neural networks with noisy labels. In: Bengio, S., Wallach, H., Larochelle, H., Grauman, K., Cesa-Bianchi, N., Garnett, R. (eds.) Advances in Neural Information Processing Systems, vol. 31, pp. 8778–8788. Curran Associates, Inc. (2018)

A Residual Correction Approach for Semi-supervised Semantic Segmentation

Haoliang Li[1,2,3] and Huicheng Zheng[1,2,3](✉)

[1] School of Computer Science and Engineering, Sun Yat-sen University, Guangzhou, China
zhenghch@mail.sysu.edu.cn

[2] Key Laboratory of Machine Intelligence and Advanced Computing, Ministry of Education, Guangzhou, China

[3] Guangdong Key Laboratory of Information Security Technology, Guangzhou, China

Abstract. Fully-supervised deep learning models have achieved a great success in complex semantic segmentation tasks. However, the segmentation annotations are prohibitively expensive, which causes a growing interest in the methods that require lower annotating cost but still achieve a competitive performance. This paper proposes a residual correction approach based on self-training for semi-supervised semantic segmentation. We train a residual correction network built on top of the segmentation network with labeled data to predict a residual of the original segmentation. For unlabeled data, the output of the residual correction network is combined with the original segmentation to form the pseudo label used to train the segmentation network. Extensive experimental results on the PASCAL VOC 2012 and the Cityscapes datasets demonstrate the effectiveness of the proposed approach.

Keywords: Semantic segmentation · Semi-supervised learning · Self-training

1 Introduction

With the emergence of deep learning, most computer vision researches have been turned towards Convolutional Neural Networks (CNNs) [13] from traditional machine learning algorithms. Current state-of-the-art deep learning models based on CNNs achieve a great success in the domains of computer vision with the availability of huge amount of annotated data. However, the acquisition of annotated data is often expensive and time-consuming, especially for segmentation asking for pixel-level annotation.

In the task of semantic segmentation, semi-supervised learning (SSL) and weakly-supervised learning (WSL) has been extensively explored to reduce the cost of labeling [14,17,22–24,28]. Compared with fully-supervised learning using

© Springer Nature Switzerland AG 2021
H. Ma et al. (Eds.): PRCV 2021, LNCS 13022, pp. 90–102, 2021.
https://doi.org/10.1007/978-3-030-88013-2_8

pixel-level annotation, semi-supervised semantic segmentation leverages unlabeled data to enhance the performance, while weakly-supervised semantic segmentation exploits weakly-annotated samples. The leading progresses consist of consistency regularization [14,23,24], adversarial training [11,25,27], self-training [16,31], and so on. The objective of consistency regularization is to enforce the model's predictions to be invariant when small perturbations are applied to the inputs. Methods based on adversarial training extend the generator of the generic Generative Adversarial Networks (GANs) [9] framework to segmentation network and enforce the discriminator to discriminate ground truths and predictions with an adversarial loss so as to adapt for SSL setting. The principle of self-training is to generate pseudo pixel-level labels for unlabeled or weakly-labeled data, which are used to train model in a supervised manner, together with the original strongly-labeled data. Self-training framework is generally more generic and simpler in contrast to hand-crafted perturbations of consistency regularization and the complex training process of adversarial training.

We propose a residual correction approach that trains semantic segmentation models in a self-training framework. The key to self-training schemes is how to generate pseudo labels. [11,22] picked pseudo labels according to the confidence of discriminator classifying the given segmentation as either real or fake, while their difference is discriminating at image-level [22] or pixel-level [11]. Moreover, [21] introduced a correction network to transform the given image-segmentation pair to a correction map of $N+1$ classes, including N original semantic classes and one additional class indicating whether the input segmentation matches the ground truth. Then the original segmentations of unlabeled data is corrected by the correction map and serve as pseudo labels. In contrast, we extend the segmentation network with an additional residual correction network which fuses the image and its segmentation more efficiently and outputs a residual instead of matching regions in [21]. It leads to an adaptive weighting scheme to solve the problem of class imbalances in [21]. Two networks of our approach work collaboratively to generate pseudo labels on unlabeled images. Main contributions of this paper are summarized as follows:

- We design a residual correction network, which fuses the information of the input image and its original segmentation efficiently and capture complementary knowledge in residual form.
- We propose a training schedule for semi-supervised semantic segmentation, where a segmentation network and a residual correction network are trained jointly to perform a self-training scheme.
- We carry out extensive and detailed experiments to demonstrate the effectiveness of our approach, achieving state-of-the-art performance on the PASCAL VOC 2012 and Cityscapes in semi-supervised settings.

2 Related Work

2.1 Supervised Semantic Segmentation

Within the scope of fully supervised segmentation, many excellent works based on CNNs emerged. Long et al. proposed the pioneering Fully Convolutional Network (FCN) [20] which has been the most widespread deep neural network for semantic segmentation. To extract long-range information, many encoder-decoder based models using different information-passing mechanism have been proposed. SegNet [1] records max-pooling indices in encoder and reuses them in the decoding process. U-Net [26] introduces skip-connections between encoder and decoder network. RefineNet [18] is a variant of U-Net, which introduces multipath refinement in the decoder. With reference of spatial pyramid pooling [15] used to capture contextual information, PSPNet [30] uses multiple pooling kernels to extract features of various scales. To increase the receptive field of the network without the lossy down-sampling, atrous convolution [29] was put forward. The series of DeepLab must be mentioned for semantic segmentation. Among which, DeepLabv2 [3] captures multi-scale information with atrous spatial pyramid pooling (ASPP), and DeepLabV3+ [4] extends the previous design with an effective decoder and applies the depthwise separable convolution to further improve the performance.

2.2 Semi-supervised Semantic Segmentation

Semi-supervised learning leverages unlabeled data to reduce the annotation cost but keep a competitive performance. Recently semi-supervised learning has been applied to semantic segmentation successfully.

Methods based on consistency regularization are aimed to enforce an invariance of the output of the model over some perturbations applied to the inputs. The effectiveness of consistency regularization depends on the cluster assumption that different classes are separated by low density regions. Thus, the decision boundary should lie in low-density regions to improve generalization performance. CutMix [8] enforce a consistency between the mixed outputs and the predictions over the mixed inputs. MixMatch [2], incorporating ideas from the dominant paradigms for semi-supervised learning, guesses low-entropy labels for data-augmented unlabeled examples. Observing that the low-density regions separating the classes are more apparent within the outputs of encoder than within the inputs, CCT [24] enforced the consistency over different forms of perturbations applied to the encoder's output.

For semi-supervised learning, pseudo labeling is a simple and effective method applied widely [16]. The paradigm of pseudo labeling is to use a small set of labeled data to generate pseudo labels for a large quantity of unlabeled data, thus reducing human labeling effort. Self-training proposed in [31] performed pseudo labeling with a teacher-student framework where a teacher model is trained with labeled samples and then generate pseudo labels for unlabeled images. As the teacher-student framework is widely studied in the literature of distillation,

[19] considered that dense prediction is a structured prediction problem and transferred the structure information from large networks to compact ones for dense prediction tasks.

Adversarial learning facilitates effective semi-supervised learning on various tasks. The architecture of GANs consists of two sub-networks, a generator and a discriminator. During training, the generator tries to trick discriminator, while discriminator is committed to distinguishing between the real and those generated by generator. Thus, these two sub-networks play a min-max game in the training process. Souly et al. [27] applied adversarial learning to semantic segmentation by keeping a generator to produce artificial samples but using a segmentation network as a discriminator which classifies each pixel as either generated or the true class it belongs to. Qi et al. [25] adopted a novel Knowledge Embedded Generative Adversarial Networks (KE-GANs) to capture semantic consistency with a knowledge graph. Different from those generators trained to generate images, Hung et al. [11] used a segmentation network as the generator and a fully convolutional discriminator to differentiate the predictions from ground truths.

Kalluri et al. [12] proposed a universal approach to learn from labeled and unlabeled data across domains, which extends the segmentation network with an entropy module using the unlabeled examples to perform alignment of pixel wise features from multiple domains. Mittal et al. [22] proposed a dual-branch approach to combine semi-supervised classification with semi-supervised segmentation, which consistently reduces both the low-level and the high-level artifacts.

3 Method

The segmentation network trained on limited data suffers from several types of failure, such as wrong object shapes, incoherent boundaries, and inaccurate semantic class, motivating our residual correction approach. Given an image-segmentation pair, some low-level information in the relation between the image and its coarse segmentation can be leveraged to make refinement. Our residual correction network is designed to capture this type of information.

The overall architecture is shown in Fig. 1. Let $D_l = \{(x_1^l, y_1^l), ..., (x_n^l, y_n^l)\}$ denotes a small set of n labeled training examples and $D_u = \{x_1^u, ..., x_m^u\}$ denotes a large set of m unlabeled training examples. Our method contains two networks, a segmentation network S and a residual correction network C. The segmentation network is optimized with labeled data to generate the original segmentation $S(x)$, which can be any standard segmentation network for generating per-pixel class prediction given an input image. The residual correction network explores the image in combination with its original segmentation to generate a residual $C(x, S(x))$. During inference, the corrected map is treated as the final prediction.

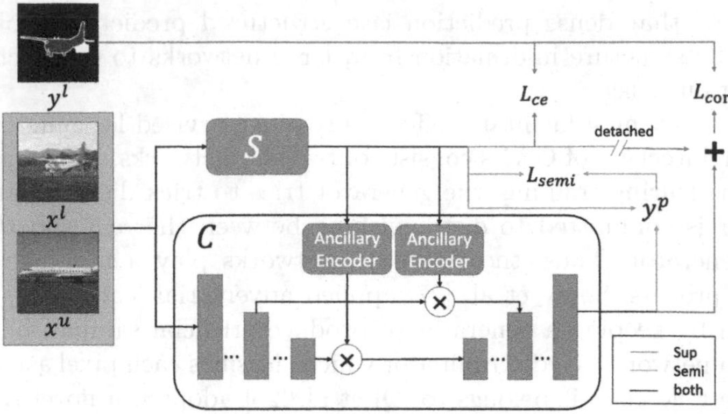

Fig. 1. Illustration of our residual correction approach. For the supervised training, the images x^l of labeled examples (x^l, y^l) are passed through the segmentation network S to obtain $S(x^l)$. Then x^l combined with $S(x^l)$ are input to the residual correction network C to output the residual. We compute the cross-entropy L_{ce} between y^l and $S(x^l)$, together with the cross-entropy L_{cor} between y^l and the corrected prediction. For unlabeled examples x^u, the segmentation network is supervised by the pseudo-label y^p generated in the residual correction process, which corresponds to L_{semi}.

3.1 Residual Correction Network

The objective of the correction training is to model the relationship between the input image and its original segmentation and then infer the residual, which is totally different from that of the original training for segmentation.

The key to the correction network is how to fuse the information of the image and its corresponding segmentation. Existing approaches [21,22] mainly concatenate them directly and feed to following convolutional layers. However, there are two issues with such concatenation. First, as the input image and its original segmentation belong to different semantic levels, it is harmful that the details of the segmentation map are lost along with those of the input images during the process of feature extraction. Second, most of encoder-decoder-based segmentation networks initialize their encoder from a classification model pretrained on large datasets (e.g., ImageNet [6]) to transfer knowledge from those datasets, which is no longer feasible in this case. To overcome these shortcomings, we take a different fusion approach by encoding the image and its original segmentation separately. The correction network is trained with the labeled data and then treated as a teacher to generate pseudo labels for unlabeled images.

As shown in Fig. 1, we extend an existing encoder-decoder segmentation model with ancillary encoders that embed the original segmentation information at different scales. The image is inputted to the backbone to extract features, and its corresponding segmentation is inputted into multiple ancillary encoders where the input tensor is resized to the target shape and passed through several convolution layers to generate an attention map. The features extracted from the backbone are element-wise multiplied by the attention map to generate weighted features that are fed to the following decoder. The fusion process is shown in Fig. 1 where the features at two scales are fused by such an element-wise multiplication parallelly.

The residual correction network is aimed to analyze the matching of the given image-segmentation pair and generate a residual map. Intuitively, setting the target of the correction network to the ground truth, identical to that of the segmentation network, can also achieve the same goal. However, experiments show that this would lead to no significant improvement compared with the segmentation network. To deal with this issue, [21] introduced an additional class indicating the semantically matched regions but led to extremely imbalanced label distribution. Though a fixed weighting scheme is adopted to balance regular semantic classes with the additional class, it introduces extra hyper parameters, which is suboptimal. Motivated by the skip connection introduced in [10], we consider this problem from another direction. We adopt a residual architecture that the correction network learns to produce a compensatory residual of the original segmentation. In this case, it is equal to assign different weights to the pixels according to the correctness of the original segmentation. Since the misclassified pixels accounting for high loss during training process, the correction network is promoted to focus on the misclassified regions. The residual correction network is only trained on the labeled data.

3.2 Supervised Training

In standard supervised semantic segmentation training, the cross-entropy loss between the prediction and the ground truth of the labeled data is minimized. For the labeled training samples, our segmentation network is trained using the cross-entropy loss as usual:

$$L_{ce} = \frac{1}{n} \sum_{(x^l, y^l) \in D^l} H(S(x^l), y^l) \tag{1}$$

where $H(.,.)$ is the cross-entropy function. Additionally, the output of the residual correction network is added with the original segmentation to fit the ground truth, which enables the residual learning of the residual correction network:

$$L_{cor} = \frac{1}{n} \sum_{(x^l, y^l) \in D^l} H(\hat{y}^l + C(x^l, S(x^l)), y^l) \tag{2}$$

For a labeled training sample, its original segmentation, detached from the segmentation network to stop backpropagation, is denoted as $\hat{y}^l$.

In contrast to the concept of adversarial learning where each network attempts to confuse the other, our segmentation network and residual correction network are working in a collaborative way. The original segmentation is improving during training and provides more accurate information for the residual correction network to focus on those misclassified. The corrected predictions of unlabeled data can be used as pseudo labels to train segmentation network in turn. The original segmentation and the corrected results will converge to about the same, while the latter is generally better.

3.3 Semi-supervised Training

The concept of residual correction learning is to capture the relation between the given image and its original segmentation and offer a residual to refine the details of the original segmentation. In semi-supervised step, the residual correction network is considered as a teacher model whose outputs of unlabeled data are used as pseudo labels. The output of segmentation network $S(x^u)$ combined with its residual $C(x^u, S(x^u))$ is transformed to discrete label representation y^p:

$$y^p_{hwc^*} = \begin{cases} 1, & \text{if } c^* = \arg\max_c (S(x^u) + C(x^u, S(x^u)))_{hwc} \\ 0, & \text{otherwise} \end{cases} \tag{3}$$

where h, w, c indicate the row, column and channel, respectively. That is to say, we choose the class having maximum predicted probability as pseudo label for every pixel of unlabeled samples. We encourage the segmentation network to learn from the pseudo labels, taking the form of cross-entropy as a self-training loss:

$$L_{semi} = \frac{1}{m} \sum_{x^u \in D^u} H(S(x^u), y^p) \tag{4}$$

The final training objective L is composed of the supervised and semi-supervised terms.

$$L = L_{ce} + L_{cor} + \lambda L_{semi} \tag{5}$$

where λ is a coefficient weighting the self-training loss. During early training, the network is initialized randomly, resulting in inaccurate pseudo labels on unlabeled data. [14,16,24] adopted ramp-up schedules with different increasing curves to overcome this issue. In order to avoid such a hyperparameter adjustment, we adopt the following pretraining strategy instead: 1) Initial training of the segmentation model with labeled samples; 2) Initial training of residual correction network with labeled samples; 3) The collaborative fine-tuning of the whole framework with labeled and unlabeled samples.

4 Experiments

4.1 Network Architecture

The segmentation network in our experiments is a DeepLabv3+ [4] with a ResNet50 backbone [10]. The residual correction network is also based on a ResNet50-DeepLabv3+ forming the encoder and decoder of the architecture described in Sec. 3.1. The ancillary encoder consists of three 3×3 convolutional layers and a sigmoid activation whose output acts as an attention map. The features of two scales that are fed to the decoder in the original DeepLabv3+ architecture, are fused with the output of an individual ancillary encoder. The only difference of DeepLabv3+ used in segmentation network and residual correction network is the introduction of ancillary encoders.

4.2 Datasets and Evaluation Metrics

PASCAL VOC 2012. The original PASCAL VOC 2012 [7] consists of 1464 training samples, 1449 validation samples and 1456 test samples with 20 foreground classes and a single background class in various resolutions. Following previous work, we augment the original training set with extra 9118 annotated samples from the Segmentation Boundaries Dataset (SBD) [9] and obtain a total training set of 10,582 samples.

Cityscapes. Cityscapes [5] is an autonomous driving dataset collected from cars driving in 50 cities during different seasons. Cityscapes contains 5000 images divided into 2975 training, 500 validation and 1525 testing samples with high quality annotations covering 19 foreground classes for the segmentation.

Evaluation Metric. The performance of our approach is evaluated with the commonly used mean Intersection-over-Union (mIoU) for all the experiments. For PASCAL VOC 2012 and Cityscapes, we report the results obtained on the validation set.

4.3 Experimental Settings

The backbones of segmentation network and residual correction network are initialized to the pre-trained ImageNet model. Both networks are trained with Stochastic Gradient Descent (SGD) with a learning rate of 1×10^{-3} on PASCAL VOC 2012 and 2.5×10^{-3} on Cityscapes. Following [21,22,24], we employ a *Poly* learning rate policy where the initial learning rate is multiplied by $1 - (\frac{iter}{max\_iter})^{pow}$ with $pow = 0.9$. As for data augmentation, we adopt random spatial scaling, horizontal flipping and color jittering during training. The PASCAL VOC 2012 images are randomly cropped with a size of 321×321 with a batch-size of 8. As with Cityscapes, we take crops of size 768×768 with a batch-size of 4. We train the whole framework for 35K iterations as in [22], before which both networks are initialized with a pretraining for 10K iterations. The weighting coefficient λ is set to 1.0. Different from DeepLabv3+ [4], multi-resolution and mirroring are not employed for validation.

4.4 Results

Ablation Studies. We carry out an ablation study to reveal the contribution of each component to the overall performance. We set up a baseline of DeepLabv3+ trained with the only 1464 samples extracted from the original training set of PASCAL VOC 2012, achieving 68.99 shown in Table 1. Further, training the two networks collaboratively improves the performance significantly even without the semi-supervised objective, which implies that the residual correction network does capture the complementary information to refine the original segmentation. The result of using the pretraining strategy described in Sec. 3.3 outperforms that of training from scratch while both of them surpass the baseline significantly. The simple pretraining strategy avoids complex hyper parameter search on λ by setting semi-supervised training to a reasonable starting point instead of a noisy initialization. In the same architecture, our fusion way yields an improvement of 2.09% (from 73.04% to 75.13%) over that using concatenation, which demonstrates the effectiveness of our fusion design. The result of complete form of our semi-supervised method is very close to that of training DeepLabv3+ with all available labeled data. Qualitative results generated by the proposed method are shown in Fig. 2. It is observed that the failure cases of the original segmentation are corrected with correction training and semi-supervised objective. The coherence of boundary and the correctness of classification are improved significantly when compared to the baseline.

Table 1. Ablation study of our method on PASCAL VOC 2012. ES: Our fusion way of encoding separately, while the default is concatenation as in [21,22]. PS: Training with pretraining strategy, while the default is training from scratch.

Method	ES	PS	Labeled examples	Unlabeled examples	mIoU
DeepLabv3+	-	-	1464	0	68.99
Ours+L_{cor}	-	-	1464	0	72.81
Ours+$L_{cor}+L_{semi}$	✓	×	1464	9118	73.55
Ours+$L_{cor}+L_{semi}$	×	✓	1464	9118	73.04
Ours+$L_{cor}+L_{semi}$	✓	✓	1464	9118	75.13
DeepLabv3+	-	-	10582	0	75.37

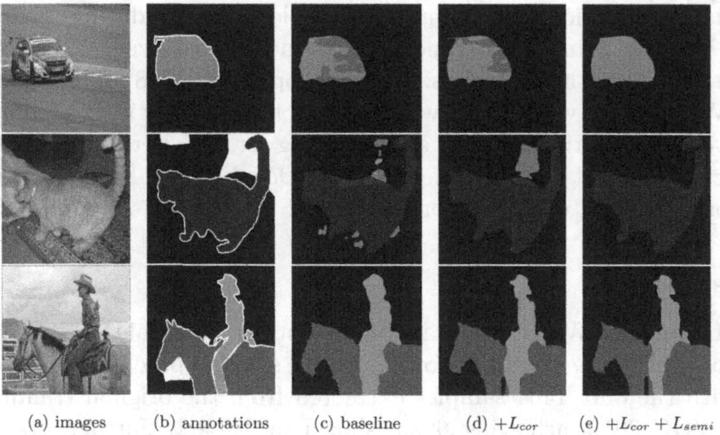

(a) images (b) annotations (c) baseline (d) $+L_{cor}$ (e) $+L_{cor}+L_{semi}$

Fig. 2. Qualitative results of our approach on the PASCAL VOC 2012 dataset with the original training set as labeled data and the SBD set as unlabeled data.

Comparison with Existing Methods. To set the upper bound for our semi-supervised results, we evaluate our implementation of DeepLabv3+ in fully-supervised case where all available labeled data are used. As shown in Table 2, we achieve 75.37 mIoU on PASCAL VOC 2012, which is lower than 78.85 of the ResNet101-DeepLabv3+ reported in [4] for the reason of a weaker backbone and lower resolution. Similarly, we get 74.45 on Cityscapes while 78.79 is achieved in [4] with an Xception style network backbone. We adopt such a backbone and resolution to reduce computational cost and focus on our intention of semi-supervised learning.

Table 2. Comparison with existing methods. The experimental results of our models trained with different proportions of training data as labeled samples and the remaining as unlabeled samples. Sup: Only use the labeled samples. Semi: Use labeled samples and the remaining unlabeled samples

Method	PASCAL VOC 2012 ($N = 10582$)							Cityscapes ($N = 2975$)				
	$N/8$		$N/4$		1464		Full	$N/8$		$N/4$		Full
	Sup	Semi	Sup	Semi	Sup	Semi	Sup	Sup	Semi	Sup	Semi	Sup
Souly et al. [27]	-	-	-	-	59.5	64.1	-	-	-	-	-	-
Hung et al. [11]	66.0	69.5	68.3	72.1	66.3	68.4	73.6	55.5	58.8	59.9	62.3	66.4
KE-GAN [25]	-	-	-	-	-	-	-	62.6	66.1	65.5	69.2	72.6
CCT [24]	-	-	-	-	-	69.4	-	-	-	-	-	-
Mittal et al. [22]	63.5	70.4	-	-	-	-	74.6	56.2	59.3	60.2	61.9	66.0
ECS [21]	65.20	70.22	69.78	72.60	-	-	76.29	63.12	67.38	67.31	70.70	74.76
Ours	65.69	71.76	69.54	74.48	68.99	75.13	75.37	62.88	67.40	67.38	71.92	74.45

The labeled samples were randomly sampled from the whole dataset as in [11,21]. Following [21], we adopt a ResNet50-DeepLabv3+ as the segmentation network and a modified ResNet50-DeepLabv3+ as the residual correction network introduced in Sec. 3.1. We achieve a result similar to [21] in fully-supervised case on Cityscapes. However, we get a relatively lower fully-supervised result on PASCAL VOC 2012 for the reason that we adopt a smaller resolution 321×321 on PASCAL VOC 2012 in contrast to 512×512 in [21]. Comparing with the published results of [21], we achieve a consistent improvement in different semi-supervised settings. Additionally, we also present the results of training on the original training set of PASCAL VOC 2012 (1,464 samples) with the SBD as unlabeled data to compare with [11,24,27]. Though other existing semi-supervised methods use different segmentation networks and distinctive training schedules, the improvement relative to the supervised results indicates the superiority of our method.

5 Conclusions

In this work, we propose a residual correction approach for semi-supervised semantic segmentation, a simple and efficient self-training method leveraging unlabeled data. Our framework consists of a segmentation network and a residual correction network that are trained collaboratively. The residual correction network is designed to generate a residual of the original segmentation and serves as a teacher model on unlabeled data. The effectiveness of our approach is demonstrated in extensive experiments on PASCAL VOC 2012 and Cityscapes.

Acknowledgments. This work was supported in part by the National Natural Science Foundation of China under Grant 61976231, Grant U1611461, Grant 61573387, and Grant 61172141, in part by the Guangdong Basic and Applied Basic Research Foundation under Grant 2019A1515011869, and in part by the Science and Technology Program of Guangzhou under Grant 201803030029.

References

1. Badrinarayanan, V., Kendall, A., Cipolla, R.: SEGNET: a deep convolutional encoder-decoder architecture for image segmentation. IEEE Trans. Pattern Anal. Mach. Intell. **39**(12), 2481–2495 (2017)
2. Berthelot, D., Carlini, N., Goodfellow, I.J., Papernot, N., Oliver, A., Raffel, C.: Mixmatch: a holistic approach to semi-supervised learning. In: Advances in Neural Information Processing Systems, pp. 5050–5060 (2019)
3. Chen, L.C., Papandreou, G., Kokkinos, I., Murphy, K., Yuille, A.L.: Deeplab: Semantic image segmentation with deep convolutional nets, atrous convolution, and fully connected CRFs. IEEE Trans. Pattern Anal. Mach. Intell. **40**(4), 834–848 (2017)
4. Chen, L.C., Zhu, Y., Papandreou, G., Schroff, F., Adam, H.: Encoder-decoder with atrous separable convolution for semantic image segmentation. In: Proceedings of the European Conference on Computer Vision, pp. 801–818 (2018)
5. Cordts, M., et al.: The cityscapes dataset for semantic urban scene understanding. In: Proceedings of the IEEE Conference on Computer Vision and Pattern Recognition, pp. 3213–3223 (2016)
6. Deng, J., Dong, W., Socher, R., Li, L.J., Li, K., Fei-Fei, L.: ImageNet: a large-scale hierarchical image database. In: Proceedings of the IEEE Conference on Computer Vision and Pattern Recognition, pp. 248–255 (2009)
7. Everingham, M., Eslami, S.A., Van Gool, L., Williams, C.K., Winn, J., Zisserman, A.: The PASCAL visual object classes challenge: a retrospective. Int. J. Comput. Vision **111**(1), 98–136 (2015)
8. French, G., Laine, S., Aila, T., Mackiewicz, M., Finlayson, G.: Semi-supervised semantic segmentation needs strong, varied perturbations. In: British Machine Vision Conference, pp. 1–14 (2020)
9. Goodfellow, I.J., et al.: Generative adversarial nets. In: Advances in Neural Information Processing Systems, pp. 2672–2680 (2014)
10. He, K., Zhang, X., Ren, S., Sun, J.: Deep residual learning for image recognition. In: Proceedings of the IEEE Conference on Computer Vision and Pattern Recognition, pp. 770–778 (2016)

11. Hung, W., Tsai, Y., Liou, Y., Lin, Y., Yang, M.: Adversarial learning for semi-supervised semantic segmentation. In: British Machine Vision Conference, pp. 1–14 (2018)
12. Kalluri, T., Varma, G., Chandraker, M., Jawahar, C.: Universal semi-supervised semantic segmentation. In: Proceedings of the IEEE International Conference on Computer Vision, pp. 5259–5270 (2019)
13. Krizhevsky, A., Sutskever, I., Hinton, G.E.: Imagenet classification with deep convolutional neural networks. In: Advances in Neural Information Processing Systems, pp. 1106–1114 (2012)
14. Laine, S., Aila, T.: Temporal ensembling for semi-supervised learning. In: International Conference on Learning Representations, pp. 1–13 (2017)
15. Lazebnik, S., Schmid, C., Ponce, J.: Beyond bags of features: spatial pyramid matching for recognizing natural scene categories. In: Proceedings of the IEEE Computer Society Conference on Computer Vision and Pattern Recognition, pp. 2169–2178 (2006)
16. Lee, D.H., et al.: Pseudo-label: the simple and efficient semi-supervised learning method for deep neural networks. In: Workshop on Challenges in Representation Learning, pp. 1–6 (2013)
17. Lee, J., Kim, E., Lee, S., Lee, J., Yoon, S.: Ficklenet: weakly and semi-supervised semantic image segmentation using stochastic inference. In: Proceedings of the IEEE Conference on Computer Vision and Pattern Recognition, pp. 5267–5276 (2019)
18. Lin, G., Milan, A., Shen, C., Reid, I.: Refinenet: multi-path refinement networks for high-resolution semantic segmentation. In: Proceedings of the IEEE Conference on Computer Vision and Pattern Recognition, pp. 1925–1934 (2017)
19. Liu, Y., Shu, C., Wang, J., Shen, C.: Structured knowledge distillation for dense prediction. IEEE Trans. Pattern Anal. Mach. Intell. **2020**, 1–15 (2020). https://doi.org/10.1109/TPAMI.2020.3001940
20. Long, J., Shelhamer, E., Darrell, T.: Fully convolutional networks for semantic segmentation. In: Proceedings of the IEEE Conference on Computer Vision and Pattern Recognition, pp. 3431–3440 (2015)
21. Mendel, R., de Souza, L.A., Rauber, D., Papa, J.P., Palm, C.: Semi-supervised segmentation based on error-correcting supervision. In: Proceedings of the European Conference on Computer Vision, pp. 141–157 (2020)
22. Mittal, S., Tatarchenko, M., Brox, T.: Semi-supervised semantic segmentation with high-and low-level consistency. IEEE Trans. Pattern Anal. Mach. Intell. **43**(4), 1369–1379 (2021)
23. Miyato, T., Maeda, S.i., Koyama, M., Ishii, S.: Virtual adversarial training: a regularization method for supervised and semi-supervised learning. IEEE Trans. Pattern Anal. Mach. Intell. **41**(8), 1979–1993 (2018)
24. Ouali, Y., Hudelot, C., Tami, M.: Semi-supervised semantic segmentation with cross-consistency training. In: Proceedings of the IEEE Conference on Computer Vision and Pattern Recognition, pp. 12674–12684 (2020)
25. Qi, M., Wang, Y., Qin, J., Li, A.: KE-GAN: Knowledge embedded generative adversarial networks for semi-supervised scene parsing. In: Proceedings of the IEEE Conference on Computer Vision and Pattern Recognition, pp. 5237–5246 (2019)
26. Ronneberger, O., Fischer, P., Brox, T.: U-net: convolutional networks for biomedical image segmentation. In: Proceedings of the International Conference on Medical Image Computing and Computer-Assisted Intervention, pp. 234–241 (2015)

27. Souly, N., Spampinato, C., Shah, M.: Semi supervised semantic segmentation using generative adversarial network. In: Proceedings of the IEEE International Conference on Computer Vision, pp. 5688–5696 (2017)
28. Wang, Y., Zhang, J., Kan, M., Shan, S., Chen, X.: Self-supervised equivariant attention mechanism for weakly supervised semantic segmentation. In: Proceedings of the IEEE Conference on Computer Vision and Pattern Recognition, pp. 12275–12284 (2020)
29. Yu, F., Koltun, V.: Multi-scale context aggregation by dilated convolutions. In: International Conference on Learning Representations, pp. 1–13 (2016)
30. Zhao, H., Shi, J., Qi, X., Wang, X., Jia, J.: Pyramid scene parsing network. In: Proceedings of the IEEE Conference on Computer Vision and Pattern Recognition, pp. 2881–2890 (2017)
31. Zhu, Y., et al.: Improving semantic segmentation via self-training (2020). arXiv preprint: arXiv:2004.14960

Hypergraph Convolutional Network with Hybrid Higher-Order Neighbors

Jiahao Huang[1,2], Fangyuan Lei[1,2](✉), Senhong Wang[3], Song Wang[4], and Qingyun Dai[1,2]

[1] Guangdong Provincial Key Laboratory of Intellectual Property and Big Data, Guangdong Polytechnic Normal University, Guangzhou 510665, China
[2] School of Electronic and Information, Guangdong Polytechnic Normal University, Guangzhou 510665, China
[3] School of Information Engineering, Guangdong University of Technology, Guangzhou 510006, China
[4] Department of Computer Science and Engineering, University of South Carolina, Columbia, SC 29208, USA

Abstract. Hypergraph-based methods can learn non-pairwise associations more efficiently in many real-world datasets. However, existing hypergraph-based methods do not consider the relationship of the hybrid neighborhood. To address this issue, we propose a hybrid higher-order neighborhood based hypergraph convolutional network (HybridHGCN). Technically, feature embeddings are generated via k-hop hypergraph convolution layers and mixed by the hybrid message operator. To evaluate the proposed HybridHGCN, we conduct experiments on the citation network datasets and the visual object datasets. The experimental results show that HybridHGCN brings significant improvements over state-of-the-art hypergraph neural network baselines.

Keywords: Hypergraph · Higher-order correlation · Hypergraph convolutional networks

1 Introduction

Graphs are widely used to model the pair-wise relationships in the real world, such as collaboration networks and co-authoring networks [5,18]. An example of such a graph is shown in Fig. 1(a), in which $a1$,..., to $a7$ are the nodes which represent the authors, and $p1$,..., to $p4$ are the edges which represent the papers connecting the co-authors. Non-pair-wise and complex relationships among entities can be more effectively and flexibly modeled by a hypergraph [6]. An example of a hypergraph is shown in Fig. 1(b), in which $p1$,..., to $p4$ are the hyperedges that connect the multiple co-authors. The number of nodes connected by a hyperedge is defined as the degree of the hyperedge. A hypergraph is simplified to a graph when the degree of the hyperedge is set to 2.

© Springer Nature Switzerland AG 2021
H. Ma et al. (Eds.): PRCV 2021, LNCS 13022, pp. 103–114, 2021.
https://doi.org/10.1007/978-3-030-88013-2_9

Graph convolutional network (GCN) [15] has been applied to citation networks and knowledge graphs, with significant improvement in the semi-supervised node classification task. Although GCN can be used for classification tasks in visual data and social networks, it is highly desired to extend it to hypergraph structure given its more flexible modeling of complex relationships in many real-world networks compared with graphs. Recently, many researchers explored the hypergraph application in GNNs [3,4,10,14,25]. Feng et al. [10] proposed a hypergraph neural network (HGNN) by using hypergraph Laplacian to learn the message of non-pair-wise relationships. Yadati et al. [25] simplified the hypergraph to a graph and then applied the GCN. However, existing hypergraph-based neural networks do not consider the k-hop neighbor relations.

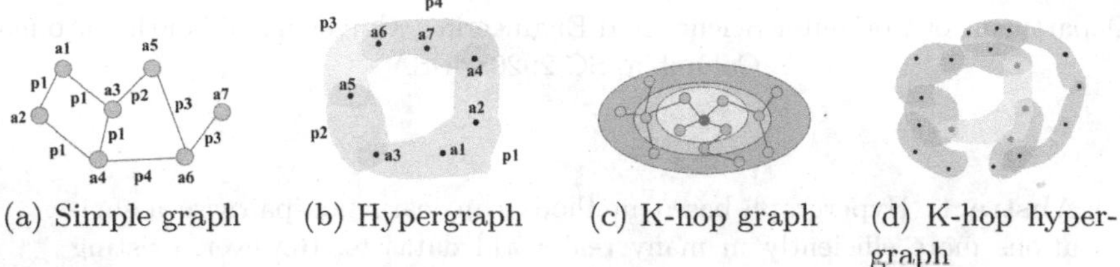

(a) Simple graph (b) Hypergraph (c) K-hop graph (d) K-hop hypergraph

Fig. 1. Illustration of the graph/hypergraph structures, higher-order graph and higher-order hypergraph. (a) A simple graph represents the pair-wise relations among authors and papers. (b) A hypergraph with 4 hyperedges that represent the non-pair-wise relations among authors and papers. (c) A k-hop graph where ovals of different colors represent different orders. (d) A k-hop hypergraph where hyperedges of different colors represent different orders (Color figure online).

Inspired by [1], to consider the k-hop neighbor in a hypergraph, we propose a hybrid higher-order neighborhood based hypergraph convolutional network (HybridHGCN). To aggregate k-hop neighbor messages, HybridHGCN is composed of k-hop hypergraph convolutional layers and a hybrid message operator. As the higher-order neighbors of a hypergraph can be described by the incidence matrix of higher-order power. An example of a k-hop graph is shown in Fig. 1(c), in which ovals of different colors represent different orders. As illustrated in Fig. 1(d), a k-hop hypergraph is represented by different-order hyperedges, shown in different colors. In the incidence matrix of different power, the receptive field of neighbors is broadened as the order increases. Updated by k-hop hypergraph convolutional layers, the generated features embedding represent the k-hop neighbor messages. In the hybrid message operator, we use an element-wise max pooling operator to mix k-hop neighbor messages. To evaluate the proposed HybridHGCN, we construct three different hop hypergraph convolutional layers and examine the node classification performance on both citation network datasets and visual object datasets.

The main contributions of this paper are summarized as follows.

- We propose HybridHGCN, a new method to capture higher-order and low-order neighbor relations and it enhance the representation capability of the hypergraph network.
- We propose the hypergraph structuration with the higher-order incidence matrix to broaden the receptive field of the hypergraph network.
- The experimental results show the proposed HybridHGCN achieve the new state-of-the-art performance on citation networks and visual object datasets.

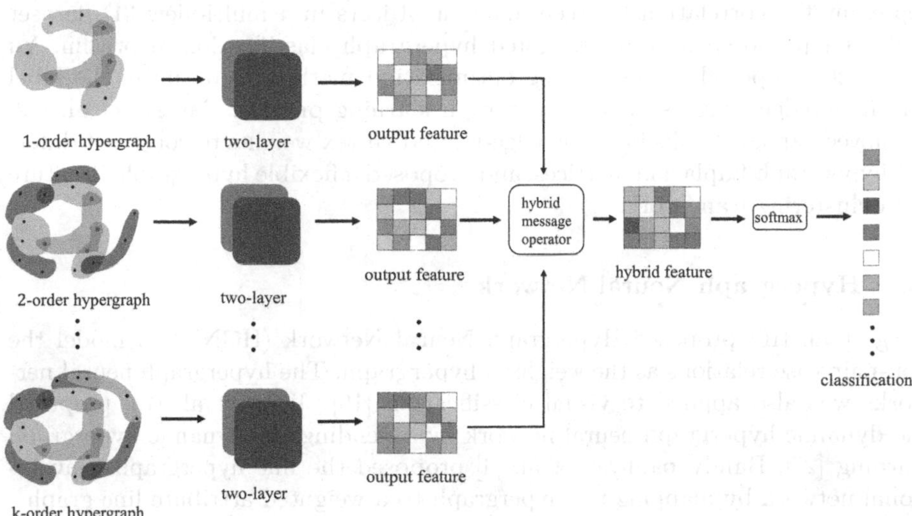

Fig. 2. Overview of the proposed hybrid higher-order neighborhood based hypergraph convolutional network (HybridHGCN). The parameters 1,..., to k denote the hypergraphs with different hops. The two-layer denotes the adopted two hypergraph convolutional layers. The output feature embedding is composeed of N-nodes with D-dimension features. Mixing by a hybrid message operator, the number of nodes and dimension of features remain unchanged.

2 Related Works

2.1 Graph Neural Networks

Due to the excellent performance of deep neural networks on structured data from various tasks, Bronstein et al. [7] extended the neural network model to the graph structure data drawn from non-Euclidean space. Kipf et al. [15] proposed Graph Convolutional Network (GCN) by learning neighboring node representations through the convolution defined by the graph Laplacian. To solve the problem of GCN's dependence on the global graph structure, Veličković et al. [22] proposed Graph Attention Network (GAT) in which the attention mechanism assigns different weights to different nodes. Abu-El-Haija et al. [1]

proposed the MixHop model to explore neighborhood mixing relationships represented by repeatedly mixing feature representations. More details about the current research of graph neural networks and graph representation can be found in excellent surveys [9,23,29].

2.2 Learning on Hypergraph

On hypergraphs, clique expansion or star expansion [2,16,28] are widely used to mine the hypergraph structure. Su et al. [21] utilized a hypergraph structure to represent the correlation between different objects in a multi-view 3D dataset and then proposed a vertex-weighted hypergraph classification algorithm. Yu et al. [26] proposed an alternating optimization method to optimize the label and hyperedge weights in the hypergraph learning process. Hayashi et al. [12] employed random walks based on edge-related vertex weights to construct different hypergraph Laplacian matrices, and proposed a flexible hypergraph structure data clustering framework.

2.3 Hypergraph Neural Network

Feng et al. [10] proposed Hypergraph Neural Network (HGNN) to model the non-pair-wise relations as the weighted hypergraph. The hypergraph neural networks was also applied to visual classification [19]. Jiang et al. [13] proposed the dynamic hypergraph neural network by extending the dynamic hypergraph learning [27]. Bandyopadhyay et al. [4] proposed the line hypergraph convolutional network by mapping the hypergraph to a weighted attribute line graph.

3 Preliminary Knowledge

3.1 Hypergraph

In this section, we briefly introduce the preliminary knowledge of hypergraphs. An edge in a simple graph connects two vertices. Compared with simple graph, a weighted hypergraph is denoted as $\mathcal{G} = (\mathcal{V}, \mathcal{E}, \mathcal{W})$, where $\mathcal{V} = \{v_1, v_2, ..., v_n\}$ is a set of n vertices, $\mathcal{E} = \{e_1, e_2, ..., e_m\}$ is a set of m hyperedges and $\mathcal{W} = \{(w(e_1), w(e_2), ..., w(e_m)\}$ is a set of hyperedge weight. The structure of hypergraph $\mathcal{G}$ can be represented by an incidence matrix $\mathbf{H} \in \mathbb{R}^{|\mathcal{V}| \times |\mathcal{E}|}$ with entries

$$h(v,e) = \begin{cases} 0 \text{ if } v \notin e, \\ 1 \text{ if } v \in e. \end{cases} \tag{1}$$

In practice, $h(v, e)$ takes continuous values in the range of $[0, 1]$ which indicates the importance of the vertex v for hyperedge e. The degree of a vertex $v \in \mathcal{V}$ is defined by

$$d(v) = \sum_{e \in \mathcal{E}} w(e) h(v, e), \tag{2}$$

where e denotes a hyperedge in the hyperedge set $\mathcal{E}$, and the degree of hyperedge $e \in \mathcal{E}$ is defined by

$$\delta(e) = \sum_{v \in \mathcal{V}} h(v, e). \tag{3}$$

Let $\mathbf{D}_v$ be the diagonal matrix of the vertex degrees, $\mathbf{D}_e$ be the diagonal matrix of the hyperdege degrees, and $\mathbf{W}$ be the diagonal matrix of the hyperedge weights, i.e., $\mathbf{D}_v = diag(d(v_1), d(v_2), ..., d(v_n))$, $\mathbf{D}_e = diag(\delta(e_1), \delta(e_2), ..., \delta(e_m))$, and $\mathbf{W} = diag(w(e_1), w(e_2), ..., w(e_m))$.

3.2 Hypergraph Convolution Network

For a hypergraph $\mathcal{G} = (\mathcal{V}, \mathcal{E}, \mathcal{W})$ and hypergraph signal $\mathbf{X}$, the hypergraph convolution layer $f(\mathbf{X}, \mathbf{W}, \boldsymbol{\Theta})$ based on the theory of spectral convolution on hypergraph is defined as

$$\mathbf{X}^{(l+1)} = \sigma(\mathbf{D}_v^{-\frac{1}{2}} \mathbf{H} \mathbf{W} \mathbf{D}_e^{-1} \mathbf{H}^T \mathbf{D}_v^{-\frac{1}{2}} \mathbf{X}^{(l)} \Theta^{(l)}), \tag{4}$$

where $\mathbf{X}^{(l)} \in \mathbb{R}^{N \times D^{(l)}}$ represents the N vertex features in the $l-th$ layer, $\Theta^{(l)}$ is a learnable parameter of filter in the $l-th$ layer and $\sigma(\cdot)$ denotes the nonlinear activation function. Hyperedge weight $\mathbf{W} \in \mathbb{R}^{N \times N}$ reflects the importance of different hyperedges in the network. A two-layer hypergraph convolutional network model can be defined by

$$\mathbf{Y} = softmax(\hat{\mathbf{H}}(\sigma(\hat{\mathbf{H}}\mathbf{X}^{(1)}\Theta^{(1)}))\Theta^{(2)})), \tag{5}$$

where $\hat{\mathbf{H}} = \mathbf{D}_v^{-\frac{1}{2}} \mathbf{H} \mathbf{W} \mathbf{D}_e^{-1} \mathbf{H}^T \mathbf{D}_v^{-\frac{1}{2}}$, and $\Theta^{(1)}$ and $\Theta^{(2)}$ represent the trainable parameter matrix in first layer and second layers respectively.

4 Method

In this section, we propose the HybridHGCN to capture k-hop neighbor relations. As shown in Fig. 2, HybridHGCN consists of k branches and a hybrid message operator that each branch takes the two-layer structure. We employ incidence matrices of different order of powers to represent the k-hop hypergraph. In the hypergraph convolutional layer, node representation is updated with the k-hop neighbor message by the incidence matrix of k-order power. To represent different-order neighbor relations, we propose a hybrid message operator to mix feature embeddings generated from each branch. Specifically, the hybrid message operator is implemented before the $softmax$ layer. The HybridHGCN consisting of k branches and a hybrid message operator can be written as

$$Y = softmax(HM(\sigma(\hat{H}^{(1)} X^{(l)} \Theta^{(l)}), \sigma(\hat{H}^{(2)} X^{(l)} \Theta^{(l)}), ..., \sigma(\hat{H}^{(k)} X^{(l)} \Theta^{(l)})), \tag{6}$$

where $HM(\cdot)$ is a hybrid message operator, $\hat{H} = D_v^{-\frac{1}{2}} HWD_e^{-1}H^T D_v^{-\frac{1}{2}}$, and $\sigma(\cdot)$ is the Relu activation function. The parameter k denotes the power of the incidence matrix, and l represents the layer of the hypergraph convolution. In $HM(\cdot)$ layer, the input feature of $(l+1)$-layer is the output of l-layer hypergraph convolution. When parameter $l = 1$, the input feature of the first hypergraph convolutional layer is the initial feature X. Specifically, $\hat{H}^{(k)}$ represents the incidence matrix of k-th order of power. The diagonal matrices of the edge degrees $D_e^{(k)}$ and vertex degrees $D_v^{(k)}$ correspond to the k-th order of hypergraph Laplacian $\hat{H}^{(k)}$, respectively. In the process of simultaneous high order and low order message propagation, we propose a hybrid message operator $HM(\cdot)$ as follows:

$$Out_{HM} = HM(Fts_{H^{(1)}}, Fts_{H^{(2)}}, ..., Fts_{H^{(k)}}), \tag{7}$$

where Out_{HM} represents the mixed feature. The features $Fts_{H^{(1)}}$, $Fts_{H^{(2)}}$ and $Fts_{H^{(k)}}$ represent the output features of hypergraph convolution layers associated with the $1st$, $2nd$ and $k-th$ orders of power incidence matrices respectively. $HM(\cdot)$ performs an element-wise operation on eigenvector matrices of different orders, which selects the max elements. In this paper, we set the parameter $l = 2$ which means the HybridHGCN has two layers and we have

$$\begin{aligned} Y = softmax(HM(&\hat{H}^{(1)}\sigma(\hat{H}^{(1)}X^{(l_1)}\Theta^{(l_1)})\Theta^{(l_2)}, \hat{H}^{(2)}\sigma(\hat{H}^{(2)}X^{(l_1)}\Theta^{(l_1)})\Theta^{(l_2)}, \\ &..., \hat{H}^{(k)}\sigma(\hat{H}^{(k)}X^{(l_1)}\Theta^{(l_1)})\Theta^{(l_2)})), \end{aligned} \tag{8}$$

where $\hat{H}$ is the normalized hypergraph Laplancian, $\Theta^{(l_1)} \in \mathbb{R}^{d_0 \times d_1}$ and $\Theta^{(l_2)} \in \mathbb{R}^{d_1 \times d_2}$ are the learnable weight parameters. For classification with q classes, we adopt cross entropy as the loss function of HybridHGCN:

$$\mathcal{L} = -\sum_{i \in \mathcal{V}_L} \sum_{j=1}^{q} \hat{Y}_{ij} \ln Y_{ij}, \tag{9}$$

where $\mathcal{V}_L$ denotes the set of labeled examples and q represents the number of classes. $\hat{Y}_{ij}$ denotes the actual label of a node in $\mathcal{V}_L$ and Y_{ij} is the predicted label computed by Eq. (8).

5 Experiments

5.1 Datasets and Baseline

In our experiments, we use classification accuracy as the evaluation criteria. To evaluate the HybridHGCN, we employ five datasets including citation networks and visual objects. Cora, Citeseer and Pumbed [17] are publicly used citation network datasets, which contain the graph structures of citations with the bags-of-words feature vector of documents. In Cora, Citeseer, and Pumbed, nodes correspond to documents and edges represent the relation between each pair of nodes. Specifics of Cora, Citeseer, and Pumbed are presented in Table 1.

Table 1. Summary of citation network datasets.

Dataset	Cora	Citeseer	Pumbed
Number of nodes	2,708	3,327	19,717
Number of edges	5,278	4,552	44,324
Length of features	1,433	3,703	500
Number of classes	7	6	3

The Priceton ModelNet40 dataset [24] contains 12,311 visual objects of 40 categories including airplane, bathtub, car, dresser, guitar, and so on. The National Taiwan University 3-D model (NTU) dataset [8] contains 2,012 visual objects of 67 categories, including chair, clock, door, frame and so on. The summary of visual object, categories, and length of MVCNN and GVCNN extracted features are given in Table 2.

Table 2. Summary of visual object datasets.

Dataset	*ModelNet*40	*NTU*
Number of object	12,311	2,012
Length of MVCNN features	4,096	4,096
Length of GVCNN features	2,048	2,048
Number of classes	40	67

We compare the following methods in our experiments. We denote HGNN as HGNN-s when HGNN adopt the same graph structure as HyperGCN [25] and LHCN [4].

- HyperGCN [25]: The method approximates the hypergraph Laplacian to graph and then performs graph convolution. 1-HyperGCN and FastHyperGCN are two variants of HyperGCN. The former approximates the hyperedge by a pair of edges and adds mediators to enhance the performance. The latter reduces computation time where the hypergraph Laplacian is computed only once before training.
- Line Hypergraph Convolution Network (LHCN) [4]: The hypergraph structure is mapped to an attributed and weighted line graph which adapts in graph convolution.
- Hypergraph Neural Network (HGNN) [10]: The method adopts the normalized hypergraph Laplacian to perform graph convolution in weighted clique expansion hypergraph.

5.2 Experimental Setting

For citation networks and visual object datasets, we construct the hypergraph from the original graph structure and Euclidean distance of visual objects, respectively. For each node in the graph of citation networks, we take it as a central node and set a hyperedge with this central node as the centroid. The other nodes that connect to the centroid are added into the hyperedge, and the entries of hypergraph structure are formulated as Eq. (1). HGNN [10] and HybridHGCN adopt the same hypergraph structure. The graph structures of HyperGCN have 1,579, 1,079 and 7,963 edges for Cora, Citeseer and Pubmed respectively.

For visual object datasets, we select Mutil-view CNN [20] and Group-view CNN [11] to extract features, which have shown excellent performance in the representation of 3D shape. Considering the feature of each visual object, we calculate its Euclidean distance with other objects, and then select the k nearest nodes to connect. In our experiments, we set the hyper-parameter k to be 10. The entries of the constructed hypergraph structure is as follows.

$$h(v,e) = \begin{cases} 0 \text{ if } v \notin e \\ exp\left(-\frac{2D_{ij}^2}{\Delta}\right) \text{ if } v \in e, \end{cases} \tag{10}$$

where D_{ij} denotes the Euclidean distance between node i and node j, and Δ denotes the average pairwise distance of all nodes.

For Cora, Citeseer, and Pubmed datasets, the dimensions of the hidden units of HybridHGCN are 32, 16, and 64com, respectively, and the orders of the incidence matrices are 1, 2, and 3 respectively.

For ModelNet40 and NTU datasets, the dimensions of the hidden units of HybridHGCN are 256, and the orders of the incidence matrices are 1, 2, and 3 respectively.

5.3 Experimental Results and Discussion

For citation networks datasets, experiment results are shown in Table 3, where performances of comparison methods are directly taken from [4,25]. The proposed HybridHGCN achieves the best testing accuracy of 81.88%, 70.96%, and 78.31% on Cora, Citeseer, and Pubmed respectively. We adopt the datasets split by using 5.2%, 4.1%, and 0.3% of data for training respectively and the rest is for testing. The train-test split is the same as HyperGCN [25] which samples the nodes of the same size from each class.

We also evaluate the specific effects of different label rates on HGNN and HybridHGCN for the citation datasets, by trying to use 5%, 10%, 20%, 30%, and 40% of data for training, respectively and the rest is for validating and testing. As shown in Table 4, compared with HGNN, the accuracy of HybridHGCN increases by 0.1% to 1.79% for different data splits on Cora, with the more obvious improvement on the low label rate. For Citeseer, as shown in Table 5, HybridHGCN shows an increase in accuracy of 0.3% to 2.0% for different data splits compared to HGCN. It's worth noting that HybridHGCN improves performance even more when the label rates are high in Citeseer. For Pubmed, from Table 6 we can see that HybridHGCN achieves 0.2% to 0.3% increase in accuracy for different data splits, which are slight performance improvements over

Table 3. Test accuracy (%) on citation networks classification. ± represents the standard deviation.

Method	Cora	Citeseer	Pubmed
HGNN-s [25]	67.59 ± 1.8	62.60 ± 1.6	70.59 ± 1.5
1-HyperGCN [25]	65.55 ± 2.1	61.13 ± 1.9	69.92 ± 1.5
FastHyperGCN [25]	67.57 ± 1.8	62.58 ± 1.7	70.52 ± 1.6
HyperGCN [25]	67.63 ± 1.7	62.65 ± 1.6	74.44 ± 1.6
LHCN [4]	73.34 ± 1.7	63.19 ± 2.2	70.76 ± 2.4
HGNN [10]	80.99 ± 0.8	69.72 ± 1.0	78.14 ± 1.7
HybridHGCN	**81.88 ± 0.2**	**70.96 ± 0.8**	**78.31 ± 1.6**

Table 4. Test accuracy (%) on Cora dataset classification. ± represents the standard deviation. 5% to 40% represent the percentage of data used for training.

Method	Cora				
	5%	10%	20%	30%	40%
HGNN [10]	79.86 ± 1.1	81.72 ± 1.6	84.60 ± 0.9	86.36 ± 1.4	88.02 ± 1.4
HybridHGCN	**81.04 ± 0.5**	**83.28 ± 0.8**	**85.20 ± 1.1**	**87.50 ± 0.9**	**89.81 ± 0.4**

HGNN. The success of HybridHGCN lies in the addition of the k-hop neighbor message to improve node representation capabilities.

For the experiment on ModelNet40 and NTU datasets, we follow the same 80%–20% dataset split for training and testing respectively as in [24]. For visual object datasets, from Table 7 we can observe that HybridHGCN performs better than the rest under most CNNs features. On the ModelNet40 dataset, compared with the MVCNN features and GVCNN features, the performance of HybridHGCN is close to HGNN. On the NTU dataset, HybridHGCN brings the gain of 2.24% and 2.93% on MVCNN features and GVCNN features respectively. The results indicate that HybridHGCN is more effective in node classification tasks than HGNN.

Table 5. Test accuracy (%) on Citeseer dataset classification. ± represents the standard deviation. 5% to 40% represent the percentage of data used for training.

Method	Citeseer				
	5%	10%	20%	30%	40%
HGNN [10]	70.22 ± 1.2	71.70 ± 0.6	**73.82 ± 1.0**	74.98 ± 0.5	75.04 ± 1.3
HybridHGCN	**70.58 ± 1.1**	**72.32 ± 0.6**	73.60 ± 0.5	**76.08 ± 1.4**	**77.02 ± 1.4**

Table 6. Test accuracy (%) on Pubmed dataset classification. ± represents the standard deviation. 5% to 40% represent the percentage of data used for training.

Method	Pubmed				
	5%	10%	20%	30%	40%
HGNN [10]	83.16 ± 0.2	83.80 ± 0.8	**84.54 ± 0.5**	84.60 ± 0.3	84.66 ± 0.5
HybridHGCN	**83.38 ± 0.3**	**84.12 ± 0.3**	84.22 ± 0.1	**84.96 ± 0.3**	**84.90 ± 0.6**

Table 7. Test accuracy (%) on ModelNet40 and NTU datasets classification. ± represents the standard deviation. MVCNN and GVCNN represent the features extracted from Multi-view CNN [20] and Group-view CNN [11] respectively.

Method	ModelNet40		NTU	
	MVCNN	GVCNN	MVCNN	GVCNN
HGNN [10]	**91.00**	92.60	75.60	82.50
HybridHGCN	90.62 ± 0.0	**92.76 ± 0.1**	**77.84 ± 0.1**	**85.43 ± 0.1**

6 Conclusions

This paper proposed a hybrid higher-order neighborhood based hypergraph convolutional network (HybridHGCN), which explores the k-hop neighbor message. We conducted extensive experiments on hypergraphs construct on citation networks and visual object datasets, and the results showed that HybridHGCN performs better than the state-of-the-art methods. For the future work, we plan to further reduce the feature redundancy in mixing the k-hop neighbor messages.

Acknowledgements. This work was supported in part by the National Natural Science Foundation of China under Grant U1701266, in part by Guangdong Provincial Key Laboratory of Intellectual Property and Big Data under Grant 2018B030322016, in part by Special Projects for Key Fields in Higher Education of Guangdong under Grant 2020ZDZX3077 and Grant 2021ZDZX1042, and in part by Qingyuan Science and Technology Plan Project under Grant 170809111721249 and Grant 170802171710591.

References

1. Abu-El-Haija, S., et al.: Mixhop: higher-order graph convolutional architectures via sparsified neighborhood mixing. In: Proceedings of the International Conference on Machine Learning, pp. 21–29 (2019)
2. Agarwal, S., Branson, K., Belongie, S.: Higher order learning with graphs. In: Proceedings of the International Conference on Machine Learning, pp. 17–24 (2006)
3. Bai, S., Zhang, F., Torr, P.H.S.: Hypergraph convolution and hypergraph attention. Pattern Recogn. **110**, 107637 (2021)
4. Bandyopadhyay, S., Das, K., Narasimha Murty, M.: Line hypergraph convolution network: Applying graph convolution for hypergraphs (2020). arXiv preprint: arXiv:2002.03392
5. Benson, A.R., Gleich, D.F., Leskovec, J.: Higher-order organization of complex networks. Science **353**(6295), 163–166(2016)

6. Bretto, A.: Hypergraph Theory. An Introduction. Mathematical Engineering. Springer, Cham (2013)
7. Bronstein, M.M., Bruna, J., LeCun, Y., Szlam, A., Vandergheynst, P.: Geometric deep learning: going beyond Euclidean data. IEEE Signal Process. Mag. **34**(4), 18–42 (2017)
8. Chen, D., Tian, X., Shen, Y., Ouhyoung, M.: On visual similarity based 3d model retrieval. Comput. Graph. Forum **22**, 223–232 (2003)
9. Chen, F., Wang, Y., Wang, B., Jay Kuo, C.-C.: Graph representation learning: a survey. APSIPA Trans. Signal Inf. Process. 9 (2020)
10. Feng, Y., You, H., Zhang, Z., Ji, R., Gao, Y.: Hypergraph neural networks. In: Proceedings of the AAAI Conference on Artificial Intelligence, Vol. 33, pp. 3558–3565 (2019)
11. Feng, Y., Zhang, Z., Zhao, X., Ji, R., Gao, Y.: GVCNN: group-view convolutional neural networks for 3d shape recognition. In: Proceedings of the IEEE Conference on Computer Vision and Pattern Recognition, pp. 264–272 (2018)
12. Hayashi, K., Aksoy, S.G., Park, C.H., Park, H.: Hypergraph random walks, laplacians, and clustering. In: Proceedings of the 29th ACM International Conference on Information & Knowledge Management, pp. 495–504 (2020)
13. Jiang, J., Wei, Y., Feng, Y., Cao, J., Gao, Y.: Dynamic hypergraph neural networks. In: Proceedings of the International Joint Conference on Artificial Intelligence, pp. 2635–2641 (2019)
14. Kim, E.-S., Kang, W.Y., On, K.-W., Heo, Y.-J., Zhang, B.-T.: Hypergraph attention networks for multimodal learning. In: Proceedings of the IEEE/CVF Conference on Computer Vision and Pattern Recognition, pp. 14581–14590 (2020)
15. Kipf, T.N., Welling, M.: Semi-supervised classification with graph convolutional networks (2016). arXiv preprint: arXiv:1609.02907
16. Li, P., Faltings, B.: Hypergraph learning with hyperedge expansion. In: Flach, P.A., De Bie, T., Cristianini, N., (eds.) Machine Learning and Knowledge Discovery in Databases. ECML PKDD 2012. LNCS, vol. 7523, pp. 410–425. Springer, Berlin (2021). https://doi.org/10.1007/978-3-642-33460-3_32
17. Sen, P., Namata, G., Bilgic, M., Getoor, L., Galligher, B., Eliassi-Rad, T.: Collective classification in network data. AI Mag. **29**(3), 93 (2008)
18. Shchur, O., Mumme, M., Bojchevski, A., Günnemann, S.: Pitfalls of graph neural network evaluation (2018). arXiv preprint: arXiv:1811.05868
19. Shi, H., et al.: Hypergraph-induced convolutional networks for visual classification. IEEE Trans. Neural Netw. Learn. Syst. **30**(10), 2963–2972 (2018)
20. Hang, S., Subhransu, M., Evangelos, K., Learned-Miller, E.: Multi-view convolutional neural networks for 3d shape recognition. In: Proceedings of the IEEE International Conference On Computer Vision, pp. 945–953 (2015)
21. Su, L., Gao, Y., Zhao, X., Wan, H., Gu, M., Sun, J.: Vertex-weighted hypergraph learning for multi-view object classification. In: Proceedings of the International Joint Conference on Artificial Intelligence, pp. 2779–2785 (2017)
22. Veličković, P., Cucurull, G., Casanova, A., Romero, A., Lio, P., Bengio, Y.: Graph attention networks (2017). arXiv preprint: arXiv:1710.10903
23. Wu, Z., Pan, S., Chen, F., Long, G., Zhang, C., Philip, S.Y.: A comprehensive survey on graph neural networks. IEEE Trans. Neural Netw. Learn. Syst. **32**, 4–24 (2020)
24. Wu, Z., et al.: 3d shapenets: a deep representation for volumetric shapes. In: Proceedings of the IEEE Conference On Computer Vision And Pattern Recognition, pp. 1912–1920 (2015)

25. Yadati, N., et al.: HyperGCN: a new method of training graph convolutional networks on hypergraphs (2018). arXiv preprint: arXiv:1809.02589
26. Jun Yu, Dacheng Tao, and Meng Wang.: Adaptive hypergraph learning and its application in image classification. IEEE Transactions on Image Processing, vol. 21, no. 7, pp. 3262–3272(2012)
27. Zhang, Z., Lin, H., Gao, Y.: KLISS BNRist.: dynamic hypergraph structure learning. In: Proceedings of the International Joint Conference on Artificial Intelligence, pp. 3162–3169 (2018)
28. Zhou, D., Huang, J., Schölkopf, B.: Learning with hypergraphs: clustering, classification, and embedding. Adv. Neural Inf. Process. Syst. **19**, 1601–1608 (2006)
29. Zhou, J., et al.: Graph neural networks: a review of methods and applications (2018). arXiv preprint: arXiv:1812.08434

Text-Aware Single Image Specular Highlight Removal

Shiyu Hou[1,2], Chaoqun Wang[1,2], Weize Quan[1,2], Jingen Jiang[1,2], and Dong-Ming Yan[1,2(✉)]

[1] National Laboratory of Pattern Recognition (NLPR), Institute of Automation, Chinese Academy of Sciences, Beijing 100190, China
{weize.quan,dongming.yan}@nlpr.ia.ac.cn

[2] School of Artificial Intelligence, University of Chinese Academy of Sciences, Beijing 100049, China

Abstract. Removing undesirable specular highlight from a single input image is of crucial importance to many computer vision and graphics tasks. Existing methods typically remove specular highlight for medical images and specific-object images, however, they cannot handle the images with text. In addition, the impact of specular highlight on text recognition is rarely studied by text detection and recognition community. Therefore, in this paper, we first raise and study the text-aware single image specular highlight removal problem. The core goal is to improve the accuracy of text detection and recognition by removing the highlight from text images. To tackle this challenging problem, we first collect three high-quality datasets with fine-grained annotations, which will be appropriately released to facilitate the relevant research. Then, we design a novel two-stage network, which contains a highlight detection network and a highlight removal network. The output of highlight detection network provides additional information about highlight regions to guide the subsequent highlight removal network. Moreover, we suggest a measurement set including the end-to-end text detection and recognition evaluation and auxiliary visual quality evaluation. Extensive experiments on our collected datasets demonstrate the superior performance of the proposed method.

Keywords: Specular highlight removal · Text-awareness · Datasets · Neural network

1 Introduction

Specular highlights often exist in real-world images due to the material property of objects and the capturing environments. It is always desired to reduce or eliminate these specular highlights to improve the visual quality and to facilitate the vision and graphics tasks, such as stereo matching [10,12], text recognition [16], image segmentation [3,6] and photo-consistency [30,31]. See Fig. 1 for examples, the performance of the end-to-end text detection and recognition drops due to

© Springer Nature Switzerland AG 2021
H. Ma et al. (Eds.): PRCV 2021, LNCS 13022, pp. 115–127, 2021.
https://doi.org/10.1007/978-3-030-88013-2_10

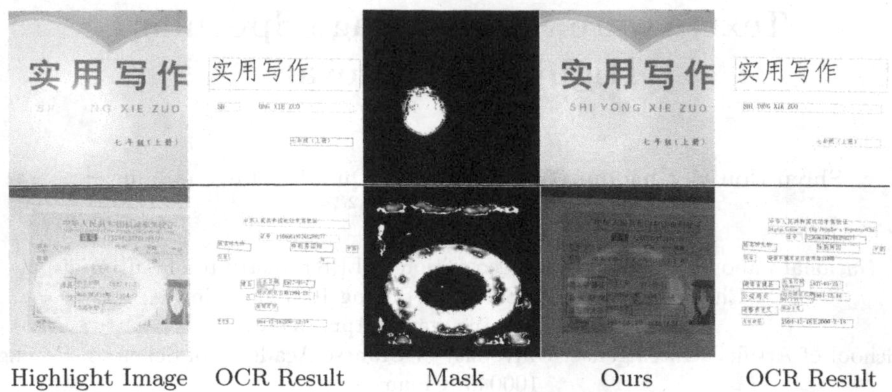

Fig. 1. Selected single image specular highlight removal results of our method. "Mask" and "Ours" separately are the outputs of our first-stage and second-stage networks.

the existence of highlight in the images, while our method is designed to detect and remove the highlight so as to improve the subsequent OCR performance.

In the last decades, many approaches have been proposed to address this challenging specular highlight removal problem. These existing works can be roughly classified into three categories: dichromatic reflection model-based methods [7,23,26,28,32], inpainting-based methods [4,18,21,27], and deep learning-based methods [8,15,20]. The dichromatic reflection model [24] linearly combines the diffuse and specular reflections, and subsequently many methods are proposed based on this model. These methods usually require some simplifying assumptions. In addition, they often need to carry out the pre-processing operations, *e.g.*, segmentation, when encountering images with diverse colors and complex textures, which results in low efficiency and weak practicability. Inpainting-based methods mainly recover the original image contents behind the highlight borrowing the techniques from the image inpainting community. This kind of methods have limited performance for the large highlight contamination. Considering the complexity of single image specular highlight removal, some recent works [8,15,20] are proposed based on the deep neural networks, *e.g.*, convolutional neural network (CNN) and generative adversarial network (GAN). With the aid of the powerful learning capacity of deep models, these deep learning-based methods usually have better performance compared with traditional optimization-based methods. However, these deep learning-based methods require the large-scale training data, especially paired real-world images with necessary annotations, which are time-consuming even difficult to collect.

Existing specular highlight removal methods mainly process the medical images, natural images, and specific-object images, however, there is no work to focus on the text images. On the other hand, for the end-to-end text detection and recognition, many approaches are proposed to handle texts with arbitrary shapes and various orientations. To our knowledge, the case of text images with specular highlight contamination is rarely studied. Therefore, in this paper, we conduct an extensive study on the text-aware single image specular highlight removal problem including dataset collection, network architecture, training losses, and evaluation metrics. The main contributions of our work are as follows:

- We first raise and study in the literature text-aware single image specular highlight removal problem. To study this challenging problem, we collect three high-quality datasets with fine-grained annotations.
- We propose a novel two-stage framework of highlight regions detection and removal implemented with two sub-networks. The highlight detection network provides the useful location information to facilitate the subsequent highlight removal network. For the training objectives, we jointly exploit detection loss, reconstruction loss, GAN loss, and text-related loss to achieve the good performance.
- For the result comparison, we suggest a comprehensive measurement set, which contains the end-to-end text detection and recognition performance and auxiliary visual quality evaluation.

2 Related Work

2.1 Dichromatic Reflection Model-Based Methods

The dichromatic reflection model [24] assumes that the image intensity can be represented by a linear combination of diffuse and specular reflections. This model have been widely used for specular highlight removal. Based on the distribution of diffuse and specular points in the maximum chromaticity-intensity space, Tan *et al.* [28] separated the reflection components by identifying the diffuse maximum chromaticity and then applying a specular-to-diffuse mechanism. Inspired by the observation that diffuse maximum chromaticity in a local patch of color images changes smoothly, Yang *et al.* [32] enhanced the real-time performance and robustness of the chromaticity estimation by applying the bilateral filtering. To exploit the global information of color images for specular reflection separation, Ren *et al.* [23] proposed a global color-lines constraint based on the dichromatic reflection model. Fu *et al.* [7] reformulated estimating the diffuse and specular images as an energy minimization with sparse constraints, which can be approximately solved. Recently, Son *et al.* [26] proposed a convex optimization framework to effectively remove the specular highlight from chromatic and achromatic regions of natural images. These dichromatic reflection model-based approaches often have limited performance for processing the images with diverse colors and complex textures.

2.2 Inpainting-Based Methods

Inpainting is to complete the missing regions of images by propagating information from the known regions, and this technique can be used to restore damaged paintings or remove specific objects [5]. Tan *et al.* [27] first proposed an inpainting-based method for highlight removal by incorporating the illumination-based constraints. Ortiz and Torres [21] designed a connected vectorial filter integrating into the inpainting process to eliminate the specular reflectance. Park and Lee [22] introduced a highlight inpainting method based on the color line projection, however, this method needs two images taken with different exposure times. Inpainting-based highlight removal methods were also proposed to handle the medical images, such as endoscopic images [4] and colposcopic images [18]. However, these inpainting-based methods are only effective for images with small areas of highlight contamination.

2.3 Deep Learning-Based Methods

Different from the aforementioned two kinds of methods, the deep learning-based methods do not require the specular highlight model assumption, and thus have the potential to handle various scenarios. Lee *et al.* [14] proposed a perceptron artificial neural network to detect the specular reflections of tooth images and then applied the smoothing spatial filter to recursively correct the specular reflections. Due to the lack of paired training data, Funke *et al.* [8] adopted the cycle GAN framework [33] and introduced a self-regularization loss aiming to reduce image modification in non-specular regions. Similarly, Lin *et al.* [15] also adopted a GAN framework and proposed a multi-class discriminator, where classifying the generated diffuse images from real ones and original input images as well. Muhammad *et al.* [20] proposed two deep models (Spec-Net and Spec-CGAN) for specularity removal from faces. The former takes the intensity channel as input while the latter takes the RGB image as input. These methods mainly proposed for the medical images, specific-object images or facial images, whereas our work pays attention to the text images.

3 Datasets

In the literature, there is no publicly available dataset for studying the text-aware single image specular highlight removal problem. Therefore, in this work, we collect three high-quality datasets including a real dataset and two synthetic datasets. The pipelines of datasets collection and an example of paired data sample are shown in Fig. 2.

3.1 Real Dataset

Figure 2(a) illustrates the pipeline of real dataset collection. For the real dataset, we collect 2,025 image pairs: image with text-aware specular highlight, the corresponding highlight-free image and binary mask image indicating the location of highlight. The image contents include ID cards and driver's licenses, which contain a lot of text information. We first put the transparent plastic film on the picture and turn on the light. Then, the camera shoots to obtain a highlight image. Correspondingly, we obtain a highlight-free image by turning off

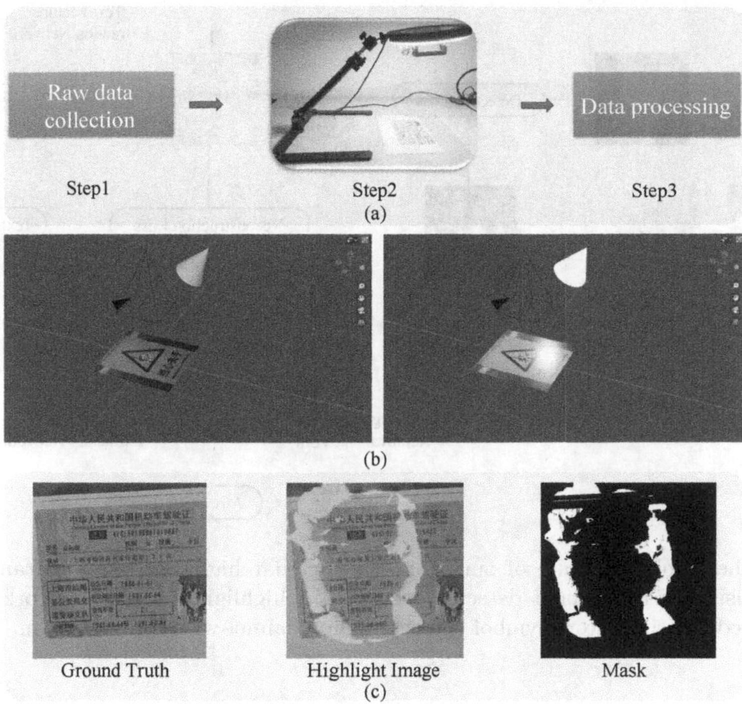

Fig. 2. The collection pipelines of real dataset (a) and synthetic dataset (b), and an example of paired data sample (c).

the light. The shapes and intensities of the highlights are various by adjusting the location of the plastic film. Binary mask image is achieved from the image with specular highlight and highlight-free image through difference and multiple threshold screening. We randomly split this dataset (named RD) into a training set (1,800 images) and a test set (225 images).

3.2 Synthetic Datasets

To further enrich the diversity of our dataset, we construct two sets of synthetic images using the 3D computer graphics software Blender. Figure 2(b) shows the pipeline of synthetic dataset collection. We first collect 3,679 images with texts from supermarkets and streets, and 2,025 images mentioned in Sec. 3.1. Then, we use the Blender with Cycles engine to automatically generate 27,700 groups of text-aware specular highlight images, the corresponding highlight-free images and highlight mask images. In particular, the highlight shapes include circles, triangles, ellipses, and rings to simulate the lighting conditions in real-world scenes. The material roughness is randomly set in the range [0.1,0.3], and the illumination intensity is randomly chosen from the range [40,70]. To force the specular highlight on the text areas of the image, we provide the Blender with

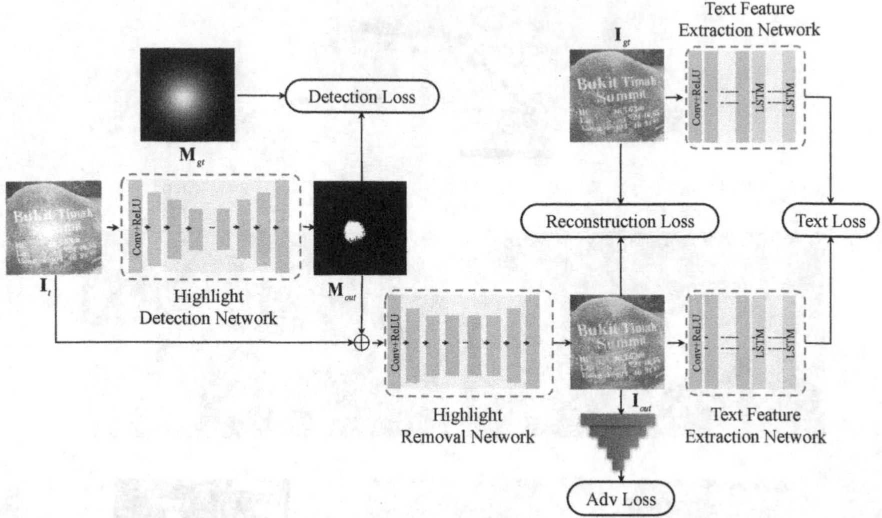

Fig. 3. The whole structure of our proposed specular highlight removal framework, which consists of a highlight detection network, a highlight removal network, and a patch-based discriminator. Symbol $\oplus$ means the channel-wise concatenation.

the location information of the text areas obtained via the text detection model CTPN [29].

Because the product or street view category contains less texts per image, while the texts in ID cards and driver's licenses are more dense. Under the same illumination condition, the difficulty of restoring the text information interfered by the specular highlight in these two kinds of images is different. Therefore, we divide the above two types of images into two datasets, namely, SD1 and SD2. SD1 contains 12,000 training sets and 2,000 test sets. SD2 contains 12,000 training sets and 1,700 test sets. Note that, the image contents of RD and SD2 are same.

4 Proposed Method

In this work, we propose a two-stage framework to detect and remove the specular highlight from text images. The whole architecture is shown in Fig. 3. In the following, we describe the details of our network architecture and the loss functions.

4.1 Network Architecture

Highlight Detection Network. The highlight detection network Net_D takes the text image $\mathbf{I}_t$ with specular highlight as input and outputs a mask $\mathbf{M}_{out}$ indicating the highlight regions. Each element of $\mathbf{M}_{out}$ is in [0,1], and a larger value stands for a higher probability that the corresponding location of image $\mathbf{I}_t$ is covered by the specular highlight. Due to the same width and height of $\mathbf{I}_t$ and $\mathbf{M}_{out}$, for this network, we adopt a fully convolutional architecture consisting of three downsampling and upsampling layers. Each downsampling layer is followed by two convolutional layers, and each upsampling layer is followed by three convolutional layers.

Highlight Removal Network. After achieving the highlight mask $\mathbf{M}_{out}$, the highlight removal network Net_R is then applied to remove the specular highlight and recover the text information. As input, Net_R accepts an input text image $\mathbf{I}_t$ and detected highlight mask $\mathbf{M}_{out}$. The output of our highlight removal network Net_R is a highlight-free image $\mathbf{I}_{out}$. Through introducing $\mathbf{M}_{out}$, network Net_R can pay more attention to the highlight regions and achieve more better removal performance. For the network architecture of Net_R, in this work, we adopt an encoder-decoder network with skip connection. This network consists of two downsampling layers, four residual blocks, and two upsampling layers. To further enhance the removal performance, we also apply a patch-based discriminator [19]. The discriminator D includes one convolutional layer and five downsampling layers with kernel size of 5 and stride of 2. The spectral normalization is utilized to stabilize the training of the discriminator.

4.2 Loss Functions

Next, we illustrate the loss functions used for training our network.

Highlight Detection Loss. For the objective function of highlight detection network, we use l_1 loss, *i.e.*, $\mathcal{L}_{Net_D} = \|\mathbf{M}_{out} - \mathbf{M}_{gt}\|_1$, where $\mathbf{M}_{gt}$ is the ground truth of highlight mask.

Reconstruction Loss. The reconstruction loss is to add constraints on the pixel and feature space. The pixel-aware loss consists of pixel-wise difference item and total varition (TV) item: $\mathcal{L}_P = 5 * \|\mathbf{I}_{out} - \mathbf{I}_{gt}\|_1 + 0.1 * (\|\mathbf{I}_{out}(i,j) - \mathbf{I}_{gt}(i-1,j)\|_1 + \|\mathbf{I}_{out}(i,j) - \mathbf{I}_{gt}(i,j-1)\|_1)$. The feature-aware loss including perceptual loss [11] and style loss [9]: $\mathcal{L}_F = 0.05 * \|\Phi(\mathbf{I}_{out}) - \Phi(\mathbf{I}_{gt})\|_1 + 120 * \|\Psi(\mathbf{I}_{out}) - \Psi(\mathbf{I}_{gt})\|_1$, where Φ is the feature maps of pre-trained VGG-16 [25] and $\Psi(\cdot) = \Phi(\cdot)\Phi(\cdot)^T$ is the Gram matrix [9]. The feature-aware loss improves the visual quality of results.

GAN Loss. In the highlight removal network, we use a patch-based discriminator D to enhance the visual realism of results. For the GAN loss, we adopt the hinge loss. Therefore, the adversarial loss for Net_R is $\mathcal{L}_G = -\mathbb{E}[D(\mathbf{I}_{out})]$. The loss used for training the discriminator D is formulated as $\mathcal{L}_D = \mathbb{E}[max(0, 1 - D(\mathbf{I}_{gt}))] + \mathbb{E}[max(0, 1 + D(\mathbf{I}_{out}))]$.

Text-Related Loss. In this work, our specular highlight removal is text-aware. This means that the highlight removal network Net_R needs to pay more attention to recover the texts hidden behind the highlights. To do this, we apply the pre-trained text detection and recognition models to provide the supervision on the text recovering. More specifically, we add the consistent constraints on the feature maps of $\mathbf{I}_{out}$ and $\mathbf{I}_{gt}$ extracted from above two pre-trained models, and the text-related loss is formulated as $\mathcal{L}_T = \sum_{c=1}^{3} \|\phi_c(\mathbf{I}_{out}) - \phi_c(\mathbf{I}_{gt})\|_1 + \|\phi_d(\mathbf{I}_{out}) - \phi_d(\mathbf{I}_{gt})\|_1$, where ϕ_c stands for the c-th layer feature map from the pre-trained CTPN model [1] and ϕ_d denotes the d-th layer feature map from the pre-trained DenseNet [1].

To this end, the total objective function of Net_D and Net_R is $\mathcal{L} = \lambda_{Net_D}\mathcal{L}_{Net_D} + \mathcal{L}_P + \mathcal{L}_F + \lambda_G\mathcal{L}_G + \mathcal{L}_T$. In all experiments, we set $\lambda_{Net_D} = 10$ and $\lambda_G = 0.01$.

5 Experiments

5.1 Implementation Settings

Our network is implemented with TensorFlow 1.15. As GPU we use a TITAN RTX from NVIDIA®. The Adam optimizer [13] with a batch size of 4 is used to train our network, where $\beta_1 = 0.5$ and $\beta_2 = 0.9$. The learning rate is initialized as 0.0001. In our experiments, all the images are of size of 512×512. Note that, the text recognition model used for result evaluation is different from the model used in text-related loss.

5.2 Qualitative Evaluation

We qualitatively compare our method with two recent advanced specular highlight removal methods: Multi [15] and SPEC (Spec-CGAN [20]) on our collected three datasets. The results are shown in Fig. 4. Among these three methods, our method can better remove the highlight and achieve the superior end-to-end text detection and recognition performance. For example, our method successfully recovers the name, address, and id number in the third row. Multi has apparent highlight remnants in the third and fourth rows due to its blind removal property, whereas our method can better perceive the highlight regions. Compared with Multi, the results of SPEC have less highlights, however, the capability of recovering the texts is limited for the cycleGAN framework as SPEC followed.

5.3 Quantitative Evaluation

In addition, we quantitatively compare the above three methods in terms of the end-to-end text detection and recognition performance and visual quality. For the end-to-end text detection and recognition evaluation, we adopt the common metrics [17]: recall, precision, and f-measure. We choose the current advanced text detection and recognition algorithm Paddle OCR [2] to calculate these three metrics. For visual quality evaluation, we utilize the PSNR and SSIM.

Table 1 reports the numerical results of the three methods on our three datasets. Due to the same image contents of RD and SD2, for real dataset (RD), we fine-tune the model trained on SD2 using the training set of RD for all three

Fig. 4. Qualitative comparisons of our method with Multi [15] and SPEC [20].

methods. From Table 1, we can find that our method achieves the best performance for end-to-end text detection and recognition (see 3–5 columns). Take the recall as an example, our method can improve the end-to-end text detection and recognition performance by 6.89% (SD1), 3.07% (SD2), and 13.65% (RD), respectively. This improvement indicates that our method can better recover the original texts hidden behind the specular highlight. In addition, the end-to-end detection and recognition performance of Multi and SPEC sometimes is lower than that of Light Image. The reason is that these two methods remove the highlight and texts as well. For PSNR and SSIM, SPEC is worst, while our method and Multi are competitive for synthetic datasets, and our method is better than Multi for real datasets. PSNR and SSIM of our method sometimes are lower than that of Multi, however, these two metrics are not exactly the same as the visual quality that the human eyes perceive. More importantly, we focus on the end-to-end text detection and recognition performance after highlight removal, and the visual quality is an auxiliary aspect.

5.4 Ablation Study

To verify the effectiveness of the text-related loss, we perform the ablation experiments and report the corresponding results in Table 2. We observe that the end-to-end text detection and recognition performance of our method with text-related loss is consistently improved for three datasets. This indicates that the text-related loss can enforce the highlight removal network to conduct the text-aware restoration. In addition, we can find that the end-to-end text detection and recognition performance of our method is already better than that of Multi and SPEC (comparing the first row of each dataset in Table 2 with the corresponding rows in Table 1), even though there is no text-related loss.

Table 1. Quantitative comparison of our method and two recent state-of-the-art methods: Multi [15] and SPEC [20]. All three methods are trained and tested on our collected three datasets separately. Recall, precision, f-measure, and SSIM are in %.

Datasets	Methods	Recall ↑	Precision ↑	F-measure ↑	PSNR ↑	SSIM ↑
SD1	Light Image	85.03	94.70	88.70	17.58	82.37
	Multi (2019)	86.28	94.76	89.30	**26.29**	**89.86**
	SPEC (2020)	82.39	93.12	86.31	15.61	68.82
	Ours	**91.92**	**96.32**	**93.57**	22.65	88.33
SD2	Light Image	80.50	**95.89**	87.10	11.79	66.42
	Multi (2019)	79.21	93.82	84.88	28.99	**91.81**
	SPEC (2020)	78.87	95.10	85.55	9.66	53.95
	Ours	**83.57**	95.00	**88.42**	**29.21**	90.67
RD	Light Image	64.85	90.60	73.49	17.05	65.04
	Multi (2019)	61.58	87.63	70.72	17.17	64.23
	SPEC (2020)	70.59	**91.62**	78.38	14.82	52.49
	Ours	**78.50**	91.34	**83.34**	**21.62**	**77.19**

Table 2. Performance of our method without and with text-related loss on our collected three datasets.

Datasets	Methods	Recall ↑	Precision ↑	F-measure ↑	PSNR ↑	SSIM ↑
SD1	w/o text loss	91.43	94.12	92.75	21.88	87.19
	Ours	**91.92**	**96.32**	**93.57**	**22.65**	**88.33**
SD2	w/o text loss	82.69	93.48	87.76	28.12	89.93
	Ours	**83.57**	**95.00**	**88.42**	**29.21**	**90.67**
RD	w/o text loss	77.04	89.66	82.87	21.38	76.11
	Ours	**78.50**	**91.34**	**83.34**	**21.62**	**77.19**

6 Conclusion and Future Work

In this work, we studied and solved the challenging specular highlight removal problem of single text image. To facilitate this study, we collected three high-quality datasets with fine-grained annotations. We proposed a two-stage framework including a highlight detection network and a highlight removal network. The output of highlight detection network is used as an auxiliary information, which guides the highlight removal network to pay more attention to the highlight regions. In addition, text-related loss was introduced to improve the recovering of texts. Our source code and datasets are available at https://github.com/weizequan/TASHR.

In the future, we would like to construct lager and richer dataset to promote the development of related research. We would also like to design more effective networks and loss functions. Furthermore, an exciting research problem is to suggest more complete and exact visual quality measurements.

Acknowledgments. This work was supported by the National Key R&D Program of China (2019YFB2204104), and the National Natural Science Foundation of China (Nos. 6210071649, 62172415 and 61772523).

References

1. Chineseocr: Ctpn plus densenet plus ctc based chinese ocr. https://github.com/YCG09/chinese_ocr. Accessed 30 Apr 2021
2. Paddleocr: Awesome multilingual ocr toolkits based on paddlepaddle. https://github.com/PaddlePaddle/PaddleOCR. Accessed 30 Apr 2021
3. Arbeláez, P., Maire, M., Fowlkes, C., Malik, J.: Contour detection and hierarchical image segmentation. IEEE Trans. Pattern Anal. Mach. Intell. **33**(5), 898–916 (2011)
4. Arnold, M., Ghosh, A., Ameling, S., Lacey, G.: Automatic segmentation and inpainting of specular highlights for endoscopic imaging. J. Image Video Process. (2010)
5. Bertalmio, M., Sapiro, G., Caselles, V., Ballester, C.: Image inpainting. In: ACM SIGGRAPH, pp. 417–424 (2000)

6. Fleyeh, H.: Shadow and highlight invariant colour segmentation algorithm for traffic signs. In: IEEE Conference on Cybernetics and Intelligent Systems (2006)
7. Fu, G., Zhang, Q., Song, C., Lin, Q., Xiao, C.: Specular highlight removal for real-world images. Comput. Graph. Forum **38**(7), 253–263 (2019)
8. Funke, I., Bodenstedt, S., Riediger, C., Weitz, J., Speidel, S.: Generative adversarial networks for specular highlight removal in endoscopic images. In: Medical Imaging 2018: Image-Guided Procedures, Robotic Interventions, and Modeling, vol. 10576, pp. 8–16 (2018)
9. Gatys, L.A., Ecker, A.S., Bethge, M.: Image style transfer using convolutional neural networks. In: IEEE Conference on Computer Vision and Pattern Recognition, pp. 2414–2423 (2016)
10. Guo, X., Chen, Z., Li, S., Yang, Y., Yu, J.: Deep eyes: binocular depth-from-focus on focal stack pairs. In: Chinese Conference on Pattern Recognition and Computer Vision, pp. 353–365 (2019)
11. Johnson, J., Alahi, A., Fei-Fei, L.: Perceptual losses for real-time style transfer and super-resolution. In: Proceedings of the European Conference on Computer Vision, pp. 694–711 (2016)
12. Khanian, M., Boroujerdi, A.S., Breuß, M.: Photometric stereo for strong specular highlights. arXiv preprint arXiv:1709.01357 (2017)
13. Kingma, D.P., Ba, J.: Adam: a method for stochastic optimization. In: International Conference on Learning Representations (2015)
14. Lee, S.T., Yoon, T.H., Kim, K.S., Kim, K.D., Park, W.: Removal of specular reflections in tooth color image by perceptron neural nets. In: International Conference on Signal Processing Systems, vol. 1, pp. V1-285-V1-289 (2010)
15. Lin, J., El Amine Seddik, M., Tamaazousti, M., Tamaazousti, Y., Bartoli, A.: Deep multi-class adversarial specularity removal. In: Image Analysis, pp. 3–15 (2019)
16. Long, S., He, X., Yao, C.: Scene text detection and recognition: The deep learning era. Int. J. Comput. Vis. **129**(1), 161–184 (2021)
17. Lucas, S., Panaretos, A., Sosa, L., Tang, A., Wong, S., Young, R.: Icdar 2003 robust reading competitions. In: International Conference on Document Analysis and Recognition, pp. 682–687 (2003)
18. Meslouhi, O.E., Kardouchi, M., Allali, H., Gadi, T., Benkaddour, Y.A.: Automatic detection and inpainting of specular reflections for colposcopic images. Central Eur. J. Comput. Sci. **1** (2011)
19. Miyato, T., Kataoka, T., Koyama, M., Yoshida, Y.: Spectral normalization for generative adversarial networks. In: International Conference on Learning Representations (2018)
20. Muhammad, S., Dailey, M.N., Farooq, M., Majeed, M.F., Ekpanyapong, M.: Spec-net and spec-cgan: Deep learning models for specularity removal from faces. Image Vis. Comput. **93**, 103823 (2020)
21. Ortiz, F., Torres, F.: A new inpainting method for highlights elimination by colour morphology. In: International Conference on Pattern Recognition and Image Analysis, pp. 368–376 (2005)
22. Park, J.W., Lee, K.H.: Inpainting highlights using color line projection. IEICE Trans. Inf. Syst. **90**(1), 250–257 (2007)
23. Ren, W., Tian, J., Tang, Y.: Specular reflection separation with color-lines constraint. IEEE Trans. Image Process. **26**(5), 2327–2337 (2017)
24. Shafer, S.A.: Using color to separate reflection components. Color. Res. Appl. **10**(4), 210–218 (1985)

25. Simonyan, K., Zisserman, A.: Very deep convolutional networks for large-scale image recognition. In: International Conference on Learning Representations (2015)
26. Son, M., Lee, Y., Chang, H.S.: Toward specular removal from natural images based on statistical reflection models. IEEE Trans. Image Process. (2020)
27. Tan, P., Lin, S., Quan, L., Shum, H.Y.: Highlight removal by illumination-constrained inpainting. In: IEEE International Conference on Computer Vision, pp. 164–169 (2003)
28. Tan, R.T., Nishino, K., Ikeuchi, K.: Separating reflection components based on chromaticity and noise analysis. IEEE Trans. Pattern Anal. Mach. Intell. **26**(10), 1373–1379 (2004)
29. Tian, Z., Huang, W., He, T., He, P., Qiao, Y.: Detecting text in natural image with connectionist text proposal network. In: European Conference on Computer Vision, pp. 56–72 (2016)
30. Wang, T.C., Efros, A.A., Ramamoorthi, R.: Occlusion-aware depth estimation using light-field cameras. In: IEEE International Conference on Computer Vision, pp. 3487–3495 (2015)
31. Wang, W., Deng, R., Li, L., Xu, X.: Image aesthetic assessment based on perception consistency. In: Chinese Conference on Pattern Recognition and Computer Vision, pp. 303–315 (2019)
32. Yang, Q., Wang, S., Ahuja, N.: Real-time specular highlight removal using bilateral filtering. In: European Conference on Computer Vision, pp. 87–100 (2010)
33. Zhu, J.Y., Park, T., Isola, P., Efros, A.A.: Unpaired image-to-image translation using cycle-consistent adversarial networks. In: IEEE International Conference on Computer Vision, pp. 2242–2251 (2017)

Minimizing Wasserstein-1 Distance by Quantile Regression for GANs Model

Yingying Chen[1,2], Xinwen Hou[1(✉)], and Yu Liu[1]

[1] Institute of Automation, Chinese Academy of Sciences, Beijing, China
{chenyingying2018,xinwen.hou,yu.liu}@ia.ac.cn

[2] School of Artificial Intelligence, University of Chinese Academy of Sciences, Beijing, China

Abstract. In recent years, Generative Adversarial Nets (GANs) as a kind of deep generative model has become a research focus. As a representative work of GANs model, Wasserstein GAN involves earth moving distance which can be applied to un-overlapped probability distributions, and promoted the stability of model training. However, the alternative optimization of the discriminative network in the Wasserstein GAN model makes it impossible to accurately calculate the Wasserstein-1 distance between the real data distribution and generated data distribution. It may result in unstable training sometimes. So we propose minimizing the Wasseerstain-1 distance by Quantile Regression algorithm which works well on minimizing the Wasserstein-1 distance between the real data score distribution and the generated data score distribution. We named our method QR-GAN. QR-GAN involves the information about data distribution instead of distinguishing data between fake and real in original GANs model. Meanwhile, QR-GAN model adds the real data information to the updating of generator network, which makes the parameter updating of generator more effective. In order to verify the effectiveness of our method, we perform experiments on MNIST, CIFAR-10, STL-10, LSUN-Tower and the results demonstrate superiority of our method.

Keywords: GANs model · Wasserstein-1 distance · Quantile regression

1 Introduction

In the past decade, deep learning has triggered a research boom of artificial intelligence technology. Deep learning models can be divided into two categories: deep generative model and deep discriminative model. Compare with the great success of deep discriminative model in computer vision, natural language processing and other fields, deep generative model has a slightly inferior prestige due to the high-dimensional probability model which is difficult to calculate. However, since Goodflow et al. propose the GANs model [1] in 2014, the deep generative model has received more and more attention.

Y. Chen—Student.

© Springer Nature Switzerland AG 2021
H. Ma et al. (Eds.): PRCV 2021, LNCS 13022, pp. 128–139, 2021.
https://doi.org/10.1007/978-3-030-88013-2_11

The GANs model avoids the difficulty of calculating the likelihood function in explicit density-based method. But there are some inherent shortcomings of the model. Training instability and mode collapsing are two basic problems of GANs model. Training instability involves the generator and discriminator oscillating rather than converging to a fixed point in training. Mode collapsing means that the generator tends to produce only a single sample or a small family of very similar samples.

GANs can be viewed as a minimax two-player game. The mechanism revealed by the game is to make the generated distribution approximate to the real distribution. The original GANs model measures the gap between the two distributions by Jensen-Shannon (JS) divergence. But JS divergence is a constant when the two distributions don't intersect. It will cause the gradient vanishing problem. In addition, the improvement to alleviate the gradient vanishing is equipped with an unreasonable objective function, which will lead to training instability [2]. Arjovsky et al. propose Wasserstein GAN model [3]. They introduce Wasserstein-1 distance into GANs model which promoted the stability of GANs model training. It makes Wasserstein GAN model become a representative improvement baseline of GANs model.

However Ostrovski et al. state that the approximate error caused by incomplete solution may aggravate the instability of training [4]. Fortunately the Quantile Regression (QR) algorithm can minimize the Wasserstein-1 distance between the distributions of two one-dimensional random variables. It serves well in distributional reinforcement learning in recent years [5]. However the data generated by the GANs model are mostly high-dimensional data. Therefore, we model the discriminative network as a scalar distribution mapping which can reflect the characteristics of data distribution. It can capture more data distribution characteristics than single valued mapping. Then the Quantile Regression algorithm is introduced into the GANs model to minimize the Wasserstein-1 distance between the generated data score distribution and the real data score distribution. In short, we provide a new idea for minimizing Wasserstein-1 distance in GANs model. Comparative experiments on MNIST, CIFAR-10, STL-10 and LSUN-Tower datasets demonstrate the effectiveness of our method and superiority to the Wasserstein GAN model.

2 Related Work

In the past few years, the GANs model has achieved great success in data generation, image restoration, image segmentation, image super-resolution and other fields. It is due to the flexibility and broad application prospect of GANs model. Improvement and extension works based on GANs model can be divided into three categories: improvement schemes based on model structure, improvement schemes based on objective function, and schemes triggered by extended application.

Researchers have evolved many variations of the GANs model by improving the model structure. Mirza et al. propose Conditional-GAN model[6].

By conditioning the model on additional information, it is possible to guide the data generation process. Such conditioning could be based on class labels, on some part of data for inpainting, or even on data from different modality. Zhang et al. propose Self-Attention GAN [7] by introducing the attention mechanism into the GANs model. It allows attention-driven, long-range dependency modeling for image generation tasks, such as the asymmetrical distribution of eyes in human face generation. Ledig et al. propose a generative adversarial network for image super resolution (SR-GAN) [8]. It is the first framework capable of inferring photo-realistic natural images for 4×upscaling factors. Zhu et al. propose Cycle-GAN [9] which combines dual structure and cycle-loss. It demonstrates the superiority of Cycle-GAN model in collection style transfer, object transfiguration, season transfer, photo enhancement.

The representative work of the improvement scheme based on objective function is Wasserstein GAN model. Arjovsky et al. find that the JS divergence corresponding to the objective function of the original GANs model is not an excellent distance metric [2]. It can not provide good gradient to guide the parameters updating at the initial stage of GANs model training. Moreover, the scheme for improving the above problem with a unstable objective function, which will result in training breakdown. In order to promote the stability of the GANs model training, they introduced Wasserstein-1 distance into the GANs model by dual transformation. Arjovsky et al. verify the effectiveness of Wasserstein GAN in promoting training stability by directly displaying visual renderings of the generated images.

Wasserstein GAN approximately minimizes Wasserstein-1 distance, and introduces Lipschitz constraint at the same time. Arjovsky et al. clip the discriminative network weight parameters to ensure the Lipschitz constraint. It is too simple to make the critic network satisfy Lipschitz constraint. Lipschitz constraint actually restricts the norm of discriminative network gradient to be less than a constant. Gulrajani et al. propose gradient penalty for Wasserstein GAN (WGAN-GP) [10]. It enforces a soft version of the constraint with a penalty on the gradient norm for the random samples. In addition, Miyato et al. propose Spectrally Normalized GAN (SN-GAN) [11]. It controls the Lipschitz constant of the discriminator function by literally constraining the spectral norm of each layer. The improved scheme to optimize Lipschitz constraint does not explore the implementation of Wasserstein-1 distance, so the performance improvement to Generation Adversarial Nets model is limited to the set range of the original WGAN framework.

In recent years, Quantile Regression (QR) algorithm performs well in the field of distributional reinforcement learning. It can minimize the Wasserstein-1 distance between two distributions. Dabney et al. put forward the concept of distributional reinforcement learning [12]. It learns value distribution information and realizes value distribution sampling. QR algorithm is used to minimize the Wasserstein-1 distance between the model distribution and the target distribution. Some researchers have tried to applied Quantile Regression algorithm to GANs models. But there is some deviation in the understanding of QR algorithm, which fixes the target distribution quantile to a certain number. In this paper, QR regression is used to minimize the Wasserstein-1 distance between the score distribution of generated data and that of real data, completely based on the principle of QR regression.

3 Background

3.1 Wasserstein GAN

The Original GANs objective function is:

$$\begin{aligned}\min_G \max_D V(G, D) &= \mathbb{E}_{\boldsymbol{x}\sim p_r(\boldsymbol{x})}[\log D(\boldsymbol{x})] \\ &+ \mathbb{E}_{\boldsymbol{x}\sim p_g(\boldsymbol{x})}[\log(1 - D(\boldsymbol{x}))]\end{aligned} \tag{1}$$

where $p_r(\boldsymbol{x})$ is the real data distribution and $p_g(\boldsymbol{x})$ is the generated data distribution with $\boldsymbol{x} = G(\boldsymbol{z})$; $\boldsymbol{z}$ is the input to generator obeying a given distribution $p_z(\boldsymbol{z})$; $D(\boldsymbol{x})$ is the output of discriminator, represents the probability that $\boldsymbol{x}$ comes from the real data rather than fake data.

GANs involves JS divergence to measure the distance between $p_r(x)$ and $p_g(x)$. Arjovsky et al. introduce Wasserstein-1 distance into GANs model to promoted the stability of model training. The Wasserstein distance is a metric defined by the concept of optimal transport:

$$W_c[p(x), q(y)] = \inf_{\zeta\in\prod(p(x),q(y))} \mathbb{E}_{(x,y)\in\zeta}[d(x, y)] \tag{2}$$

where $p(x)$ is the target distribution; $q(y)$ is an approximate constructed distribution; $\prod(p(x), q(y))$ denotes the set of all joint distributions $\zeta(x, y)$, whose marginals are respectively $p(x)$ and $q(y)$; $d(x, y)$ is the cost of moving y into x. When $d(x, y) = ||x - y||_1$, (2) denotes Wasserstein-1 distance:

$$W_1[p(x), q(y)] = \inf_{\zeta\in\prod(p(x),q(y))} \mathbb{E}_{(x,y)\in\zeta}[||x - y||_1] \tag{3}$$

The infimum in (3) is highly intractable. Arjovsky et al. use Kantorovich-Rubinstein duality to convert the infimum problem into the following form:

$$W_1[p(x), q(y)] = \sup_{||f||_L\leq K} \mathbb{E}_{x\sim p(x)}[f(x)] - \mathbb{E}_{x\sim q(x)}[f(x)] \tag{4}$$

where the supremum is over all the K-Lipschitz functions $f : \mathcal{X} \to R$. And then maximize (4) by searching some w in the parameterized family functions $\{f_w\}_{w\in\mathcal{W}}$ to approximately solve the supremum:

$$\max_{w\in\mathcal{W}} \mathbb{E}_{x\sim p_r(x)}[f_w(x)] - \mathbb{E}_{z\sim p(z)}[f_w(g_\theta(z))] \tag{5}$$

where $f_w(x)$ denotes the discriminator mapping function which satisfies K-Lipschitz constraint for some K; $p_r(\boldsymbol{x})$ is the target real data distribution; $g_\theta(z)$ denotes the generator mapping function parameterized by θ; $f_w(x)$

Wasserstein GAN model still faces limitations. Due to insufficient training of the discriminator or limitations of the function approximator, the gradient direction produced by Wasserstein GAN model can be arbitrarily bad.

3.2 Quantile Regression

The original definition of Wasserstein distance is highly intractable due to the infmum. But in some special cases, Wasserstein distance can be very concise. Bickel et al. show that the lower bound in (4) is attainable [13]; In addition, Major shows that the Wasserstein-1 distance of one-dimensional random variables is [14]:

$$W_1[X,Y] = \int_0^1 |F_1^{-1}(t) - F_2^{-1}(t)|dt \tag{6}$$

where $F_1^{-1}(t)$ and $F_2^{-1}(t)$ are the inverse function of the cumulative distribution function $F_1(x)$ and $F_2(x)$. $F(x)$ and $F^{-1}(t)$ satisfies Eq. (7), for which x is also called the t quantile of the random variable X.

$$\begin{aligned} F(x) &= p(X \leq x) \\ F^{-1}(t) &= \inf\{x \in \mathbb{R} : t \leq F(x)\} \end{aligned} \tag{7}$$

When the construction distribution $q(y)$ modeled by a mixed Dirac distribution, the Wasserstein-1 distance between X and Y is shown as:

$$W_1[X,Y_z] = \sum_{i=1}^{N} \int_{\tau_{i-1}}^{\tau_i} |F_1^{-1}(t) - z_i|dt \tag{8}$$

where z_i is the sample of a mixed Dirac distribution. The probability density function of mixed Dirac distribution is:

$$p(z) = \frac{1}{N}\sum_{i=1}^{N} \delta(z_i) \tag{9}$$

The values for $\{z_1, z_2, ..., z_N\}$ that minimize $W_1(X, Y_z)$ are given by $z_i = F_1^{-1}(\hat{\tau}_i)$. $\hat{\tau}_i$ is the quantile midpoints can be denoted by $\hat{\tau}_i = \frac{\tau_{i-1}+\tau_i}{2}$. Unfortunately, quantile parametrization leads to biased gradients. However, Quantile Regression is an unbiased stochastic approximation method for the quantile function of distributions.

For random variable X, and a given probability τ, the value of the quantile function $x_\tau = F_X^{-1}(\tau)$ can be characterized as the minimizer of the Quantile Regression loss:

$$x_\tau = \arg\min_z \left\{ \sum_{x^k \geq z_\theta} \tau|x^k - z_\theta| + \sum_{x^k < z_\theta} (1-\tau)|x^k - z_\theta| \right\} \tag{10}$$

where x^k is the the target distribution sample; z_θ is the quantile regression mapping with adjustable parameter θ, and $z^* = x_\tau$. More generally, for obtaining all quantile values $\{z_\theta^1, z_\theta^2, ..., z_\theta^N\}$ that minimize the Wasserstein-1 distance, the objective function is:

$$\sum_{i=1}^{N} \mathbb{E}_{x \in X}[\rho_{\tau_i}(x - z_\theta^i)] \tag{11}$$

where $\rho_{\tau_i}(u) = u(\tau - \delta_{(u<0)})$.

4 Our Method

The Quantile Regression algorithm provides an unbiased stochastic approximation of quantile value. By setting the probability $\{\hat{\tau}_i\}_{i=1}^{N}$, the solutions of QR loss will be the quantile values that minimize the Wasserstein-1 distance. However it is only suitable for one-dimension random variable distribution approximation. The data generated by the GANs model is usually high-dimension data. Therefore, we consider to map the high-dimension data x to one-dimension score distribution through the feature mapping network $f(x)$. It is a one-dimensional scalar distribution that can reveal the characteristics of high-dimension data. The Quantile Regression algorithm can be used to minimize the Wasserstein-1 distance between real data score distribution and generated data score distribution.

$$\sum_{i=1}^{N} \mathbb{E}_{x_r \sim p_r} \left[\rho_{\tau_i} \left(f(x_r, \tau_j) - f(x_g, \tau_i)\right)\right] \tag{12}$$

where p_r is the real data distribution; x_r is the sample of real data; x_g is the sample of generated data with $x_g = G_\theta(z), z \sim p(z)$; $f(x_r, \tau_j)$ is the score of x_r indexed by τ_j; $f(x_g, \tau_i)$ is the score of x_g index by τ_i; By optimizing (12), the score mapping network $f(x)$ outputs the real score distribution τ_i quantile indexed indexed by τ_j. In a more general case, the real score distribution indexed by $\{\tau_j\}_{j=1}^{M}$ forms M true score distributions. Then the objective function for generator is :

$$\min_{\theta \sim \Theta} \mathbb{E}_{x_g \sim p_g} \sum_{j=1}^{M} \sum_{i=1}^{N} \mathbb{E}_{x_r \sim p_r} \left[\rho_{\tau_i} \left(f(x_r, \tau_j) - f(x_g, \tau_i)\right)\right] \tag{13}$$

where p_g is the generated data distribution. The parameters θ of the generator $G_\theta(z)$ is updated by the minimization (13) so that the score distribution of the generated data approaches the score distribution of the real data. In fact, it is the optimization of Quantile Regression loss that minimize the Wasserstein-1 distance between two score distributions. (13) shows that QR-GAN model involves real data information when updating of generator network, which makes the parameter updating of generator more effective.

For the updating score mapping network $f_w(x_r, \tau_j)$, we hope it can distinguish the real data score distribution from the generated data score distribution. And in order to provide a relatively tight constraint, we train the score mapping network $f_w(x_r, \tau_j)$ by maximizing the following formula:

$$\max_{w \sim \mathcal{W}} \mathbb{E}_{x_g \sim p_g} \sum_{i=1}^{N} \mathbb{E}_{x_r \sim p_r} \left[\rho_{\tau_i} \left(f_w(x_r, \tau_i) - f_w(x_g, \tau_i)\right)\right] \tag{14}$$

That is, under the same index τ_i, the larger the difference between corresponding score distribution quantiles, the better. In order to make the score mapping network obtain the distribution characteristics effectively, we limit the parameters of the score mapping network to [−c, c]. It avoids inefficient optimization by simply maximizing the output of $f_w(\cdot, \cdot)$.

In the above optimization process, Quantile Regression algorithm is used to minimize the wasserstein-1 distance between the real score distribution and the generated score distribution. The parameters θ of the generator are updated by the gradient comes from QR regression loss function. The parameters w of the score mapping network $f_w(x, \tau)$ are updated by maximizing the weighted deviation between the two score distributions. The main purpose of $f_w(x, \tau)$ is to obtain characteristics of the data by mapping the high-dimension data to a scalar distribution. Compare with the discriminator network in the original GANs model, the score mapping network considers the information of data distribution. Instead of true and false binary classification.

For convenience, we call our method QR-GAN. The structure of QR-GAN model and Wasserstein GAN model is shown in the Fig. 1. The QR-GAN model maintains the basic structure of GANs model. The main difference is the structure of score mapping network. $\varphi : \mathcal{X} \rightarrow \mathbb{R}^d$ is the convolutional layer mapping for extracting visual features of the image. $\psi : [0, 1] \rightarrow \mathbb{R}^d$ can map the probability τ to a d-dimensional representation as shown in Eq. (15) with $T = 16$. $\varphi(x)$ and $\psi(\tau)$ are associated by element-by-element product (Hadama product). Then all the features are combined through the full connection layer $f : \mathbb{R}^d \rightarrow \mathbb{R}$ with $d = 4096$. The output of the final score mapping network can be expressed as Eq. (16).

$$\psi_j(\tau) := ReLU(\sum_{i=0}^{T-1} cos(\pi i \tau) w_{ij} + b_j) \tag{15}$$

$$f_w(x, \tau) = f(\varphi(x) \odot \psi(\tau)) \tag{16}$$

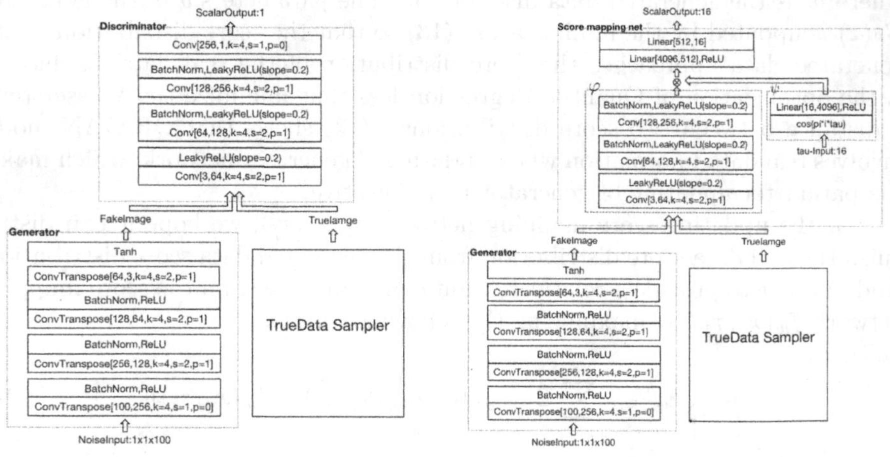

(a) The structure of Wasserstein GAN (b) The structure of QR-GAN

Fig. 1. The structure of QR-GAN model and Wasserstein GAN model

5 Experiment

5.1 Basic Setting

In order to verify the effectiveness of the QR-GAN model, we conduct a series of comparative experiments with Wasserstein GAN as the baseline model. In each training iteration, we update the score distribution mapping network n times first, and then update the generated network once. The specific operation is shown as the Algorithm 1. Where η is the learning rate; $[-c, c]$ represents the clipping interval of network weight parameters of score distribution mapping; m is mini-batch size of training data. Except for special instructions, the experiments use Adam optimizer, in which the super parameter $\beta_1 = 0.5, \beta_2 = 0.999$.

Algorithm 1. QR-GAN.

$\eta = 0.00005$, $c = 0.05$, $m = 64$, $n = 5$, $N = M = 16$

while Θ has not converged **do**
  for $t = 0, ..., n$ **do**
    Sample $\{\mathbf{x}_r^i\}_{i=1}^m \sim p_r(\mathbf{x})$ a batch of the real data.
    Sample $\{\mathbf{z}^i\}_{i=1}^m \sim p(\mathbf{z})$ a batch of prior samples, and $\{x_g^i\}_{i=1}^m = \{G(z^i)\}_{i=1}^m$.
    $g_w \leftarrow \nabla_w \left[\frac{1}{m}\sum_{k=1}^m \left[\sum_{i=1}^N \frac{1}{m}\sum_{h=1}^m \left[\rho_{\tau_i}\left(f(x_r^h, \tau_i) - f(x_g^k, \tau_i)\right)\right]\right]\right]$
    $w \leftarrow w + \eta \cdot Adam(w, g_w)$
    $w \leftarrow clip(w, -c, c)$
  end for
  Sample $\{\mathbf{z}_i\}_{i=1}^m \sim p(\mathbf{z})$ a batch of prior samples, and $\{x_g^i\}_{i=1}^m = \{G(z^i)\}_{i=1}^m$.
  $g_\theta \leftarrow \nabla_\theta \left[\frac{1}{m}\sum_{k=1}^m \left[\sum_{j=1}^M \left[\sum_{i=1}^N \frac{1}{m}\sum_{h=1}^m \left[\rho_{\tau_i}\left(f(x_r^h, \tau_j) - f(x_g^k, \tau_i)\right)\right]\right]\right]\right]$
  $\theta \leftarrow \theta - \eta \cdot Adam(\theta, g_\theta)$
end while

5.2 IS and FID Criteria Experiment

We train model on a range of datasets including MNIST, CIFAR-10, STL-10, LSUN-Tower. Figure 2 shows the generated data by QR-GAN model and Wasserstein GAN model under MNIST dataset, with a resolution of 32×32. We calculate Inception Score (IS) and Fréchet Inception Distance (FID) to quantitatively evaluate the generated images quality. The IS indicator measures the quality and diversity of the generated image at the same time. The greater the value, the better. The FID indicator calculates the Fréchet Distance between the generated data and the real data statistics. As a distance measure, the smaller the value, the better. In the following experiments, the sample number of IS calculated is 100,000, and that of FID calculated is 50,000.

Figure 3 shows the IS and FID curves of QR-GAN model and Wasserstein GAN model on CIFAR-10, STL-10 and LSUN-Tower datasets. The final IS and FID indicator values of the QR-GAN model are better than that of the Wasserstein GAN baseline model on all three datasets. However, in the early stage of

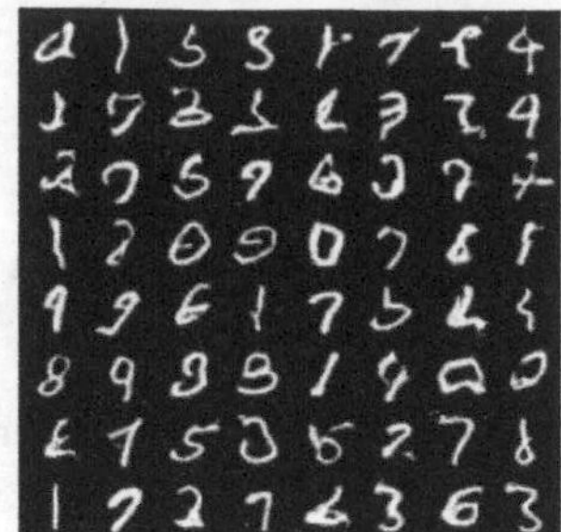

(a) Images generated by Wasserstein GAN

(b) Images generated by QR-GAN

Fig. 2. Handwritten digital images generated by QR-GAN and Wasserstein GAN models.

training (the number of generator iteration is less than 10000), the performance of QR-GAN model is poor. We think the score mapping network needs more data to learn the distribution characteristics, the score mapping network with poor capability in the early stage of training. It could not provide accurate information for the updating of the generative network quickly. With the progress of training, the ability of score mapping network is gradually enhanced, and the advantages of learning data distribution are highlighted. QR-GAN model shows more superiority than Wasserstein GAN model with single-valued mapping.

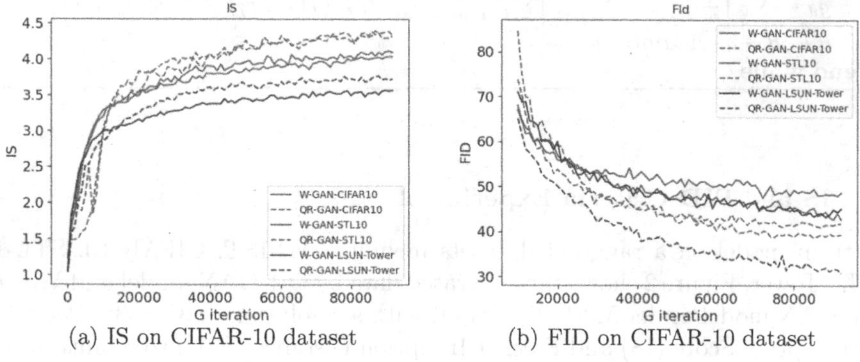

(a) IS on CIFAR-10 dataset (b) FID on CIFAR-10 dataset

Fig. 3. IS and FID indicators curves of QR-GAN model and Wasserstein GAN model on CIFAR-10, STL-10 and LSUN-Tower datasets.

The maximum value of IS indicator and the minimum value of FID indicator in the above experiments are listed in the Table 1. Under different hardware environment and parameter setting, IS and FID values are different. We do not pursue the absolute value of IS and FID, but mainly focus on the improvement of the two indicators on our model relative to the baseline model under the same experimental environment. According to the table, the IS indicator of QR-GAN model improves by an average of 7% over the Wasserstein GAN model. The FID indicator of QR-GAN model improves by an average of 17% over the Wasserstein GAN model. Based on the promotion rate, we believe that the quality and diversity of images generated by QR-GAN model are better than baseline Wasserstein GAN model.

Table 1. IS and FID indicator of QR-GAN model and Wasserstein GAN model

	Model	Dataset		
		CIFAR-10	STL-10	LSUN-Tower
IS	Wasserstein GAN	4.15	4.04	3.57
	QR-GAN	4.42	4.40	3.77
FID	Wasserstein GAN	43.38	47.43	43.15
	QR-GAN	38.64	40.90	30.75

5.3 Adam and Rmsprob Experiment

In this section, we use Adam and RMSProp algorithm to train the model on STL-10 dataset, and calculate the IS and FID indicator of the corresponding model. We believe that an algorithm with good performance should have certain adaptability. The gap between model performance under different optimization algorithms should be small. Figure 4 is the IS and FID indicators curves under different optimization algorithms. It shows the performance of QR-GAN model is better than Wasserstein GAN model. And the performance curves difference between Adam optimizer and RMSProp optimizer of QR-GAN model is smaller than that of Wasserstein GAN model.

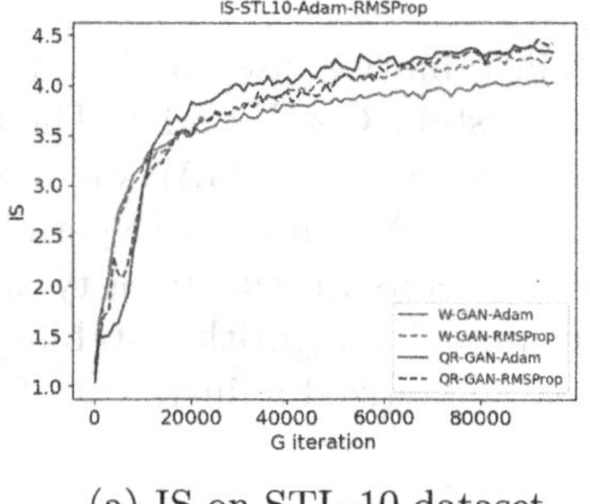

(a) IS on STL-10 dataset

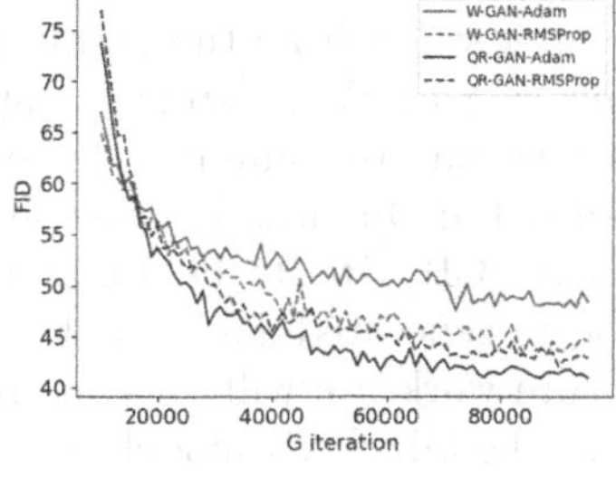

(b) FID on STL-10 dataset

Fig. 4. IS and FID indicators curves on STL-10 dataset with different optimization algorithms

5.4 Different Quantile Initialization Experiment

In the experimental process, we find that different quantile setting would affect the performance of QR-GAN model. Figure 5 shows the IS and FID indicator curves of CIFAR-10 data generated by the model under two different quantile initialization. There are differences in the performance of the QR-GAN models under two initializations, but both of them are better than the baseline model. Previously, when we demonstrate the effectiveness of QR-GAN model, we do not select the curve with the best performance in the experiment. To a certain extent, it avoids over fitting phenomenon caused by overtuning parameters. Yang et al. use parameterized τ to optimize the problems caused by τ value initialization in distributional reinforcement learning [15]. The improvement of QR-GAN model performance by parameterized τ will be one of the contents for further research in the future.

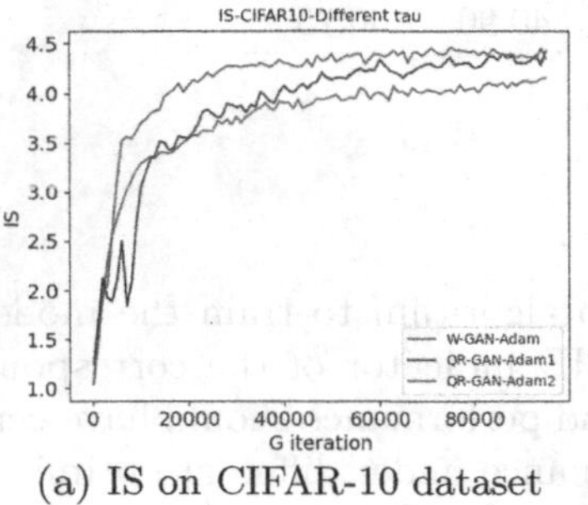

(a) IS on CIFAR-10 dataset

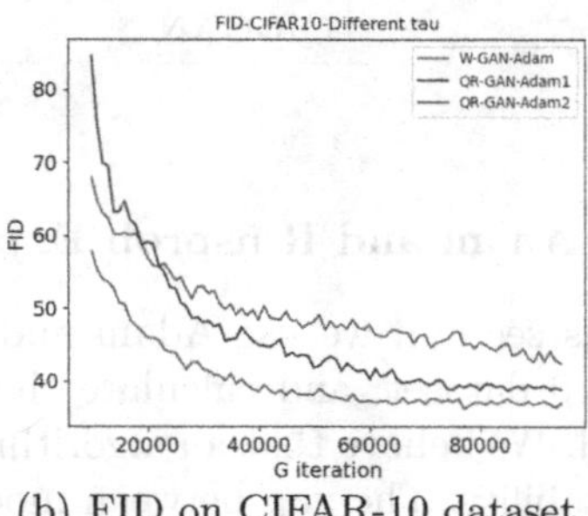

(b) FID on CIFAR-10 dataset

Fig. 5. IS and FID indicators curves on CIFAR-10 dataset with different quantile setting

6 Conclusion

This paper starts from the problem of training instability caused by incomplete optimization of Wasserstein-1 distance in Wasserstein GAN model. Then we find a new way to minimize the Wasserstein-1 distance in the GANs model by extending the Quantile Regression algorithm to the GANs model. Experiments on MNIST,CIFAR-10,STL-10, and LSUN-Tower demonstrate superiority of our method in generated data quality and multi-optimization algorithm stability. In the future work, we will do some research on parameterized adjustment of τ to improve the QR-GAN model.

Acknowledgments. We would like to acknowledgment the Strategic Priority Research Program of Chinese Academy of Sciences (XDA27000000). This paper is supported by it.

References

1. Goodfellow, I.: Generative adversarial nets. In: Advances in Neural Information Processing Systems 27 NIPS, pp. 2672–2680, Curran Associates Inc., (2014)
2. Arjovsky, M., Bottou, L.: Towards principled methods for training generative adversarial networks. In: ICLR (2017)
3. Arjovsky, M., Chintala, S., Bottou, L.: Wasserstein gan. ArXiv:1701.07875 (2017)
4. Ostrovski, G., Dabney, W., Munos, R.: Autoregressive quantile networks for generative modeling. In: International Conference on Machine Learning, pp. 3933–3942 (2018)
5. Dabney, W., Rowland, M., Bellemare, M.G., Munos, R.: Distributional reinforcement learning with quantile regression. In: AAAI (2018)
6. Mirza, M., Osindero, S.: Conditional generative adversarial nets. arXiv preprint arXiv:1411.1784 (2014)
7. Zhang, H., Goodfellow, I.J., Metaxas, D.N., Odena, A.: Self-attention generative adversarial networks. In: International Conference on Machine Learning, pp. 7354–7363 (2018)
8. Ledig, C., et al.: Photo-realistic single image super-resolution using a generative adversarial network. In: Proceedings of the IEEE Conference on Computer Vision and Pattern Recognition, pp. 4681–4690 (2017)
9. Zhu, J.-Y., Park, T., Isola, P., Efros, A.A.: Unpaired image-to-image translation using cycle-consistent adversarial networks. In: Proceedings of the IEEE International Conference on Computer Vision, pp. 2223–2232 (2017)
10. Gulrajani, I., Ahmed, F., Arjovsky, M., Dumoulin, V., Courville, A.: Improved training of wasserstein gans. In: NIPS 2017 Proceedings of the 31st International Conference on Neural Information Processing Systems, vol. 30, pp. 5769–5779 (2017)
11. Miyato, T., Kataoka, T., Koyama, M., Yoshida, Y.: Spectral normalization for generative adversarial networks. arXiv preprint arXiv:1802.05957 (2018)
12. Bellemare, M.G., Dabney, W., Munos, R.: A distributional perspective on reinforcement learning. arXiv preprint arXiv:1707.06887 (2017)
13. Bickel, P.J., Freedman, D.A.: Some asymptotic theory for the bootstrap. Ann. Statist. **9**(6), 1196–1217 (1981)
14. Major, P.: On the invariance principle for sums of independent identically distributed random variables. J. Multivariate Anal. **8**(4), 487–517 (1978)
15. Yang, D., Zhao, L., Lin, Z., Qin, T., Bian, J., Liu, T.-Y.: Fully parameterized quantile function for distributional reinforcement learning. In: Advances in Neural Information Processing Systems, vol. 32, pp. 6193–6202 (2019)

A Competition of Shape and Texture Bias by Multi-view Image Representation

Lingwei Kong, Jianzong Wang(✉), Zhangcheng Huang, and Jing Xiao

Ping An Technology (Shenzhen) Co., Ltd., Shenzhen, China
{konglingwei630,wangjianzong347,huangzhangcheng624, xiaojing661}@pingan.com.cn

Abstract. There are mainly two views on the interpretation of high efficiency of Convolutional Neural Networks (CNNs) for the task of image classification: shape bias and texture bias. This is critical to the causality and reliability of CNN models in real applications. In this work, we try to explore the power of CNNs and reconcile the hypothesis contradiction of CNNs from a multi-view image representation. Firstly, we assume an image is generated from object shape representation, object texture representation, and background information. Secondly, we segment and recombine the object shape, texture and image background through two losses: image reconstructed loss and feature discrepancy loss. Finally, the classification loss is combined by shape, texture and background contributions weighted by multi-view features. Comprehensive experiments conducted on real-world datasets show that, first, CNNs generally do not have texture or shape bias, which change with the internal bias of data; second, CNNs are learning knowledge in a lazy way, i.e., high level knowledge is learned only if low level knowledge does not satisfy the task requirements. Our findings might benefit the interpretability of CNNs and provide insight of more robust design.

Keywords: CNNs · Multi-view · Explainability · Image representation

1 Introduction

ver the last two decades, Convolutional Neural Networks (CNNs) have shown successful performance in different domains such as visual object recognition [36] and semantic segmentation [12]. This success is often attributed to its powerful ability of feature representation learned from original data to intricate high-dimensional features, which can be grouped into two categories: object shapes and object textures. However, which plays a more important role for CNNs object recognition? Which are shape feature or texture information in the complicated high-dimensional numerical features? The problems have attracted the attention of lots of researchers and related to the explainability of CNNs [1,29,34], which are important to help us understand the CNNs decisions and causality.

This paper is supported by National Key Research and Development Program of China under grant No. 2018YFB0204403, No. 2017YFB1401202 and No. 2018YFB1003500.

© Springer Nature Switzerland AG 2021
H. Ma et al. (Eds.): PRCV 2021, LNCS 13022, pp. 140–151, 2021.
https://doi.org/10.1007/978-3-030-88013-2_12

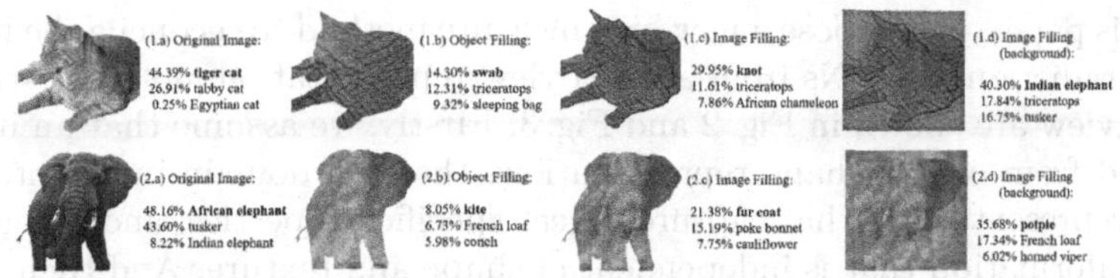

Fig. 1. Classification by a standard VGG-16 on different situations. (1.a) and (2.a) are the original images. (1.b) and (2.b) are generated by filling the special texture into each others' object. (1.a) and (2.a) are filled with the special textures to generate (1.c), (2.c) and (1.d) and (2.d). The difference is that (1.d) and (2.d) contains background content. As is shown, neither *Shape hypothesis* or *Texture hypothesis* is rigorous.

Existing explanations can be broadly categorized into two types. *Shape hypothesis* holds that CNNs combine low-level features to increasingly complex shapes until the object can be readily classified. This hypothesis indicates that shape dominates and is supported by a number of research findings [16,18,24,35]. *Texture hypothesis* considers that local textures already provide sufficient information for object recognition and play a more important role than object shapes. The findings [2,4,8,11] have provided strong evidence to support the *texture hypothesis.* These two hypotheses seem to be contradictory, because they all have their own theoretical or experimental support.

Despite a great quantity of related studies, few articulate precisely the relationship between *shape hypothesis* and *texture hypothesis.* Existing discussions on the bias of CNNs are either inadequate or not rigorous. For example, Geirhos et al. [11] supported that object textures are more important than global object shapes for CNN object recognition. The method trained on ImageNet, but tested on Stylized-ImageNet (generated by AdaIN style transfer [14]), which was contrary to the basic data hypothesis (independently and identically distributed). It was actually a domain transformation or domain adaptation problem. Incorporating Stylized-ImageNet in the training data must improve object classification performance, which not only conformed to the basic data hypothesis, but also augmented data. The results shown in Fig. 1 also validates our point of view as an example. With the continuous increase of texture area, the category of an image will belong to the category of texture. It's not the category of texture from the beginning, which does not seem to imply that CNNs have partiality for texture.

The importance of shape and texture information is also highly dependent on the application scenarios, such as medical imaging analysis. CNNs have proved the performance and accuracy in medical imaging [21], but in details, some lesions are easily detected and segmented given texture information while the others might rely more on shape feature. Interpretability determines whether people can trust the artificial intelligence to make a diagnosis or even auxiliary treatment.

In this paper, we propose a new bias-measure method to reconcile the hypothesis contradiction of CNNs from a multi-view representation [30]. The structure and overview are shown in Fig. 2 and Fig. 3. Firstly, we assume that an image is generated from object shape representations that are domain-invariant, object texture representations that capture object-specific properties, and image background information that is independent of shape and texture. And then we separate and recombine the object shape, texture and image background using end-to-end structurally constrained CNNs through two losses: image reconstructed loss that ensures the integrity of image information, and feature discrepancy loss that enforce divergence of the feature of different views. Finally, three classification losses are joined with different contribution weights based on multi-view features. The experimental datasets contain: MNIST and Fashion-MNIST that consist of more shape feature and less texture, SVHN and Deep-Fashion that include a large amount of texture information. This enables us to observe the feature of each category separately and quantify their bias for object classification task. Comprehensive and careful experiments are implemented on three datasets and the results show that CNNs don't have texture bias or shape bias. The bias of CNNs change with data internal bias. We believe this approach could be a good start to explore the interpretability of deep neural networks.

The main contributions of this work are briefly summarized as follows:

1) Separating object (foreground) and background from the original image further emphasizes the differences between texture and shape to reduce the whole image shape influence.
2) Whether in process training or testing, we do not violate the basic data assumptions or avoid the transformation of bias-measure.
3) After getting the pre-trained weights and the bias of CNNs, we just need to adjust the contribution weights to adapt to the new data, which improves the generalization and robustness of the model.

2 Multi-view Image Representations

Multi-View Image representations in our work are inspired by recent works on disentangled representation learning [22,27,37], which focuses on disentangling content from style. Ditching the disordered definition of content and style, we refer content as object shape that is the underling spatial structure and style as object texture that is the rendering of the structure. Because object and background features are firstly extracted, the remaining image only contains object. The changes of their names are widely accepted in the image style transfer literature [10]. And we assume that an image can be decomposed into shape, texture and background. Shape is global and decentralized information of object, which is associated with each category fitted human shape perception. Texture is local and regular image information and background is composed by information other than the target object.

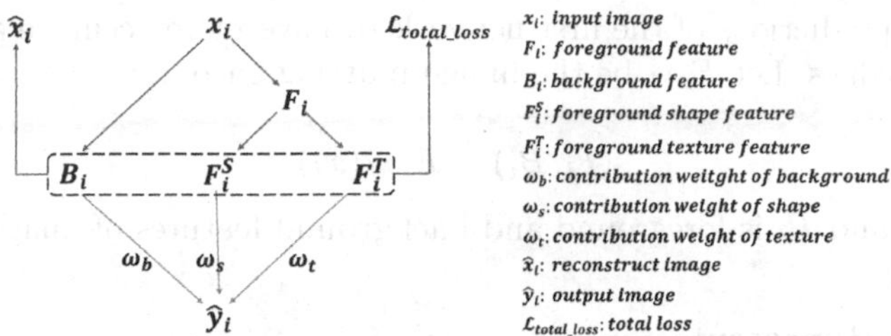

Fig. 2. The structure of the proposed Image representation and feature learning. Shape representations F_i^S, texture representations F_i^T and background feature B_i are extracted from the input data x_i. These information can form CNNs' output image $\hat{y}_i$, reconstructed images $\hat{x}_i$ and total loss $\mathcal{L}_{totalloss}$ of the process. Details are explained in Fig. 3.

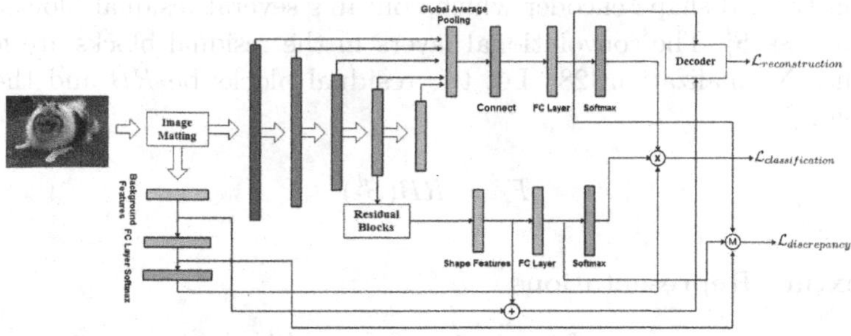

Fig. 3. Overview of the proposed Feature Learning using CNNs from Multi-View Representation framework. It consists of Image Matting, pre-trained CNNs, shape and texture feature extractor, decoder and three classifiers. Image Matting separates the foreground and background of an image. Pre-trained CNNs is regarded as object feature extractor, whose parameters are fixed. Shape and texture extractor accurately extract texture and shape information respectively from original image. Decoder restructures the image from three views features to ensure the integrity of image. Three classifiers are fed with the deep feature maps to obtain three predicted results.

2.1 Background Representations

Separating the foreground and background of an image, also named image matting, is a fundamental computer vision problem and has many applications [5,25,33]. Image matting divides an image into foreground and background, and returns the probability that it belongs to foreground or background. Extracting them separately is not the focus of our attention, so we use [33]'s method for reference which had two parts: a deep convolutional encoder-decoder network that takes an image and the corresponding *Trimap* as inputs and predict the alpha matte of the image, and a small convolutional network that refines the alpha matte predictions of the first network to have more accurate alpha values and sharper edges. Let E_{IM} be the image matting encoder:

$$(F_i, B_i) = E_{IM}(x_i) \tag{1}$$

where F_i and B_i is foreground and background features of image x_i.

2.2 Shape Representations

There is a widely accepted intuition that CNNs combine low-level features to increasingly complex shapes until the object can be readily classified [7]. When matching the content feature on a higher layer of CNNs, detailed pixel information of the image is not as strongly constraint. Hence, an image is passed through the CNNs and the shape representation S_i^l in the higher layer l is transmitted to the constrained shape encoder which contains several residual blocks [13] to further process S_i^l. The convolutional layers in the residual blocks are followed by Instance Normalization [28]. Let the residual blocks be RB and the shape feature be F_i^S:

$$F_i^S = RB(S_i^l) \tag{2}$$

2.3 Texture Representations

To obtain a representation of the texture of an object, we use a feature space designed to capture texture information [9,10]. The texture space can be built on top of the filter responses in any layer of the CNNs. It consists of the correlations between the different filter responses, where the expectation is taken over the spatial extent of the feature maps. Due to the different shape of the different layers, the feature are resized by the reshape layer, followed by a global average pooling layer and a fully connected (FC) layer. Unlike shape representations, instance normalization is not used in texture representations, which removes the original feature mean and variance that represent important style information. Let the reshape layer be RL, the global average pooling layer be GAP, and the fully connected layer be FC:

$$F_i^T = FC(GAP(\sum RL(T_i^l))) \tag{3}$$

where T_i^l is the texture representation of image x_i in layer l.

3 Loss

To reconcile hypothesis contradictions of CNNs from a multi-view representation, we jointly minimise the three *loss* functions, i.e., the *classification loss*, the *reconstruction loss*, and the *feature discrepancy loss*. *reconstruction loss* ensures

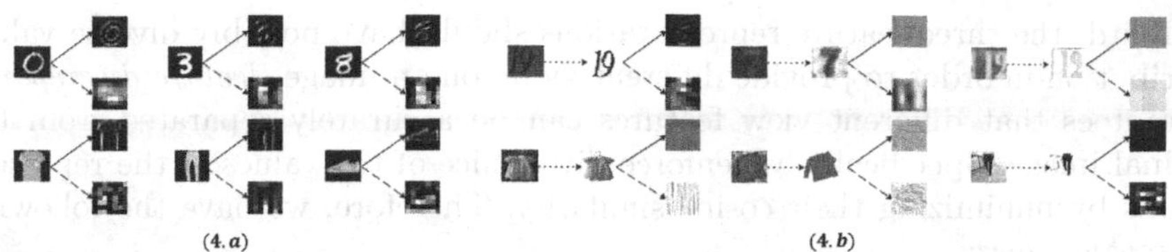

Fig. 4. Image representations of our architecture. The original images in 4.a are randomly selected from MNIST and Fashion-MNIST. The original images in 4.b are randomly selected from SVHN and DeepFashion. The input images of the four datasets are not pre-processed to Image Matting. Black solid and line dotted lines represent shape information and texture information, respectively.

the integrity of image information, *feature discrepancy loss* makes feature distribution as different as possible. Let $(x_i, y_i) \in \mathcal{X}$ be an image and its label from the style domain. The *classification loss* $\mathcal{L}_{classification}$ can be concretized as:

$$\mathcal{L}_{classification} = \sum_i CrossEntropy(y_i, \hat{y}_i) \tag{4}$$

where

$$\begin{aligned} \hat{y}_i &= \arg\max_{y \in \mathcal{Y}} w_b p_b^i + w_s p_s^i + w_t p_t^i \\ &s.t. \quad w_b + w_s + w_t = 1 \end{aligned} \tag{5}$$

where w_b, w_s, and w_t are the contribution weight of different feature representations for image classification. p_b^i, p_s^i, and p_t^i are predicted probability distributions of categories on multi-view representations for the image x_i. p_b^i is calculated from background feature representation B_i by fully connected layer and softmax layer, which is similar to p_s^i and p_t^i.

For the *second loss*, given an image sampled from the data distribution, the image should be reconstructed after multi-view representation operations and decoding and *reconstruction loss* is

$$\mathcal{L}_{reconstruction} = \sum_i \mathbb{E}_{x_i \in \mathcal{X}}[||G(B_i, F_i^S, F_i^T) - x_i||_1] \tag{6}$$

The G in Eq. 6 is a specially designed decoder, which reconstructs the input image from its background, object shape and texture. It processes the shape representation by a set of residual blocks and finally produces the reconstructed image by several upsampling and convolutional layers. Similar to the structure used in [15], and take advantages of [3] we equip the residual blocks with Adaptive Instance Normalization (AdaIN) [14,17] layers whose parameters are dynamically generated by a multi-layer perceptron (MLP) from the texture code. With the representations of multi-views of background, shape and texture, we fuse them into a common representation with global loss function $\mathcal{L}_{total}$.

Third, the three feature representations should have possibly diverse values distribution in order to provide different views on an image. *feature discrepancy* guarantees that different view features can be accurately separated from the original image. Specifically, we enforce divergence of the values of the representations by minimizing their cosine similarity. Therefore, we have the following *discrepancy loss*:

$$\mathcal{L}_{discrepancy} = \frac{\boldsymbol{B}_i \cdot \boldsymbol{F}_i^S}{\|\boldsymbol{B}_i\|\|\boldsymbol{F}_i^S\|} + \frac{\boldsymbol{B}_i \cdot \boldsymbol{F}_i^T}{\|\boldsymbol{B}_i\|\|\boldsymbol{F}_i^T\|} + \frac{\boldsymbol{F}_i^T \cdot \boldsymbol{F}_i^S}{\|\boldsymbol{F}_i^T\|\|\boldsymbol{F}_i^S\|} \tag{7}$$

With the above *loss* terms, we jointly train the representation and classification to optimize the final objective 2, which is a weighted sum of three *sub-loss*:

$$\mathcal{L}_{total} = \eta\mathcal{L}_{classification} + \alpha\mathcal{L}_{reconstruction} + \beta\mathcal{L}_{discrepancy} \tag{8}$$

where η, α, and β denote the hyper parameters that control the relative importance of the three losses.

4 Experiments

4.1 Datasets

MNIST database [19] has a training set of 60,000 examples, and a test set of 10,000 examples. And handwritten digits have been size-normalized and centered in a fixed-size 28 × 28 image. **SVHN** [23] is the abbreviation of Street View House Numbers data set, which contains 100k images (32 × 32 color) of house numbers collected by Google Street View. **Fashion-MNIST** [32] is a MNIST-like fashion product database that consists of 70k gray scale 28 × 28 images, associated with a label from 10 classes. Fashion-MNIST preferably represents modern CV tasks. **DeepFashion** [20] is a large-scale clothes dataset with comprehensive annotations, which is adapted to various CV tasks. It contains over 800,000 images, which are richly annotated with massive attributes, clothing landmarks, and correspondence of images taken under different scenarios.

4.2 Implementation Details

Image Matting separates the foreground from the background of the image, which is used to reduce the impact of the background for classification. Deep Image Matting [33] is used in our framework, consists encoder-decoder and refinement stages.

A standard **VGG16** [26] contains 13 convolutional layers, where filters with a receptive field: 3 × 3. The convolution stride is fixed to 1 pixel and the strategy of the spatial padding is the spatial resolution is preserved after convolution. Max-pooling is performed over a 2 × 2 pixel window, with stride 2. There are three fully connected layers: the first two have 4096 channels each, the third contains different channels for different datasets. What's more, each input of

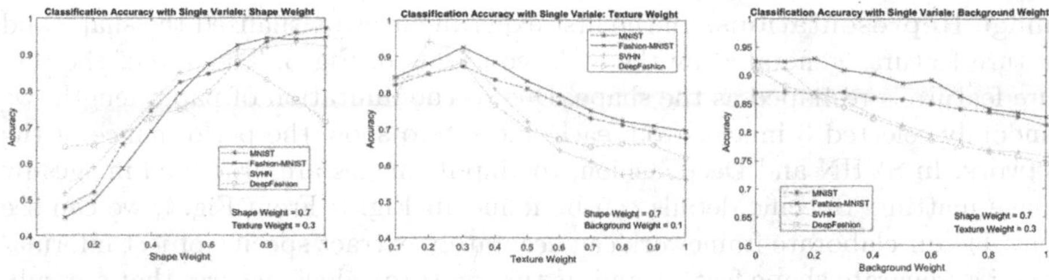

Fig. 5. The experimental results of the single variable changing. The first two figures show the classification accuracies obtained when MNIST, Fashion-MNIST, SVHN and DeepFashion change shape weight or texture weight while fixing other weights. The last figure shows the results when shape and texture weights are fixed.

VGG16 is processed by the batch normalization. The structure of pre-trained VGG16 would be slightly different from the standard one [31].

Shape Encoder consists of four residual blocks followed by Instance Normalization, whose input feature maps are selected from the *conv*4 − 2 layer of VGG16. The shape feature on a higher layer of the network, detailed pixel information of the image is not as strongly constraint. Hence, the *conv*4 − 2 layer is suitable, which is suggested by many researches.

Texture Encoder captures texture information from the top of the filter responses in any layer of the network. The purpose of this operation is to extend the spatial expression ability of feature maps. And then all feature maps are fed to a global average pooling layer to regularize the network and resize the feature maps. When classifying based on texture feature, all feature maps would be connected.

Decoder reconstructs the input image object from its shape and texture code. It processes the shape and background code by a set of residual blocks and finally produces the reconstructed image by several upsampling and convolutional layers. Inspired by recent works that use affine transformation parameters in normalization layers to represent styles [6,14], we equip the residual blocks with Adaptive Instance Normalization [14] ayers whose parameters are dynamically generated by a multilayer perceptron (MLP) from the texture code.

4.3 Results and Analysis

The main motivation behind our work was to investigate the bias of CNNs for image classification. Firstly, we visualized intermediate convnet outputs to verify the validity of the network structure of Image representations. Then, we listed the contribution weights of different feature representations on the different datasets. Finally, we observed the trend of classification accuracy changing with three weights to figure out the weight parameters that provides the best accuracy performance. More importantly, whether classification performances of CNNs depend on shape or texture information is tested among the listed datasets.

Image Representations. In the first experiment, we visualized the shape and texture features generated by the architecture as in Fig. 3. The size of the texture feature is reshaped as the shape. Due to the limitation of paper length, we randomly selected 3 images from each dataset to show the performance of the network. In SVHN and DeepFashion, the input images are processed images by image matting. Specific details can be found in Fig. 4. From Fig. 4, we can see that: 1) Our elaborate framework can accurately extract specific object information, i.g. separate shape feature and texture feature, which ensures that our subsequent experiments can be carried out as expected. 2) Compared with shape feature, the difference of texture information extraction is stronger, because global average pooling erases the difference of features.

Contribution Weights. In a second experiment, we evaluate the contribution weights of different image representations, which contained two sections: standard training and single variable changing. Standard training minimized the three loss under the whole architecture to obtain the three adaptive weights. The purpose of standard training is to find the weights suitable for the distribution of original training dataset. Single variable changing fixed the all variables except single and specific weight. And the starting point is the result getting from standard training. Note that the weights only plays a role in the integration of final classification results and the sum of three weights is not equal to 1 in the single variable changing.

Table 1. The experimental results of three weights on the four real-world datasets. '-' represented that image representations did not conclude the background representation.

	MNIST	SVHN	Fashion-MNIST	DeepFashion
w_b	-	0.0794	-	0.1487
w_s	0.813	0.6162	0.7968	0.5863
w_t	0.187	0.3044	0.2032	0.265

Table 1 presents detailed results obtained by the standard training on four real-world datasets. Based on these results, we can find that: 1) As expected, the values of shape weight w_s in MNIST and Fashion-MNIST is larger than texture weight w_t. The result suggest that CNNs has to learn global and more shape information when it faces datasets with less texture information. This results lead to explain that CNNs can effectively learn and inference from the features of the data 2) Compared to the SVHN, the result of DeepFashion shows that texture feature play a more important role for classification. It is easy to understand and accept. Although they are all real-world natural image datasets, DeepFashion is obviously more complex than SVHN, so more information needs to be considered and synthesized for image classification. We can reason from the phenomenon that CNNs can learn more information from images. 3) We compare MNIST and SVHN, Fashion-MNIST and DeepFashion, respectively, because they have similar shapes and different textures. When the information provided by the local texture is not enough to obtain a satisfactory result, the global shape information must be involved. It shows that, for images with highly complicated texture information, CNNs tend to ignore and avoid the obstacles, and prefer to learn easier knowledge from the shapes of the data. Hence, CNNs seems be 'lazy', which first learn easy features and then hard features.

As shown in Fig. 5, we can see that: 1) No matter it is MNIST, Fashion-MNIST, SVHN or DeepFashion, the classification accuracy fluctuates with the change of the weight, which indicates that no classification can completely rely on a certain type of features alone. To achieve good results, all the features should be considered, but in different proportions. 2) When the image has a large amount of texture information, the accuracy of classification is sensitive to the change of texture weight. 3) Because in most cases salient object occupies most of the whole image and provides rich texture information. Background feature have little influence, they are sometimes important.

5 Conclusion and Future Work

This study proposed a novel perspective to explore the competition of shape and texture bias based on multi-view image representations. Our method first separates the foreground and background of the image to reduce the distraction of background and then extracts shape and texture features from the foreground through a special network structure. Finally, the classification loss, reconstruction loss, and discrepancy loss are calculated to update parameters. The extensive experimental results on real-world datasets show that CNNs do not have texture bias or shape bias. CNNs is lazy to learn global shape feature if the accuracy requirement is enough.

For simplicity, we naively fixed the parameters of pre-trained VGG16 that should update in the training process. We noticed that this setting is quite simple and rough, which may lead to the non-convergence of gradients. Therefore, alleviating this setting more or less to improve further the performance of the current work and no increase training complexity is a main direction for our future work. We are at the era of advancing from data driven approaches to knowledge representation methods. This work could provide some insights of the explainability of deep neural networks and further the research of infilling knowledge to deep learning and neural networks.

Acknowledgments. This paper is supported by National Key Research and Development Program of China under grant No. 2018YFB0204403, No. 2017YFB1401202 and No. 2018YFB1003500.

References

1. Adadi, A., Berrada, M.: Peeking inside the black-box: a survey on explainable artificial intelligence (XAI). IEEE Access **6**, 52138–52160 (2018)
2. Ballester, P., Araujo, R.M.: On the performance of GoogLeNet and AlexNet applied to sketches. In: Thirtieth AAAI Conference on Artificial Intelligence (2016)
3. Bhattacharjee, D., et al.: DUNIT: detection-based unsupervised image-to-image translation. In: Proceedings of the IEEE/CVF Conference on Computer Vision and Pattern Recognition (2020)
4. Brendel, W., Bethge, M.: Approximating CNNs with bag-of-local-features models works surprisingly well on ImageNet. arXiv preprint arXiv:1904.00760 (2019)
5. Cho, D., Tai, Y.-W., Kweon, I.: Natural image matting using deep convolutional neural networks. In: Leibe, B., Matas, J., Sebe, N., Welling, M. (eds.) ECCV 2016. LNCS, vol. 9906, pp. 626–643. Springer, Cham (2016). https://doi.org/10.1007/978-3-319-46475-6_39
6. Dumoulin, V., Shlens, J., Kudlur, M.: A learned representation for artistic style. arXiv preprint arXiv:1610.07629 (2016)
7. Erhan, D., Bengio, Y., Courville, A., Vincent, P.: Visualizing higher-layer features of a deep network. Univ. Montreal **1341**(3), 1 (2019)
8. Funke, C.M., Gatys, L.A., Ecker, A.S., Bethge, M.: Synthesising dynamic textures using convolutional neural networks. arXiv preprint arXiv:1702.07006 (2017)
9. Gatys, L., Ecker, A.S., Bethge, M.: Texture sythesis using convolutional neural networks. In: Advances in Neural Information Processing Systems, pp. 262–270 (2015)
10. Gatys, L.A., Ecker, A.S., Bethge, M.: Image style transfer using convolutional neural networks. In: Proceedings of the IEEE Conference on Computer Vision and Pattern Recognition, pp. 2414–2423 (2016)
11. Geirhos, R., Rubisch, P., Michaelis, C., Bethge, M., Wich-mann, F.A., Brendel, W.: ImageNet-trained CNNs are biased towards texture; increasing shape bias improves accuracy and robustness. arXiv preprint arXiv:1811.12231 (2018)
12. Hao, S., Zhou, Y., Guo, Y.: A brief survey on semantic segmentation with deep learning. Neurocomputing **406** (2020)
13. He, K., Zhang, X., Ren, S., Sun, J.: Deep residual learning for image recognition. In: Proceedings of the IEEE Conference on Computer Vision and Pattern Recognition, pp. 770–778 (2016)
14. Huang, X., Belongie, S.: Arbitrary style transfer in real-time with adaptive instance normalization. In: Proceedings of the IEEE International Conference on Computer Vision, pp. 1501–1510 (2017)
15. Huang, X., Liu, M.-Y., Belongie, S., Kautz, J.: Multimodal unsupervised image-to-image translation. In: Proceedings of the European Conference on Computer Vision, pp. 172–189 (2018)
16. Kubilius, J., Bracci, S., de Beeck, H.P.O.: Deep neural networks as a computational model for human shape sensitivity. PLoS Comput. Biol. **12**(4), e1004896 (2016)
17. Karras, T., Laine, S., Aila, T.: A style-based generator architecture for generative adversarial networks. In: Proceedings of the IEEE/CVF Conference on Computer Vision and Pattern Recognition (2019)
18. LeCun, Y., Bengio, Y., Hinton, G.: Deep learning. Nature **521**(7553), 436 (2015)
19. LeCun, Y., Bottou, L., Bengio, Y., Haffner, P., et al.: Gradient-based learning applied to document recognition. Proc. IEEE **86**(11), 2278–2324 (1998)

20. Liu, Z., Luo, P., Qiu, S., Wang, X., Tang, X.: DeepFashion: powering robust clothes recognition and retrieval with rich annotations. In: Proceedings of IEEE Conference on Computer Vision and Pattern Recognition (2016)
21. Milletari, F., Navab, N., Ahmadi, S.-A.: V-Net: fully convolutional neural networks for volumetric medical image segmentation. In: 2016 Fourth International Conference on 3D Vision (3DV), pp. 565–571. IEEE (2016)
22. Narayanaswamy, S., et al.: Learning disentangled representations with semi-supervised deep generative models. In: Advances in Neural Information Processing Systems, pp. 5925–5935 (2017)
23. Netzer, Y., Wang, T., Coates, A., Bissacco, A., Wu, B., Ng, A.Y.: Reading digits in natural images with unsupervised feature learning (2011)
24. Ritter, S., Barrett, D.G., Santoro, A., Botvinick, M.M.: Cognitive psychology for deep neural networks: a shape bias case study. In: Proceedings of the 34th International Conference on Machine Learning, vol. 70, pp. 2940–2949 (2017). JMLR.org
25. Shen, X., Tao, X., Gao, H., Zhou, C., Jia, J.: Deep automatic portrait matting. In: Leibe, B., Matas, J., Sebe, N., Welling, M. (eds.) ECCV 2016. LNCS, vol. 9905, pp. 92–107. Springer, Cham (2016). https://doi.org/10.1007/978-3-319-46448-0_6
26. Simonyan, K., Zisserman, A.: Very deep convolutional networks for large-scale image recognition. arXiv preprint arXiv:1409.1556 (2014)
27. Tran, L., Yin, X., Liu, X.: Disentangled representation learning GAN for pose-invariant face recognition. In: Proceedings of the IEEE Conference on Computer Vision and Pattern Recognition, pp. 1415–1424 (2017)
28. Ulyanov, D., Vedaldi, A., Lempitsky, V.: Improved texture networks: maximizing quality and diversity in feed-forward stylization and texture synthesis. In: Proceedings of the IEEE Conference on Computer Vision and Pattern Recognition, pp. 6924–6932 (2017)
29. Wang, N., Chen, M., Subbalakshmi, K.P.: Explainable CNN-attention networks (C-attention network) for automated detection of Alzheimer's disease. arXiv preprint arXiv:2006.14135 (2020)
30. Wang, Q., et al.: IBRNet: learning multi-view image-based rendering. In: Proceedings of the IEEE Conference on Computer Vision and Pattern Recognition (2021)
31. Wang, R., et al.: Multi-view bearing fault diagnosis method based on deep learning. J. Phys. Conf. Ser. **1757**(1) (2021)
32. Xiao, H., Rasul, K., Vollgraf, R.: Fashion-MNIST: a novel image dataset for benchmarking machine learning algorithms. arXiv preprint arXiv:1708.07747 (2017)
33. Xu, N., Price, B., Cohen, S., Huang, T.: Deep image matting. In: Proceedings of the IEEE Conference on Computer Vision and Pattern Recognition, pp. 2970–2979 (2017)
34. Xu, F., Uszkoreit, H., Du, Y., Fan, W., Zhao, D., Zhu, J.: Explainable AI: a brief survey on history, research areas, approaches and challenges. In: Tang, J., Kan, M.-Y., Zhao, D., Li, S., Zan, H. (eds.) NLPCC 2019. LNCS (LNAI), vol. 11839, pp. 563–574. Springer, Cham (2019). https://doi.org/10.1007/978-3-030-32236-6_51
35. Zeiler, M.D., Fergus, R.: Visualizing and understanding convolutional networks. In: Fleet, D., Pajdla, T., Schiele, B., Tuytelaars, T. (eds.) ECCV 2014. LNCS, vol. 8689, pp. 818–833. Springer, Cham (2014). https://doi.org/10.1007/978-3-319-10590-1_53
36. Zhang, C., Wang, D.-H.: Exploring the prediction consistency of multiple views for transductive visual recognition. IEEE Signal Process. Lett. **28**, 668–672 (2021)
37. Zhao, B., et al.: Multi-view image generation from a single-view. In: Proceedings of the 26th ACM International Conference on Multimedia (2018)

Learning Indistinguishable and Transferable Adversarial Examples

Wu Zhang[1], Junhua Zou[1], Yexin Duan[1], Xingyu Zhou[2], and Zhisong Pan[1(✉)]

[1] Command and Control Engineering College, Army Engineering University of PLA, Nanjing, China

[2] Communication Engineering College, Army Engineering University of PLA, Nanjing, China

Abstract. The fast gradient sign method series can attack deep neural networks (DNNs) with high black-box success rates but with low image fidelity. Although the Adam iterative fast gradient tanh method breaks this limitation, its performance is not good enough. In this paper, we propose a **M**ixed-input **A**dam **I**terative **F**ast **G**radient **P**iecewise **L**inear **M**ethod (**MAI-FGPLM**) to generate adversarial examples with more indistinguishability and transferability for image classification task. Our method utilizes the piecewise linear function and the gradient regularization term to reduce the perturbation size for better image fidelity, and improves the transferability of adversarial examples via the mixed-input strategy for higher attack success rates. Extensive experiments on an ImageNet-compatible dataset show that the adversarial examples generated by our attack method have smaller perturbation size while offering higher attack success rates. Our best attack, NI-TI-DI-MAILM, evades six black-box defenses with the average perturbation size decreased by 1.11 and the average success rate increased by 2.1% compared with the state-of-the-art gradient-based attacks.

Keywords: Deep neural networks · Adversarial examples · Indistinguishability · Transferability

1 Introduction

DNNs have been used in various fields such as image classification, natural language processing and malware detection. However, recent work has shown that DNNs are vulnerable to adversarial examples, *e.g.*, inputs with human-imperceptible perturbations can make DNNs produce incorrect predictions [6,18]. More seriously, adversarial examples can generalize across network models [12], thus causing serious security threats to real-world applications such as automatic driving [5] and face recognition [15].

Foolbox [14] roughly divides existing attack methods into three branches: the gradient-based attacks [3,6,9], the score-based attacks [13] and the decision-based attacks [1,2]. In particular, the fast gradient sign method series which

© Springer Nature Switzerland AG 2021
H. Ma et al. (Eds.): PRCV 2021, LNCS 13022, pp. 152–164, 2021.
https://doi.org/10.1007/978-3-030-88013-2_13

belong to the gradient-based attacks are widely used due to good transferability. However, adversarial examples generated by these methods usually have low image fidelity [22,23]. To generate more indistinguishable adversarial examples, Zhang *et al.* [22] integrated the just noticeable difference coefficients into the the fast gradient sign method series. Although this strategy improves the indistinguishability, it has bad transferability. Besides, Zou *et al.* [23] attributes the poor image fidelity to the basic sign structure which increases the perturbation size. Hence, they proposed the Adam iterative fast gradient tanh method (AI-FGTM) to achieve smaller average perturbation size and higher attack success rates. However, adversarial examples generated by NI-TI-DI-AITM which belongs to AI-FGTM series have not good enough image fidelity from Fig. 1.

Fig. 1. The comparison of adversarial examples generated by NI-TI-DIM, NI-TI-DI-AITM and NI-TI-DI-MAILM ensemble attack method with the equal maximum perturbation size.

Therefore, in this paper, we conduct a case study on MI-FGSM to know why the classic fast gradient sign attacks generate adversarial examples with poor image fidelity. From Fig. 2(a), we find that the gradient processing steps such as the gradient normalization, the gradient accumulation and the sign function mainly increase the perturbation size of adversarial examples. In other words, the perturbation size may be reduced by modifying these gradient processing steps to improve image quality. For adversarial examples, it is also necessary to have high attack success rates, especially the black-box attack. In this paper, we find that mixing the original input with Gaussian blurred input can further improve the black-box attack success rates.

Based on the above findings, MAI-FGPLM is proposed to make adversarial examples more indistinguishable and transferable in this paper. Although we take AI-FGTM as the starting point for our research in this paper, there are several differences between our proposed method and AI-FGTM: 1) Our method replaces the tanh function with the piecewise linear function to get smaller perturbation size; 2) We employ mixed-input strategy to generate more transferable adversarial examples; 3) In the first order and the second order momentum term, our method preserves the loss gradient as regularization term to reduce the perturbation size while maintaining attack success rates.

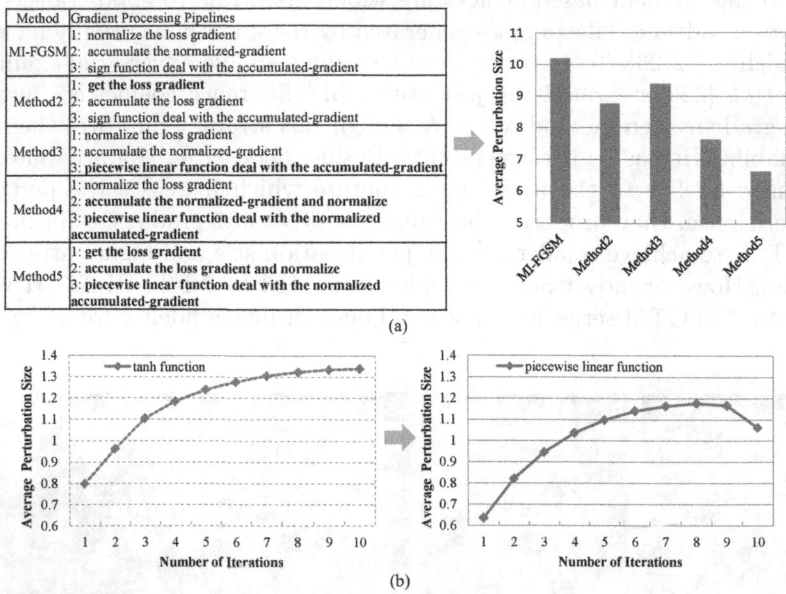

Fig. 2. Overview of the our observations.

In summary, our main contributions are listed as follows:

- We comprehensively investigate why the fast gradient sign attack series generate adversarial examples with high perturbation size.
- We propose a mixed-input Adam iterative fast gradient piecewise linear method to generate more indistinguishable and transferable adversarial examples.
- Our proposed method can be integrated into any gradient-based attacks to get smaller perturbation size and higher attack success rates.
- Our best attack achieves the average perturbation size decreased by 1.11 and the average success rate increased by 2.1% compared with the state-of-the-art gradient-based attack.

2 Related Work

2.1 Adversarial Example Generation

Given a clean input x and its corresponding ground-truth label y. For a pre-trained classifier $f(\cdot)$, it should correctly classify x to y. The attacker can construct an adversarial example x^{adv} by adding small perturbation δ to fool the pre-trained classifier, as $f(x+\delta) \neq y$. The gradient-based attack methods use L_∞ norm to constrain the perturbation δ by the threshold ε, *e.g.*, $\|\delta\|_\infty \leq \varepsilon$. Moreover, in order to generate non-targeted adversarial example, it also needs to maximize the cross-entropy loss function of the classifier. The cross-entropy loss function can be expressed as

$$J(x, y) = -1_y . \log(\text{softmax}(l(x))), \tag{1}$$

where 1_y is one-hot encoding of the ground-truth label y and $l(x)$ is the logits output.

2.2 The Fast Gradient Sign Method Series

Fast Gradient Sign Method (FGSM) [6] is the basic gradient-based method which only requires one-step gradient update to generate adversarial examples. This method increases or decreases each pixel equally according to the gradient direction of the loss function. It can be expressed as

$$x^{adv} = x + \varepsilon \cdot \text{sign}(\nabla_x J(x, y)), \tag{2}$$

where $\text{sign}(\cdot)$ is the sign function and $\nabla_x J(x, y)$ computes the loss gradient.

Iterative Fast Gradient Sign Method (I-FGSM) [9] is the iterative version of FGSM. In other words, the one-step update is decomposed into multiple-step iterative update to get smaller perturbation size and higher white-box success rates. The iterative process can be expressed as

$$x_{t+1}^{adv} = \text{Clip}_x^{\varepsilon}\{x_t^{adv} + \alpha \cdot \text{sign}(\nabla_{x_t^{adv}} J(x_t^{adv}, y))\}, \tag{3}$$

where x_t^{adv} denotes the adversarial example generated in the t-th iteration and α is the step size. $\text{Clip}_x^{\varepsilon}\{x'\}$ performs element-wise clipping of the image x' to restrict x' in the vicinity of x, that can be expressed as $\min\{255, x+\varepsilon, \max\{0, x-\varepsilon, x'\}\}$.

Momentum Iterative Fast Gradient Sign Method (MI-FGSM) [3] accumulates previous gradient information by integrating momentum term into I-FGSM, which stabilizes update directions and escapes from trapping into local optima during the iterations. It can be expressed as

$$g_{t+1} = \mu \cdot g_t + \frac{\nabla_{x_t^{adv}} J(x_t^{adv}, y)}{\left\|\nabla_{x_t^{adv}} J(x_t^{adv}, y)\right\|_1}, \tag{4}$$

$$x_{t+1}^{adv} = \text{Clip}_x^{\varepsilon}\{x_t^{adv} + \alpha \cdot \text{sign}(g_{t+1})\}, \tag{5}$$

where g_t represents the t-th accumulated-gradient and μ is the decay factor.

Nesterov Iterative Fast Gradient Sign Method (NI-FGSM) [11] combines MI-FGSM with the anticipatory update of Nesterov accelerated gradient, so as to effectively improve the transferability of adversarial examples. It can be formalized as

$$x_t^{nes} = x_t^{adv} + \alpha \cdot \mu \cdot g_t, \tag{6}$$

$$g_{t+1} = \mu \cdot g_t + \frac{\nabla_{x_t^{nes}} J(x_t^{nes}, y)}{\left\|\nabla_{x_t^{nes}} J(x_t^{nes}, y)\right\|_1}, \tag{7}$$

$$x_{t+1}^{adv} = \text{Clip}_x^{\varepsilon}\{x_t^{adv} + \alpha \cdot \text{sign}(g_{t+1})\}, \tag{8}$$

where x_t^{nes} denotes the Nesterov term of the t-th iteration. Please note that the Nesterov term will not be used in updating x_{t+1}^{adv}.

Diverse Inputs Iterative Fast Gradient Sign Method (DI^2-FGSM) [21] can get higher attack success rate by randomly resizing and padding the input image with a given probability p at each iteration as

$$D(x_t^{adv}; p) = \begin{cases} D(x_t^{adv}) & \text{with probability } p \\ x_t^{adv} & \text{with probability } 1-p, \end{cases} \tag{9}$$

where $D(\cdot)$ is the transformation function. Moreover, DI^2-FGSM can be combined with other methods to generate more transferable adversarial examples.

Translation-Invariant Iterative Fast Gradient Sign Method (TI^2-FGSM) [4] makes adversarial examples less sensitive to the discriminative regions of the substitute model by convolving the gradient with the pre-defined Gaussian kernel W. That is, TI^2-FGSM achieves higher black-box attack success rates against the defense models by applying Gaussian blurred gradient strategy.

Adam Iterative Fast Gradient Tanh Method (AI-FGTM) [23] changes the basic sign structure and generates more transferable and indistinguishable adversarial examples based on Adam [8] and the tanh function, which can be express as

$$m_{t+1} = m_t + \mu_1 \cdot \nabla_{x_t^{adv}} J(x_t^{adv}, y), \tag{10}$$

$$v_{t+1} = v_t + \mu_2 \cdot (\nabla_{x_t^{adv}} J(x_t^{adv}, y))^2, \tag{11}$$

$$x_{t+1}^{adv} = \text{Clip}_x^{\varepsilon}\{x_t^{adv} + \alpha_t \cdot \tanh(\lambda \frac{m_{t+1}}{\sqrt{v_{t+1}} + r})\}, \tag{12}$$

where m_t and v_t denote the first moment vector and the second moment vector respectively. μ_1 and μ_2 are exponential decay rates. α_t is the increasing step size, λ is the scale factor and $r = 10^{-8}$.

Ensemble Strategy Attack Method [12] uses an ensemble of multiple models as attack targets, so that the generated adversarial examples are less likely to trap into the local optima of any specific model. Besides, Dong *et al.* [3] find that attacking multiple models with logit activations can get more transferable adversarial examples. Therefore, to attack an ensemble of k models, the logits can be fused as

$$l(x) = \sum\nolimits_{i=1}^{k} w_i l_i(x), \tag{13}$$

where $l_i(x)$ is the logits output of the i-th model, w_i is the ensemble weight with $w_i \geq 0$ and $\sum_{i=1}^{k} w_i = 1$.

3 Methodology

In this paper, we propose MAI-FGPLM to generate adversarial examples with more indistinguishability and transferability, which modifies the gradient processing steps for better image quality and utilizes mixed-input strategy for higher transferability.

Algorithm 1. NI-TI-DI-MAILM ensemble attack method

Input: A clean image x and its corresponding ground-truth label y; k classifiers $f_1, f_2, ..., f_k$; ensemble weights $w_1, w_2, ..., w_k$;
Hyper-Parameter: Perturbation threshold ε; iteration number T; transformation probability p; pre-defined kernel W and V; slope ρ; regularization term factor γ_1 and γ_2; moving average factor τ; exponential decay rates μ_1 and μ_2; scale factor λ; increasing step size α_t.
Output: An adversarial example x^{adv}.

1: $x_0^{adv} = x$;
2: **for** $t = 0$ to $T - 1$ **do**
3: Get x_t^{nes} by Eq.(6);
4: Take $x_t^{mix} = \tau \cdot V * x_t^{nes} + (1 - \tau) \cdot x_t^{nes}$ as mixed-input;
5: Input x_t^{mix}, apply the transformation function Eq.(9) and output the model logits $l_i(D(x_t^{mix}))$ for $i = 1, 2, ..., k$;
6: Fuse the logits as $l(x_t^{mix}) = \sum_{i=1}^{k} w_i(l_i(D(x_t^{mix})))$;
7: Get the cross-entropy loss $J(x_t^{mix}, y)$ based on $l(x_t^{mix})$;
8: Compute the loss gradient $g = \nabla_{x_t^{mix}} J(x_t^{mix}, y)$;
9: Update m_{t+1} and v_{t+1} by applying Gaussian blurred gradient strategy and the gradient regularization term as
$m_{t+1} = m_t + \mu_1 \cdot W * g + \gamma_1 \cdot g$
$v_{t+1} = v_t + \mu_2 \cdot (W * g)^2 + \gamma_2 \cdot (g)^2$;
10: Update x_{t+1}^{adv} by applying the piecewise linear function as
$x_{t+1}^{adv} = \text{Clip}_x^{\varepsilon}\{x_t^{adv} + \alpha_t \cdot PL(\lambda \frac{m_{t+1}}{\sqrt{v_{t+1}} + r})\}$;
11: **end for**
12: **return**: $x^{adv} = x_T^{adv}$.

3.1 The Piecewise Linear Function

Compared to the sign function, the tanh function can normalize the large gradient values as well as maintaining the small gradient values. Hence, AI-FGTM improves the indistinguishability of adversarial examples by replacing the sign function with the tanh function. However, in Fig. 2(b), the piecewise linear function gets smaller perturbation size than the tanh function at each iteration for AI-FGTM by further making the small gradient values smaller. Hence, we propose an Adam Iterative Fast Gradient Piecewise Linear Method (AI-FGPLM) to generate more indistinguishable adversarial examples. That is, the Eq. (12) should be replaced with

$$x_{t+1}^{adv} = \text{Clip}_x^{\varepsilon}\{x_t^{adv} + \alpha_t \cdot PL(\lambda \frac{m_{t+1}}{\sqrt{v_{t+1}} + r})\}, \tag{14}$$

$$PL(z) = \begin{cases} \rho \cdot z_{i,j} & if\ |z_{i,j}| < 3 \\ 1 & if\ z_{i,j} \geq 3 \\ -1 & if\ z_{i,j} \leq -3 \end{cases}, \tag{15}$$

where $PL(\cdot)$ is the piecewise linear function and ρ is the slope. $z_{i,j}$ denotes the value of matrix z at position (i, j).

3.2 The Gradient Regularization Term

Furthermore, we find that AI-FGPLM can further reduce the perturbation size by preserving the loss gradient in the first order and the second order momentum term when applying Gaussian blurred gradient. So as to take the loss gradient as regularization term into AI-FGPLM, the Eq. (10) and Eq. (11) should be changed with

$$g = \nabla_{x_t^{adv}} J(x_t^{adv}, y), \tag{16}$$

$$m_{t+1} = m_t + \mu_1 \cdot W * g + \gamma_1 \cdot g, \tag{17}$$

$$v_{t+1} = v_t + \mu_2 \cdot (W * g)^2 + \gamma_2 \cdot (g)^2, \tag{18}$$

where γ_1 and γ_2 are regularization term factors, g is the loss gradient.

3.3 The Mixed-Input Strategy

Other than considering the indistinguishability of adversarial examples, achieving higher attack success rates is also equally important. In this paper, we find that mixing original input with Gaussian blurred input can reach this goal. A mixed-input crafted by that method not only maintains original feature but also has Gaussian blurred feature, so that the generated adversarial examples are more transferable. Hence, we propose a mixed-input strategy, which can be expressed as

$$x^{mix} = \tau \cdot V * x + (1 - \tau) \cdot x, \tag{19}$$

where x^{mix} is the mixed-input, τ is the moving average factor and V is predefined Gaussian kernel.

In order to make adversarial examples more indistinguishable and transferable, we naturally combine AI-FGPLM with mixed-input strategy to build a robust attack, that is, MAI-FGPLM. MAI-FGPLM can be a basic structure to be integrated with other gradient-based attacks to get smaller perturbation size and higher attack success rates. Particularly, **NI-TI-DI-MAILM** ensemble attack method is summarized in Algorithm 1 which achieves the highest black-box average attack success rate and the best indistinguishability in this paper. In addition, if we do not consider the Nesterov Accelerated Gradient in algorithm 1, NI-TI-DI-MAILM will degrade to TI-DI-MAILM.

4 Experiments

4.1 Experimental Setting

See Table 1.

Dataset. We choose an ImageNet-compatible dataset which was used in the NIPS 2017 adversarial competition to perform experiments. This dataset is comprised of 1000 images with size 299 × 299 × 3.

Table 1. Abbreviations used in the paper.

Abbreviation	Definition
TI-DIM	The combination of MI-FGSM, TI^2-FGSM and DI^2-FGSM
TI-DI-AITM	The combination of AI-FGTM, TI^2-FGSM and DI^2-FGSM
TI-DI-MAILM	The combination of MAI-FGPLM, TI^2-FGSM and DI^2-FGSM
NI-TI-DIM	The combination of MI-FGSM, NI-FGSM, TI^2-FGSM and DI^2-FGSM
NI-TI-DI-AITM	The combination of AI-FGTM, NI-FGSM, TI^2-FGSM and DI^2-FGSM
NI-TI-DI-MAILM	The combination of MAI-FGPLM, NI-FGSM, TI^2-FGSM and DI^2-FGSM

Metrics and Models. Two metrics, Attack Success Rate (ASR) and Average Perturbation Size (APS) of adversarial examples, are used to evaluate the attack performance in this paper. The ASR refers to the percentage of adversarial examples that can fool DNNs, while APS denotes image distortion. APS can be computed as $\frac{\sum_{i=1}^{N}\sum_{j=1}^{M}\left|x'_{ij}-x_{ij}\right|}{N\times M}$, where N denotes the total number of images, M is the dimensionality of clean image x and adversarial example x', x_{ij} is the pixel value of the j-th dimension of the i-th clean image, within range $[0, 255]$, and x'_{ij} is similar for adversarial example.

We consider four normally trained networks including Inception-v3 (Inc-v3) [17], Inception-v4 (Inc-v4), InceptionResnet-v2 (IncRes-v2) [16] and Resnet-v2-101 (Res-101) [7] as white-box models to generate adversarial examples. Then we select six defense models as black-box models to evaluate the transferability of generated adversarial example. Three of the six defense models are ensemble adverasarially trained models such as Inc-v3$_{\text{ens3}}$, Inc-v3$_{\text{ens4}}$ and IncRes-v2$_{\text{ens}}$ [19]. The other are high-level representation guided denoiser (HGD) [10], input transformation through random resizing and padding (R&P) [20], and NIPS-r3 in the NIPS 2017 adversarial competition.

Implementation Details. In our experiment, we set perturbation $\varepsilon = 16$, the number of iteration $T = 10$ and the momentum decay factor $\mu = 1.0$ as in [3]. Also, we set exponential decay rates $\mu_1 = 1.5$, $\mu_2 = 1.9$, the transformation probability $p = 1.0$ and scale factor $\lambda = 1.3$ as in [23]. For TI-DIM and NI-TI-DIM, the size of kernel W is setted to 15×15 as in [4]. For TI-DI-AITM and NI-TI-DI-AITM, the size of kernel W is setted to 9×9 as in [23]. For our methods, we set $\rho = 0.5$, $\gamma_1 = 0.12$, $\gamma_2 = 0.12$, $\tau = 0.5$ and $V = 9 \times 9$.

4.2 Ablation Study

In order to study the effects of the piecewise linear function, the mixed-input strategy and the gradient regularization term, we conduct an ablation experiment here. The adversarial examples are crafted for the ensemble of Inc-v3, Inc-v4, IncRes-v2 and Res-101 using the baseline method NI-TI-DI-AITM under the corresponding settings in Table 2. In other words, the baseline method NI-TI-DI-AITM will evolve into our method NI-TI-DI-MAILM after gradually applying the piecewise linear function, the gradient regularization term and the mixed-input strategy. From Table 2, we can find that the piecewise linear function and the gradient regularization term play important roles in reducing the APS of adversarial examples, *e.g.*, the APS decreases from 8.11 to 7.31 by the piecewise linear function and decreases from 7.41 to 7.00 by the gradient regularization term. We also observe that the mixed-input strategy mainly contribute to increasing the ASR though slightly making the APS get higher (Table 2).

Table 2. We show ASR and APS against six defense models. Note that PL, MIX and GR denote piecewise linear function, mixed-input strategy and gradient regularization term respectively.

PL	MIX	GR	Inc-v3$_{ens3}$	Inc-v3$_{ens4}$	IncRes-v2$_{ens}$	HGD	R&P	NIPS-r3	**Average ASR**	**APS**
×	×	×	90.5	88.8	85.5	89.8	88.6	89.0	88.7	8.11
✓	×	×	90.7	89.2	86.0	89.7	88.9	88.9	88.9	7.31
×	✓	×	92.3	91.2	88.2	91.5	90.9	90.9	90.8	8.21
×	×	✓	90.7	89.7	85.7	90.5	88.8	89.1	89.1	7.91
✓	✓	×	92.4	91.2	88.4	91.3	91.0	91.1	**90.9**	7.41
✓	✓	✓	92.0	91.1	88.3	91.5	91.0	90.7	90.8	**7.00**

4.3 The Results of Single-Model Attacks

In this section, we report the results of attacks against defense models under single-model setting. We first conduct adversarial attacks on Inc-v3, Incv4, IncRes-v2 and Res-101 respectively using our methods and the baseline methods. Then we test the generated adversarial examples on six black-box defense models. The results are present in Table 3 and Table 5.

From Table 3 and Table 5, we observe that our methods outperform all other baseline methods on the average ASR and the APS. It demonstrates that our methods can generate more transferable and indistinguishable adversarial examples. Moreover, our methods combined with the Nesterov Accelerated Gradient make the APS of adversarial examples decrease by a larger margin in Table 5, which indicates that adversarial examples can get better indistinguishability when our methods are combined with the Nesterov Accelerated Gradient.

Table 3. The ASR (%) and APS of adversarial examples crafted by AI-FGTM and MAI-FGPLM against six defense models under single-model setting.

Model	Attack	Inc-v3$_{ens3}$	Inc-v3$_{ens4}$	IncRes-v2$_{ens}$	HGD	R&P	NIPS-r3	**Average ASR**	**APS**
Inc-v3	AI-FGTM	20.0	19.6	9.4	8.6	8.8	11.6	13.0	7.65
	MAI-FGPLM (Ours)	**23.1**	**24.1**	**11.7**	**12.0**	**11.3**	**13.4**	**15.9**	**6.98**
Inc-v4	AI-FGTM	22.1	22.8	12.3	13.7	12.6	14.7	16.4	7.99
	MAI-FGPLM (Ours)	**26.7**	**28.2**	**16.0**	**19.5**	**16.1**	**19.1**	**20.9**	**7.28**
IncRes-v2	AI-FGTM	30.0	27.9	20.8	22.8	19.8	21.1	23.7	8.12
	MAI-FGPLM (Ours)	**37.7**	**35.9**	**29.2**	**29.8**	**26.6**	**28.5**	**31.3**	**7.49**
Res-101	AI-FGTM	25.8	26.4	16.4	19.6	15.5	17.5	20.2	7.58
	MAI-FGPLM (Ours)	**27.5**	**29.6**	**18.7**	**21.9**	**18.5**	**19.7**	**22.7**	**7.09**

Table 4. The ASR (%) and APS of adversarial examples crafted by NI-TI-DIM, NI-TI-DI-AITM and NI-TI-DI-MAILM against six defense models under single-model setting.

Model	Attack	Inc-v3$_{ens3}$	Inc-v3$_{ens4}$	IncRes-v2$_{ens}$	HGD	R&P	NIPS-r3	**Average ASR**	**APS**
Inc-v3	TI-DIM	44.8	45.5	34.3	36.4	37.0	39.2	39.5	10.3
	TI-DI-AITM	43.3	52.2	38.6	44.0	42.3	46.4	46.3	8.22
	TI-DI-MAILM (**Ours**)	**51.8**	**55.3**	**40.0**	**44.1**	**43.0**	**47.3**	**47.5**	**7.06**
Inc-v4	TI-DIM	47.4	47.0	37.7	39.8	40.0	41.9	42.3	10.3
	TI-DI-AITM	53.9	51.8	42.4	48.1	46.2	49.0	48.6	8.29
	TI-DI-MAILM (**Ours**)	**56.5**	**55.8**	**45.5**	**50.0**	**50.1**	**52.2**	**51.7**	**7.22**
IncRes-v2	TI-DIM	60.2	59.6	58.6	58.5	62.4	60.7	60.0	10.5
	TI-DI-AITM	65.8	62.1	61.4	63.2	64.2	64.7	63.6	8.23
	TI-DI-MAILM (**Ours**)	**68.8**	**66.7**	**65.5**	**64.5**	**68.2**	**68.7**	**67.1**	**7.03**
Res-101	TI-DIM	59.5	58.7	51.8	54.2	53.9	55.3	55.6	10.4
	TI-DI-AITM	63.4	60.5	53.7	**58.9**	**56.7**	**59.9**	58.9	7.98
	TI-DI-MAILM (**Ours**)	**65.0**	**62.4**	**53.8**	57.1	56.0	59.6	**59.0**	**6.93**

Table 5. The ASR (%) and APS of adversarial examples crafted by NI-TI-DIM, NI-TI-DI-AITM and NI-TI-DI-MAILM against six defense models under single-model setting.

Model	Attack	Inc-v3$_{ens3}$	Inc-v3$_{ens4}$	IncRes-v2$_{ens}$	HGD	R&P	NIPS-r3	**Average ASR**	**APS**
Inc-v3	NI-TI-DIM	41.3	41.7	30.5	32.2	32.4	35.8	35.7	10.3
	NI-TI-DI-AITM	52.4	50.1	37.1	**43.0**	40.0	45.1	44.6	8.16
	NI-TI-DI-MAILM (**Ours**)	**52.5**	**53.4**	**37.2**	41.6	**40.5**	**45.6**	**45.1**	**6.85**
Inc-v4	NI-TI-DIM	45.6	44.5	34.9	37.5	36.9	39.4	39.8	10.3
	NI-TI-DI-AITM	54.5	51.2	42.3	48.5	46.5	49.0	48.7	8.34
	NI-TI-DI-MAILM (**Ours**)	**55.5**	**53.6**	**43.3**	**49.9**	**47.8**	**51.3**	**50.2**	**7.06**
IncRes-v2	NI-TI-DIM	57.0	54.8	53.4	53.8	57.5	57.3	55.6	10.3
	NI-TI-DI-AITM	64.9	62.2	61.4	64.0	64.4	65.5	63.7	8.33
	NI-TI-DI-MAILM (**Ours**)	**68.2**	**65.8**	**64.8**	**64.5**	**67.8**	**68.5**	**66.6**	**6.93**
Res-101	NI-TI-DIM	57.4	57.3	49.3	53.6	51.9	54.4	54.0	10.4
	NI-TI-DI-AITM	62.4	61.0	**54.2**	**60.1**	**57.1**	**60.2**	59.2	7.88
	NI-TI-DI-MAILM (**Ours**)	**65.5**	**63.9**	53.9	60.0	56.5	59.7	**59.9**	**6.72**

4.4 The Results of Multi-model Attacks

In this section, we show the results of our methods when attacking multiple models simultaneously. We adopt the ensemble strategy [12] to attack an ensemble of four normally trained models with equal ensemble weights using TI-DIM, TI-DI-AITM, TI-DI-MAILM, NI-TI-DIM, NI-TI-DI-AITM and NI-TI-DI-MAILM respectively. The results are present in Table 6.

Table 6. The ASR (%) and APS against six defense models under multi-model setting. The adversarial examples are crafted for the ensemble of Inc-v3, Inc-v4, IncRes-v2 and Res-101 using the baseline methods and our methods.

Attack	Inc-v3$_{ens3}$	Inc-v3$_{ens4}$	IncRes-v2$_{ens}$	HGD	R&P	NIPS-r3	**Average ASR**	**APS**
TI-DIM	79.5	79.0	75.0	77.8	78.0	79.2	78.1	10.4
TI-DI-AITM	89.3	87.8	84.3	87.9	87.2	87.5	87.3	8.14
TI-DI-MAILM (**Ours**)	**91.0**	**89.8**	**87.3**	**89.8**	**89.5**	**89.4**	**89.5**	**7.24**
NI-TI-DIM	80.5	80.1	75.2	79.5	79.3	80.5	79.2	10.3
NI-TI-DI-AITM	90.5	88.8	85.5	89.8	88.6	89.0	88.7	8.11
NI-TI-DI-MAILM (**Ours**)	**92.0**	**91.1**	**88.3**	**91.5**	**91.0**	**90.7**	**90.8**	**7.00**

Fig. 3. The comparison of adversarial examples generated by NI-TI-DIM, NI-TI-DI-AITM and NI-TI-DI-MAILM ensemble attack method.

We can see that our methods can get higher success rates and smaller perturbation size than the baseline methods in Table 6. For example, our best attack method, NI-TI-DI-MAILM can fool six black-box defense models with an APS of 7.00 and an average ASR of 90.8%, while the state-of-the-art baseline method NI-TI-DI-AITM has an APS of 8.11 and an average ASR of 88.7%. In other words, our method achieves the average perturbation size decreased by 1.11 and the average success rate increased by 2.1% compared with NI-TI-DI-AITM. Furthermore, we show some adversarial examples generated by the baseline methods and NI-TI-DI-MAILM under multi-model setting in Fig. 3. The first column of each figure denotes the clean images, the second column and the third column denote the adversarial examples generated by the baseline methods, and the last column denotes the adversarial examples generated by NI-TI-DI-MAILM. As shown in Fig. 3, the adversarial example generated by our method are more similar to clean image than the baseline methods.

5 Conclusion

In this paper, we comprehensively analyze why the fast gradient sign attack series generate adversarial examples with higher perturbation size, and find that the gradient processing steps lead to the perturbation size increase. Base on this analysis, we propose a mixed-input Adam iterative fast gradient piecewise linear method to generate more indistinguishable and transferable adversarial examples. In addition, our method can be integrated into any gradient-based attack method to form stronger attack methods. The results on an ImageNet-compatible dataset show that our method can get smaller perturbation size and higher attack success rates under single-model setting and multi-model setting. Our best attack, NI-TI-DI-MAILM, can fool six classic black-box defenses with the average perturbation size of 7.0 and the average success rate of 90.8%.

References

1. Brendel, W., Rauber, J., Bethge, M.: Decision-based adversarial attacks: reliable attacks against black-box machine learning models. In: 6th International Conference on Learning Representations, ICLR (2018)
2. Chen, J., Jordan, M.I.: Boundary attack++: query-efficient decision-based adversarial attack
3. Dong, Y., et al.: Boosting adversarial attacks with momentum. In: 2018 IEEE Conference on Computer Vision and Pattern Recognition, CVPR, pp. 9185–9193 (2018)
4. Dong, Y., Pang, T., Su, H., Zhu, J.: Evading defenses to transferable adversarial examples by translation-invariant attacks. In: IEEE Conference on Computer Vision and Pattern Recognition, CVPR, pp. 4312–4321 (2019)
5. Evtimov, I., et al.: Robust physical-world attacks on machine learning models. arXiv preprint arXiv:1707.08945 (2017)
6. Goodfellow, I.J., Shlens, J., Szegedy, C.: Explaining and harnessing adversarial examples. In: 3rd International Conference on Learning Representations, ICLR (2015)
7. He, K., Zhang, X., Ren, S., Sun, J.: Identity mappings in deep residual networks. In: Leibe, B., Matas, J., Sebe, N., Welling, M. (eds.) ECCV 2016. LNCS, vol. 9908, pp. 630–645. Springer, Cham (2016). https://doi.org/10.1007/978-3-319-46493-0_38
8. Kingma, D.P., Ba, J.: Adam: a method for stochastic optimization. In: 3rd International Conference on Learning Representations, ICLR (2015)
9. Kurakin, A., Goodfellow, I.J., Bengio, S.: Adversarial examples in the physical world. arXiv preprint arXiv:1607.02533 (2016)
10. Liao, F., Liang, M., Dong, Y., Pang, T., Hu, X., Zhu, J.: Defense against adversarial attacks using high-level representation guided denoiser. In: 2018 IEEE Conference on Computer Vision and Pattern Recognition, CVPR, pp. 1778–1787 (2018)
11. Lin, J., Song, C., He, K., Wang, L., Hopcroft, J.E.: Nesterov accelerated gradient and scale invariance for adversarial attacks. In: 8th International Conference on Learning Representations, ICLR (2020)
12. Liu, Y., Chen, X., Liu, C., Song, D.: Delving into transferable adversarial examples and black-box attacks. In: 5th International Conference on Learning Representations, ICLR (2017)
13. Narodytska, N., Kasiviswanathan, S.P.: Simple black-box adversarial perturbations for deep networks. arXiv preprint arXiv:1612.06299 (2016)
14. Rauber, J., Brendel, W., Bethge, M.: Foolbox v0.8.0: a python toolbox to benchmark the robustness of machine learning models. arXiv preprint arXiv:1707.04131 (2017)

15. Sharif, M., Bhagavatula, S., Bauer, L., Reiter, M.K.: Accessorize to a crime: real and stealthy attacks on state-of-the-art face recognition. In: Proceedings of the 2016 ACM SIGSAC Conference on Computer and Communications Security, pp. 1528–1540 (2016)
16. Szegedy, C., Ioffe, S., Vanhoucke, V., Alemi, A.A.: Inception-v4, inception-ResNet and the impact of residual connections on learning. In: Proceedings of the Thirty-First AAAI Conference on Artificial Intelligence, pp. 4278–4284 (2017)
17. Szegedy, C., Vanhoucke, V., Ioffe, S., Shlens, J., Wojna, Z.: Rethinking the inception architecture for computer vision. In: 2016 IEEE Conference on Computer Vision and Pattern Recognition, CVPR, pp. 2818–2826 (2016)
18. Szegedy, C., et al.: Intriguing properties of neural networks. In: 2nd International Conference on Learning Representations, ICLR (2014)
19. Tramèr, F., Kurakin, A., Papernot, N., Boneh, D., McDaniel, P.D.: Ensemble adversarial training: attacks and defenses. arXiv preprint arXiv:1705.07204 (2017)
20. Xie, C., Wang, J., Zhang, Z., Ren, Z., Yuille, A.L.: Mitigating adversarial effects through randomization. arXiv preprint arXiv:1711.01991 (2017)
21. Xie, C., et al.: Improving transferability of adversarial examples with input diversity. In: IEEE Conference on Computer Vision and Pattern Recognition, CVPR, pp. 2730–2739 (2019)
22. Zhang, Z., Qiao, K., Jiang, L., Wang, L., Yan, B.: AdvJND: generating adversarial examples with just noticeable difference. arXiv preprint arXiv:2002.00179 (2020)
23. Zou, J., Pan, Z., Qiu, J., Duan, Y., Liu, X., Pan, Y.: Making adversarial examples more transferable and indistinguishable. arXiv preprint arXiv:2007.03838 (2020)

Efficient Object Detection and Classification of Ground Objects from Thermal Infrared Remote Sensing Image Based on Deep Learning

Falin Wu[1](✉), Guopeng Zhou[1], Jiaqi He[1], Haolun Li[1], Yushuang Liu[2], and Gongliu Yang[1]

[1] SNARS Laboratory, School of Instrumentation and Optoelectronic Engineering, Beihang University, Beijing 100191, China
falin.wu@buaa.edu.cn

[2] Beijing System Design Institute of Electro-Mechanic Engineering, Beijing 100854, China

Abstract. Wild searching and nature reserve monitoring are formidable tasks. In order to relieve the current pressure of general manpower observation, drone aerial surveillance using visible and thermal infrared (TIR) cameras is increasingly being adopted. Automatic data acquisition has become easier with advances in unmanned aerial vehicles (UAVs) and sensors like TIR cameras, which enables executives to search and detect ground objects at night. However, it's still a challenge to accurately and quickly process the large amount of TIR data generated from this. In response to the above problems, this paper designs an enhanced ground object detection network (UAV-TIR Retinanet) for the UAV thermal imaging system. The network uses the Retinanet as infrastructure, extracts shallow features according to the characteristics of thermal infrared remote sensing images, introduces an attention mechanism and adaptive receptive field mechanism. The method achieves the best speed-accuracy trade-off on the dataset, reporting 74.47% AP at 23.48 FPS.

Keywords: Ground object detection · Thermal infrared remote sensing image · Deep learning · Attention mechanism · Adaptive multiscale receptive field

1 Introduction

With the rapid development of economy and society, mankind has put forward higher requirements for wild searching and nature reserve monitoring. Thermal infrared imaging technology can transform the thermal radiation captured by sensors into thermal infrared images, and reflect the thermal radiation characteristics in the observation range through imaging. At the same time, thermal infrared imaging technology is not sensitive to light changes, which can effectively image in weak light, and can maintain good penetration in fog, rain, snow weather [1]. With the rapid development of UAV technology, its related applications have not only achieved remarkable results in the military field, but also showed strong applicability in the civil field. Especially with the development of light UAV platform, there are a large number of light UAV remote sensing loads, such as optical, infrared spectrum, lidar, synthetic aperture radar and so on [2, 3]. Combined

© Springer Nature Switzerland AG 2021
H. Ma et al. (Eds.): PRCV 2021, LNCS 13022, pp. 165–175, 2021.
https://doi.org/10.1007/978-3-030-88013-2_14

with the flexibility of UAV and the advantages of thermal infrared imaging technology, it can provide powerful information support for search and rescue, animal monitoring and other fields.

The ground image obtained by UAV thermal infrared remote sensing has the characteristics of too few object pixels, too large difference of object types observed from different angles, and difficult to distinguish objects in complex background, which also constitute the difficulty of this kind of object detection task. The use of traditional object detection algorithm, which often requires noise reduction, image enhancement, manual selection of design features, extraction of features, and binarization to obtain the object, has a high false detection rate, poor robustness, and long processing time [4]. Thanks to the algorithm of deep convolutional neural network (CNN): A series of detection algorithms based on R-CNN have emerged in academic circles, such as SPP-Net (Spatial Pyramid Potential Net) [5], Fast-RCNN [6], Faster-RCNN [7] and so on, the detection accuracy has been greatly improved. At the same time, there are end-to-end detection algorithms which are different from the R-CNN series of two-step detection methods, such as SSD (Single Shot Multi Box Detector) [8], RetinaNet [9] and Yolo (You Only Look Once) [10], the detection speed has been greatly improved.

On balance, deep learning allows the computer to find the best solution of the task as much as possible. It has strong feature learning ability, and can achieve the relative balance between detection accuracy and detection speed through reasonable design. Therefore, it has considerable potential and broad development space to study the ground object detection algorithm of thermal infrared remote sensing image based on deep learning.

2 Related Work

In the task of computer vision, the existing object detection models are widely used in the object detection of natural images [11]. The thermal infrared remote sensing image is obviously different from the ordinary natural imaging in the aspects of imaging mechanism, imaging conditions, shooting equipment, shooting angle, etc.: the thermal infrared image has only one channel and lacks color features, and the texture of the thermal infrared image is relatively weak compared with the visible image, rich texture information cannot be obtained. At the same time, compared with natural images, thermal infrared images have the characteristics of low resolution and more noise. In addition, some high temperature points can also lead to defects such as sharp changes in the brightness of thermal infrared data. These problems bring difficulties to the object detection task of thermal infrared image, so there is a certain difference between the object detection task of ordinary image and the ground object detection task of thermal infrared remote sensing image. What's more, most of the large-scale image data sets are focused on the visible light field. With the popularization of UAV technology, there are some visible light data sets of ground vehicles and pedestrians from UAV perspective, but a large number of thermal infrared data are still difficult to obtain [12].

3 Methodology

According to the application requirements of UAV thermal infrared remote sensing in the future, we designed an enhanced ground object detection network (UAV-TIR Retinanet) for the UAV thermal imaging system. The network uses the Retinanet as infrastructure. According to the low pixel characteristics of infrared small object, the shallow convolution layer features are extracted, and the shallow convolution feature output layer is constructed to improve the object detection rate. The attention mechanism is introduced to enhance the attention to the effective features of ground objects. The adaptive receptive field mechanism is designed to realize the network receptive field adaptation. Figure 1 shows algorithm flowchart.

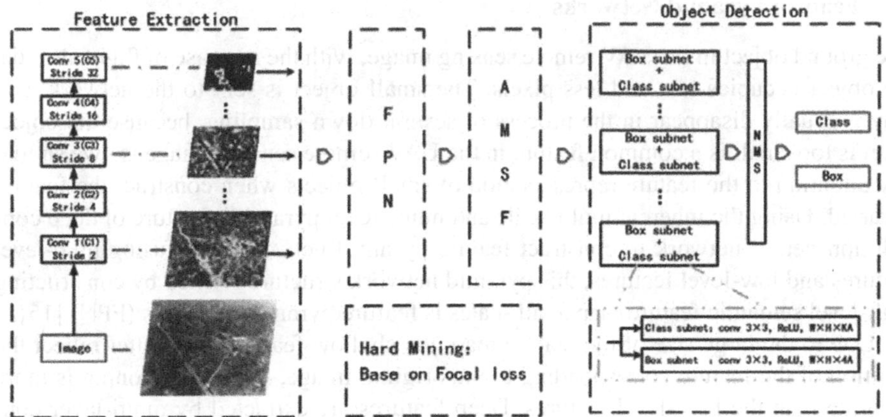

Fig. 1. Algorithm flowchart.

3.1 Backbone Network

The residual module in Resnet [13] makes the gradient dispersion disappear, which can make the network design as deep as possible, thus obtaining stronger representation ability. Resnet has two basic blocks. One is Identity Block, the input and output data dimensions are the same, so multiple blocks can be concatenated; Another basic block is Conv Block. The input and output data dimensions are different, so they cannot be connected in series. Its function is to change the dimension of feature vector. The final Resnet backbone is made up of the above two blocks. This paper selects Resnet50 as the backbone network.

An efficient channel attention module ECAM [14] is designed, as shown in Fig. 2. The input features are first processed by global average pooling (GAP) channel by channel, and cross channel interactive learning is carried out without reducing the number of channels, so as to effectively improve the representation of features at the cost of little computation. The number of cross channels K is 3. We add the feature graph weighting module of ECAM to the residual module of Resnet backbone. It is worth noting that the designed ECA module not only improves the detection performance, but also hardly affects the detection speed.

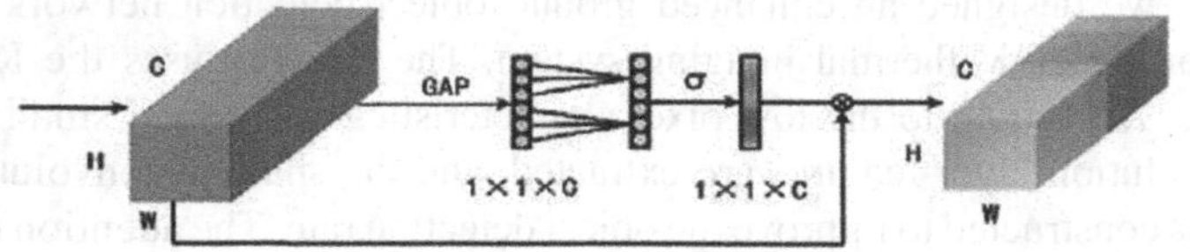

Fig. 2. ECA module in resnet.

3.2 Feature Pyramid Networks

The ground object in the UAV remote sensing image, with the increase of flight altitude, the object occupies less and less pixels. The small object is sent to the network, and may gradually disappear in the process of several down sampling, because the object pixel is too small is a common feature in the UAV remote sensing image, so we should pay attention to the feature representation of small objects when construct the feature pyramid. Using the inherent multi-scale and multi-level pyramid structure of deep convolution neural network to construct feature pyramid network, and fusing high-level features and low-level features, this pyramid network structure formed by constructing high-level semantic feature map at all scales is feature pyramid networks (FPN) [15].

Due to the large size of the feature map, the shallow features can better reflect the position of the feature corresponding to the original image, so the positioning is more accurate than the high-level features. Deep features are extracted by multi-layer convolution, and their semantic information is higher than that of the lower layer, but they cannot be mapped back to the original image domain accurately, resulting in the weak positioning ability. Therefore, we should combine the advantages of shallow features and deep features to build a feature pyramid with excellent classification judgment and positioning ability, this process can be realized by sampling on the feature map, compressing or amplifying the feature channel. Taking Resnet-50 backbone as an example to construct the feature pyramid, as shown in Fig. 3.

Although the top-down FPN designed above can fuse the shallow features and high-level features from the feature extraction network, it is also limited by the inherent one-way information flow. In order to improve the efficiency of the model, refer-ring to the idea of Bi-FPN [16], this paper designs a cross scale connection optimization method, Fig. 4 shows example of building a weighted bi-directional feature pyramid. First, delete those nodes with only one input side. If a node has only one input edge and no feature fusion, it has less contribution to the feature network aiming at fusing different features, which can greatly simplify the bidirectional network; Secondly, if they are at the same level, we add additional edges from the original input to output nodes, similar to the idea of shortcut channel, so as to fuse more features without increasing too much cost; Thirdly, each bidirectional (top-down and bottom-up) path is regarded as a feature network layer, and repeated many times in the same layer to achieve higher level feature fusion. When fusing features of different resolutions, the top-down FPN

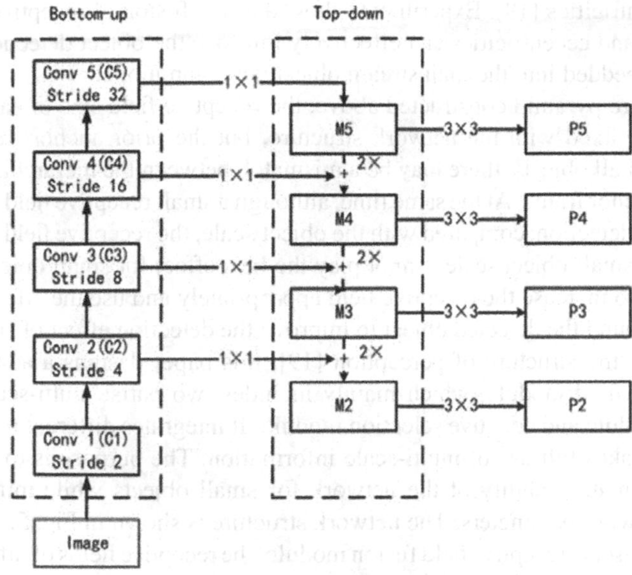

Fig. 3. Example of building feature pyramid.

designed above first adjusts them to the same resolution, and then summarizes them. Because different input features have different resolutions, their contributions to output features are usually unequal. In order to solve this problem, we consider adding an extra weight to each input to let the net- work learn the importance of each input feature.

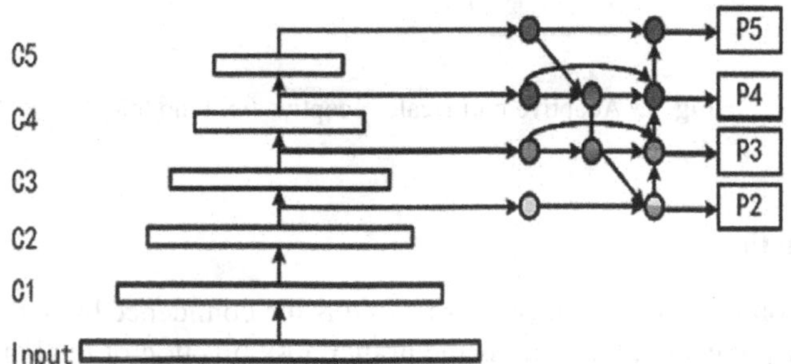

Fig. 4. Example of building a weighted bi-directional feature pyramid.

3.3 Adaptive Multiscale Receptive Field

Receptive field is the area size of the pixels on the output feature map of each layer of convolutional neural network mapped on the input image, which is similar to the human visual system [17]. Liu s imitated the structure of receptive field in human visual system, and discussed the discrimination and robustness of receptive field with different sizes and eccentricities [18]. Experiments show that the fusion of receptive fields with different sizes and eccentricities can effectively improve the object detection accuracy, and can be embedded into the mainstream object detection model.

In the feature pyramid constructed above, the receptive field size of each detection layer feature is fixed with the network structure, but the prior anchor frame scale is variable. For small objects, there may be a mismatch between the hierarchical receptive field and the anchor frame. At the same time, although a small receptive field is conducive to small object detection, compared with the object scale, the receptive field smaller than or close to the small object scale cannot play the best effect for small object detection. It is necessary to increase the receptive field appropriately and use the effective context information around the detected object to improve the detection effect of small objects.

Inspired by the structure of perception [19], this paper designs a adaptive multi-scale receptive field module, which mainly includes two parts: multi-scale receptive field fusion module and adaptive selection module. It integrates different receptive field features and makes full use of multi-scale information. The purpose is to enhance the feature representation ability of the network for small objects while minimizing the increase of network parameters, The network structure is shown in Fig. 5.

In the multi-scale receptive field fusion module, the receptive fields of different scales are expanded and fused through multiple shared convolutions. The adaptive selection module uses the attention mechanism to make effective adaptive selection for the multi-scale features of different sizes of receptive field, which makes the receptive field more realistic and closer to the biological visual system.

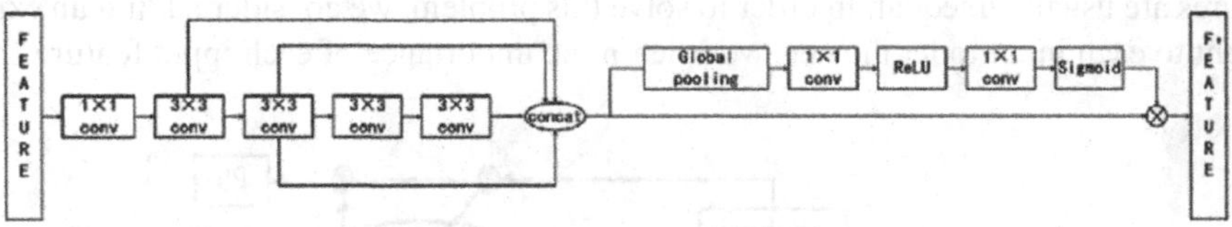

Fig. 5. Adaptive multiscale receptive field module.

3.4 Loss Function

The loss function is composed of two parts: one is the confidence branch loss function of the category prediction, the other is the branch loss function of the boundary frame network which is responsible for the shape and position prediction of the boundary frame.

For the object detection task of UAV thermal infrared remote sensing data, although the thermal radiation information can be more efficient and accurate to capture the information of ground object in the extreme environment such as weak light, night, rain and snow weather, it is difficult to detect the ground object when the back- ground environment is complex and the ambient temperature is high. When the conditions are limited, it's supposed to improve the performance of thermal infrared object detection in the midday environment by improving the algorithm as much as possible. This requires some hard mining methods. Therefore, we add the category loss in the form of focal loss in the design of loss function [9]. On the one hand, we can mine the difficult cases, on the other hand, we can adjust the imbalance of positive and negative samples in the single stage object detection task.

$$CE(\mathrm{p}, y) = \begin{cases} -\alpha(1-p)^{\gamma}\log(p), & y=1 \\ -(1-\alpha)p^{\gamma}\log(1-p), & y=0 \end{cases} \tag{1}$$

where y is the true value, and a value of 1 indicates that the boundary box contains objects. This value can be judged by predicting whether the intersection ratio between the border and the real Border exceeds the threshold value, p is the confidence prediction value. The addition of parameter γ can reduce the loss of simple samples and increase the loss of difficult samples. The addition of parameter α can balance the positive and negative samples in model training. When building the model, γ takes 2.5, α takes 0.25. What's more, the loss function of the branch of the bounding box network is the Smooth L1 loss [7, 8] between the coordinates of the center point, the size of boundary box and the true value, which will not be repeated here.

4 Experiments and Results

4.1 Dataset

The data set selected in this paper comes from a long wave thermal infrared (TIR) dataset released by Harvard University in 2020, which contains night images of animals and humans in southern South Africa [12]. After the data set is filtered, eliminated and enhanced, a total of 15850 available images were screened, with the resolution concentrated in 640 × 480. The category information in the tag includes human and animals (elephant, giraffe, lion, etc.). Some examples of data augmentation are shown in Fig. 6.

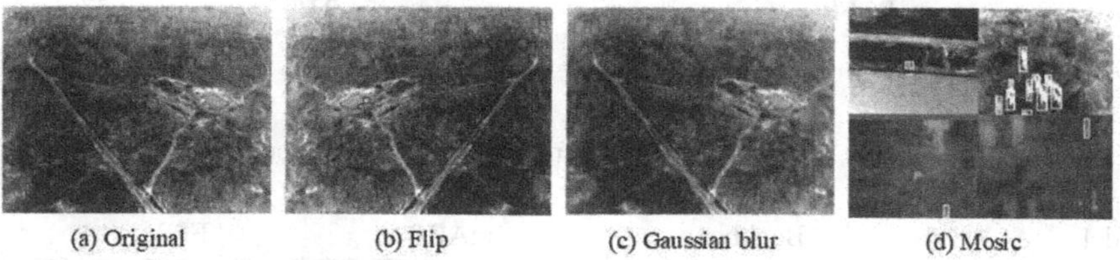

(a) Original (b) Flip (c) Gaussian blur (d) Mosic

Fig. 6. Some examples of data augmentation.

At the same time, in order to better set the anchor frame information of the network, the k-means++ [20] method is used to cluster the length and width information of the objects in the data set, as shown in Fig. 7.

4.2 Results

In object detection task, mean average precision (mAP) is usually used to evaluate the performance of a detection model. In addition, considering the application background

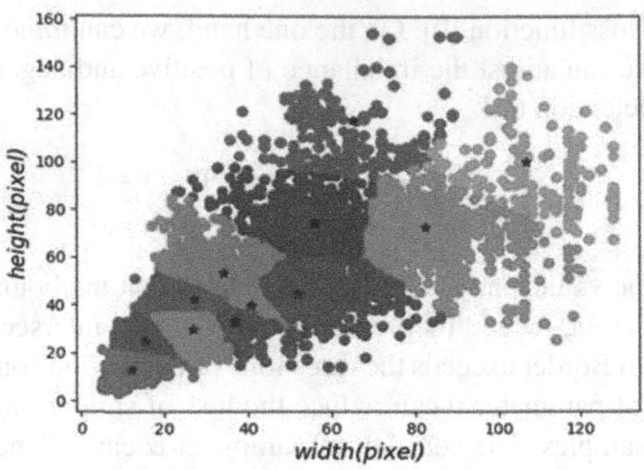

Fig. 7. The width and height distribution of objects.

of search and monitoring in the future, the number of images detected per second (FPS) is used to evaluate the detection speed [21]. In the test phase, the detection accuracy and speed of the proposed method and several general object detection algorithms are compared. The results are shown in Table 1 and Table 2.

Table 1. Test result of UAV-TIR retinanet.

Backbone	Feature fusion	AMRF	mAP	FPS
Resnet	FPN		67.94%	**24.14**
ECA-resnet	FPN		73.02%	23.73
ECA-resnet	Bi-FPN		74.38%	18.50
ECA-resnet	FPN	√	74.47%	23.48
ECA-resnet	Bi-FPN	√	**74.93%**	18.37

Table 2. Test result of general object detection model.

Model	Backbone	mAP	FPS
Faster R-CNN	Resnet	**43.64%**	12.00
SSD	Resnet	31.11%	33.10
YOLO	Resnet	28.20%	**38.32**

Compared with several popular general detection models, the accuracy of the model designed in this paper is improved by about 30%, and has a certain detection speed. Part of the detection results are shown in Fig. 8, all objects are detected and correctly identified.

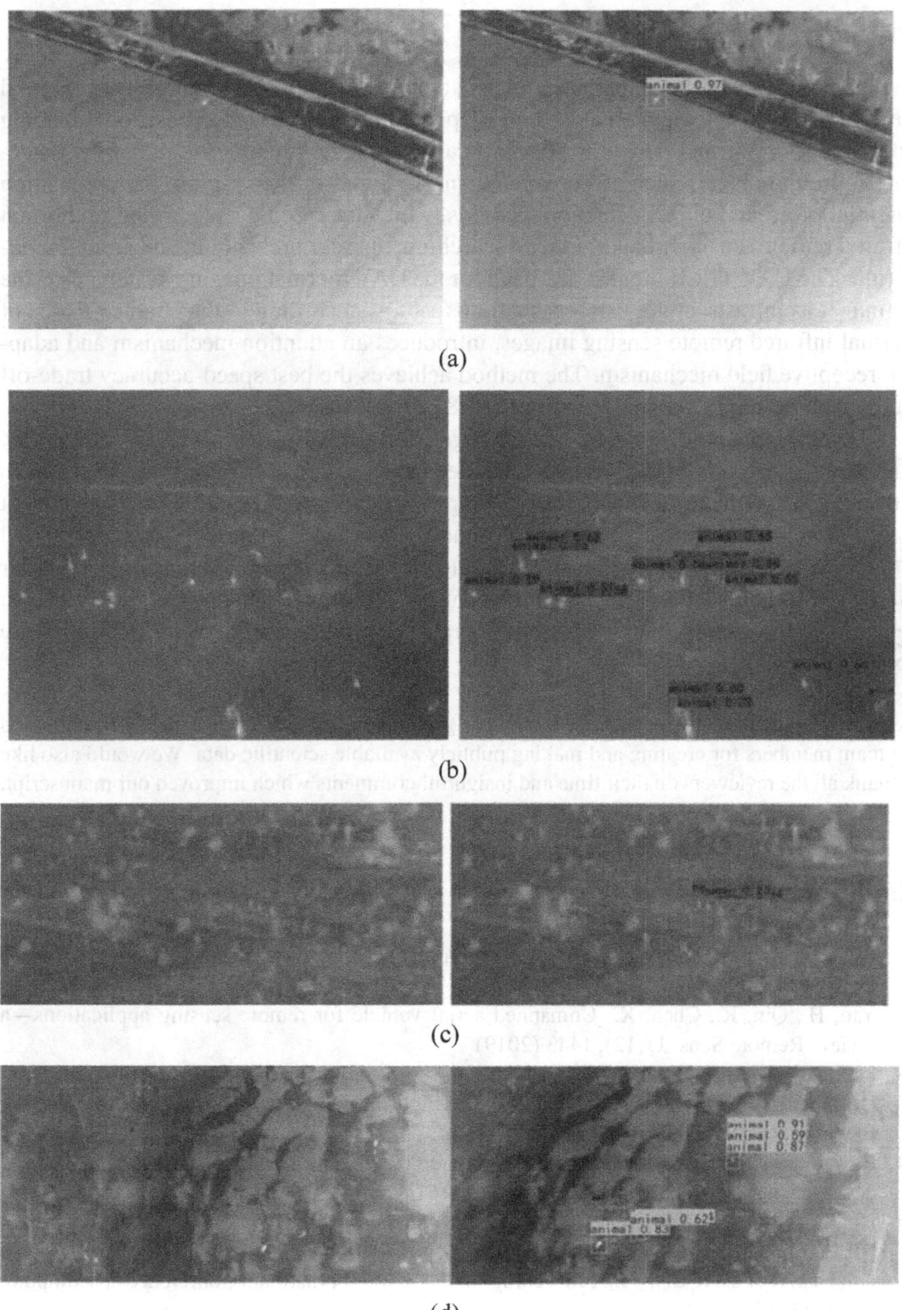

(a)

(b)

(c)

(d)

Fig. 8. Test result: the left side is the original image, and the right side is the model output.

5 Conclusions

The main purpose of this paper is to design an object detection method of UAV thermal infrared scene during the night based on deep learning theory. On the basis of balancing detection accuracy and detection speed, it can realize the function of automatic detection of ground objects such as human and animals, and further explore the application potential of ground object detection methods, which based on deep learning in thermal infrared remote sensing images, in wild searching, disaster prevention, and animal monitoring. The UAV-TIR Retinanet designed for the UAV thermal imaging system, uses the Retinanet as infrastructure, extracts shallow features according to the characteristics of thermal infrared remote sensing images, introduces an attention mechanism and adaptive receptive field mechanism. The method achieves the best speed-accuracy trade-off on the dataset, reporting 74.47% AP at 23.48 FPS.

The development of object detection algorithm is changing with each passing day. Sometimes, specific remote sensing tasks need to customize the algorithm in depth in order to achieve the established goal. Taking this paper as an example, the subsequent UAV thermal infrared remote sensing ground object detection model can be improved in the direction of lighter weight, but the detection performance remains unchanged or even improved, so as to achieve the purpose of UAV real-time data processing. It can also be explored in Anchor Free direction to liberate the limitation of detector in multi-scale object detection.

Acknowledgements. We would like to express gratitude to the efforts of Bondi, Elizabeth and her team members for creating and making publicly available scientific data. We would also like to thank all the reviewers on their time and insightful comments which improved our manuscript.

References

1. He, Y., et al.: Infrared machine vision and infrared thermography with deep learning: a review. Infrared Phys. Technol. **2021**, 103754 (2021)
2. Yao, H., Qin, R., Chen, X.: Unmanned aerial vehicle for remote sensing applications—a review. Remote Sens. **11**(12), 1443 (2019)
3. Feng, L., et al.: A comprehensive review on recent applications of unmanned aerial vehicle remote sensing with various sensors for high-throughput plant phenotyping. Comput. Electron. Agricult. **182**, 106033 (2021)
4. Rawat, S.S., Verma, S.K., Kumar, Y.: Review on recent development in infrared small target detection algorithms. Procedia Comput. Sci. **167**, 2496–2505 (2020)
5. He, K., et al.: Spatial pyramid pooling in deep convolutional networks for visual recognition. IEEE Trans. Pattern Anal. Mach. Intell. **37**(9), 1904–1916 (2015)
6. Girshick, R.: Fast R-CNN. In: Proceedings of the IEEE International Conference on Computer Vision (2015)
7. Ren, S., et al.: Faster R-CNN: towards real-time object detection with region proposal networks. Adv. Neural Inf. Process. Syst. **28**, 91–99 (2015)
8. Liu, W., et al.: SSD: single shot multibox detector. In: Leibe, B., Matas, J., Sebe, N., Welling, M. (eds.) Computer Vision – ECCV 2016. ECCV 2016. LNCS, vol 9905, pp. 21–37. Springer, Cham (2016). https://doi.org/10.1007/978-3-319-46448-0_2

9. Lin, T.-Y., et al.: Focal loss for dense object detection. In: Proceedings of the IEEE International Conference on Computer Vision (2017)
10. Redmon, J., et al.: You only look once: unified, real-time object detection. In: Proceedings of the IEEE Conference on Computer Vision and Pattern Recognition (2016)
11. Kundid Vasić, M., Papić, V.: Multimodel deep learning for person detection in aerial images. Electronics **9**(9), 1459 (2020)
12. Bondi, E., et al.: BIRDSAI: a dataset for detection and tracking in aerial thermal infrared videos. In: The IEEE Winter Conference on Applications of Computer Vision (2020)
13. Wu, Z., Shen, C., Van Den Hengel, A.: Wider or deeper: revisiting the resnet model for visual recognition. Pattern Recognit. **90**, 119–133 (2019)
14. Wang, Q., et al.: ECA-Net: efficient channel attention for deep convolutional neural networks. In: 2020 IEEE in CVF Conference on Computer Vision and Pattern Recognition (CVPR). IEEE (2020)
15. Lin, T.-Y., et al.: Feature pyramid networks for object detection. In: Proceedings of the IEEE Conference on Computer Vision and Pattern Recognition (2017)
16. Tan, M., Pang, R., Le, Q.V.: Efficientdet: Scalable and efficient object detection. In: Proceedings of the IEEE/CVF Conference on Computer Vision and Pattern Recognition (2020)
17. Luo, W., et al.: Understanding the effective receptive field in deep convolutional neural networks. In: Proceedings of the 30th International Conference on Neural Information Processing Systems (2016)
18. Liu, S., Huang, D., Wang, Y.: Receptive Field Block Net for Accurate and Fast Object Detection. In: Ferrari, V., Hebert, M., Sminchisescu, C., Weiss, Y. (eds.) ECCV 2018. LNCS, vol. 11215, pp. 404–419. Springer, Cham (2018). https://doi.org/10.1007/978-3-030-01252-6_24
19. Szegedy, C., et al.: Inception-v4, inception-resnet and the impact of residual connections on learning. In: Thirty-first AAAI Conference on Artificial Intelligence (2017)
20. Liu, J., et al.: High precision detection algorithm based on improved RetinaNet for defect recognition of transmission lines. Energy Rep. **6**, 2430–2440 (2020)
21. Cartucho, J., Ventura, R., Veloso, M.: Robust object recognition through symbiotic deep learning in mobile robots. In: 2018 IEEE/RSJ International Conference on Intelligent Robots and Systems (IROS). IEEE (2018)

MEMA-NAS: Memory-Efficient Multi-Agent Neural Architecture Search

Qi Kong[1], Xin Xu[2(✉)], and Liangliang Zhang[1]

[1] Autonomous Driving Division, JD.com American Technologies Corporation, Mountain View, CA 94043, USA
{qi.kong,liangliang.zhang}@jd.com

[2] Autonomous Driving Division, JD.com, Beijing, China
xuxin178@jd.com

Abstract. Object detection is a core computer vision task that aims to localize and classify categories for various objects in an image. With the development of convolutional neural networks, deep learning methods have been widely used in the object detection task, achieving promising performance compared to traditional methods. However, designing a well-performing detection network is inefficient. It consumes too much hardware resources and time to trial, and it also heavily relies on expert knowledge. To efficiently design the neural network architecture, there has been a growing interest in automatically designing neural network architecture by Neural Architecture Search (NAS). In this paper, we propose a Memory-Efficient Multi-Agent Neural Architecture Search (MEMA-NAS) framework in end-to-end object detection neural network. Specifically, we introduce the multi-agent learning to search holistic architecture of the detection network. In this way, a lot of GPU memory is saved, allowing us to search each module's architecture of the detection network simultaneously. To find a better tradeoff between the precision and computational costs, we add the resource constraint in our method. Search experiments on multiple datasets show that MEMA-NAS achieves state-of-the-art results in search efficiency and precision.

1 Introduction

Deep learning has achieved promising results on a variety of tasks, such as image classification and object detection. However, most current neural networks are designed manually, which is time-consuming. Because of this, there has been a growing interest in automatically designing the neural network architecture by Neural Architecture Search (NAS).

Zoph et al. [20] proposed the first NAS framework for the image classification task, which frames neural network search as a reinforcement learning problem. The key idea of their work is that they specified the architecture and connectivity of a neural network by using a configuration string. To speed up the search, Zoph

Q. Kong and X. Xu—Equal contribution.

© Springer Nature Switzerland AG 2021
H. Ma et al. (Eds.): PRCV 2021, LNCS 13022, pp. 176–187, 2021.
https://doi.org/10.1007/978-3-030-88013-2_15

et al. [21] then put forward a new search framework, named NAS-Net. Unlike previous work searches on the global search space, NAS-Net only searches for the architecture of the cell and then stacks searched cells together to generate a deep neural network. Then Liu et al. [11] proposed PNASNet to further improve the search efficiency. Besides these RL-based methods, some researchers attempt to adopt the evolutionary algorithm to search the neural network architecture. Real E et al. [14] proposed a novel search framework based on the evolutionary algorithm, named AmoebaNet. AmobebaNet uses the same search space as the NAS-Net, searching for the architectures of the normal cell and the reduction cell. To ensure search efficiency, Chen et al. [4] introduce the reinforcement learning into the search framework based on evolutionary algorithm. They design a mutation controller based on the reinforcement learning to learn the effects of slight modifications and produce mutation actions.

Despite the success of RL-based methods and EA-based methods, the huge search cost is still not acceptable. To further improve the search efficiency and reduce search costs, some NAS works try to use gradient optimization methods to search optimal architectures. DARTS [12] is the first gradient-based NAS approach, which relaxes the search space to be continuous so that the architecture can be optimized with respect to its validation set performance by gradient descent. Then some variants of DARTS, such as P-DARTS [3] and PC-DARTS [17], are proposed to further optimize remaining problems of DARTS.

Although NAS works for the image classification task have achieved great success and searched models outperform human exports in classification accuracy, NAS for object detection is still poorly explored. The backbone is responsible for extracting semantic features of an image, which is an important module in a detection network. Most detectors directly take the network designed for image classification tasks such as ResNet [7] or ResNeXt [15] as the backbone network. There is a gap between the classification task and the object detection task. Therefore, directly using the network designed for image classification tasks might be sub-optimal. To address the above issue, Chen et al. [19] proposed Det-NAS that applies NAS to design better backbone architecture for object detection. They pre-trained a super-net which contains all candidate architectures on the ImageNet dataset. Then they fine-tuned the pre-trained super-net on the object detection dataset and conducted architecture search on trained super-net with an evolutionary algorithm (EA). However, in general, Batch Normalization (BN) cannot work well in the small batch size. To address this issue, Det-NAS replaces the batch normalization with Synchronized Batch Normalization (SyncBN) [2] when training the super-net.

High-level features have strong semantic information and low resolution, and low-level features are opposite. In general, strong semantic information is beneficial to classification and high-resolution is beneficial to localization. Thus, FPN is proposed to fuse high-level features and low-level features to generate the feature representations with strong semantic information and high-resolution. Some research works [8,9,13] proposed various cross-scale connections to fuse features to generate better feature representations. However, the FPN architecture of these works might not be optimal. Thus, Golnaz et al. [6] proposed an FPN search framework named NAS-FPN. NAS-FPN designs the search space that can cover all possible cross-scale connections to generate better feature fusion representations. Xu et al. [16] proposed an architecture search framework named Auto-FPN. Auto-FPN consists of two auto search modules for object detection: Auto-fusion module aims at fusing the multi-level features and Auto-head module aims at searching for an efficient RCNN head architecture for classification and regression. However, Auto-FPN adopts the gradient-based algorithm to search for the network architecture, which is memory-inefficient for object detection. Since Auto-FPN consumes a large number of GPU memory, it only searches for architectures of FPN and RCNN head one by one.

Current NAS techniques face two challenges when applied to object detection: (1) Searching a detection network consumes too much GPU memory and time, which fails to enable an end-to-end search for the whole detection network; (2) The ImageNet pre-training requirement makes it hard to directly search for the architecture of the backbone. To address above problems, we propose a novel neural architecture search framework named Memory-Efficient Multi-Agent NAS (MEMA-NAS). Specifically, during the search stage, we model the search process as a multi-agent learning problem. Multiple agents are established to supervise a set of candidate operations and all agents work together to find the optimal architecture. In this way, the GPU memory usage can be reduced to at least half of the gradient-based NAS method, ensuring that we have enough GPU memory to search the architecture simultaneously.

In summary, the contributions of this paper are as follows:

- We propose a novel end-to-end neural network architecture search framework for object detection, named MEMA-NAS, which is more computationally efficient compared to prior works. We introduce the multi-agent learning to solve the typical problem of the memory explosion in gradient-based NAS frameworks. Our method can complete a search of the whole detection network within 10 GPU days on the large-scale COCO dataset.
- We prove the effectiveness of MEMA-NAS with extensive experiments. It works well on different backbones (ResNet and ResNeXt) and various datasets (COCO and BDD dataset). Besides, our method demonstrates a strong generalization ability when we transfer the searched models to other datasets (VOC dataset).

2 MEMA-NAS Framework

In this section, we mainly introduce components of our end-to-end object detection neural network architecture search framework named Memory-Efficient Multi-Agent NAS (MEMA-NAS), including search algorithm, and the resource constraint we used.

Despite the success in the image classification task, the gradient-based method (DARTS) is memory-inefficient for object detection. The search space of the whole detection network-composed is much larger than the classification network. Naively including all the candidate operations into a hyper-net and allowing all candidate operations to participate in the computation in per iteration will easily lead to GPU memory explosion. We attempt to address the above issue by converting the NAS problem into a multi-agent learning problem. The proposed method obviously reduces GPU memory usage compared to DARTS, ensuring that architectures of the whole detection network can be searched simultaneously.

2.1 Multi-Agent Search Algorithm

To alleviate the problem of the huge computational complexity in DARTS, inspired by previous NAS work [1] for image classification, we frame the NAS problem as a multi-agent learning problem. Each agent is responsible for controlling a set of candidate operations and sequentially samples different candidate operations based on the learned sample strategy. Agents interact with an environment, receiving feedback (In our work, the loss is used as the feedback) to update their sampling strategy over associated operations and all agents work together to find the optimal architecture. Theoretically, since each agent samples one candidate operation in per iteration, it saves $\frac{K-1}{K}$(K is the number of candidate operations) GPU memory compared to DARTS [1].

Neural Architecture Search as Multi-Agent Learning. As shown in Fig. 1, in the multi-agent search algorithm, the search space is represented as a DAG with N nodes and V edges. We assign an agent for each edge (i, j) to select an operation according to its sample strategy (action distribution) $a_t^{(A_i)} \sim \pi_t^{(A_i)}\left(a_t^{(A_i)}\right)$ in iteration t, where $i \in \{1, \ldots, V\}$ and $a_t^{(A_i)} \in \{1, \ldots, K\}$. Thus, we obtain a decision sequence $\mathbf{a_t} = \left\{a_t^{(A_1)}, \ldots, a_t^{(A_V)}\right\}$ and use its loss $\mathcal{L}_t = (\mathbf{a}_t, w_t)$ to update the sample strategy (action distribution).

Sample Strategy. We denote the contribution of the operation k belonging to the agent A_i as $c_t^{A_i}[k]$ (similar to the architecture parameters α in DARTS) [1]. Each agent A_i samples an operation from a softmax distribution in per iteration, which is formulated as:

$$c_t^{A_i}[k] = \frac{\exp\left(c_t^{A_i}[k]\right)}{\sum_{j=1}^{K} \exp\left(c_t^{A_i}[j]\right)}, \tag{1}$$

where $k \in \{1, \ldots K\}$ and $c_t^{A_i} \in \mathbb{R}^{|K|}$.

Update Strategy. In our method, each agent A_i directly associates the quality of its taken action with the loss $\mathcal{L}_t\left(a_t^{(A_1)}, \ldots, a_t^{(A_V)}\right)$ and the update strategy is given by:

$$c_t^{(A_i)}[k] = \begin{cases} c_{t-1}^{(A_i)}[k], a_t^{(A_i)} \neq k, \\ (1-\mu)c_{t-1}^{(A_i)}[k] - \mu\mathcal{L}_t(\mathbf{a}_t), a_t^{(A_i)} = k, \end{cases} \tag{2}$$

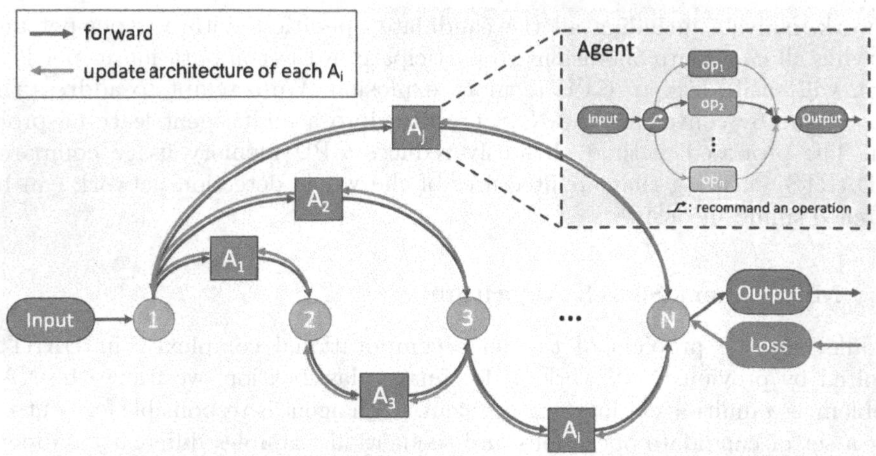

Fig. 1. An illustration of the multi-agent search algorithm, a directed acyclic graph (DAG) consists of N nodes, each edge (m, n) is assigned an agent A_i to explore and supervise all candidate operations, each agent A_i recommends one in iteration t according the current sample policy $\pi_t^{A_i}$, the loss is used as the feedback to update its policy, and repeat the above process until the model converges.

where $\mathbf{a_t} = \left(a_t^{(A_1)}, \ldots, a_t^{(A_V)}\right)$ and μ is a momentum coefficient. After search stage, each agent selects the optimal operation: $o^{*(i)} = \arg\max_k c^{A_i}[k]$, where $k \in \{1, \ldots K\}$, to generate the final architecture.

Optimization. The parameters of our method can be divided into two types of parameters: Model parameters w and architecture parameters $\alpha = \{\alpha_B, \alpha_N, \alpha_H\}$, where $\alpha_B, \alpha_N, \alpha_H$ denote the architecture parameters for Backbone, FPN neck and RCNN head, respectively. We split the training dataset into training data to optimize w by $\nabla_w \mathcal{L}_{\text{train}}(w, \alpha)$ and validation data to optimize α using Eq. 2. Following DARTS, we iteratively optimize w and α until the search model converges.

2.2 Resource Constraint

Considering that the efficiency is a crucial factor for a detection system, we further add a resource constraint in our method. Specifically, we consider three metrics for the resource constraint $C(\alpha_B, \alpha_N, \alpha_H)$: parameter size; floating-point operations (FLOPs); and memory access cost (MAC), and the resource constraint is calculated:

$$C(\alpha_B, \alpha_N, \alpha_H) = \sum_i C\left(O\left(\alpha_B^i\right)\right) + \sum_j C\left(O\left(\alpha_N^j\right) + \sum_k C\left(O\left(\alpha_H^k\right)\right)\right), \quad (3)$$

where $C\left(O\left(\alpha_B^i\right)\right), C\left(O\left(\alpha_N^j\right)\right)$ and $C\left(O\left(\alpha_H^k\right)\right)$ are computational costs of operations sampled from agent α_B^i, α_N^j, and α_H^k respectively, and the computational cost is a sum of normalized parameter size, FLOPs, and MAC. In this work, we add $C\left(\alpha_B, \alpha_N, \alpha_H\right)$ as a regularization term into the loss function to control the computational complexity of the searched model:

$$\mathcal{L}(w, \alpha) = \mathcal{L}_{\text{model}}(w, \alpha) + \lambda C\left(\alpha_B, \alpha_N, \alpha_H\right), \tag{4}$$

where λ is a hyper-parameter to control the importance of $C\left(\alpha_B, \alpha_N, \alpha_H\right)$.

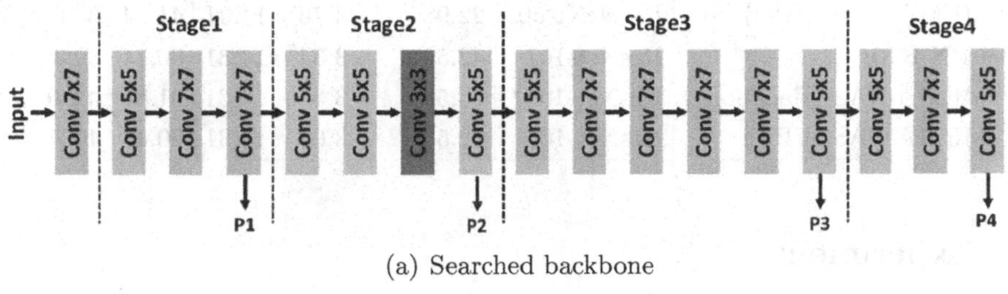

(a) Searched backbone

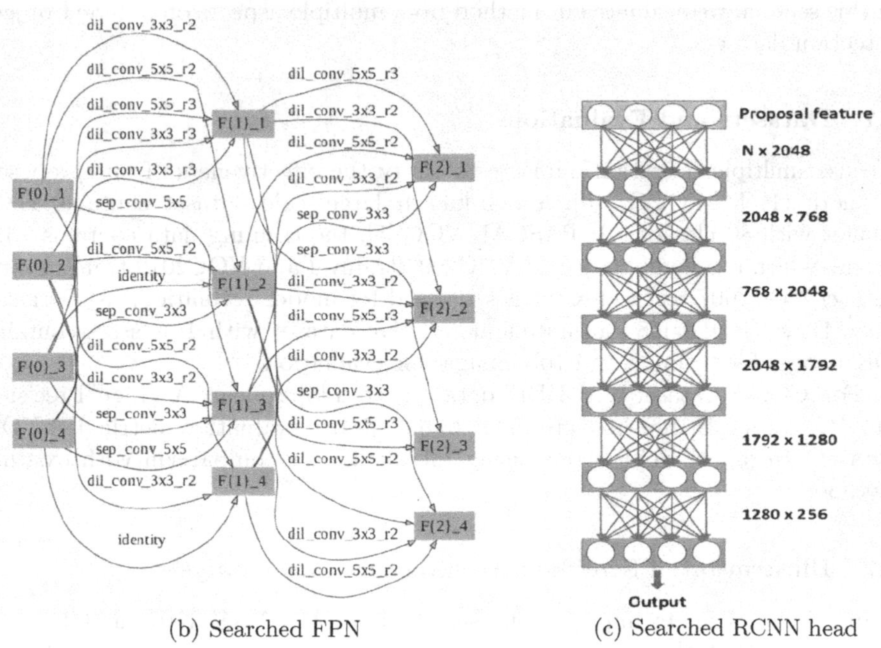

(b) Searched FPN (c) Searched RCNN head

Fig. 2. The illustration of the searched MEMA-NAS-R50$_M$ architecture.

Table 1. Individual module search experimental results on COCO mini-val dataset. MEMA-NAS (Backbone) and MEMA-NAS (FPN) denote the separate search results of backbone and FPN respectively. * refers to the corresponding searched backbones.

Model	Backbone	Parameters				AP
		Backbone	Neck	Head	Total	
FPN-R50	ResNet-50	23.51	3.34	14.31	41.76	37.4
MEMA-NAS (Backbone)	ResNet-50*	34.65	3.34	14.31	52.90	**39.1**
MEMA-NAS (FPN)	ResNet-50	23.51	3.13	14.31	41.54	38.5
FPN-X50	ResNeXt-50	22.98	3.34	14.31	41.23	38.2
MEMA-NAS (Backbone)	ResNeXt-50*	26.09	3.34	14.31	44.34	**39.6**
MEMA-NAS (FPN)	ResNeXt-50	22.98	3.76	14.31	41.64	38.9
FPN-R101	ResNet-101	42.50	3.34	14.31	60.74	39.4
MEMA-NAS (Backbone)	ResNet-101*	73.56	3.34	14.31	91.81	**41.0**
MEMA-NAS (FPN)	ResNet-101	42.50	3.02	14.31	60.43	40.7

3 Experiments

In this section, we evaluate our method from multiple aspects on different object detection datasets.

3.1 Datasets and Evaluations

We use multiple detection datasets to verify the effectiveness of our proposed method: (1) MSCOCO [10]: a well-known large-scale dataset contains 118K images with 80 classes; (2) PASCAL VOC [5]: the training data contains $10K$ image, which is a combination of VOC2007 trainval and VOC2012 trainval, and dataset VOC2007 test (4.9K images) is used for model evaluation; (3) Berkeley Deep Drive (BDD) [18]: an autonomous drive dataset with 10 classes contains 70K images for training and 10K images for evaluation.

For COCO dataset and BDD dataset, we adopt mean Average Precision (mAP) across IoU thresholds from 0.5 to 0.95 as our evaluation metric. For VOC dataset, we report mAP scores using IoU at 0.5 for comparison with existing methods.

3.2 Illustration of Searched Architecture and Analysis

Figure 2 shows an example of our searched MEMA-NAS-R50$_{\mathrm{M}}$ architecture. We can see that the model tends to use convolutions with large kernel sizes in backbone, and experimental results show that models searched by MEMA-NAS achieve significant improvements in large scale object detection. Besides, the model tends to use dilated convolutions in the 2nd layer of MEMA-NAS FPN module, demonstrating that the large receptive field is very important for feature fusing.

Table 2. Evaluation results on BDD dataset. MEMA-NAS are our searched models. * refers to the corresponding searched backbones.

Model	Backbone	Parameters				FLOPs	AP
		Backbone	Neck	Head	Total	(G)	
FPN-R50	R50	23.51	3.34	13.95	41.39	197.4	34.0
MEMA-NAS-R50	R50*	52.25	3.17	32.96	88.96	330.2	**35.6**
FPN-X50	X50	22.98	3.34	13.95	40.87	200.0	34.3
MEMA-NAS-X50	X50*	27.08	3.50	37.68	68.85	250.5	**35.6**
FPN-R101	R101	42.50	3.34	13.95	60.38	269.3	35.4
MEMA-NAS-R101	R101*	112.56	3.55	33.42	150.12	501.3	**37.4**
FPN-X101	X101	86.74	3.34	13.95	104.63	439.2	36.2
MEMA-NAS-X101	X101*	111.65	3.84	38.20	154.28	574.9	**37.3**

3.3 Ablation Experiments for Individual Module Search

To verify the effectiveness of our method for individual module search and investigate the contribution of each searched component in MEMA-NAS, we conduct more search experiments. We search for backbone and FPN module individually based on multiple prototype backbones. The results are shown in Table 1. We find that both searched backbones and FPNs bring AP gains compared to the baseline model FPN. Searching backbones can bring more performance improvements, and searching FPN is able to boost the AP while slightly cuts down the model size.

3.4 Generalization Performance Evaluation

Search on More Datasets. We conduct more searching experiments under the similar setting on BDD dataset to evaluate the generalization performance of our proposed method. Table 2 shows the evaluation results using $\lambda = 0.02$. We can observe that the searched models achieve significant improvements compared with baseline models (at least 1% boost in AP), demonstrating that our proposed method can work well on other detection datasets.

Architecture Transfer. In order to further evaluate the generalization performance of our proposed method, we transfer models searched on COCO dataset to VOC dataset, and evaluation results are shown in Table 3. All transferred models show noticeable performance improvements on VOC dataset, which proves the great generalization ability of searched models.

Table 3. Transfer results on VOC dataset. * denotes the corresponding searched backbones.

Model	Backbone	Params (M)	AP
FPN-R50	ResNet-50	41.44	79.7
MEMA-NAS-R50	ResNet-50*	96.60	**80.4**
FPN-X50	ResNeXt-50	40.92	79.5
MEMA-NAS-X50	ResNeXt-50*	62.82	**80.2**
FPN-R101	ResNet-101	60.43	81.6
MEMA-NAS-R101	ResNet-101*	135.42	**83.6**
FPN-X101	ResNeXt-101	104.68	82.6
MEMA-NAS-X101	ResNeXt-101*	150.06	**83.7**

Table 4. Comparison between MEMA-NAS and other NAS-based detection methods. Our efficient search method takes only 10 GPU days to finish a search of the whole detection network, outperforming all other NAS-based detection works in search efficiency.

Model	Search part	Backbone	Search cost	AP	Search method
Det-NAS	Backbone	DetNASNet	43.4	41.8	Evolutionary
NATS	Backbone	NATS-X101	20	41.4	Gradient-based
NAS-FPN	FPN	ResNeXt-101	100	44.8	RL
MEMA-NAS-X101	Whole	ResNeXt-101*	10	43.5	Multi-agent

3.5 Comparison with NAS-Based Detection Works

We compare more NAS-based detection methods and show more details in Table 4. Our method is the first NAS framework that is capable of searching for a whole detection network. Our method achieves a 43.5% AP on COCO dataset with a search cost of only 10 GPU days, which is efficient enough to out perform all existing counterparts. The searched model surpasses Det-NAS and NATS by 1.7% and 2.1%, respectively, and reaches a comparable AP with NAS-FPN, whose search cost is 10× than ours.

Table 5. The GPU memory consumption comparison between MEMA-NAS and DATRS. We use the same search space for both DARTS and MEMA-NAS. All experiments are conducted with batch size 1 and input size 1333×800.

Search part	Method	Memory usage (M)	Δ
–	FPN-R50	3627	–
Backbone	DARTS	5797	2148
	MEMA-NAS	4709	**1082**$^{-50\%}$
FPN	DARTS	31771	28144
	MEMA-NAS	8779	**5152**$^{-82\%}$
RCNN head	DARTS	5447	1820
	MEMA-NAS	4491	**864**$^{-53\%}$
Overall	DARTS	Exploded (more than 32G)	More than 32G
	MEMA-NAS	10191	**6564**$^{-76\%}$

3.6 GPU Memory Consumption Evaluation

In order to further evaluate the GPU memory usage efficiency of our method, we compare the average GPU memory consumption for the search of each component between our method and the gradient-based method (DARTS) with the same search space. The results are shown in Table 5. Compared to DARTS, our method can save 50%, 82% and 53% GPU memory usage for the search of backbone, FPN, and RCNN head, respectively. When conducting the search for the whole detection network, DARTS results in a memory explosion while our method is able to complete the joint search with a considerable low resource requirement.

4 Conclusion

In this paper, we put forward an end-to-end framework, named MEMA-NAS, which is memory-efficient and has the capability to search the holistic architecture of the detection network. We use a more efficient search algorithm to search network architecture. To find a better tradeoff between the precision and computational costs, we add a resource constraint in our method. We compare our MEMA-NAS with different baselines and show its superiority under various conditions both on different datasets.

References

1. Carlucci, F.M., et al.: MANAS: multi-agent neural architecture search. arXiv preprint arXiv:1909.01051 (2019)
2. Chao, P., Xiao, T., Li, Z., Jiang, Y., Jian, S.: MegDet: a large mini-batch object detector. In: 2018 IEEE/CVF Conference on Computer Vision and Pattern Recognition (2018)

3. Chen, X., Xie, L., Wu, J., Tian, Q.: Progressive differentiable architecture search: bridging the depth gap between search and evaluation. In: Proceedings of the IEEE/CVF International Conference on Computer Vision, pp. 1294–1303 (2019)
4. Chen, Y., et al.: Reinforced evolutionary neural architecture search. arXiv preprint arXiv:1808.00193 (2018)
5. Everingham, M., Gool, L.V., Williams, C., Winn, J., Zisserman, A.: The pascal visual object classes (VOC) challenge. Int. J. Comput. Vision **88**(2), 303–338 (2010)
6. Ghiasi, G., Lin, T.Y., Le, Q.V.: NAS-FPN: learning scalable feature pyramid architecture for object detection. In: 2019 IEEE/CVF Conference on Computer Vision and Pattern Recognition (CVPR) (2019)
7. He, K., Zhang, X., Ren, S., Sun, J.: Deep residual learning for image recognition. In: Proceedings of the IEEE Conference on Computer Vision and Pattern Recognition, pp. 770–778 (2016)
8. Kim, S.-W., Kook, H.-K., Sun, J.-Y., Kang, M.-C., Ko, S.-J.: Parallel feature pyramid network for object detection. In: Ferrari, V., Hebert, M., Sminchisescu, C., Weiss, Y. (eds.) ECCV 2018. LNCS, vol. 11209, pp. 239–256. Springer, Cham (2018). https://doi.org/10.1007/978-3-030-01228-1_15
9. Kong, T., Sun, F., Huang, W., Liu, H.: Deep feature pyramid reconfiguration for object detection. In: Ferrari, V., Hebert, M., Sminchisescu, C., Weiss, Y. (eds.) ECCV 2018. LNCS, vol. 11209, pp. 172–188. Springer, Cham (2018). https://doi.org/10.1007/978-3-030-01228-1_11
10. Lin, T.-Y., et al.: Microsoft COCO: common objects in context. In: Fleet, D., Pajdla, T., Schiele, B., Tuytelaars, T. (eds.) ECCV 2014. LNCS, vol. 8693, pp. 740–755. Springer, Cham (2014). https://doi.org/10.1007/978-3-319-10602-1_48
11. Liu, C., et al.: Progressive neural architecture search. In: Ferrari, V., Hebert, M., Sminchisescu, C., Weiss, Y. (eds.) ECCV 2018. LNCS, vol. 11205, pp. 19–35. Springer, Cham (2018). https://doi.org/10.1007/978-3-030-01246-5_2
12. Liu, H., Simonyan, K., Yang, Y.: DARTS: differentiable architecture search. arXiv preprint arXiv:1806.09055 (2018)
13. Liu, S., Qi, L., Qin, H., Shi, J., Jia, J.: Path aggregation network for instance segmentation. In: Proceedings of the IEEE Conference on Computer Vision and Pattern Recognition, pp. 8759–8768 (2018)
14. Real, E., Aggarwal, A., Huang, Y., Le, Q.V.: Regularized evolution for image classifier architecture search. In: Proceedings of the AAAI Conference on Artificial Intelligence, vol. 33 (2018)
15. Xie, S., Girshick, R., Dollár, P., Tu, Z., He, K.: Aggregated residual transformations for deep neural networks. In: Proceedings of the IEEE Conference on Computer Vision and Pattern Recognition, pp. 1492–1500 (2017)
16. Xu, H., Yao, L., Zhang, W., Liang, X., Li, Z.: Auto-FPN: automatic network architecture adaptation for object detection beyond classification. In: Proceedings of the IEEE/CVF International Conference on Computer Vision, pp. 6649–6658 (2019)
17. Xu, Y., et al.: PC-DARTS: partial channel connections for memory-efficient architecture search. arXiv preprint arXiv:1907.05737 (2019)
18. Yu, F., et al.: BDD100K: a diverse driving video database with scalable annotation tooling. arXiv preprint arXiv:1805.04687 **2**(5), 6 (2018)

19. Zhao, Z.Q., Zheng, P., Xu, S.T., Wu, X.: Object detection with deep learning: a review. IEEE Trans. Neural Netw. Learn. Syst. **30**(11), 3212–3232 (2019)
20. Zoph, B., Le, Q.V.: Neural architecture search with reinforcement learning. arXiv preprint arXiv:1611.01578 (2016)
21. Zoph, B., Vasudevan, V., Shlens, J., Le, Q.V.: Learning transferable architectures for scalable image recognition. In: Proceedings of the IEEE Conference on Computer Vision and Pattern Recognition, pp. 8697–8710 (2018)

Adversarial Decoupling for Weakly Supervised Semantic Segmentation

Guoying Sun[1], Meng Yang[1,2](✉), and Wenfeng Luo[1]

[1] School of Computer Science and Engineering, Sun Yat-sen University, Guangzhou, China
yangm6@mail.sysu.edu.cn

[2] Key Laboratory of Machine Intelligence and Advanced Computing (SYSU), Ministry of Education, Guangzhou, China

Abstract. Image semantic segmentation has been widely used in medical image analysis, autonomous driving and other fields. However, the fully-supervised semantic segmentation network requires a lot of labor cost to label pixel-level training data, so weakly supervised semantic segmentation (WSSS), which requires much easily available supervision, has become a new research hotspot. This paper focuses on tackling the semantic segmentation problem under weak supervision of image-level labels. To estimate more accurate pseudo masks, this paper proposes to jointly explore sub-category clustering, context decoupling augmentation and adversarial climbing to mine more object-related regions. With sub-categories of k-means clustering, model can learn better feature representations, which breaks the dependency of object on the context by decoupling augmentation. The image is perturbed away from the classification boundary to further increase the classification score with adversarial climbing method. In order to verify the effectiveness of the method in this paper, we conduct a large number of experiments on the PASCAL VOC 2012 dataset obtained an excellent performance of 69.8% mIoU on the verification set and 69.5% mIoU on the test set, which surpassed many advanced models of the same level supervision.

Keywords: Weakly supervised semantic segmentation · Context decoupling · Adversarial climbing · K-means clustering

1 Introduction

Image semantic segmentation aims at assigning a class label to each pixel, offering fine-grained object compositions in the image. Due to its soaring success recently, it has found practical application in many fields, including medical

This work is partially supported by National Natural Science Foundation of China (Grants no. 61772568), Guangdong Basic and Applied Basic Research Foundation (Grant no. 2019A1515012029), and Youth science and technology innovation talent of Guangdong Special Support Program.

© Springer Nature Switzerland AG 2021
H. Ma et al. (Eds.): PRCV 2021, LNCS 13022, pp. 188–200, 2021.
https://doi.org/10.1007/978-3-030-88013-2_16

diagnosis and autonomous driving. However, these segmentation models require huge amount of pixel-level annotations, whose acquisition is label-intensive and time-consuming. Therefore, researchers attempt to explore weak supervisions, such as image-level information, to tackle semantic segmentation task.

Compared to pixel-level masks whose annotation takes 4 to 90 min [1,2], it only requires around 20 s [1] to provide image-level labels. Thus this paper focuses on the weakly supervised semantic segmentation (WSSS) under image-level label, which is the most easily available annotation among all weak supervisions. Existing WSSS methods via image-level labels usually adopt three individual stages: 1) train a normal classifier to produce class activation maps to coarsely locate the target objects; 2) propose an expansion strategy to mine more object-related regions before generating the final pseudo labels; 3) learn a segmentation network based on the pseudo labels. This paper mainly makes its contributions in the first and second stages.

Although there are various object expansion methods, they are all based on the class activation map (CAM) [3]. There are mainly two aspects worth considering for CAM. Firstly, the CAM trained by classification network usually only high-lights the distinguishing area. Secondly, since only image-level labels are provided, when the objects in the image are tightly coupled with the background or co-occurrence category, such as "boat" and "water", "aircraft" and "sky", "train" and "track", "horse" and "people", CAM will mistakenly identify background and foreground objects due to context interference [4].

Most methods use CAM of the classification network to generate initial predictions for each class [3]. However, the CAM generated by the weighted feature map of the classification network usually only focuses on the part of the target object. The classification network can distinguish different categories better through the most distinguishing features, so the overall object is hardly located. In order to solve the seed sparseness problem, many excellent methods have been proposed [5–7], which can effectively obtain initial predictions with better coverage. However, those methods do not consider the context, ignoring the influence of the co-occurrence category and background. If most images containing horses with people riding, the classification model will mistakenly believe that most horses appear with people, so the boundary between people and horses is ambiguous. The pairs of train and track, boat and water, aircraft and sky also have the same problems that need to be resolved.

Regarding the two above-mentioned aspects of CAM, we first adopt sub-category clustering [8] to mine more object-related region, which maps the original label space to a higher-dimensional label space. This essentially adds K category maps for each category with k-means clustering, which can solve the problem of seed sparseness.

As traditional data augmentation methods do not consider the association of object and context, we adopt the context decoupling augmentation method that randomly pastes the selected foreground objects into the other image to obtain the enhanced image, which breaks the dependency of the object on the context. Through the perturbation methods of sub-category clustering and context decoupling augmentation, the classification network can finally cover the target object more completely with more features in each category, and decouple the target object from the context.

In order to further decrease the wrong bias, we additionally adopt the adversarial climbing method as post-analysis and optimization of the classifier to decouple the object with other co-occurrence category objects by keeping the image away from the decision boundary, in which the image is perturbed along the pixel gradient to improve the classification score of the target class [9]. We ultimately improve the performance of the initial class activation map and expand the seed region to generate better pseudo labels by refinement network of IRNet [10] for the downstream segmentation task. The conceptual description of our method in image processing is shown in Fig. 1.

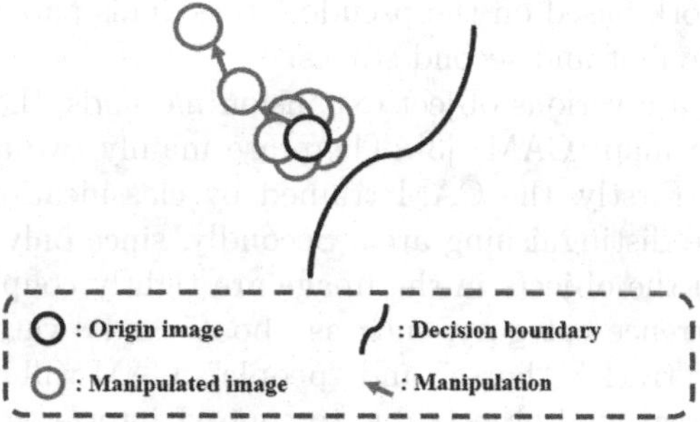

Fig. 1. Conceptual description of image processing method for CAM.

The main contributions of this paper are three-fold:

- We propose the SDA-CAM method to explore **S**ub-category clustering, context **D**ecoupling augmentation, **A**dversarial climbing to refine the initial **CAM**, which improves the feature representation and identifies more regions of the object.
- The method in this paper effectively alleviates the impact of co-occurrence problems on image-level weakly supervised semantic segmentation.
- Our method produces significantly better performance than existing methods in weakly supervised semantic segmentation. In particular, it achieves 69.8% and 69.5% mIoU scores on val and test set of PASCAL VOC 2012 dataset.

2 Related Work

2.1 Initial Prediction for WSSS

The initial prediction can provide reliable prior information and approximate position for generating the pseudo labels. Many methods usually use CAM [3] as an initial prediction. Since the CAM model is trained by the classification task, it tends to activate small and distinct parts of the object, resulting in an incomplete initial mask. There are currently several directions to alleviate this problem.

One way is to erase [11,12], which removes the discernible area of the object, forcing the model to look for more different parts. However, the erasure methods require modification of the network structure, repeated execution of the training model and response aggregation steps. There are also proposed methods that improve the original erasure method [13,14], which extend the initial response through end-to-end training against erasure strategies. The SeeNet method [15] adopts a self-erasing strategy to encourage the network to use both the object and the background cues, which prevents the attention from containing background areas. The erasing method has certain effects, but it is difficult to provide reliable termination conditions for iterative erasing. Besides, eliminating the identification area of the image will cause the network to misclassify the image.

There is also a way which suppresses the most distinctive areas [16], so that the classification network can cover the target more comprehensively. Our work additionally uses a certain degree of suppression. There is another way to perturb. The SC-CAM method [8] obtains the sub-categories under each parent category through unsupervised clustering, and learns to obtain more comprehensive features. The AdvCAM method [4] uses adversarial climbing method to perturb the image along the pixel gradient to increase the classification score.

2.2 Response Refinement for WSSS

Many methods have been proposed to refine the initial clues by expanding the initial seed. The SEC method [17] proposes a loss function that constrained global weighted rank pooling and low-level boundaries to expand localized mapping. The MCOF method [18] alternately expands the target area and optimizes the segmentation network by the iterative bottom-up and top-down framework. The MDC method [19] expands the seed by using multiple branches of the convolutional layer with different dilation rates. The DSRG method [20] refines the initial prediction when training the segmentation network with the seed region growth method. Other methods are developed through affinity learning. AffinityNet [21] considers pixel-level affinity and propagates local response to nearby areas. The IRNet method [10] refines the class activation map to obtain the pseudo labels with affinity learning through the class boundary map and the displacement field.

However, the initial seed still base on the CAM method. If these seeds only come from the distinguishing part of the object, it is difficult to extend the area to the non-distinctive part. In addition, if the initial prediction produces an incorrect attention area, applying the refinement step will cover the more inaccurate area. In this paper, we focus on improving the initial prediction to make the target positioning more accurate, which is conducive to the refinement steps.

3 Method

In this section, we elaborate on the technical details of the proposed SDA-CAM method, which consists of three individual modules: sub-category clustering, context decoupling augmentation and adversarial climbing. The joint training strategy takes into account the seed sparseness and co-occurrence issues, which synergistically improves the segmentation performance.

The Overview of the proposed framework is shown in Fig. 2. Firstly, we adopt unsupervised clustering to explore sub-category for increasing the difficulty of the classification network, so that it can automatically learn more features in each category. Then we decouple the class object from the image context, which can break the dependency between the object and the context. Finally, we disturb the image to a certain extent via the iterative adversarial climbing method to obtain the final SDA-CAM, in which the image is moved away from the classification boundary to increase the classification score.

We present a technical description of our method. We denote the space of images and image-level labels by $\hat{X}$ and $\hat{Y}$. Any image X $\in \hat{X}$ has the corresponding image-level label Y $\in \hat{Y}$. The semantic labels belong to a set $C' =$ C $\cup\{c_{bg}\}$, where C is a set of foreground labels and c_{bg} is the background label. We assume that the training data $\{(X_i, Y_i)\}_{i=1}^{N}$, consists of N images, $X_i \in \hat{X}$, where each image is weakly labeled by $Y_i \in \{0,1\}^C$ of foreground labels.

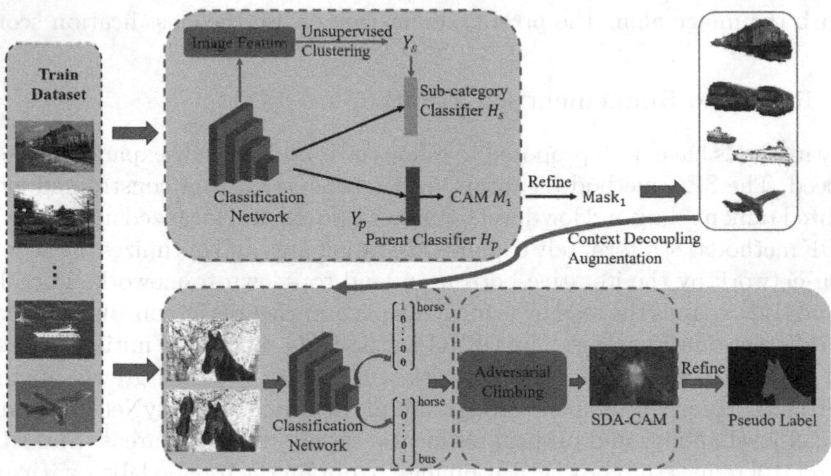

Fig. 2. Overview of the proposed framework for generating the SDA-CAM.

3.1 Sub-category Clustering

We first train a normal classification network using the available image-level labels $Y_p \in \{0,1\}^C$. Let $F \in R^{h \times w \times d}$ denote the output feature maps before the Global Averaging Pooling (GAP) layer. Then the initial CAM for class c could be computed as the weighted sum of feature maps:

$$CAM = ReLU\left(\sum_k F^k \times \omega_c^k\right) \tag{1}$$

where $F^k \in R^{h \times w}$ represents the k-th channel of F and $\omega_c \in R^d$ are weights from the classification layer for class c. The initial CAM tends to focus on the most discriminative regions, leading to incomplete object mask for the downstream segmentation task. Motivated by [8], we propose to perform sub-category clustering to discover more object-related pixels.

Sub-category clustering maps the original class label space to a high dimensional one. The training images are first divided into semantic subsets, each of which contains images with the same class label. Specifically, we extract image representation $f \in R^d$ for each training image, which is obtained by performing GAP on the output feature maps:

$$f = \frac{1}{hw} \sum_i \sum_j F_{i,j} \tag{2}$$

Then k-means clustering is applied on the image representations $\sum_{i=1}^{N} f \in R^{N \times d}$ to re-label the original training images with pseudo sub-categories $Y_s \in \{0,1\}^{KC}$, as visually presented in Fig. 3. Consequentially, the original parent class label $Y_p \in \{0,1\}^C$ is mapped to $Y_s \in \{0,1\}^{KC}$ with K sub-categories.

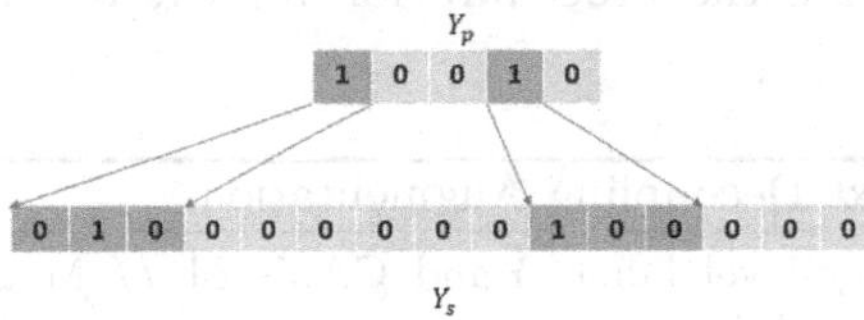

Fig. 3. Sub-category clustering. Here we demonstrate that each parent class is mapped to K = 3 sub-categories.

To utilize the pseudo label $Y_s \in \{0,1\}^{KC}$ we add a parallel classification layer which shares the backbone network with the existing one, as shown in Fig. 2. The original classifier H_p is trained by the parent class label $Y_p \in \{0,1\}^C$ while the sub-category classifier H_s is supervised by $Y_s \in \{0,1\}^{KC}$. So the overall training objective is defined as:

$$L_{cls} = \frac{1}{N} \sum_{i}^{N} L_{CE}\left(H_p\left(f_i\right), Y_p\right) + \gamma L_{CE}\left(H_s\left(f_i\right), Y_s\right) \tag{3}$$

where L_{CE} represents the cross entropy loss and γ is a hyper-parameter controlling the relative importance of two terms.

With the attached sub-category classifier, we essentially introduce extra K CAMs for each class, significantly diversifying the response regions. Since these two parallel classifiers share the same input features, so the responsive regions are also reflected in the parent classifier. As a result, we are able to estimate more complete object mask from M_1.

3.2 Context Decoupling Augmentation

Traditional WSSS data augmentation methods usually adopt geometric transformation, random cropping and horizontal flip. However, simply adding the same context data bring less benefit to the network for distinguishing objects. The image-level classification may not only be owing to the recognition of the object itself, but also related to its co-occurrence context, which will cause the model to pay less attention to the features of the object and lead to blurring pseudo-label boundaries. Motivated by [4], we propose to perform the context decoupling augmentation method by randomly pasting objects into the new image, which increases the diversity of objects in the image and reduces the dependence of the same object in the inherent scene.

When two images with the same background have different objects, they tend to leave a deep impression. By jointly training the original image and the context-decoupled augmentation image, the network can further identify the target, and alleviate the impact of the co-occurrence to a certain extent. As most objects are located in the middle or prominent position of the image, we paste the context-decoupled object to the eccentric position of the image for ensuring the augmentation quality. Although the phenomenon of occluding the original image objects may occur, the augmentation method generally improves performance. Algorithm 1 summarizes the procedure for context decoupling augmentation method.

Algorithm 1. Context Decoupling Augmentation

Input: Images $\hat{X}$, image-level labels $\hat{Y}$and CAMs M // M generated by the sub-category clustering module
Output: Classifier H
for i in {1,2,. . . ,N} **do** // Step1: Inferring
  if $Is\_single\,(Y_i)$ **then** // only chose image $X_i \in R^{h_1 \times w_1 \times 3}$ with single category to get object
    $Mask_i \leftarrow Refining\,(X_i, Y_i, M_i)$ // refining by IRNet, $Mask_i \in R^{h_1 \times w_1}, Y_i \in \{0,1\}^C$
    Object O_i decoupled from context $\leftarrow Mask_i \cdot X_i$ // $O_i \in R^{h_2 \times w_2 \times 3}$
  end if
end for
for j in {1,2,. . . ,N} **do** // Step 2: Online Augmentation
  i $\leftarrow Choose\_Random\,(Y_j)$ // random choose category not appear in the original image
  $X_j^{Aug}, Y_j^{Aug} \leftarrow Paste\,(X_j, Y_j, O_i, i)$ // paste O_i into image X_j appropriately by Gaussian smoothing, randomly scaling and rotating
  H $\leftarrow ClassifyNet\left(X_j, Y_j, X_j^{Aug}, Y_j^{Aug}\right)$ // adopt ResNet-50 [22] as classification network
end for

3.3 Adversarial Climbing

Both sub-category clustering and context decoupling augmentation modules act on the classification network to yield a better CAM output. In this section, we instead explore adversarial climbing [4] as the post-processing of the classifier H to perturb the input image X for generating better CAM. Adversarial climbing was an anti-attacking technique that modified the input X in a direction to disturb the image away from the classification boundary. Let X^t be the perturbed image after t-th update. Then the iterative update procedure can be formulated as follows:

$$X^t = X^{t-1} + \varepsilon \bigtriangledown_{X^{t-1}} s_c^{t-1} \tag{4}$$

where s_c^{t-1} is the classification score, ε is the step size and $\bigtriangledown_{X^{t-1}} s_c^{t-1}$ is the gradient with respect to the image. This treatment encourages the network to become activated in the previously no-discriminative regions, thus capable of mining more foreground pixels.

However, there are two issues concerning the aforementioned update procedure: 1) the updated version X^t might cause other non-existing classes to be recognized; 2) it could simply reinforce those regions that already have a relatively large activation value. To avoid such trivial update, we introduce two extra regularization terms to constrain the update procedure:

$$L = s_c^{t-1} - \sum_{k \in C \backslash c} s_k^{t-1} - \delta \parallel Q_r \odot \mid CAM\left(X^{t-1}\right) - CAM\left(X^0\right) \mid \parallel_1 \tag{5}$$

$$X^t = X^{t-1} + \varepsilon \bigtriangledown_{X^{t-1}} L \tag{6}$$

The hyper-parameter δ represents the degree of suppression. The first regularization term $\sum_{k \in C \backslash c} s_k^{t-1}$ takes into consideration all the classification scores so classes other than c will be suppressed during the updating process. Moreover, the second term achieves the goal of partial enhancement through the introduction of suppression mask Q_r, which takes the form of:

$$Q_r = \frac{CAM\left(X^{t-1}\right)}{max\{CAM\left(X^{t-1}\right)\}} > \beta \tag{7}$$

where β is a threshold value. As a result, regions indicated by Q_r tends to stay the same. Ultimately, the perturbed image X^t of last step is utilized to generate class activation map SDA-CAM with more comprehensive coverage for the downstream segmentation task.

4 Experiments

4.1 Evaluated Dataset and Metric

We evaluated the proposed method on the PASCAL VOC 2012 [23] semantic segmentation benchmark, which contains 20 foreground classes and one background class. Following the previous WSSS methods, we enhance the train set (1,464 images) to trainaug set with 10,582 images by [24]. For all experiments, we use the mean Intersection-over-Union (mIoU) as the evaluation metric. The results of the test set are obtained from the official PASCAL VOC evaluation website.

4.2 Ablation Study and Analysis

As only evaluating the CAM and the pseudo-mask with the mIoU to compare the performance of different methods has certain limitations, we additionally perform the ablation experiments compared with the final segmentation models performance. For fair comparison, we adopt the IRNet [10] as the refined network and the DeepLab-v2 network [25] of the ResNet-101 [22] backbone as segmentation model for all comparative experiments in Table 1. Baseline is the method that does not use any optimization into the CAM. Through the ablation experiment, it can be seen that the three modules we adopted have certain effects on the promotion of the CAM. Our SDA-CAM combined the three methods has achieved the best effect.

Table 1. CAM ablation experiments.

Baseline	Self-supervision	Context decoupling augmentation	Adversarial climbing	CAM	Pseudo masks	Val
√				48.3	65.6	66.2
√	√			49.6	67.1	66.7
√		√		49.9	66.5	67.9
√			√	55.6	69.9	68.1
√	√	√		50.6	67.7	68.8
√	√		√	53.7	67.5	69.0
√		√	√	56.4	69.6	69.5
√	√	√	√	**56.6**	**70.0**	**69.8**

4.3 Semantic Segmentation Performance

For fair comparisons with other WSSS methods, we adopt DeepLab-v2 [25] with the backbone of ResNet-101 [22] as the supervised semantic segmentation model.

Improvement on Initial Response. Figure 4 shows the initial response of our method and the SC-CAM method [8] proposed by Chang et al. Our SDA-CAM often generates the response map that covers larger region of the object compared to SC-CAM. It is worth mentioning that our method also can activate less the background region, as shown in the last column. Because the proposed method better decouple from the context.

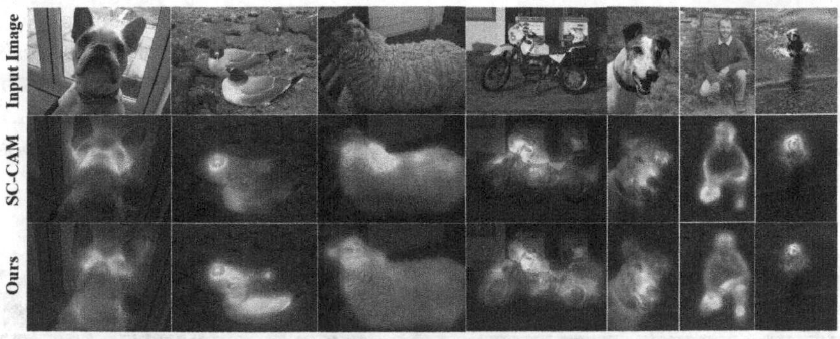

Fig. 4. Sample results of initial responses.

Quality of the Mask. Table 2 compares the initial seeds (CAM) and the pseudo labels obtained by our method and other recent methods. Both seeds and masks were generated from training images of the PASCAL VOC12 dataset [23]. It can be seen that our proposed SDA-CAM can provide the more accurate initial seed and obtain the highest pseudo-mask performance.

Table 2. mIoU (%) of the initial seed (CAM), and the pseudo labels on PASCAL VOC 2012 train images.

Method	Seed	Pseudo labels
$\text{PSA}_{\text{CVPR'18}}$ [26]	48.0	61.0
$\text{IRNet}_{\text{CVPR'19}}$ [10]	48.3	66.5
$\text{Mixup-CAM}_{\text{BMVC'20}}$ [5]	50.1	61.9
$\text{SC-CAM}_{\text{CVPR'20}}$ [8]	50.9	63.4
$\text{SEAM}_{\text{CVPR'20}}$ [6]	55.4	63.6
$\text{CONTA}_{\text{CVPR'20}}$ [21]	48.8	67.9
$\text{AdvCAM}_{\text{CVPR'21}}$ [9]	55.6	69.9
CDA_{21} [4]	50.8	67.7
SDA-CAM (Ours)	**56.6**	**70.0**

Weakly Supervised Semantic Segmentation. With the refinement of CRF and ResNet-101 [22] backbone, our method achieves the mIoU results of 69.8% on val set and 69.5% on the test set. The result on test set is available on the website (http://host.robots.ox.ac.uk:8080/anonymous/GSAW9D.html). In Fig. 5 we visualize some examples of the final semantic segmentation results, which can be seen that our results are close to ground truth. Our WSSS method with image-level labels can segment and recognize the target object well whether it is the single-category image or the complex multi-category image. However, the segmentation results are not fine enough, especially in the bicycle category. The reason is that we adopt the DeepLab-v2 [25] segmentation network with ResNet-101 [22] backbone for fair comparison with other WSSS methods, which has been down sampled by eight times and lost certain pixel prediction information. If a more advanced semantic segmentation network is adopted, performance boost is expected [27].

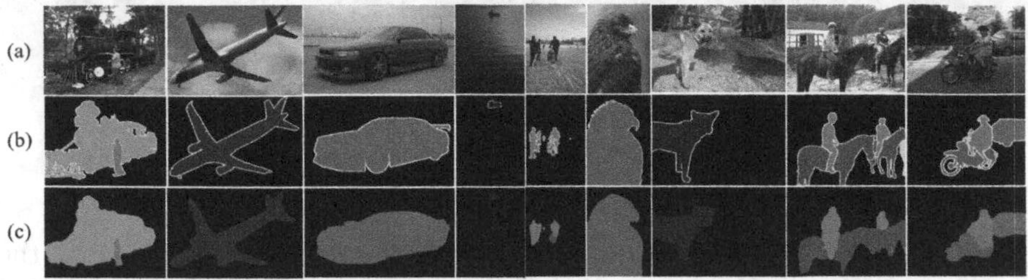

Fig. 5. Qualitative results on the PASCAL VOC 2012 validation set. (a) Input images. (b) Ground truth. (c) Our results.

We compare our method with the recent WSSS methods adopted ResNet backbone segmentation network in Table 3. Our method surpasses many current advanced WSSS methods with the same level supervision. In addition, methods such as FickleNet [7] and ICD [28] extract the background cues from an external saliency detector, which requires additional pixels for training. Our method does not require the additional external saliency detector, and only uses image-level classification labels, which achieves better performance.

Table 3. WSSS performance on PASCAL VOC 2012 val and test set.

Method	Backbone	Saliency	Val	Test
$\text{DCSP}_{\text{BMVC}'17}$ [5]	ResNet-101	√	60.8	61.8
$\text{MCOF}_{\text{CVPR}'18}$ [18]	ResNet-101	√	60.3	61.2
$\text{DSRG}_{\text{CVPR}'18}$ [20]	ResNet-101	√	61.4	63.2
$\text{AffinityNet}_{\text{CVPR}'18}$ [21]	ResNet-38	–	61.7	63.7
$\text{FickleNet}_{\text{CVPR}'19}$ [7]	ResNet-101	√	64.9	65.3
$\text{IRNet}_{\text{CVPR}'19}$ [10]	ResNet-50	–	63.5	64.8
$\text{SC−CAM}_{\text{CVPR}'20}$ [8]	ResNet-101	–	66.1	65.9
$\text{SEAM}_{\text{CVPR}'20}$ [6]	ResNet-38	–	64.5	65.7
$\text{ICD}_{\text{CVPR}'20}$ [28]	ResNet-101	√	67.8	68.0
CDA_{21} [4]	ResNet-50	–	65.8	66.4
$\text{AdvCAM}_{\text{CVPR}'21}$ [9]	ResNet-101	–	68.1	68.0
Ours	ResNet-101	–	**69.8**	**69.5**

5 Conclusion

In this paper, we propose a method to improve the class activation map via sub-category clustering, context decoupling augmentation and adversarial climbing tasks, which effectively alleviates the impact of co-occurrence on image-level WSSS. The SDA-CAM we proposed learns better feature representations through unsupervised clustering of subcategories, reduces the confusion bias of WSSS under image-level labels via the context decoupling augmentation, and is further optimized by the method of anti-climbing. Due to the high cost of labeling for fully-supervised semantic segmentation, WSSS has gradually developed and narrowed the gap with fully-supervised semantic segmentation, which is expected to play a huge role in medical diagnosis and other fields in the future.

References

1. Bearman, A., Russakovsky, O., Ferrari, V., Fei-Fei, L.: What's the point: semantic segmentation with point supervision. In: Leibe, B., Matas, J., Sebe, N., Welling, M. (eds.) ECCV 2016. LNCS, vol. 9911, pp. 549–565. Springer, Cham (2016). https://doi.org/10.1007/978-3-319-46478-7_34
2. Cordts, M., et al.: The cityscapes dataset for semantic urban scene understanding. In: CVPR (2016)
3. Zhou, B., et al.: Learning deep features for discriminative localization. In: CVPR (2016)
4. Su, Y., et al.: Context decoupling augmentation for weakly supervised semantic segmentation. CoRR abs/2103.01795 (2021)
5. Chaudhry, A., Dokania, P.K., Torr, P.: Discovering class-specific pixels for weakly-supervised semantic segmentation. In: BMVC (2017)
6. Wang, Y., et al.: Self-supervised equivariant attention mechanism for weakly supervised semantic segmentation. In: CVPR, pp. 12272–12281 (2020)
7. Lee, J., et al.: FickleNet: weakly and semi-supervised semantic image segmentation using stochastic inference. In: CVPR (2019)
8. Chang, Y.T., et al.: Weakly-supervised semantic segmentation via sub-category exploration. In: CVPR (2020)
9. Lee, J., Kim, E., Yoon, S.: Anti-adversarially manipulated attributions for weakly and semi-supervised semantic segmentation. In: CVPR (2021)
10. Ahn, J., Cho, S., Kwak, S.: Weakly supervised learning of instance segmentation with inter-pixel relations. In: CVPR, pp. 2209–2218 (2019)
11. Singh, K.K., Yong, J.L.: Hide-and-seek: forcing a network to be meticulous for weakly-supervised object and action localization. In: ICCV (2017)
12. Wei, Y., et al.: Object region mining with adversarial erasing: a simple classification to semantic segmentation approach. In: CVPR (2017)
13. Zhang, X., et al.: Adversarial complementary learning for weakly supervised object localization. CoRR abs/1804.06962 (2018)
14. Li, K., et al.: Tell me where to look: guided attention inference network. In: CVPR (2018)
15. Hou, Q., et al.: Self-erasing network for integral object attention. CoRR abs/1810.09821 (2018)
16. Kim, B., Kim, S.: Discriminative region suppression for weakly-supervised semantic segmentation. CoRR abs/2103.07246 (2021)

17. Kolesnikov, A., Lampert, C.H.: Seed, expand and constrain: three principles for weakly-supervised image segmentation. In: Leibe, B., Matas, J., Sebe, N., Welling, M. (eds.) ECCV 2016. LNCS, vol. 9908, pp. 695–711. Springer, Cham (2016). https://doi.org/10.1007/978-3-319-46493-0_42
18. Wang, X., et al.: Weakly-supervised semantic segmentation by iteratively mining common object features. In: CVPR (2018)
19. Wei, Y., et al.: Revisiting dilated convolution: a simple approach for weakly- and semi-supervised semantic segmentation. In: CVPR, pp. 7268–7277 (2018)
20. Huang, Z., et al.: Weakly-supervised semantic segmentation network with deep seeded region growing. In: CVPR (2018)
21. Ma, T., Zhang, A.: AffinityNet: semi-supervised few-shot learning for disease type prediction. CoRR abs/1805.08905 (2018)
22. He, K., et al.: Deep residual learning for image recognition. In: CVPR, pp. 770–778 (2016)
23. Everingham, M., et al.: The pascal visual object classes challenge. Int. J. Comput. Vis. **88**(2), 303–338 (2010)
24. Hariharan, B., et al.: Semantic contours from inverse detectors. In: ICCV (2011)
25. Chen, L.C., et al.: DeepLab: semantic image segmentation with deep convolutional nets, atrous convolution, and fully connected CRFs. IEEE Trans. Pattern Anal. Mach. Intell. **40**(4), 834–848 (2018)
26. Ahn, J., Kwak, S.: Learning pixel-level semantic affinity with image-level supervision for weakly supervised semantic segmentation. In: CVPR (2018)
27. Li, Y., et al.: Learning dynamic routing for semantic segmentation. CoRR abs/2003.10401 (2020)
28. Fan, J., et al.: Learning integral objects with intra-class discriminator for weakly-supervised semantic segmentation. In: CVPR (2020)

Towards End-to-End Embroidery Style Generation: A Paired Dataset and Benchmark

Jingwen Ye, Yixin Ji, Jie Song, Zunlei Feng, and Mingli Song(✉)

Zhejiang University, Hangzhou, China
{yejingwen,jiyixin,sjie,zunleifeng,brooksong}@zju.edu.cn

Abstract. Despite the numerous developments in image to image translation, further improvement and applications are limited by monotonous datasets, especially the lack of the datasets with aligned image pairs. In this paper, we present the first dedicated paired embroidery dataset, which contains 9k sets of the input sketches and the corresponding output embroidery images. Specialized on this dataset, we propose a new image-based generative approach as the benchmark for automatically generating a preview of the image produced by an expert on an embroidery machine. The key idea is to segment the input image and use the two-stage generation. The first stage trains a sub-generator function within each segmentation region, while the second stage fine-tunes the output of the first stage with a global generator function. Experimental results demonstrate that our proposed benchmark handles this task best, in terms of both qualitative and quantitative measures.

Keywords: Image-to-image translation · GAN · Benchmark

1 Introduction

Apparel customization is a new trend fashion industry that aims to efficiently deliver unique garments to customers. One typical type of customization is the embroidery customization, which has seen increasing demand through retailers such as CapBeast. Providing the customers with a real-time preview of the finished product is an essential aspect of the customization experience. However, it takes tremendous effort to simulate embroidery and produce an accurate preview and there does not currently exist such an automatic embroidery preview system. In this paper, we investigate the problem of automatic embroidery preview, where a customer gives a sketch image as input and receives as output the embroidery-style preview.

Electronic supplementary material The online version of this chapter (https://doi.org/10.1007/978-3-030-88013-2_17) contains supplementary material, which is available to authorized users.

© Springer Nature Switzerland AG 2021
H. Ma et al. (Eds.): PRCV 2021, LNCS 13022, pp. 201–213, 2021.
https://doi.org/10.1007/978-3-030-88013-2_17

Traditional embroidery generation methods [35,38,41] require expert knowledge and graphics technology. They present several issues: how to extract the image content, how to apply various stitching styles, how to simulate artistic effects, and how to generate the stitch sequence used by the embroidery machine. These issues make the process of embroidery preview time-consuming and user-unfriendly. For example, the work of [41] proposes a stitch neighborhood graph to model the interactions among neighboring stitches and adopts several reaction-diffusion procedures with high-level layout parameters.

The appearance of style transfer [17] makes it possible to transfer an embroidery style to an input image. Gatys et al. [7] propose to model the content of an image as the feature responses of a pre-trained CNN, and to model the style of an artwork as a set of summary feature statistics. However, applying style transfer directly to generate embroidery fails to learn the elaborate selection of different stitching patterns to achieve aesthetic and robustness goals.

With the appearance of generative adversarial networks (GAN), image-to-image translation has been applied to problems such as image colorization and transferring segmentation maps. Conditional GAN-based image translation [2,15,26,42] has shown remarkable success at taking an abstract user input, such as an edge map or a semantic segmentation map, and translating it to a real image. We propose a new GAN-based embroidery generation benchmark that works in two stages. We subdivide the input image into regions. In the first stage, we generate locally coherent embroidery preview in each region, and in the second stage, we fine-tune the samples generated in the first stage.

(a) PEmD-Chara (b) PEmD-Cartn (c) PEmD-Sketch (d) PEmD-Real (e) PEmD-Com

Fig. 1. Sample image pairs from the paired embroidery style dataset PEmD.

To summarize, this paper makes the following contributions. We propose a new generative network framework for embroidery style image generation. The training process iterates between the first local generator for each region and then the global generator for fine-tuning. Our proposed approach outperforms other state-of-the-art approaches in all evaluation metrics on an embroidery dataset

(PEmD), shown in Fig. 1, containing over 9000 unique image pairs (input image and corresponding embroidery output produced by a human expert).

2 Related Work

2.1 Traditional Stitching Generation

Focusing on the physical medium simulation problem and based on the field of the computer graphics, a significant number of works aimed at simulating the appearance of various kinds of textiles, including batik [34], knitwear [18], and woven materials [1]. Also, this problem can be treated as a kind of art rendering [5,9,12,23]. Based on this, the related works can be classified into two types: filter-based method and stroke-based method.

There are mainly two kinds of strategies in the traditional stitching generation: greedy and optimization-based. In greedy methods [10,21,22], at each step the algorithm determines the current stroke according to certain goals or image features. The optimization-based methods [6,36] compute the entire strokes together to achieve a global optimal energy or desired statistics.

2.2 Style Transfer

Recently, inspired by the power of Convolutional Neural Networks (CNNs), Gatys et al. [7] firstly study how to use a CNN to reproduce famous painting styles on natural images. Style transfer has been applied into multiple fields, including text effects transfer [31], data augmentation [40] and color sketch generation [39]. After the pioneer work, numerous researchers [13,20,32] are devoted to accelerate the speed of the style transfer process.

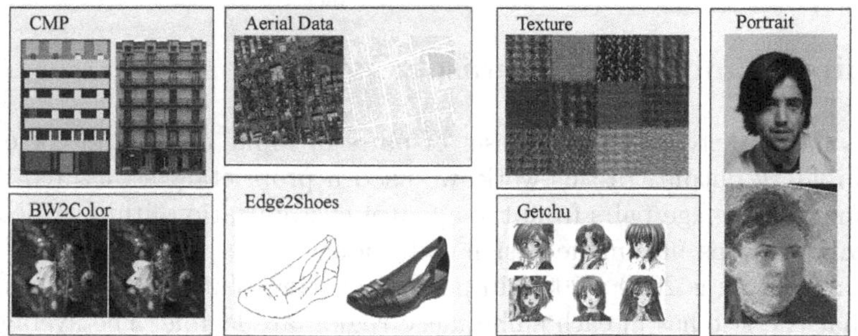

Fig. 2. The samples from the 7 related datasets.

Table 1. A comparison of publicly available datasets for image-to-image translation.

Dataset	Pair	Scale	Description
CMP [28]	✓	606	Architecture label maps to real facade images
Aerial Data	✓	1096	Map to aerial, which are scraped from Google Maps
Edge2Shoes [37]	✓	50k	Zappos50k dataset and edges are computed by HED
BW2Color [25]	✓	1.2M	Data from ImageNet is used for image colorization
Textures	×	120/c	The Oxford dataset [4] composed of various textures
Getchu [16]	×	3.1k	The images contains anime character face
Portrait [19]	×	1.1k/6.5k	CelebA dataset + painting images from Wikiart

2.3 Image-to-Image Translation

With the popularity of generative adversarial networks (GANs) proposed by Goodfellow et al. [8], it has been applied into generating samples in various fields. Especially, Isola et al. [14] investigate conditional adversarial networks (cGAN) as a general-purpose solution to image-to-image translation problems. For synthesizing high-resolution photo-realistic images, Wang et al. [29] present a novel adversarial loss, as well as new multi-scale generator and discriminator architectures. In order to handle more than two domains, Choi et al. [3] propose StarGAN to simultaneously train multiple datasets with different domains within a single network. Note that the above methods study the general image-to-image translation, the uniqueness of embroidery image is not considered.

2.4 Related Datasets

Here we review some common datasets in image-to-image translation. The detailed information are concluded in Table 1 and Fig. 2.

3 Paired Embroidery Dataset Overview

There is no publicly available dataset of pairs of input image and corresponding embroidery output. In this work, we used a proprietary structured dataset consisting of 9k image pairs from the apparel customization firm CapBeast.

PEmD contains 9k unique design-embroidery pairs. More than half of the images' resolution is 2000×2000. In practice, this resolution is enough to guarantee that the stitches in each embroidery region are legible. The average sizes of the input and output image are about 76.9 and 239.5 KB, respectively (a total of over 2.8 GB for the entire dataset).

According to the types of the input images, we split the whole dataset into five subsets, named as PEmD-Chara, PEmD-Cartn, PEmD-Real, PEmD-Sketch and PEmD-Com, the details of which are displayed in Table 2. The five input image categories can be ranked according to the difficulty of preview generation: PEmD-Real > PEmD-Com > PEmD-Cartn > PEmD-Sketch > PEmD-Chara.

Table 2. Detailed descriptions of different sub-datasets in PEmD.

Subset	Prop.	Description
PEmD-Chara	38%	The pairs with characters as input, including numbers, alphabets et al.
PEmD-Cartn	3%	The pairs with the cartoon images as input
PEmD-Real	1%	The pairs with real images as input, usually are the human portraits
PEmD-Sketch	21%	The pairs with sketch input, including simple color blocks and strokes
PEmD-Com	37%	The pairs with the mixture input of the above 4 types

4 Automatic Embroidery Generation

In order to automatically synthesize reliable embroidery-style images, we build the generative network specialized for embroidery translation based on the conditional GAN, as shown in Fig. 3. The main idea of our work is to decompose the whole generation process into 2 stages. In the first local texture generation process, regular and clear stitches are generated by the local generator (Sub G) within each non-overlapping sub areas, which are then grouped into the primary embroidery $\mathcal{I}_{loc}$. Then in the second global fine-tuning stage, the whole image is fed into the global generator (Global G) to fine-tune $\mathcal{I}_{loc}$ to be the final $\mathcal{I}_{out}$.

4.1 Local Texture Generation

As can be seen in Fig. 1, the input images $\mathcal{I}_{in}$ are composed of several color blocks, which often turn out to be of different stitch types in the corresponding embroidery $\mathcal{I}_{gt}$. When using the dataset to directly train the vanilla GAN (e.g. condition GAN), the regular and clear stitches are hard to learn within each unique regions. With this consideration, in the local texture generation, we use a set of sub generators to synthesize the sub embroideries for each regions.

Given an input image $\mathcal{I}_{in}$ with the resolution of $H \times W$, several independent regions are segmented firstly. Note that in most cases, the pixel values of the input images are concrete, it comes out with the satisfying results with the unsupervised segmentation algorithms [24]. After segmentation, the input image $\mathcal{I}_{in}$ is separated into S non-overlapping areas with the masks $\{B^1, B^2, \ldots, B^S\}$, where the s-th region is donated as $\mathcal{I}_{in}^s = B^s \cdot \mathcal{I}_{in}$ for all $s \in [1, S]$. Then in the local generation stage, the sub generator G_{sub} is constructed to transfer the segmented region $\mathcal{I}_{in}^s$ into the regular embroidery block $\mathcal{I}_{loc}^s$:

$$\mathcal{I}_{loc}^s \leftarrow G_{sub}(\mathcal{I}_{in}^s, z, glob(\mathcal{I}_{in})) \quad s \in \{1, 2, ..., S\}, \tag{1}$$

where z is the random noise. In addition to the random noise and $\mathcal{I}_{loc}^s$, we use a global encoder module ($glob(\cdot)$) to add the global information as a part of joint input to G_{sub}, which is consisted of several convolutional layers and global pooling layers. The detailed architecture of the proposed global encoder module is in the supplementary.

Note that for a total of S regions, the sub generator G_{sub} processes the input S times to get all the S generated sub embroideries $\mathcal{I}_{loc}^s$. And for each generated

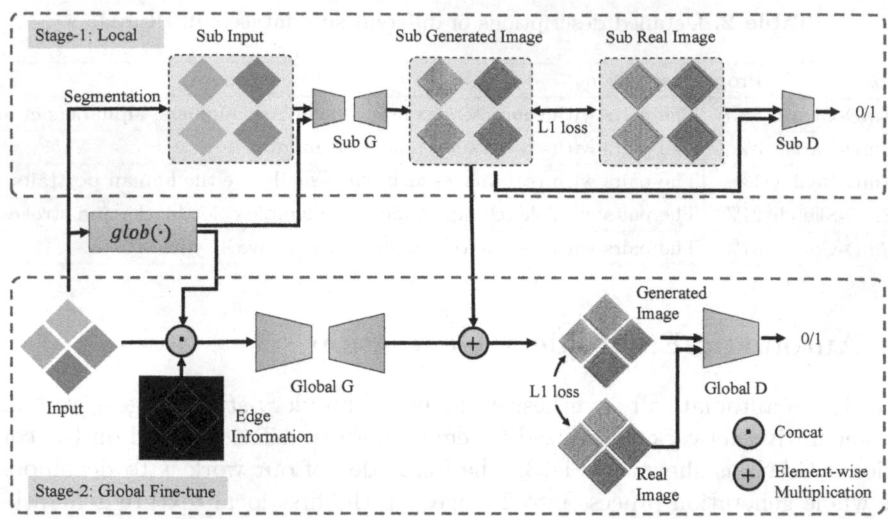

Fig. 3. The two-stage generation of embroidery style image. At the first stage, we train the sub generators (Sub G) within each local segmentation regions. At the second stage, fine-tune the output of the first stage with global generator (Global G).

$\mathcal{I}_{loc}^{s}$, a sub discriminator D_{sub} is applied to distinguish them from the real ones $B^s\mathcal{I}_{gt}$, $s \in \{1, 2, ..., S\}$. Then the adversarial loss $\mathcal{L}_{GAN}^{1}$ in the first local texture generation stage can be concluded as:

$$\mathcal{L}_{GAN}^{1}(G_{sub}, D_{sub}) = \frac{1}{S}\sum_{s} \mathbb{E}_{z\sim p_z(z)}[\log(1 - D_{sub}(B^s\mathcal{I}_{loc}^{s}))] + \frac{1}{S}\sum_{s} \mathbb{E}_{\mathcal{I}_{gt}\sim p_{data}(\mathcal{I}_{gt})}[\log D_{sub}(B^s\mathcal{I}_{gt})], \quad (2)$$

where the discriminator D_{sub} tries to maximize the output confidence score from real samples and minimize the output confidence score from fake samples generated by G_{sub}. On contrast, the aim of G_{sub} is to maximize the D_{sub} evaluated score for its outputs, which can be viewed as deceiving the discriminator.

In addition to the adversarial loss, the L1 norm loss is added to ensure that the generated samples are not only able to fool the discriminator, but also approach the corresponding ground truth $\mathcal{I}_{gt}$. The loss is formulated as:

$$\mathcal{L}_{L1}(G_{sub}) = \mathbb{E}[||\mathcal{I}_{gt} - \sum_{s} B^s\mathcal{I}_{loc}^{s}||_1]. \quad (3)$$

Thus, the final objective for the first stage generation is:

$$\mathcal{L}_{s1} = \arg\min_{G_{sub}}\max_{D_{sub}} \mathcal{L}_{GAN}^{1} + \mathcal{L}_{L1}. \quad (4)$$

Finally at the first local texture generation stage, the complete generated embroidery $\mathcal{I}_{s1}$ is regrouped as $\mathcal{I}_{s1} = \sum_{s=1}^{S} B^s \cdot \mathcal{I}_{loc}^{s}$.

4.2 Global Fine-Tuning

In the local texture generation stage, the aim is to synthesize the elegant stitches within each unique segmentation areas, where the global information is not carefully considered (although we have added the global information as input). With the consideration of revising the primary output $\mathcal{I}_{s1}$, we build a global generator G_{glob} to fine-tune the output of the first stage, especially the connection areas between each sub embroideries $\mathcal{I}_{loc}^{s}$.

In order to acquire the confidence of the generated $\mathcal{I}_{s1}$, we train an efficient patch discriminator to distinguish $\mathcal{I}_{s1}$ from $\mathcal{I}_{gt}$. To be specific, we utilize a convolutional "PatchGAN" classifier, the $L \times Q$ patch discriminator $D_{\lambda\mu}$ $(1 \leq \lambda \leq L$ and $1 \leq \mu \leq M)$, followed the work of [15]. Then the discriminator can be optimized with the objective below:

$$\mathcal{L}_p = \frac{1}{LQ}\sum_{\lambda,\mu}\mathbb{E}[\log(1 - D_{\lambda\mu}(\mathcal{I}_{s1}))] + \frac{1}{LQ}\sum_{\lambda,\mu}\mathbb{E}[\log D_{\lambda\mu}(\mathcal{I}_{gt})], \tag{5}$$

where the optimal discriminator $D^{*}_{\lambda\mu}$ is obtained by updating the parameters to maximize $\mathcal{L}_p$.

After this step, the reliability of the generated $\mathcal{I}_{s1}$ can be measured by first feeding $\mathcal{I}_{s1}$ to $D^{*}_{\lambda\mu}$ and then resizing the output $D^{*}_{\lambda\mu}(\mathcal{I}_{s1})$ to the size of $\mathcal{I}_{s1}$, which is donated as β_{ij} $(1 \leq i \leq H$ and $1 \leq i \leq W)$. Finally the filtering mask M which marks down the unreliable pixels of the generated sample $\mathcal{I}_{s1}$ from the first stage can be calculated as:

$$M(i,j) = \begin{cases} 1 & \beta_{ij} \leq \rho \\ 0 & \beta_{ij} > \rho \end{cases}, \tag{6}$$

where we set $\rho = 0.3$ in the experiments by the cross validation. Thus, the unreliable areas $M\mathcal{I}_{s1}$ are pointed out with mask M and need to be re-processed in the global generator G_{glob}, with the left part of $M\mathcal{I}_{s1}$ unchanged. So the final output embroidery $\mathcal{I}_{s2}$ is the combination of: $\mathcal{I}_{s2} = (1 - M)\mathcal{I}_{s1} + M\mathcal{I}_{glob}$, where $\mathcal{I}_{glob}$ is the generated target in the global fine-tuning stage (the lower part of Fig. 3) with the global generator G_{glob}:

$$\mathcal{I}_{glob} \leftarrow G_{glob}(M\mathcal{I}_{in}, z, glob(\mathcal{I}_{in}), C), \tag{7}$$

where the input of G_{glob} is consisted of 4 parts, the random noise z, the global information tensor $glob(\mathcal{I}_{in})$, the masked input $M\mathcal{I}_{in}$ and the edge map C. The random noise z and the global tensor $glob(\mathcal{I}_{in})$ are in the same definition as Eq. 1. Specifically, in order to concentrate more on the unknown pixels, not the whole input image $\mathcal{I}_{in}$ is fed into the generator. Instead, the filtering mask M masks out the key areas that needs to be focused on by G_{glob}, which shows up as $M\mathcal{I}_{in}$. Recall that the global generator is leveraged mainly to fine-tune $\mathcal{I}_{s1}$, especially boundary and connection regions, we add the edge information by attaching the edge detection map C to intensify it.

Then the adversarial loss for the global stage is rewritten as:

$$\mathcal{L}_{GAN}^2(G_{glob}, D_{glob}) = \mathbb{E}[\log(1 - D_{glob}(M\mathcal{I}_{glob}))] + \mathbb{E}[\log D_{glob}(M\mathcal{I}_{gt})]. \quad (8)$$

Then the optimal generator G_{glob} can be learned by the objective function:

$$\mathcal{L}_{s2} = \arg \min_{G_{glob}} \max_{D_{glob}} \mathcal{L}_{GAN}^2 + \mathcal{L}_{L1}(G_{glob}), \quad (9)$$

where $\mathcal{L}_{L1}(G_{glob}) = \mathbb{E}[M \cdot ||\mathcal{I}_{gt} - \mathcal{I}_{glob}||_1]$, which is the L1 norm loss defined in Eq. 3. The loss of the second global fine-tuning stage $\mathcal{L}_{s2}$ is calculated based on the unknown pixels left in the first stage.

After obtaining the optimal generator in the first and the second stage (G_{sub}^* and G_{glob}^*), the final output is produced by these two generators as:

$$\mathcal{I}_{out} = \mathcal{I}_{s2} = (1 - M)G_{sub}^* + MG_{glob}^*, \quad (10)$$

by which, the generated embroidery not only has local consistent stitches but also clear boundaries. The whole algorithm of the two stage embroidery style generation will be given in the supplementary.

5 Experiments

In this section, we first describe our experimental settings and then show the results with the ablation study and the comparisons with other methods. And more details and experimental results are in the supplementary.

5.1 Experimental Setting

All the experiments are done on the proposed PEmD dataset, which is split into the training set with 8k pairs and the testing set with 1k pairs. The images in PEmD are not in the same resolution, and we resize them to 256 × 256 in the implementation. We build the two-stage generation architecture modified from condition GAN. The entire network is trained on the TensorFlow platform with an NVIDIA M6000 GPU of 24G memory. All models are optimized using Adam optimizer. During the training process, we use a batch size of 16. The learning rate is initialized to 0.0002 and exponentially decease after 50k iterations of training for both the two stages of generation. The numbers of training iterations of the first local texture generation stage and the second global fine-tuning stage are set to be 50k and 80k, respectively.

5.2 Evaluation Metrics

PSNR. (higher is better) Peak Signal-to-Noise Ratio (PSNR) is used to measure the similarity between the generated image $\mathcal{I}$ and the corresponding ground-truth $\mathcal{I}_{gt}$. **SSIM.** (higher is better) The Structural similarity metric (SSIM) [33] is used to measure the similarity between generated image $\mathcal{I}$ and ground truth $\mathcal{I}_{gt}$. **FID Evaluation.** (lower is better) To evaluate the quality of the generated images, the FID [11] metric is utilized, the main idea of which is to measure the distance between the generated distribution and the real one through features extracted by Inception Network [27].

5.3 Experimental Results

Compare with SOTA. We compare the performance of the proposed benchmark with three popular image translation methods, which are: **Pix2pix** [15], the original conditional adversarial networks; **CycleGAN** [42], the network that learns unpaired image-to-image translation; **Pix2pixHD** [30], the network for synthesizing high-resolution photo-realistic images.

Table 3. Quantitative comparisons with state-of-the-art methods evaluated on using three different criterions. From the top to bottom the results are evaluated on PEmD-Chara, PEmD-Cartn, PEmD-Real, PEmD-Sketch, PEmD-Com and the whole PEmD.

	Pix2pix	CycleGAN	Pix2pixHD	Ours
PSNR(db)↑	20.73	19.46	22.27	**24.34**
SSIM↑	0.7345	0.7537	0.8234	**0.8902**
FID↓	16.29	15.48	12.34	**11.07**
PSNR(db)↑	15.59	12.68	18.30	**19.08**
SSIM↑	0.6734	0.3248	0.6923	**0.7155**
FID↓	21.33	20.90	**18.71**	18.85
PSNR(db)↑	12.39	10.58	**14.90**	14.59
SSIM↑	0.5456	0.4385	**0.6738**	0.6766
FID↓	22.35	21.48	**20.56**	20.88
PSNR(db)↑	20.67	19.01	21.98	**25.30**
SSIM↑	0.6989	0.6885	0.7537	**0.8605**
FID↓	18.43	19.99	15.36	**11.52**
PSNR(db)↑	18.43	17.86	20.94	**22.20**
SSIM↑	0.6883	0.6325	0.7210	**0.7359**
FID↓	20.08	21.29	19.11	**15.75**
PSNR(db)↑	19.63	18.48	21.52	**23.49**
SSIM↑	0.7062	0.6791	0.7654	**0.8194**
FID↓	18.35	18.77	15.75	**13.22**

Table 4. Ablation study on the proposed two-stage generation model. And we show the effectiveness of the components in the benchmark.

	Baseline	o/Edge	o/Glob	Benchmark
PSNR(db)↑	20.42	23.42	20.80	23.49
SSIM↑	0.7338	0.8138	0.7563	0.8149
FID↓	17.27	13.81	18.92	13.22

The quantitative results comparing with the above three methods are shown in Table 3, where all the methods for comparison are performed in the same setting. As shown in the table, we evaluate the quality of the generated images first on the 5 sub datasets separately and then the whole PEmD dataset. And the proposed method outperforms other methods on the whole PEmD dataset with the 3 criterions by a large margin. Specifically, on the PEmD-Sketch, the superiority of our method is remarkable. The benchmark proposed in this paper does well in all the sub datasets except for the most challenging PEmD-Real, the performance of which can be further improved as one future direction.

The visualization results are depicted in Fig. 4, and our method outperforms the other methods. Specifically, for the samples on the second row, our method shows the extraordinary performance on keeping the shape of the centering characters. And for the input images without the pure white background (samples in the third row), the output embroideries are failed with 'Pix2pix', 'CycleGAN' and 'Pix2pixHD', while our benchmark ignores the unless information of the background and produces satisfying results. Also, we zoom in the samples in the last row, which demonstrate the effectiveness further.

Ablation Study. Also, we have done the ablation study to analyze the components of the proposed method on the whole PEmD dataset. The results are shown in Table 4, where the experiments are conducted with the following settings: 'Baseline' is conducted with the vanilla one-stage condition GAN; 'o/Edge' denotes the model that does not include the edge information at the second stage; 'o/Glob' denotes the model does not include the global information at the first and the second stage; 'Benchmark' denotes the proposed method in the paper with the full setting.

As shown in Table 4, the proposed method ('Benchmark') improves the baseline method a lot in all the 3 criterions, including PSNR(db), SSIM and FID. Another observation is that the add of edge information does not show

Fig. 4. The qualitative comparison. We show visualization results of 'Pix2pix', 'CycleGAN', 'Pix2pixHD' and 'Ours'. Each row represents one testing sample.

significant improvement in this quantitative comparison ('o/Edge' vs 'Benchmark'), but it plays an vital role in the visualization results. And comparing the results of 'o/Glob' and 'Benchmark', the proposed global encoder module is prove to be of vital importance.

6 Conclusion

In this paper, we present the first paired embroidery dataset (PEmD) consisted of 9k sets of the input design and the corresponding output embroidery, which gives a new challenge in the field of image-to-image translation. Based on this dataset, we propose a benchmark embroidery preview method that works in two stages. In the first stage, we train the sub-generators within each segmentation regions; in the second stage, we fine-tune the output of the first stage with a global generator. Experimental results show that our benchmark method solves the embroidery problem much better than others—by measuring PSNR, SSIM, and FID scores on a dataset containing 9k pairs input image and expert-produced embroidery.

Acknowledgement. This work is supported by National Key Research and Development Program (2016YFB1200203), National Natural Science Foundation of China (61572428, U1509206), Key Research and Development Program of Zhejiang Province (2018 C01004), and the Startup Funding of Stevens Institute of Technology and the Fundamental Research Funds for the Central Universities (2021FZZX001-23).

References

1. Adabala, N., Magnenat-Thalmann, N., Fei, G.: Real-time rendering of woven clothes. In: VRST (2003)
2. Beg, M.A., Yu, J.Y.: Generating embroidery patterns using image-to-image translation. In: SAC (2020)
3. Choi, Y., Choi, M.J., Kim, M., Ha, J.W., Kim, S., Choo, J.: StarGAN: unified generative adversarial networks for multi-domain image-to-image translation. In: CVPR, pp. 8789–8797 (2017)
4. Cimpoi, M., Maji, S., Kokkinos, I., Mohamed, S., Vedaldi, A.: Describing textures in the wild, pp. 3606–3613 (2014)
5. Deussen, O., Hiller, S., van Overveld, C.W.A.M., Strothotte, T.: Floating points: a method for computing stipple drawings. CGF **19**, 41–50 (2000)
6. Gansner, E.R., Hu, Y., North, S.C.: A maxent-stress model for graph layout. TVCG **19**, 927–940 (2012)
7. Gatys, L.A., Ecker, A.S., Bethge, M.: Image style transfer using convolutional neural networks. In: CVPR, pp. 2414–2423 (2016)
8. Goodfellow, I.J., et al.: Generative adversarial nets. In: NIPS (2014)
9. Hausner, A.: Simulating decorative mosaics. In: SIGGRAPH (2001)
10. Hays, J., Essa, I.: Image and video based painterly animation. In: NPAR, pp. 113–120 (2004)
11. Heusel, M., Ramsauer, H., Unterthiner, T., Nessler, B., Hochreiter, S.: GANs trained by a two time-scale update rule converge to a local nash equilibrium. In: NIPS (2017)

12. Huang, H., Fu, T., Li, C.F.: Painterly rendering with content-dependent natural paint strokes. TVC **27**, 861–871 (2011)
13. Huang, X., Belongie, S.J.: Arbitrary style transfer in real-time with adaptive instance normalization. In: ICCV, pp. 1510–1519 (2017)
14. Isola, P., Zhu, J.Y., Zhou, T., Efros, A.A.: Image-to-image translation with conditional adversarial networks. In: CVPR, pp. 5967–5976 (2016)
15. Isola, P., Zhu, J., Zhou, T., Efros, A.A.: Image-to-image translation with conditional adversarial networks. In: CVPR, pp. 5967–5976 (2017)
16. Jin, Y., Zhang, J., Li, M., Tian, Y., Zhu, H., Fang, Z.: Towards the automatic anime characters creation with generative adversarial networks. In: NIPS (2017)
17. Jing, Y., Yang, Y., Feng, Z., Ye, J., Song, M.: Neural style transfer: a review. In: TVCG (2017)
18. Kaldor, J.M., James, D.L., Marschner, S.: Simulating knitted cloth at the yarn level. In: SIGGRAPH (2008)
19. Lee, H.-Y., Tseng, H.-Y., Huang, J.-B., Singh, M., Yang, M.-H.: Diverse image-to-image translation via disentangled representations. In: Ferrari, V., Hebert, M., Sminchisescu, C., Weiss, Y. (eds.) ECCV 2018. LNCS, vol. 11205, pp. 36–52. Springer, Cham (2018). https://doi.org/10.1007/978-3-030-01246-5_3
20. Li, Y., Fang, C., Yang, J., Wang, Z., Lu, X., Yang, M.H.: Universal style transfer via feature transforms. In: NIPS (2017)
21. Litwinowicz, P.: Processing images and video for an impressionist effect. In: SIGGRAPH (1997)
22. Lu, J., Sander, P.V., Finkelstein, A.: Interactive painterly stylization of images, videos and 3d animations. In: I3D (2010)
23. Martín, D., Arroyo, G., Luzón, M.V., Isenberg, T.: Scale-dependent and example-based grayscale stippling. Comput. Graph. **35**, 160–174 (2011)
24. Prewitt, J.M., Mendelsohn, M.L.: The analysis of cell images. ANN NY ACAD **128**(3), 1035–1053 (1966)
25. Russakovsky, O., et al.: ImageNet large scale visual recognition challenge. IJCV **115**(3), 211–252 (2015)
26. Sangkloy, P., Lu, J., Chen, F., Yu, F., Hays, J.: Scribbler: controlling deep image synthesis with sketch and color. In: CVPR (2017)
27. Szegedy, C., et al.: Going deeper with convolutions. In: CVPR, pp. 1–9 (2015)
28. Tylecek, R., Sára, R.: Spatial pattern templates for recognition of objects with regular structure. In: GCPR (2013)
29. Wang, T.C., Liu, M.Y., Zhu, J.Y., Tao, A., Kautz, J., Catanzaro, B.: High-resolution image synthesis and semantic manipulation with conditional GANs. In: CVPR, pp. 8798–8807 (2017)
30. Wang, T.C., Liu, M.Y., Zhu, J.Y., Tao, A., Kautz, J., Catanzaro, B.: High-resolution image synthesis and semantic manipulation with conditional GANs. In: CVPR (2018)
31. Wang, W., Liu, J., Yang, S., Guo, Z.: Typography with decor: intelligent text style transfer. In: CVPR, pp. 5882–5890 (2019)
32. Wang, X., Oxholm, G., Zhang, D., fang Wang, Y.: Multimodal transfer: a hierarchical deep convolutional neural network for fast artistic style transfer. In: CVPR, pp. 7178–7186 (2016)
33. Wang, Z., Bovik, A.C., Sheikh, H.R., Simoncelli, E.P.: Image quality assessment: from error visibility to structural similarity. TIP **13**(4), 600–612 (2004)
34. Wyvill, B., van Overveld, C.W.A.M., Carpendale, M.S.T.: Rendering cracks in batik. In: NPAR (2004)

35. Xu, X., Zhang, L., Wong, T.T.: Structure-based ASCII art. TOG **29**(4), 1 (2010)
36. Yang, Y., Wang, J., Vouga, E., Wonka, P.: Urban pattern: layout design by hierarchical domain splitting. TOG **32**, 181:1–181:12 (2013)
37. Yu, A., Grauman, K.: Fine-grained visual comparisons with local learning. In: CVPR, pp. 192–199 (2014)
38. Zeng, K., Zhao, M., Xiong, C., Zhu, S.C.: From image parsing to painterly rendering. TOG **29**(1), 1–11 (2009)
39. Zhang, W., Li, G., Ma, H., Yu, Y.: Automatic color sketch generation using deep style transfer. CG&A **39**, 26–37 (2019)
40. Zheng, X., Chalasani, T., Ghosal, K., Lutz, S., Smolic, A.: STADA: style transfer as data augmentation (2019)
41. Zhou, J., Sun, Z., Yang, K.: A controllable stitch layout strategy for random needle embroidery. J. Zhejiang Univ. Sci. C **15**(9), 729–743 (2014). https://doi.org/10.1631/jzus.C1400099
42. Zhu, J., Park, T., Isola, P., Efros, A.A.: Unpaired image-to-image translation using cycle-consistent adversarial networks. In: ICCV, pp. 2242–2251 (2017)

Efficient and Real-Time Particle Detection via Encoder-Decoder Network

Yuanyuan Wang, Ling Ma(✉), Lihua Jian, and Huiqin Jiang

School of Information Engineering, Zhengzhou University, Zhengzhou, China
{ielma,ielhjian,iehqjiang}@zzu.edu.cn

Abstract. Particle detection aims to locate and count valid particles in pad images accurately. However, existing methods fail to achieve both high detection accuracy and inference efficiency in real applications. In order to keep a good trade-off between inference efficiency and accuracy, we propose a computation-efficient particle detection network (PAD-Net) with an encoder-decoder architecture. For the encoder part, MobileNetV3 is tailored to greatly reduce parameters at a little cost of accuracy drop. And the decoder part is designed based on the light-weight RefineNet, which further boosts particle detection performance. Besides, the proposed network is equipped with the adaptive attention loss (termed AAL), which improves the detection accuracy with a negligible increase in computation cost. Finally, we employ a knowledge distillation strategy to further boost the final detection performance of PAD-Net without increasing its parameters and floating-point operations (FLOPs). Experimental results on the real datasets demonstrate that our methods can achieve high-accuracy and real-time detection performance on valid particles compared with the state-of-the-art methods.

Keywords: Particle detection · Knowledge distillation · Light-weight neural networks · PAD-Net

1 Introduction

Conductive particle detection is the key step in the circuit inspection of liquid crystal modules and its main task is to accurately locate and count valid particles in pad images, then determine whether a good conductive circuit is formed between IC and glass substrate [5,8,14,20,21]. In addition, in real industrial inspection, it is almost equivalently important to achieve an acceptable accuracy and to obtain a fast inference speed. Many light-weight networks have been designed for various application fields [3,7,13,16,18,22]. However, the light-weight particle detection network has been rarely studied, despite its importance in industrial inspection.

This work is supported by the National Natural Science Foundation of China (No. U1604262 and U1904211).

© Springer Nature Switzerland AG 2021
H. Ma et al. (Eds.): PRCV 2021, LNCS 13022, pp. 214–226, 2021.
https://doi.org/10.1007/978-3-030-88013-2_18

In our work, a light-weight and effective network is proposed for particle detection. This network adopts the encoder-decoder architecture, achieving a good trade-off between detection accuracy and speed. The encoder part is designed based on MobileNetV3-Small [3] by using few convolution layers (6 bnecks instead of 11 bnecks) and few feature channels. And the decoder part is designed based on the light-weight RefineNet [13]. Additionally, we use AAL and knowledge distillation to improve the final detection accuracy of PAD-Net. Experiment results show that our network dramatically reduces parameters and FLOPs and can achieve comparable performance with state-of-the-arts. The main contributions are summarized as follows:

- An efficient network (PAD-Net) is specifically designed for real-time particle detecting. The MobileNetV3-based encoder and light-weight RefineNet-based decoder are tailored to achieve a good balance between inference speed and detection accuracy.
- A target adaptive attention loss function (AAL) is proposed to enforce the network to learn semantic features of valid particles.
- Knowledge distillation strategy is employed to transfers a teacher model's information to our PAD-Net. By using this strategy, it can further improve the final performance of PAD-Net without increasing parameters and FLOPs.

2 Related Work

In this section, we will introduce the related works from four aspects: (1) Particle detection methods; (2) Decoder architectures; (3) Light-weight model designs; (4) Knowledge distillation (KD).

2.1 Particle Detection Methods

According to the forms of extracting features, particle detection methods can be divided into two categories: (1) the handcrafted feature-based methods [5,14,21]; (2) the convolutional neural networks (CNNs)-based methods [8,19,20]. The handcrafted feature-based methods attempt to design appropriate descriptors for valid particles. Through the handcrafted features, semantic information extracted is simple and can't well describe detection targets. Moreover, many parameters in handcrafted rules need to be adjusted manually, resulting in inconvenience in industrial inspection [8,20]. The mainstream methods are based on CNNs, which can offer more discriminative features compared with the handcrafted features. For instance, Liu et al. [8] propose the U-ResNet network to detect particles, which obtains better results than traditional methods. Similarly, Ma et al. [19] propose a compact U-shape structure to accurately estimate valid particles, utilizing semantic features at multi-scales. Based on the work [19], GAN [20] is introduced in the detection model, in which the discriminator is used to correct high-order inconsistencies between predicted particles and ground truth, further improving the detection results.

Compared with the existing CNNs for particle detection, our encoder-decoder network is specifically designed for high-accuracy real-time particle detection on industrial devices with limited computation resources. In Sect. 4, the proposed network is evaluated in detail.

2.2 Decoder Architectures

The decoder aims to recover high-resolution spatial information while the encoder models low-resolution category information, and it has been widely used for image segmentation. For instance, fully convolutional network (FCN) [11] forms a decoder structure through simple skip connections, making CNNs transition from classification networks to segmentation networks. Later, FCN networks with different decoders appear one after another, such as U-Net [15], RefineNet [6], etc. In U-Net [15], symmetric decoder (SD) is introduced to integrate shallow-layer and deep-layer information, achieving fine segmentation accuracy. The decoder of RefineNet [6] improves the segmentation accuracy via a multi-path refinement module. In order to achieve real-time segmentation speed, Light-Weight RefineNet decoder [13] is proposed based on RefineNet [6]. In addition, researchers also designed other decoder architectures based on neural architecture search (NAS), such as [12]. As a kind of pixel-wise task, CNNs-based particle detection network also needs a decoder to generate high-quality maps. In our work, PAD-Net uses a light-weight decoder based on the work [13] and greatly improves the detection performance.

2.3 Light-Weight Networks

Light-weight networks mainly focus on how to tune deep neural architectures to make a good trade-off between accuracy and performance. Many effective light-weight networks are based on efficient CNNs architectures designing. For instance, MobileNetV1 [4], using depthwise separable convolutions to design a small network, achieves high classification accuracy. Comparing with [4], ShuffleNet [22] achieves higher efficiency by reducing computation cost based on channel shuffle and group convolution. Based on the inverted residual structure with liner bottleneck, MobileNetV2 [16] builds light-weight deep networks and obtains great performance. After [16], MobileNetV3-Small [3] further utilizes AutoML technology achieving better classification performance. Benefiting from previous effective CNNs architectures designing, our PAD-Net adopts a fast and effective encoder based on MobileNetV3-Small [3].

2.4 Knowledge Distillation

Knowledge distillation (KD) aims to transfer knowledge from a complex network to improve the performance of a light-weight network [1,2,9,10]. For instance, Hinton et al. [2] transfer knowledge of a large network to a small network. In [1], the authors transfer the knowledge embedded in layer-wise features of the complex network to optimize the segmentation accuracy of the small network. In [9], the authors transfer the distinguishing features from the large network to improve the counting performance of the compact network. In our work, we introduce KD into the particle detection task. The structured knowledge extracted from the complex networks is utilized to optimize the PAD-Net, which further boosts the detection performance of PAD-Net without increasing its parameters and FLOPs.

3 The Proposed Method

In this section, we will describe the proposed PAD-Net, including network framework, loss function, and our KD strategy.

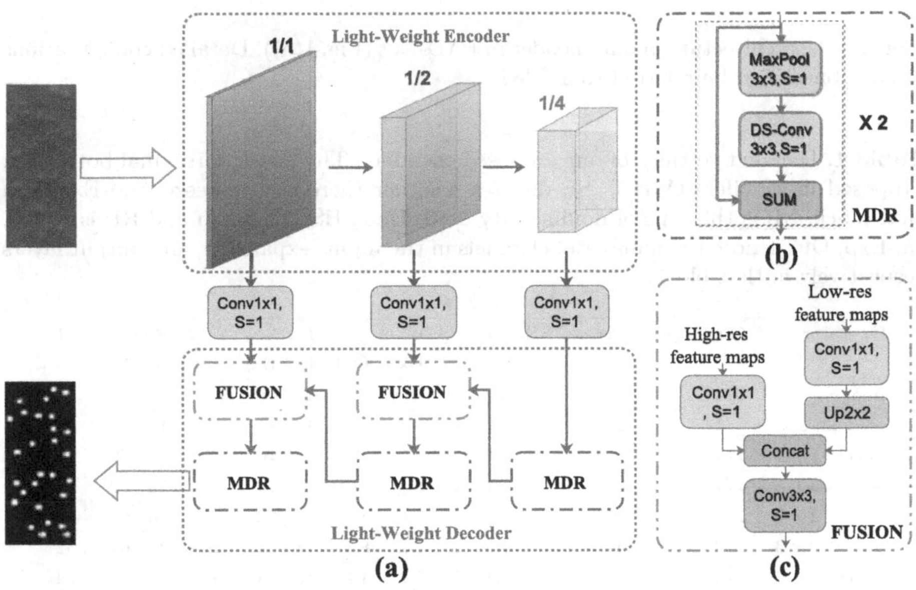

Fig. 1. Overall framework of PAD-Net. (a) PAD-Net consists of encoder and decoder. (b) MaxPool-DSConv-Residual chain (MDR). (c) FUSION module for integrating low-res features and high-res features. (b) and (c) together constitute the decoder in (a).

3.1 Network Framework

The PAD-Net adopts the light-weight encoder-decoder framework, as shown in Fig. 1. The encoder MobileNetV3-Small [3] is specifically designed for real-time classification, with significantly reduced memory footprint and improved classification accuracy. To reduce both parameters and FLOPs to satisfy the demands of real industrial detection, we choose MobileNetV3-Small [3] as the encoder and adjust it specifically for particle detection. Through experiments, we find that using 6 bnecks instead of 11 can obtain a better trade-off between accuracy and parameters. Specifically, compared with MobileNetV3-Small-11bnecks (Mv3-11BN), MobileNetV3-Small-6bnecks (Mv3-6BN) reduces 50% parameters and over 55% FLOPs with a trivial drop of accuracy. In addition, we further compress Mv3-6BN by reducing the number of channels to find an optimal balance between inference performance and accuracy. Comparing with the encoder Mv3-6BN, Our encoder in PAD-Net reduces over 95% parameters and over 90% FLOPs with a tolerable drop of accuracy. The detail of the encoder in PAD-Net is shown in Fig. 2.

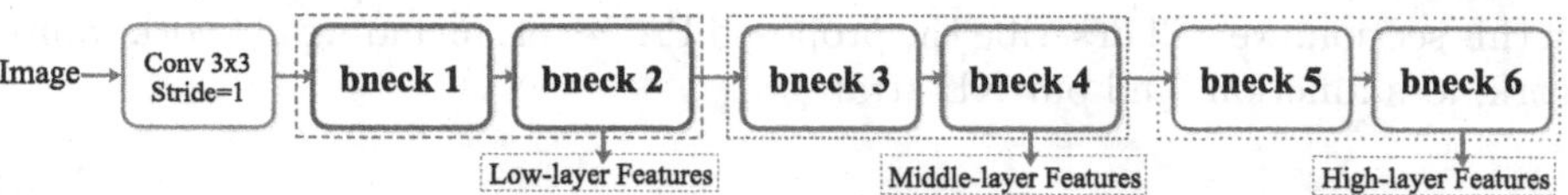

Fig. 2. The architecture of our encoder in PAD-Net (Fig. 1(a)). Detailed configurations of each bneck can be referred to Table 1.

Table 1. Different settings of our proposed encoders. The bneck is residual bottleneck proposed in MobileNetV3 [3]. SE denotes whether there is a Squeeze-And-Excite in that block. NL is the type of nonlinearity used. Here, HS is h-swish and RE is ReLU. In, Exp, Out denote the number of channels in the input, expansion, and output layers respectively in that block.

Operator	OutputSize	Stride	SE	NL	PAD-Net			PAD-Net×2			PAD-Net×4		
					In	Exp	Out	In	Exp	Out	In	Exp	Out
Image	1/1	–	–	–	1	–	–	1	–	–	1	–	–
conv2d, 3 × 3	1/1	1	–	HS	1	–	2	1	–	4	1	–	8
bneck, 3 × 3	1/1	1	✓	RE	2	8	4	4	16	8	8	32	16
bneck, 3 × 3	1/1	1	–	RE	4	8	4	8	16	8	16	32	16
bneck, 3 × 3	1/2	2	✓	HS	4	16	8	8	32	16	16	64	32
bneck, 3 × 3	1/2	1	✓	HS	8	16	8	16	32	16	32	64	32
bneck, 3 × 3	1/4	2	✓	HS	8	32	16	16	64	32	32	128	64
bneck, 3 × 3	1/4	1	✓	HS	16	32	16	32	64	32	64	128	64

In our decoder, we incorporate multi-scale semantic features to distinguish valid particles. The high-layer semantic features, middle-layer features, and low-layer spatial details from the encoder are integrated into the decoder for improving the detection performance. Inspired by [13], our decoder consists of three MDR and two FUSION modules, as shown in Fig. 1(a). The decoding process of PAD-Net starts with the last output of the encoder. High-layer semantic features are fed into MDR through conv1×1 operation (Fig. 1). The subsequent results are sent into a FUSION module along with middle-layer features. Inside FUSION module (Fig. 1(c)), each path is convolved with conv1×1. Then, the semantic features with low-resolution are up-sampled to the high-resolution and merge with spatial details with high-resolution by Concat operation. Two paths are then convolved with conv3×3, and analogously further propagated through subsequent MDR and FUSION modules until the desired resolution is reached. Compared with the light-weight RefineNet decoder, our decoder can obtain better detection performance with lower FLOPs and fewer parameters. In addition, we also try to use different decoder sizes by changing the number of feature channels to find a better balance between efficiency and accuracy. The number of channels in our decoder is all set to 4. And the number of channels in our decoder+ is 4 times that of our decoder.

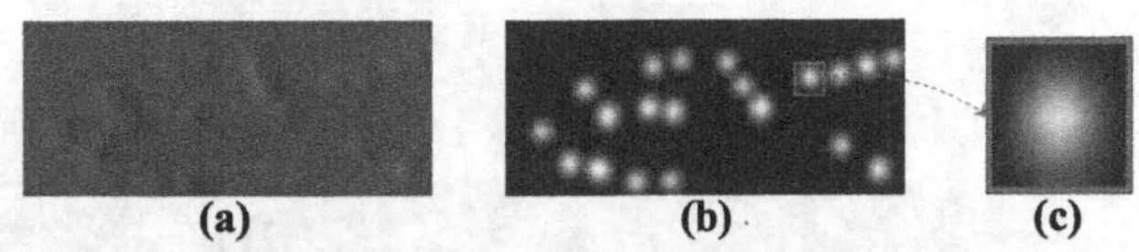

Fig. 3. The visualization of the adaptive coefficient matrix M. (a) Input image. (b) The global value distribution of M, corresponding to the distribution of particles in (a). (c) The local magnification of M: the attention at the particle center is the strongest.

3.2 Loss Function

To solve the unbalanced number of pixels between particles and background, the AAL is proposed to make the model put more focus on the particle regions. AAL loss is defined as: $L = \alpha_1 \cdot L_{CE} + \alpha_2 \cdot L_{IoU}$, where α_1, α_2 are weight coefficients.

The first item in AAL loss, is cross-entropy loss, which is defined as:

$$L_{CE} = -\frac{1}{wh} \sum_{x=0}^{w-1} \sum_{y=0}^{h-1} \left(p\left(x,y\right) \log\left(\hat{p}\left(x,y\right)\right) + \left(1 - p\left(x,y\right)\right) \log\left(1 - \hat{p}\left(x,y\right)\right)\right) \quad (1)$$

where h, w denote the size of image, $\hat{p}\left(x,y\right)$ and $p\left(x,y\right)$ are the output at a specific location (x,y) of the prediction and ground truth, respectively.

The second item in AAL loss, is pixel-level IoU loss with the target adaptive attention coefficient matrix M. L_{IoU} is defined as:

$$L_{IoU} = \frac{1}{wh} \sum_{x=0}^{w-1} \sum_{y=0}^{h-1} M_{x,y} \left(1 - \frac{p(x,y) \cdot \hat{p}(x,y) + \varepsilon}{p(x,y) + \hat{p}(x,y) - p(x,y) \cdot \hat{p}(x,y) + \varepsilon}\right) \quad (2)$$

and M is defined as: $M = ones_{matrix} + AvgPool\left(P\right)$. $M_{x,y}$ is the coefficient value at (x,y) of M; $AvgPool$ is an average pooling operation with size of 5×5 and step size of 1; P is ground truth, in which each pixel is either 0 or 1; $ones_{matrix}$ has the same size as P, and its all values are 1.

In the training, the coefficients in M are adjusted adaptively according to two aspects: (1) the global distribution of particles in P; (2) the local distribution of particle center. At the global level, as shown in Fig. 3(b), the value distribution in M is self-adaptive to the spatial distribution of valid particles in the input image, that is, the coefficients of particle region are larger than that of background, which alleviates the imbalance pixels between the particles and background. At the local level, as shown in Fig. 3(c), the value distribution in M is also self-adaptive to the location distribution of particle center, that is, the closer to the particle center, the greater the coefficient. The coefficient at the particle center is the largest, which can strengthen the penalty for the location deviation of the predicted particle. In addition, we also use other classical loss functions for comparison. Compared with these classical loss functions, our AAL achieves the best particle detection performance. The quantitative comparison in Sect. 4.

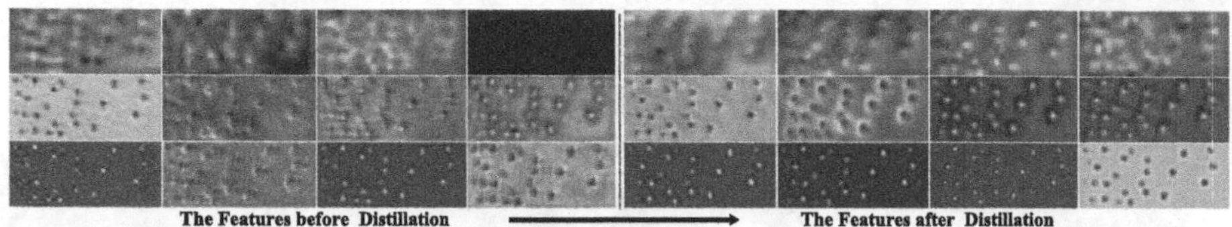

Fig. 4. Comparison of the features before and after KD. High-layer (first row), Middle-layer (second row), and Low-layer (last row) feature maps are from three MDR units of PAD-Net's decoder, respectively. The left feature maps are obtained before KD, while the right feature maps are extracted after KD. We can observe that the features after distillation contain clearer and more effective information. Best viewed in color. (Color figure online)

3.3 Structured Knowledge Distillation

Considering the particularity of particle detection, we need a method to transfer the structured knowledge of discriminative semantics and spatial details of particles. Since the intra-layer and cross-layer knowledge distillation [9] can more effectively transfer the structured knowledge of semantics and spatial details, we directly use this special knowledge distillation strategy for optimizing our PAD-Net. First, we build a complex teacher network, in which the encoder employs the original MobileNetV3-Small [3] without the last classification structure. And the decoder uses the original light-weight RefineNet decoder [13], in which the SUM operation of FUSION module is replaced with Concat and Conv3×3 operations for fully integrating low-res and high-res features.

In KD training, the teacher model is first trained to generate accurate feature labels. Then we obtain different level feature maps after each MDR unit of PAD-Net, as shown in Fig. 4, which are used to calculate intra-layer and cross-layer knowledge losses with the feature labels generated by the teacher model respectively. The total loss is the sum of the two types of losses and used for optimizing the PAD-Net. In the test phase, compared with the PAD-Net before KD, PAD-Net after KD does not increase the parameters and FLOPs, but the detection performance is further improved. In order to clearly show the good effect of KD on particle detection performance, the visualization comparison of feature maps is shown in Fig. 4. In addition, a detailed quantitative comparison is given in Sect. 4.3.

4 Experiments

In this section, we firstly introduce the dataset, implementation details, and evaluation metrics. Then, we evaluate the different encoders, different decoders, different loss functions, and the knowledge distillation strategy. Finally, we compare the three settings of our models with other detection methods.

4.1 Datasets and Implementation Details

As we know, there are no public particle datasets for real detection tasks. We collect pad images containing effective particles from real assembly lines. Pad images are taken by a line scan camera and the size of pad image is 112×48. Our dataset includes 2952 pad images with a total of 73819 valid particles, in which training data has 1952 images and testing data has 1000 images. In addition, input images need to be normalized before being fed into the network.

The training is performed on PyTorch framework and a workstation with Intel Xeon E5-2630 v4 CPU,128G RAM NVIDIA, Tesla K80×8 GPU. In our experiment, we use Adam optimization with a batch size of 8 and a weight decay rate of 1×10^{-3}. The number or training epoch is set to 100. The initial learning rate is set to 1×10^{-4}, β_1 is set to 0.9, and β_2 is set to 0.99.

4.2 Evaluation Metrics

MAE and RMSE: For particle detection tasks, mean absolute error (MAE) and root mean square error (RMSE) are used to evaluate our model, more details refer to former works [9,17].

Precision and Recall: In order to more accurately evaluate the detection performance, *Precision* and *Recall* are also adopted to evaluate our models, which is the same as former works [8,20].

4.3 Results and Analysis

Comparison of Different Encoders. Under a fixed decoder, we evaluate the encoder of PAD-Net against four different encoders, including the MobileNetV2 [16] with 7 bottlenecks (denoted as Mv2-7BN) and 4 bottlenecks (denoted as Mv2-4BN), the MobileNetV3-Small [3] with 11 bnecks (denoted as Mv3-11BN) and 6 bnecks (denoted as Mv3-6BN). Besides, our encoder is also evaluated with different channels (i.e. PAD-Net, PAD-Net×2, PAD-Net×4, as shown in Table 1). From Table 2, we can observe that PAD-Net can obtain a better trade-off between detection accuracy and the number of parameters and FLOPs. Specifically, compared with Mv3-11BN, PAD-Net reduces 98% parameters and over 97% FLOPs with a roughly 7.2% reduction of Precision and 4.0% reduction of Recall. In Table 2, compared with other encoders, the encoder of PAD-Net is more suitable for high-speed particle detection.

Comparison of Different Decoders. Under a fixed encoder, we compare different decoders for fusing multi-scale features, including SD, the proposed decoder (our decoder), and another version with more feature channels (our decoder+). Besides, light-weight Refine decoder [13] with the same number of channels as our decoder+ is also involved in the comparison (denoted as LWRD). From Table 3, we can find that the proposed decoders perform better than other decoders in terms of the MAE, RMSE, Precision, and Recall. Specifically, the computation complexity of SD is more than two times larger than our decoder, but its detection performance is slightly worse. Moreover, compared with LWRD in Table 3, our decoder achieves better particle detection performance with fewer parameters and fewer FLOPs. In addition, compared with our decoder+, our decoder reduces the parameters and computational complexity, but its performance is still close to our decoder+. Hence, our decoder achieves a better trade-off between computational efficiency and accuracy.

Comparison of Different Loss Functions We make a comparison of AAL and other loss functions. From Table 4, we can observe that AAL performs better than other loss functions in terms of MAE, RMSE, Precision, and Recall. Among these loss functions, AAL achieves the best detection performance, which verifies the effectiveness of AAL.

Comparison Before and After Knowledge Distillation. We choose a complex network with high detection accuracy as the teacher network (the details in Sect. 3.3). The structured knowledge of the discriminative semantics and spatial details from the teacher model is transferred into the PAD-Net. The performance comparison of PAD-Net before and after KD is shown in Table 5. From Table 5, we can see the performance of PAD-Net after KD (denoted as PAD-Net(KD)) is better than the one before KD. Particularly, PAD-Net(KD) decreases the MAE by over 0.29, the RMSE by over 0.34, and increases the Precision by 4.93% against the PAD-Net. Experimental results in Table 5 show that knowledge distillation can further improve the detection performance of PAD-Net.

Comparison with State-of-the-Arts. We compare state-of-the-art detection approaches with our proposed models (i.e. PAD-Net, PAD-Net×2, and PAD-Net×4), as shown in Table 6. From Table 6, it can be shown that PAD-Net achieves an optimized trade-off between detection accuracy and computation speed. Specifically, the total number of parameters in PAD-Net is only 0.0057M while the Precision and Recall of PAD-Net can reach 0.8858 and 0.9210 respectively. PAD-Net's detection performance is still competitive. What's more, after knowledge distillation, the final performance of PAD-Net has been further improved, which reaches the Precision of 0.9351 and the Recall of 0.9244, without the increase of parameters and FLOPs. Visualization comparison of detection results of different models is shown in Fig. 5, which indicates that our networks can obtain high-quality detection results, especially PAD-Net(KD), as shown in Fig. 5(m). In addition, compared with the models with higher accuracy, our model achieves a better trade-off between detection accuracy and inference efficiency. As shown in Table 7, we compare the forward inference time of models, for input images (112 × 48), on three types of platforms (GTX 1060, Tesla K80, and GTX 2080), and with two batch sizes (128 and 256). From Table 7, our PAD-Net(KD) is significantly faster than the compared models. It arrives at 0.082ms on GTX 2080 with batch size equals 256.

Table 2. Comparison of different encoders under a fixed decoder, in terms of Params(↓), MFLOPs(↓), MAE(↓), RMSE(↓), Precision(↑), and Recall(↑).

Encoder	Params (MB)	MFLOPs	MAE	RMSE	Precision	Recall
Mv2-7BN	1.82	1484.5	1.1025	1.5489	0.9536	0.9586
Mv2-4BN	0.25	228.8	1.5494	2.1021	0.9185	0.9445
Mv3-11BN	0.44	319.6	**1.0833**	**1.5341**	**0.9545**	**0.9594**
Mv3-6BN	0.22	142.4	1.5230	2.0746	0.9212	0.9490
PAD-Net	**0.0057**	**8.6**	1.9380	2.5938	0.8858	0.9210
PAD-Net×2	0.016	18.5	1.8978	2.4970	0.8965	0.9397
PAD-Net×4	0.052	52.6	1.7930	2.2790	0.9098	0.9403

Table 3. Comparison of different decoders using the same encoder (PAD-Net×4), in terms of Params(↓), MFLOPs(↓), MAE(↓), RMSE(↓), Precision(↑), and Recall(↑).

Encoder	Params (MB)	MFLOPs	MAE	RMSE	Precision	Recall
SD	0.11	173.6	1.9361	2.5812	0.8896	0.9243
LWRD	0.057	61.7	1.8851	2.3693	0.9002	0.9204
Our decoder	**0.052**	**52.6**	1.7932	2.2792	0.9098	0.9403
Our decoder+	0.065	92.0	**1.7441**	**2.2221**	**0.9137**	**0.9428**

Table 4. Comparison of AAL and other loss functions in terms of MAE(↓), RMSE(↓), Precision(↑), and Recall(↑). We use the same detection model (PAD-Net).

Loss functions	MAE	RMSE	Precision	Recall
IoU-loss	2.4783	3.4178	0.8350	0.8976
Dice-loss	2.0006	2.6561	0.8818	0.9130
MSE-loss	2.0247	2.7171	0.8844	0.9203
BCE-loss	1.9468	2.5989	0.8814	0.8841
AAL (ours)	**1.9380**	**2.5938**	**0.8858**	**0.9210**

Table 5. Comparison of PAD-Net model before and after knowledge distillation.

Models	Params (MB)	MFLOPs	MAE	RMSE	Precision	Recall
Teacher Net	0.4697	422.5	**0.8539**	**1.2884**	**0.9673**	**0.9797**
PAD-Net	**0.0057**	**8.6**	1.9380	2.5938	0.8858	0.9210
PAD-Net (KD)	**0.0057**	**8.6**	1.6453	2.2480	0.9351	0.9244

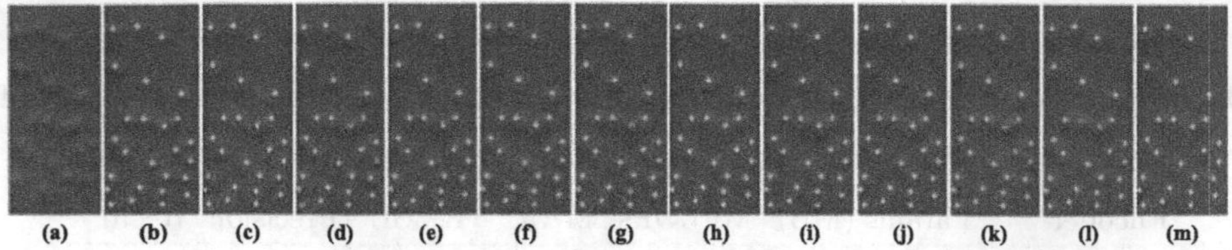

Fig. 5. Examples of particle detection results from different models. (a) Input image; (b) Particle center in Ground truth; (c) U-Net; (d) U-ResNet; (e) U-MultiNet; (f) MV2-7BN; (g) MV2-4BN; (h) MV3-11BN; (i) MV3-6BN; (j) PAD-Net×4; (k) PAD-Net×2; (l) PAD-Net; (m) PAD-Net(KD). Best viewed in color. (Color figure online)

Table 6. Comparison of different detection methods in terms of Params(↓), MFLOPs(↓), MAE(↓), RMSE(↓), Precision(↑), and Recall(↑).

Models	Params (MB)	MFLOPs	MAE	RMSE	Precision	Recall
U-Net	0.0086	4.4	2.4935	3.2949	0.8502	0.8913
U-ResNet [8]	0.0125	7.3	2.1873	2.9012	0.8685	0.8929
U-MultiNet [20]	0.0297	48.4	1.9358	2.5780	0.8874	0.9333
Mv2-7BN	1.82	1484.5	1.1025	1.5489	0.9536	0.9586
Mv2-4BN	0.25	228.8	1.5494	2.1021	0.9185	0.9445
Mv3-11BN	0.44	319.6	**1.0833**	**1.5341**	**0.9545**	**0.9594**
Mv3-6BN	0.22	142.4	1.5230	2.0746	0.9212	0.9490
PAD-Net	**0.0057**	**8.6**	1.9380	2.5938	0.8858	0.9210
PAD-Net×2	0.016	18.5	1.8978	2.4970	0.8965	0.9397
PAD-Net×4	0.052	52.6	1.7930	2.2790	0.9098	**0.9403**
PAD-Net (KD)	**0.0057**	**8.6**	**1.6453**	**2.2480**	**0.9351**	0.9244

Table 7. Comparison of the forward inference times of different models on three types of platforms (GTX 1060, Tesla K80, and GTX 2080).

Models	GTX1060 (ms)		Tesla K80 (ms)		GTX2080 (ms)	
	batchsize128	batchsize256	batchsize128	batchsize256	batchsize128	batchsize256
Mv2-7BN	5.270	5.336	7.269	7.228	1.755	1.758
Mv2-4BN	1.516	1.514	1.970	1.976	0.496	0.494
Mv3-11BN	2.674	2.671	3.505	3.502	0.903	0.901
Mv3-6BN	1.202	1.199	1.444	1.440	0.424	0.422
PAD-Net×4	0.693	0.689	0.854	0.842	0.243	0.241
PAD-Net×2	0.404	0.400	0.496	0.487	0.137	0.135
PAD-Net	**0.264**	**0.259**	**0.332**	**0.324**	**0.086**	**0.082**
PAD-Net (KD)	**0.264**	**0.259**	**0.332**	**0.324**	**0.086**	**0.082**

5 Conclusion

In this paper, we present a light-weight encoder-decoder network for efficient and real-time particle detection, named PAD-Net. The encoder and decoder of PAD-Net are designed to strike an optimal balance between detection accuracy and inference speed. Besides, we propose a target Adaptive Attentional Loss function to train the PAD-Net, which makes the network concentrate on learning the features of valid particles. In addition, the knowledge distillation method is introduced into the training model, which further boosts the final detection performance of PAD-Net without increasing parameters and FLOPs. Extensive experiments demonstrate that our method achieves comparable particle detection performance by using fewer computation resources.

References

1. He, T., Shen, C., Tian, Z., Gong, D., Sun, C., Yan, Y.: Knowledge adaptation for efficient semantic segmentation. In: IEEE Conference on Computer Vision and Pattern Recognition, CVPR 2019, Long Beach, CA, USA, 16–20 June 2019, pp. 578–587 (2019)
2. Hinton, G.E., Vinyals, O., Dean, J.: Distilling the knowledge in a neural network. CoRR arXiv:abs/1503.02531 (2015)
3. Howard, A., et al.: Searching for mobilenetv3. In: 2019 IEEE/CVF International Conference on Computer Vision (ICCV) (2020)
4. Howard, A.G., et al.: MobileNets: efficient convolutional neural networks for mobile vision applications. CoRR arXiv:abs/1704.04861 (2017)
5. Lin, C.S., Lu, K.H.H., Lin, T.C., Shei, H.J., Tien, C.L.: An automatic inspection method for the fracture conditions of anisotropic conductive film in the TFT-LCD assembly process. Int. J. Optomechatronics **5**(9), 286–298 (2011)
6. Lin, G., Milan, A., Shen, C., Reid, I.D.: RefineNet: multi-path refinement networks for high-resolution semantic segmentation. In: 2017 IEEE Conference on Computer Vision and Pattern Recognition, CVPR 2017, Honolulu, HI, USA, 21–26 July 2017, pp. 5168–5177 (2017)
7. Lin, P., Sun, P., Cheng, G., Xie, S., Li, X., Shi, J.: Graph-guided architecture search for real-time semantic segmentation. In: 2020 IEEE/CVF Conference on Computer Vision and Pattern Recognition, CVPR 2020, Seattle, WA, USA, 13–19 June 2020, pp. 4202–4211 (2020)
8. Liu, E., Chen, K., Xiang, Z., Zhang, J.: Conductive particle detection via deep learning for ACF bonding in TFT-LCD manufacturing. J. Intell. Manuf. **31**(4), 1037–1049 (2020)
9. Liu, L., Chen, J., Wu, H., Chen, T., Li, G., Lin, L.: Efficient crowd counting via structured knowledge transfer. In: Proceedings of the 28th ACM International Conference on Multimedia, pp. 2645–2654 (2020)
10. Liu, Y., Chen, K., Liu, C., Qin, Z., Luo, Z., Wang, J.: Structured knowledge distillation for semantic segmentation. In: IEEE Conference on Computer Vision and Pattern Recognition, CVPR 2019, Long Beach, CA, USA, 16–20 June 2019, pp. 2604–2613 (2019)
11. Long, J., Shelhamer, E., Darrell, T.: Fully convolutional networks for semantic segmentation. In: Proceedings of the IEEE Conference on Computer Vision and Pattern Recognition, pp. 3431–3440 (2015)

12. Nekrasov, V., Chen, H., Shen, C., Reid, I.D.: Fast neural architecture search of compact semantic segmentation models via auxiliary cells. In: IEEE Conference on Computer Vision and Pattern Recognition, CVPR 2019, Long Beach, CA, USA, 16–20 June 2019, pp. 9126–9135 (2019)
13. Nekrasov, V., Shen, C., Reid, I.: Light-weight refineNet for real-time semantic segmentation. In: British Machine Vision Conference 2018, BMVC 2018, Newcastle, UK, 3–6 September 2018, p. 125 (2018)
14. Ni, G., Liu, L., Du, X., Zhang, J., Liu, J., Liu, Y.: Accurate AOI inspection of resistance in LCD anisotropic conductive film bonding using differential interference contrast. Optik **130**, 786–796 (2017)
15. Ronneberger, O., Fischer, P., Brox, T.: U-Net: convolutional networks for biomedical image segmentation. In: Navab, N., Hornegger, J., Wells, W.M., Frangi, A.F. (eds.) MICCAI 2015. LNCS, vol. 9351, pp. 234–241. Springer, Cham (2015). https://doi.org/10.1007/978-3-319-24574-4_28
16. Sandler, M., Howard, A., Zhu, M., Zhmoginov, A., Chen, L.C.: MobileNetV 2: inverted residuals and linear bottlenecks. In: 2018 IEEE/CVF Conference on Computer Vision and Pattern Recognition (CVPR) (2018)
17. Tian, Y., Lei, Y., Zhang, J., Wang, J.Z.: PaDNet: pan-density crowd counting. IEEE Trans. Image Process. **29**, 2714–2727 (2020)
18. Wang, Y., et al.: LedNet: a lightweight encoder-decoder network for real-time semantic segmentation. In: 2019 IEEE International Conference on Image Processing, ICIP 2019, Taipei, Taiwan, 22–25 September 2019, pp. 1860–1864 (2019)
19. Wang, Y., Ma, L., Jiang, H.: Detecting conductive particles in TFT-LCD with U-multinet. In: 2019 8th International Symposium on Next Generation Electronics (ISNE), pp. 1–3. IEEE (2019)
20. Wang, Y., Ma, L., Jiu, M., Jiang, H.: Detection of conductive particles in TFT-LCD circuit using generative adversarial networks. IEEE Access **PP**(99), 1 (2020)
21. Yu-ye, C., Ke, X., Zhen-xiong, G., Jun-jie, H., Chang, L., Song-yan, C.: Detection of conducting particles bonding in the circuit of liquid crystal display. Chinese J. Liq. Cryst. Disp. **32**(7), 553–559 (2017)
22. Zhang, X., Zhou, X., Lin, M., Sun, J.: ShuffleNet: an extremely efficient convolutional neural network for mobile devices. In: 2018 IEEE Conference on Computer Vision and Pattern Recognition, CVPR 2018, Salt Lake City, UT, USA, 18–22 June 2018, pp. 6848–6856 (2018)

Flexible Projection Search Using Optimal Re-weighted Adjacency for Unsupervised Manifold Learning

Yuting Tao[1(✉)], Haifeng Zhao[1,2], and Yan Zhang[1]

[1] School of Software Engineering, Jinling Institute of Technology, Nanjing 211169, China
tao_yuting@jit.edu.cn

[2] Jiangsu HopeRun Software Co. Ltd., Nanjing 210012, China

Abstract. Graph-based manifold learning plays an important role in clustering and classification tasks. Regarding the unsupervised case, the local structure of each sample is vital to the quality of clustering results. Many state-of-the-art methods seek the low-dimensional projection matrix for graph embedding, ignoring the contortion of original local structure in the projected space, which impairs the quality of clustering. To remedy this shortcoming, we propose an iterative leaning approach in this paper, aiming at preserving the original locality in each iteration. During iterative steps, adjacency weights of each currently projected sample are optimally defined by quadratic programming with equality constraints, and in return the upcoming projection matrix that attempts to keep the original locality is flexibly determined based on the current weights. Such iteration proceeds until the objective function value converges. In particular, the proposed approach requires very few parameters, leading to simple operation in experiments. Further, local distances of projected samples could be directly obtained from their inner products, with no explicit calculation of projection matrix in each iteration. We repeat k-means clustering many times *w.r.t* these samples after convergence, and experimental results reveal the obvious better clustering quality of the proposed approach on average, compared to the state-of the-art ones.

Keywords: Unsupervised manifold leaning · Quadratic programming · Flexible projection · Re-weighted adjacency · k-means clustering

1 Introduction

In machine learning field, unsupervised learning is the case with no prior label information to guild how to distinguish or build up relationships among samples.The typical way for this case is clustering [1], aiming at separating samples into groups based on their similarities, i.e. intra-group similar and inter-group dissimilar. Samples' relations interpreted by graph are constructed under the assumption that data lies in the manifold where local ambience of each sample is as flat as Euclidean (linear) space, but global structure is nonlinear. Original samples e.g. images, however, are generally of too high dimensions to tackle with, leading to the curse of dimensionality. In order to facilitate the

© Springer Nature Switzerland AG 2021
H. Ma et al. (Eds.): PRCV 2021, LNCS 13022, pp. 227–239, 2021.
https://doi.org/10.1007/978-3-030-88013-2_19

tasks of computer vision and pattern recognition, dimensionality reduction technique is required, to pursue compact representation of samples and their relations' preservation, i.e. graph embedding [2].

In terms of graph-based manifold learning, there are several state-of-the-art unsupervised methods for dimensionality reduction and graph embedding, such as principle component analysis (PCA) [3, 4], laplacian eigenmap (LE) [5], locality preserving projection (LPP) [6], local linear embedding (LLE) [7], neighbor preserving embedding (NPE) [8] and etc. Yan et al. [2] pointed out that PCA belong to the special case of manifold learning, since it assumes the global data structure lie in the Euclidean space, while others take structure as linear locally but nonlinear globally. LE seeks k nearest neighbors of each sample and attempts to find a low-dimensional space for the preservation of the local structure. LPP takes linear space to best depict the reduced space of LE. Rather than LE which defines adjacency weights by Gaussian kernel as $\exp\{-\|x_i - x_j\|^2/2\sigma^2\}$, LLE determines the weights by assuming that each sample is approximated by the linear combination of its k nearest neighbors, and maps such locality into low dimensional space. NPE is the linear approximation to the space derived by LLE, which therefore can be generalized to the out-of-sample problems. Apart from these, spectral clustering (SC) [9] conducts the dimensional reduction using the technique of LE over the graph built by local adjacency, and operates k-means clustering on it thereafter in the reduced space.

Different from the methods introduced above, some scholars in this area designed linear regression model that approximate the nonlinear low-dimensional projected samples. For example, Dornaika et al. [10, 11] took such model, proposing joint learning framework for semi-supervised manifold learning. Also using this model, Nie et al. [12] proposed projective unsupervised flexible embedding (PUFE). Wang et al. [13] pointed out that original data was likely contaminated by noise, and proposed projective unsupervised flexible embedding models with optimal graph (PUFE-OG), by integrating optimal adjustment of adjacency weights and the update of linear low-dimensional projection. Compared to PUFE with no weight adjustment, PUFE-OG achieved better clustering results.

In recent years, deep learning has achieved a great success in the tasks of recognition. Especially, convolutional neural network (CNN) performs excellently for image classification, which originated from the LeNet-5 model proposed by LeCun et al. [14] in 1998. Inspired by this, Chen et al. [15] combined manifold learning with CNN, where manifold that interprets data structure was embedded through convolutional layers for training process, enhancing CNN's discriminative power for action recognition. Despite of superiority of deep learning, it does not work well for unsupervised case.

From the viewpoint of metric learning, Liu et al. stated in [16] that manifold learning are confronted with a problem in common, i.e. it is no longer the Euclidean distance *w.r.t.* local samples in the projected space, instead is the so-called Mahalanobis. It indicates that some sample's nearest neighbor in the original space will be possibly second or third nearest in the projected space, since the projection matrix could scale the original distances (stretch or shrink), leading to the contortion of original local structure. Hence, Liu et al. [16] provided a joint learning of adjacency weights and distance metric (i.e. projection matrix) for label propagation in semi-supervised learning.

In this paper, we take account of the potential local structure contortion *w.r.t.* projected data, and propose an innovative unsupervised manifold learning approach, i.e. flexible projection search using optimal re-weighted adjacency (FPSORA). It adopts the joint learning framework by integrating the updated projection matrix and the re-weighted local adjacency into iterative steps. To be exact, in each iteration, adjacency weights of each sample in the current projected space are optimally updated by quadratic programming with equality constraints [17], and in return the upcoming projection matrix that attempts to preserve the original locality is flexibly determined based on the current adjacency weights.

The contribution of FPSORA are as follows:

(1) Instead of taking many parameters in some traditional manifold learning methods, the objective function of FPSORA does not need many parameters, leading to much simpler operation in experiment.
(2) Orthogonality *w.r.t.* the vectors of $\boldsymbol{P}$ is not imposed, i.e. such constraint as $\boldsymbol{P}^T\boldsymbol{P} = \boldsymbol{I}$ is not required, where $\boldsymbol{P}$ is the projection matrix.
(3) The updated $\boldsymbol{P}$ in each iteration requires no explicit calculation, since the local distances among newly projected samples can be directly obtained from their inner products.
(4) $\boldsymbol{P}$ calculated by many state-of-the-art methods are model-driven (i.e. eigen-decomposition), but FPSORA seeks $\boldsymbol{P}$ iteratively using result-driven strategy, assuming that the upcoming $\boldsymbol{P}$ is supposed to preserve the original locality without changing the current objective function value.

After convergence, we repeat k-means clustering many times *w.r.t* these samples in the eventually projected space, and take clustering accuracy (Acc) and normalized mutual information (NMI) [18] for evaluation, which reveal the obvious better clustering quality of FPSORA on average, compared to the state-of-the-art unsupervised ones, like PCA, LPP, NPE, SC, PUFE and PUFE-OG.

The rest of the paper is arranged as follows: Sect. 2 introduces the related knowledge of graph construction and metric learning. Section 3 presents the details of the proposed FPSORA. Section 4 conducts experiments and gives clustering results. Section 5 draws the final conclusion.

2 Graph Construction and Metric Learning

2.1 Graph-Based Affinity Matrix

Suppose there are totally n samples represented by $\boldsymbol{X} = [\boldsymbol{x}_1,\ldots,\boldsymbol{x}_n]$, where $\boldsymbol{X} \in \mathbf{R}^{p\times n}$, and p is the original samples' dimension. Let us recall the construction of affinity matrix $\boldsymbol{W} \in \mathbf{R}^{n\times n}$, based on the local adjacency of each sample in the set $\boldsymbol{X}$.

$$w_{ij} = \begin{cases} \exp\left(-\frac{\|\boldsymbol{x}_i-\boldsymbol{x}_j\|^2}{2\sigma^2}\right) & \text{if } \boldsymbol{x}_j \in N_k(\boldsymbol{x}_i) \\ 0 & \text{otherwise} \end{cases} \tag{1}$$

where $N_k(\boldsymbol{x}_i)$ is the realm of k nearest neighbor of $\boldsymbol{x}_i$, and w_{ij} is the i-th row and j-th column of $\boldsymbol{W}$. Besides, it indicates from Eq. (1) that the smaller the local distance $\|\boldsymbol{x}_i - \boldsymbol{x}_j\|^2$ is, the larger the weight w_{ij} will be.

Let $\boldsymbol{D} \in \mathbf{R}^{n\times n}$ be the diagonal matrix, where D_{ii} is the summation of the i-th row of $\boldsymbol{W}$, i.e. $D_{ii} = \sum_j w_{ij}$, standing for the summation of local adjacency weights of $\boldsymbol{x}_i$. Therefore, the following formula holds:

$$\operatorname{trace}\left(\mathbf{XLX}^{\mathrm{T}}\right) = \frac{1}{2}\sum_i \sum_j w_{ij}\|\boldsymbol{x}_i - \boldsymbol{x}_j\|^2 \tag{2}$$

where $\boldsymbol{L} = \boldsymbol{D} - \boldsymbol{W}$ is the so-called graph Laplacian.

2.2 Graph Embedding

If we project $\boldsymbol{X}$ into the low-dimensional space $\boldsymbol{P}$, then $\boldsymbol{Y} = \boldsymbol{P}^{\mathrm{T}}\boldsymbol{X}$ is the projected sample set where $\boldsymbol{Y} = [\boldsymbol{y}_1, \ldots, \boldsymbol{y}_n] \in \mathbf{R}^{d\times n}$. The state-of-the-art manifold learning methods attempt to seek such space $\boldsymbol{P}$, i.e.

$$\min_{\boldsymbol{P}} \operatorname{trace}\left(\boldsymbol{P}^T\boldsymbol{XLX}^{\mathrm{T}}\boldsymbol{P}\right) = \min \frac{1}{2}\sum_i \sum_j w_{ij}\|\boldsymbol{y}_i - \boldsymbol{y}_j\|^2 \tag{3}$$

In Eq. (3), the graph Laplacian $\boldsymbol{L}$ representing the local adjacency is supposed to be preserved as much as possible, and $\boldsymbol{YLY}^{\mathrm{T}}$ is called graph embedding [2].

2.3 Distance Metric Learning

Let $\boldsymbol{M} = \boldsymbol{X}^T\boldsymbol{PP}^T\boldsymbol{X}$, then it is easy to get that:

$$\|\boldsymbol{y}_i - \boldsymbol{y}_j\|^2 = \boldsymbol{M}_{ii} + \boldsymbol{M}_{jj} - \boldsymbol{M}_{ij} - \boldsymbol{M}_{ji} \tag{4}$$

From the viewpoint of metric learning, $\|\boldsymbol{y}_i - \boldsymbol{y}_j\|^2$ in Eq. (4) is no longer the square of Euclidian distance between $\boldsymbol{x}_i$ and $\boldsymbol{x}_j$. Instead, it is the Mahalanobis distance[16], since $\|\boldsymbol{y}_i - \boldsymbol{y}_j\|^2 = \|\boldsymbol{x}_i - \boldsymbol{x}_j\|_{\boldsymbol{P}}^2$. In fact, $\boldsymbol{PP}^T$ in $\boldsymbol{M}$ is not the identity matrix $\boldsymbol{I}$, indicating that $\boldsymbol{P}$ scale the original Euclidean distances between $\boldsymbol{x}_i$ and $\boldsymbol{x}_j$ (stretch or shrink). Therefore, the original distances among $\boldsymbol{x}_i$ and its k nearest neighbors, are possibly scaled to different degrees after projection. Such phenomenon leads to the contortion of original local structure, e.g. the nearest neighbor of $\boldsymbol{x}_i$ becomes the second or third nearest after projection.

3 Flexible Projection Search Using Optimal Re-weighted Adjacency (FPSORA)

As discussed in Sect. 2.2, 2.3, the target of graph embedding is to seek the projection matrix $\boldsymbol{P}$, in which the local structure of original ambiance may be contorted. In this section, we propose a new approach, i.e. FPSORA, trying to remedy this shortcoming. To be exact, we build up an iterative framework by integrating adjacency weights' update using quadratic programming and flexible projection search for original locality preservation.

3.1 Quadratic Programming for Updating Adjacency Weights

Projected in $\boldsymbol{P}$, the adjacency weight of $\boldsymbol{x}_i$ and $\boldsymbol{x}_j$ is still w_{ij}, as shown in Eq. (3), which is defined based on the original Euclidean distance in Eq. (1). In the proposed approach, w_{ij} can be optimally re-weighted in the given projected space $\boldsymbol{P}$, to further minimize Eq. (3). To begin with, we consider that Eq. (3) is equivalent to:

$$\min_{\boldsymbol{W}} \frac{1}{2}\sum_i \sum_j w_{ij}\left\|\boldsymbol{y}_i - \boldsymbol{y}_j\right\|^2 = \sum_i^n \min_{w_{ij}} \frac{1}{2}\sum_{x_j \in N_k(x_i)} w_{ij}\left\|\boldsymbol{y}_i - \boldsymbol{y}_j\right\|^2 \tag{5}$$

As in Eq. (5), adjacency weights for k nearest neighbors of $\boldsymbol{x}_i$ ($i = 1,\ldots,n$) can be reformulated to the following form:

$$\min_{\mu_{ij}} \frac{1}{2}\sum_i \sum_{x_j \in N_k(x_i)} \mu_{ij}^2 d_{ij}, \quad s.t. \sum_j \mu_{ij} = 1 \tag{6}$$

where $d_{ij} = \|\boldsymbol{y}_i - \boldsymbol{y}_j\|^2$.

Lemma 1. The imposed linear constraint $\sum_j \mu_{ij} = 1$ in Eq. (6) does not impair the local structure composed of the k nearest neighbors of $\boldsymbol{x}_i$.

Proof. If $\sum_j \sqrt{w_{ij}} = C$, then $\mu_{ij} = \frac{\sqrt{w_{ij}}}{C}$, so $\mu_{ij}^2 = \frac{w_{ij}}{C^2}$ and such constraint scales the original adjacency weights of $\boldsymbol{x}_i$ to the same extent, i.e. divide by C^2. □

To be further, Eq. (6) can be optimized by quadratic programming with equality constraint [17], i.e.

$$f_i = \min_{\boldsymbol{\mu}_i} \frac{1}{2}\mathrm{trace}(\boldsymbol{\mu}_i^T \boldsymbol{\Lambda}_i \boldsymbol{\mu}_i) + \lambda(\boldsymbol{\mu}_i^T \boldsymbol{e} - 1) \tag{7}$$

where $\boldsymbol{\Lambda}_i = \begin{pmatrix} d_{i1} & \cdots & 0 \\ \vdots & \ddots & \vdots \\ 0 & \cdots & d_{ik} \end{pmatrix} \in \mathbf{R}^{k \times k}$ is the diagonal matrix where the diagonal elements denote the k local distances of $\boldsymbol{x}_i$ projected in the given space $\boldsymbol{P}$. $\boldsymbol{\mu}_i = [\mu_{i1}, \ldots, \mu_{ik}]^T$ and $\boldsymbol{e} \in \mathbf{R}^k$ is the column vector with all the elements 1.

Since f_i in Eq. (7) is the convex function *w.r.t.* $\boldsymbol{\mu}_i$, its optimal solution could be got by letting the first derivative be $\mathbf{0}$, i.e.

$$\frac{\partial f_i}{\partial \boldsymbol{\mu}_i} = \boldsymbol{\Lambda}_i \boldsymbol{\mu}_i + \lambda \boldsymbol{e} = 0. \tag{8}$$

Combining Eq. (8) and $\sum_j \mu_{ij} = 1$, we define.

$$\boldsymbol{A} = \begin{bmatrix} \boldsymbol{\Lambda}_i & \boldsymbol{e} \\ \boldsymbol{e}^T & 0 \end{bmatrix}, \ \boldsymbol{b} = \begin{bmatrix} \mathbf{0} \\ 1 \end{bmatrix}, \ \boldsymbol{x} = \begin{bmatrix} \boldsymbol{\mu}_i \\ \lambda \end{bmatrix} \tag{9}$$

In Eq. (9), $\boldsymbol{A} \in \mathbf{R}^{(k+1)\times(k+1)}$ and $\boldsymbol{b} \in \mathbf{R}^{k+1}$ are known beforehand, where $\boldsymbol{b}$ is the vector with all 0 but the last element 1. $\boldsymbol{x} \in \mathbf{R}^{k+1}$ is the vector consisting of $k + 1$ variables to be determined, in which the optimal $\boldsymbol{\mu}_i$ along with the parameter λ will be obtained by solving the linear equation $\boldsymbol{Ax} = \boldsymbol{b}$.

3.2 Flexible Projection Search for Preservation of Original Locality

Let L_A and L_o denote the graph Laplacian constructed by original weights $\frac{w_{ij}}{C^2}$ (to ensure that $\sum_j \mu_{ij} = 1$ always hold) and the optimally updated ones, respectively. We know from Sect. 3.1 that $\text{trace}\left(P_{t-1}^T X L_{o\_t} X^{\mathrm{T}} P_{t-1}\right) \leq \text{trace}\left(P_{t-1}^T X L_A X^{\mathrm{T}} P_{t-1}\right)$ at the t-th iteration. Our target now is to seek the unknown space P_t, in which we attempt to preserve L_A, meanwhile to keep the value of $\text{trace}\left(P_{t-1}^T X L_{o\_t} X^{\mathrm{T}} P_{t-1}\right)$ by constructing the following equation:

$$L_A^{1/2} X^T P_t P_t^T X L_A^{1/2} = L_{o\_t}^{1/2} X^T P_{t-1} P_{t-1}^T X L_{o\_t}^{1/2} \tag{10}$$

In Eq. (10), taking singular value decomposition (SVD), i.e. $L_A = U_A \Sigma_A^2 U_A^T$ and $L_{o\_t} = U\Sigma^2 U^T$, we get $L_A^{1/2} = U_A \Sigma_A U_A^T$, and likewise $L_{o\_t}^{1/2} = U \Sigma U^T$. Furthermore, Eq. (10) can be deducted into the new metric as below:

$$M_t = X^T P_t P_t^T X = (L_A^{1/2})^+ L_{o\_t}^{1/2} X^T P_{t-1} P_{t-1}^T X L_{o\_t}^{1/2} (L_A^{1/2})^+ \tag{11}$$

where $(L_A^{1/2})^+$ is the pseudo-inverse of $L_A^{1/2}$, because L_A is of rank-deficiency.

The local distance between x_i and x_j projected in P_t can be calculated directly from M_t in Eq. (11), ready for the weights' update in the upcoming $t + 1$-th iteration to construct L_{o_t+1}. Please note that the exact P_t requires no computation, because M_t is known from the rightmost side of Eq. (11).

3.3 Complete Workflow of the Proposed FPSORA

Here the whole procedure of the proposed FPSORA is detailed in Table 1.

Summary. The proposed FPSORA's objective function i.e. $\text{trace}\left(P^T X L X^{\mathrm{T}} P\right)$ in Eq. (3), deceases monotonously as the iteration proceeds. In fact, $\text{trace}\left(P^T X L X^{\mathrm{T}} P\right)$ shrinks after the weights' update scheme, and it is unchanged after X are projected into the space to be searched i.e. P_t in the current iteration t, i.e.

$$\text{trace}(P_t^T X L_A X^T P_t) = \text{trace}(P_{t-1}^T X L_{o\_t} X^T P_{t-1}) \leq \text{trace}(P_{t-1}^T X L_A X^T P_{t-1}) \tag{12}$$

After convergence, the eventual projection matrix shown in Table 1 is:

$$P = (X^T)^+ (L_A^{1/2})^+ L_{o\_ts}^{1/2} \ldots (L_A^{1/2})^+ L_{o\_1}^{1/2} X^T P_0 \tag{13}$$

where ts is the total number of iterations before convergence. As a matter of fact, we directly take the projected data $P^T X$, i.e. $P_0^T X L_{o_1}^{1/2} (L_A^{1/2})^+ \ldots L_{o\_ts}^{1/2} (L_A^{1/2})^+$ for clustering quality evaluation after convergence. It has to explicitly calculate P only in the case of out-of-sample problem.

Table 1. Complete workflow of the proposed FPSORA

Input: The original data set $\boldsymbol{X}$ (**Note:** SVD is conducted to keep 100% energy, if $p > n$)
parameters k, σ, reduced dimension d, and tolerance $\boldsymbol{tol} = 10^{-3}$

Step 1: Construct $\boldsymbol{L_A}$ based on the original local structure, and seek the initial low-dimensional projection matrix $\boldsymbol{P_0}$ using LE[5].
Objective function value $F_0 = \text{trace}\left(\boldsymbol{P_0^T X L_A X^T P_0}\right)$
Loop $\boldsymbol{M_0} = \boldsymbol{X^T P_0 P_0^T X}$, iteration $t = 0$,
$t \leftarrow t+1$
Step 2: Given $\boldsymbol{M_{t-1}}$, calculate local distances among samples projected in $\boldsymbol{P_{t-1}}$ using Eq.(4).
Step 3: Based on distances obtained by Step.2, build up quadratic programming optimization formula as in Eq.(7) for each sample $\boldsymbol{x_i}$ (i=1,...,n), update its adjacency weights using Eq.(9) , to construct $\boldsymbol{L_{o\_t}}$
Step 4: given $\boldsymbol{L_{o\_t}}$, $F_t = \text{trace}(\boldsymbol{P_t^T X L_A X^T P_t}) = \text{trace}(\boldsymbol{P_{t-1}^T X L_{o\_t} X^T P_{t-1}})$
$F_{t-1} = \text{trace}(\boldsymbol{P_{t-1}^T X L_A X^T P_{t-1}})$
if $F_{t-1} - F_t < \boldsymbol{tol}$ or $t > 200$
exit loop
end
end Loop

Output: the eventual projected samples $\boldsymbol{P^T X}$

4 Experiments and Analysis

4.1 Evaluation Metrics

For the unsupervised feature extraction, we cluster the projected samples using k-means clustering by 100 times for each method. After that, we evaluate the average clustering quality using two metrics, i.e. Clustering Accuracy (Acc) and normalized mutual information (NMI) [18].

Clustering Accuracy (Acc). It measures the degree to which the ground truth classes are consistent to the clustering results. Let $\boldsymbol{\Omega} = \{\omega_1, \ldots, \omega_c\}$ be the ground truth classes, and $\boldsymbol{G} = \{g_1, \ldots, g_c\}$ be the clusters. Suppose s_i is the cluster label of the i-th sample and t_i is its ground truth class label, then the accuracy is

$$Acc(\Omega, G) = \frac{1}{n}\sum\nolimits_{i=1}^{n} \delta(s_i, t_i) \tag{14}$$

where $\delta(s_i, t_i) = 1$ if $s_i = t_i$, and $\delta(s_i, t_i) = 0$ if $s_i \neq t_i$.

Normalized Mutual Information (NMI). It measures the similarity between ground truth classes and the clustering results, from the viewpoint of joint probability. Let n_i and $\hat{n}_j$ denote the number of samples contained in class ω_i ($1 \le i \le c$) and the number of samples belonging to cluster g_j $(1 \leq j \leq c)$, respectively. Given a clustering result, NMI is defined by

$$NMI = \frac{\sum_{i=1}^{c} \sum_{j=1}^{c} n_{i,j} \log n \frac{n_{i,j}}{n_i \hat{n}_j}}{\sqrt{\left(\sum_{i=1}^{c} n_i \log \frac{n_i}{n}\right)\left(\sum_{i=1}^{c} \hat{n}_j \log \frac{\hat{n}_j}{n}\right)}} \quad (15)$$

where $n_{i,j}$ represents the number of samples in the intersection between cluster g_j and class ω_i.

4.2 Experimental Setup

Here we introduce three datasets taken in the experiment, i.e. JAFFE Dataset,Yale Face Dataset and ETH80 Object Category Dataset, as well as the parameter settings. for these datasets.

JAFFE Dataset. http://www.kasrl.org/jaffe.html It contains 10 Japanese female models, with 7 posed facial expressions (6 basic facial expressions + 1 neutral) for each model, as shown in Fig. 1. There are several images of each expression, therefore the whole data set is composed of 213 images in total [19]. Each image's resolution is of 256 × 256 pixels, and we resize to 26 × 26 in the experiment.

Fig. 1. The 7 posed facial expressions for one female model, i.e. neural, joy, surprise, anger, fear, disgust and sadness from left to right.

Yale Face Dataset. It is constructed by the Yale Center for Computational Vision and Control http://cvc.yale.edu/projects/yalefaces/yalefaces.html. It contains 165 Gy scale images of 15 individuals. The image demonstrates variations in lighting condition, facial expression (normal, happy, sad, sleepy, surprised and wink). Each person has 11 images with the size 32 × 32, as shown in Fig. 2.

Fig. 2. Image samples of one person from the Yale Face Dataset

ETH80 Object Category Dataset. It includes 8 categories (classes) of biological and artificial objects. For each category, there are 10 objects, with each represented by 41 images from viewpoints spaced equally over the upper viewing hemisphere (at distances of 22.5–26°), as shown in Fig. 3. Therefore, there are totally 41 × 10 = 410 for each

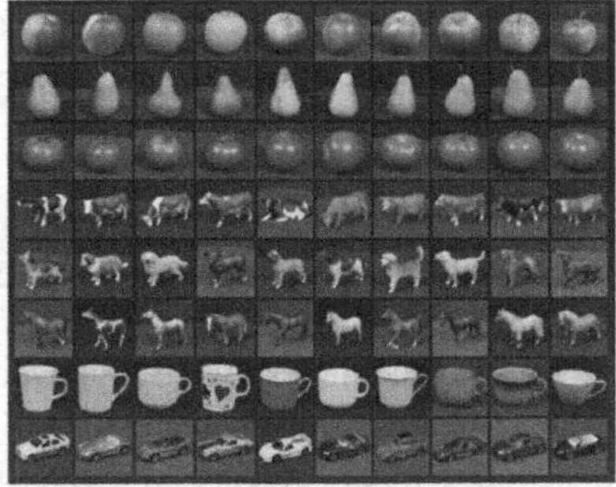

Fig. 3. The example of 8 categories of objects in the ETH80 Dataset

category. More details can be found in [20, 21]. All images of the size 128 × 128 are reduced to 64 × 64 in this experiment. For the computational efficiency, we only select the first 50 samples from each category, so there are 200 in total.

Parameter Settings

Reduced Dimension. The selected dimension d varies within the range [10,20,…,210] for JAFFE dataset, [10,20,…,160] for Yale dataset and [10,20,…,200] for ETH80 dataset, all of which are at the interval of 10.

Manifold Parameters. As shown in Eq. (1), the three datasets, i.e. JAFFE, Yale and ETH80 take the basic parameters $k = 10$ $\sigma = 1$, $k = 2$ $\sigma = 10$, and $k = 5$ $\sigma = 10$ respectively.

Besides, the objective function of PUFE is:

$$\min_{w,b,F} tr\left(\boldsymbol{F}^T\boldsymbol{L}_A\boldsymbol{F}\right) + \mu\|\boldsymbol{X}^T\boldsymbol{W} + 1\boldsymbol{b}^T - \boldsymbol{F}\|_F^2 + \gamma\|\boldsymbol{W}\|_F^2 s.t.\boldsymbol{F}^T\boldsymbol{F} = \boldsymbol{I} \tag{16}$$

And PUFE-OG takes the following objective form:

$$\min_{s,w,b,F} \|\boldsymbol{S} - \boldsymbol{A}\|_F^2 + \lambda tr\left(\boldsymbol{F}^T\boldsymbol{L}_s\boldsymbol{F}\right) + \mu\|\boldsymbol{X}^T\boldsymbol{W} + 1\boldsymbol{b}^T - \boldsymbol{F}\|_F^2 + \gamma\|\boldsymbol{W}\|_F^2 \tag{17}$$

where $\boldsymbol{F}^T\boldsymbol{F} = \boldsymbol{I}$ and $\boldsymbol{S}\boldsymbol{I} = \boldsymbol{I}, \boldsymbol{S} \geq 0$. $\boldsymbol{L}_s$ is the graph Laplacian built by the weight matrix $\boldsymbol{S}$, in which the summation of each row equals to 1.

In terms of all the three datasets, the parameters $\lambda = 1$, $\mu = 1$ and $\gamma = 1$ are taken for PUFE and PUFE-OG in the experiments.

4.3 Experiments and Analysis

After k-means clustering for 100 times, we compare Acc and NMI among PCA, LPP, NPE, PUFE, PUFE-OG and FPSORA as the dimension varies, shown in Fig. 4.

The curves in Fig. 4 tell that PCA is robust to the dimensional variation, and NPE, PUFE and PUFE-OG perform better as dimension reduces. In particular, PUFE-OG outperforms PUFE at very small dimension for all the three dataset, but falls behind when dimension goes up. LPP achieves slightly better clustering quality with dimension going up for JAFFE and Yale, but it takes on the opposite trend for ETH80. FPSORA yields the best results for all the three datasets, which surpasses PCA and LPP for JAFFE and Yale, respectively, as dimension increases. As of ETH80, FPSORA always overwhelms the others.

The best result (mean%± std) of each method is listed in Table 2, with what in the parentheses being the dimension at which each best result is achieved. The bold font denotes the best clustering quality among these methods weighed by the same evaluation metric for the same dataset. Please note that the dimension of spectral clustering (SC) is always fixed, since it directly clusters the n rows of eigenvector set $\boldsymbol{P} = [\boldsymbol{p}_1, \ldots, \boldsymbol{p}_c]$ into c groups, where $\boldsymbol{P} \in \boldsymbol{R}^{n \times c}$ (c is the class number).

Regarding FPSORA, the monotonous decrease of objective function values along with the iterative steps are demonstrated in Fig. 5, consisting with the theoretical foundation stated in Sect. 3.

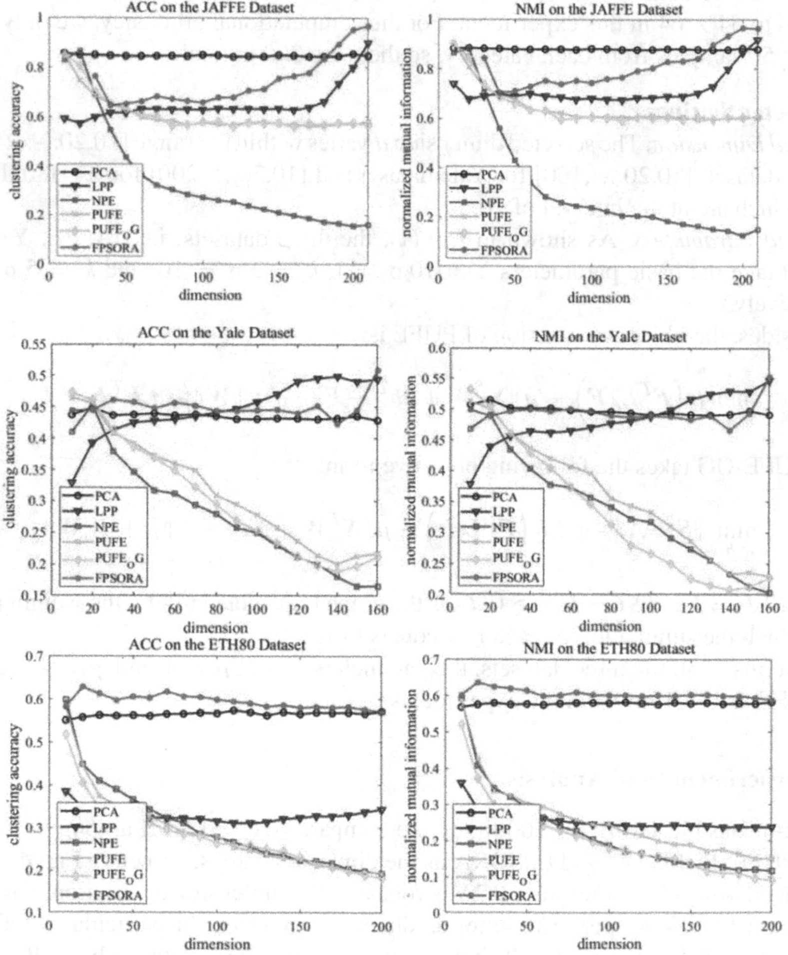

Fig. 4. Clustering quality comparison along with the varying dimension among PCA, LPP, NPE, PUFE, PUFE_OG and FPSORA. Acc (left) and NMI (right) with JAFFE on the 1st row, Yale on the 2nd row and ETH80 on the 3rd row.

Table 2. Comparison of best performance (mean clustering result % ± standard deviation) with the corresponding dimension in the parentheses (**Note:** the dimension of spectral clustering (SC) is always fixed)

Method	JAFFE dataset		Yale dataset		ETH80 dataset	
	Acc	NMI	Acc	NMI	Acc	NMI
SC[9]	76.41 ± 3.15	84.87 ± 1.55	44.65 ± 1.70	51.42 ± 1.48	59.99 ± 0.80	62.65 ± 0.31
PCA[3, 4]	85.34 ± 4.35 (200)	88.43 ± 2.09 (20)	44.83 ± 2.67 (20)	51.50 ± 2.23 (20)	57.04 ± 2.52 (200)	58.21 ± 1.85 (200)
LPP[6]	79.82 ± 2.69 (200)	86.49 ± 1.53 (200)	49.39 ± 2.96 (160)	54.68 ± 2.40 (160)	38.42 ± 0.27 (10)	35.91 ± 0.16 (10)
NPE[8]	86.47 ± 4.24 (20)	88.28 ± 3.23 (20)	45.25 ± 2.34 (20)	49.13 ± 2.01 (20)	59.77 ± 3.61 (10)	59.32 ± 2.98 (10)
PUFE[12]	85.15 ± 1.86 (10)	90.54 ± 1.33 (10)	46.52 ± 1.32 (10)	51.29 ± 1.26 (10)	58.35 ± 2.23 (10)	58.98 ± 2.93 (10)
PUFE-OG[13]	84.98 ± 0.01 (10)	90.04 ± 0.02 (10)	47.25 ± 1.26 (10)	53.22 ± 0.96 (10)	51.62 ± 2.59 (10)	51.89 ± 3.14 (10)
FPSORA	**96.55 ±1.13 (210)**	**96.50 ± 2.16 (200)**	**50.86 ± 3.33 (160)**	**55.24 ± 3.07 (160)**	**62.71 ± 0.44 (20)**	**63.55 ± 0.56 (20)**

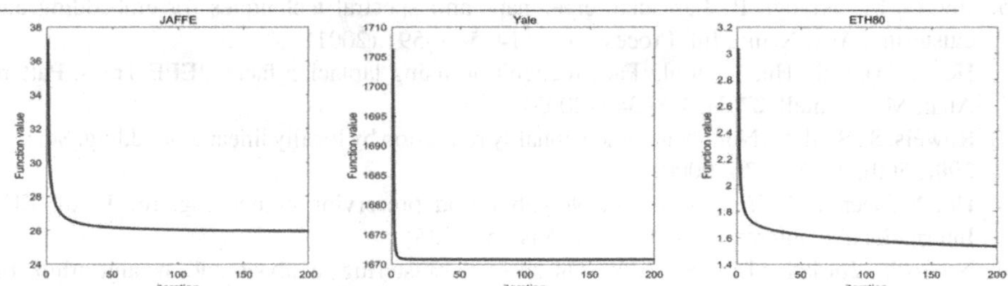

Fig. 5. Objective function value of FPSORA monotonously decreases as iteration proceeds, i.e. JAFFE, Yale, ETH80 from left to right.

5 Conclusion

In this paper, we propose a new unsupervised manifold learning approach named FPSORA, taking account of the potential contortion of original local structure after projection in each iteration. In order to decrease the objective function value in the given projected space, FPSORA updates the adjacency weights by quadratic programming with equality constraints for each sample. In return, FPSORA seeks new projected space that is supposed to preserve the original local structure without changing the current function value. Such iterative steps proceed until it achieves convergence. In particular, the space to be updated needs no exact calculation, since local distances among the upcoming projected samples can be directly obtained from their inner products. Experimental results show that FPSORA achieves better clustering quality than that of other traditional methods, since it attempts to shorten local distances in the reduced space while keep original local structure as much as possible. The most time-consuming part of FPSORA is weights' update, as it is operated sample by sample. In the future work, we plan to adopt parallel computing for computational efficiency, since such update could be independently operated among samples.

Acknowledgements. This work was supported by the International Science and Technology Cooperation Project of Jiangsu Province under grant BZ2020069, Research Foundation for Advanced Talents and Incubation Foundation of Jingling Institute of Technology under grant JIT-B-201717, JIT-B-201617, JIT-FHXM-201808, and JIT-FHXM-201911.

References

1. Chong, Y., Ding, Y., Yan, Q., et al.: Graph-based semi-supervised learning: a review. Neurocomputing **408**(30), 216–230 (2020)
2. Yan, S., Xu, D., Zhang, B., et al.: Graph embedding and extensions: a general framework for dimensionality reduction. IEEE Trans. Pattern Anal. Mach. Intell. **29**(1), 40–51 (2007)
3. Jolliffe, I.T.: Principal Component Analysis. Springer-Verlag (2005)
4. Turk, M.A., Pentland, A.P.: Face recognition using eigenfaces. In: IEEE Computer Society Conference on Computer Vision and Pattern Recognition, pp. 586–591 (1991)
5. Belkin, M., Niyogi, P.: Laplacian eigenmaps and spectral techniques for embedding and clustering. Adv. Neural Inf. Process. Syst. 14, 585–591 (2001)
6. He, X., Yan, S., Hu, Y., et al.: Face recognition using laplacian faces. IEEE Trans. Pattern Anal. Mach. Intell. **27**(3), 328–340 (2005)
7. Roweis, S., Saul, L.: Nonlinear dimensionality reduction by locally linear embedding. Science **290**(5500), 2323–2326 (2000)
8. He, X., Deng, C., Yan, S., et al.: Neighborhood preserving embedding. In: Tenth IEEE International Conference on Computer Vision (2005)
9. Ng, A.Y., Jordan, M.I., Weiss, Y.: On spectral clustering: analysis and an algorithm. In: Advances in Neural Information Processing System, p. 849–856 (2001)
10. Dornaika, F., Traboulsi, Y.E.: Learning flexible graph-based semi-supervised embedding. IEEE Trans. Cybernet. **46**(1), 206–218 (2016)
11. Dornaika, F., Traboulsi, Y.E., Assoum, A.: Inductive and flexible feature extraction for semi-supervised pattern categorization. Pattern Recogn. **60**, 275–285 (2016)
12. Nie, F., Xu, D., Tsang, W.H., et al.: Flexible manifold embedding: a framework for semi-supervised and unsupervised dimension reduction. IEEE Trans. Image Process. **19**(7), 1921–1932 (2010)
13. Wang, W., Yan, Y., Nie, F., et al.: Flexible manifold learning with optimal graph for image and video representation. IEEE Trans. Image Process. **27**(6), 2664–2675 (2018)
14. Lecun, Y., Bottou, L., Haffner, P.: Gradient-based learning applied to document recognition. Proc. IEEE **86**(11), 2278–2324 (1998)
15. Xin, C., Jian, W., Wei, L., et al.: Deep manifold learning combined with convolutional neural networks for action recognition. IEEE Trans. Neural Netw. Learn. Syst. **29**(9), 3938–3952 (2018)
16. Liu, B., Meng, W., Hong, R., et al.: Joint learning of labels and distance metric. IEEE Trans. Syst. Man Cybernet. Part B Cybernet. **40**(3), 973–978 (2010)
17. Boyd, S., Vandenberghe, L.: Convex Optimization. Cambridge University Press (2004)

18. Strehl, A., Ghosh, J.: Cluster ensembles – a knowledge reuse framework for combining multiple partitions. J. Mach. Learn. Res. **3**(3), 583–617 (2002)
19. Lyons, M.J., Kamachi, M., Gyoba, J.: The Japanese Female Facial Expression (JAFFE) Database. In: IEEE International Conference on Face and Gesture Recognition, pp.14–16, (1998)
20. Leibe, B., Schiele, B.: Analyzing appearance and contour based methods for object categorization. In: International Conference on Computer Vision and Pattern Recognition (2003)
21. Leibe, B.: The ETH-80 Image Set. http://www.mis.informatik.tu-darmstadt.de/Research/Projects/categorization/eth80-db.html

Fabric Defect Detection via Multi-scale Feature Fusion-Based Saliency

Zhoufeng Liu(✉), Ning Huang, Chunlei Li, Zijing Guo, and Chengli Gao

Zhongyuan University of Technology, Zhengzhou, Henan, China
lzf@zut.edu.cn

Abstract. Automatic fabric defect detection plays a key role in controlling product quality. Salient object detection (SOD) based on convolutional neural network has been proven applicable in fabric defect detection, but how to learn powerful features and feature fusion for saliency are still challenging tasks due to the complex texture of fabric image. In this paper, a novel visual saliency based on multi-scale feature fusion is proposed for fabric defect detection. First, a Multi-scale Feature Learning Module (MFLM) by simulating the parallel processing mechanism of multi-receptive is proposed to efficiently characterize the complex fabric texture. In addition, Feedback Attention Refinement Fusion Module (FARFM) is designed to selectively aggregate multi-level features for enhancing the feature fusion. In the end, fabric defect detection is localized by segmenting the generated saliency map. Experimental results demonstrate that the proposed method can localize the defect region with high accuracy, and outperform the 5 state-of-the-art methods.

Keywords: Fabric defect detection · Salient object detection · Multi-scale feature learning · Feedback attention refinement fusion

1 Introduction

Many fabric defects maybe occur during the production process of fabrics, such as broken weft, double weft, thin and dense paths, broken warps and jumping flowers, etc. These defects have negative impacts on the appearance and comfort of the fabric. Therefore, fabric defect detection plays an important role in the quality control of textile production. It is traditionally conducted through visual inspections by the skilled workers. The manual detection method can only achieve a detection rate of 40%–60%, and is easily affected by subjective factors [1,2]. Consequently, to meet the high-quality requirements of fabric products, it is necessary to develop an automatic fabric defect detection method based on machine vision and image processing technology.

The traditional computer vision-based fabric defect detection methods can be categorized into structural methods [3], statistical methods [4], spectrum methods [5], model-based methods [6]. Structure-based methods regards texture as a combination of texture primitives, the defect region can be localized by

© Springer Nature Switzerland AG 2021
H. Ma et al. (Eds.): PRCV 2021, LNCS 13022, pp. 240–251, 2021.
https://doi.org/10.1007/978-3-030-88013-2_20

identifying the irregular primitives. But this method can be only applied for the fabric with structural texture. Statistical methods usually adopt the statistical features, such as first-order and second-order statistics to detect the fabric, but they fail to detect the tiny defects or the defects with low contrast. Spectral methods use spectral features to conduct the fabric defect detection in the spectrum domain. However, the computational complexity is high and the detection results depends on the selected filters. The model-based methods model the fabric texture as a random process, and the defect detection is treated as a hypothesis testing problem based on the model. Nevertheless, these methods often have high computational complexity, and poor performance for the defects with small size.

The biological visual system can quickly search and locate significant objects [7], and thus the visual saliency has been widely applied into object detection [8], image segmentation [9] and visual tracking [10], etc. Although the fabric texture and defects are complex and diversity, the defective regions are outstanding in the complex background. Therefore, several saliency-based methods for fabric defect detection have been proposed [11–13]. However, these methods adopted the traditional pattern recognition technology to model the visual saliency, the detection performance mainly depend on the extracted hand-crafted features, and it lacks of self-adaptivity. Therefore, it is necessary to further improve the existing methods and build a robust detection model.

Fully convolutional network (FCNs) based on deep learning has successfully broken the limitations of traditional hand-crafted features [14]. With the powerful feature representation ability that can simultaneously characterize the semantic information and detail texture feature, FCNs has been proved to be effective in salient object detection. Based on these characteristics, some novel architectures have been designed to further improve the performance of salient object detection. Wang et al. [15] developed a weakly supervised learning method for saliency detection using image-level tags only. Li et al. [16] proposed an end-to-end deep contrast network for generating better boundary. Pang et al. [17] considered both encoder and decoder for multi-level contextual information integration. Although these methods have made great progress at present, two issues in fabric defect detection still need to be paid attention to how to extract more robust features from the data of scale variation and how to integrate them effectively.

To address the above challenges, a novel visual saliency based on multi-scale feature fusion is proposed for fabric defect detection. The proposed network consists of three components: Backbone used to extract features, Multi-scale feature learning module (MFLM) and Feedback attention refinement fusion module (FARFM). First, four side outputs are generated by backbone network. And the MFLM module which is proposed to extract multi-scale features by simulating the parallel processing mechanism of multi-receptive, is designed to solve the scale variation problem. Furthermore, FARFM module is proposed to selectively aggregate multi-level features for enhancing the feature fusion at each stage. The module is based on the observations that: 1) deeper layers encode high-level knowledge contain rich contextual information, which can help to locate objects; 2) shallower layers capture more spatial details. Therefore, the proposed method can improve the detection performance for the fabric defect.

To demonstrate the performance of the proposed method, we report experiment results and visualize some saliency maps. We conduct a series of ablation studies to evaluate the effect of each module. Quantitative indicators and visual results show that the proposed method can obtain significantly better local details and improve saliency maps. Ours main contributions as follows:

1. We propose the multi-scale feature learning module to efficiently characterize the complex fabric texture by simulating the parallel processing mechanism of multi-receptive, which can solve the scale variation problem.
2. We design a feedback attention refinement fusion module to selectively aggregate multi-level features for enhancing the feature fusion, which can feedback features of both high resolutions and high semantics to previous ones to improve them for generating better saliency maps.
3. We compare the proposed methods with 5 state-of-the-art methods on our datasets in terms of seven metrics. The results demonstrate that the effectiveness and efficiency of the proposed method.

2 Proposed Method

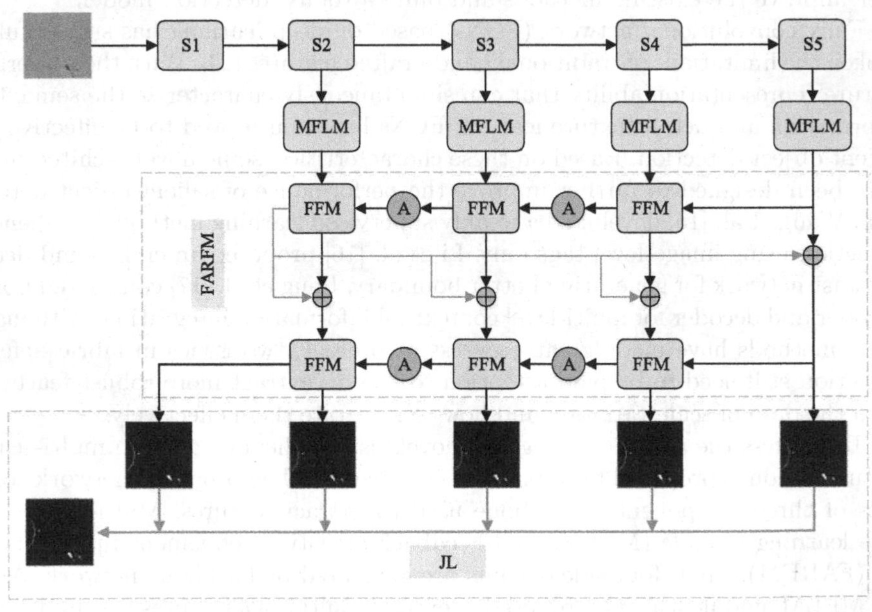

Fig. 1. The overall framework of the proposed model.

In this section, a novel fabric defect detection method via multi-scale feature fusion-based saliency is proposed. ResNet-50 is used as the backbone encoder. MFLM is proposed to efficiently characterize the complex fabric texture by simulating the parallel processing mechanism. FARFM is designed to selectively aggregate multi-level features for enhancing the feature fusion. Finally, five prediction maps are obtained. The final saliency map is generated by the sum of the five prediction maps after the joint loss, and the defect region is localized by threshold segmentation. The overall architecture of the proposed method is illustrated in Fig. 1. And the specific modules can be described as follows.

2.1 Multi-scale Feature Learning Module

The fabric texture and defect are complex and diversity in scale, shape and position, the original CNN network composed of convolution kernels with the same size cannot efficiently characterize the fabric texture feature. Inspired by the visual receptive field, a multi-scale feature learning module is proposed to solve this issue by simulating the parallel processing mechanism of multi-receptive.

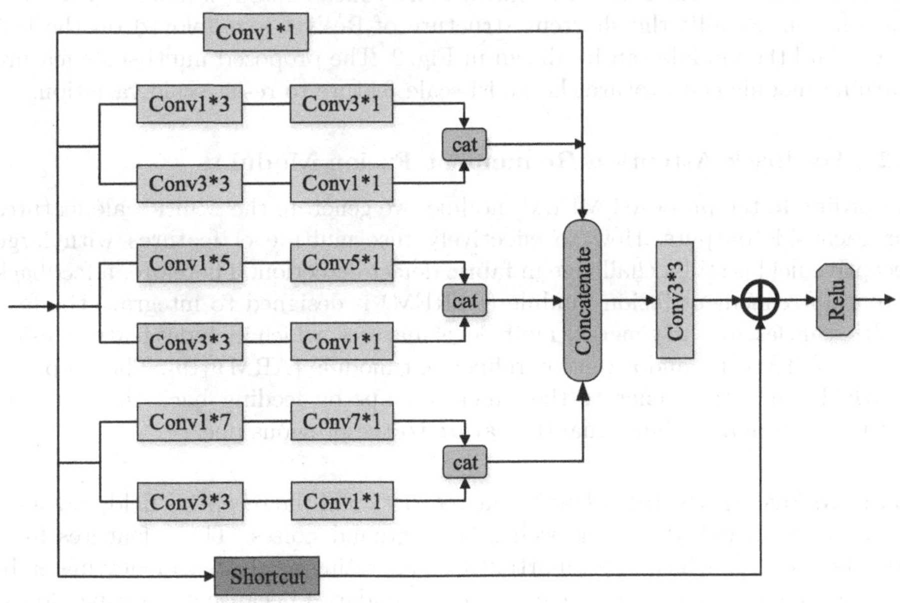

Fig. 2. Multi-scale feature learning module.

Receptive field is one of the important concepts of convolutional neural network. It originated from human neural system and was introduced into the field of computer vision. In CNN, receptive field is used to represent the receptive range of different neurons in the network to the image, or the region size of the pixels on the feature map output by each layer of the network mapped on the image. The larger the receptive field is, the larger the image range it can touch, which means that it contains more global information; On the contrary, it contains more local and detailed features.

Specifically, we remove the original global average pooling, fully connected and softmax layers and maintain the previous five convolutional blocks in ResNet-50 network to efficiently characterize the fabric texture, and denote as $\{f_i|i = 1, \ldots, 5\}$ with resolutions $[\frac{H}{2^{i-1}}, \frac{W}{2^{i-1}}]$. Since the lowest level features is vulnerable to the noises, and have adverse effects on the final detection result, the last four convolutional blocks are used to extract multi-level features as side outputs. For each side outputs, we proposed the multi-scale feature learning module to characterize the fabric texture. And the multi-scale feature learning module have five branches. A convolution with 1×1 kernel is applied on the first branch. Then we adopt the following two ways to assist each other on the 2, 3 and 4 branches respectively. It aims to realize a convolution operation with kernel size of $n \times n$: (i) A original convolution with kernel size of $n \times n$ is replaced by a combination of $1 \times n$ and $n \times 1$ kernels. (ii) Two successive convolutions with kernel size of $n \times n$ to obtain the same channel number and cascaded with the first way. Further, the first four branches are concatenated, followed by a 3×3 convolution. Finally, the shortcut structure of ResNet is employed on the last layer. And the module can be shown in Fig. 2. The proposed multi-scale feature learning module can capture the multi-scale feature to resist scale variation.

2.2 Feedback Attention Refinement Fusion Module

According to the proposed MFLM module, we generate the Multi-scale features for each side outputs. How to effectively fuse multi-level features with large receptive field is still a challenge in fabric defect detection. Therefore, a feedback attention refinement fusion module (FARFM) is designed to integrate the four multi-scale features to generate multi-level features, which includes feature fusion module (FFM) [18] and attention refinement module (ARM) [19]. The proposed FARFM can better generate the saliency maps by feeding back the low-level texture feature and high semantic feature to the previous ones.

Feature Fusion Module. Due to the restriction of the receptive field, low-level features retain rich details as well as background noises. These features have clear boundaries, which are important for generating accurate saliency maps. In contrast, high-level features are coarse on boundaries because of multiple downsampling, high-level features still have consistent semantics, and is important for localizing the defect region.

FFM performs cross-fusion of high-level features and low-level features to reduce the discrepancy between features. Firstly, it extracts the common part between low-level features and high-level features by element-wise multiplication, and then combines them with the original low-level features and high-level features by element-wise addition, respectively. Compared with the direct addition or concatenation, FFM avoids the redundant information of low-level features and high-level features, thus can efficiently characterize the texture feature for generate the better saliency maps.

Specifically, FFM consists of two branches, one is high-level features and the other is low-level features, as shown in Fig. 3(a). First, we conduct convolution

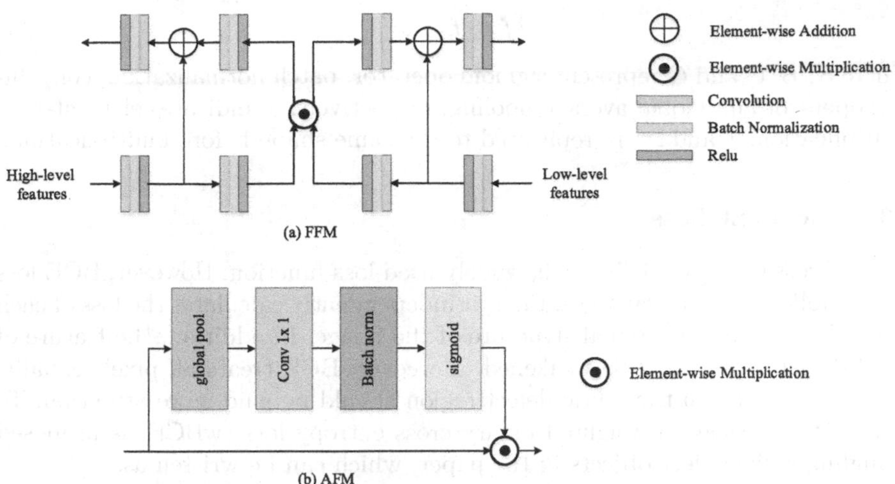

Fig. 3. Two components of Feedback attention refinement fusion module.

on the two layers of features. Then these features are transformed and fused by multiplication. Finally, the fused features is appended into the original low-level features and high-level features as output, and it is shown in Eq. 1 and Eq. 2.

$$f_l = f_l + G_l(G_l(G_l(f_l)) * G_h(G_h(f_h))) \tag{1}$$

$$f_h = f_h + G_h(G_l(G_l(f_l)) * G_h(G_h(f_h))) \tag{2}$$

Where f_l and f_h are low-level features and high-level features, respectively. $G_l(\cdot)$, $G_h(\cdot)$ are the combination of convolution, batch normalization and relu operator of low-level features and high-level features, respectively. After obtaining the fused features, a 3×3 convolution is applied to restore the original dimension. The proposed module is a symmetrical structure, where f_l embeds its details into f_h, and f_h filters the background noises of f_l.

Attention Refinement Module. The layers with different depth can represent different scale information. For the fabric image, we should selectively utilize the feature layer information for suppressing non-information branches and automatically promoting differentiated branches. Therefore, we propose an attention refinement module (ARM) to refine the features of each FFM, and it is shown in Fig. 3(b).

ARM employs global average pooling to capture global context information and computes an attention vector to guide the feature learning by a series of convolution, BN and sigmoid layers. This module can optimize the output features between FFMs. It easily integrates the global context information without any up-sampling operation, and has a small computation. The calculation equation can be described as follows,

$$\omega = S(B(C(G(f)))) \tag{3}$$

$$f = f \otimes \omega \tag{4}$$

Where S, B, C and G represent sigmoid operator, batch normalization, convolution operator and global average pooling, respectively. $\otimes$ indicates element-wise multiplication, f and ω are replicated to the same shape before multiplication.

2.3 The Joint Loss

Binary cross entropy (BCE) is the widely used loss function. However, BCE loss has the following disadvantages. First, it independently calculates the loss of each pixel, thus ignores the global structure of the image. In addition, the feature of small defect object may be weakened. Moreover, BCE treats all pixels equally. In fact, the pixels in the fabric defect region should be paid more attention. To address these issues, a weighted binary cross entropy loss (wBCE) is proposed to highlight the defect objects in the paper, which can be written as,

$$L^{s}_{\mathrm{wBCE}} = -\frac{\sum\limits_{i=1}^{H}\sum\limits_{j=1}^{W}(1+\gamma\alpha_{ij})\sum\limits_{l=0}^{1}1(g^{s}_{ij}=l)\log \Pr(p^{s}_{ij}=l|\Psi)}{\sum\limits_{i=1}^{H}\sum\limits_{j=1}^{W}\gamma\alpha_{ij}} \tag{5}$$

Where $1(\cdot)$ is an indication function and γ is a hyperparameter. $l \in \{0,1\}$ is the labels of defect and background. p^{s}_{ij} and g^{s}_{ij} are the prediction and ground truth of pixels at position (i,j) in the image. Ψ indicates all the parameters of the model and $\Pr(p^{s}_{i,j}=l|\Psi)$ represents the predicted probability.

For L^{s}_{wBCE}, each pixel is assigned a weight α, which can be regarded as an indicator of the importance of pixels, which is calculated based on the difference between the center pixel and its surroundings, as shown in Eq. 6.

$$\alpha^{s}_{ij} = \left|\frac{\sum\limits_{m,n\in A_{ij}} g^{s}_{mn}}{\sum\limits_{m,n\in A_{ij}} 1} - g^{s}_{ij}\right| \tag{6}$$

Where A_{ij} represents the neighborhood of the pixel (i,j). For all pixels, the larger $\alpha^{s}_{ij} \in [0,1]$ means that the pixel at (i,j) is quite different from its surroundings, otherwise, the pixel (i,j) is prone to be in the background.

In addition, in order to efficiently characterize the global structure feature, a weighted IoU (wIoU) loss which has been widely used in image segmentation is adopted in our method. It is a complementation of wBCE. Unlike IoU loss, the wIoU loss assigns more weight to distinguished pixels, which could be denoted as:

$$L^{s}_{\mathrm{wIoU}} = 1 - \frac{\sum\limits_{i=1}^{H}\sum\limits_{j=1}^{W}(g^{s}_{ij} * p^{s}_{ij}) * (1+\gamma\alpha^{s}_{ij})}{\sum\limits_{i=1}^{H}\sum\limits_{j=1}^{W}(g^{s}_{ij} + p^{s}_{ij} - g^{s}_{ij} * p^{s}_{ij}) * (1+\gamma\alpha^{s}_{ij})} \tag{7}$$

The joint loss which is combined wBCE with wIoU can be described as Eq. 8. The joint loss integrates the local texture and the global structure information, which can better highlight the defect region.

$$L_{\mathrm{J}}^{s} = L_{\mathrm{wBCE}}^{s} + L_{\mathrm{wIoU}}^{s} \tag{8}$$

3 Experiments

In this section, we firstly present the experimental setup, including datasets, the evaluation criteria, and implementation details of the proposed method. Then, experiments are conducted to evaluate and compare the proposed network with the 5 state-of-the-art methods. Finally, we provide a rigorous analysis of the experimental results.

3.1 Dataset and Evaluation Metrics

Dataset. We evaluated the proposed model on our fabric image dataset, which contains 1,600 images with scratches, stains, holes, and many other types of defects. We divide the dataset into two parts: 1100 images are used for training, and the remaining 500 images are used for testing.

Evaluation Metrics. In this paper, we evaluate the performance of the proposed network and existing state-of-the-art salient object detection methods by using seven widely-used evaluation metrics, including the precision-recall (PR) curves, F-measure curves, Max F- measure (maxF), mean F-measure (meanF), mean absolute error (MAE), structural similarity measure ($\mathrm{S_m}$) and E-measure ($\mathrm{E_m}$).

3.2 Implementation Details

During the training stage, we apply horizontal flip for the training data augmentation, which aims to avoid overfitting. To ensure model convergence, our network is trained for 50 epochs with an NVIDIA GTX 1080 Ti GPU. Our model is implemented in PyTorch. The parameters of the backbone are initialized by the ResNet-50 and the remaining convolution layers are initialized by the default settings of PyTorch. The whole network adopts stochastic gradient descent (SGD) optimizer with a weight decay of 5e−4, a maximum learning rate of 5e−3 and a momentum of 0.9 to train our model. Warm-up and linear decay strategies are utilized to adjust the learning rate.

3.3 Comparison with State-of-the-Arts

We compare the proposed algorithm with 5 state-of-the-art saliency detection methods, including the NLDF [20], DSS [21], PiCANet [22], CPD [23], BASNet [24]. For fair comparisons, all saliency maps of these methods are computed by running their released codes under the default parameters.

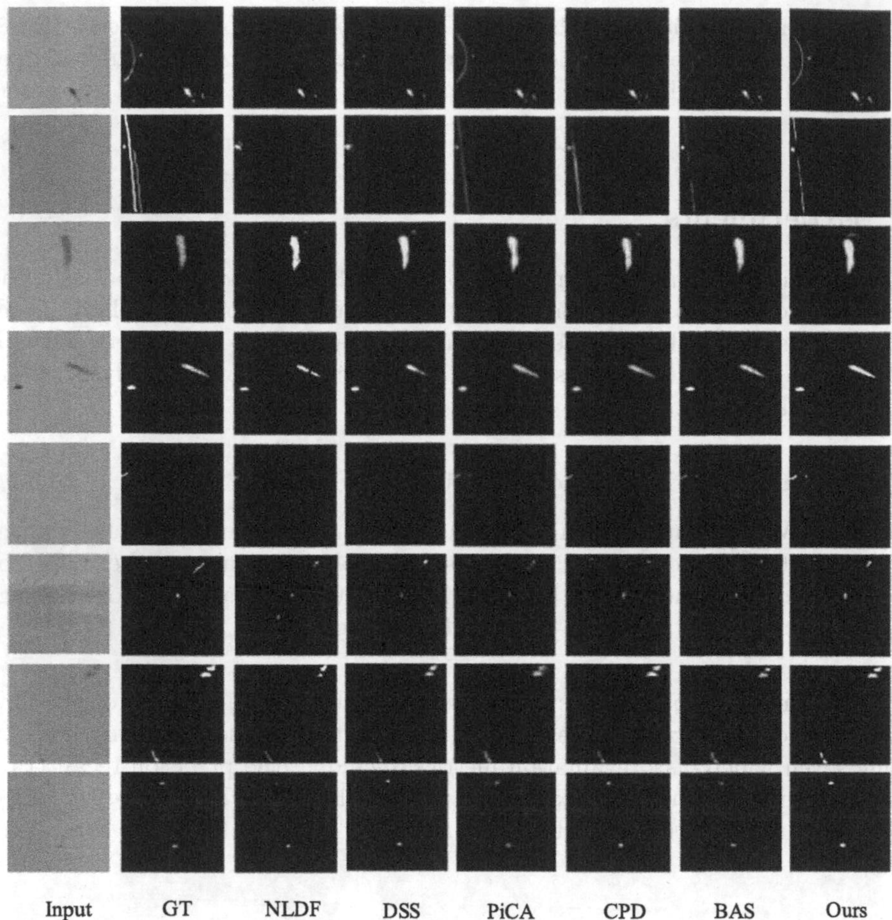

Fig. 4. Visual comparison of the proposed method and several state-of-the-art saliency object detection methods.

Visual Comparison. Figure 4 shows the visual comparison of the proposed method and several state-of-the-art saliency object detection methods. The first column is the test image, the second column is GT, the third column is the detection results using NLDF, the fourth column is the detection results using DSS, the fifth column is the detection results using PiCA, the sixth column is the detection results using CPD, the seventh column is the detection results using BAS and the last column is the detection results of our method. From this figure, we can see that our method is able to accurately detect the fabric defects, and highlight the defect objects with clear boundaries, such as some slender strip defects (1st and 2nd rows), dot defects (4th, 5th, 6th, 7th and 8th rows), etc.

Quantitative Evaluation. To further illustrate the performance of our method, we give the quantitative evaluation, and the comparisons are shown in Table 1.

Table 1. Quantitative evaluation. The best results on our dataset are highlighted in boldface.

Method	maxF	meanF	MAE	Sm	Em
NLDF	0.5632	0.4661	**0.0041**	0.6986	**0.7838**
DSS	0.5923	0.3134	0.0045	0.6854	0.5949
PiCANet	0.5985	0.1519	0.0069	0.6634	0.4016
CPD	0.6064	0.2410	0.0052	0.6869	0.5028
BASNet	0.6058	0.4195	0.0107	0.7078	0.7150
Ours	**0.6233**	**0.4886**	0.0047	**0.7241**	0.7624

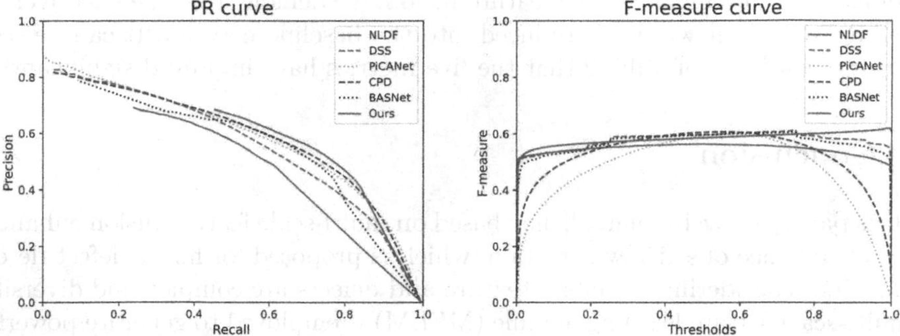

Fig. 5. Quantitative comparisons of the proposed method and several state-of-the-art saliency object detection methods.

The evaluation metrics include Max F-measure (max F, larger is better), Mean F-measure (meanF, larger is better), Mean Absolute Error (MAE, smaller is better), S-measure (S_m, larger is better) and E-measure (E_m, larger is better). As can be seen from the Table 1, the overall performance of our proposed model is outperform the existing methods. In addition, the PR curves and the F-measure curves are demonstrated in Fig. 5. From these curves, we can conclude that our model outperforms most other models at different thresholds, which demonstrates that our method has better performance in fabric defect detection.

3.4 Ablation Study

In this section, we conduct extensive ablation studies to validate the effectiveness of the proposed components in our model. ResNet-50 is adopted as the backbone network on our model.

Performance of MFLM. The MFLM model can efficiently characterize the complex fabric texture by simulating the parallel processing mechanism of multi-receptive, which is able to improve the ability of solving scale variation problem. We install the MFLM on the baseline network and evaluate its performance. The results are shown in Table 2. It can be seen that the module achieves significant performance improvement over the baseline.

Table 2. Ablation analysis for the main architecture.

Baseline	MFLM	FARFM	maxF	meanF	MAE	Sm	Em
√			0.6069	0.4571	0.0049	0.7253	0.7396
√	√		0.6136	0.4682	0.0053	0.7222	0.7456
√		√	0.6158	0.4756	**0.0046**	**0.7293**	0.7547
√	√	√	**0.6233**	**0.4886**	0.0047	0.7241	**0.7624**

Performance of FARFM. FARFM is proposed to selectively aggregate multi-level features for enhancing the feature fusion. To demonstrate the effectiveness of FARFM, only it will be introduced into the baseline network. It can be seen from the third row of Table 2 that the five metrics have improved significantly.

4 Conclusion

In this paper, a novel visual saliency based on multi-scale feature fusion enhances the performance of saliency detection, which is proposed for fabric defect detection. First, considering the fabric texture and defects are complex and diversity, a multi-scale feature learning module (MFLM) is employed to generate powerful features, which is able to improve the ability of solving scale variation problem. Besides, feedback attention refinement fusion module (FARFM) is designed to generate 5 prediction maps by the selective fusion of multi-level features. In addition, we obtain the final saliency map by the adopting joint loss (JT). We comprehensively validate the effectiveness of each component of our network in ablation study. Subsequently, extensive experimental results demonstrate that the proposed method outperforms 5 state-of-the-art methods under different evaluation metrics.

Acknowledgement. This work was supported by NSFC (No. 61772576, No. 62072489, U1804157), Henan science and technology innovation team (CXTD2017091), IRTSTHN (21IRTSTHN013), Program for Interdisciplinary Direction Team in Zhongyuan University of Technology, ZhongYuan Science and Technology Innovation Leading Talent Program (214200510013).

References

1. Srinivasan, K., Dastoor, P.H., Radhakrishnaiah, P., et al.: FDAS: a knowledge-based framework for analysis of defects in woven textile structures. J. Text. Inst. **83**(3), 431–448 (1992)
2. Zhang, Y.F., Bresee, R.R.: Fabric defect detection and classification using image analysis. Text. Res. J. **65**(1), 1–9 (1995)
3. Abouelela, A., Abbas, H.M., Eldeeb, H., et al.: Automated vision system for localizing structural defects in textile fabrics. Pattern Recogn. Lett. **26**(10), 1435–1443 (2005)

4. Behravan, M., Tajeripour, F., Azimifar, Z., et al.: Texton-based fabric defect detection and recognition. Journal, 57–69 (2011)
5. Chan, C., Pang, G.K.H.: Fabric defect detection by Fourier analysis. IEEE Trans. Ind. Appl. **36**(5), 1267–1276 (2000)
6. Bu, H., Wang, J., Huang, X.: Fabric defect detection based on multiple fractal features and support vector data description. Eng. Appl. Artif. Intell. **22**(2), 224–235 (2009)
7. Guan, S.: Fabric defect detection using an integrated model of bottom-up and top-down visual attention. J. Text. Inst. **107**(2), 215–224 (2016)
8. He, H.: Saliency and depth-based unsupervised object segmentation. IET Image Proc. **10**(11), 893–899 (2016)
9. Zhang, G., Yuan, Z., Zheng, N.: Key object discovery and tracking based on context-aware saliency. Int. J. Adv. Rob. Syst. **10**(1), 15 (2013)
10. Mahadevan, V., Vasconcelos, N.: Saliency-based discriminant tracking. In: IEEE (2009)
11. Liu, Z., Li, C., Zhao, Q., et al.: A fabric defect detection algorithm via context-based local texture saliency analysis. Int. J. Cloth. Sci. Technol. (2015)
12. Li, C., Yang, R., Liu, Z., et al.: Fabric defect detection via learned dictionary-based visual saliency. Int. J. Cloth. Sci. Technol. (2016)
13. Zhang, H., Hu, J., He, Z.: Fabric defect detection based on visual saliency map and SVM. In: IEEE (2017)
14. Lee, G., Tai, Y.W., Kim, J.: Deep saliency with encoded low level distance map and high level features. In: IEEE (2016)
15. Wang, L., Lu, H., Wang, Y., et al.: Learning to detect salient objects with image-level supervision. In: IEEE (2017)
16. Li, G., Yu, Y.: Deep contrast learning for salient object detection. In: IEEE (2016)
17. Pang, Y., Zhao, X., Zhang, L., et al.: Multi-scale interactive network for salient object detection. In: IEEE (2020)
18. Wei, J., Wang, S., Huang, Q.: F^{3}Net: fusion, feedback and focus for salient object detection. In: AAAI (2020)
19. Yu, C., Wang, J., Peng, C., Gao, C., Yu, G., Sang, N.: BiSeNet: bilateral segmentation network for real-time semantic segmentation. In: Ferrari, V., Hebert, M., Sminchisescu, C., Weiss, Y. (eds.) ECCV 2018. LNCS, vol. 11217, pp. 334–349. Springer, Cham (2018). https://doi.org/10.1007/978-3-030-01261-8_20
20. Luo, Z., Mishra, A., Achkar, A., et al.: Non-local deep features for salient object detection. In: IEEE (2017)
21. Hou, Q., Cheng, M.M., Hu, X., et al.: Deeply supervised salient object detection with short connections. In: IEEE (2017)
22. Liu, N., Han, J., Yang, M.H.: PicaNet: learning pixel-wise contextual attention for saliency detection. In: IEEE (2018)
23. Wu, Z., Su, L., Huang, Q.: Cascaded partial decoder for fast and accurate salient object detection. In: IEEE/CVF (2019)
24. Qin, X., Zhang, Z., Huang, C., et al.: BASNet: boundary-aware salient object detection. In: IEEE/CVF (2019)

Improving Adversarial Robustness of Detector via Objectness Regularization

Jiayu Bao[1,2], Jiansheng Chen[1,2,3(✉)], Hongbing Ma[1], Huimin Ma[2], Cheng Yu[1], and Yiqing Huang[1]

[1] Department of Electronic Engineering, Tsinghua University, Beijing 100084, China
[2] School of Computer and Communication Engineering, University of Science and Technology Beijing, Beijing 100083, China
jschen@ustb.edu.cn
[3] Beijing National Research Center for Information Science and Technology, Tsinghua University, Beijing 100084, China

Abstract. Great efforts have been made by researchers for achieving robustness against adversarial examples. However, most of them are confined to image classifiers and only focus on the tiny global adversarial perturbation across the image. In this paper, we are the first to study the robustness of detectors against vanishing adversarial patch, a physically realizable attack method that performs vanishing attacks on detectors. Based on the principle that vanishing patches destroy the objectness feature of attacked images, we propose objectness regularization (OR) to defend against them. By enhancing the objectness of the whole image as well as increasing the objectness discrepancy between the foreground object and the background, our method dramatically improves the detectors' robustness against vanishing adversarial patches. Compared with other defense strategies, our method is more efficient but robust to adaptive attacks. Another benefit brought by our method is the improvement of recall on hard samples. Experimental results demonstrate that our method can generalize to adversarial patches of different strengths. We reduce the vanishing rate (VR) on YOLOv3 and YOLOv4 under the vanishing attack by 49% and 41% respectively, which is state-of-the-art.

Keywords: Adversarial defense · Vanishing patch · Object detection · Objectness regularization

1 Introduction

Deep neural networks (DNNs) have achieved remarkable success on object detection [10,19,23] and fueled the development of many applications. However, DNNs are found to be easily fooled by adversarial examples [21]. In the computer vision field, adversarial examples are maliciously crafted images that aim at misleading the predictions of DNNs. Typically, for an input image x and a model $F(.)$, the goal of adversarial attacks is to find the adversarial example x' which satisfies Eq. (1), where Δ is a metric to measure the difference between x and x'. In most

© Springer Nature Switzerland AG 2021
H. Ma et al. (Eds.): PRCV 2021, LNCS 13022, pp. 252–262, 2021.
https://doi.org/10.1007/978-3-030-88013-2_21

of studies [17,24,29], Δ is the p-norm ($p = 2$ or ∞) metric, and the perturbation is restricted to be within the p-norm ball of radius ϵ, which means the adversarial perturbation is imperceptible to humans.

$$F(x) \neq F(x') \wedge \Delta(x, x') < \epsilon \tag{1}$$

Object detection is wildly used in many security critical areas like autonomous driving and medical diagnosis. Hence the robustness of deep detectors has attracted great attention. Many attack methods [20,22,30] have been proposed to study the robustness of detectors. DAG [26] misleads the classification of all the bounding boxes, while RAP [14] also includes regression loss in attacks. TOG [8] designs different objectness loss functions to conduct three types of adversarial attacks. However, detectors are wildly used in the real world while attacks with global tiny perturbations are not realizable in the physical world. Among those physically realizable attacks, adversarial patches [4,6,12,16] are the most common attacks which misleading networks with localized image patches. Like what shows in Fig. 1, localized adversarial patches can mislead the object detector to detect nothing. Attackers can implement those patches in the real world and poses real threats to detectors [6,13,30]. So we pay attention to the physically realizable adversarial patch in this work.

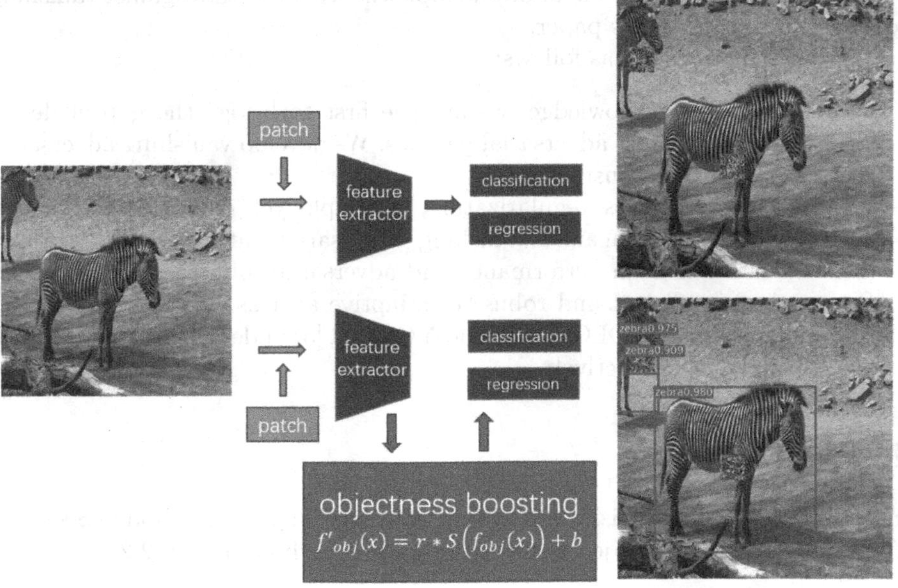

Fig. 1. Illustration of our objectness regularization method. The objectness regularization module is inserted into the detector. We regenerate adversarial patch for the model with objectness regularization.

Defenses against adversarial patches, such as LGS [18] and DW [11], are designed originally for classifiers. Besides, those strategies are proved to be easily circumvented [7] by exploiting BPDA [1] to approximate gradients. By contrast, much less work has been done to improve the adversarial robustness of detectors. It has proven to be an effective way for classifiers to achieve robustness by adversarial training (AT) [17]. AT continuously generates adversarial examples and optimizes the model on these samples in the training phase. By such min-max optimizations, AT can achieve a classifier with a very smooth decision boundary, thus it's more difficult for a benign example to cross the decision boundary with only an imperceptible perturbation. Therefore, AT is extremely time-consuming and usually serves as a trade-off between clean accuracy and adversarial robustness [29]. However, when applying to object detectors, AT can even cause a 25.8 mAP drop on clean images [28], which is far from satisfactory. AT methods are robust to adaptive attacks [1] but only effective to adversarial perturbations of small l_2 or l_∞ norm, which is inappropriate for defending against physically realizable perturbations (often have large l_∞ norm and small l_0 norm).

The vanishing attack [2,8] is the most frequently used adversarial attack on detectors that allowing the object to evade detection. This type of attack is harmful for it is natural-style [25,27] but can be catastrophic to security-critical systems like automatic driving [6,30]. And the adversarial patch that performing vanishing attacks poses security concerns for the employment of detectors in the real world. Hence we shine a light on the robustness of detectors against vanishing adversarial patches in this paper.

Our contributions are as follows:

- To the best of our knowledge, we are the first to bridge the gap of detection robustness against adversarial patches. We develop vanishing adversarial patch to judge the robustness.
- We propose objectness regularization, a simple yet effective method for achieving robustness against vanishing adversarial patches, with a proper trade-off between clean performance and adversarial robustness.
- Our method is efficient and robust to adaptive attacks. We reduce the vanishing rate (VR) on YOLOv3 [10] and YOLOv4 [3] under the adaptive attack by 49% and 41% respectively.

2 Method

In this section, we first revisit the vanishing adversarial patch method in Sect. 2.1. Then we introduce our objectness regularization method in Sect. 2.2.

2.1 Vanishing Adversarial Patch

For an input image x, the object detector outputs bounding box predictions $b(x)$ and classification predictions $c(x)$. The objectness scores of bounding boxes are denoted as $o(x)$, representing the confidence of containing objects. In some detectors [3,10], objectness is directly defined. While in detectors of other structures [19,23], objectness can be represented by the sum of all foreground object probabilities. Objectness plays an import role in distinguishing the foreground objects and the background. So it is often attacked by vanishing attacks [8].

The most import aspects of the vanishing patch are the positions of patches and the vanishing loss function. We choose the positions of patches in an empirical way for attack efficiency. The center of objects are proven to be good choices for vanishing attacks in TOG [8] and SAA [2], so we add vanishing patches at the centers of corresponding objects. Specifically, for an input image x, we get the detection result $F(x)$ and choose patch locations using bounding box positions in $F(x)$. Since it is difficult to optimize the l_0 perturbation directly, we exploit a predefined location mask m with bool values to restrict the adversarial perturbation positions. The adversarial example x' is then denoted as Eq. (2). Here x' denotes the image with perturbation, $\odot$ is the element-wise multiplication operator and p is the vanishing patch we want to get.

$$x' = x \odot (1 - m) + p \odot m \tag{2}$$

We optimize patch p using stochastic gradient descent (SGD) with properly designed loss function and step length. The loss function we employ here is as what exactly used in SAA [2] as Eq. (3). Here $o(x')$ is the objectness predictions of x' and the loss function erases all the predictions with a high objectness. The step length of adversarial attack is fixed in most of cases [5,9,17]. However, we find exponential decay step length will create more powerful adversarial examples under the same attack budgets (e.g. iterations, time). So we use both fixed step length and decay step length attacks to evaluate the adversarial robustness.

$$loss = max(o(x')) \tag{3}$$

Like many other works [17,24,29], we consider the attack budgets in evaluating the robustness of detectors. In this work, we use three indicators to indicate the attack strength, the total pixels of patches (l_0 norm), the maximum iteration numbers (resource constraints), and the step length (optimization strategy).

2.2 Objectness Regularization

The vanishing adversarial patch in the previous Sect. 2.1 is an objectness gradient based attack. To erase objects in detections, vanishing attacks have to fool the objectness of the victim object. In a clean image, foreground objects often have much higher objectness than the background. However, the vanishing patch changes this situation. Compared to clean images, adversarial images with vanishing patches often have much lower objectness. Like what shows in Fig. 2(b), the highest value of objectness feature map is far less than 0, and is far less than 0.1 even after the *sigmoid* activation. We conclude the impacts of the vanishing patch as follows. First, the vanishing patch reduces the whole objectness of the image. Second, the vanishing patch compresses the objectness to a

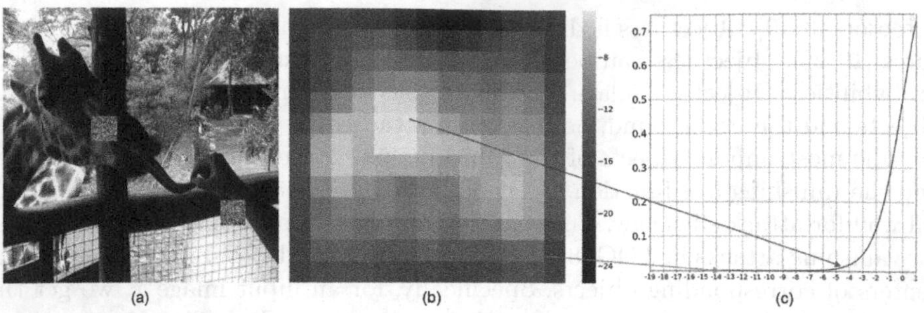

Fig. 2. The objectness distribution of an adversarial image. (a) is an image with vanishing patches and (b) is the objectness distribution of the image. (c) is the sigmoid function. We mark the objectness of the object and the background with blue arrows in (c).

small range, where the discrepancy between the foreground and the background becomes smaller.

To defend against such vanishing attacks, we have to boost the objectness of the image. However, there are two problems we have to solve. First, we should consider the robustness to adaptive attacks. That is, when attackers know our defense strategy and regenerate adversarial examples for attacks, our defense method should be still effective. Second, since the discrepancy between the foreground and the background is smaller, it is of vital importance to avoid too many false predictions when boosting the objectness of the whole image. To solve these problems, we design an objectness boosting function with the post-process parameter of the detector included (to defend adaptive attacks). Before the final classification and regression, we apply our objectness boosting function to correct the objectness feature, like what shows in Fig. 1. We describe the function design in the following.

The basic idea of our method is to make it more difficult for attackers to reduce the objectness of foreground objects. We observe that the foreground object still remains a slightly higher objectness than the background due to the feature discrimination, though the vanishing patch reduces the objectness of the whole victim image to a large scale. So we boost the objectness of the whole image as well as increase the discrepancy between the foreground and the background. We denote the objectness feature of an image x as $f_{obj}(x)$, and the objectness feature after regularization can be formulated by Eq. (4).

$$f'_{obj}(x) = r * S(f_{obj}(x)) + b \tag{4}$$

Here r serves as a range control, b is a necessary balancing bias and $S(.)$ denotes the boosting function which has the form of Eq. (5).

$$S(t) = \frac{1}{1 + e^{-t}} \tag{5}$$

We choose the boosting function $S(.)$ as the *sigmoid* function. The *sigmoid* function can map the objectness feature to the range of 0 and 1 while maintaining the internal relative numerical size relationship in it. The object attacked by the vanishing patch has low objectness but is often slightly higher than that of the background. We choose the *sigmoid* function for it also increases the objectness discrepancy between the attacked object and the background when boosting the objectness. As can be seen from Fig. 2, the objectness of the attacked object and that of the background are in different segments of the *sigmoid* function (indicates with blue arrows). In our method, higher objectness results in a greater gain due to the attacked image typically has all values of objectness feature lower than 0. Therefore, we increase the objectness of the foreground object and avoiding too high objectness of the background. That is, our method can enhance object detection under vanishing adversarial attacks without generating too many unreasonable bounding boxes.

The regularization parameters r and b are closely related to the objectness threshold τ. The τ is used in the post process of the detector to erase redundant bounding boxes. We argue that a larger tangent slope in the *sigmoid* function corresponding to τ is supposed to have a smaller range r. So we define r as the reciprocal of the *sigmoid* derivative. Due to the convenience of *sigmoid* derivative calculation, we can easily get r as Eq. (6). We introduce a constant product factor 1/4 into Eq. (6) to avoid too high objectness.

$$r = \frac{1}{4\tau(1-\tau)} \tag{6}$$

The b is an essential bias that control the lowest prediction objectness. We must ensure that the lowest objectness after regularization is high enough for achieving robustness against adaptive adversarial attacks. However, considering the time consumption of post-process, the lowest objectness after regularization should not be higher than $S^{-1}(\tau)$ (otherwise there will be too many redundant bounding boxes with prediction objectness higher than threshold τ). Therefore we design the b as Eq. (7), where $S^{-1}(.)$ is the inverse function of the *sigmoid* function and ϵ is a small constant to filter redundant bounding boxes with relative low objectness. We choose the value of ϵ quite empirically and will study the effect of it in Sect. 3.

$$b = S^{-1}(\tau) - \epsilon = \ln(\frac{\tau}{1-\tau}) - \epsilon \tag{7}$$

3 Experiment

In this section, we evaluate the proposed objectness regularization (OR) method. Both standard object detection and adversarial object detection are investigated.

3.1 Experimental Setup

We introduce our experimental setup in this section. For standard object detection and adversarial object detection, we use different settings accordingly.

Datasets. For standard object detection, we evaluate the performance of detectors on COCO2014 [15] validation set. However, many tiny objects are contained in COCO dataset and will be covered by patches directly. For a fair judgment, we generate adversarial examples on 1000 images chosen from the COCO dataset. All the objects in the chosen 1000 images are large enough to not be covered by patches directly.

Models. We evaluate our method on YOLOv3 [10] and YOLOv4 [3] that are both pre-trained on COCO2014 [15]. The input size of both detectors is 416 * 416 pixels in our experiments. The performances of detectors on clean images are evaluated on COCO validation set with the objectness threshold of 0.001 for non-max suppression (NMS). While the objectness threshold τ of detectors is set to be the most frequently used 0.5 in all our robustness evaluations.

Patches. The method in Sect. 2.1 is exploited to generate adversarial patches. We evaluate our defense method under patches with different strengths. The attacks are strong enough that the iteration number of patches is set to be at least 100. We generate adversarial patches for every single image independently. And we evaluate our method under defense aware adversarial patches. That is, we regenerate vanishing patches for models equipped with objectness regularization.

Metrics. The mAP is chosen to demonstrate the performance on clean images. For convenience, we use mAP-50 in experiments. While the vanishing rate (VR) is introduced to demonstrate the performance under vanishing attacks. The lower the VR, the better robustness of detectors against vanishing patches. The VR is calculated as Eq. (8), where $B(x)$ and $B(x')$ denote the prediction of the clean image x and the adversarial image x' severally. The $IOU(.)$ is a function that calculates the reasonable detections in $B(x')$ where $B(x)$ serves as the ground truth result.

$$VR = 1 - \frac{IOU(B(x), B(x'))}{B(x)} \tag{8}$$

3.2 Experimental Result

The performance of detectors on clean images and adversarial images is reported in this section.

Resilience to Adaptive Attacks. We investigate the VR of detectors under attacks with different strengths. We exploit adversarial patches of various sizes (2500, 3000, and 3500 total pixels respectively) to attack detectors. For each size of the patch, we design three iteration number budgets (100, 200, and 255 respectively) for robustness evaluation. A constant update step of 1/255 is used in all attacks of 100 and 200 iterations. While a decaying update step with initial update step 8/255, decay rate 1/2 and decay point at 30, 90, 190 is employed in all attacks of 255 iterations.

The VR on YOLOv3 and YOLOv4 under attacks with different budgets are presented in Table 1. The hyper-parameter ϵ in experiments of Table 1 is 0.01 for YOLOv3 and 0.05 for YOLOv4. From Table 1, adversarial patches using

Table 1. The VR on YOLOv3 and YOLOv4 (with and without OR defense) under attacks of different strengths. Attacks to defense models are all adaptive attacks in this table.

Patch pixels	Attack iters	YOLOv3	YOLOv3_OR	YOLOv4	YOLOv4_OR
2500	100	34.5%	20.4% (↓ 14.1%)	28.3%	25.4% (↓ 2.9%)
	200	48.1%	22.1% (↓ 26.0%)	37.5%	27.6% (↓ 9.9%)
	255	79.7%	31.5% (↓ 48.2%)	59.5%	32.0% (↓ 27.5%)
3000	100	41.3%	21.9% (↓ 19.4%)	34.4%	26.5% (↓ 7.9%)
	200	56.2%	23.9% (↓ 32.3%)	45.7%	29.0% (↓ 16.7%)
	255	85.2%	37.4% (↓ 47.8%)	70.1%	34.5% (↓ 35.6%)
3500	100	48.8%	23.1% (↓ 25.7%)	38.3%	27.3% (↓ 11.0%)
	200	64.4%	26.0% (↓ 38.4%)	52.5%	30.0% (↓ 22.5%)
	255	91.0%	42.2% (↓ **48.8%**)	78.3%	37.0% (↓ **41.3%**)

strategies of SAA greatly increase the VR on the two detectors, with even 91% and 78% of objects evade detection. Our method reduces the VR on YOLOv3 and YOLOv4 by 48.8% and 41.3% respectively under the strongest attack in Table 1. As also can be seen from Table 1, the OR method is particularly effective against strong adversarial attacks, which is more representative of the real robustness of models.

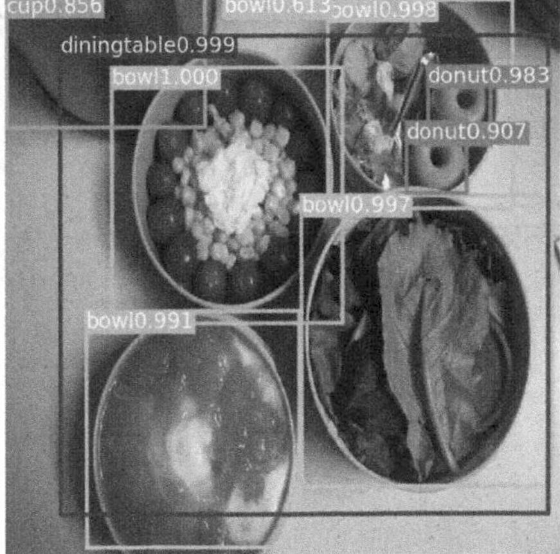

Fig. 3. Detection results on a clean image. *left*: detection results of YOLOv3, *right*: detection results of YOLOv3_OR.

Effects on Clean Images. Our method changes the original objectness for achieving detection robustness. However, the method only causes a decrease of 2.67 mAP on clean images in YOLOv3, as demonstrated in Table 2. The performance of YOLOv4 on clean images only has a slight drop from 56.74 mAP to 56.45 mAP. Despite the comprehensive performance drop on clean images, our method improves the recall of weak-feature objects significantly. It can be observed from Table 2 that the recall of tiny objects like spoon and baseball glove has an increase of over 5% when using OR. The recall of the refrigerator even reaches 96.3% with our method. As demonstrated in Fig. 3, our method is helpful to detect small objects like donuts and hard samples like the dining-table and the cup.

Table 2. The recall of some COCO dataset categories in YOLOv3 with and without OR.

Category	YOLOv3 (54.30 mAP)	YOLOv3_OR (51.63 mAP)
Stop sign	88.1%	90.5%(↑ 2.4%)
Baseball glove	67.6%	72.7%(↑ 5.1%)
Spoon	62.5%	71.1%(↑ **8.6%**)
Banana	70.9%	76.6%(↑ 5.7%)
Refrigerator	90.7%	**96.3%**(↑ 5.6%)

Ablation Study. The effects of the hyper-parameter ϵ are presented in Table 3. The adversarial attack used in Table 3 has a strength of pixel 3000 and iteration number 255. It's obvious that a smaller ϵ typically results in a better performance on adversarial images and a slightly worse performance on clean images, at the expense of inference speed. The negative values of ϵ are abandoned by us in experiments due to the explosion of inference time. We choose ϵ as 0.01 for balance in most of the experiments.

Table 3. The effects of ϵ on clean mAP (mAP on clean images of COCO validation set), VR, and inference time per image (test on GTX 2080 Ti) in YOLOv3_OR.

ϵ	Clean mAP	VR (%)	Time (ms)
0.3	50.32	76.2	23.6
0.1	51.69	58.3	23.9
0.01	51.63	37.4	27.0
0.001	51.63	28.9	41.8
0.0001	51.63	27.4	96.0

4 Conclusion

In this paper, we propose a defense method called objectness regularization (OR) against vanishing adversarial patch attacks. The *sigmoid* function is chosen to enhance the image objectness as well as increase the objectness discrepancy between the foreground object and the background. Our method is efficient (compared to adversarial training methods) but effective against adaptive adversarial attacks. The experimental results on YOLOv3 and YOLOv4 demonstrate that OR can generalize to attacks of different strengths. This method significantly improves the recall of hard samples on clean images with only little mAP degradation. We will further generalize our method to detectors of other structures and adjust it to resist different types of adversarial attacks.

Acknowledgement. This work is supported by the National Natural Science Foundation of China (No. 61673234, No. U20B2062), and Beijing Science and Technology Planning Project (No. Z191100007419001).

References

1. Athalye, A., Carlini, N., Wagner, D.: Obfuscated gradients give a false sense of security: circumventing defenses to adversarial examples. In: International Conference on Machine Learning, pp. 274–283 (2018)
2. Bao, J.: Sparse adversarial attack to object detection. arXiv preprint arXiv:2012.13692 (2020)
3. Bochkovskiy, A., Wang, C.Y., Liao, H.Y.M.: YOLOv4: optimal speed and accuracy of object detection. arXiv preprint arXiv:2004.10934 (2020)
4. Brown, T.B., Mané, D., Roy, A., Abadi, M., Gilmer, J.: Adversarial patch. arXiv preprint arXiv:1712.09665 (2017)
5. Carlini, N., Wagner, D.: Towards evaluating the robustness of neural networks. In: 2017 IEEE Symposium on Security and Privacy (SP), pp. 39–57. IEEE (2017)
6. Chen, S.-T., Cornelius, C., Martin, J., Chau, D.H.P.: ShapeShifter: robust physical adversarial attack on faster R-CNN object detector. In: Berlingerio, M., Bonchi, F., Gärtner, T., Hurley, N., Ifrim, G. (eds.) ECML PKDD 2018. LNCS (LNAI), vol. 11051, pp. 52–68. Springer, Cham (2019). https://doi.org/10.1007/978-3-030-10925-7_4
7. Chiang, P.y., Ni, R., Abdelkader, A., Zhu, C., Studor, C., Goldstein, T.: Certified defenses for adversarial patches. In: International Conference on Learning Representations (2019)
8. Chow, K.H., et al.: Adversarial objectness gradient attacks in real-time object detection systems. In: 2020 Second IEEE International Conference on Trust, Privacy and Security in Intelligent Systems and Applications (TPS-ISA), pp. 263–272. IEEE (2020)
9. Dong, Y., et al.: Boosting adversarial attacks with momentum. In: Proceedings of the IEEE Conference on Computer Vision and Pattern Recognition, pp. 9185–9193 (2018)
10. Farhadi, A., Redmon, J.: YOLOv3: an incremental improvement. Computer Vision and Pattern Recognition, cite as (2018)
11. Hayes, J.: On visible adversarial perturbations & digital watermarking. In: Proceedings of the IEEE Conference on Computer Vision and Pattern Recognition Workshops, pp. 1597–1604 (2018)
12. Karmon, D., Zoran, D., Goldberg, Y.: LaVAN: localized and visible adversarial noise. In: International Conference on Machine Learning, pp. 2507–2515 (2018)

13. Komkov, S., Petiushko, A.: AdvHat: real-world adversarial attack on ArcFace face ID system. In: 2020 25th International Conference on Pattern Recognition (ICPR), pp. 819–826. IEEE (2021)
14. Li, Y., Tian, D., Bian, X., Lyu, S.: Robust adversarial perturbation on deep proposal-based models
15. Lin, T.-Y., et al.: Microsoft COCO: common objects in context. In: Fleet, D., Pajdla, T., Schiele, B., Tuytelaars, T. (eds.) ECCV 2014. LNCS, vol. 8693, pp. 740–755. Springer, Cham (2014). https://doi.org/10.1007/978-3-319-10602-1_48
16. Liu, X., Yang, H., Liu, Z., Song, L., Chen, Y., Li, H.: DPatch: an adversarial patch attack on object detectors. In: SafeAI@ AAAI (2019)
17. Madry, A., Makelov, A., Schmidt, L., Tsipras, D., Vladu, A.: Towards deep learning models resistant to adversarial attacks. In: International Conference on Learning Representations (2018)
18. Naseer, M., Khan, S., Porikli, F.: Local gradients smoothing: defense against localized adversarial attacks. In: 2019 IEEE Winter Conference on Applications of Computer Vision (WACV), pp. 1300–1307 (2019)
19. Ren, S., He, K., Girshick, R., Sun, J.: Faster R-CNN: towards real-time object detection with region proposal networks. In: Proceedings of the 28th International Conference on Neural Information Processing Systems-Volume 1, pp. 91–99 (2015)
20. Song, D., et al.: Physical adversarial examples for object detectors. In: 12th USENIX Workshop on Offensive Technologies (WOOT 2018) (2018)
21. Szegedy, C., et al.: Intriguing properties of neural networks. arXiv preprint arXiv:1312.6199 (2013)
22. Thys, S., Van Ranst, W., Goedemé, T.: Fooling automated surveillance cameras: adversarial patches to attack person detection. In: Proceedings of the IEEE Conference on Computer Vision and Pattern Recognition Workshops (2019)
23. Tian, Z., Shen, C., Chen, H., He, T.: FCOS: fully convolutional one-stage object detection. In: Proceedings of the IEEE/CVF International Conference on Computer Vision, pp. 9627–9636 (2019)
24. Wu, D., Xia, S.T., Wang, Y.: Adversarial weight perturbation helps robust generalization. Advances in Neural Information Processing Systems 33 (2020)
25. Wu, Z., Lim, S.-N., Davis, L.S., Goldstein, T.: Making an invisibility cloak: real world adversarial attacks on object detectors. In: Vedaldi, A., Bischof, H., Brox, T., Frahm, J.-M. (eds.) ECCV 2020. LNCS, vol. 12349, pp. 1–17. Springer, Cham (2020). https://doi.org/10.1007/978-3-030-58548-8_1
26. Xie, C., Wang, J., Zhang, Z., Zhou, Y., Xie, L., Yuille, A.: Adversarial examples for semantic segmentation and object detection. In: Proceedings of the IEEE International Conference on Computer Vision, pp. 1369–1378 (2017)
27. Xu, K., et al.: Adversarial T-shirt! Evading person detectors in a physical world. In: Vedaldi, A., Bischof, H., Brox, T., Frahm, J.-M. (eds.) ECCV 2020. LNCS, vol. 12350, pp. 665–681. Springer, Cham (2020). https://doi.org/10.1007/978-3-030-58558-7_39
28. Zhang, H., Wang, J.: Towards adversarially robust object detection. In: Proceedings of the IEEE International Conference on Computer Vision, pp. 421–430 (2019)
29. Zhang, H., Yu, Y., Jiao, J., Xing, E., El Ghaoui, L., Jordan, M.: Theoretically principled trade-off between robustness and accuracy. In: International Conference on Machine Learning, pp. 7472–7482. PMLR (2019)
30. Zhao, Y., Zhu, H., Liang, R., Shen, Q., Zhang, S., Chen, K.: Seeing isn't believing: towards more robust adversarial attack against real world object detectors. In: Proceedings of the 2019 ACM SIGSAC Conference on Computer and Communications Security, pp. 1989–2004 (2019)

IPE Transformer for Depth Completion with Input-Aware Positional Embeddings

Bocen Li[1], Guozhen Li[1], Haiting Wang[1], Lijun Wang[1](✉), Zhenfei Gong[2], Xiaohua Zhang[1], and Huchuan Lu[1]

[1] Dalian University of Technology, Dalian, China
ljwang@dlut.edu.cn

[2] Guangdong OPPO Mobile Telecommunications Corp. Ltd., Dongguan City, China

Abstract. In contrast to traditional transformer blocks using a set of pre-defined parameters as positional embeddings, we propose the input-aware positional embedding (IPE) which is dynamically generated according to the input feature. We implement this idea by designing the IPE transformer, which enjoys stronger generalization powers across arbitrary input sizes. To verify its effectiveness, we integrate the newly-designed transformer into NLSPN and GuideNet, two remarkable depth completion networks. The experimental result on a large scale outdoor depth completion dataset shows that the proposed transformer can effectively model long-range dependency with a manageable memory overhead.

Keywords: Transformer · Positional embeddings · Depth completion

1 Introduction

Depth information implies the geometric relationships, but is lost during the projection from real word 3D scenes to 2D images. Depth estimation aims to recover the 3D geometric relationships, providing richer perceptual cues of the 3D environment, and thus plays an important role in downstream applications, like 3D reconstruction, autonomous driving, etc.

The acquisition of depth values often requires specific sensors, e.g., Lidar and Kinect. However, the depth maps produced by these hardware sensors are often extremely sparse, especially under outdoor scenarios. For instance, in the large-scale autonomous driving data set KITTI [1], the accurate depth values after screening and verification often only account for 35% of the total number of pixels in the entire image, which is far from the demand of real-word applications. To address this issue, a number of depth completion algorithms have been proposed in the literature, which are able to reconstruct the dense depth map using only 5% of the valid depth values delivered by hardware sensors. Though much progress has been achieved, it is currently still a challenging task and attracts progressively more attention from the community.

© Springer Nature Switzerland AG 2021
H. Ma et al. (Eds.): PRCV 2021, LNCS 13022, pp. 263–275, 2021.
https://doi.org/10.1007/978-3-030-88013-2_22

With the development of deep learning techniques, fully convolutional networks (FCNs) [2] have achieved impressive performance in many pixel-level prediction tasks, like semantic segmentation, saliency detection, etc. Its tremendous learning capabilities have also been successfully transferred to the depth completion area by recent works [3–7] which surpass traditional methods with a significant margin. As one of the key advantages, FCNs can handle input images with arbitrary sizes due to its fully convolutional architecture, serving as an efficient solution for pixel-level tasks.

There is also a recent surge of interests in exploring transformers [8–12] for vision tasks. Compared to FCNs, transformers can better model long-range dependencies, which enables the network to render more accurate depth completion results based on the relationships among pixels with/without valid depth values. Nonetheless, most of the traditional transformers [11–13] employ a set of pre-defined parameters as the positional embeddings. As a consequence, they are only applicable to input images with a pre-fixed size, and are shown to suffer from performance degeneration when input sizes at training and inference are inconsistent. In light of this issue, we propose to generate the positional embedding adaptively based on the input feature. Based on this idea, we design a new transformer with input-aware positional embeddings. As opposed to traditional transformers, ours is able to effectively tackle input images with arbitrary sizes without performance drop. By integrating our newly designed transformer with FCN networks, we combine the best of both worlds, i.e., effective long-range dependency modeling and high flexibility in handling arbitrary input sizes. To verify its effectiveness, we apply the proposed transformer to the depth completion task, yielding promising results.

The major contribution of this paper can be summarized as follows:

(1) We propose a new method to generate positional embeddings, which enables transformers to better generalize across arbitrary input sizes.
(2) We implement the above idea by designing a new transformer with input-aware positional embeddings, which can be easily plugged into FCN architectures and shows superior performance in the depth completion task.

To the best of our knowledge, we are the first to apply Transformer to the depth completion task. Extensive experiments on a large scale benchmark dataset demonstrate the effectiveness of our proposed method.

2 Related Work

MSG-CHN [7] addresses the need for global or semi-global information in depth completion by utilizing multi-scale Hourglass [14] structure to extract features, so that the feature map contains large-scale information and fine-grained local information. SPN (Spatial Propagation Network) [15] proposed that image A can be transformed by Laplace matrix to obtain image B, and this transformation process is standard anisotropic diffusion process. Compared with image A, B has clearer object boundary, less noise, and stronger similarity within the same object, which is the same demand in dense depth map. The article [16] uses spatial propagation to further smooth the depth of the same target and highlight the edges of different targets. This propagation is achieved by spreading information from pixels with known depth value to their surrounding regions according to affinity matrix between any pixel and its eight neighbors. Based on that, CSPN++ [17] introduces multi-scale affinity matrix to tackle the problems of small receptive field of the affinity matrix in CSPN [16], resulting in more accurate dense depth.

NLSPN [18] believes that CSPN and CSPN++ calculate affinity matrix within a fixed neighbor region is not conducive for the network to learn more flexible features within a local region, and replace convolution with deformable convolution [19,20] in spatial propagation process. Meanwhile it introduces a new local normalization method, which aims to further strengthen the relationship between features of a point and its neighbor region.

Transformer was first proposed by the Google team [21] and applied to natural language processing. Later it was gradually applied to computer vision. ViT [22] and DETR [23] use transformer blocks after a convolutional encoder to extract global features, which are applied to image classification and object detection tasks, respectively. In addition, self-attention is an important part of the transformer block. Prajit Ramachandran et al. [24] uses this attention mechanism to construct a fully self-attention network and achieves better results than convolutional networks in object detection. For pixel-level tasks, such as segmentation, SETR [25] follows ViT and cuts the input image into several patches, and these patches are then fed into the transformer blocks as tokens. Beyond that, Swin [8] divides the input image into more patches, performs self-attention within each patch, and uses shifted patch partition to model the relationship among patches.

Positional embedding, as a set of pre-defined learnable parameter in recent vision transformers, plays an important role in modeling spatial information and acts as coordinate index. It has different names such as relative index, positional encoding or relative position and so on. Different transformers treat it as different component. Such as in Swin, position encoding is a pair-wise parameters for each token inside the window, and is directly added to relation map in Eq. 1. In ViT, positional embedding is a pair of patch-level parameters interpreting which patch is more likely to contain useful information. Besides, it is added to patch tokens directly, which is different Swin. And in axial-attention [9], relation map is multiplied by positional encoding. In another word, positional embeddings in axial-attention act more like weight but in Swin and ViT more like bias.

But we should notice that a set of predefined parameters will cause the following drawbacks:

(1) if shape of input images changes, common method to handle with the shape of positional encoding is resize [10,22], which will cause artifact.
(2) A set of pre-defined parameter can model distribution of spatial information in data set well, but is shared for all images which harms the ability to model specific object distribution.

In summary, taking these factors into account, we propose a new transformer with input-aware positional embedding, named IPE transformer, which can feat the variation of input size and get better result. Besides, it can be embedded into any other network.

3 Method

In this section, we first introduce the idea of generating positional embedding according to input feature, and then explain how to incorporate it into transformers, leading to transformers with Input-aware Positional Embeddings (called IPE transformers). Finally, we apply the IPE transformers to the depth completion task.

3.1 Input-Aware Positional Embedding

The core component of transformer block is self-attention module. This module aims to compute attention among every pixel in input feature map, which can also be interpreted as relation or affinity matrix among all pixels. The basic flow of self-attention mechanism is to calculate relation map among pixels using K and Q deriving from input feature map X and then to perform matrix multiplication between relation map and V. This procedure can be described as follows:

$$R(X, X) = \phi(conv_K(X), conv_Q(X)) \tag{1}$$

$$\phi(A, B) = softmax(AB^T) \tag{2}$$

$$A(X) = R(X, X)conv_V(X) \tag{3}$$

$$out = FFN(attention(X)) \tag{4}$$

$$m = conv_m(X), \ m = Q, K, V \tag{5}$$

where $conv_m$ aims to calculate Key, Query and Value from the input tensor X in convolution way repectively and $conv_m$ is implemented as 1×1 convolution. The $R(X, X)$ is the realtion map and can be regarded as similarity matrix or affinity matrix among pixels. For example, given two point i and j in X, the corresponding point (i, j) in $R(X, X)$ matrix means how close this point pair is. As for $A(X)$, it can be seen as the weighted X using the relation map calculated by Eq. 1. $FFN(\cdot)$ is a feed forward network to further fuse the result.

Positional embedding can be learned from dataset during training process, and acts more like prior knowledge during inference and test process. Considering its drawbacks discussed above, we propose a new method to calculate positional embedding dynamically according to the input feature.

Convolution can keep spatial information in feature map according to pixel position even in the deepest level. So we conjecture that it do not have to learn a set of parameters additionally, and we can get spatial information directly from feature map. On the basis of this idea, given a feature map $X \in R^{B \times C \times H \times W}$, we can get spatial information directly after 1×1 convolution using Eq. (6), which can be seen as positional embedding.

$$*_{embed} = Conv1 \times 1_{*\_embed}(X), * = Q, K, V \quad (6)$$

Using Eq. (5) and Eq. (6), we can get Q, K, V and its corresponding positional embedding. Q, Q_{embed} and K, K_{embed} is with shape of $R^{B\times C\times H\times W}$ but V, V_{embed} with the shape of $R^{B\times 2C\times H\times W}$.

The input tensor is with shape of $R^{B\times C\times L}$, where $L = H \times W$, which can be regarded as number of tokens. In the other self-attention modules, their positional embedding is with shape of $R^{C\times L\times L}$ which can be added to relationship map by using unsqueeze operation on batch dimention or added to token feature directly. In our input-aware positional embedding, it has the same shape with their counterpart $\in R^{B\times C\times L}$, which means different images have their own specific positional embedding and can model their unique spatial information better.

3.2 IPE Transformer

Traditional self-attention module tends to flatten the input tensor with shape $R^{B\times C\times H\times W}$ into $R^{B\times C\times L}$, which will cost extra memory to finish this calculation. One way to alleviate this notorious out-of-CUDA-memory problem is to cut an image into several patches [8,22,25], and the other way axial attention [9].

In axial attention, it does not calculate the relationship between one point and other points directly, but reaches this goal in two steps, calculating the relationship of one point among its corresponding row and column sequentially, namely width step and height step respectively. As shown in Fig. 1, information will propagate from A to C in two step, from A to B in column direction and then from B to C in row direction.

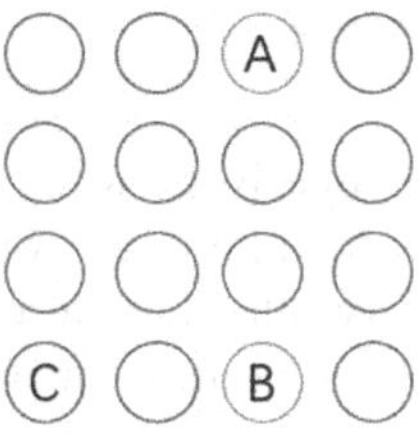

Fig. 1. An example of how information propagates from one point to another.

The input of axial-attention block is different from other self-attention modules. Assuming that $X \in R^{B\times C\times H\times W}$ is the input tensor and then flattened into shape of $X' \in R^{B\times C\times (H\times W)}$, where B,C,H,W is batch size, number of channels, height and width of the input feature map. In axial-attention, the input tensor is re-organized into shape of $R^{(B\times H)\times C\times W}$ or $R^{(B\times W)\times C\times H}$ for width step or height step respectively. In another word, in width step or height step, different rows or columns are treated as different image and concatenated in batch dimension.

Due to its efficiency and effectiveness, we design our IPE transformer based on the axial attention structure [9]. In order to produce more positional-sensitive relation map in Eq. (1), we combine our input-aware positional embeddings with axial-attention not by directly addition but matrix multiplication between Q, K, V and their corresponding positional embeddings which has the same shape of its counter part, according to Eq. 7.

$$attention = softmax(\theta(K, K_{embed}) + \theta(Q, Q_{embed}) + \theta(K, Q))(V + V_{embed}) \tag{7}$$

where $\theta(A, B)$ denotes matrix multiplication, which can be re-written as follows:

$$\theta(A, B)_{b,i,j} = AB^T{}_{b,i,j} = \sum_c A_{b,c,i} \cdot B_{b,c,j} \tag{8}$$

For any point (b, i, j) in $\theta(A, B) \in R^{(B\times W\times W)}$ or $R^{B\times H\times H}$ for width step or height step respectively, we can calculate its value by multiplying corresponding point in A and B image by image. In this formulation, we can model pixel's relationship in arbitrary image shape and pay more attention to unique object distribution in every different image.

In order to feat the variation of input size, in our IPE transformer, positional encoding is generated from input feature map. As shown in Fig. 2, the red box represents our IPE transformer and the yellow box represents one step of this two step mechanism talked above. Every step has two input, one of which is all-embeddings that contains different positional embedding for K,Q and V, and the other is used to calculate K,Q and V that comes from the input tensor or last step result. Besides, we use the same positional embedding for both width step and height step to keep that these two step share the same spatial information.

3.3 Network Structure

In this section, we will show the effectiveness of our attention module and combine it with NLSPN [18] network. The core component in NLSPN is spatial propagation module. It uses affinity information which can be learned from RGB to propagate known information to the unknown.

In this procedure, affinity matrix model local information within a small region which results in losing long range generality. Our IPE transformer can help this procedure to capture long range information.

The network structure is showed in Fig. 3. RGB and sparse depth are concatenated and then fed into encoder-decoder structure. Owing to limited memory condition, we embed our IPE transformer into the middle of this structure to model global information among all pixels in one image and its sparse depth. After that, there are three part in the output of decoder, namely initial depth, affinity matrix and confidence. In this network, spatial propagation takes affinity

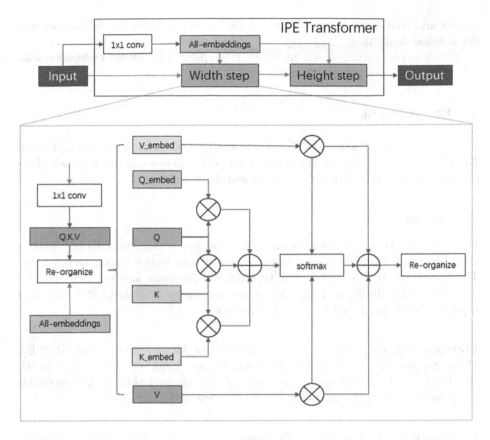

Fig. 2. Structure of IPE transformer. ⊗ denotes matrix multiplication and ⊕ denotes elemental-wise summation. Firstly, the input tensor X with shape of $R^{B\times H\times C\times W}$ is fed into 1×1 convolution and then re-organized into shape of $R^{(B\times H)\times C\times W}$ or $R^{(B\times W)\times C\times H}$ for width step or height step respectively. Q, K and their corresponding positional embedding are in this shape, but V and its embedding has $2C$ channels. (Color figure online)

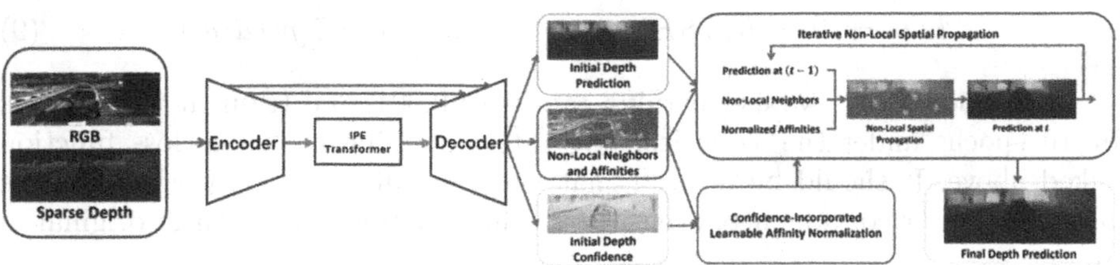

Fig. 3. Structure of NLSPN combined with IPE transformer

matrix and confidence as input to refine initial depth iteratively. At last, we will get a dense depth map.

Furthermore, owing to our module's convenience, it can be embedded into any other encoder-decoder structure.

4 Experiment

In order to verify effectiveness of our proposed transformer, we combine it with NLSPN [18] and GuideNet [5], apply them to the depth completion task. This section will present the detailed experimental results.

4.1 Setup

Dataset. We train our network on KITTI dataset, which contians $86k$ images with 35% and 5% valid points in groundtruth and sparse depth respectively. The image size is 375×1242, but top-cropped 96 pixels and random cropped into 256×1216 during training. As for testing, image is of size 352×1216 and top-cropped 96 pixels before fed into network.

Metrics. Following prior works, we choose Root Mean Square Error (RMSE), Mean Square Error (MAE), Root Mean Square Error of the inverse depth (iRMSE) and inverse Mean Square Error of the inverse depth (iMAE) as evaluation metrics to verify our module's effectiveness and flexibility.

Implementation Details. We train our NLSPN with IPE-transformer (NLSPN-IPE) on KITTI dataset for 40 epochs. Initial learning rate is 0.001, and it will drop to $4e-4$, $1.6e-4$, $6.4e-5$ at 15, 25 and 35 epoch. Following NLSPN, RMSE and MAE are choosen as our loss funciton and their weight is the same as shown in Eq. (9). It should be noticed that, all of networks are trained with top-crop but tested with (marked as -crop in the following experiment) and without top-crop.

$$Loss = 1.0 \times RMSE(pred, gt) + 1.0 \times MAE(pred, gt) \tag{9}$$

In ablation study, we use learning rate with 0.001, and train those networks for 10 epochs under the same learning rate and using the same loss function talked above. It should be noticed that we train all of the networks with the same setting for convenience, even if it is different from the settings original in paper.

4.2 Experiment Results

In order to enlarge receptive field, traditional convolution neural network stacks more convolution layers, which means long-range dependency is more likely overwhelmed in deeper structure by local information. Transformer uses self-attention to model global information directly, and can model large or long object's feature more easily and accurately.

As shown in Fig. 4, the first row is input image with shape of 352×1216. The prediction is separated into two part. The input size in blue box is 352×1216, and 256×1216 in the red one which is top cropped for 96 pixels before fed into network. In blue box, object depth in yellow box is more complete and reasonable with our IPE transformer than the other network, which denotes that long-range dependency can help networks to learn and infer object feature better.

Table 1. Result of NLSPN and NLSPN-IPE on KITTI selective validiton set

	RMSE (mm)	MAE (mm)	iRMSE (1/km)	iMAE (1/km)
NLSPN	771.81	197.33	2.03	0.83
GuideNet	1007.47	251.05	2.74	1.07
NLSPN-IPE	769.47	199.88	2.05	0.85
NLSPN-crop	771.25	197.24	2.03	0.83
GuideNet-crop	777.11	221.29	2.33	0.99
NLSPN-IPE-crop	768.88	199.45	2.04	0.84

In order to verify our module's ability of handling variation of different input size, we conduct a comparison experiment of different input size while testing, 352×1216 and 256×1216 respectively, but with same size of 256×1216 while training. The result is shown in red box. At the boundary of this trunk, both NLSPN and GuideNet do not perform as well as our IPE transformer given larger input size while testing. In another word, our IPE transformer can help networks to model relationship within longer distance, which will benefit handling with the problem of variation of input size. Quantitative result is shown in Table 1. With help of our IPE transformer, it further improves the accuracy of modeling feature.

4.3 Ablation Study

In this section, we verify the effectiveness and flexibility of our IPE transformer. We train four different models, NLSPN, NLSPN with IPE transformer (NLSPN-IPE), GuideNet and GuideNet with IPE transformer (GuideNet-IPE). We simply embed our module into the middle of encoder-decoder structure of NLSPN and GuideNet to implement their IPE transformer counterpart. The training process use the setting talked above. Quantitative result is shown in Table 2. It proves that our module is effective and easy to embed into other network.

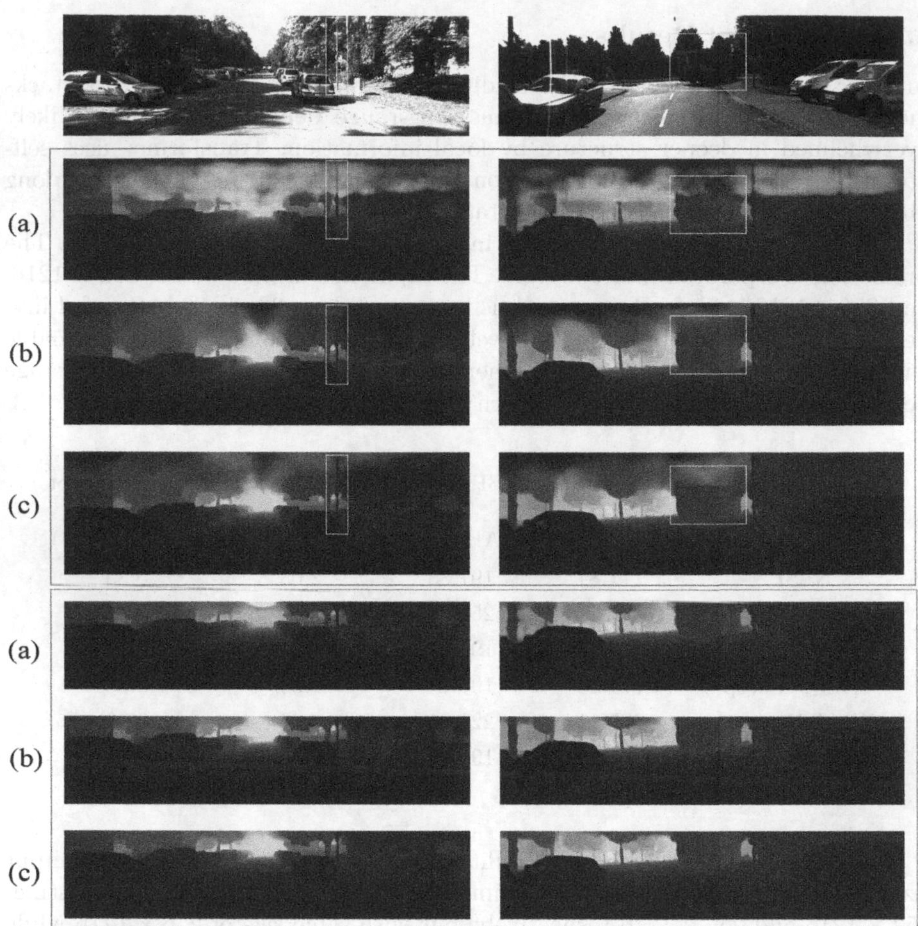

Fig. 4. Experiment result. (a), (b) and (c) are GuideNet, NLSPN, NLSPN-IPE respectively (Color figure online)

Table 2. Result of NLSPN and NLSPN-IPE on KITTI selective validiton set

	RMSE (mm)	MAE (mm)	iRMSE (1/km)	iMAE (1/km)
NLSPN	809.98	207.52	2.23	0.87
NLSPN-IPE	808.18	207.31	2.25	0.87
GuideNet	824.50	236.69	2.75	1.03
GuideNet-IPE	819.35	235.80	2.72	1.03

Table 3. Result of different transformers

	RMSE (mm)	MAE (mm)	iRMSE (1/km)	iMAE (1/km)
NLSPN	809.98	207.52	2.23	0.87
NLSPN-Swin	814.62	209.25	2.30	0.88
NLSPN-ViT	819.14	210.55	2.33	0.89
NLSPN-AA	812.67	209.03	2.31	0.91
NLSPN-IPE	808.18	207.31	2.25	0.87

Then we combine different transformers with NLSPN by embedding these modules into the middle of encoder-decoder structure and experiment result is shown in Table 3. These transformers include axial-attention, Swin, ViT and marked with AA, Swin and ViT respectively. Compared with other transformers, our IPE transformer shows superiority over the others. Swin needs to pad the input feature to feat the change of input size but without resizing positional embeddings. ViT and Axial-attention need to resize positional embedding to appropriate size. Our IPE transformer is input-aware and can generate positional embedding dynamically. We conjecture that this is the reason why our model can bypass the others.

5 Conclusion

In this paper, we propose a new method to generate input-aware positional embeddings and design a new transformer with it, named IPE transformer. Then we embed this transformer into NLSPN and GuideNet, remarkable networks in depth completion. Comparison experiment and ablation study show that our proposed IPE transformer can model long-range dependency better and is easy to transfer to other network by simply embedding it into the middle of encoder-decoder structure.

Acknowledgement. We thank all editors and reviewers for their helpful suggestions. This work is supported by National Natural Science Foundation of China (No.61906031), and Fundamental Research Funds for Central Universities (No. DUT21RC(3)025).

References

1. Geiger, A., Lenz, P., Stiller, C., Urtasun, R.: Vision meets robotics: The KITTI dataset. Int. J. Robot. Res. **32**(11), 1231–1237 (2013)
2. Long, J., Shelhamer, E., Darrell, T.: Fully convolutional networks for semantic segmentation. In: Proceedings of the IEEE Conference on Computer Vision and Pattern Recognition, pp. 3431–3440 (2015)

3. Hu, M., Wang, S., Li, B., Ning, S., Fan, L., Gong, X.: Penet: towards precise and efficient image guided depth completion. arXiv preprint arXiv:2103.00783 (2021)
4. Liu, L., et al.: FCFR-net: feature fusion based coarse-to-fine residual learning for monocular depth completion. arXiv preprint arXiv:2012.08270 (2020)
5. Tang, J., Tian, F.P., Feng, W., Li, J., Tan, P.: Learning guided convolutional network for depth completion. IEEE Trans. Image Process. **30**, 1116–1129 (2020)
6. Zhao, S., Gong, M., Fu, H., Tao, D.: Adaptive context-aware multi-modal network for depth completion. arXiv preprint arXiv:2008.10833 (2020)
7. Li, A., Yuan, Z., Ling, Y., Chi, W., Zhang, C.: A multi-scale guided cascade hourglass network for depth completion. In: The IEEE Winter Conference on Applications of Computer Vision, pp. 32–40 (2020)
8. Liu, Z., et al.: Swin transformer: Hierarchical vision transformer using shifted windows. arXiv preprint arXiv:2103.14030 (2021)
9. Wang, H., et al.: Axial-DeepLab: stand-alone axial-attention for panoptic segmentation. In: Vedaldi, A., Bischof, H., Brox, T., Frahm, J.-M. (eds.) ECCV 2020. LNCS, vol. 12349, pp. 108–126. Springer, Cham (2020). https://doi.org/10.1007/978-3-030-58548-8_7
10. Ranftl, R., Bochkovskiy, A., Koltun, V.: Vision transformers for dense prediction. arXiv preprint arXiv:2103.13413 (2021)
11. Li, S., Sui, X., Luo, X., Xu, X., Liu, Y., Goh, R.S.M.: Medical image segmentation using squeeze-and-expansion transformers. arXiv preprint arXiv:2105.09511 (2021)
12. Wang, Y., et al.: End-to-end video instance segmentation with transformers. arXiv preprint arXiv:2011.14503 (2020)
13. Wu, B., et al.: Visual transformers: Token-based image representation and processing for computer vision. arXiv preprint arXiv:2006.03677 (2020)
14. Newell, A., Yang, K., Deng, J.: Stacked Hourglass Networks for Human Pose Estimation. In: Leibe, B., Matas, J., Sebe, N., Welling, M. (eds.) Computer Vision, ECCV 2016. ECCV 2016. LNCS, vol. 9912, pp. 483–499. Springer, Cham (2016). https://doi.org/10.1007/978-3-319-46484-8_29
15. Liu, S., De Mello, S., Gu, J., Zhong, G., Yang, M.H., Kautz, J.: Learning affinity via spatial propagation networks. In: Advances in Neural Information Processing Systems, pp. 1520–1530 (2017)
16. Cheng, X., Wang, P., Yang, R.: Learning depth with convolutional spatial propagation network. arXiv preprint arXiv:1810.02695 (2018)
17. Cheng, X., Wang, P., Guan, C., Yang, R.: Cspn++: Learning context and resource aware convolutional spatial propagation networks for depth completion. In: AAAI, pp. 10615–10622 (2020)
18. Park, J., Joo, K., Hu, Z., Liu, C.K., Kweon, I.S.: Non-local spatial propagation network for depth completion. arXiv preprint arXiv:2007.10042 3(8) (2020)
19. Dai, J., et al.: Deformable convolutional networks. In: Proceedings of the IEEE International Conference on Computer Vision, pp. 764–773 (2017)
20. Zhu, X., Hu, H., Lin, S., Dai, J.: Deformable convnets v2: more deformable, better results. In: Proceedings of the IEEE Conference on Computer Vision and Pattern Recognition, pp. 9308–9316 (2019)
21. Vaswani, A., et al.: Attention is all you need. Adv. Neural Inf. Proces. Sys. **30**, 5998–6008 (2017)
22. Dosovitskiy, A., et al.: An image is worth 16x16 words: transformers for image recognition at scale. arXiv preprint arXiv:2010.11929 (2020)

23. Carion, N., Massa, F., Synnaeve, G., Usunier, N., Kirillov, A., Zagoruyko, S.: End-to-end object detection with transformers. arXiv preprint arXiv:2005.12872 (2020)
24. Parmar, N., Ramachandran, P., Vaswani, A., Bello, I., Levskaya, A., Shlens, J.: Stand-alone self-attention in vision models. arXiv preprint arXiv:1906.05909 (2019)
25. Zheng, S., et al.: Rethinking semantic segmentation from a sequence-to-sequence perspective with transformers. arXiv preprint arXiv:2012.15840 (2020)

Enhanced Multi-view Matrix Factorization with Shared Representation

Sheng Huang, Yunhe Zhang, Lele Fu, and Shiping Wang(✉)

College of Mathematics and Computer Science, Fuzhou University, Fuzhou 350108, China

Abstract. Multi-view data is widely used in the real world, and traditional machine learning methods are not specifically designed for multi-view data. The goal of multi-view learning is to learn practical patterns from the divergent data sources. However, most previous researches focused on fitting feature embedding in target tasks, so researchers put forward with the algorithm which aims to learn appropriate patterns in data with associative properties. In this paper, a multi-view deep matrix factorization model is proposed for feature representation. First, the model constructs a multiple input neural network with shared hidden layers for finding a low-dimensional representation of all views. Second, the quality of representation matrix is evaluated using discriminators to improve the feature extraction capability of matrix factorization. Finally, the effectiveness of the proposed method is verified through comparative experiments on six real-world datasets.

Keywords: Deep learning · Matrix factorization · Shared representation · Multi-view clustering

1 Introduction

In recent decades, matrix factorization has been widely used in image processing [2], clustering analysis [12] and recommendation systems [10]. Nowadays computers need to process a large amount of data, and it becomes crucial to find the hidden low-dimensional representation in the huge amount of data. Earlier, many kinds of matrix decomposition methods have been proposed, such as singular value decomposition (SVD). Another approach, called non-negative matrix factorization (NMF), is classical and usually used for non-negative inputs. After that, more extensions were proposed and a typical example is convex and semi-nonnegative matrix factorization [3].

The first author is a student. This work is in part supported by the National Natural Science Foundation of China (Grant No. U1705262), the Natural Science Foundation of Fujian Province (Grant Nos. 2020J01130193 and 2018J07005).

© Springer Nature Switzerland AG 2021
H. Ma et al. (Eds.): PRCV 2021, LNCS 13022, pp. 276–287, 2021.
https://doi.org/10.1007/978-3-030-88013-2_23

In order to improve the feature extraction capability of matrix factorization, deep matrix factorization is proposed [9] to obtain strong feature characterization ability by successive decomposition of representation matrix. Previous deep matrix factorization methods are optimized by matrix iteration, and it is necessary to design a new computational method specifically for different restrictions [15]. This situation leads to the dilemma of designing distinct algorithms for different constraints, which constitutes a great challenge for the practical use of matrix factorization. Thus, this inspires us to explore a method to make matrix factorization general. Deep learning is a generalized machine learning method that aims to discover rich hierarchical features, which inspires us to combine deep learning and matrix decomposition to construct a generalized algorithm to solve the matrix factorization problem.

Generative Adversarial Networks (GAN) is a network consisting of a generator and a discriminator [4], which improves the generative ability of the generator and the discriminative ability of the discriminator through an adversarial process [7]. The discriminator has a superior power on the generating ability of the generator. Inspired by the above, we believe that the discriminator will have a large improvement on the matrix factorization problem.

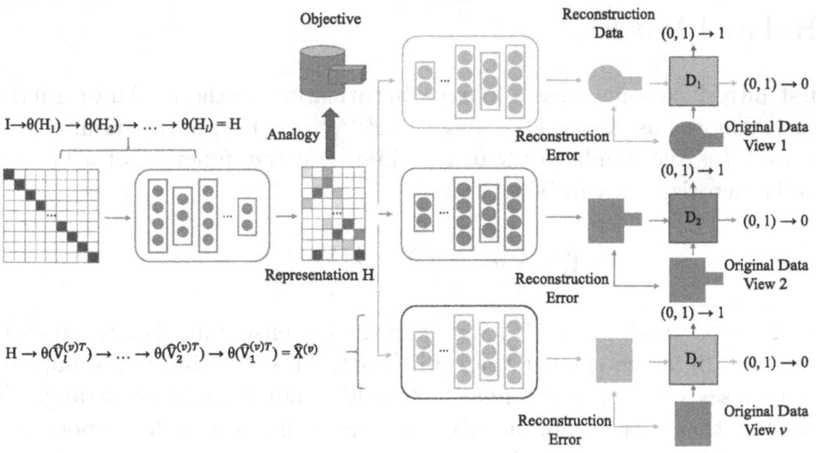

Fig. 1. The architecture of the proposed model. Our model uses an identity matrix as the input of the model, and the representation matrix is generated by the encoders, which can be analogized to the objective. Then, the shared representation matrix is projected differently to each view reconstruction data. $\theta(\cdot)$ is the ReLU nonlinear activation function.

In this paper, we propose a multi-view deep matrix factorization model with enhanced discriminators. The framework diagram of this model is shown in Fig. 1. First, our model uses a shared representation layer. And a multi-layer neural network is employed to enhance the feature extraction capability. We project each layer of the network onto a different space to achieve a nonlinear feature decomposition and use projected gradient descent to optimize the model. Then, in order to map the shared representation layers onto the space of different perspectives, various multi-layer of nonlinear projection matrices are used in the model, and we optimize the shared representation by reconstruction errors. Finally, we use a set of discriminators to optimize the generation of shared representation. These reconstructed data not only calculate the reconstruction error with the original data, but also are transmitted to the discriminator, thereby optimizing the representation matrix and obtaining a better shared representation. In the meantime, the discriminators are also trained. The proposed method is compared with several outstanding multi-view clustering algorithms to verify its performance, and we perform ablation studies to validate the effect of each module. In summary, our main contributions are as follows:

- Use a neural network to solve the matrix factorization, which builds a bridge between deep learning and traditional matrix factorization.
- Construct a shared representation matrix to extract features from multi-view data matrices.
- Apply discriminators to matrix decomposition tasks to improve the feature extraction capability.

2 Related Work

We first introduce some classic matrix factorization methods. An original data matrix is denoted as $\mathbf{X} = [x_1, \cdots, x_n]^T \in \mathbb{R}^{n \times d}$, where n is the number of data points and d is the number of features. The objective function of a basic form of matrix factorization can be written as

$$\min_{\mathbf{H},\mathbf{V}} \mathcal{L}_{MF} = \left\|\mathbf{X} - \mathbf{H}\mathbf{V}^T\right\|_F^2, \tag{1}$$

where $\mathbf{H} \in \mathbb{R}^{n \times k}$ and $\mathbf{V} \in \mathbb{R}^{d \times k}$. Here k is the dimension number to be reduced, and k is usually much smaller than $\min\{n,d\}$. This is a simple decomposition, and some researchers have extended it to additional forms of constraints. NMF is a method that takes a non-negative matrix as input and decomposes it into two non-negative matrices. Under the non-negative constraints, the optimization objective of NMF can be written as the following minimization problem

$$\begin{aligned} \min_{\mathbf{H},\mathbf{V}} \mathcal{L}_{NMF} &= \left\|\mathbf{X} - \mathbf{H}\mathbf{V}^T\right\|_F^2, \\ s.t.\ &\mathbf{H} \geq \mathbf{0}, \mathbf{V} \geq \mathbf{0}. \end{aligned} \tag{2}$$

To enhance the feature extraction capability of matrix decomposition and due to the non-linear property caused by the non-negative constraint, matrix factorization is extended to structures with more hierarchies, named deep matrix factorization. The deep matrix factorization takes the form as

$$\begin{aligned}\mathbf{X} &\approx \mathbf{H}_1\mathbf{V}_1^T,\\ \mathbf{X} &\approx \mathbf{H}_2\mathbf{V}_2^T\mathbf{V}_1^T,\\ \mathbf{X} &\approx \mathbf{H}_3\mathbf{V}_3^T\mathbf{V}_2^T\mathbf{V}_1^T,\\ &\vdots\\ \mathbf{X} &\approx \mathbf{H}_l\mathbf{V}_l^T\ldots\mathbf{V}_3^T\mathbf{V}_2^T\mathbf{V}_1^T,\end{aligned} \tag{3}$$

where $\mathbf{H}_i$ is the representation matrix of the output of i-th layer, which is decomposed from $\mathbf{H}_{i-1}$. To associate with the NMF, here we make $\mathbf{H}_i \geq 0$. But in practice, it is not necessary to force $\mathbf{H}_l$ to be a non-negative matrix. $\mathbf{V}_i$ can be considered as a projection matrix that maps the representation matrix $\mathbf{H}_i$ into the original space. By continuously decomposing the representation matrix, the matrix factorization can extract more potential features.

3 Proposed Method

3.1 Multi-view Matrix Factorization with Shared Representation

First of all, we define the symbols for ease of explanation. Given multi-view data $\mathcal{X} = \{\mathbf{X}^{(1)}, \ldots, \mathbf{X}^{(p)}, \ldots, \mathbf{X}^{(P)}\}$ and P is the total number of views. Here $\mathbf{X}^{(p)} \in \mathbb{R}^{n\times d_p}$ is the input data of the p-th view. For each view of data $\mathbf{X}^{(p)}$, an intuitive idea is to decompose them into two matrices groups $\mathbf{H}$ and $\mathbf{V}$.

But this is not our ultimate goal, for that is actually not fundamentally different from the single-view methods, and data of each view is still not correlated with each other as independent individuals. So we associate that the essence of multi-view data is to collect information from the same object in different views. Each view should have the same representation in the potential space, therefore, we decompose the data matrices of different views into a common representation matrix as the following equations

$$\begin{aligned}\mathbf{X}^{(1)} &\approx \mathbf{H}_l\mathbf{V}_l^{(1)T}\ldots\mathbf{V}_3^{(1)T}\mathbf{V}_2^{(1)T}\mathbf{V}_1^{(1)T},\\ &\vdots\\ \mathbf{X}^{(P)} &\approx \mathbf{H}_l\mathbf{V}_l^{(P)T}\ldots\mathbf{V}_3^{(P)T}\mathbf{V}_2^{(P)T}\mathbf{V}_1^{(P)T},\\ &s.t.\ \mathbf{H}_i^{(p)} \geq 0, i \in [1, 2, \ldots, l-1],\end{aligned} \tag{4}$$

where $\mathbf{H}_l$ is the shared representation of all views. They can be reconstructed to the source data of each view respectively with different perspectives under corresponding mappings of the projection matrices $\mathbf{V}^{(p)} = \mathbf{V}_1^{(p)}\mathbf{V}_2^{(p)}\mathbf{V}_3^{(p)}\ldots\mathbf{V}_l^{(p)}$. To solve this matrix factorization problem, we formulate the objective function as the following

$$\begin{aligned}\mathcal{L}_R &= \sum_{p=1}^{P} dist\left(\mathbf{X}^{(p)}, \mathbf{H}\mathbf{V}^{(p)T}\right),\\ &s.t.\ \mathbf{H}_i^{(p)} \geq 0, i \in [1, 2, \ldots, l-1],\end{aligned} \tag{5}$$

where $dist(\cdot,\cdot)$ means a distance function that can be instantiated to a specific function, such as mean square error or binary cross entropy. This is a minimization problem that aims to make the reconstructed data matrices approach the source matrices as closely as possible. Thus, this allows the proposed model to automatically learn a shared representation and extract the features of all views into a unified matrix.

To solve the above optimization problem, we can use an auto-encoder to instantiate the problem. An auto-encoder is a model that can map features to other spaces. Its mathematical expression is $\hat{\mathbf{X}} = g(f(\mathbf{X}))$ that $f(\cdot)$ is encoder, $g(\cdot)$ is decoder, $\mathbf{X}$ is the input data and $\hat{\mathbf{X}}$ is the output. It expressed in terms of matrix is $\hat{\mathbf{X}} = \mathbf{XED}^T$ where $\mathbf{E}$ is the weighted matrix of encoder and $\mathbf{D}$ is the weighted matrix of decoder. We can use an identity matrix as the input to the auto-encoder, so that the formula is $\hat{\mathbf{X}} = \mathbf{IED}^T = \mathbf{ED}^T$. In this way, we convert the matrix decomposition problem into an auto-encoder model.

3.2 Enhancement of Feature Extraction Capability

In order to enhance the feature extraction ability of matrix factorization, we use a discriminator module to evaluate the matrices reconstructed by matrix decomposition. In our model, matrix decomposition not only contains the reconstruction error, but also introduces the discriminators to investigate the quality of reconstruction. The discriminators force our model to extract more representative feature to deceive the discriminators.

In our model, the p-th discriminator is $D_p(\hat{\mathbf{X}}^{(p)})$. Each reconstructed matrix has an independent discriminator to judge separately. The aim of the discriminators is to make each reconstructed matrix be judged as false, and each original data matrix is judged as true. In this way, the matrix factorization model is prompted to find better features to reconstruct the data, so as to improve the accuracy. Typically, the loss function of the discriminators is

$$\mathcal{L}_{Dis} = \sum_{p=1}^{P} \left(\mathbb{E}_{x^{(p)} \sim p_{real}} \left[\ln \left(D_p \left(x^{(p)} \right) \right) \right] + \mathbb{E}_{\hat{x}^{(p)} \sim p_{ae}} \left[\ln \left(1 - D_p \left(\hat{x}^{(p)} \right) \right) \right] \right), \tag{6}$$

where x is one of original data and $\hat{x}$ is one of reconstructed data. We define the distribution of original data as p_{real} and reconstructed data as p_{ae}. Expectation is continuous rather than discrete, but in practice the probability distribution of the data can only be obtained by sampling. So that we use the following objective function to optimize the discriminators:

$$\mathcal{L}_D = \sum_{p=1}^{P} \left(\frac{1}{n} \sum_{j=1}^{n} \ln \left(D_p \left(x_j^{(p)} \right) \right) + \frac{1}{n} \sum_{j=1}^{n} \ln \left(1 - D_p \left(\hat{x}_j^{(p)} \right) \right) \right). \tag{7}$$

This loss function indicates that the discriminators are trained to distinguish the real from the fake. Due to the existence of the discriminators, the goal of matrix factorization is not only to reconstruct the matrix, but also to find key features in the data. This puts stronger pressure on matrix factorization and can improve its feature extraction capability. When the reconstructed data is expected to cheat the discriminators, its objective function can be represented as the following form

$$\mathcal{L}_{RD} = -\sum_{p=1}^{P}\left(\frac{1}{n}\sum_{j=1}^{n}\ln\left(D_p\left(\hat{x}_j^{(p)}\right)\right)\right). \tag{8}$$

The objective function is to make the discriminators tend to determine the reconstructed data as true. In turn, the reconstruction loss term in the total loss function ensures that the model does a better job on the premise of completing the target of matrix factorization, instead of deceiving the discriminators with tricks without any boundary.

In view of the above, the objective function of our proposed model is shown as follows

$$\mathcal{L}_1 = \mathcal{L}_R + \lambda_d \mathcal{L}_{RD}, \tag{9}$$

$$\mathcal{L}_2 = \mathcal{L}_D. \tag{10}$$

These objective functions consist of two components: reconstruction loss $\mathcal{L}_1$ and discriminators loss $\mathcal{L}_2$. λ_d is the parameter to adjust the influence of two loss terms. We summarize Algorithm 1 to train our model and output the shared representation $\mathbf{H}_l$.

4 Experiments

In this section, we conduct comparative experiments with other clustering algorithms to verify the effectiveness of our model. The datasets and experimental setups are introduced and the experimental results are analyzed.

Algorithm 1. Enhanced Multi-view Matrix Factorization with Shared Representation

Input: Multi-view data $\mathcal{X} = \{\mathbf{X}^{(1)}, \dots, \mathbf{X}^{(p)}, \dots, \mathbf{X}^{(P)}\}$, parameter λ_d and the number of iterations max_iter.

Output: The shared representation $\mathbf{H}_l$.

```
for t = 1 → max_iter do
    Forward propagation in the model using the identity matrix as input;
    Compute the reconstruction loss L1 by Equation 9;
    Optimize the auto-encoder by backward propagation the reconstruction loss L1;
    Compute the discriminators loss L2 by Equation 10;
    Optimize the discriminators by backward propagation the loss L2;
end for
return The shared representation Hl.
```

4.1 Datasets

To verify the effectiveness of our proposed method, we perform comparative experiments on six real-world datasets.

MSRC-v1[1] is a dataset of 210 object images from 7 classes. It contains 24-D colour moments, 576-D HOG features, 512-D GIST features, 256-D local binary patterns, and 254-D CENTRIST features.

Wikipedia[2] is an article dataset that consists of 693 documents with 10 categories, and we extract each entry as two feature representations. They are two-view data sources come with 10-D and 128-D low-dimensional features.

ALOI[3] is an 1,079 images dataset of object from 10 classes. Each image is extracted four types of features, including 64-D RGB color histograms, 64-D HSV color histograms, 77-D color similarities, and 13-D Haralick texture features.

NUS-WIDE[4] is a web images dataset of 1,600 images from 8 classes. This dataset is extracted as 6 views of features: 64-D color histograms, 144-D color correlograms, 73-D edge direction histograms, 128-D wavelet textures, 225-D block-wise color moments, and 500-D bag of words.

MNIST[5] is a digit images dataset that contains 2,000 handwritten numbers '0'-'9'. There are six views of features in them, including 30 features of IsoProjection, 9 features of linear discriminant analysis, and 9 features of neighborhood preserving embedding.

Caltech101[6] is an object image dataset of 9,144 images from 101 classes, including cellphone, brain, face, etc. There are about 40 to 800 images per category on average and most categories have about 50 images. Each image is roughly scaled to 300×200 pixels.

We summarize these datasets in Table 1. The table contains the number of samples, views, features and classes.

Table 1. A summary of datasets

Dataset ID	Datasets	# Samples	# Views	# Total features	# Classes	Data types
1	MSRC-v1	210	5	1,622	7	Object image
2	Wikipedia	693	2	138	10	Documents
3	ALOI	1,079	4	218	10	Object image
4	NUS-WIDE	1,600	6	1,134	8	Web image
5	MNIST	2,000	3	48	10	Digit image
6	Caltech101	9,144	6	3,766	101	Object image

[1] http://riemenschneider.hayko.at/vision/dataset/task.php?did=35.
[2] http://lig-membres.imag.fr/grimal/data.html.
[3] http://aloi.science.uva.nl/.
[4] https://lms.comp.nus.edu.sg/wp-content/uploads/2019/research/nuswide.
[5] http://yann.lecun.com/exdb/mnist/.
[6] http://www.vision.caltech.edu/Image_Datasets/Caltech101/Caltech101.html.

4.2 Experimental Setup

We will show our experimental setup in this section. First we introduce the clustering methods used as comparison algorithms, including a single-view clustering method k-means and eight multi-view clustering algorithms. They are MLAN [8] (Multi-view Learning with Adaptive Neighbours), MVKSC [5] (Multi-view Kernel Spectral Clustering), MLSSC [1] (Multi-view Low-rank Sparse Subspace Clustering), MSC-IAS [13] (Multi-view Subspace Clustering with Intactness-Aware Similarity), MCGC [14] (Multi-view Consensus Graph Clustering), BMVC [16] (Binary Multi-view Clustering), GMC [11] (Graph-based Multi-view Clustering) and AMCDMD [6] (Auto-weighted Multi-view Clustering via Deep Matrix Decomposition).

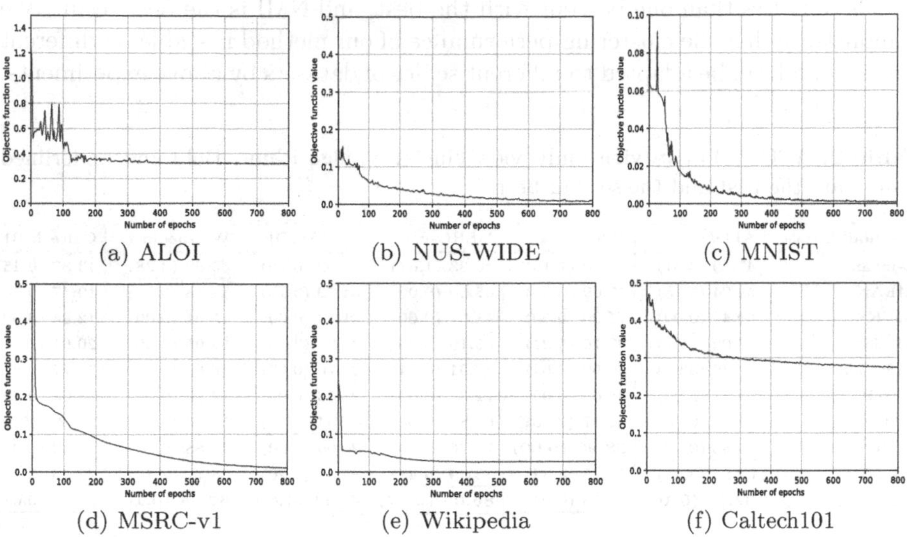

(a) ALOI (b) NUS-WIDE (c) MNIST

(d) MSRC-v1 (e) Wikipedia (f) Caltech101

Fig. 2. Convergence curves of the objective function value. The proposed method almost converges within 800 iterations on each dataset.

We use the default parameters on the comparison algorithms and run them on all datasets. For our proposed method, we use a fully connected layer network to generate the representation matrix with the neuron numbers of {1000, 500, 200, k}. And a symmetric fully connected layer network is used as a generator. Our discriminators also use fully connected layers with the neuron numbers of {200, 100, 50, 1}. We use k-means on the representation matrix to obtain the clustering results.

For the parameter λ_d, we adjust the optimal value by a hyperparameter optimization method. We use the ReLU activation function to activate each layer. For all algorithms, we perform 10 repetitions of the experiments and calculate their means and standard deviations. Finally, we report three evaluation criteria, including accuracy (ACC), normalized mutual information (NMI) and adjusted rand index (ARI).

4.3 Experimental Results

In this section, we show the detailed results of the experiments performed by our algorithm. First, the convergence curves of our method on the six datasets are shown in Fig. 2. From figures we can see that our method converges to a relatively stable loss value by 500 iterations on the majority of datasets.

In Tables 2, 3 and 4, we show the multi-view clustering performance of all the algorithms used for comparison. From the table we can see that our method achieves the best clustering accuracy performance on four of the six datasets, and the second best performance on two datasets. And on MNIST, ACC and ARI is only less than one percent with the best, and NMI is the best result. We demonstrate that the clustering performance of our method is stable on different datasets and can be adapted to different scales of datasets by above experiments.

Table 2. ACC (%) of varying multi-view clustering algorithms. Bold and underlined results are the best and the second best.

Method\Dataset	ALOI	MNIST	MSRC-v1	NUS-WIDE	Wikipedia	Caltech101
k-means	47.49 (3.31)	73.90 (7.16)	46.33 (1.67)	32.02 (0.70)	<u>55.82 (3.28)</u>	13.37 (0.45)
MLAN	58.94 (5.18)	77.09 (0.53)	68.10 (0.00)	34.72 (3.17)	18.18 (0.00)	19.47 (0.64)
MVKSC	60.43 (0.00)	75.20 (0.00)	48.57 (0.00)	31.13 (0.00)	15.01 (0.00)	12.34 (0.00)
MLSSC	63.02 (9.51)	83.76 (5.21)	65.19 (8.99)	33.28 (2.25)	52.05 (9.00)	20.61 (7.60)
MSC-IAS	61.39 (3.98)	80.59 (3.04)	67.91 (6.64)	29.70 (0.67)	46.85 (1.19)	20.77 (0.84)
MCGC	55.51 (0.00)	88.65 (0.00)	72.38 (0.00)	21.56 (0.00)	14.00 (0.00)	23.63 (0.00)
BMVC	59.59 (0.00)	62.57 (2.15)	63.81 (0.00)	<u>36.64 (1.32)</u>	54.83 (0.00)	**28.78 (0.00)**
GMC	<u>64.88 (0.00)</u>	**88.90 (0.00)**	74.76 (0.00)	20.06 (0.00)	44.88 (0.00)	19.50 (0.00)
AMCDMD	62.83 (3.24)	76.28 (3.32)	<u>83.19 (6.43)</u>	35.38 (1.20)	54.72 (2.36)	22.43 (2.36)
Ours	**82.14 (0.10)**	<u>88.73 (0.04)</u>	**86.05 (0.37)**	**40.11 (1.00)**	**62.38 (0.16)**	<u>25.33 (0.68)</u>

Table 3. NMI (%) of varying multi-view clustering algorithms. Bold and underlined results are the best and the second best.

Method\Dataset	ALOI	MNIST	MSRC-v1	NUS-WIDE	Wikipedia	Caltech101
k-means	47.34 (2.14)	68.05 (2.27)	40.18 (1.48)	17.53 (0.74)	<u>53.97 (1.11)</u>	30.30 (0.17)
MLAN	59.37 (4.31)	75.51 (0.70)	62.99 (0.00)	**22.84 (1.96)**	5.89 (0.01)	25.87 (1.56)
MVKSC	58.40 (0.00)	63.29 (0.00)	36.79 (0.00)	14.43 (0.00)	0.00 (0.00)	9.82 (0.00)
MLSSC	63.43 (9.89)	74.61 (2.13)	52.99 (15.74)	19.98 (1.59)	47.19 (7.17)	40.76 (3.81)
MSC-IAS	<u>70.05 (1.79)</u>	74.49 (0.93)	49.55 (1.70)	<u>21.05 (0.62)</u>	43.39 (1.43)	40.61 (0.34)
MCGC	55.41 (0.00)	77.39 (0.00)	61.52 (0.00)	11.79 (0.00)	1.12 (0.00)	26.27 (0.00)
BMVC	54.70 (0.00)	56.22 (0.89)	57.37 (0.00)	19.01 (0.37)	43.80 (0.00)	<u>48.58 (0.00)</u>
GMC	61.81 (0.00)	<u>77.90 (0.00)</u>	<u>74.22 (0.00)</u>	12.23 (0.00)	36.14 (0.00)	23.79 (0.00)
AMCDMD	62.93 (4.03)	71.34 (2.09)	74.09 (4.46)	20.29 (2.02)	47.87 (2.46)	41.65 (2.58)
Ours	**86.28 (0.12)**	**78.06 (0.05)**	**77.49 (0.93)**	20.41 (0.63)	**55.53 (0.07)**	**49.18 (0.68)**

Table 4. ARI (%) of varying multi-view clustering algorithms. Bold and underlined results are the best and the second best.

Method\Dataset	ALOI	MNIST	MSRC-v1	NUS-WIDE	Wikipedia	Caltech101
k-means	32.98 (2.89)	63.87 (4.28)	26.93 (1.70)	9.02 (0.71)	39.82 (2.68)	**28.89 (0.35)**
MLAN	34.54 (5.55)	68.85 (0.95)	50.39 (0.00)	13.76 (3.5)	0.48 (0.01)	−0.39 (0.12)
MVKSC	43.77 (0.00)	61.69 (0.00)	23.12 (0.00)	10.42 (0.00)	0.00 (0.00)	3.63 (0.00)
MLSSC	54.77 (9.50)	73.28 (4.68)	44.92 (9.22)	12.80 (1.75)	37.46 (9.22)	16.01 (9.98)
MSC-IAS	53.24 (3.49)	67.32 (0.81)	31.00 (1.98)	11.44 (0.65)	30.11 (1.63)	12.68 (0.80)
MCGC	35.42 (0.00)	78.75 (0.00)	52.23 (0.00)	3.49 (0.00)	−0.21 (0.00)	0.38 (0.00)
BMVC	40.77 (0.00)	47.75 (2.12)	48.75 (0.00)	13.52 (0.42)	32.76 (0.00)	22.38 (0.00)
GMC	32.90 (0.00)	**79.17 (0.00)**	64.00 (0.00)	4.24 (0.00)	14.48 (0.00)	−0.42 (0.00)
AMCDMD	40.46 (5.02)	55.80 (2.06)	67.81 (6.89)	13.15 (1.13)	30.62 (4.72)	20.84 (4.23)
Ours	**78.47 (0.14)**	78.33 (0.06)	**73.16 (0.93)**	**16.51 (1.01)**	**44.77 (0.18)**	21.88 (0.97)

Besides, the clustering results of compared algorithms on MNIST dataset are exhibited in Fig. 3, where the t-SNE method is adopted to map the original data onto a 2-dimensional subspace. The data points are colored by the output labels from each compared algorithm to compare the effectiveness of each algorithm. It is apparent that the proposed method acquires encouraging clustering performance on the MNIST dataset from the above figures.

4.4 Ablation Study

In order to verify whether adding discriminators has an improvement on the performance of matrix factorization, we conduct ablation experiments. In this subsection, we show the performance with and without adding discriminators. We complete this experiment on real-world datasets. The experimental results are shown in Table 5. We can see that after adding the discriminators, the performance of our model is improved on all tested datasets, from the large scale to the small scale. This proves the validity of the enhancement of our proposed model.

Table 5. Ablation study of the proposed model on six real-world datasets

Method\Dataset	ALOI	MNIST	MSRC-v1	NUS-WIDE	Wikipedia	Caltech101
Ours without Discriminators	60.98	81.74	64.29	28.22	51.95	21.43
Ours with Discriminators	82.14	88.73	86.05	40.11	62.38	25.33

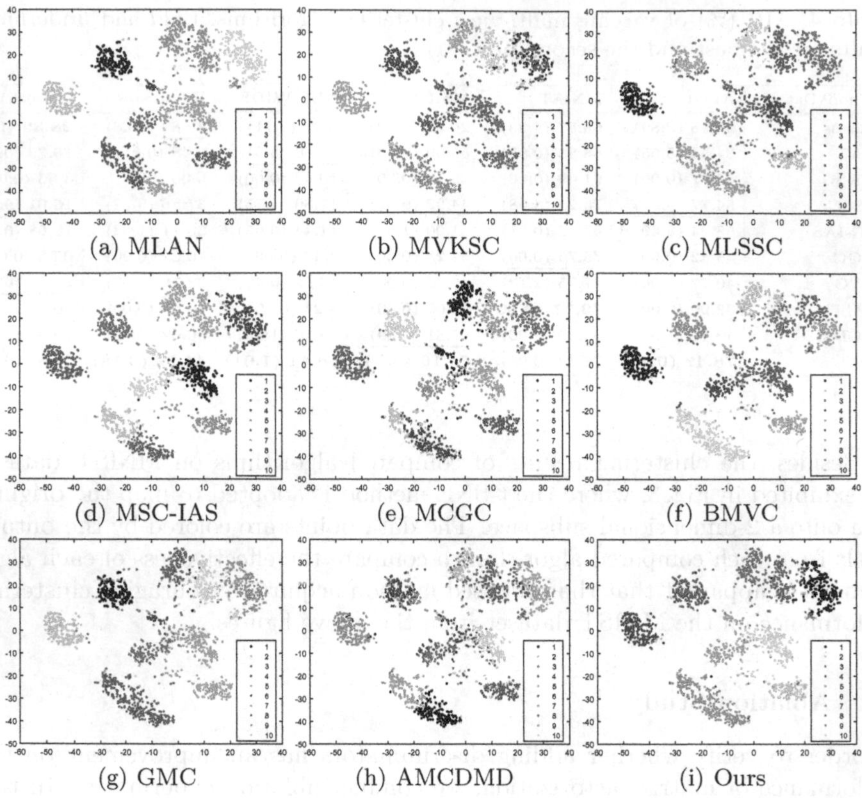

Fig. 3. Visualizations of the learned clustering results for eight compared algorithms on MNIST dataset using t-SNE.

5 Conclusion

This paper proposed a multi-view matrix factorization method that used a shared representation matrix to represent multi-view data and extracted features from all views. We used discriminators to enhance the feature extraction capability of matrix factorization and demonstrated the effectiveness of the modality. We conducted experiments on six real-world datasets to show the superiority of the performance of our approach relative to other multi-view clustering methods. In the future work, we will further focus on exploring the connection between shared representation matrices and feature representations thus providing higher quality features for subsequent tasks.

References

1. Brbic, M., Kopriva, I.: Multi-view low-rank sparse subspace clustering. Patt. Recogn. **73**, 247–258 (2018)
2. Chen, W., Lu, X.: Unregistered hyperspectral and multispectral image fusion with synchronous nonnegative matrix factorization. In: Proceedings of the Third Chinese Conference on Pattern Recognition and Computer Vision, pp. 602–614 (2020)
3. Ding, C.H.Q., Li, T., Jordan, M.I.: Convex and semi-nonnegative matrix factorizations. IEEE Trans. Patt. Anal. Mach. Intell, **32**(1), 45–55 (2010)
4. Goodfellow, I.J., et al.: Generative adversarial nets. In: Proceedings of the Twenty-eighth Conference on Neural Information Processing Systems, pp. 2672–2680 (2014)
5. Houthuys, L., Langone, R., Suykens, J.A.K.: Multi-view kernel spectral clustering. Inf. Fus. **44**, 46–56 (2018)
6. Huang, S., Kang, Z., Xu, Z.: Auto-weighted multi-view clustering via deep matrix decomposition. Pattern Recogn. **97**, 107015 (2020)
7. Li, Z., Wang, Q., Tao, Z., Gao, Q., Yang, Z.: Deep adversarial multi-view clustering network. In: Proceedings of the Twenty-Eighth International Joint Conference on Artificial Intelligence, pp. 2952–2958 (2019)
8. Nie, F., Cai, G., Li, X.: Multi-view clustering and semi-supervised classification with adaptive neighbours. In: Proceedings of the Thirty-First AAAI Conference on Artificial Intelligence, pp. 2408–2414 (2017)
9. Sun, G., Cong, Y., Zhang, Y., Zhao, G., Fu, Y.: Continual multiview task learning via deep matrix factorization. IEEE Trans. Neural Netw. Learn. Syst. **32**(1), 139–150 (2021)
10. Wang, H., Ding, S., Li, Y., Li, X., Zhang, Y.: Hierarchical physician recommendation via diversity-enhanced matrix factorization. ACM Trans. Knowl. Discov. Data **15**(1), 1:1–1:17 (2021)
11. Wang, H., Yang, Y., Liu, B.: Gmc: graph-based multi-view clustering. IEEE Trans. Knowl. Data Eng **6**, 1116–1129 (2020)
12. Wang, S., Chen, Z., Du, S., Lin, Z.: Learning deep sparse regularizers with applications to multi-view clustering and semi-supervised classification. IEEE Trans. Patt. Anal. Mach. Intell. (2021). https://doi.org/10.1109/TPAMI.2021.3082632
13. Wang, X., Lei, Z., Guo, X., Zhang, C., Shi, H., Li, S.: Multi-view subspace clustering with intactness-aware similarity. Patt. Recogn. **88**, 50–63 (2018)
14. Zhan, K., Nie, F., Wang, J., Yang, Y.: Multiview consensus graph clustering. IEEE Trans. Image Process. **28**(3), 1261–1270 (2019)
15. Zhao, H., Ding, Z., Fu, Y.: Multi-view clustering via deep matrix factorization. In: Proceedings of the Thirty-First AAAI Conference on Artificial Intelligence, pp. 2921–2927 (2017)
16. Zheng, Z., Li, L., Shen, F., Shen, H.T., Shao, L.: Binary multi-view clustering. IEEE Trans. Patt. Anal. Mach. Intell. **41**(7), 1774–1782 (2019)

Multi-level Residual Attention Network for Speckle Suppression

Yu Lei[1,2], Shuaiqi Liu[1,2,3(✉)], Luyao Zhang[1,2], Ling Zhao[1,2], and Jie Zhao[1,2]

[1] College of Electronic and Information Engineering, Hebei University, Baoding 071002, China
[2] Machine Vision Technology Innovation Center of Hebei Province, Baoding 071000, China
[3] National Laboratory of Pattern Recognition (NLPR), Institute of Automation, Chinese Academy of Sciences, Beijing 100190, China

Abstract. In order to achieve effective speckle suppression, we propose a multi-level residual attention network by combining with multi-level block and residual channel attention network, which is suitable for speckle suppression. Firstly, the network model performs a simple shallow feature extraction for the input noise image through two convolution layers. Then, the residual attention network is used to extract the deep features. Finally, a convolution layer and residual learning are used to generate the final denoised image. Experimental results show that the proposed method can effectively suppress the noise and preserve the edge details of the image.

Keywords: Speckle suppression · Deep learning · Residual attention

1 Introduction

Synthetic aperture radar (SAR) [1] is a kind of imaging radar with high resolution. The removal of speckle noise in SAR image is very important for the subsequent application of SAR image. These methods are mainly divided into two categories: spatial filtering algorithm and frequency-domain filtering algorithm. Spatial filtering algorithms mainly use local adjacent pixels to suppress noise, among which typical denoising algorithms include Frost filter [2] and Lee filter [3]. In order to better perform image denoising, Buades et al. [4] proposed the idea of non-local means (NLM). Later, Dabov et al. [5] extended this idea to the transform domain, and proposed matching adjacent pixel images and integrating similar blocks in a three-dimensional matrix called block-matching and 3D filtering (BM3D). Obviously, SAR images also have non-local similarity, so the idea of non-local denoising can also be applied to the field of speckle suppression. For example, the SAR image denoising algorithm which combines non-local ideas with the transform domain (SAR-BM3D) [6].

The first author is a student.

This research was funded by National Natural Science Foundation of China under grant 62172139, the Post-graduate's Innovation Fund Project of Heibei University under grant HBU2021ss002, Natural Science Foundation of Hebei Province under grant F2018210148, F2019201151 and F2020201025, Science Research Project of Hebei Province under grant BJ2020030.

© Springer Nature Switzerland AG 2021
H. Ma et al. (Eds.): PRCV 2021, LNCS 13022, pp. 288–299, 2021.
https://doi.org/10.1007/978-3-030-88013-2_24

Based on speckle suppression algorithm in the frequency domain, the noisy image is transformed from the spatial domain to the frequency domain, and the coefficients in the transform domain are processed, then the processed image is inversely transformed back to the spatial domain, finally achieving the purpose of removing the noise. The denoising algorithm based on transform domain mainly realizes image denoising through statistical priori in wavelet domain and multi-scale geometric transform domain, such as SAR image denoising in Shearlet domain [7]. Although the methods based on the spatial domain and the transform domain have certain denoising effects on SAR images, in the process of denoising, many algorithms will produce other image quality problems, for example, the image is too blurred, the edge detail information is lost too much, and artifacts are introduced, etc.

In recent years, convolutional neural networks (CNN) have been widely used in various image processing problems, such as image classification, image segmentation, edge detection and image denoising. Therefore, scholars have also done a lot of research and applied the method based on CNN to the field of speckle suppression. Compared with traditional non-CNN denoising methods, CNN-based methods are superior to traditional methods in denoising and image detail preservation. Inspired by the model framework of feature fusion attention network [8], we construct a new subnetwork by using residual and channel attention ideas, and propose a novel speckle suppression network: multi-level residual attention denoising network (MRANet). Experimental results show that the proposed algorithm has a good denoising effect on simulated and real SAR images. The contributions of proposed algorithm are as follows: (1) The multi-layer recursive blocks are introduced to facilitate the extraction of more feature information. (2) The residual channel attention network is proposed, which can effectively improve the denoising performance of the model through local residuals learning and global residuals learning. (3) Embedding a channel attention block at the end of the entire network can effectively maintain the details of the image while denoising, thereby avoiding the denoised image from being too smooth or over-sharpened.

2 Related Work

Many CNN methods have been applied to the denoising problem of SAR images and achieved good results. Chierchia et al. [9] proposed a speckle suppression algorithm (SAR-CNN) based on residual learning, and the whole network contains 17 convolutional layers. The algorithm first performs a homomorphic transformation on the input image, and then uses residual learning to reduce speckle from the extracted noise to restore a clean image. Although the denoising ability of this algorithm is very strong, it cannot keep the detailed information of the image very well. In addition, since logarithmic transformation and corresponding exponential transformation are required during CNN model training, the network cannot be trained end-to-end.

Wang et al. [10] proposed a GAN-based SAR denoising algorithm. This method combines three different loss functions for end-to-end training to achieve a better effect of suppressing speckle. Later, Wang et al. [11] proposed an image speckle suppression convolutional neural network (ID-CNN). The whole network has 8 layers. This model can be processed end-to-end without the need to transform the input image. Compared with SAR-CNN, ID-CNN combines Euclidean loss and TV loss for training, which can obtain a better denoising effect, but still lose some details. In order to expand the receptive field, Zhang et al. [12] proposed a SAR despekling algorithm (SAR-DRN) based on dilated convolution, combined skip connection and residual learning to carry out the design of the network framework, so that the denoising network performance has been improved. The method of SAR images denoising based on deep learning enables the network to extract image features from training data, and better learn noise models to achieve better speckle suppression performance than traditional methods, and the running time is less than traditional methods. Therefore, based on the study of SAR image speckle model and CNN theory, we also propose a new type of network model suitable for speckle suppression--MRANet.

3 Proposed Method

The framework of MRANet is mainly divided into three parts, including shallow feature extraction block (SFB), deep feature extraction block (DFB) and reconstruction block. As shown in Fig. 1, SFB consists of two 3 × 3 convolutional layers, and DFB is composed of recursive group (RG), skip connection and channel attention (CA) in the form of cascade. The reconstruction block is only implemented by a 3 × 3 convolution operation.

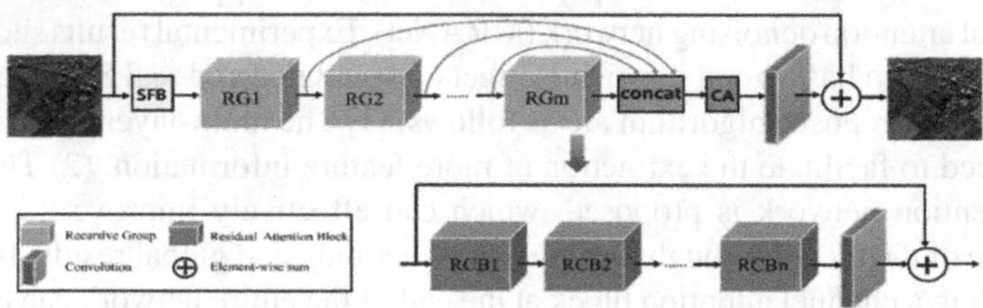

Fig. 1. Overall framework of the proposed MRANet.

Let x denotes the input of the network. As shown in Fig. 1, the input noise image x is first extracted by two convolutional blocks for shallow feature extraction, that is

$$f_o = H_{C2}(x) \tag{1}$$

where f_o represents the output after shallow extraction, which is used as the input of the second part. H_{C2} represents the function of two convolution block.

Continuous blocks can reduce the depth and computational complexity of the network model, and the introduction of skip connections can also improve the training speed of network. Therefore, the middle deep feature extraction block is designed in a cascade way. The DFB block is composed of m RGs and a CA through skip connection, and each RG is realized by cascading n residual attention blocks (RCBs). Let the output of the ith RG block be f_{rgi}

$$f_{rgi} = RG_i(RG_{i-1} \cdots (RG_1(f_0))) \tag{2}$$

where f_0 denotes the input of the second part, and RG_i represents the realization function of the RG block. The RG block denotes composed of n RCBs, a 3 × 3 convolution operation and local residual learning, which can be expressed as

$$RG_i = C(B_n(B_{n-1} \cdots (B_1(f_{rg(i-1)})))) + f_{rg(i-1)} \tag{3}$$

where B_n represents the nth RCB implementation function, C denotes the convolution operation, and $f_{rg(i-1)}$ represents the input of the ith RG.

The RCB block is composed of parametric rectified linear unit (PReLU), convolution, rectified linear unit (ReLU), CA and residual learning. It can allow a small amount of unimportant information is passed, so as to focus on effective information and further improve network performance. In the experiment, $m = 3$ in RG and $n = 10$ in RCB were set, and 64 filter coefficients were output in each RG. The output of each RG is fused, that is

$$f_{RG} = concat(f_{rg1}, f_{rg2}, f_{rg3} \cdots f_{rgm}) \tag{4}$$

Then f_{RG} is fed back to the reconstruction block through a channel attention block, and the reconstruction module is realized by only a convolution, which can be expressed as

$$z = C(H_{CA}(f_{RG})) \tag{5}$$

where z represents the obtained residual map (ie, noise), C represents the convolution operation, and H_{CA} denotes the realization function of the channel attention module. Finally, the final clean image y ($y = x - z$) is obtained through residual learning.

The proposed RCB model are shown in Fig. 2. Firstly, the input feature map is put into two residual attention blocks for feature extraction, and then the global residual attention is performed by PReLU, convolution, ReLU activation function and CA. Through the overall feature analysis and extraction, the output feature map is obtained.

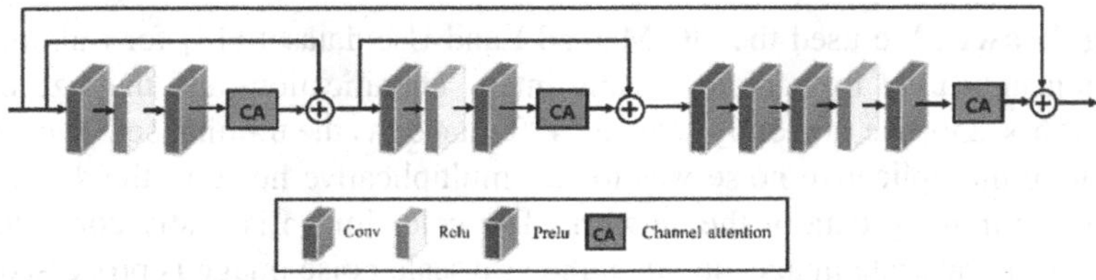

Fig. 2. Architecture of the proposed residual channel network.

Since the general CNN processing feature mapping treats each channel equally, it will reduce the learning ability between channels, thereby inhibiting the representation ability of the deep network. Therefore, we introduce the channel attention model and put it at the end of the residual block to form a residual channel attention network, and CA is added in the reconstruction stage, so that the network can ignore irrelevant information, and pay more attention to noise information to facilitate the final generation of high-quality images. The channel attention module is shown in Fig. 3.

The loss function is mainly used to guide the training of the model and to estimate the relationship between the predicted value and the true value. If the two deviate far away, the loss function will get a very large value, and the parameters will be updated through back propagation. Further reduce te value of the loss function to achieve the purpose of continuous learning. Conversely, the smaller the loss function, the closer the

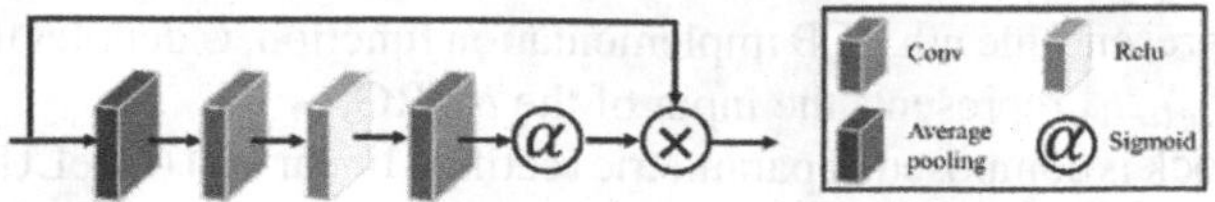

Fig. 3. Channel attention module.

predicted value and the true value, and the better the robustness of the model. In this paper, L1 loss is selected for model training. Given a training set with N pair of images $\{x^i_{noise}, y^i_{gt}\}_{i=1}^N$ and the loss function can be expressed as

$$L(\Phi) = \frac{1}{N}\sum_{i=1}^{N} ||y^i_{gt} - MRANet(x^i_{noise})||_1 \quad (6)$$

where N represents the number of noise-free image pairs, Φ denotes the set of network parameters, y_{gt} represents the noise free image, x_{noise} denotes the input noise image of the network, and *MRANet* represents the output of the entire network model.

4 Experimental Results

In order to verify the effectiveness of the proposed residual attention network, we conduct experimental verification on synthetic data and real data sets, as described below.

4.1 Datasets and Evaluation Index

Training datasets. We used the UC Merced Land Use dataset [13] for training. This dataset is mainly used for remote sensing image classification, and the size of each image is 256 × 256. We randomly selected 400 images as the training set. The artificial simulation of multiplicative noise was to add multiplicative noise to the 400 training images as the training data of the network. The color image is firstly converted to a single-channel grayscale image, and then the grayscale noise image is processed to get the final clean image.

Test datasets. The test data are divided into simulated and real image. For simulated images, on the one hand, a noise image with four looks (L = 2, 4, 8 and 10) is randomly selected in the Set12 data set for testing. For the denoising test of real SAR images, four real SAR images are used to evaluate the proposed algorithm visually, as shown in Fig. 4. All the images in Fig. 4 are 256 × 256. These real SAR images are available at www.sandia.gov. For the convenience of description, the four images are named SAR1, SAR2, SAR3 and SAR4.

In order to verify the effectiveness of the proposed algorithm, in the simulation data, due to the existence of clear original images, we use peak signal-to-noise ratio (PSNR) and structural similarity index (SSIM) [14] to measure the denoising effect of various denoising algorithms. The larger the SSIM value, the more the details of the denoised image are restored and the closer it is to the original image. The larger the PSNR value, the stronger the denoising ability of the denoising algorithm and the clearer the image.

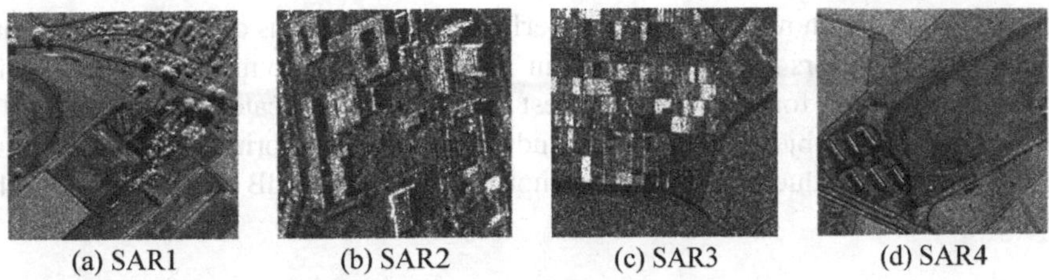

(a) SAR1 (b) SAR2 (c) SAR3 (d) SAR4

Fig. 4. Original images used in the test experiments. (a)–(d) are real SAR images.

For real image denoising, since there is no clear image, we choose the following four indicators to measure the denoising effect: equivalent numbers of looks (ENL) [15], edge preservation degree based on the ratio of average ratio (EPD-ROA) (horizontal (HD) and vertical direction (VD)) [16], unassisted measure of the quality (UM) [17] and TIME. ENL is used to measure the smoothness of the image. The larger the value, the smoother the flat area of the image. It is also used to reflect the degree of contamination of the image by coherent speckle noise. The higher the ENL, the less noise in the image. EPD-ROA is used to evaluate the ability of image detail edge preservation, which can be divided into horizontal and vertical parts. The closer the value is to 1, the stronger the image detail and edge preservation ability. UM is used to test the overall denoising ability of the image. The smaller the UM value, the better the denoising ability.

Then, in order to verify the effectiveness of the proposed algorithm for speckle suppression, we test it on simulated and real SAR images and compare it with the following seven methods: Non-local SAR image denoising algorithm based on wavelet domain (SAR-BM3D) [6], Frost filter [2], Shearlet domain Bayesian threshold shrinkage denoising algorithm based on sparse representation (BSS-SR) [7], fast and flexible based on non-subsampled clipping domain Denoising algorithm (FFDNet) [18], SAR image denoising algorithm based on FFDNet and continuous cyclic translation (FFDNet-CCS) [19], SAR image denoising algorithm based on convolutional neural network and guided filtering (CNN-GFF) [20] and SAR image denoising algorithm based on CNN prior (IRCNN) [21]. Finally, the performance of the proposed algorithm is analyzed in objective indicators and subjective vision.

The training environment used in the experiment is Windows 10 system. Model framework is Pytorch. The GPU of the machine is NVIDIA GeForce RTX 2080 Ti. CUDA10.1 and CUDNN10.1 are used to accelerate GPU computing power and speed up training. It takes about 13 h to train the complete model. The entire network is trained 40,000 times, using the ADAM [22] optimization method for training. $\beta 1 = 0.9$, $\beta 2 = 0.999$, batch-size is 2, and the initial learning rate (lr) is set to 0.0001. In the training process, the training image with a size of 256×256 is cropped into image patch with a size of 64×64, and random rotation and horizontal flipping are performed at 90, 180, and 270° to achieve data enhancement.

4.2 Experiment on Synthetic Speckled Image

For the simulated image, we randomly select an image in Set12, and add coherent noises of different look numbers to the clean image for testing. The looks are 2, 4, 8, and 10 respectively. Table 1 shows the denoising performance of various denoising algorithms. The objective indicators PSNR and SSIM in Table 1 are used to measure the denoising performance. The red font indicates the best and the blue indicates the second best. It can be seen that the objective evaluation indicators of our algorithm are basically the best, and the PSNR value is significantly improved by about 1 dB compared with other CNN methods.

Table 1. Quantitative evaluation results for simulated SAR image.

Looks	Index	SAR-BM3D	BSS-SR	Frost	IRCNN	FFDNet	FFDNet-CCS	CNN-GFF	Proposed
L=2	PSNR	29.54	27.76	27.62	27.63	27.67	27.55	27.43	29.67
	SSIM	0.6832	0.6611	0.4785	0.3831	0.3749	0.3934	0.3066	0.6643
L=4	PSNR	30.48	29.04	28.68	28.54	28.54	28.50	28.15	31.59
	SSIM	0.7299	0.7186	0.5911	0.5351	0.5076	0.5301	0.4289	0.7927
L=8	PSNR	31.88	30.31	29.91	29.60	29.88	29.84	29.03	32.92
	SSIM	0.7725	0.7425	0.6912	0.6601	0.6682	0.6819	0.5601	0.7956
L=10	PSNR	32.18	30.56	30.33	29.82	30.42	30.36	29.34	33.08
	SSIM	0.7798	0.7486	0.7257	0.6875	0.7195	0.7336	0.6023	0.7984

4.3 Experiment on Real Image

Four real SAR images were selected to test the corresponding denoising algorithm to verify the effectiveness of the proposed algorithm. Figure 5 shows the denoising effect of each denoising algorithm on the SAR1 image.

As can be seen from the magnification area in Fig. 5, the denoising images of SAR-BM3D and BSS-SR are blurred with too much detail loss. The SAR-BM3D has a strong denoising effect on smooth areas, but the edge details are lost seriously. The magnification region of CNN-GFF is very similar to that of the original SAR1, indicating that the denoising effect of the algorithm is poor. The denoising effect of IRCNN is good, but false edges appear in flat areas. Frost and FFDNet-CCS have some denoising effects, but introduce some artificial textures. The denoised image of the proposed algorithm can retain more details, and the edge details can be fully preserved while the speckle is effectively suppressed.

Table 2 shows the objective evaluation index results obtained by each denoising algorithm when denoising SAR1 image. It can be seen from the Table 2 that our ENL value is second only to SAR-BM3D, but much higher than other denoising methods. Our algorithm also has the lowest UM value, which indicates that the proposed algorithm has the strongest comprehensive denoising ability. The EPD-ROA index of our algorithm is higher than other algorithms, which indicates that our algorithm has better image edge retention ability. In terms of running time, the proposed algorithm also has the shortest running time compared with other algorithms.

Figures 6 and 7 respectively show the renderings after denoising of SAR2 and SAR3 images by each denoising algorithm. As can be seen from Figs. 6 and 7, when denoising SAR2, the images denoised by SAR-BM3D, BSS-SR and Frost were blurred, and the details of the original image were completely lost. However, other speckle suppression

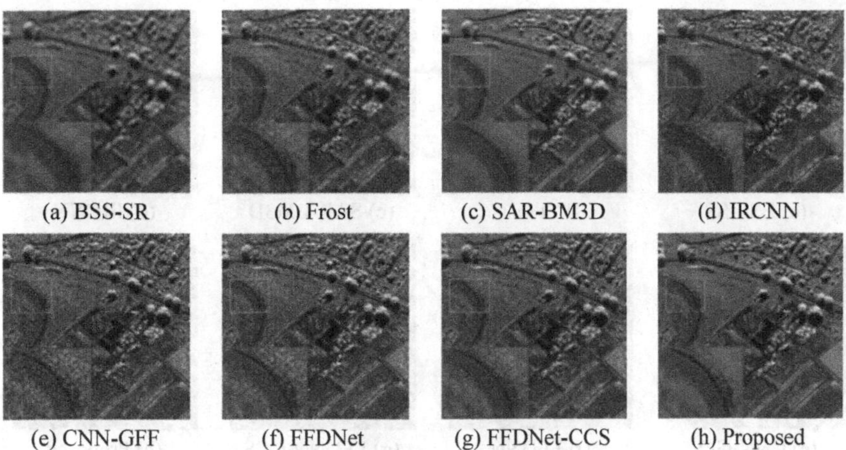

(a) BSS-SR (b) Frost (c) SAR-BM3D (d) IRCNN

(e) CNN-GFF (f) FFDNet (g) FFDNet-CCS (h) Proposed

Fig. 5. Despeckling results on the real SAR1.

Table 2. Quantitative evaluation results for real SAR1.

Method	ENL ↑	UM ↓	EPD-ROA		TIME(s) ↓
			HD ↑	VD ↑	
SAR-BM3D	166.5003	51.0335	0.8081	0.7725	68.2135
BSS-SR	86.6347	63.3830	0.4350	0.5065	6.3939
Frost	40.1545	35.5885	0.7732	0.7819	7.8311
IRCNN	25.9335	32.5849	0.8663	0.8502	2.1575
FFDNet	18.6832	88.7781	0.9063	0.8833	2.8121
FFDNet-CCS	28.4617	148.3835	0.8260	0.8141	2.7841
CNN-GFF	12.4384	100.6929	0.9075	0.8923	5.6132
Proposed	145.6307	28.5329	0.9141	0.9040	0.2754

algorithms based on CNN also have a certain amount of noise points in the amplification region. The proposed algorithm can effectively suppress the speckle while preserving the edge and detailed texture information of the image.

Table 3 presents the objective evaluation index results obtained by each denoising algorithm in SAR2 images. As can be seen from Table 3, the ENL value of our algorithm is poor, but compared with other CNN-based speckle suppression algorithms, the ENL value of our algorithm is the highest. In the UM index, the value of the proposed algorithm is the lowest, which also indicates that the proposed algorithm has stronger comprehensive denoising ability. In terms of EPD-ROA index, the proposed algorithm is also the highest, which indicates that our algorithm has a better ability of image edge preservation. In terms of running time, compared with other algorithms, our algorithm also has the shortest running time.

Table 4 shows the objective evaluation index results obtained by each denoising algorithm in SAR3 images. As can be seen from Table 4, the ENL value of the proposed algorithm is poor, but compared with other CNN-based speckle suppression algorithms, the ENL value of the proposed algorithm is the highest. The ENL and EPD-ROA values of the proposed algorithm are also the highest, which indicates that the proposed algorithm

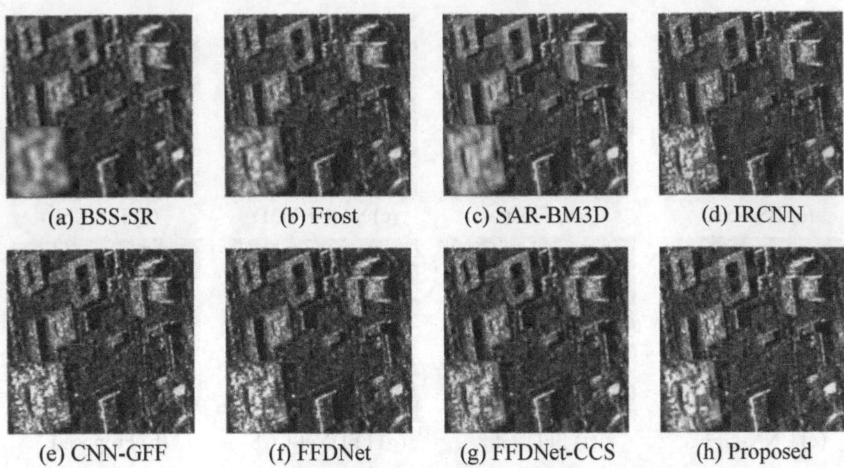

(a) BSS-SR (b) Frost (c) SAR-BM3D (d) IRCNN

(e) CNN-GFF (f) FFDNet (g) FFDNet-CCS (h) Proposed

Fig. 6. Despeckling results on the real SAR2.

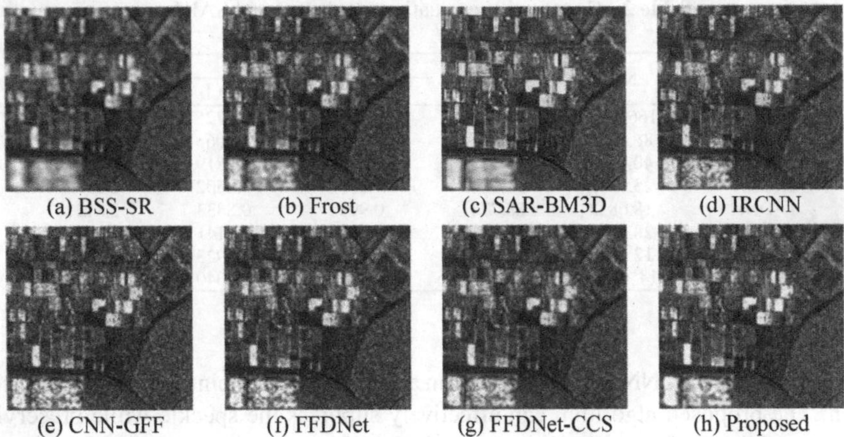

(a) BSS-SR (b) Frost (c) SAR-BM3D (d) IRCNN

(e) CNN-GFF (f) FFDNet (g) FFDNet-CCS (h) Proposed

Fig. 7. Despeckling results on the real SAR3.

Table 3. Quantitative evaluation results for real SAR2.

Method	ENL ↑	UM ↓	EPD-ROA		TIME(s) ↓
			HD ↑	VD ↑	
SAR-BM3D	3.7011	92.3219	0.7431	0.8340	65.4424
BSS-SR	4.4846	63.1376	0.5678	0.6083	2.3139
Frost	3.2515	28.8393	0.8373	0.8402	7.4867
IRCNN	2.3433	12.0083	0.8355	0.8635	2.7126
FFDNet	1.9762	37.8296	0.8923	0.9014	2.9386
FFDNet-CCS	2.3706	23.6286	0.7968	0.8443	2.2009
CNN-GFF	1.8382	56.5609	0.9012	0.9087	2.3969
Proposed	2.9261	11.2305	0.9106	0.9249	0.2504

can not only effectively suppress the speckle, but also fully preserve the edge and texture information of the image. Compared with other denoising algorithms, the running time of our algorithm is much less than that of other denoising algorithms.

Table 4. Quantitative evaluation results for real SAR3.

Method	ENL ↑	UM ↓	EPD-ROA		TIME(s) ↓
			HD ↑	VD ↑	
SAR-BM3D	4.9058	39.0508	0.5707	0.6800	62.6117
BSS-SR	5.4611	38.1924	0.3399	0.4146	2.1841
Frost	4.1862	49.2760	0.6061	0.6429	8.2414
IRCNN	3.3376	39.0926	0.7030	0.7455	1.9533
FFDNet	2.7059	380.1645	0.7354	0.7910	2.5625
FFDNet-CCS	3.2829	305.6754	0.6106	0.6796	2.2588
CNN-GFF	2.2515	176.5678	0.7385	0.7821	2.8814
Proposed	3.5132	35.5219	0.7560	0.8071	0.2370

Figure 8 shows the effect of denoising the SAR4 image by each denoising algorithm. As can be seen from the visual diagram in Fig. 8, the proposed algorithm can effectively suppress the speckle and has a strong ability to restore the texture details of the image. From the amplification area in Fig. 8, it can be seen that Frost, CNN-GFF and FFDNet cannot effectively suppress speckle. Over-smooth phenomenon exists in the image denoised by SAR-BM3D and BSS-SR. FFDNet, IRCNN and CNN-GFF have insufficient noise suppression capability, while FFDNet-CCS has artificial texture. The proposed algorithm can not only suppress the speckle effectively, but also preserve the edge and texture information of the image well.

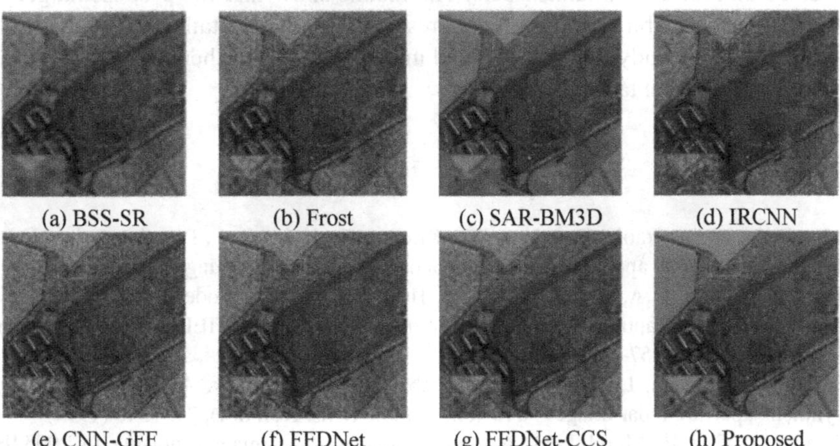
(a) BSS-SR (b) Frost (c) SAR-BM3D (d) IRCNN
(e) CNN-GFF (f) FFDNet (g) FFDNet-CCS (h) Proposed

Fig. 8. Despeckling results on the real SAR4.

Table 5 shows the objective evaluation index results obtained by each denoising algorithm in SAR4 images. As can be seen from Table 5, for SAR4, the indicators of our algorithm are the best, and compared with other denoising algorithms, our algorithm is significantly improved. Because SAR4 has less texture information, the EPD-ROA is generally lower, but our algorithm is still the best. Therefore, in general, the proposed algorithm has a better comprehensive denoising effect.

Table 5. Quantitative evaluation results for real SAR4.

Method	ENL ↑	UM ↓	EPD-ROA		TIME(s) ↓
			HD ↑	VD ↑	
SAR-BM3D	31.3483	35.5472	0.4717	0.5071	58.4861
BSS-SR	33.9264	76.3399	0.1321	0.2290	2.4597
Frost	22.3186	34.5700	0.4546	0.5735	7.2027
IRCNN	21.5150	51.2553	0.5370	0.6335	1.7841
FFDNet	15.7984	41.4648	0.6558	0.6890	2.4043
FFDNet-CCS	21.9737	34.7462	0.5887	0.6145	2.1708
CNN-GFF	11.9831	76.5049	0.6503	0.6812	2.3497
Proposed	34.8494	19.2200	0.6651	0.6970	0.2529

5 Conclusion

In this paper, we propose an end-to-end SAR denoising network, which achieves denoising by cascading multiple blocks and combining the residual channel attention network. On the one hand, more block recursive cascade can keep the diversity of features. On the other hand, the channel module can focus on the characteristics of need, while ignoring unimportant information. Therefore, in the part of depth extraction, we use local and global residual channel attention to analyze and process the noise information, so as to generate high quality images in the reconstruction stage. Finally, the proposed algorithm is validated on real and simulated data. The results show that the proposed algorithm has strong denoising ability and can fully preserve the image details. In the future work, we will continue to study this problem and improve it, and further apply the denoising task to other high-level tasks.

References

1. Moreira, A., Prats-Iraola, P., Younis, M., Krieger, G., Hajnsek, I., Papathanassiou, K.P.: A tutorial on synthetic aperture radar. IEEE Geosci. Remote Sens. Mag. **1**(1), 6–43 (2013)
2. Frost, V.S., Stiles, J.A., Shanmugan, K.S., Holtzman, J.C.: A model for radar images and its application to adaptive digital filtering of multiplicative noise. IEEE Trans. Pattern Anal. Mach. Intell. **4**(2), 157–166 (1982)
3. Lee, J.S., Jurkevich, L., Dewaele, P., Wambacq, P., Oosterlinck, A.: Speckle filtering of synthetic aperture radar images : a review. Remote Sens. Rev. **8**(4), 313–340 (1994)
4. Buades, A., Coll, B., Morel, J.-M.: A non-local algorithm for image denoising. In: 2005 IEEE Computer Society Conference on Computer Vision and Pattern Recognition (CVPR 2005), vol. 2, pp. 60–65 (2005)
5. Dabov, K., Foi, A., Katkovnik, V., Egiazarian, K.: Image denoising with block-matching and 3D filtering. In: Image Processing: Algorithms and Systems, Neural Networks, and Machine Learning, vol. 6064, p. 606414 (2006)

6. Parrilli, S., Poderico, M., Angelino, C.V., Verdoliva, L.: A nonlocal SAR image denoising algorithm based on LLMMSE wavelet shrinkage. IEEE Trans. Geosci. Remote Sens. **50**(2), 606–616 (2012)
7. Liu, S.Q., Hu, S.H., Xiao, Y., An, Y.L.: Bayesian Shearlet shrinkage for SAR image denoising via sparse representation. Multidimension. Syst. Signal Process. **25**(4), 683–701 (2013). https://doi.org/10.1007/s11045-013-0225-8
8. Qin, X., Wang, Z., Bai, Y., Xie, X., Jia, H.: FFA-Net: feature fusion attention network for single image dehazing. Proceedings of the AAAI Conference on Artificial Intelligence **34**, 11908–11915 (2020)
9. Chierchia, G., Cozzolino, D., Poggi, G., Verdoliva, L.: SAR image despeckling through convolutional neural networks. In: 2017 IEEE International Geoscience and Remote Sensing Symposium (IGARSS), pp. 5438–5441 (2017)
10. Wang, P., Zhang, H., Patel, V.M.: Generative adversarial network-based restoration of speckled SAR images. In: 2017 IEEE 7th International Workshop on Computational Advances in Multi-Sensor Adaptive Processing (CAMSAP), pp. 1–5 (2017)
11. Wang, P., Zhang, H., Patel, V.M.: SAR image despeckling using a convolutional neural network. IEEE Signal Process. Lett. **24**(12), 1763–1767 (2017)
12. Zhang, Q., Yuan, Q., Li, J., Yang, Z., Ma, X.: Learning a dilated residual network for SAR image despeckling. Remote Sens. **10**(2), 196 (2018)
13. Yang, Y., Newsam, S.: Bag-of-visual-words and spatial extensions for land-use classification. In: Proceedings of the 18th SIGSPATIAL International Conference on Advances in Geographic Information Systems, pp. 270–279 (2010)
14. Wang, Z., Bovik, A.C., Sheikh, H.R., Simoncelli, E.P.: Image quality assessment: from error visibility to structural similarity. IEEE Trans. Image Process. **13**(4), 600–612 (2004)
15. Lee, J.-S.: Speckle analysis and smoothing of synthetic aperture radar images. Comput. Graph. Image Process. **17**(1), 24–32 (1981)
16. Ma, X., Shen, H., Zhao, X., Zhang, L.: SAR image despeckling by the use of variational methods with adaptive nonlocal functionals. IEEE Trans. Geosci. Remote Sens. **54**(6), 3421–3435 (2016)
17. Gomez, L., Ospina, R., Frery, A.C.: Unassisted quantitative evaluation of despeckling filters. Remote Sens. **9**(4), 389 (2017)
18. Zhang, K., Zuo, W., Zhang, L.: FFDNet: toward a fast and flexible solution for CNN-based image denoising. IEEE Trans. Image Process. **27**(9), 4608–4622 (2018)
19. Liu, S., et al.: SAR speckle removal using hybrid frequency modulations. IEEE Trans. Geosci. Remote Sens. **59**, 3956–3966 (2021)
20. Liu, S., et al.: Convolutional neural network and guided filtering for SAR image denoising. Remote Sens. **11**(6), 702 (2019)
21. Zhang, K., Zuo, W., Gu, S., Zhang, L.: Learning deep CNN denoiser prior for image restoration. In: 2017 IEEE Conference on Computer Vision and Pattern Recognition (CVPR), pp. 2808–2817 (2017)
22. Kingma, D.P., Ba, J.L.: Adam: a method for stochastic optimization. In: ICLR 2015 : International Conference on Learning Representations 2015 (2015)

Suppressing Style-Sensitive Features via Randomly Erasing for Domain Generalizable Semantic Segmentation

Siwei Su[1], Haijian Wang[1], and Meng Yang[1,2(✉)]

[1] School of Computer Science and Engineering, Sun Yat-sen University, Guangzhou, China
[2] Key Laboratory of Machine Intelligence and Advanced Computing (SYSU), Ministry of Education, Guangzhou, China
yangm6@mail.sysu.edu.cn

Abstract. Domain generalization aims to enhance robustness of models to different domains, which is crucial for safety-critical systems in practice. In this paper, we propose a simple plug-in module to promote the ability of generalization for semantic segmentation networks without extra loss function. Firstly, we rethink the relationship between semantics and style in the sight of feature maps, and divide the channels of them into two kinds (i.e. style-sensitive channels and semantic-sensitive channels) via the variance of Gram matrix. Secondly, with the assumption that the domain shift mainly lies in style, a random erasure method is proposed to style-sensitive-channel features with the hope of learning domain invariant features and preventing model from over-fitting to specific domain. Extensive experiments demonstrate that the generalization of our proposed method outperforms existing approaches.

Keywords: Domain generalization · Semantic segmentation

1 Introduction

Deep convolution neural networks (DCNN) have seen its soaring success in many visual understanding tasks concerning their performance on the benchmark datasets. However, when applied on the real-world unseen data, DCNN models often fail to perform at their best due to the discrepancy between the training and test samples. Thus it is of great significance to reduce the performance gap between the target and source domains, especially for those safety-critical systems, i.e. autonomous driving. In response to such issues, an intuitive way is to collect and label data as many samples as possible. However, it is prohibitively expensive and impractical to manually label more unseen samples, especially for densely classification tasks, e,g. semantic segmentation. Recently, researchers instead tend to focus on developing more robust models to mitigate the domain gap issue without plenty of manually labeling.

© Springer Nature Switzerland AG 2021
H. Ma et al. (Eds.): PRCV 2021, LNCS 13022, pp. 300–311, 2021.
https://doi.org/10.1007/978-3-030-88013-2_25

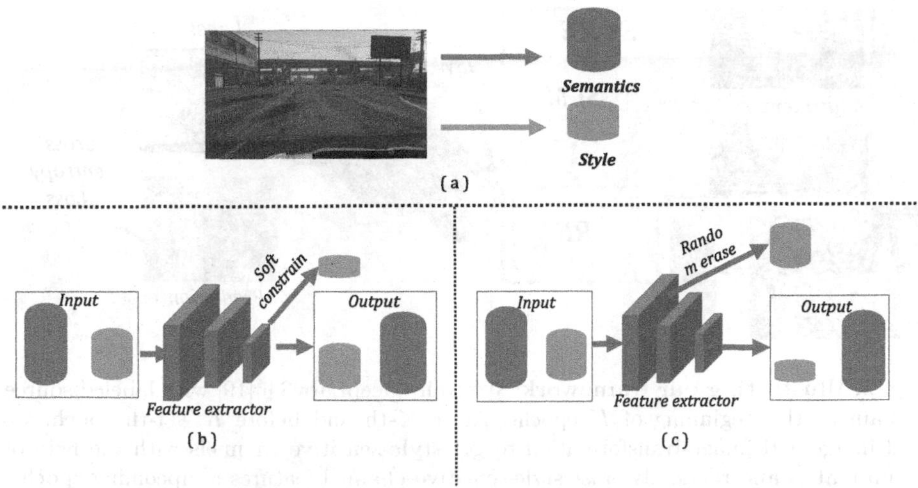

Fig. 1. Illustrating differences between ours and others: (a) An image always includes semantic information and style information. (b) Other works apply soft constrain. (c) Our work applies random erasure.

Domain adaptation (DA) is expected to align distribution on the setting of source (synthetic) domain with labels and target (real-world) domain without labels, which greatly relieves the tediousness of labeling real-world data. However, despite best efforts, we are unable to exhaustively collect all real-world data due to its massive complexity and unpredictability. Therefore, once DA network is applied in agnostic environment, their accuracy will drop significantly.

Recently, Domain generalization (DG) have drawn increasing attention due to its ability to overcome the above inadequacy. In DG, no target samples and labels are available, and its goal is to learn a robust model that can learn domain invariant feature, generalizing well to all unseen new data. A study [3] has shown that it is a preferable choice to normalize features for generalization networks. However, the normalization standardizes the whole features in an image, ignoring adverse impact of style information in them during training. An existing state-of-the-art method [7] applies selected whitening loss (ISW loss) to suppress style element in images. However, ISW loss is just soft constrain during training, which can't prevent style information from feeding into network explicitly and still potentially leads to over-fitting in specific domain. As shown in Fig.1, in order to reduce style information as possible and strengthen the semantic information in model learning, we present a strongly restrictive plug-in module in semantic segmentation network for domain generalization. To the best of our knowledge, our method is the first attempt to decouple the channels of features into two categories via Gram matrix [28]: semantic-sensitive channels and style-sensitive channels. As mentioned above, we are motivated to train a robust network by removing the features of style-sensitive channels and preserving semantic information in images. Thus how to distinguish semantics and style information is

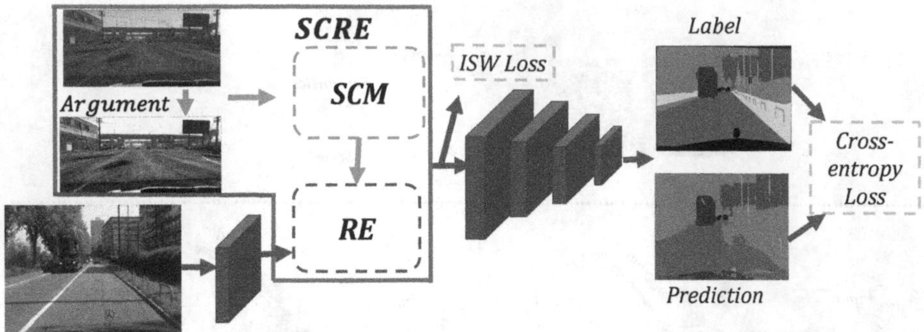

Fig. 2. Illustrating our framework: We train DeepLabv3+ [19] with labeled source domain at the beginning of K epochs. After K-th and before $K+1$-th epoch, we feed image and image-transformation to get style-sensitive channels with the help of Gram matrix and randomly erase style-sensitive-channel features in upcoming epochs. Following [7], we apply ISW Loss and Cross-entropy loss to supervise our training network. SCRE, SCM and RE in figure represent randomly erasing style-sensitive-channel features module, getting style-sensitive channels and randomly erasing respectively.

the key issue. We feed the model with image and image-relevant style transformation to calculate the differences between channel-dimensions. With these differences, we filter style-sensitive channels of feature maps and randomly erase partial feature values on these channels. Overall, our main contribution can be concluded as follows:

- We are the first to explicitly decouple the style-sensitive-channel and semantic-sensitive-channel features. Therefore, the latter, which are widely considered to be domain invariant in domain generalization, can be better preserved.
- We relief the model learning from over-fitting to domain-specific style features and enhance the domain invariant features by a plug-in module, which randomly erases style-sensitive-channel features.
- Extensive experiments and ablation studies are conducted to illustrate the effectiveness and superiority of our proposed method.

2 Related Work

In this section, we give a brief review to the related work in the paper, i.e. semantic segmentation and domain generalization.

2.1 Semantic Segmentation

Semantic Segmentation is a basic branch in computer vision, receiving wide attention in recent year, since Fully Convolutional Network (FCN) [12] is first transform convolutional classification network to fully convolutional network for semantic segmentation. Based on FCN, current models employing either encoder-decoder [13,14] or spatial pyramid pooling [15–17] greatly boost the accuracy of the task. For instance, PSPNet [17] applies pooling kernels to capture representations at various resolutions. DeepLab Family [15,18,19] employs an Atrous Spatial Pyramid Pooling (ASPP) module rather than reducing resolutions, with dilated convolutions [20] to expand convolution perspective. Up to now, although other semantic segmentation networks emerge in an endless stream, DeepLabv3+ [19] is still a classical semantic segmentation architecture, which is widely in downstream work. As our domain generalization method is proposed for semantic segmentation, we adopt DeepLabv3+ as well as other related works.

2.2 Domain Generalization

Blanchard et al. [1] is the pioneer of domain generalization, which essentially solves out-of-distribution problem. Thereafter, researchers have developed numerous outstanding algorithms to promote the development of domain generalization. For instance, Instance Normalization [8] and batch normalization [9] are utilized in parallel by Pan et al. [3] to modify the marginal architecture and prevent features from falling into specific styles. Li et al. [6] achieves distribution alignment in the hidden representation of an auto-encoder using maximum mean discrepancy. Li and Gong et al. [5] resorted to adversarial learning with auxiliary domain classifiers to learn domain-agnostic features. And Ghifary et al. [10] introduces multi-task auto-encoders to learn feature robust to invariant domain. Furthermore, Muandet et al. [11] presented a kernel-based optimization algorithm, called Domain-Invariant Component Analysis, to learn an invariant transformation by minimizing the dissimilarity across domains. Inconsistently, our method does not require extra networks, layers and complex adversarial training strategy (e.g. domain classifiers) for learning robustness models. Our method is just a plug-in module with negligible calculation and we wish our proposed can be a supplement to any domain generalization task, despite just applied for segmentation in this paper.

3 Method

In this section, we first introduce the overview in Subsect. 3.1 and framework in Subsect. 3.2 of our method in outline. We then detail our plug-in module in Subsect. 3.3 involving how to select the style-sensitive channels and how to randomly erase the features in them. At last, we show our training loss in Subsect. 3.4.

3.1 Overview

We argue that the channels of learning features should be divided into style-sensitive channels and semantic-sensitive channels due to the indisputable fact that the networks always fall into over-fitting when trained with single style data. In respond to such issue, our method are concluded as followed: firstly, we detect style differences between image and it transformation and then find out the style-sensitive channels. After that, we randomly erase the features of the style-sensitive channels to prevent the model from over-fitting in specific domains, thereby enhancing the domain generalization ability of segmentation models. Furthermore, by erasing style-sensitive-channel features, the model will be forced to pay more attention to other semantic-sensitive-channel channels.

3.2 Framework

Given source-domain images X_s with pixel-wise labels Y_s and a set of unseen target domain $D_t = \{D_1, \ldots, D_K\}$. Our goal is to generalize segmentation models $\mathcal{M}$ training with source domain images X_s to unseen target domains. To achieve this, we extract feature map $f = \mathcal{M}(x) \in \mathbb{R}^{C \times H \times W}$ of an image x; and based on the assumption that the style shifts in domain includes color and blurriness, we employ augmentation function $\tau(x)$, e.g. color jittering and Gaussian blurring, widely used in fully-supervised tasks, to change the style of images without changing its semantics; then we feed $\tau(x)$ to $\mathcal{M}$ to get feature map, i.e. $f' = \mathcal{M}(\tau(x)) \in \mathbb{R}^{C \times H \times W}$. After that we combine f and f' to explore the style-sensitive channels. And then, we can randomly erase the feature of the corresponding style-sensitive channels in the upcoming learning. Additionally, our network is trained under supervision of ISW loss and Cross-entropy loss. The overall framework is illustrated in Fig. 2.

3.3 Randomly Erasing Style-sensitive-Channel Features

In this section, we will introduce our proposed plug-in module of randomly erasing style-sensitive-channel features comprehensively, as shown in Fig. 3. As mentioned above, we feed an original image and its transformation to model respectively to obtain the features $f \in \mathbb{R}^{C \times H \times W}$ and $f' \in \mathbb{R}^{C \times H \times W}$ respectively. Next, we flatten them to $\bar{f} = flatten(f) \in \mathbb{R}^{C \times HW}$ and $\bar{f}' = flatten(f') \in \mathbb{R}^{C \times HW}$ respectively. In the above notation, C denotes the number of channels, H and W are the spatial dimensions of the feature maps. For convenience, we will use $\bar{F}$ as the unified notation of $\bar{f}$ and $\bar{f}\prime$. In the style transfer, Gram matrix is often used to represent the style of images [28]. Just like them, we measure the style of our images by Gram matrix:

$$Gram = \bar{F} \circ \bar{F}^{\mathrm{T}} \in \mathbb{R}^{C \times C} \quad (1)$$

We standardize the learning features $\bar{F}$ to $\bar{F}_s$ through an instance normalization shown in [8]. It is very worthy of our reminding that normalization does not change the distribution of values, that is, larger values are still larger and the smaller values are still smaller after regularization. Therefore, the standardization does not affect our purpose of obtaining style-sensitive channels:

$$\bar{F}_s = (diag\,(Gram_{\mu}))^{-\frac{1}{2}} \odot (\bar{F} - \mu \odot \mathbf{1}^{\mathrm{T}}) \quad (2)$$

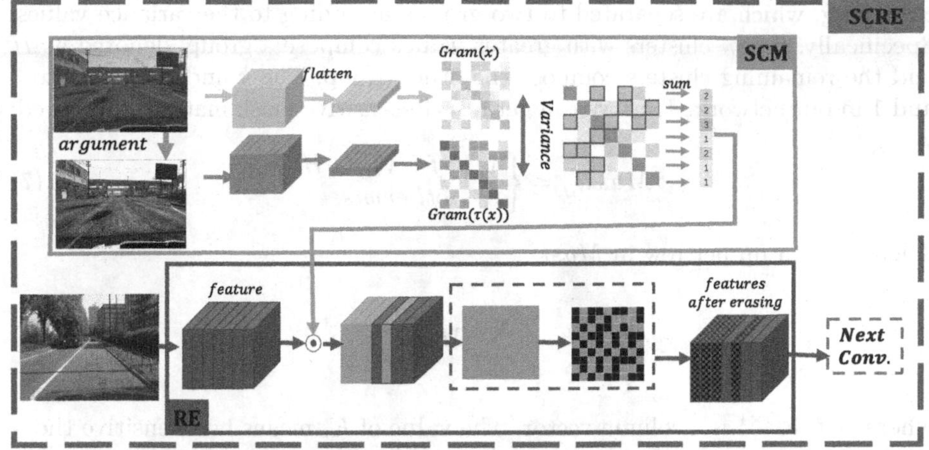

Fig. 3. Illustrating of our plug-in module. The orange solid box indicates the stream of getting style-sensitive channels by feeding image and its transformation. The red solid box shows the stream of erasing style-sensitive-channel features and the red dashed box in it represents erasing features on one channel. SCRE, SCM and RE in figure represent randomly erasing style-sensitive-channel features module, getting style-sensitive channels and randomly erasing respectively. (Color figure online)

where $\odot$ is element-wise multiplication, and $diag\left(G_{\mu}\right) \in \mathbb{R}^{C\times 1}$ denotes the column vector consisting of diagonal elements in *Gram*. Note that each diagonal element is copied along with the spatial dimension HW for element-wise multiplication. Therefore, we can get the normalized Gram matrix:

$$Grams = \bar{F}_s \circ \bar{F}_s^{\mathrm{T}} \in \mathbb{R}^{C\times C} \tag{3}$$

Specifically, we denote the normalized Gram matrix from $\bar{F}_s$ as $Grams$ and from $\bar{F'}_s$ as $Grams'$. And then we calculate the variance matrix between $Grams$ and $Grams'$ to catch differences between them, as shown the orange solid box in Fig. 3. Formally, the variance matrix $V \in \mathbb{R}^{C\times C}$ is defined as:

$$V = 1/N \sum_{i=1}^{N} \Delta_i^2 \tag{4}$$

from mean M_{G_i} and Δ_i^2 for i-th image from two normalized Gram matrices, i.e.

$$M_{G_i} = \frac{1}{2}(Grams_i + \ Grams'_i) \tag{5}$$

$$\Delta_i^2 = \frac{1}{2}(Grams_i - M_{G_i})^2 + (Grams'_i - M_{G_i})^2 \tag{6}$$

where N is the number of samples. As a result, V can include all style shifts in our argumentation technology. Following [7], V is split into k clusters with $K{-}means$

clustering, which are separated to two groups according to the variance values. Specifically, the m clusters with greater values compose a group, denoted as H and the remaining clusters compose the other group. The k and m are set to 3 and 1 in our network. Thus we can get a style-sensitive mask matrix as followed:

$$Mask_{i,j} = \begin{cases} 1 & if \quad V_{i,j} \in H \\ 0 & otherwise \end{cases} \tag{7}$$

Then we sum up per row in $Mask$:

$$K_i = \sum_{j=0}^{C} Mask_{i,j} \tag{8}$$

where $K \in \mathbb{R}^{C \times 1}$ is a column vector. The value of K_i means how sensitive the i-th channel is to style. We set a parameter $\rho \in (0, 1)$ to determine the proportion of style-sensitive channels:

$$SSC_i = \begin{cases} 1 \; if K_i \in \; top(\rho|K|) \\ 0 \qquad otherwise \end{cases} \tag{9}$$

where $topk(\cdot)$, $|K|$ represent the top $\cdot$ largest values in K and the length of K. Specially, $SSC_i = 1$ means that the i-th channel is a style-sensitive channel. Finally, we erase the style-sensitive-channel features with the motivation of removing style information:

$$E_{i,j} \in [0, 1] \sim Bernouli(p) \tag{10}$$

$$F_e = F \odot SSC \odot E + \; F \odot (1 - SSC) \tag{11}$$

where $Bernouli(p)$ denotes taking 1 with probability p under Bernouli Distribution, otherwise 0. And F_e, $F \odot SSC \odot E$ and $F \odot (1 - SSC)$ denote feature maps, style-sensitive-channel features with random erasure and semantic-sensitive-channel features respectively. $\odot$ is an element-wise multiplication and SSC is coped to the dimension as $F \in \mathbb{R}^{C \times H \times W}$. After that, we feed F_e to model and get its prediction $\hat{Y}$.

3.4 Training Loss

Training our model requires two losses, one is Cross-entropy loss commonly used in full-supervised segmentation, and the other is ISW loss from [7]. Overall, our loss function can be recorded as:

$$L = \frac{1}{HW} \sum_{h,w} \sum_{c} -y^{(h,w,c)} \log \hat{y}^{(h,w,c)} + \mathbb{E}\left[||Grams \odot M||\right] \tag{12}$$

where H and W is the height and weight of the image, and $\hat{y}^{(\cdot)}$ is the prediction of a pixel. And $\mathbb{E}$ denotes the arithmetic mean.

4 Experiment

In this section, we conduct extensive experiments on simulation-to-others and real-to-others domain generalization for semantic segmentation task. We compare our method with state-of-the-art methods on several datasets: Cityscapes [22], BDD-100K [23], Mapillary [24], SYNTHIA [25] and GTAV [26]. Specially, Cityscapes [22], BDD-100K [23] and Mapillary [24] are real-world datasets, while GTAV [26] and SYNTHIA [25] are synthetic datasets. And we discuss the advantage of our method through ablation studies with the setting of randomly erasing all style-sensitive-channel features and randomly erasing features. Following common practice in semantic segmentation, the mean intersection over union (mIoU) will be reported in the all experiments.

4.1 Datasets

Cityscapes [22] consists of 5000 fine-annotated and 20000 coarse-annotated real-world urban traffic scene images, which is widely used in semantic segmentation. We only use the fine-annotated images for our experiments, 2975, 500, and 1525 for training, validation, and test respectively.
BDD-100K [23] is a real-world dataset that contains diverse urban driving scene videos. The videos are split into training (70K), validation (10K) and testing (20K) sets. The frame at the 10-th second in each video is annotated for image tasks.
Mapillary [24] contains 25000 high resolution images annotated into 66 object categories all around the world. Specially, it is captured at various conditions regarding weather, season, and daytime.
SYNTHIA [25] is the subset of SYNTHIA-RAND-CITYSCAPES, which contain 9400 pixel-level annotated images synthesized from a virtual.
GTAV [26] is another synthetic dataset with 24966 driving-scene images generated from Grand Theft Auto V game engine. Specially, It contains 12403, 6382, and 6181 images for training, validation, and test.

4.2 Implementation Details

We implement our framework in PyTorch [21], and our experiments are conducted on NVIDIA GetForce 1080Ti GPU, the memory of which is 11 GB. In all experiments, we adopt DeepLabv3+ as our segmentation architecture and Resnet-50 as backbone, following [7]. The optimization of our network is Stochastic Gradient Descent with a initial learning late of 1e–2, momentum of 0.9 and the decay of polynomial learning scheduling [27] is set to 0.9. Besides, The maximum training iterations is 40K in all experiments. We conducted common augmentations such as color-jitering, Gaussian blur, random cropping, random horizontal flipping, and random scaling with the range of [0.5, 2.0] to prevent the over-fitting. For the argumentation function in inferring style-sensitive channels, we apply color jittering and Gaussian blur, due to the style shifts in different domain rose by color and blurriness. It is worth noted that we empirically get style-sensitive channels between 5-th epoch and 6-th epoch in the training stage. The reason for choosing this timing is that the network has learned most of the semantic in images, and it has not been over-fitted. Moreover, we train DeepLabV3+ with instance normalization layers in the first five epochs and after that, we add Selected Whitening Loss [7] and our random erasure of style-sensitive-channel features to train model.

As for the selection of the sensitive channel parameter ρ and probability p in *Bernouli*, we randomly set it to 0.3 and 0.8. Therefore, The random erasure is conducted to $0.3 \times C$ channels and approximately 20% of style-sensitive features are erased.

4.3 Performance Comparison

We compare our approach to the current state-of-the-art methods on two domain generation scenarios: real (Cityscapes) to others (BDD-100K, Mapillary, GTAV and SYNTHIA) in Table 1, simulation (GTAV) to others (Cityscapes, BDD-100K, Mapillary and SYNTHIA) in Table 2.

Real to others in Table 1. Here, training dataset is Cityscapes, validation datasets are BDD-100K, Mapillary, GTAV and SYNTHIA. Our method achieves a improvement over the best published results of the same backbone (ResNet-50), demonstrating the generalization of our method. In detail, we achieve state-of-the-art accuracy in Mapillary, GTAV and SYNTHIA. However, the accuracy in BDD-100K in our method has fallen slightly, with only −0.20.

Table 1. The comparision of Semantic segmentation performance **mIoU** on real-world dataset **Cityscapes** without accessing to others. Resnet-50 and DeepLabV3+ are basic architectures in all models for fair comparision.

Model (Cityscapes)	BDD-100K	Mapillary	GTAV	SYNTHIA	Cityscapes
Baseline	44.96	51.68	42.55	23.29	**77.51**
IBN-Net [3]	48.56	57.04	45.06	26.14	76.55
RobustNet [7]	**50.73**	58.64	45.00	26.20	76.41
Ours	50.53	**58.85**	**45.95**	**26.75**	76.20

Simulation to others in Table 2. As mentioned above, GTAV is a synthetic dataset, which can demonstrate the generalization when our network trains with synthetic images. As shown in Table 2, our method achieves the best results compared to other domain generalization methods in all datasets. Specifically, our method get improvement of +1.02, +0.44, +1.54 and +0.91 respectively in Cityscapes, BDD-100K, Mapillary and SYNTHIA. This proves the superioty of our method in synthetic datasets. It is noted that the performance on GTAV itself has a slight drop, about 1.37 to Baseline, 0.82 to IBN-Net [3] and 0.02 to RoubustNet [7].

Table 2. The comparision of Semantic segmentation performance **mIoU** on synthetic dataset **GTAV** without accessing to others. Resnet-50 and DeepLabV3+ are basic architectures in all models for fair comparision.

Model (GTAV)	Cityscapes	BDD-100K	Mapillary	SYNTHIA	GTAV
Baseline	28.95	25.14	28.18	26.23	**73.45**
IBN-Net [3]	33.85	32.30	37.75	27.90	72.90
RobustNet [7]	36.58	35.20	40.33	28.30	72.10
Ours	**37.60**	**35.64**	**41.54**	**29.21**	72.08

4.4 Ablation Study

To analyze the effectiveness of our proposed model, we conduct ablation studies on the following setting: erasing all style-sensitive-channel features to prove the rationality of our random erasure and randomly erasing all channels features to show the necessity of selecting style-sensitive channels. As Table 3 shown, erasing all style-sensitive-channel features drop the accuracy sharply, the reason of which is that style-sensitive channels contain more style information, and does not mean that they don't have semantic information. This is why we call style-sensitive channels not style channels. About randomly erasing the all channels, although its performance does not drop as much as the above setting, the decline of its accuracy shows that it doesn't make sense due to its erasing semantic features. This is because randomly erasing all features is easy to remove semantic features, which has a large proportion in channels.

Table 3. Ablation study of our method. SCRE represents **R**andomly **E**rasing **S**tyle-sensitive-**C**hannel features, SCAE means **E**rasing **A**ll **S**tyle-sensitive-**C**hannel features and ACRE is noted for **R**andomly **E**rasing the features of **A**ll **C**hannels.

Model (GTAV)	Cityscapes	BDD-100K	Mapillary	SYNTHIA	GTAV
RobustNet [7]	36.58	35.20	40.33	28.30	**72.10**
Ours (RobustNet[7]+SCRE)	**37.60**	**35.64**	**41.54**	**29.21**	72.08
RobustNet [7]+SCAE	32.99	30.64	35.48	25.64	71.49
RobustNet [7]+ACRE	35.59	33.65	39.84	27.48	70.7

5 Conclusion

In this work, we rethink the composition of learning features: style-sensitive-channel features and semantic-sensitive-channel features. In order to enhance the generalization ability of network, we propose a plug-in module to erase the features of style-sensitive channels randomly without additional loss function. And a lot experiments on two setting (i.e., simulation to real and real to simulation) demonstrate the advantage of our method when comparing with other state-of-the-art methods.

Acknowledgement. This work is partially supported by National Natural Science Foundation of China (Grants no. 61772568), Guangdong Basic and Applied Basic Research Foundation (Grant no. 2019A1515012029), and Youth science and technology innovation talent of Guangdong Special Support Program.

References

1. Blanchard, G., Lee, G., Scott, C.: Generalizing from several related classification tasks to a new unlabeled sample. Adv. Neural Inf. Process. Syst. **24**, 2178–2186 (2011)
2. Yue, X., Zhang. Y., Zhao, S., et al.: Domain randomization and pyramid consistency: simula-tion-to-real generalization without accessing target domain data. In: Proceedings of the IEEE/CVF International Conference on Computer Vision, pp. 2100–2110 (2019)
3. Pan, X., Luo, P., Shi, J., et al.: Two at once: enhancing learning and generalization capacities via ibn-net. In: Proceedings of the European Conference on Computer Vision (ECCV), pp. 464–479 (2018)
4. Volpi, R., Murino, V.: Addressing model vulnerability to distributional shifts over image transformation sets. In: Proceedings of the IEEE/CVF International Conference on Computer Vision, pp. 7980–7989 (2019)
5. Li, Y., Tian, X., Gong, M., et al.: Deep domain generalization via conditional invariant adver-sarial networks. In: Proceedings of the European Conference on Computer Vision (ECCV), pp. 624–639 (2018)
6. Li, H., Pan, S.J., Wang, S., et al.: Domain generalization with adversarial feature learning. In: Proceedings of the IEEE Conference on Computer Vision and Pattern Recognition, pp. 5400–5409 (2018)
7. Choi, S., Jung, S., Yun, H., et al.: RobustNet: improving domain generalization in urban-scene segmentation via instance selective whitening. In: Proceedings of the IEEE/CVF Conference on Computer Vision and Pattern Recognition, pp. 11580–11590 (2021)
8. Ulyanov, D., Vedaldi, A., Lempitsky, V.: Instance normalization: the missing ingredient for fast stylization. arXiv preprint arXiv:1607.08022 (2016)
9. Ioffe, S, Szegedy, C.: Batch normalization: accelerating deep network training by reducing internal covariate shift. In: International Conference on Machine Learning, pp. 448–456. PMLR (2015)
10. Ghifary, M., Kleijn, W.B., Zhang, M., et al.:Domain generalization for object recognition with multi-task autoencoders. In: Proceedings of the IEEE International Conference on Computer Vision, pp. 2551–2559 (2015)
11. Muande, K., Balduzzi, D., Schölkopf, B.: Domain generalization via invariant feature representation. In: International Conference on Machine Learning, pp. 10–18. PMLR (2013)
12. Long, J., Shelhamer, E., Darrell, T.: Fully convolutional networks for semantic segmenta-tion. In: Proceedings of the IEEE Conference on Computer Vision and Pattern Recognition, pp. 3431–3440 (2015)
13. Ronneberger, O., Fischer, P., Brox, T.: U-Net: convolutional networks for biomedical image segmentation. In: Navab, N., Hornegger, J., Wells, W.M., Frangi, A.F. (eds.) MICCAI 2015. LNCS, vol. 9351, pp. 234–241. Springer, Cham (2015). https://doi.org/10.1007/978-3-319-24574-4_28

14. Badrinarayanan, V., Kendall, A., Cipolla, R.: Segnet: a deep convolutional encoder-decoder architecture for image segmentation. IEEE Trans. Patt. Anal. Mach. Intell. **39**(12), 2481–2495 (2017)
15. Chen, L.C., Papandreou, G., Kokkinos, I., et al.: Deeplab: semantic image segmentation with deep convolutional nets, atrous convolution, and fully connected CRFS. IEEE Trans. Patt. Aanal. Mach. Intell. **40**(4), 834–848 (2017)
16. He, K., Zhang, X., Ren, S., et al.: Spatial pyramid pooling in deep convolutional networks for visual recognition. IEEE Trans. Pattern Anal. Mach. Intell. **37**(9), 1904–1916 (2015)
17. Zhao, H., Shi, J., Qi, X., et al.: Pyramid scene parsing network. In: Proceedings of the IEEE Conference on Computer Vsion and Pattern Recognition, pp. 2881–2890 (2017)
18. Chen, L.C., Papandreou, G., Schroff, F., et al.: Rethinking atrous convolution for semantic image segmentation. arXiv preprint arXiv:1706.05587 (2017)
19. Chen, L.C., Zhu, Y., Papandreou, G., et al.: Encoder-decoder with atrous separable convolution for semantic image segmentation. In: Proceedings of the European Conference on Computer Vision (ECCV), pp. 801–818 (2018)
20. Yu, F., Koltun, V.: Multi-scale context aggregation by dilated convolutions. arXiv pre-print arXiv:1511.07122 (2015)
21. Paszke, A., Gross, S., Massa, F., et al.: Pytorch: an imperative style, high-performance deep learning library. arXiv preprint arXiv:1912.01703 (2019)
22. Cordts, M., Omran, M., Ramos, S., et al.: The cityscapes dataset for semantic urban scene understanding. In: Proceedings of the IEEE Conference on Computer Vision and Pattern Recognition, pp. 3213–3223 (2016)
23. Yu, F., Chen, H., Wang, X., et al.: Bdd100k: a diverse driving dataset for heterogeneous multitask learning. In: Proceedings of the IEEE/CVF Conference on Computer Vision and Pattern Recognition, pp. 2636–2645 (2020)
24. Neuhold, G., Ollmann, T., Rota Bulo, S., et al.: The mapillary vistas dataset for semantic understanding of street scenes. In: Proceedings of the IEEE International Conference on Computer Vision, pp. 4990–4999 (2017)
25. Ros, G., Sellart, L., Materzynska, J., et al.: The synthia dataset: a large collection of synthetic images for semantic segmentation of urban scenes. In: Proceedings of the IEEE Conference on Computer Vision and Pattern Recognition, pp. 3234–3243 (2016)
26. Richter, S.R., Vineet, V., Roth, S., Koltun, V.: Playing for data: ground truth from computer games. In: Leibe, B., Matas, J., Sebe, N., Welling, M. (eds.) ECCV 2016. LNCS, vol. 9906, pp. 102–118. Springer, Cham (2016). https://doi.org/10.1007/978-3-319-46475-6_7
27. Liu, W., Rabinovich, A., Berg, A.C.: Parsenet: looking wider to see better. arXiv preprint arXiv:1506.04579 (2015)
28. Li, Y., Fang, C., Yang, J., et al.: Universal style transfer via feature transforms. arXiv preprint arXiv:1705.08086 (2017)

MAGAN: Multi-attention Generative Adversarial Networks for Text-to-Image Generation

Xibin Jia, Qing Mi, and Qi Dai(✉)

Beijing University of Technology, Beijing 100124, China
daiqi@emails.bjut.edu.cn

Abstract. Although generative adversarial networks are commonly used in text-to-image generation tasks and have made great progress, there are still some problems. The convolution operation used in these GANs-based methods works on local regions, but not disjoint regions of the image, leading to structural anomalies in the generated image. Moreover, the semantic consistency of generated images and corresponding text descriptions still needs to be improved. In this paper, we propose a multi-attention generative adversarial networks (MAGAN) for text-to-image generation. We use self-attention mechanism to improve the overall quality of images, so that the target image with a certain structure can also be generated well. We use multi-head attention mechanism to improve the semantic consistency of generated images and text descriptions. We conducted extensive experiments on three datasets: Oxford-102 Flowers dataset, Caltech-UCSD Birds dataset and COCO dataset. Our MAGAN has better results than representative methods such as AttnGAN, MirrorGAN and ControlGAN.

Keywords: Text-to-image generation · Generative adversarial networks · Attention mechanism

1 Introduction

The task of Text-to-image (T2I) generation is to input a text description and output an image. This task has great potential in many fields. As GANs [1] have made great progress in generating real images, T2I generation has also made great progress.

In 2016, Reed et al. [2] used GANs for the T2I generation task. They used recurrent neural networks (RNNs) [3] to encode natural language descriptions into text vectors, and controlled the generated content through text vectors. They also added CNN to the network, which improved the overall authenticity of the generated images and the speed of network convergence. Most existing methods [4–12] are based on this idea. However, they have the following problems.

One problem is that GANs are not effective in generating objects with a certain structure, and the objects in the generated images have incomplete structures. This problem is caused by the dependence of GANs on CNN, CNN mainly acts on the local area of each position of the image, and the long-distance dependence between disjoint regions in an

© Springer Nature Switzerland AG 2021
H. Ma et al. (Eds.): PRCV 2021, LNCS 13022, pp. 312–322, 2021.
https://doi.org/10.1007/978-3-030-88013-2_26

image needs to be achieved by a multi-layer CNN. The multi-layer CNN will cause the problem of excessive calculation, so GANs may have a very bad effect on the generation of objects with a certain structure. For this reason, we add the self-attention module to achieve long-distance dependency modeling and make generated images more realistic and believable.

Another problem is that these methods do not take into account related words well when generating image subregions. Although AttnGAN [7] used the attention mechanism for the first time in T2I generation, so that when generating a subregion of the image, it will consider the influence of different words on the subregion, but each word has a different meaning from a different perspective. AttnGAN may only consider the impact of some words on a certain subregion when generating images, and does not consider the impact of other words on the subregion from different perspectives. For this reason, we propose a multi-head attention module that enables model to comprehensive consider all words, and enhances the consistency of generated images and text descriptions.

The main contributions are summarized as follows:

(1) We propose a self-attention mechanism in the network. The self-attention mechanism helps images establish long-distance dependence, which can further improve the overall authenticity of the image.
(2) We propose a multi-head mechanism in the network. The multi-head mechanism helps model to focus on different aspects of text information and improves the consistency of generated images and text descriptions.

2 Related Work

2.1 Text-to-Image Generation

In 2016, Reed et al. [2] proposed GAN-INT-CLS based on CGAN [14] and DCGAN [15], which inputs a text as a condition vector into the network to control the generation of image. Reed et al. [4] also proposed GAWWN. Because of GAWWN can only generate a resolution of 64 × 64 images, Zhang et al. [5] proposed StackGAN. StackGAN includes two stages. A multi-stage network can be used to obtain images with a resolution of 256 × 256. Since the StackGAN could not train completely, Zhang et al. [6] proposed the StackGAN++. StackGAN++ includes three stages and could train completely. Xu et al. [7] proposed the AttnGAN. AttnGAN used the attention mechanism that will pay attention to related words when generating different areas of the image, thereby synthesizing fine-grained details. Qiao et al. [8] proposed MirrorGAN, which converts the generated image into a new text, and compares it with the original text as a reconstruction loss to improve the consistency of generated images and text descriptions.

2.2 Attention Mechanism

The attention mechanism has been used in target machine translation [16] and image captioning [17]. Transformer [13] used the self-attention mechanism to calculate the influence of other words in the same sequence on the word when encoding a word. Tranformer achieved the most advanced results in the machine translation model at the time. SAGAN [18] first used the self-attention mechanism for GANs. GANs are good at generating images with less structural constraints. The self-attention mechanism can build long-distance dependencies between different regions of the image so that GANs can generate images with higher structural constraints. SAGAN has also achieved the most advanced results on ImageNet [19]. In response to the problem of excessive calculation of the self-attention module in SAGAN, Cao et al. [20] simplified the self-attention mechanism and reduced the amount of calculation when the improvement effect was the same.

2.3 Multi-head Mechanism

AttnGAN [7] is one of the classic networks of multi-stage GANs. Many T2I works are modified on AttnGAN. The three stages of the network generate images with different resolutions. A word-level attention mechanism is used between each two stages, so that the generator will pay attention to different words. However, a subregion can be very related to multiple texts from different perspectives. In order to make the model pay attention to different aspects of text information, we combine the multi-head mechanism of the encoder in Transformer [13] with the attention mechanism in AttnGAN. Different heads consider the words related to the subregion from different perspectives, and finally summarize the information under the multi-head, so that the model can comprehensively consider the relevant text information when generating a subregion.

3 Multi-Attention Gan (MAGAN)

3.1 Model Overview

As shown in Fig. 1. Given a text description, we first use a pre-trained RNN [7] to encode this description into sentence-level features $s \in R^D$ and word-level features $w = \{w^l | l = 0, \ldots, L-1\} \in R^{D*L}$, D is the dimension of the feature, L is the number of words, then we apply conditioning augmentation (CA) [5] to sentence-level features, then the conditionally augmented sentence-level features and random noise sampled in the Gaussian distribution are input into the first stage of the network. The overall process can be expressed as:

$$V_0 = F_0(z, s_{ca}), \tag{1}$$

$$H_{i-1} = F_{SA_{i-1}}(V_{i-1}), i \in \{1, 2, \ldots, m-1\}, \tag{2}$$

$$X_i = G_i(H_{i-1}), i \in \{0, 1, 2, \ldots, m-1\}, \tag{3}$$

$$V_i = F_i\big(H_{i-1}, F_{MH_{i-1}}(H_{i-1}, w)\big), i \in \{1, 2, \ldots, m-1\}, \tag{4}$$

Where z is a random noise, V_i is the i-stage visual feature, F_{SA_i} is the self-attention module, F_{MH_i} is the multi-head attention module, X_i is the i-stage generated image, F_i is the visual feature transformers.

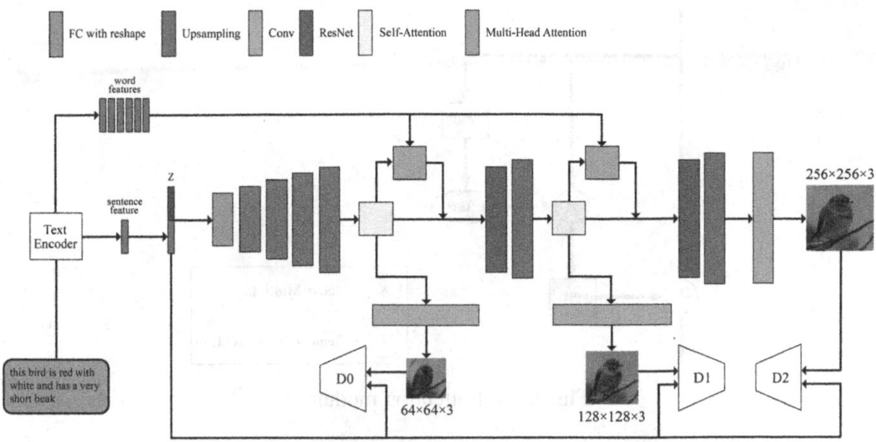

Fig. 1. The architecture of MAGAN.

The network has three stages. The visual features V_i obtained at each stage will first pass through a self-attention module F_{SA_i}, and then the visual features H_i after the self-attention module will be input to different generators G_i to generate images with corresponding resolutions. H_i will obtain the visual features weighted by the attention mechanism through the multi-head attention module F_{MH_i}. Then H_i is combined with the visual features weighted by the multi-head attention mechanism. The visual feature V_i after fusion will be used as the input of the next stage of the network.

3.2 Self-attention Module

The visual features obtained after upsampling at each stage will first pass through a self-attention module. NLNet [21] obtains the attention map by calculating the relationship between each location, and calculates the importance of other location features to the current location feature through the softmax function. Finally the attention map assigned with the weight is aggregated with the features of all positions. Here we use the simplified self-attention mechanism in GCNET [20].

As shown in Fig. 2. We calculate the visual features V_i directly through a convolutional layer to obtain a global attention map f_i:

$$f_i = W_k(V_i), \tag{5}$$

f_i use softmax function to assign a weight to the feature of each position to get p_i:

$$p_i = softmax(f_i), \tag{6}$$

Then we multiply p_i and the visual feature V_i to obtain the visual feature, and then use a convolutional layer to convert this visual feature to obtain the feature t_i, so that the final feature t_i is consistent with the input V_i dimension:

$$t_i = W_v(V_i p_i), \tag{7}$$

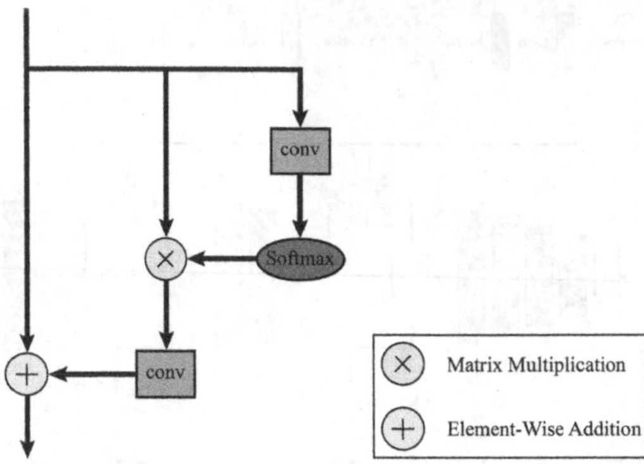

Fig. 2. Self-attention module.

Finally, the element-wise add operation is used to integrate the global attention map into the features of each location to complete the modeling of long-distance dependencies:

$$F_{SA_i}(V_i) = V_i + t_i, \tag{8}$$

3.3 Multi-head Attention Module

As shown in Fig. 3. We combine the multi-head mechanism [13] in the transformer with AttnGAN's attention mechanism [7] as a multi-head attention module. The module contains two inputs: word-level features w and visual features V_i. The word-level feature w is first changed in dimension, w is changed from $D \times L$ to $C \times L$. We obtain the attention map by calculating the word-level feature w after the dimension transformation and the visual feature V_i, then we normalize the attention map through the softmax function and matrix transpose. Finally, we obtain the attentive word-context feature by calculating the word-level feature w after the dimension transformation and the normalized attention map:

$$Att_{i-1}^{j} = \sum\nolimits_{l=0}^{L-1} (U_j w^l)(softmax(V_{i-1}^T (U_j w^l)))^T, j \in \{1, 2, \ldots, n\}, \tag{9}$$

The multi-head mechanism calculates the attentive word-context feature of multiple attention mechanisms in multiple spaces, and uses the element-wise add operation for the attentive word-context features in these multi-head spaces:

$$F_{MH_i}(V_{i-1}, w) = \sum\nolimits_{j=0}^{n-1} Att_{i-1}^{j}, , j \in \{1, 2, \ldots, n-1\}, \tag{10}$$

Finally, concatenation with V_{i-1} to obtain the visual features V_i, and V_i will be used as the input of the next stage of the network.

Through the attention mechanism, the generator can take into account the correlation of different words when generating the subregion of the image. However, a word has different meanings from different angles. When generating the subregion of the image, we comprehensively consider more word information through the multi-head mechanism, and finally summarize the word information in different spaces through the add operation, so that the generated images are more in line with the text descriptions.

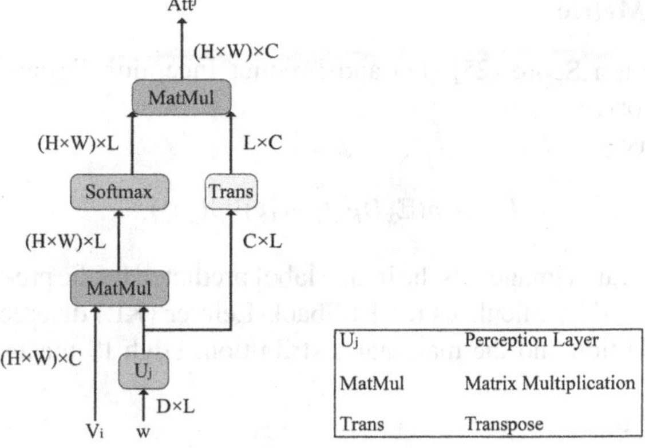

Fig. 3. Multi-head attention module.

3.4 Objective Functions

The overall loss function of generator G is defined as:

$$L_G = \sum\nolimits_i L_{G_i} + \lambda_1 L_{DAMSM}, \tag{11}$$

The generator loss function includes adversarial loss and the text-image matching loss DAMSM [7]. λ_1 is the hyperparameter used to balance these two losses. In the i-th stage, the adversarial loss of the corresponding generator is defined as:

$$L_{G_i} = -\frac{1}{2}[\mathbb{E}_{x \sim P_{G_i}} logD_i(x) + \mathbb{E}_{x \sim P_{G_i}} logD_i(x, s)], \tag{12}$$

Where x is the image generated by the generator, s is the given text, the first part is the unconditional adversarial loss which makes the image more realistic, and the latter part is the conditional adversarial loss which makes the image match the text description.

The overall loss function of the discriminator D is defined as:

$$L_D = \sum\nolimits_i L_{D_i}, \tag{13}$$

In the i-th stage, the adversarial loss of the corresponding discriminator is defined as:

$$L_{D_i} = -\frac{1}{2}[\mathbb{E}_{x \sim P_{data}} logD_i(x) + \mathbb{E}_{x \sim P_{G_i}} log(1 - D_i(x)),$$

$$+ \mathbb{E}_{x \sim P_{data}} logD_i(x, s) + \mathbb{E}_{x \sim P_{G_i}} log(1 - D_i(x, s))], \tag{14}$$

Same as the generator, the first part is the unconditional loss, and the latter part is the conditional loss.

4 Experiments

4.1 Datasets

We use Caltech-UCSD Birds dataset [22], Oxford-102 Flowers dataset [23] and COCO dataset [24]. Each image has many descriptions.

4.2 Evaluation Metric

We choose Inception Score [25] (IS) and Fréchet Inception Distance [26] (FID) as evaluation indicators.

IS is defined as:

$$I = exp(\mathbb{E}_x D_{KL}(p(y|x)||p(y))), \tag{15}$$

Where x is the generated image, y is the image label predicted by the pre-trained Inception V3 network [27], and IS calculates the Kullback-Leibler (KL) divergence between the conditional distribution and the marginal distribution. High IS means that images are well generated.

FID is defined as:

$$F(r, g) = \|\mu_r - \mu_g\|^2 + trace\left(\Sigma_r + \Sigma_g - 2(\Sigma_r \Sigma_g)^{1/2}\right), \tag{16}$$

Where r is the real data, g is the generated data, μ_r, μ_g, Σ_r, Σ_g are the means and covariance matrixs of real data distribution and generated data distribution, respectively. Low FID means that images are well generated.

4.3 Implementation Details

The optimizers all use Adam [28] optimizer, which β_1 is set to 0, β_2 is set to 0.999. Training 600 epochs.

4.4 Quantitative Results

As shown in Table 1. Compared with AttnGAN [7], the IS of MAGAN on Oxford-102 dataset has increased from 3.75 to 4.11, the IS of MAGAN on CUB dataset has increased from 4.36 to 4.63, and the IS of MAGAN on COCO dataset increased from 25.89 to 26.27. As shown in Table 2. Compared with AttnGAN, the FID of MAGAN on CUB dataset has dropped from 23.98 to 19.25, and the FID of MAGAN on COCO dataset dropped from 35.49 to 27.53. Compared with other methods, we can see that our method has obtained higher IS and lower FID on three datasets.

4.5 Qualitative Results

We first compare the images generated by representative methods and our proposed MAGAN on CUB dataset and Oxford-102 dataset. The results in Fig. 4 and Fig. 5 have a resolution of 256 × 256.

In general, these mothods can generate images with higher resolution, which can basically match the natural language description. You can see that the birds generated by our proposed MAGAN have more real and clear details, such as the third column, for the text description, in the image generated by our method, the bird's neck has black stripes, and the color of the neck is clearly generated, while other methods such as AttnGAN [7] do not clearly generate black stripes.

Table 1. IS of representative methods and MAGAN on Oxford-102, CUB and COCO datasets.

Methods	Oxford-102	CUB	COCO
GAN_CLS_INT [2]	2.66 ± 0.03	2.88 ± 0.04	7.88 ± 0.07
GAWWN [4]	–	3.62 ± 0.07	–
StackGAN [5]	3.20 ± 0.01	3.70 ± 0.04	8.45 ± 0.03
StackGAN++ [6]	3.26 ± 0.01	4.04 ± 0.05	–
HDGAN [11]	3.45 ± 0.07	4.15 ± 0.05	11.86 ± 0.18
AttnGAN [7]	3.75 ± 0.02	4.36 ± 0.03	25.89 ± 0.47
MirrorGAN [8]	–	4.56 ± 0.05	**26.47 ± 0.41**
ControlGAN [9]	–	4.58 ± 0.09	24.06 ± 0.60
LeicaGAN [10]	3.92 ± 0.02	4.62 ± 0.06	–
Ours	**4.11 ± 0.06**	**4.63 ± 0.06**	26.27 ± 0.58

Table 2. FID of representative methods and MAGAN on CUB and COCO datasets.

Methods	CUB	COCO
StackGAN++ [6]	35.11	33.88
AttnGAN [7]	23.98	35.49
DMGAN [12]	**16.09**	32.64
Ours	19.25	**27.53**

Intuitively, there are three bird's feet in the image generated by MirrorGAN [8] in the sixth column, and our method does not have this problem. Overall, it looks better than other methods. The background of the image is also more natural, such as the first column and fourth column. The image background we generate is more delicate than other image background.

Then we compared the images generated by several methods on the Oxford-102 dataset. It can be seen from the Fig. 5 that the colors of the flowers generated by methods such as AttnGAN are not bright enough, the petals have no sense of hierarchy, and the stamens are not clear. Our method can capture details, and the generated image is more layered and background is more realistic.

The above proves the generation effect of our method, the generated image is more realistic and reasonable, the semantic consistency corresponding to the text description is higher.

Fig. 4. Examples results by StackGAN++, AttnGAN, MirrorGAN and MAGAN on CUB dataset.

Fig. 5. Examples results by StackGAN++, AttnGAN, MirrorGAN and MAGAN on Oxford-102 dataset.

4.6 Ablation Studies

We conduct ablation studies to verify the effectiveness of the two modules in MAGAN. As shown in Table 3. Baseline stands for AttnGAN, SA stands for self-attention module, MH stands for multi-head attention module. Compared with the basic network, the IS of the CUB dataset has increased to 4.48 and 4.50 respectively, and the IS of the Oxford-102 dataset has increased to 3.93 and 3.90 respectively. This shows that the two modules both play a positive role in image generation. Combining the two modules can increase the

IS of the CUB dataset to 4.63 and the IS of the Oxford-102 dataset to 4.11. Combining the two modules can make the generators generate higher quality images.

Table 3. The performance of different components of our module on CUB and Oxford-102 datasets.

Architecture	CUB	Oxford-102
Baseline	4.36 ± 0.03	3.75 ± 0.02
SA	4.48 ± 0.05	3.93 ± 0.04
MH	4.50 ± 0.04	3.90 ± 0.03
(SA) + (MH)	$\mathbf{4.63 \pm 0.06}$	$\mathbf{4.11 \pm 0.06}$

5 Conclusion

We propose a new architecture called MAGAN for T2I generation tasks. Our proposed the self-attention module helps non-adjacent regions to build long-distance correlation, which helps generators to generate higher quality image. Our proposed multi-head attention module can consider all text information, which improves the semantic consistency. Experiment results demonstrate our MAGAN has excellent performance in text-to-image generation.

Acknowledgement. This work is supported by Beijing Natural Science Foundation under No. 4202004.

References

1. Goodfellow, I., Xu, B., et al.: Generative adversarial nets. In: NIPS, pp. 2672–2680 (2014)
2. Reed, S., Akata, Z., et al.: Generative adversarial text to image synthesis. In: ICML, pp. 1060–1069 (2016)
3. Cho, K., Gulcehre, C., Schwenk, H., et al.: Learning phrase representations using RNN encoder-decoder for statistical ma-chine translation. In: EMNLP (2014)
4. Reed, S., Akata, Z., et al.: Learning what and where to draw. In: NIPS, pp. 217–225 (2016)
5. Zhang, H., Xu, T., Li, H., et al.: StackGAN: text to photo-realistic image synthesis with stacked generative adversarial networks. In: ICCV, pp. 5907–5915 (2017)
6. Zhang, H., Xu, T., Li, H., et al.: StackGAN++: realistic image synthesis with stacked generative adversarial networks. In: TPAMI, pp. 1947–1962 (2018)
7. Xu, T., Zhang, P., Huang, Q., et al.: AttnGAN: fine-grained text to image generation with attentional generative adversarial networks. In: CVPR, pp. 1316–1324 (2018)
8. Qiao, T., Zhang, J., Xu, D., et al.: MirrorGAN: learning text-to-image generation by redescription. In: CVPR, pp. 1505–1514 (2019)
9. Li, B., Qi, X., et al.: Controllable text-to-image generation. In: NIPS, pp. 2065–2075 (2019)
10. Qiao, T., Zhang, J., et al.: Learn, imagine and create: text-to-image generation from prior knowledge. In: NIPS, pp. 885–895 (2019)

11. Zhang, Z., Xie, Y., Yang, L.: Photographic text-to-image synthesis with a hierarchical-ly-nested adversarial network. In: CVPR, pp. 6199–6208 (2018)
12. Zhu, M., Pan, P., Chen, W., et al.: DM-GAN: dynamic memory generative adversarial networks for text-to-image synthesis. In: CVPR, pp. 5802–5810 (2019)
13. Shazeer, N., Jones, L., et al.: Attention is all you need. In: NIPS, pp. 5998–6008 (2017)
14. Mirza, M., Osindero, S.: Conditional generative adversarial nets. arXiv preprint arXiv:1411.1784 (2014)
15. Radford, A., Metz, L., Chintala, S.: Unsupervised representation learning with deep convolutional generative adversarial networks. In: ICLR (2016)
16. Bahdanau, D., Cho, K., Bengio, Y.: Neural machine translation by jointly learning to align and translate. In: ICLR (2015)
17. Xu, K., Ba, J., Kiros, R., et al.: Show, attend and tell: neural image caption generation with visual attention. In: ICML (2015)
18. Zhang, H., Goodfellow, I., Metaxas, D., et al.: Self-attention generative adversarial networks. In: ICML, pp. 7354–7363 (2019)
19. Russakovsky, O., Deng, J., Su, H., et al.: ImageNet large scale visual recognition challenge. In: IJCV, pp. 211–252 (2015)
20. Cao, Y., Xu, J., Lin, S., et al.: GCNet: non-local networks meet squeeze-excitation networks and beyond. In: ICCV (2019)
21. Wang, X., Girshick, R., Gupta, A., et al.: Non-local neural networks. In: CVPR (2018)
22. Wah, C., Branson, P., Welinder, P., et al.: The Caltech-UCSD Birds-200-2011 Da-taset. California Institute of Technology, Technical Report CNS-TR-2011-001 (2011)
23. Nilsback, M., Zisserman, A.: Automated flower classifification over a large number of classes. In: ICVGIP, pp. 722–729 (2008)
24. Lin, T.-Y., et al.: Microsoft COCO: common objects in context. In: Fleet, D., Pajdla, T., Schiele, B., Tuytelaars, T. (eds.) ECCV 2014. LNCS, vol. 8693, pp. 740–755. Springer, Cham (2014). https://doi.org/10.1007/978-3-319-10602-1_48
25. Salimanx, T., Goodfellow, I., Zaremba, W., et al.: Improved techniques for training GANs. In: NIPS, pp. 2226–2234 (2016)
26. Heusel, M., Ramsauer, H., et al.: GANs trained by a two time-scale update rule con-verge to a local nash equilibrium. In: NIPS, pp. 6626–6637 (2017)
27. Szegedy, C., Ioffe, S., Shlens, J., et al.: Rethinking the inception architecture for com-puter vision. In: CVPR, pp. 2818–2826 (2016)
28. Kingma. D., Ba, J.: Adam: a method for stochastic optimization. In: ICLR (2015)

Dual Attention Based Network with Hierarchical ConvLSTM for Video Object Segmentation

Zongji Zhao and Sanyuan Zhao(✉)

School of Computer Science and Technology, Beijing Institute of Technology, Beijing, China
zhaosanyuan@bit.edu.cn

Abstract. Semi-supervised Video object segmentation is one of the most basic tasks in the field of computer vision, especially in the multi-object case. It aims to segment masks of multiple foreground objects in given video sequence with annotation mask of the first frame as prior knowledge. In this paper, we propose a novel multi-object video segmentation model. We use the U-Net architecture to obtain multi-scale spatial features. In the encoder part, the spatial attention mechanism and channel attention is used to enhance the spatial features simultaneously. We use the recurrent ConvLSTM module in the decoder to segment different object instances in one stage and keep the segmentation object consistent over time. In addition, we use three loss functions for joint training to improve the model training effect. We test our network on the popular video object segmentation dataset DAVIS2017. The experiment results demonstrate that our model achieves state-of-art performance. Moreover, our model achieves faster inference runtimes than other methods.

Keywords: Video object segmentation · ConvLSTM · Attention

1 Introduction

Video object segmentation is one of the most important tasks in the field of computer vision. With the wide application and rapid development of deep learning in the field of computer vision, video object segmentation methods based on convolutional neural networks have achieved better results on video object segmentation benchmark. Traditional video object segmentation methods usually require manual design and capture appearance features such as color, brightness, texture, and temporal features such as optical flow and pixels matching, while the method based on CNN uses the feature representation learned from the large-scale video object segmentation dataset to build the appearance model and the motion model in the video sequence.

This work was supported by the National Natural Science Foundation of China (61902027).

© Springer Nature Switzerland AG 2021
H. Ma et al. (Eds.): PRCV 2021, LNCS 13022, pp. 323–335, 2021.
https://doi.org/10.1007/978-3-030-88013-2_27

We tackle the video object segmentation problem in the semi-supervised setting, where the ground truth mask of the first frame is given and the aim is to estimate multiple objects masks in each subsequent frames. The recent semi-supervised video object segmentation methods can be mainly categorized into three classes: 1) online learning based; 2) feature matching based and 3) mask propagation based approaches. For the first class, the annotation mask is used to online fine-tune the pretrianed object segmentation network in the test phase. Although online learning methods can achieve impressive performance, the process of fine-tuning takes up a lot of computing resources. The second class uses pixels similarities to match the object in the video frame with the object in the first frame but often neglects both the object structure and appearance information due to unordered pixels.

In order to lighten the model and increase the runtime speed while maintaining performance, we choose a method based on mask propagation, and use the prediction result of the previous frame to enhance the features of the current frame. In response to the problems in the mask propagation methods, we propose that spatial attention and channel attention act on different features to obtain valuable information in the feature maps, and use the recurrent ConvLSTM decoder to gradually restore the scale of the feature maps. At the same time, we use temporal information such as the prediction of the previous frame and the mask of the other objects to predict the mask of the current object in the current frame.

The main contributions of our work are listed below:

- We use the criss-cross attention module to obtain the spatial context information of the input frame at low computational cost, and use the channel attention module to obtain the channel semantic dependencies in the high-level feature, to obtain an enhanced spatial representation of the feature.
- We propose a intra-frame self IOU loss function, which is used to evaluate the difference of the mask of different objects in the same frame, and jointly train the model with two other common loss functions.
- We test our model on the DAVIS2017 [10], demonstrating that our model achieves state-of-art performance. Our model can achieve real-time speed of 45.5 fps on GTX 1080Ti GPU.

2 Related Work

2.1 Semi-supervised Video Object Segmentation

Online Learning. Online Learning based methods fine-tune the pre-trained network by using the first annotated frame to fine-tune the pre-training network during the test phase. For example, Caelles et al. proposed OSVOS [1] based on FPN, which is still a static segmentation method in essence that learns the appearance feature of the object in the video sequence through an online learning process. In addition, OSVOS use object-specific appearance information to expand the object's mask, which greatly improves the result. Since the temporal information contained in the video sequence is not considered, rapid changes in the object scale and shape will cause large errors. In order to overcome the limitations of OSVOS, OnAVOS [13] updates the network online using training examples selected based on the confidence of the network and the spatial configuration. Maninis et al. [6] combined the instance-level semantic information by using instance proposals to improve segmentation performance.

Feature Match Based. Feature matching based method calculates the similarity matrix by using the features of the reference pixel and the target pixel, and further predicts these target pixels according to the learned similarity relationship. Such as Yoon et al. [16] use the siamese network to extract features from the reference frame and prediction frame, obtain the pixel-level similarity through the fully connected layer. VideoMatch [3] simultaneously match the foreground features and background features in the reference frame and the target frame to make the prediction result better. Seoung et al. [8] proposed a memory networks, the past frames with object masks form an external memory, and the current frame as the query is segmented using the mask information in the memory.

Mask Propagation Based. The method based on mask propagation uses the initial reference frame and previous frame information to maintain the temporal and spatial consistency of the segmentation results. MaskTrack [9] combines the segmentation result of the previous frame with the current frame to form a four-channel input feature to guide the segmentation network to predict. The deep siamese encoder-decoder network [7] makes full use of the advantages of mask propagation and object detection, and can predict stably without any online learning and post-processing procedures.

3 Method

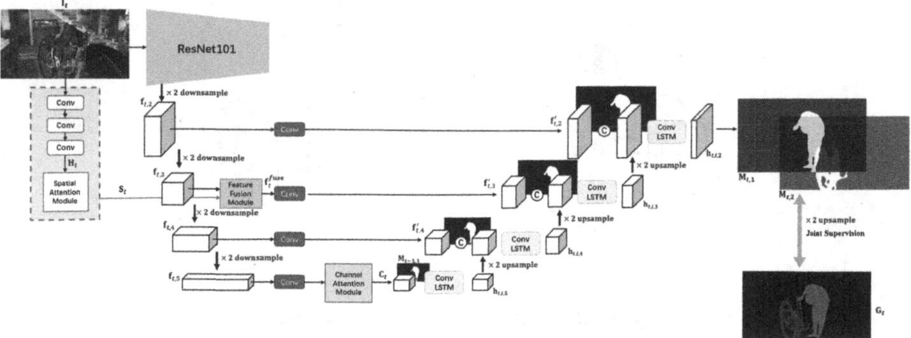

Fig. 1. The Framework. For each frame of a video sequence, it is processed by the following modules: the feature extraction network, the spatial context Branch (consists of three convolution layer and spatial attention module), the skip-connection (includes a channel attention module), and the recurrent ConvLSTM decoder.

3.1 Framework

The basic encoder-decoder architecture of video object segmentation model our proposed is based on RVOS [12]. The encoder uses ResNet50 [2] as the backbone, which is responsible for extracting high-level image semantic features. Let $\{\mathbf{I}_t \in \mathbb{R}^{W \times H \times 3}\}_{t=1}^{T}$ denotes the input video with T frames. ResNet will obtain multi-scale features for each frame $\mathbf{f}_t = \{\mathbf{f}_{t,2}, \mathbf{f}_{t,3}, \mathbf{f}_{t,4}, \mathbf{f}_{t,5}\}$, at the same time, the spatial context branch extract the shallow spatial features $\mathbf{H}_t$ of T input video frames, and use the spatial attention mechanism to focus on the contextual information $\mathbf{S}_t$. The feature fusion module merges the middle level features $\mathbf{f}_{t,3}$ obtained by the ResNet with the spatial context feature $\mathbf{S}_t$ to obtain the fusion feature $\mathbf{f}_t^{fuse}$. The fusion feature and other feature maps of the ResNet are reduced the number of channels by the skip-connection convolution and sent into decoder. Notice that the channel attention module is applied to the fifth layer feature $\mathbf{f}'_{t,5}$ of the feature extraction network to capture semantic dependencies of feature channels and obtain the channel attention feature $\mathbf{C}_t$. The decoder is based on the hierarchical recurrent ConvLSTM module, using features obtained by the encoder $\mathbf{f}'_t = \{\mathbf{f}'_{t,2}, \mathbf{f}'_{t,3}, \mathbf{f}'_{t,4}, \mathbf{C}_t\}$, predict a set of object segmentation masks for each frame$\{\mathbf{M}_{t,1}, ..., \mathbf{M}_{t,N}\}$. The overall framework is shown in Fig. 1.

3.2 Encoder

Spatial Context Branch. In order to obtain spatial context information while reducing the computational overhead,we use a simple spatial context branch, which contains three convolutional layers with the stride 2. In this way, the feature map $\{\mathbf{H}_t\}_{t=1}^{T}$ with a size of 1/8 of the input frame will be obtained, which has a larger spatial size than the deep feature map of the feature extraction module, so it will contain richer spatial details information, while having fewer feature channels.

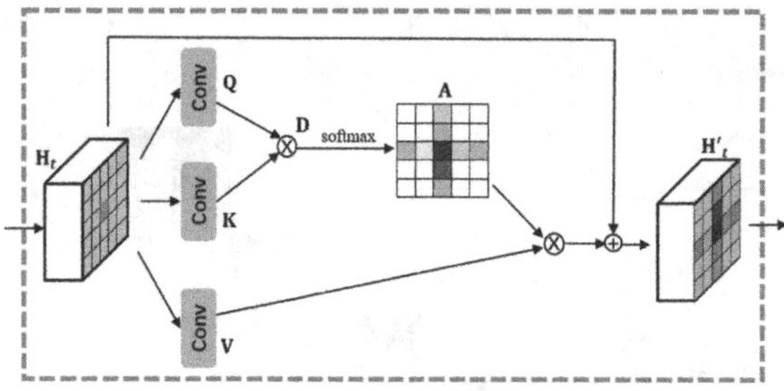

Fig. 2. Spatial Attention Module.

Spatial Attention Module. The spatial feature will focus on the effective part of the feature through the spatial attention module to obtain global context information. In order to further reduce the amount of parameters and calculations of the spatial attention module, we use the criss-cross attention module [4] to collect contextual information between pixels in both horizontal and vertical directions, and iteratively diffuse the horizontal and vertical context to the global context feature. As shown in Fig. 2, for the spatial feature $\mathbf{H}_t \in \mathbb{R}^{c \times w \times h}$ in t-th frame, firstly, two feature maps $\mathbf{Q} \in \mathbb{R}^{c' \times w \times h}$ and $\mathbf{K} \in \mathbb{R}^{c' \times w \times h}$ are generated through two 1×1 convolutions respectively to reduce the dimension of the input feature map. Next, the correlation matrix $\mathbf{A} \in \mathbb{R}^{(h+w-1)\times(w \times h)}$ is obtained from $\mathbf{Q}$ and $\mathbf{K}$. Specifically, the vector $\mathbf{Q_u} \in \mathbb{R}^{c'}$ of each position $\mathbf{u}$ in the feature map $\mathbf{Q}$ is combined with the feature vector $\boldsymbol{\Omega}_\mathbf{u} \in \mathbb{R}^{(h+w-1)\times c'}$ of the points which are in the same row or the same column of position $\mathbf{u}$ on the feature map $\mathbf{K}$ by matrix multiplication to get the degree of correlation $d_{i,\mathbf{u}} \in \mathbf{D}$:

$$d_{i,\mathbf{u}} = \mathbf{Q_u} \boldsymbol{\Omega}_{i,\mathbf{u}}^{\mathsf{T}} \tag{1}$$

where $i = [1, 2, ..., h + w - 1]$, and $\mathbf{D} \in \mathbb{R}^{(h+w-1)\times(w \times h)}$. Then, after $\mathbf{D}$ passes a softmax layer, the correlation matrix $\mathbf{A}$ is obtained. Next, we use the correlation matrix to update the input feature $\mathbf{H}_t$.

$$\mathbf{H}'_\mathbf{u} = \sum_{i=0}^{h+w-1} \mathbf{A}_{i,\mathbf{u}} \boldsymbol{\Phi}_{i,\mathbf{u}} + \mathbf{H_u} \tag{2}$$

where $\boldsymbol{\Phi}_\mathbf{u} \in \mathbb{R}^{(h+w-1)\times c}$ is the set of points which are in the same row or the same column with the position $\mathbf{u}$ in feature $\mathbf{H}_t$, $\mathbf{H}'_\mathbf{u}$ is the vector of the position $\mathbf{u}$ in the updated feature map $\mathbf{H}'$.

Each position in the feature $\mathbf{H}'$ obtained by the above steps gathers the context information of the points in the same row and the same column. We iterate the criss-cross attention module twice to obtain richer spatial features including global context information. Specifically, we input the output feature $\mathbf{H}'$ of the first criss-cross attention module into the second one, and after the same steps, obtain the spatial context feature $\mathbf{S}$, so that, Each position $\mathbf{u}'$ in $\mathbf{H}'$ can aggregate the feature information of other position $\boldsymbol{\Omega}'_\mathbf{u}$ in the same row and the same column. In the previous criss-cross attention module, these points have been aggregated to obtain the context information of position in the same row and the same column. Compared with the non-local module that is also used to extract global context dependencies, iterating twice the criss-cross attention module can achieve similar functions, and can greatly reduce the amount of calculation required by the spatial attention module.

Finally, for the input video frame of the t-th frame, the output feature $\mathbf{S}_t$ of the spatial context branch will be fused with the features obtained by the feature extraction network through a feature fusion module as shown in Fig. 3.

Channel Attention Module. We use a channel attention module on highest level feature $\mathbf{f}_{t,5}$ of the ResNet to mine the dependencies between channels,

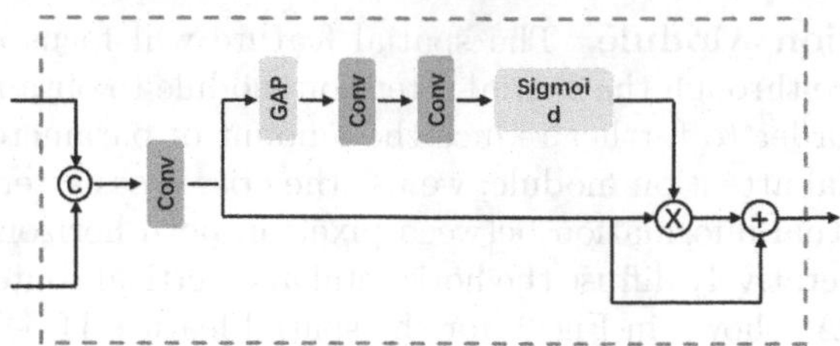

Fig. 3. Feature fusion module.

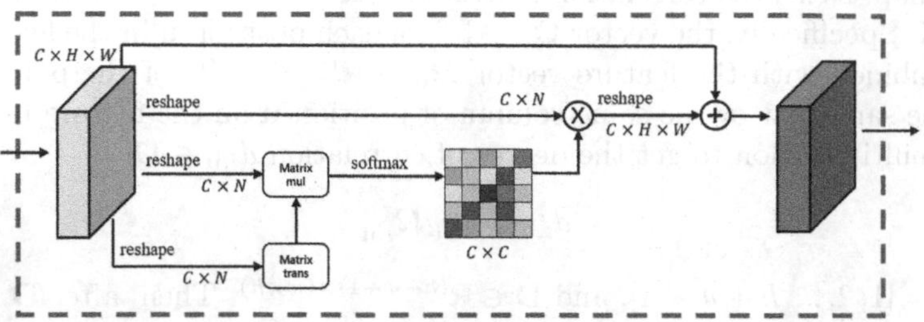

Fig. 4. Channel attention module.

because each channel of high-level features contains rich semantic information, and the dependencies between channels can enhance the semantic feature representation of high-level features. First, the input feature $\mathbf{f}'_{t,5} \in \mathbb{R}^{C_5 \times H_5 \times W_5}$ of the channel attention module is reshaped to $\mathbf{B} \in \mathbb{R}^{C_5 \times N}$, where $N = H_5 \times W_5$, C_5, H_5, W_5 respectively indicate the number of channels, height and width of the input feature $\mathbf{f}'_{t,5}$. Then obtain the channel correlation matrix by performing a matrix multiplication between $\mathbf{B}$ and the transpose of $\mathbf{B}$. Finally, we apply a softmax layer to obtain the channel attention map $\mathbf{X} \in \mathbb{R}^{C_5 \times C_5}$:

$$x_{ji} = \frac{exp(B_i \cdot B_j)}{\Sigma_{i=1}^{C_5} exp(B_i \cdot B_j)} \tag{3}$$

where x_{ji} denotes i-th channel's impact on the j-th channel. In addition, we use matrix multiplication between the transpose of the attention map $\mathbf{X}$ and $\mathbf{B}$ and shape result to $\mathbb{R}^{C_5 \times H_5 \times W_5}$. Finally, sum with the original feature map after weighting to get the final output result $\mathbf{C} \in \mathbb{R}^{C_5 \times H_5 \times W_5}$:

$$\mathbf{C}_j = \beta \sum_{i=1}^{C_5} (x_{ji} B_i) + B_j \tag{4}$$

where β is a learnable weight. As shown in Eq. 4, the final feature of each channel is obtained by the weighted sum of the feature of each channel and the original feature, so the long-range semantic dependencies of the channel dimension is obtained.

3.3 Recurrent ConvLSTM Decoder

Our decoder is a hierarchical recurrent ConvLSTM network. The ConvLSTM [11] module recursively in spatial and temporal dimensions. The recurrence in the spatial dimension aims to predict multiple objects, and the recurrence in temporal dimensions can make the prediction of the same object on different frames have the same index. The structure is shown in Fig. 1, which consists of concatenate and upsampling operation of the feature maps, alternately placed with the ConvLSTM module.

For the features of the encoder $\mathbf{f}'_t = \{\mathbf{f}'_{t,2}, \mathbf{f}_t^{fuse}, \mathbf{f}'_{t,4}, \mathbf{C}_t\}$, the decoder outputs a set of objects segmentation masks $\{\mathbf{M}_{t,1}, ..., \mathbf{M}_{t,i}, ..., \mathbf{M}_{t,N}\}$, where $\mathbf{M}_{t,i}$ denotes the segmentation mask of the i-th object in the t-th frame. For each video sequence, the object number of segmentation results obtained by the decoder is fixed. If the object disappears in the video sequence, the value of the prediction will be 0 in the subsequent frame. In the prediction process, the index of different object in the spatial recurrence is not specified in the first frame, but the optimal match between the predicted mask and annoted mask is obtained by calculating the difference between those.

Compared with the traditional ConvLSTM network in the temporal domain, the recurrent ConvLSTM module acting in the temporal domain and the spatial domain can predict multi-objects based on more input information. The input of the k-th layer ($k \in \{5, 4, 3, 2\}$) ConvLSTM module for the i-th object in the t-th frame $\mathbf{h}_{t,i,k}$ depends on the following input feature: (1) The feature $\mathbf{f}'_{t,i,k}$ extracted by the encoder part from the t-th frame, (2) The output state of ConvLSTM of the $(k+1)$-th layer, (3) The hidden state $\mathbf{h}_{t,i-1,k}$ of the previous object in the same frame of the current ConvLSTM layer, (4) The hidden state of the same object in the previous frame $\mathbf{h}_{t-1,i,k}$, (5) The prediction mask $\mathbf{M}_{t-1,i}$ of the same object in the previous frame:

$$\begin{aligned} \mathbf{h}_{input} &= [UP_2(h_{t,i,k+1}), \mathbf{f}'_{t,k}, \mathbf{M}_{t-1,i}] \\ \mathbf{h}_{state} &= [\mathbf{h}_{t,i-1,k}, \mathbf{h}_{t-1,i,k}] \end{aligned} \tag{5}$$

Notice that the input of the ConvLSTM corresponding to the fifth level feature $\mathbf{h}_{input}$ is defined as:

$$\mathbf{h}_{input} = [\mathbf{C}_t, \mathbf{M}_{t-1,i}] \tag{6}$$

We use the annoted mask of the first frame as the prior knowledge, so that the network can track and segment multiple objects corresponding to the annotation label in subsequent frames. The input of the ConvLSTM module of the k-th layer is the feature obtained by concatenate the $\times 2$ upsampled hidden state of the upper ConvLSTM layer, the spatial feature map of the current layer, and the label mask $\mathbf{y}_{i,k}$ with the corresponding scale:

$$\mathbf{h}_{input} = [UP_2(\mathbf{h}_{t,i,k+1}), \mathbf{f}'_{t,k}, \mathbf{y}_{i,k}] \tag{7}$$

And the input state $\mathbf{h}_{state}$ of the first object in each frame is:

$$\mathbf{h}_{state} = [\mathbf{Z}, \mathbf{h}_{t-1,i,k}] \tag{8}$$

Through N recurrences, the decoder generates N object segmentation results for each frame, and each result corresponds to a reference object in the first video frame, where the value of the object that does not appear in the video is 0 in the prediction result.

3.4 Loss Function

In this paper, we use the IOU loss, the Balanced Binary Cross-Entropy loss, and the intra-frame self IOU loss to joint supervise the training process. We takes the IOU loss as one of the loss functions, aims to punish the inconsistency between the predicted object and the ground truth mask. We also use the Balanced BCE loss to pay attention to the sparse foreground pixels by calculating the ratio of the number of foreground pixels to the number of pixels in the ground truth as the weight, and weighting the obtained Cross-Entropy loss. In order to avoid too much overlap between the predicted masks, we propose the intra-frame self IOU loss function $LOSS_{self}$, the loss uses the IOU between the prediction results of objects in the same frame as a penalty, and implements self-supervised on the difference between objects in a frame.

$$LOSS_{self} = \sum_{i,j=0;i\neq j}^{n} \frac{\mathbf{M}_{t,i} \cap \mathbf{M}_{t,j}}{\mathbf{M}_{t,i} \cup \mathbf{M}_{t,j}} \tag{9}$$

Finally, our loss function is the weighted sum of the IOU loss, Balanced Binary Cross-Entropy loss and the intra-frame self IOU loss:

$$LOSS = \alpha LOSS_{IOU} + \beta LOSS_{BalancedBCE} + \gamma LOSS_{self} \tag{10}$$

4 Experiments

4.1 Implementation Details

We choose the ResNet50 [2] with a pre-trained weight on ImageNet as the feature extraction network. In order to reduce the amount of network parameters and calculations, we apply the 3×3 depth-wise separable convolutions for other modules, except for the ResNet network.

We resize the input video frame to 240×427, The batchsize of the training process is set to 2, that is, two video sequences are input for each batch, and each sequence has 8 frames. We choose the Adman optimizer, the learning rate of the ResNet is set to $1e-6$, and the learning rate of other parts is $1e-3$. We apply rotation, translation, shearing and scaling on the original image for data augmentation. According to the experiment, the weight of each loss function is set as $\alpha = 1, \beta = 2, \gamma = 0.2$.

4.2 Dataset

We measured the effect of our model on the recent video object segmentation dataset DAVIS 2017 [10]. DAVIS 2017 consists of 60 videos in the training set, 30 videos in the validation set and 30 videos in the test-dev set. Each video sequence contains multiple objects, and the video duration is 3–6 s.

4.3 Ablation Study

Encoder. To test the effectiveness of the modules used in the encoder, this section conducts ablation study on the spatial context branch and the channel attention module. Table 1 illustrates the impact of spatial context branch and channel attention mechanism on model performance. We use ResNet50 with a decoder based on one layer recurrent ConvLSTM as the baseline. The training process uses weighted sum of three loss functions. From the results, it can be found that adding the spatial attention module and the channel attention module respectively, the average value of $\mathcal{J}$ and $\mathcal{F}$ have improved compared with the baseline. Specifically, the second row of Table 1 shows that applying spatial context branch, $\mathcal{J}\&\mathcal{F}$ mean has a 1.2 point improvement compared to the baseline. Adding feature fusion module and sptial attention module on this basis can further improve network performance. What's more, the fifth row of Table 1 shows that after the channel attention module is added separately, $\mathcal{J}\&\mathcal{F}$ mean is improved by 1.4 compared with the baseline. Finally, the joint use of the spatial context branch with spatial attention module and the channel attention module achieves the highest performance. The $\mathcal{J}\&\mathcal{F}$ mean is 2.0 higher than the baseline network.

Table 1. Ablation study on DAVIS2017 validation set with different spatial modules. **SCB†**:spatial context branch with only conv layers, **FFM**:feature fusion module, **SCB**:spatial context branch with sptial attention module, **CAM**:channel attention module

Method	$\mathcal{J}\&\mathcal{F}$	$\mathcal{J}$			$\mathcal{F}$		
	Mean↑	Mean↑	Recall↑	Decay↓	Mean↑	Recall↑	Decay↓
Baseline	80.1	75.8	84.5	–3.9	84.3	89.4	–4.4
+SCB†	81.3	77.0	85.4	**–4.3**	85.6	90.4	–4.3
+SCB†+FFM	81.9	77.6	85.6	**–4.3**	86.2	90.6	–4.1
+SCB+FFM	82.0	77.6	85.7	**–4.3**	86.3	90.6	–4.4
+CAM	81.5	77.2	85.5	–4.2	85.9	90.8	**–4.7**
+SCB+FFM+CAM	**82.1**	**77.8**	**85.8**	**–4.3**	**86.5**	**90.8**	–4.1

Loss Function. As shown in the Table 2, the first row and the second row represent the case of using the IOU loss and the Balanced BCE loss respectively, and IOU loss is significantly better than Balanced BCE loss. The third and fourth rows in the Table 2 are added to the intra-frame self IOU loss we proposed as the auxiliary loss on the basis of the use of IOU loss and Balanced BCE loss. After the auxiliary loss is added, the performance is improved. Compared with only using the IOU loss, $\mathcal{J}$ mean and $\mathcal{F}$ mean of $LOSS_{IOU} + LOSS_{self}$ improves 0.9 and 1.3 respectively. The two results of $LOSS_{BalanceBCE} + LOSS_{self}$ improved by 2.5 and 1.5 compared with only using the Balanced BCE loss. The fifth row of the Table 2 shows the results of using three loss functions at the same time, and

Table 2. Ablation study of the three loss functions on the DAVIS2017 validation set

$LOSS_{IOU}$	$LOSS_{BalanceBCE}$	$LOSS_{self}$	$\mathcal{J}$ Mean	$\mathcal{F}$ Mean
√			76.6	85.2
	√		64.3	73.9
√		√	77.5	86.5
	√	√	66.8	75.4
√	√	√	**77.8**	**86.5**

the $\mathcal{J}$ mean and $\mathcal{F}$ mean reach 81.8 and 90.5 respectively. This shows that the joint supervision of three loss function during the training process can improve the performance of the model.

As shown in Table 3, that the parameters and the number of floating-point operation of the criss-cross attention module we used are 0.005M and 0.067GFLOPS, respectively, which are both 1/3 of the non-local module under the same setting, meanwhile, the $\mathcal{J}$ mean and $\mathcal{F}$ mean are similar to the results obtained by the non-local module. By executing the criss-cross attention module twice in succession, the global context dependence of each pixel position can be obtained without increasing the parameter amount.

Table 3. Comparative experiment results of the influence of criss-cross attention module and non-local module on model parameters

Module	Parameters	FLOPs	$\mathcal{J}$ Mean	$\mathcal{F}$ Mean
Criss-Cross attention module	0.005M	0.067G	77.6	86.3
Non-local module	0.017M	0.215G	77.5	85.5

4.4 Semi-supervised Video Object Segmentation

Table 4 gives the overall results of our method on the DAVIS 2017 validation set. We set the same structure as the model of the last row of Table 1. The other methods in the Table 4 are all obtained from the DAVIS2017 benchmark. Our $\mathcal{J}\&\mathcal{F}$ mean are 82.2, which surpasses other methods in the benchmark. And our model inference speed is also faster than the SSM-VOS. The inference speed of SSM-VOS reach 22.3 fps, while our method with ResNet50 can reach 45.5 fps on the NVIDIA GTX1080Ti. This is due to the fact that our model adopts strategies such as criss-cross attention module and depth-wise separable convolution to control the amount of model parameters and calculations.

4.5 Visualization

Figure 5 shows the visual effect of the qualitative evaluation of the DAVIS2017 dataset. The segmentation results of each video sequence in the figure show that

Table 4. Quantitative comparison of other methods on the DAVIS2017 val sets.

Method	$\mathcal{J}\&\mathcal{F}$	$\mathcal{J}$			$\mathcal{F}$			Runtime (fps)
	Mean↑	Mean↑	Recall↑	Decay↓	Mean↑	Recall↑	Decay↓	
CFBI [15]	81.9	79.1	-	-	84.6	-	-	-
STM [8]	81.75	**79.2**	**88.7**	8.0	84.3	**91.8**	10.5	-
PReMVOS [5]	77.85	73.9	83.1	16.2	81.8	88.9	19.5	-
MHP-VOS [14]	76.15	73.4	83.5	17.8	78.9	87.2	19.1	-
SSM-VOS [17]	77.6	75.3	-	11.7	79.9	-	15.3	22.3
Ours	**82.1**	77.8	85.8	**–4.3**	**86.5**	90.8	**–4.1**	**45.4**

our model can deal with various challenging scenarios of semi-supervised video object segmentation tasks, such as the serious occlusion between the objects in the second and fifth rows, the rapid changes in the shape and scale of the object in the first and fourth row, the blurred background of the fish tank in the third row.

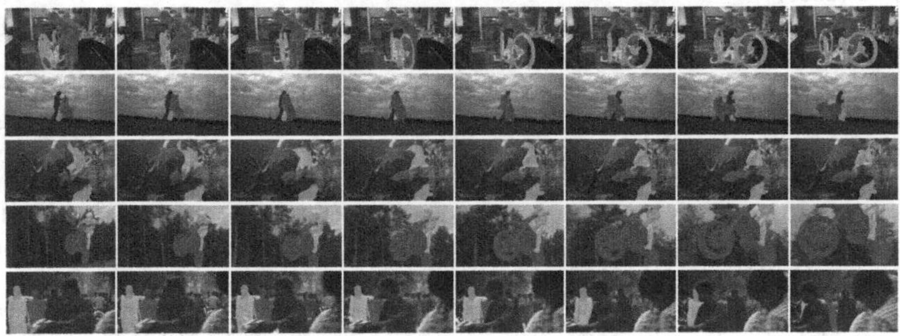

Fig. 5. The visualization results of the semi-supervised video object segmentation task on the DAVIS2017 dataset.

5 Conclusion

We propose an end-to-end framework for real-time video multi-object segmentation. We set up a spatial context branch with spatial attention module to obtains the long range context dependencies in the features and to avoid the global spatial attention module from occupying too much computing resources. In addition, we also use the channel attention mechanism for the highest level features of the feature extraction network to obtain the semantic dependencies between channels. Finally, the feature with different scale are sent to the recurrent ConvLSTM decoder through the skip-connection conv, and the multi-object video segmentation mask is obtained through step-wise upsample of the feature map. In the DAVIS2017 benchmark, our model has achieved the best results compared with the latest methods in semi-supervised tasks. At the same time, the model inference speed is 45.5 fps.

References

1. Caelles, S., Maninis, K., Pont-Tuset, J., Leal-Taixé, L., Cremers, D., Gool, L.V.: One-shot video object segmentation. In: 2017 IEEE Conference on Computer Vision and Pattern Recognition (CVPR 2017), pp. 5320–5329. IEEE Computer Society (2017)
2. He, K., Zhang, X., Ren, S., Sun, J.: Deep residual learning for image recognition. In: 2016 IEEE Conference on Computer Vision and Pattern Recognition (CVPR 2016), pp. 770–778. IEEE Computer Society (2016)
3. Hu, Y.-T., Huang, J.-B., Schwing, A.G.: VideoMatch: matching based video object segmentation. In: Ferrari, V., Hebert, M., Sminchisescu, C., Weiss, Y. (eds.) ECCV 2018. LNCS, vol. 11212, pp. 56–73. Springer, Cham (2018). https://doi.org/10.1007/978-3-030-01237-3_4
4. Huang, Z., Wang, X., Huang, L., Huang, C., Wei, Y., Liu, W.: Ccnet: criss-cross attention for semantic segmentation. In: 2019 IEEE/CVF International Conference on Computer Vision (ICCV 2019), pp. 603–612. IEEE (2019)
5. Luiten, J., Voigtlaender, P., Leibe, B.: Premvos: proposal-generation, refinement and merging for the Davis challenge on video object segmentation 2018. In: The 2018 DAVIS Challenge on Video Object Segmentation-CVPR Workshops, vol. 1, p. 6 (2018)
6. Maninis, K., et al.: Video object segmentation without temporal information. IEEE Trans. Pattern Anal. Mach. Intell. **41**(6), 1515–1530 (2019)
7. Oh, S.W., Lee, J., Sunkavalli, K., Kim, S.J.: Fast video object segmentation by reference-guided mask propagation. In: 2018 IEEE Conference on Computer Vision and Pattern Recognition (CVPR 2018), pp. 7376–7385. IEEE Computer Society (2018)
8. Oh, S.W., Lee, J., Xu, N., Kim, S.J.: Video object segmentation using space-time memory networks. In: 2019 IEEE/CVF International Conference on Computer Vision, ICCV 2019. pp. 9225–9234. IEEE (2019)
9. Perazzi, F., Khoreva, A., Benenson, R., Schiele, B., Sorkine-Hornung, A.: Learning video object segmentation from static images. In: 2017 IEEE Conference on Computer Vision and Pattern Recognition (CVPR 2017), pp. 3491–3500. IEEE Computer Society (2017)
10. Pont-Tuset, J., Perazzi, F., Caelles, S., Arbelaez, P., Sorkine-Hornung, A., Gool, L.V.: The 2017 DAVIS challenge on video object segmentation. CoRR abs/1704.00675 (2017)
11. Shi, X., Chen, Z., Wang, H., Yeung, D., Wong, W., Woo, W.: Convolutional LSTM network: a machine learning approach for precipitation nowcasting, pp. 802–810 (2015)
12. Ventura, C., Bellver, M., Girbau, A., Salvador, A., Marqués, F., Giró-i-Nieto, X.: RVOS: end-to-end recurrent network for video object segmentation. In: IEEE Conference on Computer Vision and Pattern Recognition (CVPR 2019), pp. 5277–5286. Computer Vision Foundation/IEEE (2019)
13. Voigtlaender, P., Leibe, B.: Online adaptation of convolutional neural networks for video object segmentation. In: British Machine Vision Conference 2017 (BMVC 2017). BMVA Press, London (2017)
14. Xu, S., Liu, D., Bao, L., Liu, W., Zhou, P.: MHP-VOS: multiple hypotheses propagation for video object segmentation. In: IEEE Conference on Computer Vision and Pattern Recognition (CVPR 2019), pp. 314–323. Computer Vision Foundation/IEEE (2019)

15. Yang, Z., Wei, Y., Yang, Y.: Collaborative video object segmentation by foreground-background integration. In: Vedaldi, A., Bischof, H., Brox, T., Frahm, J.-M. (eds.) ECCV 2020. LNCS, vol. 12350, pp. 332–348. Springer, Cham (2020). https://doi.org/10.1007/978-3-030-58558-7_20
16. Yoon, J.S., Rameau, F., Kim, J., Lee, S., Shin, S., Kweon, I.S.: Pixel-level matching for video object segmentation using convolutional neural networks. In: IEEE International Conference on Computer Vision (ICCV 2017), pp. 2186–2195. IEEE Computer Society (2017)
17. Zhu, W., Li, J., Lu, J., Zhou, J.: Separable structure modeling for semi-supervised video object segmentation. IEEE Trans. Circuits Syst. Video Technol. **99**, 1–1 (2021)

Distance-Based Class Activation Map for Metric Learning

Yeqing Shen[1], Huimin Ma[2(✉)], Xiaowen Zhang[1], Tianyu Hu[2], and Yuhan Dong[1,3]

[1] Tsinghua University, Beijing, China
{shenyq18,zhangxw18}@mails.tsinghua.edu.cn
[2] University of Science and Technology Beijing, Beijing, China
{mhmpub,tianyu}@ustb.edu.cn
[3] Tsinghua Shenzhen International Graduate School, Shenzhen, China
dongyuhan@sz.tsinghua.edu.cn

Abstract. The interpretability of deep neural networks can serve as reliable guidance for algorithm improvement. By visualizing class-relevant features in the form of heatmap, the Class Activation Map (CAM) and derivative versions have been widely exploited to study the interpretability of softmax-based neural networks. However, CAM cannot be adopted directly for metric learning, because there is no fully-connected layer in metric-learning-based methods. To solve this problem, we propose a **Distance-based Class Activation Map (Dist-CAM)** in this paper, which can be applied to metric learning directly. Comprehensive experiments are conducted with several convolutional neural networks trained on the ILSVRC 2012 and the result shows that Dist-CAM can achieve better performance than the original CAM in weakly-supervised localization tasks, which means the heatmap generated by Dist-CAM can effectively visualize class-relevant features. Finally, the applications of Dist-CAM on specific tasks, i.e., few-shot learning, image retrieval and re-identification, based on metric learning are presented.

Keywords: Neural network interpretability · Class activation map · Metric learning

1 Introduction

The past few years have witnessed a major development in deep learning, and impressive achievements have been made in several tasks, e.g., recognition, detection and reinforcement learning. However, current deep neural networks are facing the problem of interpretability. Specifically, deep neural networks contain a large number of learnable parameters, which must be trained on a grand scale of data using gradient descent strategy, and thus the prediction results of the neural network are less possible to be appropriately interpreted based on the parameters

© Springer Nature Switzerland AG 2021
H. Ma et al. (Eds.): PRCV 2021, LNCS 13022, pp. 336–347, 2021.
https://doi.org/10.1007/978-3-030-88013-2_28

of the network. Many studies [2,12,21] have been trying to solve this problem of network interpretability, and one representative approach is to visualize the output of the neural network, of which Class Activation Map (CAM) [20] has made significant progress. To be more specific, CAM is applied to the classification network based on Convolutional Neural Network (CNN). This classification network extracts the features of images through CNN, and the features will then be combined through fully connected layer to obtain the prediction results. To visualize the classification network, CAM combines the feature map of CNN with the weights of fully connected layers, based on which the heatmap of the image to be recognized can be generated. However, this approach relies heavily on the fully connected layers of the classification network, thereby making it difficult to be applied to metric learning which lacks fully connected layer.

Metric learning aims at learning a representation function which maps objects into a CNN network. The object's similarity should be reflected in the distance of the CNN network, i.e., the distance between similar objects is as reduced as possible while dissimilar objects are far from each other. This approach has been extensively applied in image retrieval [1,4,15,18], re-ID [5,9,10,17] and few-shot learning [3,6–8,14], etc. Therefore, it is of great value to interpret the neural networks in metric learning. Facing this problem of interpretability, we propose a Dist-CAM to achieve better interpretability of neural networks in metric learning. In particular, the current study focuses on solving the problem of CAM in its limited applicability to broader network architectures, and tries to extend CAM to metric learning based on the idea of class activation.

As shown in Fig. 1, in a recognition network with fully connected layer, the feature maps of different channels combine with the weights of the fully connected layer. The class with the highest probability in the output is considered as the final prediction result. On the other hand, different regions of the heatmap generated by CAM have distinct responses. Particularly, a region with a higher response indicates that the features of this area have more contributions to the output. Therefore, CAM actually establishes a relationship between the output of the classification network and different regions of the original image in which a stronger response implies a greater relevance.

By contrast, in a metric learning network without fully connected layer in Fig. 2, the features of the sample are firstly extracted by CNN, and then the distance between the features of the test sample and those of the training sample is calculated in the metric module. The class of the training sample which has the smallest distance from the test sample is considered as the prediction result. Following this idea of class prediction in metric learning, the Dist-CAM proposed by the current study establishes a relationship between the prediction results of metric learning and different locations of the original image. To be more specific, the main idea is to calculate the distance between the feature maps of the training sample and those of the test sample in different channels, in order to evaluate their relevance. The obtained relevance score is used as the weights corresponding to the different channels of the feature maps of the test sample, in which a channel with a higher relevance score has a greater weight.

The relevance between features of the test sample in a particular location and the class of the training sample is reflected in the responses of different locations in the generated heatmap, and a higher response suggests a greater relevance between the feature and the training set.

The main contribution of the current paper is that we propose the Dist-CAM which can be employed in the interpretation of the neural networks in metric learning. To evaluate the quality of heatmaps generated by Dist-CAM, comprehensive experiments have been conducted on weakly-supervised localization tasks in ImageNet [13]. The results show that the regions with higher responses in the heatmaps generated by Dist-CAM are indeed the class-relevant features, which clearly indicates that Dist-CAM can be used in metric learning to effectively interpret neural networks. Additionally, this paper also compares the performance of CAM and Dist-CAM in weakly-supervised localization tasks, and the results show that Dist-CAM with the same backbone network as CAM can achieve more accurate localization. To the best of our knowledge, this is the first method that can be used to generate class activation map for metric learning. In order to evaluate the applicability of Dist-CAM, the visualization results in several metric learning tasks are also presented in Sect. 5.

2 Distance-Based Class Activation Map

Details on CAM in softmax-based methods and Dist-CAM in metric learning as well as their comparison will be introduced in this section.

Class Activation Map

Softmax-based learning refers to neural networks with fully-connected(FC) layers, which calculates probabilities of different classes, and predicts the final result with the softmax layer. The operation of softmax layer is shown in Eq. 1, in which $\hat{y}$ is the prediction of softmax and v_i is the value of vector generated by FC layers.

$$\hat{y} = \frac{e^{v_i}}{\sum_j e^{v_i}} \tag{1}$$

The architecture of CAM [20] for the softmax-based classification networks is shown in Fig. 1(a), in which FC means FC layer. Test feature map $Q \in \mathbf{R}^{W \times H \times K}$ is encoded by a convolutional neural network (CNN) backbone with test sample as input. The width and height of feature map are denoted as W and H, and the number of its channels is denoted as K. Furthermore, the feature map of the k-th channel are denoted as $Q_k \in \mathbf{R}^{W \times H}$. Then Global Average Pooling (GAP) calculates the average of feature map in each channel, which is denoted as $\mathcal{GAP}(\cdot)$. Finally, as shown in Eq. 2, the output of the GAP is combined with weight of FC layers to obtain the confidence of each class. For a specific class c, w_k^c is the FC layer weight of the k-th channel and y^c is the class confidence.

$$y^c = \sum_k w_k^c \mathcal{GAP}(Q_k) \tag{2}$$

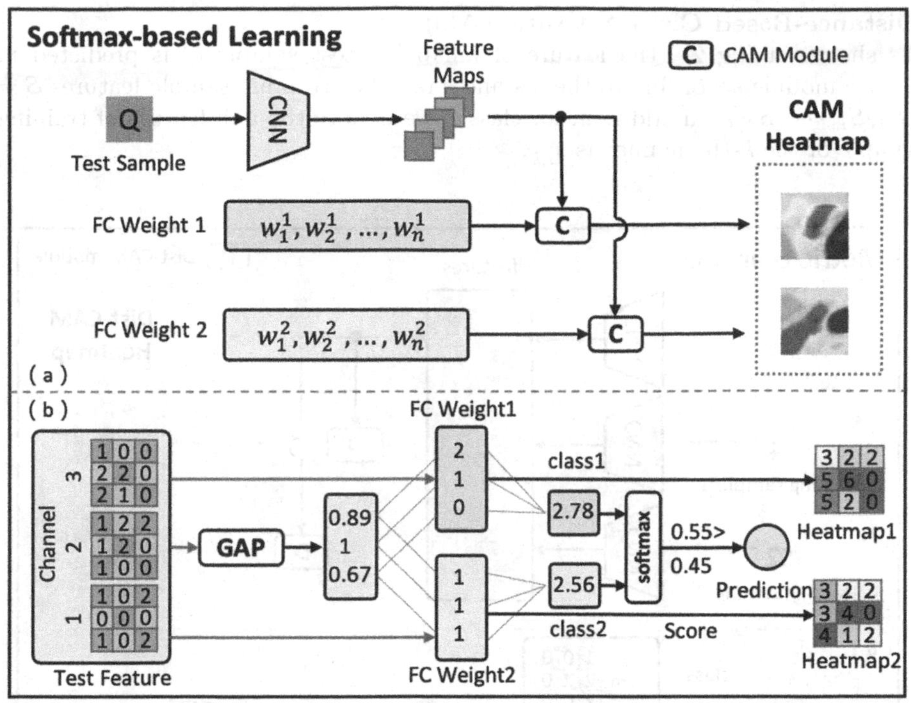

Fig. 1. Class activation map. In softmax-based learning, CAM combines the feature maps with FC weight to generate heatmaps. (a) The framework of softmax-base learning with CAM module. (b) A simplified illustration of CAM generation process.

As Eq. 3 shows, heatmap of class c is obtained by combining test feature maps with FC layers weight of class c in the CAM module. Different regions of the heatmap have distinct response. A larger response indicates a greater correlation between the region and the class c. High response region can be regarded as activation, so the heatmap of class c is the class c activation map.

$$M_{cam}^{c} = \sum_{k} w_k^c Q_k \tag{3}$$

As Fig. 1(b) shows, the final prediction is class 1, because the score of class 1 is 0.55 and the score of class 2 is 0.45. Heatmap 1 and heatmap 2 are generated by combining test feature maps with FC weight 1 and FC weight 2. A higher response in heatmap c indicates a greater correlation between the region and the class c.

However, due to the dependence on the weight of the FC layer, CAM can only be applied in the softmax-based methods, and cannot be used in metric learning. To solve this problem, the distance-based Class Activation Map is designed to analyze the models in metric learning.

Distance-Based Class Activation Map
As shown in Fig. 2 , the feature of unlabeled test sample Q is predicted in metric module according to the distances to other training sample features $\mathcal{S} = \{S_0, S_1, \cdots, S_N\}$. In addition, for class c, we denote the i-th feature of training sample of the k-th channel as $s_{i,k}^c$.

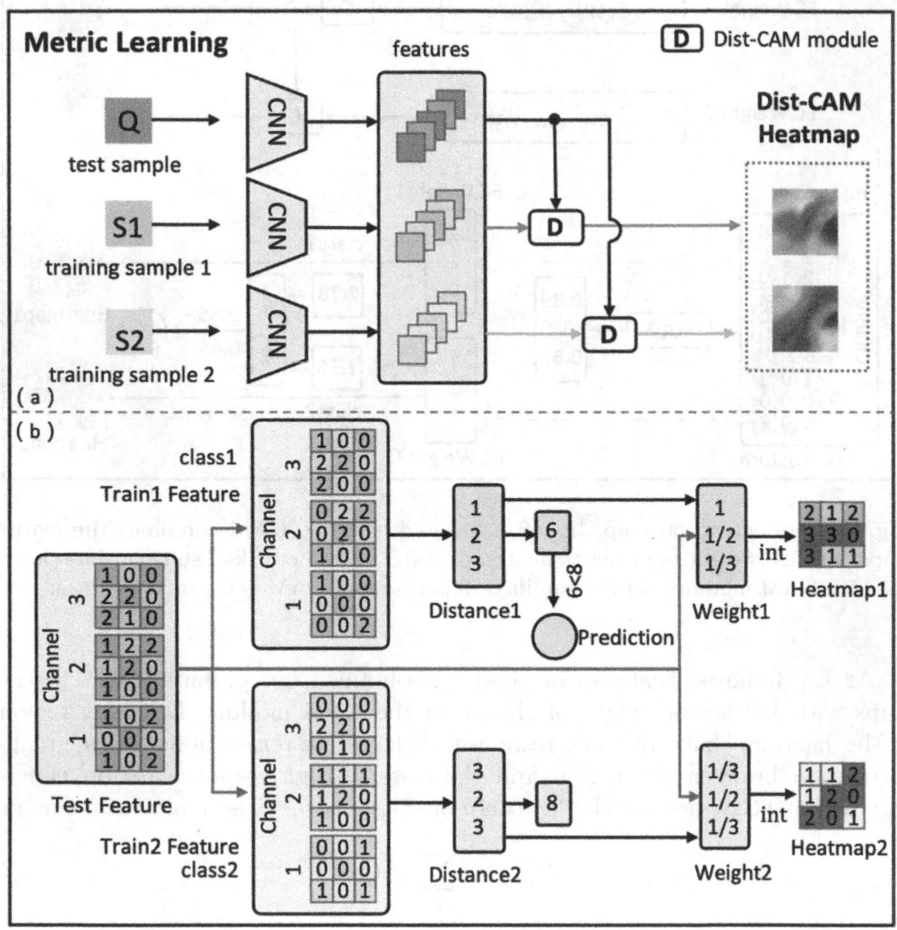

Fig. 2. Distance-based class activation map. In metric learning, Dist-CAM combines the feature maps with weight to generate heatmaps. (a) The framework of metric learning with Dist-CAM module. (b)A simplified illustration of Dist-CAM generation process.

As Eq. 4 shows, the distance D^c is calculated between the feature of training sample S^c and that of test sample Q via the GAP layer, where the operation $\mathcal{L}_1(\cdot)$ refers to element-wise 1-norm. The k-th dimension in the vector D^c represents the difference between S^c and Q in the k-th channel. It is clear that the difference is positively correlated with the distance value. Therefore, the smaller value of D^c_k is, the closer Q_k is to S^c_k. If the feature is closer to the training sample c in the channel k, it is supposed that the k-th channel plays a more important role in the prediction.

$$D^c = \mathcal{L}_1(\mathcal{GAP}(S^c) - \mathcal{GAP}(Q)), \quad D^c \in \mathbf{R}^K \tag{4}$$

Similar to the combination of the GAP outputs in Eq. 2, the output is obtained by the summation of D^c in metric learning. However, the largest response of class confidence y^c by the combination in Eq. 2 determines the output class c, while the smallest summation of D^c determines the output class c. Therefore, we transform D^c to W^c as shown in Eq. 5, where $norm(\cdot)$ is the operation of element-wise normalization. Thus the coefficient W reflects the distances from the different channels of Q to training sample S^c. The bigger the weight W^c_k is, the more relevant the k-th channel is with the class c.

$$W^c = norm(\frac{1}{D^c}), \quad W^c \in \mathbf{R}^K \tag{5}$$

$$M^c_{DistCAM} = \sum_k W^c_k Q^k \tag{6}$$

$M^c_{DistCAM}$ is calculated by combining Q^k with weight vector W^c_k as shown in Eq. 6. The different responses in Dist-CAM heatmap reflect distinct level of class activation. High response region can be regarded as activation, so the heatmap of class c is the class c activation map. As shown in Fig. 2(b), the prediction is class 1, because the distance in feature space between test sample and training sample 1 is 6, and the distance in feature space between test sample and training sample 2 is 8. In the Dist-CAM module, weight of class W^c is reciprocal of distance vector D^c. Heatmap 1 and heatmap 2 are generated by combining test feature maps with weight 1 and weight 2. A higher response in Dist-CAM heatmap c indicates a greater correlation between the region and the class c.

In Dist-CAM heatmap, a red pixel represents a large activation value, and a blue pixel represents a small activation value. The region with a large activation value suggests that feature of this region has a large contribution to the final prediction. As shown in Fig. 3, the response regions of Dist-CAM heatmaps generated with different categories of prototypes are also different. The input image contains a cat and a dog. The Dist-CAM modules measure the feature with the prototypes of cat, dog, bird, and table respectively. Among visualization results, the Dist-CAM heatmaps of cat class and dog class respond significantly at the locations of the two objects, while the other two activation regions are chaotic and scattered, which means Dist-cam effectively activates the class-relevant regions.

$$P^c_k = \frac{1}{N}\sum_i S^c_{(i,k)}, \quad P^c_k \in \mathbf{R}^{W\times H} \tag{7}$$

In some metric learning applications, the prediction of test sample is determined by the nearest class prototype, instead of the nearest training sample.

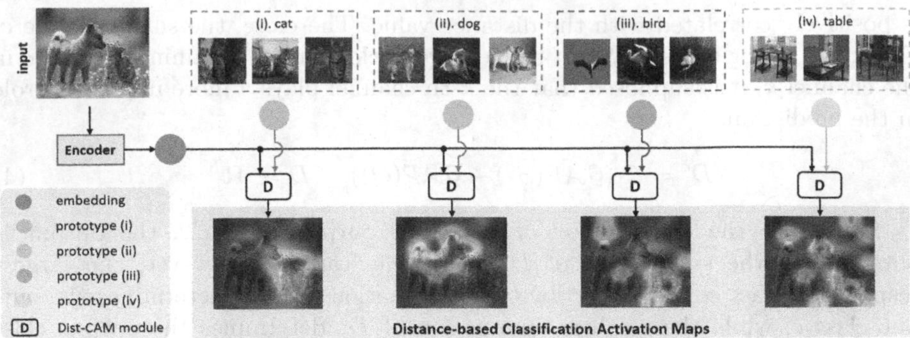

Fig. 3. Framework of Distance-based class activation Map. Different colors represent the corresponding images and prototypes of different categories (i)–(iv). The input image is encoded by a feature encoder, and the features are fed to Dist-CAM modules to class-wise calculate the distance-based Class Activation Maps with different prototypes. The Dist-CAM heatmaps of cat class and dog class respond significantly at the locations of the two objects, while the other two activation regions are chaotic and scattered.

The prototype of class c is denoted as P^c, which is obtained by calculating the mean value of features of all training samples in class c. The way to calculate prototype P^c is shown in Eq. 7, in which N is the number of training samples. In these applications, the prototype P^c replaces the training sample S^c to calculate the distance D^c and generate the Dist-CAM heatmap $M^c_{DistCAM}$.

3 Experiments

Weakly-supervised localization task is chosen for the evaluating the performance of Dist-CAM for the following reasons. On the one hand, neural networks in classification task and those in weakly-supervised localization task share the same kind of label, i.e., both are trained with class label. On the other, both weakly-supervised localization task and class activation task focus on localizing class-relevant regions. Therefore, weakly-supervised localization task is appropriate to be used in the experiments.

Experiments are conducted to quantitatively evaluate the weakly-supervised localization ability of Dist-CAM on the ILSVRC 2012 benchmark [13]. We adopt two main CNN backbones: ResNet and DenseNet. For each backbone, we have trained the model on ILSVRC 2012 training set to obtain softmax-based models with FC layers and distance-based metric learning models, respectively.

In order to ensure the fairness of the experiment, N in Eq. 7 is set to the number of training samples of each class when calculating the prototype in metric learning. Besides, we drop the last GAP layer and the FC layer of models to obtain a multi-channel feature map with spatial position information for metric learning experiments. For example, the input image with the size of $224 \times 224 \times 3$ is encoded by a modified ResNet backbone into a feature map with the size of

Table 1. Localization error (top-1) of the Dist-CAM on ILSVRC2012 *val* sets.

Backbone	Method	Top-1 error
ResNet-18	CAM	59.5
ResNet-18	**Dist-CAM**	**56.7**
ResNet-50	CAM	56.2
ResNet-50	**Dist-CAM**	**54.7**
ResNet-101	CAM	56.6
ResNet-101	**Dist-CAM**	**54.9**
DenseNet-161	CAM	62.4
DenseNet-161	**Dist-CAM**	**57.6**
DenseNet-169	CAM	62.3
DenseNet-169	**Dist-CAM**	**56.6**
DenseNet-201	CAM	62.5
DenseNet-201	**Dist-CAM**	**56.4**

$2048 \times 7 \times 7$. When predicting the class, the feature map is transformed into a 2048-dimensional feature of test sample by the GAP layer. Then the network calculates the distances between the 2048-dimensional feature and each prototype and selects the nearest one as the prediction. When calculating the Dist-CAM, the network measures the channel-wise distances of the 2048-dimensional feature and the nearest prototype and obtains the channel weighting coefficients by reciprocal and normalization. Finally, a weighted summation of the original $2048 \times 7 \times 7$ feature map with the coefficients is performed to obtain the Dist-CAM with the size of 7×7.

To compare with the original CAM, we evaluate the localization ability of Dist-CAM with the same error metric (top-1) on the ILSVRC 2012 [13] *val* set. The intersection of union (IoU) threshold is set to generate bounding boxes on the positions with strong responses. Compared with groundtruth, when the IoU between them is lower than 0.5, the prediction is considered as a wrong localization.

As shown in Table 1, Dist-CAM has achieved a lower top-1 error than the original CAM, which indicates the effectiveness of our method. Without the FC layer, Dist-CAM has achieved accurate localization of discriminative features, which is effective to interpret the model in metric learning. Meanwhile, the Dist-CAM can also be regarded as a promotion of CAM, which can be used in the softmax-based methods by dropping the last FC layer.

4 Metric-Based Applications

Dist-CAM is applied to three main tasks of metric learning, including few-shot learning, image retrieval and re-identification. Experiments are conducted to show the visualization results to explore network interpretability. Note that in few-shot learning, support sample refers to training sample mentioned in Sect. 2 and query sample refers to test sample. In image retrieval and re-identification, training sample mentioned in Sect. 2 is defined as gallery sample and test sample is defined as probe sample.

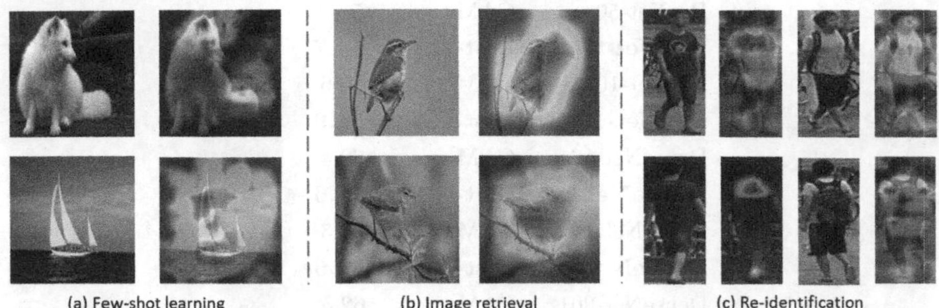

Fig. 4. Dist-CAM visualization for metric-based applications. (a) Dist-CAM heatmaps for few-shot learning on miniImageNet; (b) Dist-CAM heatmaps for image retrieval on CUB2011; Dist-CAM heatmaps for pedestrian re-identification on Market-1501.

4.1 Few-Shot Learning

Few-shot learning is one of the most significant applications for metric learning [3,6–8,14]. Studies on few-shot learning aim to overcome the lack of support samples to obtain a useful recognition model. Inspired by the idea of meta-learning, most of the current approaches adopt a number of tasks similar to the target one to train a meta-learner. Specifically, the majority of current mainstream methods are based on metric learning frameworks. To predict the class of unlabeled query sample, the metric learning frameworks measure the distances among the unlabeled query sample and the class prototypes, which are calculated from the labeled support samples.

As mentioned in Sect. 1, the lack of FC layers limits the original CAM methods to analyze the model performance. To explore the network interpretability of meta-learning, Dist-CAM is used to localize the discriminative features and analyze the advantages of metric-based few-shot learning.

We adopt ResNet-12 as a backbone and train the model [7] by meta-learning strategy. The performance has achieved a state-of-the-art performance with 77.14 ± 0.42 in the-5-way-1-shot task. Figure 4(a) shows Dist-CAM for few-shot learning on mini-Imagenet [11] dataset. According to the setting of the one-shot task, only one support sample is used to calculate the prototype. It can be seen that the activation location of the fox in the above image is concentrated on the ears and tail, and the activation location of the sailboat in the image below is concentrated on the sail and hull. These are indeed the class-defining features related to these classes. Results show that Dist-CAM is a useful tool to analyze the metric-based few-shot learning, which can also be used to improve the training strategies by analyzing failure cases.

4.2 Image Retrieval

Metric learning is widely used in image retrieval to search images by images. For softmax-based methods, it is exhausting to retrain the model when a novel class sample appears. By contrast, there is no need to retrain the model in metric learning when adding a novel class. Therefore, image retrieval is an important application of metric learning, trying to retrieve the same object or class as the probe sample from the existing gallery samples [1,4,15,18]. Different from the classification algorithm with fixed output classes, the metric learning algorithm increases the inter-class interval and reduces the intra-class variance by designing the loss function during the training process. Images are encoded by backbone and retrieved according to distance calculated by metric module. In the application stage of image retrieval, even if new categories are added, the trained backbone can be used for prediction in metric learning, which is difficult for classification algorithms with a fixed number of classes.

Dist-CAM is used to analyze an image retrieval model trained on the CUB2011 [16], a dataset containing 200 categories of birds, of which ResNet-50 is used as the backbone. According to the settings of the image retrieval task, only one gallery sample that is the closest to the probe sample is used to calculate the Dist-CAM heatmaps. It can be seen from Fig. 4(b) that Dist-CAM heatmaps have a good weakly supervised localization capability. The activation location is concentrated on the region of the birds. Therefore, it clearly shows that Dist-CAM can be used to analyze the results and failure cases of the image retrieval model.

4.3 Re-identification

As a sub-problem of image retrieval, re-identification aims to find the expected target in the image library [5,9,10,17]. During the test phase, the probe images to be retrieved are used to calculate feature distances with gallery images. Then top-k images are retrieved according to feature distances. Plenty of re-identification algorithms are based on metric learning to avoid retraining the model when adding a novel class as mentioned in previous section.

We adopt the ResNet-50 as a backbone and train the model with center loss and reranking strategy [10]. The rank-1 accuracy achieves 94.5 and the average precision achieves 85.9 on the Market-1501 [19]. According to the settings of the re-identification, only one gallery sample that is the closest to the probe sample is used to calculate the prototype. Figure 4(c) shows Dist-CAM of the probe samples in the Market-1501 dataset for pedestrian re-identification. It can be seen that the discriminative features are concentrated on the human clothes. The Dist-CAM heatmaps in Fig. 4(c) reflect that clothes are an important feature for re-identification in these probe samples.

5 Conclusion

In this paper, we propose **Distance-based Class Activation Map** for deep metric learning to explore the interpretability of metric-based networks. On weakly supervised object localization tasks on ILSVRC 2012 [13], comprehensive experiments are conducted and the result shows that Dist-CAM is better than the original CAM with ResNet or DenseNet as backbones. Besides, we demonstrate the visualization of Dist-CAM in specific applications of metric learning, including few-shot learning, image retrieval and re-identification. In the future, it is worthwhile to adopt the Dist-CAM to guide the innovation and improvement of metric learning methods.

Acknowledgments. This work was supported by the National Natural Science Foundation of China (No.U20B2062), the fellowship of China Postdoctoral Science Foundation (No.2021M690354), the Beijing Municipal Science & Technology Project (No.Z191100007419001).

References

1. Cakir, F., He, K., Xia, X., Kulis, B., Sclaroff, S.: Deep metric learning to rank. In: 2019 IEEE/CVF Conference on Computer Vision and Pattern Recognition (CVPR), pp. 1861–1870 (2019)
2. Chattopadhay, A., Sarkar, A., Howlader, P., Balasubramanian, V.N.: Grad-CAM++: generalized gradient-based visual explanations for deep convolutional networks. In: 2018 IEEE Winter Conference on Applications of Computer Vision (WACV), pp. 839–847 (2018)
3. Chu, W., Wang, Y.F.: Learning semantics-guided visual attention for few-shot image classification. In: 2018 25th IEEE International Conference on Image Processing (ICIP), pp. 2979–2983 (2018). https://doi.org/10.1109/ICIP.2018.8451350
4. Ge, W., Huang, W., Dong, D., Scott, M.R.: Deep metric learning with hierarchical triplet loss. In: Proceedings of the European Conference on Computer Vision (ECCV), pp. 272–288 (2018)
5. Hao, Y., Wang, N., Li, J., Gao, X.: Hsme: Hypersphere manifold embedding for visible thermal person re-identification. In: Proceedings of the AAAI Conference on Artificial Intelligence, vol. 33, pp. 8385–8392 (2019)
6. Li, X., et al.: Learning to self-train for semi-supervised few-shot classification. In: 33rd Conference on Neural Information Processing Systems. vol. 32, pp. 10276–10286 (2019)
7. Liu, J., Song, L., Qin, Y.: Prototype rectification for few-shot learning. In: ECCV, vol. 1. pp. 741–756 (2019)
8. Liu, L., Zhou, T., Long, G., Jiang, J., Yao, L., Zhang, C.: Prototype propagation networks (PPN) for weakly-supervised few-shot learning on category graph. In: Proceedings of the Twenty-Eighth International Joint Conference on Artificial Intelligence, pp. 3015–3022 (2019)
9. Liu, W., Wen, Y., Yu, Z., Li, M., Raj, B., Song, L.: Sphereface: deep hypersphere embedding for face recognition. In: 2017 IEEE Conference on Computer Vision and Pattern Recognition (CVPR), pp. 6738–6746 (2017)
10. Luo, H., Gu, Y., Liao, X., Lai, S., Jiang, W.: Bag of tricks and a strong baseline for deep person re-identification. In: 2019 IEEE/CVF Conference on Computer Vision and Pattern Recognition Workshops (CVPRW), pp. 0–0 (2019)
11. Rusu, A.A., Rao, D., Sygnowski, J., Vinyals, O., Pascanu, R., Osindero, S., Hadsell, R.: Meta-learning with latent embedding optimization. In: International Conference on Learning Representations (2018)

12. Selvaraju, R.R., Cogswell, M., Das, A., Vedantam, R., Parikh, D., Batra, D.: Grad-CAM: visual explanations from deep networks via gradient-based localization. Int. J. Comput. Vis. **128**(2), 336–359 (2020)
13. Simonyan, K., Zisserman, A.: Very deep convolutional networks for large-scale image recognition. In: International Conference on Learning Representations 2015 (ICLR 2015) (2015)
14. Snell, J., Swersky, K., Zemel, R.S.: Prototypical networks for few-shot learning. Adv. Neural Inf. Process. Syst. **30**, 4077–4087 (2017)
15. Song, H.O., Jegelka, S., Rathod, V., Murphy, K.: Deep metric learning via facility location. In: 2017 IEEE Conference on Computer Vision and Pattern Recognition (CVPR), pp. 2206–2214 (2017)
16. Wah, C., Branson, S., Welinder, P., Perona, P., Belongie, S.: The Caltech-UCSD Birds-200-2011 Dataset. Tech. Rep. CNS-TR-2011-001, California Institute of Technology (2011)
17. Wang, H., Zhu, X., Xiang, T., Gong, S.: Towards unsupervised open-set person re-identification. In: 2016 IEEE International Conference on Image Processing (ICIP), pp. 769–773 (2016). https://doi.org/10.1109/ICIP.2016.7532461
18. Wang, J., Zhou, F., Wen, S., Liu, X., Lin, Y.: Deep metric learning with angular loss. In: 2017 IEEE International Conference on Computer Vision (ICCV), pp. 2612–2620 (2017)
19. Zheng, L., Shen, L., Tian, L., Wang, S., Wang, J., Tian, Q.: Scalable person re-identification: a benchmark. In: IEEE International Conference on Computer Vision (2015)
20. Zhou, B., Khosla, A., Lapedriza, A., Oliva, A., Torralba, A.: Learning deep features for discriminative localization. In: 2016 IEEE Conference on Computer Vision and Pattern Recognition (CVPR). IEEE Computer Society (2016)
21. Zhou, Y., Zhu, Y., Ye, Q., Qiu, Q., Jiao, J.: Weakly supervised instance segmentation using class peak response. In: 2018 IEEE/CVF Conference on Computer Vision and Pattern Recognition, pp. 3791–3800 (2018)

Reading Pointer Meter Through One Stage End-to-End Deep Regression

Zhenzhen Chao[1], Yaobin Mao[1](✉), and Yi Han[2]

[1] Nanjing University of Science and Technology, Nanjing 210094, China
maoyaobin@njust.edu.cn

[2] Zhejiang Huayun Information Technology Co., LTD., Hangzhou 310008, China

Abstract. The recognition of analog pointer meters under nature environment is commonly a challenge task due to many influences like types of meters, shooting angle, lighting condition, etc. Most existing recognition algorithms consist of multiple steps including the detection and extraction of dial, scale marks and pointers followed by reading calculation, which is complex and sensitive to image quality. To address this issue, a one-stage, end-to-end recognition method for pointer meter based on deep regression is proposed in this paper. The proposed method simultaneously locates the position of the end point of a pointer, obtains a meter reading and determines whether the pointer exceeds the normal range through a fully convolutional neural network. Without complicated image pre-processing and post-processing, the algorithm can read multiple meters in one image just through a simple one-round forward inference. Experimental results show that the recognition accuracy achieves 92.59% under ±5% reading error, and the processing speed reaches approximately 25 FPS on a NVIDIA GTX 1080 GPU.

Keywords: Pointer meter · Automatic meter reading · Deep regression

1 Introduction

In power stations there exist numerous analogy pointer meters that need manually read and monitor periodically which is a cumbersome work since this manual data collection is of low efficiency, high labor intensity, and being easily impacted by external factors. Therefore, it is of crucial importance to develop a reliable method to automatically read in those pointer meters' indications.

Multiple methods have been proposed and applied in automatic meter reading [1, 2], however, most of them need two stage operations, namely recognition after detection. Those methods require the extraction of dials, scale marks and pointers which is not easily obtained and severely affected by image quality, thus could not suit for practical applications. The method proposed in this paper integrates detection and recognition into one neural network model and accomplishes the tasks via just one round inference.

Since the endpoint of a gauge's pointer represents the value of the meter which contains most important information, in our method, we just locate it and needn't detect

© Springer Nature Switzerland AG 2021
H. Ma et al. (Eds.): PRCV 2021, LNCS 13022, pp. 348–360, 2021.
https://doi.org/10.1007/978-3-030-88013-2_29

meter dials and scales. To reliably extract the endpoint on a meter, the CenterNet [27] is employed, as we know object can be detected through keypoint estimation by regression. As mentioned in Mask R-CNN [32], multi-task design leads to the uniformity and the consistency of the entire network model which outperforms single task design in performance.

All above considerations lead to the outcome of a one-stage, end-to-end pointer meter recognition method that is based on a deep neural network. By utilizing the multi-task learning capability of the deep network, three different output modules are conducted after a backbone network. Those three modules act simultaneously and respectively perform pointer location, meter reading regression, and measuring range checking. As an end-to-end model, the proposed method needn't image pre-processing usually used in most others. The main contributions of this paper are summarized as follows:

(1) A simultaneous meter locating and reading recognition model is designed through deep regression which is robust against environment noise.
(2) The proposed model regresses a normalized value in [0, 1] instead of the absolute meter value by compressing measure range, which makes it easier to converge.
(3) A classification module is set up for outrange checking. In this way, an extra constrain is imposed that significantly improves the accuracy of the reading regression.

The remaining of the paper is organized as follows: Sect. 2 reviews related work on pointer meter recognition. Section 3 details the method proposed in the paper. Section 4 reports the experimental results. At last, the paper is concluded in Sect. 5.

2 Related Work

Generally, existing meter reading algorithms can be catalogued into three classes, namely recognition by dial detection [3–18], recognition by keypoint detection [19–22] and direct reading through regression [23–26].

The first two classes of methods need the extraction of objects like dial, pointer and scale marks as human doing, while the third one regresses the indications of the meters by deep neural networks. No matter which kind of the method needs explicit dial region detection before reading the indication. Therefore, if DNN is used, at least two networks are required respectively for detection and recognition.

2.1 Recognition by Dial Detection

The majority of current researches belongs to this paradigm, which can be sub-divided into two categories: algorithms based on traditional image processing technology and methods based on deep learning.

Traditional Image Processing Based Algorithms. The traditional image processing based algorithms usually first perform pre-process followed by template matching [5, 7, 9] or Hough transform [3, 4, 6, 8, 10] to extract the dial regions. Then the Hough line detection or line fitting methods are employed to find pointers and scale marks on the binarized images. Even those algorithms operate fast, they suffer from noise and image degradation, therefore are less robust and unusable in practical applications.

Deep Learning Based Algorithms. To make the algorithms more robust, in recent years, deep learning is widely applied to pointer meter recognition. Liu [11], Zhang [12] and Wang [13] respectively use Faster R-CNN to detect meter regions then utilize image processing algorithms to extract pointer and scales to get meter readings. Alternatively, Jiaqi He [14] and Zengguang Zhang [15] use MASK R-CNN to identify meter region followed by a Hough transformation to detect the positions of pointers. Even deep learning is used in above methods, they still rely on traditional image-processing algorithms in value reading.

Recently, some researches begin to apply deep learning on both dial detection and pointer detection. Jilin Wan et al. [16] used Faster R-CNN to detect dial region and pointer region, followed by an improved U-Net model to segment the pointer and scale marks. Jiale Liu, etc. [17] used MASK R-CNN to detect meter region and pointer position, however, the raw image needs to be carefully pre-processed. Peilin He [18] has improved the MASK R-CNN model by PrRoIPooling and used it to detect the dial and the pointer. Due to the complexity of the DNN, those algorithms generally are time and memory consuming and only can be run on specific environments with powerful computational capability.

2.2 Recognition by Keypoint Detection

Sometimes meter as a whole is difficult to detect especially in clutter environment, however keypoints contain useful information and may be easier to detect which are drawn much attention to some researchers. Junkai Wang [19] uses a multi-task convolutional network to detect meter and four kinds of keypoints, which is followed by pointer detection and reading calculation. Yixiao Fang [20] uses a Mask R-CNN to simultaneously detect meter and keypoints, then works out meter reading through the calculation of the pointer angle. Ni Tao et al. [21] first use SSD to detect an instrument front, then extract keypoints to calculate the reading. Xiaoliang Meng et al. [22] use an optimized two-stage convolutional network to detect the keypoints like starting points, ending points of indicators and the rotation center of the meter pointer. A rotating virtual pointer algorithm is utilized to obtain the final reading through pointer's angle.

Above mentioned methods can process a variety of meters without complex image pre-processing, however they are heavily relied on exact keypoint detection that could not be applied on blur images.

2.3 Direct Recognition Through Deep Regression

Some researchers start to utilize deep neural networks to directly perform reading regression on detected and calibrated meter images. Cheng Dai, etc. [23] use a four-layer CNN to regress meter reading, however their method needs complex image pre-processing. Weidong Cai, etc. [24] expand the dataset by rotating the pointers in meter images which is subject to regression by use of a CNN. The proposed method has a complex training process since it requires pre-training a classification model and fine-tuning a regression model.

Kunfun Peng [25] first utilizes an improved Faster R-CNN to detect the dial region and then calibrates the meter image by G-RMI algorithm. A CNN is used for pointer direction regression as well as reading calculation. Hao Zhang, etc. [26] utilize YOLOv4 to detect the dial region and then regress the meter reading based on a deep neural network. All those methods will train multiple deep neural networks that increases the complexity of the algorithm and leads to large computational consumption.

3 Method Proposed in the Paper

As the position of the pointer uniquely corresponds to a meter reading, we can find that the most crucial information for meter recognition is the location of the endpoint of a pointer. Given that the measure ranges of variant pointer meters vary greatly, it is difficult to directly regress an absolute reading via a DNN. In this paper, the meter range is first scaled into [0, 1] then subject to regression. Suppose the absolute indication of a meter is V, the relationship of V and the normalized reading value is described in formula (1), where, S_1 is the starting point and S_2 is the end point of the scale, and p represents the normalized reading.

$$V = p(S_2 - S_1) + S_1 \tag{1}$$

Sometimes, the pointer may fall out of the measurement range or dial region due to error. Therefore, we design a network branch to check the outrange of the pointer.

The overall architecture of the network is illustrated in Fig. 1, where a resized image is fed into a CNN backbone for feature extraction which followed by three output branches that are established respectively to locate the end point of the pointer, directly regress the normalized meter reading and perform outrange checking.

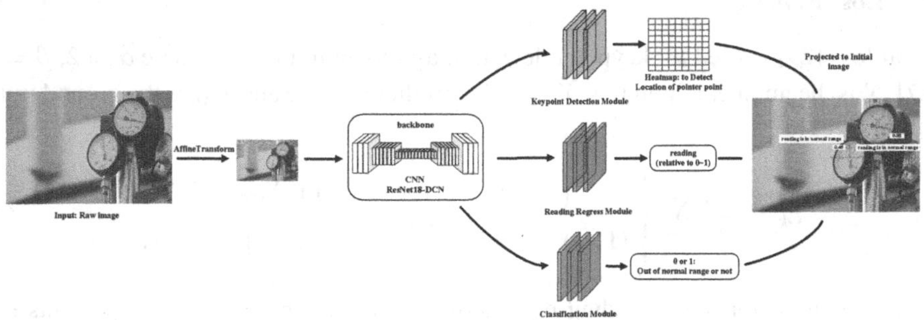

Fig. 1. The overall structure of our framework

3.1 Backbone Network

The network backbone used here is ResNet18-DCN [27], which consists of ResNet [28] and a deformable convolution network [33].

ResNet is widely used in feature extraction which consists of a series of residual block. The backbone network of our model consists of ResNet18 layers followed by three layers of deformable convolution and transposed convolution to improve the accuracy of the feature extraction as shown in Fig. 2.

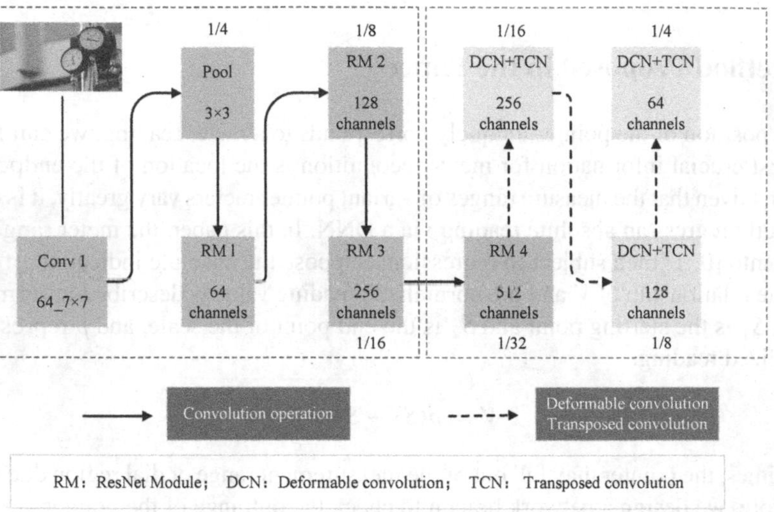

Fig. 2. Backbone framework. The numbers above or under the boxes are the resize factors relative to the input image.

3.2 Loss Function

Focal loss [29] is used for keypoint detection as shown in Eq. (2), where $\alpha = 2$, $\beta = 4$ [27]. N is the number of pointers, $\widehat{Y}_{xyc}$ is the predicted value and Y_{xyc} is the ground truth value.

$$L_k = \frac{-1}{N}\sum_{xyc}\begin{cases} \left(1-\widehat{Y}_{xyc}\right)^{\alpha}\log\left(\widehat{Y}_{xyc}\right) \text{ if } Y_{xyc}=1 \\ \left(1-Y_{xyc}\right)^{\beta}\left(\widehat{Y}_{xyc}\right)^{\alpha}\log\left(1-\widehat{Y}_{xyc}\right) \text{ otherwise} \end{cases} \quad (2)$$

L1 loss is used for meter reading regression. As shown in Eq. (3), p_k represents the pointer point k, $\widehat{R}_{p_k}$ is the predicted relative reading of p_k, R_k is actual reading and N is the number of pointers.

$$L_{\text{reading}} = \frac{1}{N}\sum_{k=1}^{N}\left|\widehat{R}_{p_k} - R_k\right| \quad (3)$$

The outrange checking is a binary classification process, therefore a binary cross-entropy loss function is used as shown in Eq. (4), where C_k represents the state of the k-th pointer point, whether it exceeds the normal range or not. $\widehat{C}_k$ is the prediction output of the classification module and N is the number of pointers.

$$L_{classify} = -\frac{1}{N}\sum_{k=1}^{N}\left[C_k * \log\left(\widehat{C}_k\right) + (1 - C_k) * \log\left(1 - \widehat{C}_k\right)\right] \tag{4}$$

The total loss is the weighted summation of above three losses as shown in Eq. (5), where, $\lambda_{reading}$ represents the weight of the regression loss and $\lambda_{classify}$ represents the weight of the classification loss. We set $\lambda_{reading} = 2$ and $\lambda_{classify} = 1$ in all the following experiments.

$$L_{\text{total}} = L_k + \lambda_{reading} L_{reading} + \lambda_{classify} L_{classify} \tag{5}$$

3.3 Model Training

For keypoint detection, a two-dimensional Gaussian function is used to make the ground truth labels of a heatmap, as shown in Eq. (6), where (x, y) is the location of each pixel, and (x_t, y_t) is the position of the pointer's endpoint, σ_P is a standard deviation which is set to 1 in our experiments.

$$Y_{xyc} = \exp\left(-\frac{(x - x_t)^2 + (y - y_t)^2}{2\sigma_p^2}\right) \tag{6}$$

Suppose there are N meters in an image, therefore N-dimensional mask labels respectively for regressing module and classification module are set. They are denoted as $\mathbf{M_{reg}}$ and $\mathbf{M_{clas}}$, in which element $M_{reg}[k]$ and $M_{clas}[k]$ are set to 1 and the remain elements are set to 0. With the help of mask labels, the model updates only when there exist pointers during the calculation of the regressing loss and the classification loss. The down-sampling layers of the Resnet-18 are initialized with ImageNet pretrained weights whilst the up-sampling layers are initialized randomly.

The input image resolution is set to 544 × 960 with the original aspect ratio unchanged for both training and testing. The data are augmented with random scaling (scale factor in between [0.6, 1.4]), random shifting (shift distance in between [−0.2, 0.2]), random rotating (rotation angle in between [−45°, 46°]), and color jittering. To keep the image contents not changed significantly, the operation probability is set to 0.4. Other training parameters are itemized as follows: batch-size is set to 20, learning rate is 1.25e−4 for 200 epochs with 10 times drops at 160 and 180 epochs respectively.

Table 1 gives hardware and software configuration for both training and testing.

Table 1. Hardware and software environment for training and testing

Item	Specification
CPU	Intel(R) Core(TM) i7-7700
GPU	GTX 1080
RAM	32G
GPU memory	8G
OS	Ubuntu 18.04.5 LTS
Deep learning framework	Pytorch
CUDA	10.2.89
cudnn	7.6.5

4 Experimental Results

4.1 Dataset

Most images of the dataset used in this paper are from the "2018 Global Artificial Intelligence Application Competition (NanJing)" [31], which contains more than 20 types of meters captured in different view angles and light conditions. The other images are captured from some substations. Our dataset contains total 813 training images and 114 test images. Several typical examples are shown in Fig. 3.

Fig. 3. Typical samples from our dataset

All endpoints of the pointers in dataset are tagged by software Labelme, and manually correspond to normalized reading values that finally are saved in json format.

4.2 Experiments

Model Testing. 114 different kinds of meter images with variants of shooting angels and lighting conditions are subject to testing. To quantitatively evaluate the performance, three metrics including precision (P), recall (R), and F-value are used which are defined in formula (7) to (9).

$$P = \frac{TP}{(TP + FP)} \tag{7}$$

$$R = \frac{TP}{(TP + FN)} \tag{8}$$

$$F = \frac{2 \times P \times R}{(P + R)} \tag{9}$$

Where TP denotes true positive, FP denotes false positive and FN denotes false negative. To determine correct detection, a distance measure is defined in formula (10), in which T is a threshold and L is the length of the pointer.

$$T = 0.14 \times L \tag{10}$$

The detection results for endpoints of pointers are shown in Table 2.

Table 2. Detection results for endpoints of pointers

Metrics	TP	FP	FN	R/%	P/%	F/%
Endpoints	134	1	1	99.26	99.26	99.26

To evaluate the accuracy of the meter recognition, allowance error is respectively set to ±5% and ±10% of the full range of the meter. Results of the reading accuracy are shown in Table 3.

Table 3. Meter reading accuracy

	#Meters	#Correct reading (±5%)/(±10%)	Accuracy (±5%)/%	Accuracy (±10%)/%
Reading	135	125/132	92.59	97.78

For outrange checking, if the output of the binary classification is higher than 0.8 while the ground-truth is 1, or the output is lower than 0.5 while the ground-truth is 0, the classification is judged as correct. Final results of the classification test are shown in Table 4.

Table 4. Accuracy of classification

	#Meters	#Correct classification	Accuracy/%
Classification	135	134	99.26

Table 5. Model size and operation speed

Model	Speed	Model size
Resnet18-DCN	25 FPS	166M

We also tested the inference speed and recorded the model size, which are shown in Table 5. Notice that the inference was performed on an NVDIA GTX 1080 GPU with 8G memory.

Comparative Experiment. We have compared our method with a template matching method [30] and a keypoint detection based method [22] on the same testing dataset. The testing results are shown in Table 6.

Table 6. Comparison among different methods

Method	End-to-end	Accuracy (±5%)/%	Accuracy (±10%)/%
Template matching [30]	No	68.42	72.28
Keypoint detection [22]	No	82.98	86.10
Our method	Yes	92.59	97.78

As reported in Table 6, compared with other methods, our method achieves the highest recognition accuracy at 92.59% under ±5% reading error. Some typical results are shown in Fig. 4, from which one can find that even under clutter scenes and uneven illumination our method still can get stable results.

4.3 Additional Experiments

Different Output Modules. To demonstrate the necessity of the outrange checking module, we trained two kinds of frameworks, one with the classifier while the other without. The experimental result is shown in Table 7. As one can see, the configuration of the outrange checking module improves the performance significantly.

With or Without DCN Module. To demonstrate the necessity of DCN module, two network architectures respectively with and without DCN are subject to reading recognition. The experiment results recorded in Table 8 show that ResNet-DCN performs better than ResNet, from which we can infer that the irregular feature extraction yields better accuracy on reading regression.

Different Keypoint Detection. We chose different kinds of key points as feature to regress meter reading, one is the endpoint of the pointer, another is the center point of the meter. Models using different keypoints are trained and subject to test, the final result

(a)Meter1 Predicted:0.56; Truth:0.56
Meter2 Predicted:0.92; Truth:0.93

(b)Meter 1 Predicted:0.58; Truth:0.59
Meter 2 Predicted:0.03; Truth:0.03

(c)Predicted:0.01; Truth:0.00

(d)Predicted:0.32; Truth:0.31

(e)Predicted:0.13; Truth:0.15

(f)Predicted:0.18; Truth:0.21

Fig. 4. Some typical recognition results

Table 7. The necessity of the outrange checking module

Method	Accuracy (±5%)/%
Keypoint + reading regress	82.63
Keypoint + reading regress + classification	92.59

is shown in Table 9. We can perceive that there is an approximately 7% improvement with the use of the endpoint, which suggests that the endpoint provides more crucial information.

Different Function Transformation. The meter readings are normalized to [0, 1], thus the regressing loss is relatively lower than other parts. We use variants of functions to increase the regressing loss. The testing results are shown in Table 10, where we can

Table 8. The improvement of DCN module

Model	Accuracy (±5%)/%
ResNet18	88.15
ResNet18-DCN	92.59

Table 9. Regression with different kinds of keypoints

Method	Accuracy (±5%)/%
Center point of meter	85.27
Endpoint of pointer	92.59

Table 10. Accuracy under different function transformation

Function transformation	Accuracy (±5%)/%
$1/(\widehat{R}_{p_k}, R_k)$	80.85
$-\log(\widehat{R}_{p_k}, R_k)$	89.88
$4 * (\widehat{R}_{p_k}, R_k)$	92.59

see the function transformation of $4 * (\widehat{R}_{p_k}, R_k)$ has the highest accuracy of reading recognition.

5 Conclusion

In this paper, a one-stage, end-to-end recognition method for multiple types of pointer meters is proposed. The method can perform the multi-task inference through a single deep neural network. Fully utilizing the fitting and learning capabilities of the deep network, our model is capable of locating the endpoint of the pointer, and obtaining the meter reading as well as making a outrange checking simultaneously just with one round inference. The experimental results show that the proposed method can achieve a high recognition accuracy at a running speed of 25 FPS on an NVDIA GTX 1080 GPU. Furthermore, the proposed method is of good versatility and adapted to different image quality, thus has potential application in complex real-world industrial scenarios.

References

1. Xiong, G.L., Xiao, W.M., Wang, X.M.: Review of pointer meter detection and recognition method based on vision. Transducer Microsyst. Technol. **39**(346(12)), 6–8+14 (2020)

2. Han, S.C., Xu, Z.Y., Yin, Z.C.: Research review and development for automatic reading recognition technology of pointer instruments. Comput. Sci. **45**(6), 54–57 (2018)
3. Liu, Y., Shi, K., Zhang, Z., Hu, Z., Liu, A.: A stable and reliable self-tuning pointer type meter reading recognition based on gamma correction. In: Liang, Q., Wang, W., Liu, X., Na, Z., Jia, M., Zhang, B. (eds.) CSPS 2019. LNEE, vol. 571, pp. 2448–2458. Springer, Singapore (2020). https://doi.org/10.1007/978-981-13-9409-6_297
4. Li, X., Yin, P., Duan, C.: Analog gauge reader based on image recognition. J. Phys. Conf. Ser. **1650**(3), 032061 (2020). 8p.
5. Zhang, M.L.: pointer instrument recognition based on Halcon template matching optimization. Artif. Intell. Robot. Res. **09**(2), 123–130 (2020)
6. Lai, H.W., Kang, Q., Pan, L.: A novel scale recognition method for pointer meters adapted to different types and shapes. In: 15th International Conference on Automation Science and Engineering (CASE). IEEE (2019)
7. Zhang, X.F., Huang, S.: Research on pointer identifying and number reading algorithm of multi-class pointer instruments. Electr. Meas. Instrum. **57**(16), 147–152 (2020)
8. Zhang, Z.F., Wang, F.Q., Tian, E.L.: Reading recognition method of pointer meter on the basis of machine vision. Control Eng. China **3**, 581–586 (2020)
9. Shen, Y.Q., Xiong, W.H., Huang, W.M., Xu, W.: Instrument recognition based on template matching and hough circle detection, vol. 31, no. 4, pp. 69–73 (2021)
10. Gao, L.: Discussion on improving the accuracy of automatic recognition algorithm for circular pointer instrument. Instrumentation **28**(04), 5–8 (2021)
11. Liu, K.: Recognition of the Analog Display Instrument Based on Deep Learning. Huazhong University of Science and Technology, China (2017)
12. Zhang, X., Dang, X., Lv, Q.: A pointer meter recognition algorithm based on deep learning. In: 3rd International Conference on Advanced Electronic Materials, Computers and Software Engineering (AEMCSE) (2020)
13. Wang, L., Wang, P., Wu, L.: Computer vision based automatic recognition of pointer instruments: data set optimization and reading. Entropy **23**(3), 272 (2021)
14. He, J.Q.: Research and Application of Automatic Recognition of Dial Instrument Based on Deep Learning. Beijing University of Posts and Telecommunications, China (2020)
15. Zhang, Z.G.: Research on the Method of Pointer Instrument Reading Recognition Based on Deep Learning. Harbin Engineering University, China (2020)
16. Wan, J.L., Wang, H.F., Guan, M.Y.: an automatic identification for reading of substation pointer-type meters using faster R-CNN and U-Net. Power Syst. Technol. **44**(08), 3097–3105 (2020)
17. Liu, J., Wu, H.Y., Chen, Z.H.: Automatic identification method of pointer meter under complex environment. In: 12th International Conference on Machine Learning and Computing, ICMLC (2020)
18. He, P.L.: Deep Learning-Based Recognition Algorithm for Industry Meters and Its Applications. University of Electronic Science and Technology of China (2020)
19. Wang, J.K.: A Thesis Submitted in Partial Fulfillment of the Requirements for the Degree for the Master of Engineering. Huazhong University of Science & Technology, China (2019)
20. Yang, Y.X.: Research and application of pointer Meter Reading Recognition Algorithm Based on Key point detection. Zhejiang University, China (2020)
21. Ni, T., Miao, H., Wang, L.: Multi-meter intelligent detection and recognition method under complex background. In: 39th Chinese Control Conference (CCC) (2020)
22. Meng, X., Cai, F., Wang, J.: Research on reading recognition method of pointer meters based on deep learning combined with rotating virtual pointer. In: 5th International Conference on Information Science, Computer Technology and Transportation (ISCTT) (2020)

23. Dai, C., Gan, Y., Zhuo, L.: Intelligent ammeter reading recognition method based on deep learning. In: IEEE 8th Joint International Information Technology and Artificial Intelligence Conference (ITAIC) (2019)
24. Cai W., Ma B., Zhang L.: A pointer meter recognition method based on virtual sample generation technology. Measurement **163**, 107962 (2020).
25. Pen, H.F.: Research on Pointer Meter Reading Recognition Method based on Deep Learning. University of Science and Technology of China (2020)
26. Zhang, H., Zhou, G.J., Wang, F.L.: Deep learning-based instrument recognition technology for sea ascending pressure station. Ind. Control Comput. **34**(03), 56–57+60 (2021)
27. Zhou, X., Wang, D., Krähenbühl, P.: Objects as points. arXiv preprint arXiv:1904.07850 (2019)
28. He K., Zhang X., Ren S.: Deep residual learning for image recognition. IEEE (2016)
29. Lin T.Y., Goyal P., Girshick R.: Focal loss for dense object detection. In: Proceedings of the IEEE International Conference on Computer Vision, pp. 2980–2988 (2017)
30. Weng, Z.H.: Research on Remote Reading Recognition and Location of Single Pointer and Digital Instrument. University of Electronic Science and Technology of China (2019)
31. https://www.kesci.com/home/competition/5b387f92257415006c47183a
32. He, K., Gkioxari, G., Dollár, P.: Mask R-CNN. IEEE Trans. Pattern Anal. Mach. Intell. **39**, 128–140 (2017)
33. Zhu, X., Hu, H., Lin, S., Dai, J.: Deformable ConvNets v2: more deformable, better results. In: Proceedings of the IEEE/CVF Conference on Computer Vision and Pattern Recognition, pp. 9308–9316 (2019)

Deep Architecture Compression with Automatic Clustering of Similar Neurons

Xiang Liu[1,2], Wenxue Liu[1], Li-Na Wang[1], and Guoqiang Zhong[1(✉)]

[1] College of Computer Science and Technology, Ocean University of China, Qingdao, China
gqzong@ouc.edu.cn

[2] Innovation Center, Ocean University of China, Qingdao, China

Abstract. The more complex the deep neural networks (DNNs) are, the more diverse the learning tasks they can be applied to. However, for complex DNNs, it is difficult to deploy them on to the edge devices, which have limited computation and storage resources. In this paper, we propose an automatic neurons clustering (ANC) approach for deep architecture compression, it can reduce the computation and storage consumption without degrading the model performance. Specifically, an automatic clustering algorithm is used to discover similar neurons in each layer of the deep architecture, then the similar neurons and the corresponding connections are merged based on the results of automatic clustering. After fine-tuning, a more compact and less storage space occupied neural network is obtained, with no performance degradation compared to the original deep architecture. This compression method is fully applicable to fully connected layer and convolutional layer, both of which are common modules of popular DNNs. The analysis of neuron redundancy in DNNs is performed on a deep belief network (DBN), and it is verified that there is great redundancy among neurons in DNNs. To verify the effectiveness of the proposed ANC, we conducted experiments on DBN and VGGNet-16 using MNIST, CIFAR-10 and CIFAR-100 datasets. The experimental results demonstrate that our method can effectively perform deep architecture compression without losing network performance. After fine-tuning, it can even obtain higher accuracy than the original network. In addition, the superiority of ANC is further demonstrated by comparing it with related network compression methods.

Keywords: Deep architecture compression · Compact neural network · Automatic neurons clustering.

1 Introduction

Deep learning have made breakthroughs in many fields, such as speech recognition, computer vision, and natural language processing. Recently, many excellent deep learning models have been proposed, such as Transformer [26,27] and multilayer perceptron (MLP) [3,25], however, the architecture that dominates learning

© Springer Nature Switzerland AG 2021
H. Ma et al. (Eds.): PRCV 2021, LNCS 13022, pp. 361–373, 2021.
https://doi.org/10.1007/978-3-030-88013-2_30

tasks is still convolutional neural network (CNN). The residual networks [10] successfully overcome the problem of gradient collapse and disappearance in ultra-deep networks, enabling CNNs to became deeper to cope with increasingly complex and difficult tasks. The consequence is that increasingly large computation and storage resources are required. For example, AlexNet [16] has 60M parameters, VGGNet-16 [24] has 138M parameters, and Gpipe [14] even reaches 556M.

Although the high accuracy is often delivered by large DNNs, the requirements for computation resource and storage space make them difficult to be directly deployed on resource-constrained devices. At the same time, in the era of 5G and IoT (Internet of Things), edge AI becomes more and more significant. Hence how to deploy high-performance DNNs on these edge devices becomes a critical problem. In this paper, we propose an automatic neurons clustering method for deep architecture compression, which aims to compress the scale of DNNs' parameters without degrading model performance, thus reducing the computational consumption and ultimately facilitating the development of edge AI.

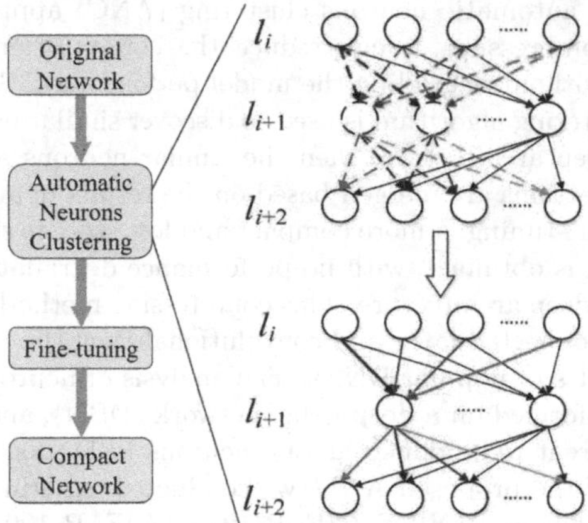

Fig. 1. The left flow chart shows the overall process of our work. Note that the "Original Network" is trained sufficiently, and the step of "Automatic Neurons Clustering" is illustrated as the right diagram.

In this work, a DNN is first trained sufficiently. We then use an **automatic clustering algorithm** to adaptively determine the number of clusters of neurons in each layer, and those neurons with the same clustering center are considered to be similar neurons. These similar neurons and their connections are then merged to reduce the redundancy degree in the network. Finally, after fine-tuning, a compact neural network can be obtained without any loss of model performance. The overall flow chart and the neuron clustering diagram are illustrated as Fig. 1. Comparing to previous similar network compression methods, the main innovation of ANC is that similar neurons can be merged automatic and adaptively, without any manual operations.

The following sections are organized as below. In Sect. 2, some of the mainstream network compression methods are introduced. In Sect. 3, we analyze the redundancy of neurons in DNNs and explain how to perform automatic neuron clustering. In Sect. 4, a large number of experiments with comparison to related approaches are reported to show the effectiveness and superiority of ANC approach. Finally in Sect. 5, this paper is concluded, and the possible directions for further research are discussed.

2 Related Work

[8] systematically summarizes the effective methods for deep neural network compression, such as low-rank decomposition, pruning, Huffman coding and weight quantization. Subsequently, more novel network compression approaches such as knowledge distillation [11,22] and structural re-parameterization [3,4] have been proposed one after another. A series of network compression methods that are of high relevance to this paper are introduced in this section.

2.1 Pruning

Pruning approach achieves network compression by reducing the number of parameters, and it can be divided into two types: unstructured pruning [9] and structured pruning. Unstructured pruning sets the unimportant parameters to zero without removing them, while structured pruning removes the information of the whole filter directly. Since the unstructured pruning approach does not remove those zeroed weights and corresponding connections, it cannot significantly improve the computational efficiency of the network, Therefore, structured pruning approach is considered as the more effective implementation.

In 2016, Lebedev et al. proposed the Improved Brain Damage method [17]. The group sparse regularization is added to the standard training process in this method, therefore filters smaller than a given threshold can be pruned in the form of neuron groups. For CNNs, judging the importance of the convolution kernels by the van value of the parameters is a well-tested method. Li et al. measured the importance of convolutional kernels by the weight parameter after L1 regularization and these kernels were removed in their entirety [18].

2.2 Knowledge Distillation

Hinton et al. argued that the output of a network with superior performance might contain some hidden but valid information, and proposed the concept of Knowledge Distillation (KD) in 2015 [11]. KD approach using both the real labels and the softmax output from a complex network (Teacher) as learning targets for a simple one (Student) to induce Students to learn something that the real labels cannot provide.

Remero et al. proposed FitNet based on KD [22], an approach that introduces not only the output of final layer, but also the feature representation of middle layers of the teacher network as knowledge to train the student network. Liu et al. [19] further implemented layers resection for DNNs using middle layer knowledge distillation. Chen et al. [1] combined Generative Adversarial Networks (GAN) [7] and teacher-student networks to propose a data-free KD method that does not require the involvement of raw training data. Zagoruyko et al. [28] proposed a mechanism for transferring attention as knowledge, allowing the student network to learn a spatial attention map similar to that of the teacher network, thereby improving the performance of the student network.

2.3 Lightweight Network Architecture Design

The main idea of lightweight network architecture design is to design compact computational module to replace the modules with large number of parameters. For example, SqueezeNet extensively uses 1×1 convolution instead of 3×3 to achieve the performance of AlexNet while reducing the computational complexity and memory consumption of the networks [15]. The MobileNet family [12,13,23] and ShuffleNet family [21,29] use deep separable convolution and pointwise group convolution instead of standard convolution respectively, reducing the computation and storage consumption of the neural networks while keeping the performance unchanged.

3 Automatic Neurons Clustering

In this section, we first analyze the redundancy of neurons based on DBN to establish a practical basis for neurons clustering. Then the automated neuron clustering algorithm is introduced in detail.

3.1 Neurons Redundancy Analysis

Based on visualization method, we analyze the redundancy of neurons in deep belief networks (DBN). The architecture of DBN is shown in Table 1.

Table 1. Network architecture of DBN.

Layers	Number of input nodes	Number of output nodes
Layer 1	784	500
Layer 2	500	500
Layer 3	500	2000
Layer 4	2000	10

Training this DBN on MNIST dataset, and after trained sufficiently, we analyze the distribution of its neurons using the t-SNE method. The result is plotted in Fig. 2. As it is illustrated in Fig. 2, the distribution of neurons in DBN is very dense. For example, in Fig. 2(c), many scattered points are clustered together and there are many very dense regions. This proves that after training, many neurons in the network learn similar features, i.e., there is redundancy among the neurons.

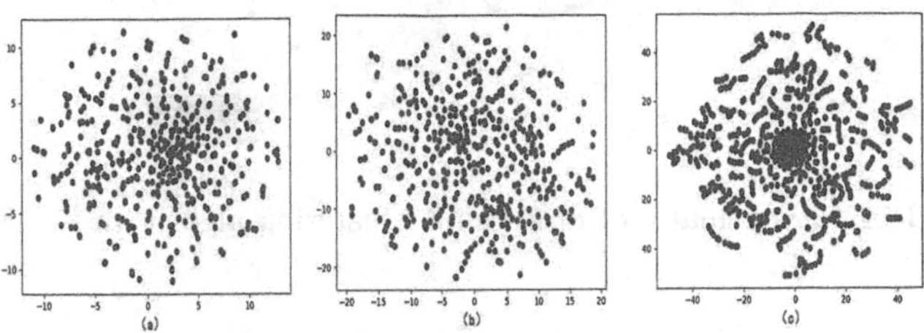

Fig. 2. The neurons distribution of original DBN trained sufficiently on MNIST dataset. (a), (b) and (c) separately show the first, second and third hidden layer.

3.2 Automatic Neurons Clustering Algorithm

A consensus should be established that those neurons learned similar features can be merged as one to reduce the network's consumption of computation and storage with no damage of performance. Determining and merging those similar neurons efficiently, is exactly the problem that this subsection is trying to solve.

Define the i th neuron in the l layer as the set of weights $\boldsymbol{w}$ and bias $\boldsymbol{b}$:

$$neu_i^l =< \boldsymbol{w}_{i,1}^l, \boldsymbol{w}_{i,2}^l, \cdots, \boldsymbol{w}_{i,n_{l-1}}^l, \boldsymbol{b}_i^l > . \tag{1}$$

In Eq. (1), $\boldsymbol{w}_{i,j}^l$ is the weight connecting the i th neuron in l th layer and the j th neuron in *l-1* th layer, b_i^l is the bias of the i th neuron in l th layer, and n_{l-1} stands for the amount of neurons in the *l-1* th layer. To facilitate operations on neurons in the l th layer, these neurons are merged into a set:

$$S_l =< neu_1^l, neu_2^l, \cdots, neu_{n_l}^l > . \tag{2}$$

Before being merged, these neurons in the set S_l are first clustered via the automatic clustering algorithm: **mean shift**, which is proposed by Fukunaga [6].

As illustrated in Fig. 3 [5], the main concepts involved in the mean shift clustering algorithm are region of interest, center of mass, and mean shift vector. the key of the algorithm is to calculate the mean shift vector of the centroids based on the density of data points in the region of interest, and then shift the centroids based on the mean shift vector the key is to calculate the mean drift vector of the centroids based on the density of data points in the region of interest, and then shift the centroids based on the mean drift vector and iterate until the centroids no longer change. During this process, the number of

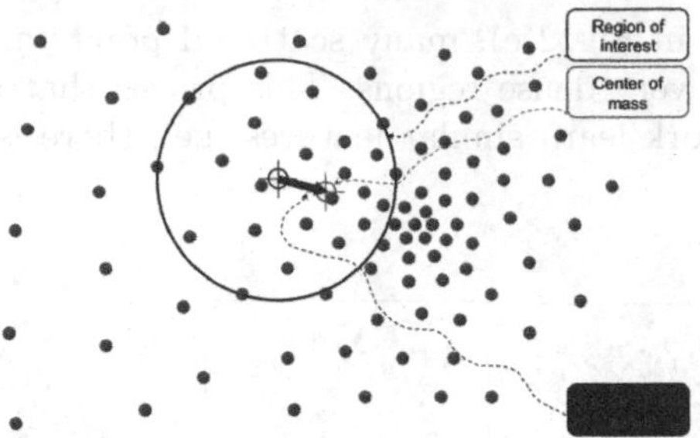

Fig. 3. Schematic of mean shift clustering algorithm [5].

occurrences of data points in each region of interest is counted, and this number is used as the basis for the final clustering.

The main process of mean shift algorithm is: for a data point x in the dataset, there are many points x_i in its region of interest, and the sum of the offsets required to move the point x to each point x_i is calculated and averaged, so that the mean shift vector is obtained (the direction of the vector is the direction of the dense distribution of surrounding points). Then the point x is moved according to the mean shift vector. The above process is iterated until certain conditions are met.

The number of clustering centers in each layer, that is, the number of groups into which the neurons can be divided, is obtained adaptively by means shift algorithm. The k_l is used to denote the number of clustering centers in the l th layer that are automatically obtained, then the set of all clustering centers in the l th layer is:

$$P_l =< p_1^l, p_2^l, \cdots, p_{k_l}^l >, \tag{3}$$

in which p_i^l denotes the i th cluster center in the l th layer. Also, the cluster partitioning information of neurons in the l th layer is expressed as:

$$R_l =< r_1^l, r_2^l, \cdots, r_{n_l}^l >, \tag{4}$$

in which r_i^l denotes the cluster to which the i th neuron in the l th layer is automatically clustered. In the l th layer, neurons assigned to the same cluster are merged into the clustering center of such cluster.

Assuming that the neurons divided into the same cluster by the mean shift method can be considered as identical within the acceptable error (the "acceptable error" is decided by the number of clustering centroids), i.e. there is $neu_i^l = neu_j^l$ if r_i^l is equal to r_j^l, the activation value of the i th neuron in the *l+1* layer can be recalculated as:

$$a_i^{l+1} = f\left(\sum_{j=1}^{n_l} \boldsymbol{w}_{i,j}^{l+1} a_j^l + \boldsymbol{b}_i^{l+1}\right), \tag{5}$$

$$= f\left(\sum_{p=1}^{k_l} (\sum_{r_j=p} \boldsymbol{w}_{i,j}^{l+1} a_j^l) + \boldsymbol{b}_i^{l+1}\right), \tag{6}$$

$$\approx f\left(\sum_{p=1}^{k_l} (\sum_{r_j=p} \boldsymbol{w}_{i,j}^{l+1} \hat{a}_p^l) + \boldsymbol{b}_i^{l+1}\right), \tag{7}$$

$$= f\left(\sum_{p=1}^{k_l} \hat{\boldsymbol{w}}_{i,p}^{l+1} \hat{a}_p^l + \boldsymbol{b}_i^{l+1}\right). \tag{8}$$

In the derivation of Eq. (7) to Eq. (8), $\hat{\boldsymbol{w}}_{i,p}^{l+1} = \sum_{r_j=p} \boldsymbol{w}_{i,j}^{l+1}$ then denotes the merging process of the relevant connections in the network. $\hat{a}_p^l$ in Eq. (7) and (8) denotes the activation value of the p th clustering center in the l layer. Note that since the above derivation is based on the assumption that the neurons assigned to the same cluster are considered as identical within the acceptable error, the obtained result in Eq. (8) is an approximation. However, also due to the errors leading to this approximation are within acceptable limits, the network after neurons clustering can be quickly restored to the initial level with simple fine-tuning.

4 Experiment and Analysis

In this section, the feasibility and effectiveness of ANC method for deep architecture compression proposed in this paper will be experimentally verified. Based on three dataset, i.e. MNIST, CIFAR-10, and CIFAR-100, the proposed approach was deployed on three networks including the fully connection network (DBN), and the VGGNet-16.

4.1 Experiment on the Fully Connected Network

This experiment was performed on the MNIST dataset using a DBN, where the benchmark network's architecture is shown in Table 1, and its error percentage in validation set was 1.03%. First, the bandwidth parameter of the mean shift algorithm was adjusted to 0.004 (the closer the parameter is to 0, the more the clusters centroids are obtained). With this parameter, a compressed network A with compression ratio of 75.45% was obtained. This compressed network's error percentage in validation set was 0.99% after 40 epochs of fine-tuning. The scatter plot of the neuron distribution of this compressed network is illustrated in Fig. 4 with the same method as Fig. 2. It can be seen that the distribution of neurons in the compressed DBN is more dispersed than in Fig. 2, and many dense areas have become sparse.

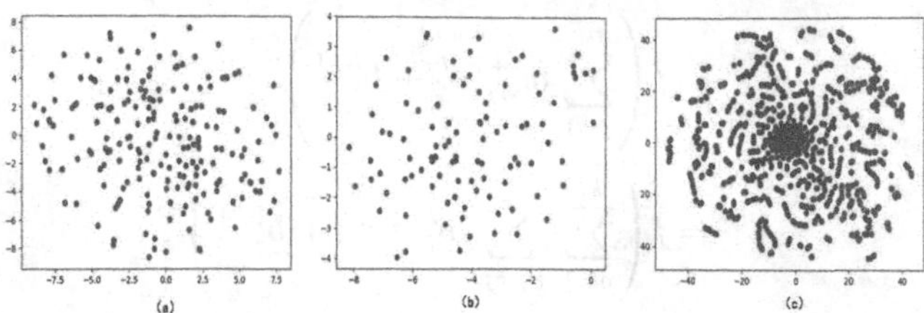

Fig. 4. The neurons distribution of compressed DBN with 75.45% parameter compression ratio comparing to the original. (a), (b) and (c) separately show the first, second and third hidden layer.

By setting the bandwidth parameter to 0.1, a compression network B with a parameter compression ratio of 92.81% was obtained. After 60 epochs of fine-tuning, the compressed network B was restored to the same accuracy as the original network. To investigate whether the good performance of the above-

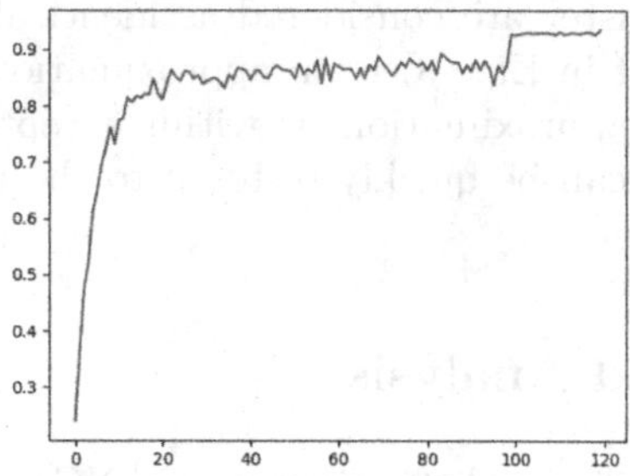

Fig. 5. The epoch-accuracy curve in validation set of reconstructed tiny DBN. The horizontal axis is epoch and the vertical axis is the accuracy in validation set.

obtained compressed network was caused by the tiny structure, a tiny DBN with the same architecture as the compressed network B was reconstructed. It was trained after being initialized, and the curve of its validation set accuracy during training is plotted as Fig. 5. The reconstructed net's validation set error rate was 3.21%, which was higher than all the above results. This proved that the good performance of the compressed network originates from our ANC method.

To further demonstrate the advantage of ANC method, we replace the clustering algorithm with the k-means, which is used by MSN [30], and specify the same number of cluster centroids for each layer of the network as in the mean shift method. For a fair comparison, the compressed network was fine-tuned with the same epoch as that obtained by the mean shift method after being compressed. finally, the results of this comparison are summarized with the results of the other experiments in this subsection into Table 2. Table 2 proved that with the same compression ratio, compressing network by using ANC method outperforms the

Table 2. The Comparison Experimental results obtained by ANC, MSN, and reconstructed net on the MNIST dataset. The "# of *A*" means the "compressed network A" which is obtained from original DBN by using our method, and it is same for the "# of *B*". The "# of K-means" is the compressed network obtained from MSN method, which has the same architecture with the "compressed network B". Finally, the "# of Re-cons" is the reconstructed tiny DBN.

Comparative idicators	Benchmark	# of *A*	# of *B*	# of K-means [30]	# of Re-cons
Amount of params (M)	1.67	0.41	0.12	0.12	0.12
Compression ratio (%)	-	75.45	92.81	92.81	92.81
Error rate in val (%)	1.03	**0.99**	1.03	1.56	3.21

reconstructed tiny network and manually confirming the number of clustering centroids via k-means. This is a preliminary demonstration of the effectiveness and superiority of the compression method proposed in this paper.

4.2 Experiment on Convolutional Networks

Table 3. The comparison experimental results obtained by ANC, and k-means on the CIFAR-10 dataset. The "# of *A*" means the "compressed VGGNet-16 A" which is obtained from original VGGNet-16 by using our method, and it is same for the "# of *B*". The "*K* of *A*" is the compressed VGGNet-16 A obtained by using k-means method, and it is same for the "*K* of *B*".

Comparative idicators	Benchmark	# of *A*	# of *B*	*K* of *A*	*K* of *B*
Amount of params (M)	33.65	3.15	2.43	3.15	2.43
Compression ratio of params (%)	-	90.64	**92.78**	90.64	92.78
FLOPS ($\times 10^8$)	6.65	4.19	4.00	4.19	4.00
Compression ratio of FLOPS (%)	-	36.99	39.85	36.99	39.85
Error rate in val (%)	6.38	6.35	**6.27**	6.41	6.97

The experiments in the previous subsection demonstrate the effectiveness of the ANC method when compressing fully connected networks. To further verify the effectiveness on more complex datasets and CNNs, we conducted validation experiments and comparison experiments on the CIFAR-10/CIFAR100 dataset using the VGGNet-16. The error rate in validation set of the fully trained VGGNet-16 on the CIFAR-10 dataset was 6.38%, which was used as the benchmark.

By setting the bandwidth of mean shift to 0.05, a compressed VGGNet-16 A with 90.64% parameters compression ratio and 36.99% FLOPs compression ratio was obtained. The validation set error rate of Compressed VGGNet-16 A without fine-tuning was 7.93%, with almost no performance loss comparing to the benchmark. After only 20 epochs of fine-tuning, the validation set error rate of the compressed network A dropped to 6.35%, which was lower than that of the benchmark.

The compressed VGGNet-16 B with the parameters compression ratio of 92.78% was obtained by setting the bandwidth parameter to 0.2. After 60 epochs of fine-tuning, its validation set error rate decreased 0.11% compared to the benchmark.

Also, for VGGNet-16, we conducted comparison experiments with the k-means method (MSN) [30]. The comparison experiments were performed on the CIFAR-10 dataset and the experimental results are summarized in Table 3.

The experimental results show that the compressed network obtained by using k-means clustering loses some accuracy relative to the benchmark at both compression rates, while the ANC method even improves the accuracy. This experiment proved that the ANC method still maintains effectiveness and stability when deploy on large CNNs.

Further, experiments on the CIFAR-100 dataset were conducted, and the results are shown in Table 4.

Finally, Table 5 shows the results of the comparison experiments between ANC and the three other network compression methods on the CIFAR-10 and CIFAR-100. To be fair, the exact same network architecture as in the paper [18] was used in the experiments. It was easy to see from Table 5 that the compressed models obtained by our method deliver higher accuracy relative to the that obtained by the other methods in the case of very similar compression rates. It was worth mentioning that during the experiments, we found that ANC has less damage to the original network than the other three methods. Specifically, after using ANC to compress the networks without fine-tuning and testing it directly on the CIFAR-10, the accuracy of validation set was 81.77%. The same test using the method proposed in paper [18] yielded an accuracy of 32.54% . This further demonstrated that ANC can compress the networks more safely and efficiently than other methods [2,18,20], and with little damage to the original network at low compression rates.

Table 4. Results of VGGNet-16 with different compression ratios obtained on CIFAR-100.

Models	Error	Params	P-Compression	FLOPS	F-Compression
VGGNet16	26.38%	34.02 M	-	6.65×10^8	-
Compressed Net A	26.20%	8.95 M	73.69%	5.58×10^8	16.09%
Compressed Net B	**26.33%**	5.68 M	**83.30%**	4.56×10^8	**31.43%**

Table 5. Comparison of ANC and two correlation network compression methods on the CIFAR-10/100 dataset. # in table stands for "Compression ratio", while Δ stands for "Change of accuracy"

Methods	# on CIFAR-10	Δ on CIFAR-10	# on CIFAR-100	Δ on CIFAR-100
Net slimming [20]	88.5%	+0.14%	76.0%	+0.22%
Pruning filters [18]	88.5%	−0.54%	75.1%	−1.62%
GSM [2]	88.5%	+0.19%	76.5%	+0.08%
Ours	88.5%	**+0.19%**	75.9%	**+0.25%**

5 Conclusion and Discussion

In this paper, a novel deep architecture compression method is proposed. The assumption that there is redundancy in neurons is obtained by visualizing and analyzing the distribution of neurons in DNNs. Based on this assumption, we design an automatic neurons clustering algorithm to obtain and merge similar neurons in networks. Experimental results demonstrate that the compressed models obtained by our method achieve better performance. Moreover, since the problem of optimal initialized cluster centroids selection is avoided, the ANC method always achieves better performance at the same compression ratio comparing to those neural networks compression methods that manually specify the cluster centroids (e.g., k-means based methods [30]). And the more complex the networks are, the better results can be achieved by ANC.

The compressed method in this paper focuses on the convolutional neural networks, but there are still many other networks with different architectures, such as RNN, LSTM, and Transformer, which are also widely used in the field of deep learning. How to implement the ANC method specifically in these networks and whether it has good results still need to be verified. Therefore, future work can explore how to perform deep architecture compression by the ANC method in those non-convolutional neural networks.

Acknowledgement. This work was supported by the National Key Research and Development Program of China under Grant No. 2018AAA0100400, the Joint Fund of the Equipments Pre-Research and Ministry of Education of China under Grant No. 6141A0 20337, the Science and Technology Program of Qingdao under Grant No. 21-1-4-ny-19-nsh, the Natural Science Foundation of Shandong Province under Grant No. ZR2020MF131, and the Open Fund of Engineering Research Center for Medical Data Mining and Application of Fujian Province under Grant No. MDM2018007. Thanks to Zhaoxu Ding for his assistance in writing this paper.

References

1. Chen, H., et al.: Data-free learning of student networks. In: 17 International Conference on Computer Vision, Seoul, pp. 3513–3521. IEEE Computer Society (2019)

2. Ding, X., Ding, G., Zhou, X., Guo, Y., Han, J., Liu, J.: Global sparse momentum SGD for pruning very deep neural networks. In: 32nd Annual Conference on Neural Information Processing Systems, Vancouver, pp. 6379–6391 (2019)
3. Ding, X., Zhang, X., Han, J., Ding, G.: Repmlp: re-parameterizing convolutions into fully-connected layers for image recognition. CoRR abs/2105.01883 (2021)
4. Ding, X., Zhang, X., Ma, N., Han, J., Ding, G., Sun, J.: Repvgg: making vgg-style convnets great again. CoRR abs/2101.03697 (2021)
5. of Electronic Engineering, D., Computer Science, U.o.M.: senmentation and clustering. [EB/OL] (2012). https://www.eecs.umich.edu/vision/teaching/EECS442_2012/lectures/seg_cluster.pdf
6. Fukunaga, K., Hostetler, L.D.: The estimation of the gradient of a density function, with applications in pattern recognition. IEEE Trans. Inf. Theory **21**(1), 32–40 (1975)
7. Goodfellow, I.J., et al.: Generative adversarial networks. CoRR abs/1406.2661 (2014)
8. Han, S., Mao, H., Dally, W.J.: Deep compression: Compressing deep neural network with pruning, trained quantization and huffman coding. In: 4th International Conference on Learning Representations (ICLR), San Juan (2016)
9. Hassibi, B., Stork, D.G.: Second order derivatives for network pruning: Optimal brain surgeon. In: 5th Advances in Neural Information Processing Systems, Denver, Colorado, pp. 164–171. Morgan Kaufmann, Denver (1992)
10. He, K., Zhang, X., Ren, S., Sun, J.: Deep residual learning for image recognition. In: 4th IEEE Conference on Computer Vision and Pattern Recognition, Las Vegas, pp. 770–778. IEEE Computer Society (2016)
11. Hinton, G.E., Vinyals, O., Dean, J.: Distilling the knowledge in a neural network. CoRR abs/1503.02531 (2015)
12. Howard, A., et al.: Searching for mobilenetv3. In: 17th International Conference on Computer Vision, Seoul, pp. 1314–1324. IEEE Computer Society (2019)
13. Howard, A.G., et al.: Mobilenets: efficient convolutional neural networks for mobile vision applications. CoRR abs/1704.04861 (2017)
14. Huang, Y., et al.: Efficient training of giant neural networks using pipeline parallelism. In: 33rd Annual Conference on Neural Information Processing Systems (NIPS), Vancouver, pp. 103–112 (2019)
15. Iandola, F.N., Moskewicz, M.W., Ashraf, K., Han, S., Dally, W.J., Keutzer, K.: Squeezenet: Alexnet-level accuracy with 50x fewer parameters and ¡1mb model size. CoRR abs/1602.07360 (2016)
16. Krizhevsky, A., Sutskever, I., Hinton, G.E.: Imagenet classification with deep convolutional neural networks. In: 26th Advances in Neural Information Processing Systems, Lake Tahoe. pp. 1106–1114 (2012)
17. Lebedev, V., Lempitsky, V.S.: Fast convnets using group-wise brain damage. In: 4th IEEE Conference on Computer Vision and Pattern Recognition, Las Vegas, pp. 2554–2564. IEEE Computer Society (2016)
18. Li, H., Kadav, A., Durdanovic, I., Samet, H., Graf, H.P.: Pruning filters for efficient convnets. In: 5th International Conference on Learning Representations (ICLR), Toulon (2017)
19. Liu, X., Wang, L., Liu, W., Zhong, G.: Incremental layers resection: a novel method to compress neural networks. IEEE Access **7**, 172167–172177 (2019)
20. Liu, Z., Li, J., Shen, Z., Huang, G., Yan, S., Zhang, C.: Learning efficient convolutional networks through network slimming. In: 16th International Conference on Computer Vision, Venice, pp. 2755–2763. IEEE Computer Society (2017)

21. Ma, N., Zhang, X., Zheng, H.-T., Sun, J.: ShuffleNet V2: practical guidelines for efficient CNN architecture design. In: Ferrari, V., Hebert, M., Sminchisescu, C., Weiss, Y. (eds.) Computer Vision – ECCV 2018. LNCS, vol. 11218, pp. 122–138. Springer, Cham (2018). https://doi.org/10.1007/978-3-030-01264-9_8
22. Romero, A., Ballas, N., Kahou, S.E., Chassang, A., Gatta, C., Bengio, Y.: Fitnets: hints for thin deep nets. In: 3rd International Conference on Learning Representations (ICLR), San Diego (2015)
23. Sandler, M., Howard, A.G., Zhu, M., Zhmoginov, A., Chen, L.: Mobilenetv 2: Inverted residuals and linear bottlenecks. In: 6th IEEE Conference on Computer Vision and Pattern Recognition, Salt Lake City, pp. 4510–4520. IEEE Computer Society (2018)
24. Simonyan, K., Zisserman, A.: Very deep convolutional networks for large-scale image recognition. In: 3rd International Conference on Learning Representations (ICLR), San Diego (2015)
25. Tolstikhin, I.O., et al.: Mlp-mixer: An all-mlp architecture for vision. CoRR abs/2105.01601 (2021)
26. Vaswani, A., et al.: Attention is all you need. In: 31st Annual Conference on Neural Information Processing Systems, Long Beach, pp. 5998–6008 (2017)
27. Wu, B., et al.: Visual transformers: token-based image representation and processing for computer vision. CoRR abs/2006.03677 (2020)
28. Zagoruyko, S., Komodakis, N.: Paying more attention to attention: improving the performance of convolutional neural networks via attention transfer. In: 5th International Conference on Learning Representations, Toulon. OpenReview.net (2017)
29. Zhang, X., Zhou, X., Lin, M., Sun, J.: Shufflenet: an extremely efficient convolutional neural network for mobile devices. In: 6th IEEE Conference on Computer Vision and Pattern Recognition, Salt Lake City, pp. 6848–6856. IEEE Computer Society (2018)
30. Zhong, G., Liu, W., Yao, H., Li, T., Sun, J., Liu, X.: Merging similar neurons for deep networks compression. Cogn. Comput. **12**(3), 577–588 (2020)

Attention Guided Spatio-Temporal Artifacts Extraction for Deepfake Detection

Zhibing Wang[1,2], Xin Li[1,2], Rongrong Ni[1,2(✉)], and Yao Zhao[1,2]

[1] Institute of Information Science, Beijing Jiaotong University, Beijing 100044, China
{19120311,rrni}@bjtu.edu.cn

[2] Beijing Key Laboratory of Advanced Information Science and Network Technology, Beijing 100044, China

Abstract. Recently, deep-learning based model has been widely used for deepfake video detection due to its effectiveness in artifacts extraction. Most of the existing deep-learning detection methods with the attention mechanism attach more importance to the information in the spatial domain. However, the discrepancy of different frames is also important and should pay different levels of attention to temporal regions. To address this problem, this paper proposes an Attention Guided LSTM Network (AGLNet), which takes into consideration the mutual correlations in both temporal and spatial domains to effectively capture the artifacts in deepfake videos. In particular, sequential feature maps extracted from convolution and fully-connected layers of the convolutional neural network are receptively fed into the attention guided LSTM module to learn soft spatio-temporal assignment weights, which help aggregate not only detailed spatial information but also temporal information from consecutive video frames. Experiments on FaceForensics++ and Celeb-DF datasets demonstrate the superiority of the proposed AGLNet model in exploring the spatio-temporal artifacts extraction.

Keywords: Spatio-temporal artifacts · Attention · Deepfake detection

1 Introduction

Advances in deep learning technology have made it increasingly easier for generative models to synthesize compelling face forgery videos which are even indistinguishable for human eyes. These forgery videos are likely to be abused by malicious users to cause severe societal problems or political threats [10]. The potential threats may include pornographic videos of a victim whose face is synthesized, a chief executive officer who comments on his company's performance

This work was supported in part by the National Key Research and Development of China (2018YFC0807306), National NSF of China (U1936212), Beijing Fund-Municipal Education Commission Joint Project (KZ202010015023).

© Springer Nature Switzerland AG 2021
H. Ma et al. (Eds.): PRCV 2021, LNCS 13022, pp. 374–386, 2021.
https://doi.org/10.1007/978-3-030-88013-2_31

that may exert certain influence on the stock market, or even realistically looking videos of state leaders who seem to make inflammatory comments they have never actually made. Therefore, the ability of detecting whether a face has been manipulated in a video sequence is crucial to social stability.

With the increasing concerns over face forgery videos, there has been a surge of interest in developing deepfake detection methods with significant progress in the past two years. Generally speaking, the existing work can be divided into hand-crafted feature based method [7,12,22] and deep learning based method [1,13–15,18]. The hand-crafted feature based method mainly focuses on the visual artifacts in forgery videos. Most of these methods detect face forgery videos depending on prior knowledge of face manipulation methods. Although they have achieved great results in specific dataset [14], they are not optimal due to the visual artifacts which are easily removed with the development of generative technology. The deep learning methods which directly treat deepfake detection tasks as a binary classification can automatically learn features from a huge number of labeled data, and perform better than traditional approaches relying on manually-designed features. Early deep learning based methods mainly focused on spatial information. Some methods [4,24,25] introduce attention mechanism, but they mainly focus on the more important region in the spatial domain, lacking the attention in the temporal domain.

In recent years, recurrent neural network (RNN) based approaches have attracted tremendous attention. Many variants of RNN are widely employed in deepfake detection, such as Long Short-Term Memory (LSTM) [5], and convolutional LSTM (Conv-LSTM) [21]. The RNN like LSTM which exploits possible inter-frame dissimilarities is effective for processing face manipulation because the forgery videos are generated frame by frame. Despite the promising progress, the existing methods still have a lot of room for improvement. In previous research, the knowledge embedded in different-level layers of CNN was not fully exploited in face manipulation detection. What's more, the existing LSTM based solutions lack learning capacity of discriminative spatio-temporal feature representation without explicitly extracting the most informative information in spatial and temporal dimensions of the videos, for they usually learn the temporal features by equally treating the consecutive frames. However, in practice, different frames might convey quite different information for deepfake detection. Similarly, along with the spatial dimension, the differences between the visual information from different position are usually undistinguished in the existing LSTM solutions.

In this paper, we propose an Attention Guided LSTM Network (AGLNet) for deepfake video detection. Our AGLNet model is constructed by face feature extraction module and the attention guided LSTM module. The face feature extraction module is based on pretrained EfficienNet-B4 network, which extracts high-level features from the fully-connected layer and spatial features from the middle-level convolution layer. The extractd feature maps are respectively fed into the fully-connected LSTM (FC-LSTM) and the convolutional LSTM (Conv-LSTM) learn the spatio-temporal information. Afterwards, the temporal attention module and spatio-temporal attention module are designed to focus on the critical artifacts information in videos. For the high-level fully connected feature with semantic information, our temporal attention module can adaptively learn frame-level attention features at each step of FC-LSTM. For the middle-level convolution features with detailed artifacts, our spatio-temporal attention module can explicitly allocate content and temporal dependent attention to the output of each deep feature in the video sequence. Finally, we concatenate the outputs from two attention module and feed them to the fully connected layer for binary classification. A large-scale evaluation is conducted across two large datasets which consist of thousands of real and deepfake videos. Its results show that our approach is highly effective in detecting deepfake videos.

2 Related Work

Hand-Crafted Feature-Based Approach. In traditional approaches of deepfake detection, suitable hand-crafted features play a critical role in training a high-performance classifier. Li et al. [7] proposed a method based on abnormal eye-blinking to identify deepfake videos which usually do not have closed eyes. The work of [22] found that the creation of deepfake videos leads to inconsistencies between head poses estimated with all facial landmarks and those estimated with the central region. In [12], some visual artifacts such as the defects of reflection details near eyes, and the imprecise geometry of both nose and teeth were exploited to determine whether a video was a deepfake video. [6] presented the Face X-ray to detect the trace of manipulation around the boundary regions of fake faces. Li et al. [8] proposed a detection method based on post processing artifacts from the generation process. The Face Warping Artifacts (FWA) was employed to capture the clues in generated videos. However, when there exist no obvious specific artifacts in deepfake videos with the development of generative technologies, these methods might be invalidated.

Deep Learning-Based Approach. In recent years, with the development of deep learning, many deep learning networks have been proposed and applied for deepfake detection. These deep learning based methods usually be categorized into two groups: methods that employ inter-frame features and those that explore intra-frame features. The methods based on inter-frame features mainly explore visual artifacts within single frames to obtain discriminant features. Afchar et al. [1] proposed two detection methods which focus on the mesoscopic features, including Meso-4 and MesoInception-4. In work of [14], XceptionNet was introduced for deepfake detection, which could extract effective features for this task. Nguyen et al. [13] proposed a model which leverages capsule network to detect fabricated images and videos. Unlike the approaches based on inter-frame features, the methods based on intra-frame features capture high-level features from the temporal domain by using deep neural network. Sabir et al. [15] presented a detection approach which extracts features from CNN and passes the features to Recurrent Neural Network to capture the temporal information. Tariq et al. [18] proposed a Convolutional LSTM based Residual Network (CLRNet) model using Convolutional LSTM cells, which can capture the spatio-temporal information directly from an input image sequence. Masi et al. [11] presented a method for deepfake detection based on a two-branch network structure that isolates digitally manipulated faces by learning to amplify artifacts while suppressing the high-level face content.

Attention Mechanism-Based Approach. To explore manipulated regions of deepfake detection in frames, Dang et al. [4] introduced an attention mechanism to process and improve the feature maps for the classification task. Zi et al. [25] proposed to exploit a CNN structure together with an attention mask to better differentiate between the realand the fake faces. In work of [24], a multi-attentional network for deepfake detection was introduced to pay attention to different local regions in images. Chen et al. [3] proposed a method based on spatial and frequency domain combination and attention mechanism. However, all of these attention models above are mainly based on spatial domain, which didn't utilize the temporal information. According to this, we propose an attention guided LSTM network for deepfake video detection. It is beneficial for artifacts extraction to put more efforts to develop spatio-temporal attention model which can learn different focusing weights for different frames in the temporal dimension and different focusing weights for different locations in the spatial dimension.

3 The Proposed Method

To detect deepfake videos, we present an Attention Guided LSTM Network. Our proposed model as shown in Fig. 1 consists of the face feature extraction module and the attention guided LSTM module and classification.

3.1 Face Feature Extraction Module

In our proposed method, we utilize EfficienNet-B4 network [17] pretrained on ImageNet as a feature extraction network. The EfficienNet-B4 network is a conventional convolutional neural network using 7 stages of the convolutional and identity blocks to classify the image into 1000 classes for image classification. We modify the pretrained Efficient-B4 network by eliminating the last layer and inserting the new fully-connected layer with 1024 dimensions for face feature extraction. Inspired by the complementarity of feature representation in different CNN layers, each frame is fed into EfficienNet-B4 to extract the high-level fully-connected features and middle-level convolutional features from the last fully-connected layer and convolutional layer in the fifth stage, respectively. The extracted features will be used as the input of the subsequent Attention Guided LSTM Module.

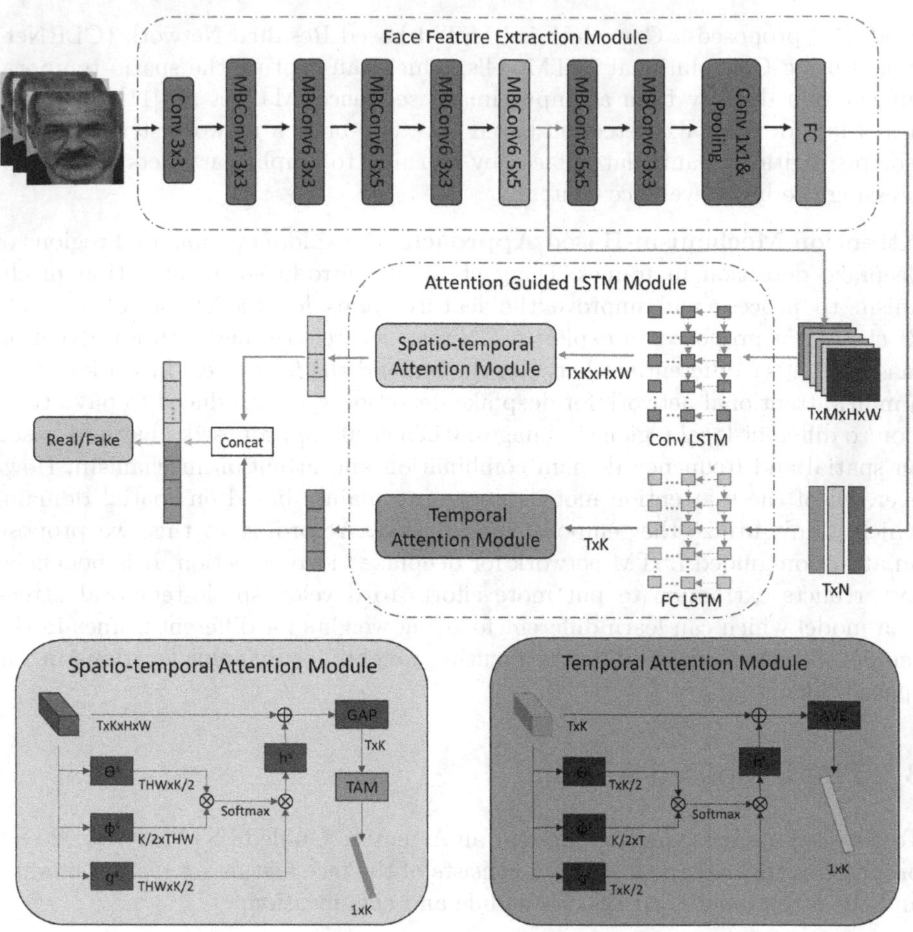

Fig. 1. An overall architecture of the Attention Guided LSTM Network. The effective CNN is employed to extract features in videos, and followed by the attention guided LSTM module with temporal attention module (TAM) and spatio-temporal attention module (STAM), where ⊗ denotes matrix multiplication, and ⊕ denotes the matrix sum. GAP and AVE respectively denote global average pooling and average operation.

3.2 Attention Guided LSTM Module

Thanks to the memory mechanism and forgetting mechanism, LSTM can weigh the contribution of current and previous observations, and automatically update itself to determine the amount of information needed to be forgotten and remembered at each time step. Therefore, LSTM is capable of acquiring the discriminative information and learning the dependency in sequential features. Because the features from different layers have different dimensions, we introduce convolutional LSTM and fully-connected LSTM to model spatio-temporal information for the extracted features. Due to the small convolution filter and the weak attention ability of LSTM, the convolutions can only rely on the local information contained in the small receptive field in the spatial domain and the short consecutive frame sequence in the temporal domain. This leads to the severe loss of the spatio-temporal correlations without considering the global information in the whole feature maps and the whole frame sequence. To address this problem, we introduce an attention mechanism for our spatio-temporal model, which can generate more discriminative feature maps by transforming the original feature maps along the temporal and spatial dimension.

Temporal Attention Module. We first elaborate on the attention mechanism along the temporal dimension and show an efficient capture of the long-range temporal dependencies across multiple frames. Specifically, inspired by self-attention mechanism [19], the relationship between any two points in the input feature maps proves to be helpful to convey the long-range information. Therefore, we design a temporal attention module (TAM), which can compute the attention response at each position in the input feature maps by taking all other positions and their weighted average into consideration. Formally, we re-denote the feature maps $\mathbf{x}_t$ as $\mathbf{x}_t = [x_1, x_2, \cdots, x_T] \in \mathbb{R}^{T \times K}$, which are convolved with kernel W_θ and W_ϕ to generate attention features,

$$\theta^t(\mathbf{x}_t) = W_\theta * \mathbf{x}_t, \quad \phi^t(\mathbf{x}_t) = W_\phi * \mathbf{x}_t, \tag{1}$$

where $*$, W_θ and W_ϕ respectively denote convolution operation and the weight matrices with K/2 channels. Then the attention map can be calculated as:

$$\sigma^t(s) = \frac{exp(s)}{\sum_i^C exp(s)}, \quad s = \theta^t(\mathbf{x}_t)^T \phi^t(\mathbf{x}_t) \tag{2}$$

where $\sigma^t(s) \in \mathbb{R}^{K/2 \times K/2}$ is the attention map, which indicates the weights of all positions in the attention features. We define the temporal attention module as:

$$\mathbf{F}^t = h^t(\sigma^t(\mathbf{x}_t) g^t(\mathbf{x}_t)) + \mathbf{x}_t, \tag{3}$$

$$g^t(\mathbf{x}_t) = W_g * \mathbf{x}_t, \quad h^t(\mathbf{x}_t) = W_h * \mathbf{x}_t, \tag{4}$$

where shape of $\mathbf{F}^t$ is $T \times K$, W_g is a 1D trainable kernel with the same size as W_ϕ. W_h are the weight matrices with K channels. $\sigma(s)$ has the form of softmax function. Thus the formulation of temporal attention module can be rewritten as:

$$\mathbf{F}^t = h^t(softmax(\theta^t(\mathbf{x}_t)^T \phi^t(\mathbf{x}_t)) g^t(\mathbf{x}_t) + \mathbf{x}_t. \tag{5}$$

Then we use average operation for $\mathbf{F}^t$ to get the final temporal feature $\mathbf{G}^t$, $\mathbf{G}^t \in \mathbb{R}^{1 \times K}$.

Spatio-Temporal Attention Module. We design a spatio-temporal attention module (STAM) according to the temporal and spatial characteristics of the features from Conv-LSTM. Instead of directly employing two similar attention mechanisms which capture temporal and spatial attention separately, we focus our attention simultaneously on a single module, which learns the attention weights adaptively in spatial and temporal domain. Similarly, we can also give the definition of the spatio-temporal attention module:

$$\mathbf{F}^s = h^s(softmax(\theta^s(\mathbf{x}_s)^T \phi^s(\mathbf{x}_s))g^s(\mathbf{x}_s) + \mathbf{x}_s, \quad \mathbf{F}^s \in \mathbb{R}^{T\times K\times H\times W}, \tag{6}$$

where the input feature maps are denoted as: $\mathbf{x}_s = [x_1, x_2, \cdots, x_T] \in \mathbb{R}^{T\times K\times H\times W}$, θ^s, g^s and ϕ^s are $1\times 1\times 1$ 3D convolution operations to reduce the number of input channel to K/2 for efficient computation, h^s is 3D convolution operation with K channels. To better aggregate the key informative locations of feature map, a new feature vector $\mathbf{H}^s \in \mathbb{R}^{T\times K}$ is simply produced by generated by dealing with the feature maps of each frame through global average pooling operation. This feature vector will be feed into the temporal attention module to obtain the spatio-temporal feature $\mathbf{G}^s$, $\mathbf{G}^s \in \mathbb{R}^{1\times K}$.

3.3 Classfication

To integrate the temporal, spatial and semantic information of videos, we concatenate the outputs from TAM and STAM and feed them to the fully connected layer for binary classification. In the test stage, the final prediction of the network will merge the outputs of the two branches as follows:

$$\mathbf{G} = \mathbf{concat}\{\mathbf{G}^s, \mathbf{G}^t\}, \tag{7}$$

For the deepfake detection classification, we use the cross-entropy loss as follows:

$$L = -\frac{1}{N}\sum_{i=1}[y_i \cdot log(p_i) + (1-y_i)\cdot log(1-p_i)], \tag{8}$$

where y_i is the one-hot vector of the ground-truth of video, p_i is the predicted probability vector.

4 Experiments

In this section, we first introduce the datasets used in the experiments. Then we describe our experimental setup and some implementation details. Next, We present the experimental results and compare them with those of other state-of-the-art methods.

4.1 Datasets

We conduct experiments on two datasets: FaceForensics++ [14], Celeb-DF [9]. FaceForensics++ dataset consists of 1000 real videos and four sub-databases that produce 1000 face forgery videos via different methods respectively, i.e. DeepFake (DF), FaceSwap (FS), Face2Face (F2F) and NeuralTexture (NT). Since each sub-database contains 1,000 videos, we split it into a training and a test set, which consist of 950 and 50 videos respectively. Celeb-DF [9] dataset is one of the largest deepfake video datasets, which is composed of more than 5,000 manipulated videos taken from celebrities. In this experiment, we use the train a dataset which consists of 1000 fake videos and 500 real videos. For test dataset, we use 50 fake videos and 50 real videos.

4.2 Setup and Implementation Details

In our experiment, first of all, we extracted 9 samples which contains ten consecutive frames for each video. Then, we used multi-task CNN (MTCNN) [23] to crop the face from the frame. All the frames are resized to a 224×224 resolution. The convolutional features from the fifth stage of the EfficienNet-B4 network are extracted as the middle level representations. The fully connected features are extracted from the last fully connected layer as high level representations. For each frame, the output size of the feature maps is $160 \times 14 \times 14$ and 1×1024 respectively. In Conv LSTM, the convolutional kernels for input-to-state and state-to-state transitions are of size 3×3 with 512 channels. In addition, the two-layer FC-LSTM structure is employed and has the hidden size of 1024. The network is trained using Stochastic Gradient Descent (SGD) algorithm. The training epochs are set to 20. The batch size is set to 8. The weight decay is set to 0.0001. The initial learning rate is set to 0.01. After every 3 epochs on the training set, the learning rate decays to a tenth of original. We choose the one which has best performance on the test set. The model is implemented with PyTorch framework using two GeForce RTX 2080Ti GPUs. We evaluate the performance of the methods in terms of their accuracy: the higher the accuracy is, the better the performance is.

Table 1. Quantitative results (Acc (%)) on Celeb-DF dataset and FaceForensics++ dataset with four different manipulation methods, i.e. DeepFake (DF), Face2Face (F2F), FaceSwap (FS), NeuralTextures (NT).

Methods	DF	F2F	FS	NT	Celeb-DF
Afchar et al. [1]	82.67	80.22	78.78	66.00	53.78
Rossler et al. [14]	95.56	93.89	94.22	84.89	86.56
Nguyen et al. [13]	94.11	96.44	97.67	90.22	83.33
Li and Lyu [8]	96.78	97.22	96.33	91.67	69.89
Wang et al. [20]	95.89	93.56	94.78	85.11	95.44
Bonettini et al. [2]	98.33	97.44	98.67	93.56	96.89
Ours	**99.44**	**99.33**	**99.78**	**94.44**	**98.78**

4.3 Comparison with State-of-the-Art Methods

We compare our AGLNet with recent deep learning based detection methods, including XceptionNet [14], FWA [8], I3D [20] and the other state-of-the-art methods [1,2,13] in Table 1. Firstly, to evaluate the proposed AGLNet's ability to capture defects introduced by different manipulation methods, the model is trained and tested on different manipulation methods in FaceForensics++ [14]. The experimental results indicate that the proposed method achieves state-of-the-art performance, which demonstrates that the AGLNet is capable of capturing various kinds of defects introduced by different manipulation methods. Then the Celeb-DF [9] dataset is also tested. As the results shown in Table 1, although the Celeb-DF dataset is very realistic, the proposed model can effectively capture the defects. The results show that our best result outperforms many methods, which indicates the importance of attention mechanism and demonstrates the effectiveness of AGLNet. Meanwhile, we can find that there is a performance gap between our method and the state-of-the-arts. We conjecture that there are two reasons for this phenomenon. First, the combination of feature maps in different CNN layers is useful, which can enrich the video representation to help artifact extraction. Second, temporal attention module and spatio-temporal attention module play an important role in our model, which can guide LSTM to learn more important area. Different from the methods [2], our attention mechanism can exploit both long-range temporal dependencies across multiple frames and long-distance spatial dependencies within each frame, thus enabling the extracting of the discriminative global information at both inter-frame and intra-frame levels.

Table 2. Componet study of Attention Guided LSTM Network (AGLNet) on Celeb-DF dataset. TAM and STAM denote temporal attention module and spatio-temporal attention module, respectively.

XceptionNet	EfficienNet	Conv-LSTM	FC-LSTM	TAM	STAM	Acc (%)
√						86.56
	√					89.67
	√	√				96.44
	√		√			96.78
	√		√	√		97.56
	√	√			√	97.44
	√	√	√	√	√	98.78

4.4 Ablation Study

Component Analysis. As shown in Table 2, the effectiveness of each part of our proposed framework is evaluated. To give a more comprehensive comparison, a variety of models are implemented. First, we evaluate the performance of the XceptionNet and EfficienNet-B4 to choose better backbone. Besides, to verify whether different level features and cooperation of spatio-temporal domains can improve the performance, we separately train FC-LSTM and Conv-LSTM, which respectively handle the fully-connected features and middle-level convolution features. The fully-connected features contain global information and the middle-level features contain more detail information. From the experimental results listed in Table 2, we can see that our model achieves better performance through combining different level information. Moreover, the attention modules play an important role in our approach, which are designed to integrate spatio-temporal information for different-level features. The ablation studies verify the performance of separate attention modules in AGLNet. We can conclude that the AGLNet model exhibits higher accuracy than those without any attention modules, which can guide the model to find key information for better classification.

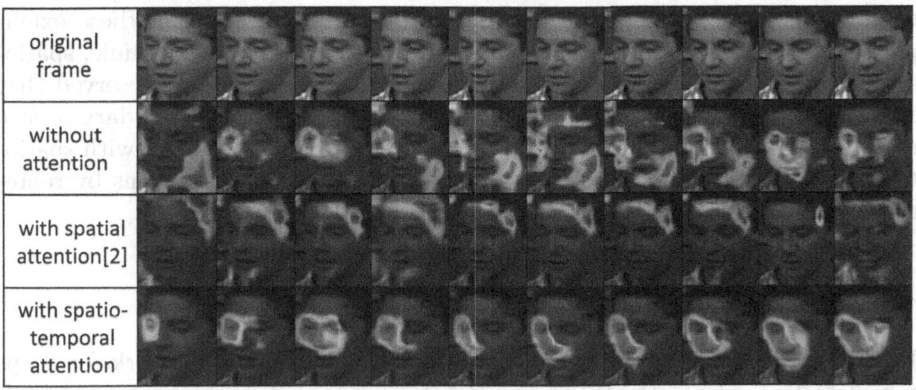

Fig. 2. Grad-CAM results: Ten frames are overlayed with the important attention regions highlighted using Grad-CAM. [16].

Table 3. Results on using different video clip length.

	5	10	15
Acc (%)	97.44	98.78	97.78

Input Video Clip Length. The AGLNet model works over an input video clip to capture the spatio-temporal attentions. Therefore, it is important to see the connections between the input video clip length and the performance of AGLNet model. In Table 3 we compare the performance using different lengths including 5, 10 and 15 respectively on the Celeb-DF dataset. It is obvious that with a small input length, our AGLNet model can provide much worse performance on the Celeb-DF dataset. This is because the short input frame sequence conveys less spatio-temporal information. Besides, the experiment result shows the long input length also reduces the performance of model, which is mainly because LSTM models are less effective in learning high-level video representations or capturing long-term relations.

4.5 Visualization

Besides the above mentioned quantitative and qualitative evaluations, the generated attention maps at each prediction step are also visualized in Fig. 2. Because fully-connected feature is not convenient to mapped to the corresponding frames for temporal attention visualization, we only illustrate the attention maps computed by spatio-temporal attention module. These illustrated examples reveal tremendous effect of our spatio-temporal attention. As shown in these examples, Fig. 2 visualizes features characterized by spatial attention module, spatio-temporal attention module on the Celeb-DF dataset. It can be observed that EfficienNet with spatial attention module [2] focuses more on boundary of face region. Compared spatial attention module, our proposed AGLNet with spatio-temporal attention module better characterizes face artifacts regions by representing feature maps that cover the multi frame.

5 Conclusion

In this paper, we propose a novel Attention Guided LSTM Network for deepfake detection, which attempts to exploit the discriminative information at both spatial domain and temporal domain. The key advantage of our architecture is the attention mechanism. We present an attention guided LSTM module with the temporal attention module and the spatio-temporal attention module, which improves the artifacts extraction based on different layers of the feature extraction networks. The former aims to pay more attention to the high-level features with semantic information, while the latter can adaptively distinguish key information for middle-level convolution features with detailed artifacts. Our AGLNet simultaneously distinguishes the characteristics in temporal and spatial dimensions, and further improves the capability of the LSTM with more powerful artifacts extraction. The experiments on several state-of-the-art methods and two different datasets have demonstrated that our AGLNet can obtain the state-of-the-art performance for deepfake detection.

References

1. Afchar, D., Nozick, V., Yamagishi, J., Echizen, I.: MesoNet: a compact facial video forgery detection network. In: 2018 IEEE International Workshop on Information Forensics and Security (WIFS), pp. 1–7. IEEE (2018)
2. Bonettini, N., Cannas, E.D., Mandelli, S., Bondi, L., Bestagini, P., Tubaro, S.: Video face manipulation detection through ensemble of CNNs. In: 2020 25th International Conference on Pattern Recognition (ICPR), pp. 5012–5019. IEEE (2021)
3. Chen, Z., Yang, H.: Manipulated face detector: joint spatial and frequency domain attention network. arXiv e-prints, arXiv-2005 (2020)
4. Dang, H., Liu, F., Stehouwer, J., Liu, X., Jain, A.K.: On the detection of digital face manipulation. In: Proceedings of the IEEE/CVF Conference on Computer Vision and Pattern Recognition, pp. 5781–5790 (2020)

5. Hochreiter, S., Schmidhuber, J.: Long short-term memory. Neural Comput. **9**(8), 1735–1780 (1997)
6. Li, L., et al.: Face X-ray for more general face forgery detection. In: Proceedings of the IEEE/CVF Conference on Computer Vision and Pattern Recognition, pp. 5001–5010 (2020)
7. Li, Y., Chang, M.C., Lyu, S.: In ictu oculi: exposing AI created fake videos by detecting eye blinking. In: 2018 IEEE International Workshop on Information Forensics and Security (WIFS), pp. 1–7. IEEE (2018)
8. Li, Y., Lyu, S.: Exposing deepfake videos by detecting face warping artifacts. arXiv preprint arXiv:1811.00656 (2018)
9. Li, Y., Yang, X., Sun, P., Qi, H., Lyu, S.: Celeb-DF: a large-scale challenging dataset for deepfake forensics. In: Proceedings of the IEEE/CVF Conference on Computer Vision and Pattern Recognition, pp. 3207–3216 (2020)
10. Lyu, S.: DeepFake detection: current challenges and next steps. In: 2020 IEEE International Conference on Multimedia & Expo Workshops (ICMEW), pp. 1–6. IEEE (2020)
11. Masi, I., Killekar, A., Mascarenhas, R.M., Gurudatt, S.P., AbdAlmageed, W.: Two-branch recurrent network for isolating deepfakes in videos. In: Vedaldi, A., Bischof, H., Brox, T., Frahm, J.-M. (eds.) ECCV 2020. LNCS, vol. 12352, pp. 667–684. Springer, Cham (2020). https://doi.org/10.1007/978-3-030-58571-6_39
12. Matern, F., Riess, C., Stamminger, M.: Exploiting visual artifacts to expose deepfakes and face manipulations. In: 2019 IEEE Winter Applications of Computer Vision Workshops (WACVW), pp. 83–92. IEEE (2019)
13. Nguyen, H.H., Yamagishi, J., Echizen, I.: Capsule-forensics: using capsule networks to detect forged images and videos. In: ICASSP 2019–2019 IEEE International Conference on Acoustics, Speech and Signal Processing (ICASSP), pp. 2307–2311. IEEE (2019)
14. Rossler, A., Cozzolino, D., Verdoliva, L., Riess, C., Thies, J., Nießner, M.: FaceForensics++: learning to detect manipulated facial images. In: Proceedings of the IEEE/CVF International Conference on Computer Vision, pp. 1–11 (2019)
15. Sabir, E., Cheng, J., Jaiswal, A., AbdAlmageed, W., Masi, I., Natarajan, P.: Recurrent convolutional strategies for face manipulation detection in videos. Interfaces (GUI) **3**(1), 80–87 (2019)
16. Selvaraju, R.R., Cogswell, M., Das, A., Vedantam, R., Parikh, D., Batra, D.: Grad-CAM: visual explanations from deep networks via gradient-based localization. In: Proceedings of the IEEE International Conference on Computer Vision, pp. 618–626 (2017)
17. Tan, M., Le, Q.: EfficientNet: rethinking model scaling for convolutional neural networks. In: International Conference on Machine Learning, pp. 6105–6114. PMLR (2019)
18. Tariq, S., Lee, S., Woo, S.S.: A convolutional LSTM based residual network for deepfake video detection. arXiv preprint arXiv:2009.07480 (2020)
19. Wang, X., Girshick, R., Gupta, A., He, K.: Non-local neural networks. In: Proceedings of the IEEE Conference on Computer Vision and Pattern Recognition, pp. 7794–7803 (2018)
20. Wang, Y., Dantcheva, A.: A video is worth more than 1000 lies. Comparing 3DCNN approaches for detecting deepfakes. In: 2020 15th IEEE International Conference on Automatic Face and Gesture Recognition (FG 2020), pp. 515–519. IEEE (2020)
21. Xingjian, S., Chen, Z., Wang, H., Yeung, D.Y., Wong, W.K., Woo, W.C.: Convolutional LSTM network: a machine learning approach for precipitation nowcasting. In: Advances in Neural Information Processing Systems, pp. 802–810 (2015)

22. Yang, X., Li, Y., Lyu, S.: Exposing deep fakes using inconsistent head poses. In: ICASSP 2019–2019 IEEE International Conference on Acoustics, Speech and Signal Processing (ICASSP), pp. 8261–8265. IEEE (2019)
23. Zhang, K., Zhang, Z., Li, Z., Qiao, Y.: Joint face detection and alignment using multitask cascaded convolutional networks. IEEE Sig. Process. Lett. **23**(10), 1499–1503 (2016)
24. Zhao, H., Zhou, W., Chen, D., Wei, T., Zhang, W., Yu, N.: Multi-attentional deepfake detection. In: Proceedings of the IEEE/CVF Conference on Computer Vision and Pattern Recognition, pp. 2185–2194 (2021)
25. Zi, B., Chang, M., Chen, J., Ma, X., Jiang, Y.G.: WildDeepfake: a challenging real-world dataset for deepfake detection. In: Proceedings of the 28th ACM International Conference on Multimedia, pp. 2382–2390 (2020)

Learn the Approximation Distribution of Sparse Coding with Mixture Sparsity Network

Li Li[1], Xiao Long[2,3], Liansheng Zhuang[1,2](✉), and Shafei Wang[4]

[1] School of Data Science, USTC, Hefei, China
lszhuang@ustc.edu.cn
[2] School of Information Science and Technology, USTC, Hefei, China
[3] Peng Cheng Laboratory, Shenzhen, China
[4] Northern Institute of Electronic Equipment, Beijing, China

Abstract. Sparse coding is typically solved by iterative optimization techniques, such as the ISTA algorithm. To accelerate the estimation, neural networks are proposed to produce the best possible approximation of the sparse codes by unfolding and learning weights of ISTA. However, due to the uncertainty in the neural network, one can only obtain a possible approximation with fixed computation cost and tolerable error. Moreover, since the problem of sparse coding is an inverse problem, the optimal possible approximation is often not unique. Inspired by these insights, we propose a novel framework called Learned ISTA with Mixture Sparsity Network (LISTA-MSN) for sparse coding, which learns to predict the best possible approximation distribution conditioned on the input data. By sampling from the predicted distribution, LISTA-MSN can obtain a more precise approximation of sparse codes. Experiments on synthetic data and real image data demonstrate the effectiveness of the proposed method.

Keywords: Sparse coding · Learned ISTA · Mixture Sparsity Network

1 Introduction

Sparse coding (SC) has shown great success in uncovering global information from noisy and high dimensional data such as image super-resolution [17], image classification [15], and object recognition [13]. The main goal of SC is to find the sparse representation from over-complete dictionary. To solve this problem, classic methods are based on high dimensional optimization theory, such as proximal coordinate descent [9], Least Angle Regression [8] and proximal splitting methods [2]. Among these methods, Iterative Shrinkage-Thresholding Algorithm (ISTA) [5] is the most popular one, which belongs to proximal-gradient method. It has been proven that ISTA converges with rate $1/t$, where t is the number of the iterations/layers, and its computational complexity is too high. To address this issue,

L. Li and X. Long—Contributed equally.

© Springer Nature Switzerland AG 2021
H. Ma et al. (Eds.): PRCV 2021, LNCS 13022, pp. 387–398, 2021.
https://doi.org/10.1007/978-3-030-88013-2_32

Beck and Teboulle proposed the FISTA [3] algorithm converges more rapidly in 2009. The major difference with ISTA is the introduction of a "momentum" term. The algorithms mentioned above belong to traditional iterative approaches. However, even though the FISTA accelerates the speed of convergence a lot, these algorithms are still too slow for practical applications such as real-time object recognition.

To further increase the speed of ISTA, Gregor and LeCun proposed a trainable version of ISTA called Learned ISTA (LISTA) [11] by unfolding ISTA structure into a recurrent neural network (RNN). Unlike the traditional iterative approaches, LISTA is highly computationally efficient during the inference period. Once the learnable parameters of the neural network are trained, it can quickly estimate a solution of sparse codes by passing the input through a fixed recurrent neural network rather than solving a series of convex optimization problems. Moreover, LISTA yields better estimation result than ISTA on new samples for the same number of iterations/layers. This idea has led to a profusion of literature [6,18]. For one thing, they follow the idea of LISTA and modify the structure to use more historical information. For another, some works change shared weights to layer-wise weights and get better performance. All these methods have achieved impressive performance in solving sparse coding.

But the existing neural network-based methods have suffered from the following drawbacks. First, they ignore the fact that the LASSO problem is an inverse problem and the optimal solution may be not unique. For example, in a super resolution task [12] a low-resolution image could be explained by many different high-resolution images. In this case, the neural network designed to predict a specific value is not effective. Second, due to the uncertainty of deep learning, it is hard to get a unique accurate solution of sparse codes with fixed iterations. In fact, neural network-based methods (e.g., LISTA) can only obtain a possible approximation of sparse codes with fixed computational cost and tolerable error [11]. Therefore, the best possible approximation of sparse codes should satisfy some kind of distribution. We argue that, it is more reasonable to predict the distributions of possible approximation of sparse codes instead of the specific value of best possible approximation.

Inspired by the above insights, this paper proposes a novel framework called Learned ISTA with Mixture Sparsity Network (LISTA-MSN) for sparse coding. The key idea is to introduce a novel module called Mixture Sparsity Network (MSN) to predict the distribution of best possible approximation of sparse codes. Specifically, the proposed framework first uses the popular LISTA network to obtain an initial estimate solution of sparse coding. The LISTA framework can be replaced by any other neural networks such as ALISTA [14], Coupled-LISTA (LISTA-CP) [6], etc. Then, our framework introduces the Mixture Sparsity Network to predict the distribution of the best possible approximations according to the initial estimate solution. At last, the proposed framework samples the final optimal results of sparse coding from the distribution. Note that, it is a challenging problem to model the conditional probability density function of the target sparse vectors conditioned on the input vector. To address this problem,

Mixture Sparsity Network adds an additional penalty to the popular framework of Mixture Density Network [4] so that it can ensure the sparsity of network's outputs as we hope. Experiments on synthetic data and real image data have shown that the proposed LISTA-MSN framework can significantly improve the accuracy and convergence speed of sparse coding.

In summary, our main contributions are as follows:

- A novel framework called LISTA-MSN is proposed to learn fast approximations of sparse codes. Different from previous works (such as LISTA [11], SC2Net [18] and ALISTA [14]), the proposed framework learns to predict the distribution of the best possible approximation of sparse codes instead of the best possible approximation. To the best of our knowledge, this is the first work to learn a trainable neural network to predict the distribution of the optimal solution of sparse coding. Moreover, the proposed framework is very flexible, where the LISTA can be replaced with any other neural network for sparse coding.
- Mixture Sparsity Network is proposed to model the conditional probability density function of the target sparse vectors conditioned on the input vector. It ensures that the data sampling from the predicted distribution is sparse enough, which makes the final results meaningful.

2 The Proposed Method

In this section, we will introduce the LISTA-MSN framework. The architecture of LISTA-MSN is shown in Fig. 1. Specifically, it first uses the LISTA network to obtain a coarse estimation of sparse codes. Then, the framework introduces the mixture sparsity network to predict the distribution of the best possible approximations according to the initial estimation. Finally, the framework samples the final optimal sparse codes from the distribution. Note that, the proposed method adds penalty to the mixture density network [4] to ensure the sparsity of results.

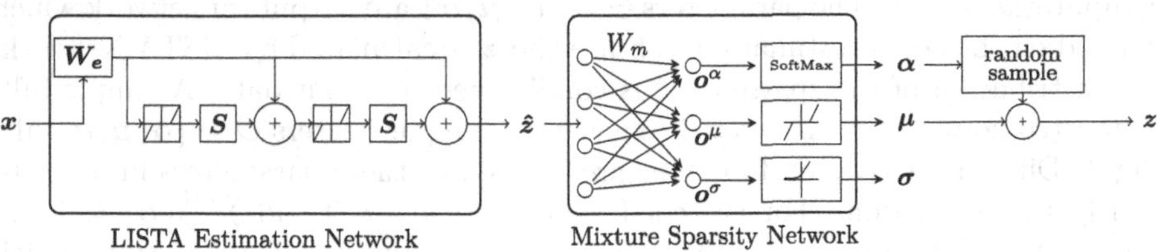

Fig. 1. The architecture of LISTA-MSN.

2.1 LISTA Network

Given the input data $\boldsymbol{X} = [\boldsymbol{x}_1, \boldsymbol{x}_2, ..., \boldsymbol{x}_N] \in \mathbb{R}^{n \times N}$, sparse coding aims to learn the over-complete dictionary $\boldsymbol{D} = [\boldsymbol{d}_1, \boldsymbol{d}_2, ..., \boldsymbol{d}_m] \in \mathbb{R}^{n \times m}$ and the sparse representation $\boldsymbol{Z} = [\boldsymbol{z}_1, \boldsymbol{z}_2, ..., \boldsymbol{z}_N] \in \mathbb{R}^{m \times N}$. And the goal of LISTA Network is to calculate the coarse estimation $\hat{\boldsymbol{Z}} = [\hat{\boldsymbol{z}}_1, \hat{\boldsymbol{z}}_2, ..., \hat{\boldsymbol{z}}_N] \in \mathbb{R}^{m \times N}$, where $\hat{\boldsymbol{z}}_q$ is the coarse estimation of sparse codes of $\boldsymbol{x}_q$ with limited iterations. Specifically, LISTA is:

$$\boldsymbol{z}^{(t+1)} = h_{\boldsymbol{\theta}}(\boldsymbol{W}_e \boldsymbol{x} + \boldsymbol{S} \boldsymbol{z}^{(t)}) \quad t = 0, ..., K-1 \tag{1}$$

$\hat{\boldsymbol{z}} = \boldsymbol{z}^{(K)}$, and K is fixed number of steps. $\boldsymbol{\theta} = [\theta_1, ..., \theta_m]$ is a trainable vector. The variables $\boldsymbol{W}_e$, $\boldsymbol{S}$ and $\boldsymbol{\theta}$ are learned by the given training data. So, the LISTA can be replaced by any other neural networks such as ALISTA [14], Coupled-LISTA (LISTA-CP) [6], etc.

2.2 Mixture Sparsity Network

Having the coarse estimation $\hat{\boldsymbol{z}}$ generated from LISTA Network, in this stage, the mixture sparsity network is proposed to model the conditional distribution of sparse codes $\boldsymbol{z}$ on the coarse estimation $\hat{\boldsymbol{z}}$ as the linear combination of kernel function:

$$P(\boldsymbol{z}|\hat{\boldsymbol{z}}) = \sum_{i=1}^{M} \alpha_i(\hat{\boldsymbol{z}}) \phi_i(\boldsymbol{z}|\hat{\boldsymbol{z}}) \tag{2}$$

where M is the number of kernel function, ϕ_i is the kernel function, $\alpha_i(\hat{\boldsymbol{z}})$ is the mixture coefficients, which can be regarded as prior probability of the sparse code $\boldsymbol{z}$ being generated from i^{th} kernel given the coarse estimation $\hat{z}$. In practice, the Gauss density function is often chosen as the kernel function:

$$\phi_i(\boldsymbol{z}|\hat{\boldsymbol{z}}) = \frac{\exp}{(2\pi)^{\frac{m}{2}} \prod_{j=1}^{m} \sigma_{ij}(\hat{\boldsymbol{z}})} \left\{ -\sum_{j=1}^{m} \frac{(z_j - \mu_{ij}(\hat{\boldsymbol{z}}))^2}{2\sigma_{ij}(\hat{\boldsymbol{z}})^2} \right\} \tag{3}$$

where z_j is the jth element of target data $\boldsymbol{z}$, μ_{ij} and σ_{ij} denote the jth element of mean and standard deviation of the ith kernel. A diagonal matrix is used instead of the covariance matrix of Gauss density function from the concern of computational cost. The parameters $\Theta = \{\boldsymbol{\alpha}, \boldsymbol{\mu}, \boldsymbol{\sigma}\}$ are outputs of network which depend on the coarse estimation $\hat{\boldsymbol{z}}$. Since the $\hat{\boldsymbol{z}}$ is calculated by LISTA Network, the distribution of the sparse code is conditioned on input data. A simple full-connected network is constructed to generate the parameters $\Theta = \{\boldsymbol{\alpha}, \boldsymbol{\mu}, \boldsymbol{\sigma}\}$ like Fig. 1. Different activation functions are applied to these parameters in order to satisfy the restrictions. For the coefficient $\boldsymbol{\alpha}(\hat{\boldsymbol{z}})$, $\alpha_i > 0$ and $\sum_{i=1}^{M} \alpha_i = 1$, we use the SoftMax function [10]. For the standard deviation of kernel $\boldsymbol{\sigma}(\hat{\boldsymbol{z}})$ which should be positive, we choose a modified Elu function [7]:

$$f(t) = \begin{cases} t+1, & \text{if } t \geq 0; \\ \gamma[exp(t) - 1] + 1, & \text{otherwise} \end{cases} \tag{4}$$

where γ is a scale parameter.

Next, to ensure the sparsity of the final result, it is noteworthy that the element of $\boldsymbol{\mu}$ which corresponds to zero elements in sparse codes should be very close to zero when the network was trained. So, we use the coordinate-wise shrinking function h_ϵ as sparsity restriction of $\boldsymbol{\mu}$ to keep it sparse:

$$h_\epsilon(t) = sign(t)(|t| - \epsilon)_+ \tag{5}$$

Here, ϵ is a hyperparameter with the positive value which could be set to a small number *e.g.*, 0.01. The shrinking function h_ϵ could change the small number to zero. If the output of linear layer id denoted as $\boldsymbol{o} \in \mathbb{R}^{(2m+1)M} = \{o_i^\alpha, o_{i1}^\mu, ..., o_{im}^\mu, o_{i1}^\sigma, ..., o_{im}^\sigma\}_{i=1}^M$, the parameters $\boldsymbol{\Theta}$ are:

$$\alpha_i = \frac{exp(o_i^\alpha)}{\sum_{j=1}^M exp(o_j^\alpha)} \quad \mu_{ij} = h_\epsilon(o_{ij}^\mu) \quad \sigma_{ij} = Elu(o_{ij}^\sigma) \tag{6}$$

The whole network is optimized by using the negative log-likelihood loss (NLL) of (4) and (5), the loss function is defined as:

$$\begin{aligned} E &= -\sum_{q=1}^N E^q \\ E^q &= -ln(\sum_{i=1}^M \alpha_i(\hat{\boldsymbol{z}}_q)\phi_i(\boldsymbol{z}_q|\hat{\boldsymbol{z}}_q)) \end{aligned} \tag{7}$$

So, the derivatives of E^q with respect to output of linear layer $\boldsymbol{o}$ are calculated as follows:

$$\begin{aligned} \pi_i &= \frac{\alpha_i\phi_i}{\sum_{j=1}^M \alpha_j\phi_j} \\ \frac{\partial E^q}{\partial o_j^\alpha} &= \alpha_i - \pi_i \end{aligned} \tag{8}$$

$$\frac{\partial E^q}{\partial o_{ij}^\sigma} = \pi_i \left\{ \frac{1}{\sigma_{ij}} - \frac{(z_j - \mu_{ij})^2}{\sigma_{ij}^3} \right\} f'(o_{ij}^\sigma) \tag{9}$$

$$\frac{\partial E^q}{\partial o_{ij}^\mu} = \pi_i \left\{ \frac{(\mu_{ij} - z_j)}{\sigma_{ij}^2} \right\} \delta(|o_{ij}^\mu| > \lambda) \tag{10}$$

where f' denotes the derivative of function f, $\delta(t)$ is defined as follow:

$$\delta(t) = \begin{cases} 1, & \text{if } t \text{ is true;} \\ 0, & \text{otherwise} \end{cases} \tag{11}$$

So, the standard back-propagation is guaranteed, and the algorithm is shown in Algorithm 1 and Algorithm 2.

Finally, after getting the parameters Θ, we need to sample the final results from the learned distribution. Luckily, we get the mixture of Guass density function by which the sampling approach can be easily implemented. The location is obtained by randomly sampling according to $\boldsymbol{\alpha}$ and the corresponding center is the result of sampling. Actually, what interested us more is the most likely value of the output. The most likely value for output vector is calculated by maximum the conditional distribution, but this procedure might be computationally costly. A faster approximation is to use the center of kernel function which has highest probability of being sampled, from (4) and (5):

$$ind = \arg\max_i \{\alpha_i\} \tag{12}$$

The corresponding center μ_{ind} is the most likely output. And the result of sample will be sparse as long as the h_ϵ activation for $\boldsymbol{\mu}$ is used.

Algorithm 1. LISTA-MSN: fprop and bprop

fprop($\boldsymbol{x}, \boldsymbol{z}, \boldsymbol{W}_e, \boldsymbol{S}, \boldsymbol{\theta}$)
  Variable $Z(t), C(t), B, \boldsymbol{\Theta}$ are stored for bprop
  $B = \boldsymbol{W}_e\boldsymbol{x};\ \ Z(0) = h_{\boldsymbol{\theta}}(B)$
  for t=1 to K **do**
    $C(t) = B + \boldsymbol{S}Z(t-1)$
    $Z(t) = h_{\boldsymbol{\theta}}(C(t))$
  end for
  $\hat{\boldsymbol{z}} = Z(K)$
  $\boldsymbol{o} = \boldsymbol{W}_m\hat{\boldsymbol{z}}$
  $\alpha_i = \frac{exp(\hat{o}_i^\alpha)}{\sum_{j=1}^M exp(\hat{o}_j^\alpha)}\quad \mu_{ij} = h_\epsilon(\hat{o}_{ij}^\mu)\quad \sigma_{ij} = f(\hat{o}_{ij}^\sigma)$
  $\boldsymbol{\Theta} = \{\boldsymbol{\alpha}, \boldsymbol{\mu}, \boldsymbol{\sigma}\}$

bprop ($\boldsymbol{z}^*, \boldsymbol{x}, \boldsymbol{W}_e, \boldsymbol{S}, \boldsymbol{W}_m, \boldsymbol{\theta}, \delta\boldsymbol{W}_e, \delta\boldsymbol{S}, \delta\boldsymbol{W}_m, \delta\boldsymbol{\theta}$)
  $Z(t)$, $C(t)$, B and $\boldsymbol{\Theta}$ were stored in fprop
  Initialize: $\delta B = 0;\ \ \delta\boldsymbol{S} = 0;\ \ \delta\boldsymbol{\theta} = 0$
  $\delta\boldsymbol{o}$ is calculated by (10) – (12)
  $\delta\boldsymbol{W}_m(t) = \delta\boldsymbol{o}\hat{\boldsymbol{z}}^T;\ \ \delta\hat{\boldsymbol{z}} = \boldsymbol{W}_m^T\delta\boldsymbol{o};\ \ \delta Z(K) = \delta\hat{\boldsymbol{z}}$
  for $t = K$ down to 1 **do**
    $\delta C(t) = h_\theta{}'(C(t)) \odot \delta Z(t))$
    $\delta\theta = \delta\theta - sign(C(t)) \odot \delta C(t)$
    $\delta B = \delta B + \delta C(t)$
    $\delta\boldsymbol{S} = \delta\boldsymbol{S} + \delta C(t)Z(t-1)^T$
    $\delta Z(t-1) = \boldsymbol{S}^T\delta C(t)$
  end for
  $\delta B = \delta B + h_\theta{}'(B) \odot \delta Z(0)$
  $\delta\theta = \delta\theta - sign(B) \odot h_\theta(B)\delta Z(0)$
  $\delta W_e = \delta BX^T$

3 Experiment

In this section, we evaluate the performance of the proposed framework on synthetic data and real image data, and compare it with other state-of-the-art algorithms, including ISTA, FISTA, LISTA, ALISTA, and Coupled-LISTA. Similar to previous works [1,3,11], we adopt Prediction error and Function value error as the criteria. Prediction error is the squared error between the input data and predicted codes in a certain dictionary. And cost function error is the cost between current prediction and best prediction. These criteria can evaluate the accuracy and convergence of the algorithm. During the experiments, we find that all the evaluated methods perform stable when λ ranges between 0.1 and 0.9. So, the sparsity parameter $\lambda = 0.5$ is fixed in all the experiments, which means the difference during experiments is just the algorithms themselves. All the algorithms are implemented by python and pytorch, and run the experiments on a DGX-1v server.

3.1 Synthetic Experiments

For synthetic case, the dictionary $D \in \mathbb{R}^{n \times m}$ of standard normal distribution is generated. Once D is fixed, a set of Gaussian i.i.d. samples $\{x_i\}_{i=1}^{N} \in \mathbb{R}^n$ are draw. In this case, we set $m = 256$, $n = 64$, $N_{train} = 40000$ and $N_{test} = 10000$.

In this subsection, two experiments are carried out to verify the performance of the proposed method. First, we compare the LISTA-MSN with several traditional algorithms by measuring their prediction error to verify whether LISTA-MSN outperforms the traditional iterative approaches. Figure 2 shows the prediction error of several algorithms for different iterations or layers (For ISTA and FISTA, the number of iterations changes. For LISTA and LISTA-MSN, the number of layers changes.) From Fig. 2, we can observe that LISTA-MSN can always achieve the lowest prediction error in different depth compared with other algorithms. Even a 10 layers LISTA-MSN can achieve the same error as the five times depth of LISTA or FISTA. Furthermore, in order to verify whether the proposed framework is effective under different estimation network structures. So, we use the proposed framework for verification under the two network structures (ALISTA and Coupled-LISTA) respectively. Figure 3 and Fig. 4 show that for different estimation network structures, the proposed framework also outperforms the original network structure. And it can decrease the prediction error nearly by 10% at the same network depth and structure.

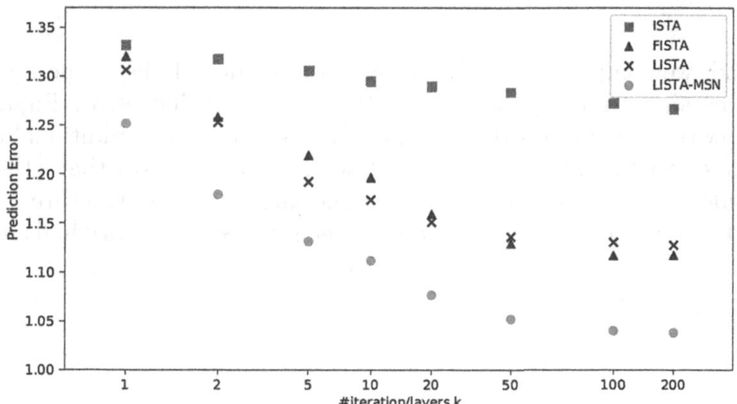

Fig. 2. Evolution of prediction error in ISTA, FISTA, LISTA, LISTA-MSN on simulated data

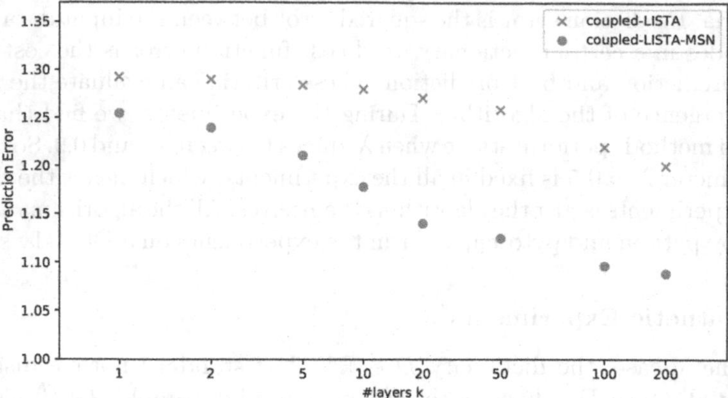

Fig. 3. Evolution of prediction error in Coupled-LISTA, Coupled-LISTA-MSN on simulated data

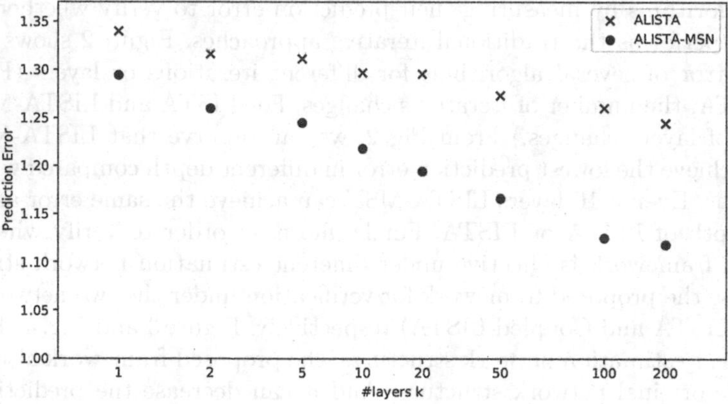

Fig. 4. Evolution of prediction error in ALISTA, ALISTA-MSN on simulated data

Second, we compare the convergence performance of the proposed method with other algorithms by calculating the function value error. Figure 5 and Fig. 6 show that the proposed method converges faster than traditional iterative approaches (ISTA and FISTA) and reaches a lower overall cost than other methods. Besides, we can also find that under the same network structure, using the proposed framework can improve the convergence speed of the original algorithm.

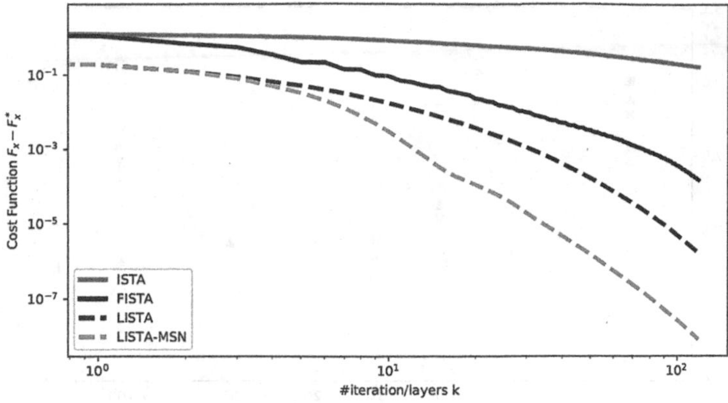

Fig. 5. Evolution of the function value error in ISTA, FISTA, LISTA, LISTA-MSN on simulated data

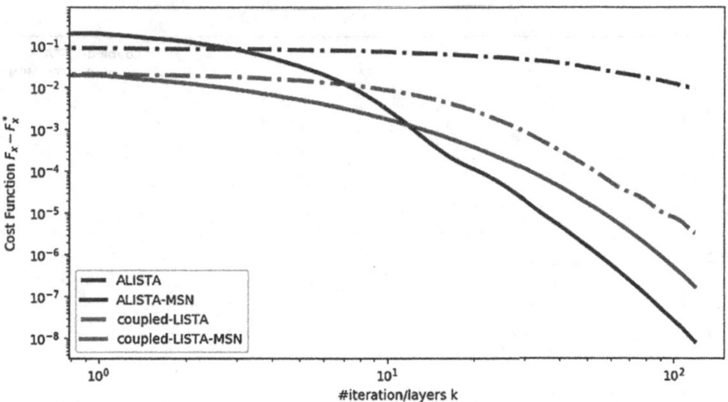

Fig. 6. Evolution of the function value error in four algorithms on simulated data

3.2 Digit Data Experiments

About real image data, we use the handwritten digits dataset from scikit-learn [Pedregosa et al., 2011]. The digits dataset contains 60,000 training images and 10,000 test images, where each image size is 8×8 and sampled from digits (0 to 9). We randomly sample $m = 256$ samples from dataset and normalize it to generate the dictionary D. Besides the above, all the image data is processed to remove its mean and normalize its variance.

In the digit dataset, we also compare several algorithms with the proposed method by measuring their prediction error. From Fig. 7, 8 and Fig. 9, wc can observe that the results are very similar to the synthetic data. The proposed method outperforms the traditional iterative approaches. And under different estimation network structures (LISTA, ALISTA and Coupled-LISTA) with the use of our framework, the prediction error can also decrease. The interesting

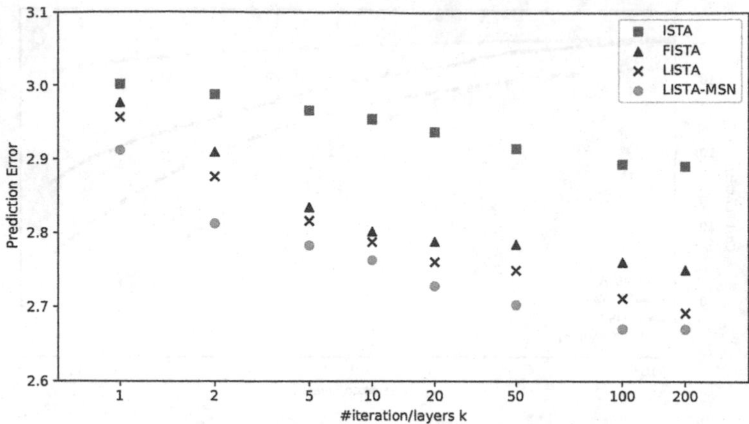

Fig. 7. Evolution of prediction error in ISTA, FISTA, LISTA, LISTA-MSN on digit data

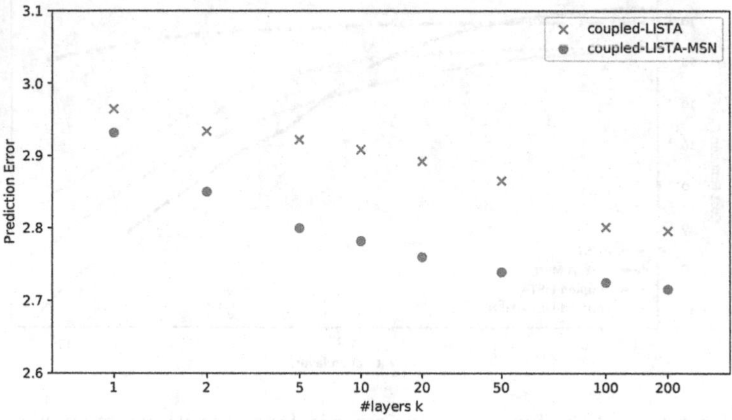

Fig. 8. Evolution of prediction error in Coupled-LISTA, Coupled-LISTA-MSN on digit data

thing observed is that all the algorithms perform better on synthetic dataset than digit dataset. For this result, the dictionary D of the digit data has a much richer correlation structure than the simulated Gaussian dictionary, which is known to impair the performance of learned algorithms [16].

3.3 Sparsity Analysis

As mentioned earlier, how to guarantee the sparsity of results from the learned distribution is a very important thing. And the sparse regulation is put forward to solve this problem. Therefore, we experimented to prove the importance of sparse regulation to MSN by comparing the sampling results' sparsity of the

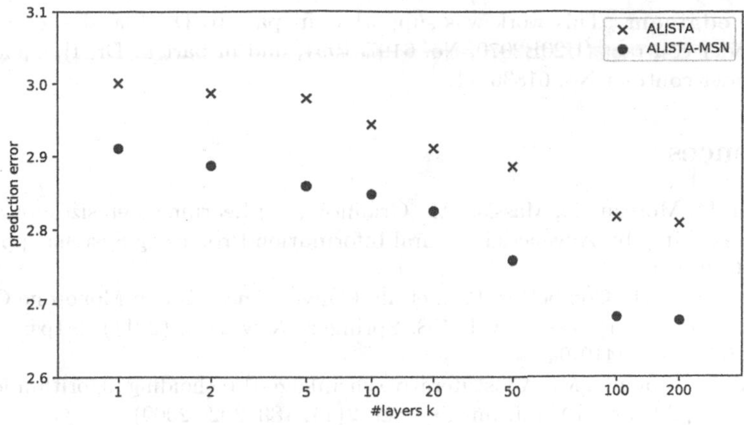

Fig. 9. Evolution of prediction error in ALISTA, ALISTA-MSN on digit data

proposed method with or without sparse regulation under the same estimation network structure. We calculate the proportion of zero elements in the final results. Table 1 shows that no matter how the dataset changes, under a certain estimation network structure with sparse regulation can always keep the sparsity of the results. This also guarantees that the final results are meaningful.

Table 1. The sparsity of the results whether use sparse regulation under a certain network structure

Datasets	Whether use sparse regulation	LISTA-MSN	ALISTA-MSN	Coupled-LISTA-MSN
Synthetic data	Without	35.67%	38.52%	40.28%
	With	**97.57%**	**94.31%**	**95.46%**
Digit data	Without	34.30%	33.60%	37.59%
	With	**94.67%**	**93.69%**	**93.55%**

4 Conclusion

This paper proposes a novel framework called LISTA-MSN for sparse coding, which significantly improves the accuracy of sparse coding. Different from existing neural network-based methods, the proposed framework learns the approximation distribution of sparse codes, then obtains the final optimal solution by sampling from the learned distribution. Furthermore, the proposed framework is very flexible. Mixture sparsity network can be combined with various neural networks as estimation networks for sparse coding, including LISTA, ALISTA, and Coupled-LISTA. Experimental results show that the proposed framework can significantly improve the accuracy of sparse coding.

Acknowledgment. This work was supported in part to Dr. Liansheng Zhuang by NSFC under contract (U20B2070, No. 61976199), and in part to Dr. Houqiang Li by NSFC under contract No. 61836011.

References

1. Ablin, P., Moreau, T., Massias, M., Gramfort, A.: Learning step sizes for unfolded sparse coding. In: Advances in Neural Information Processing Systems, pp. 13100–13110 (2019)
2. Bauschke, H.H., Combettes, P.L., et al.: Convex Analysis and Monotone Operator Theory in Hilbert Spaces, vol. 408. Springer, New York (2011). https://doi.org/10.1007/978-1-4419-9467-7
3. Beck, A., Teboulle, M.: A fast iterative shrinkage-thresholding algorithm for linear inverse problems. SIAM J. Imaging Sci. **2**(1), 183–202 (2009)
4. Bishop, C.M.: Mixture density networks (1994)
5. Blumensath, T., Davies, M.E.: Iterative thresholding for sparse approximations. J. Fourier Anal. Appl. **14**(5–6), 629–654 (2008). https://doi.org/10.1007/s00041-008-9035-z
6. Chen, X., Liu, J., Wang, Z., Yin, W.: Theoretical linear convergence of unfolded ISTA and its practical weights and thresholds. In: Advances in Neural Information Processing Systems, pp. 9061–9071 (2018)
7. Clevert, D.A., Unterthiner, T., Hochreiter, S.: Fast and accurate deep network learning by exponential linear units (ELUs) (2015)
8. Efron, B., Hastie, T., Johnstone, I., Tibshirani, R., et al.: Least angle regression. Ann. Stat. **32**(2), 407–499 (2004)
9. Friedman, J., Hastie, T., Höfling, H., Tibshirani, R., et al.: Pathwise coordinate optimization. Ann. Appl. Stat. **1**(2), 302–332 (2007)
10. Gold, S., Rangarajan, A., et al.: Softmax to softassign: neural network algorithms for combinatorial optimization. J. Artif. Neural Netw. **2**(4), 381–399 (1996)
11. Gregor, K., LeCun, Y.: Learning fast approximations of sparse coding. In: Proceedings of the 27th International Conference on International Conference on Machine Learning, pp. 399–406 (2010)
12. Ledig, C., et al.: Photo-realistic single image super-resolution using a generative adversarial network. In: Proceedings of the IEEE Conference on Computer Vision and Pattern Recognition (CVPR), July 2017
13. Lee, H., Ekanadham, C., Ng, A.Y.: Sparse deep belief net model for visual area V2. In: NIPS (2007)
14. Liu, J., Chen, X., Wang, Z., Yin, W.: ALISTA: analytic weights are as good as learned weights in LISTA. In: International Conference on Learning Representations (2019)
15. Mairal, J., Bach, F.R., Ponce, J., Sapiro, G., Zisserman, A.: Discriminative learned dictionaries for local image analysis. In: 2008 IEEE Conference on Computer Vision and Pattern Recognition, pp. 1–8 (2008)
16. Moreau, T., Bruna, J.: Understanding trainable sparse coding via matrix factorization. Stat **1050**, 29 (2017)
17. Yang, J., Wright, J., Huang, T.S., Ma, Y.: Image super-resolution via sparse representation. IEEE Trans. Image Process. **19**(11), 2861–2873 (2010). https://doi.org/10.1109/TIP.2010.2050625
18. Zhou, J.T., et al.: SC2Net: sparse LSTMs for sparse coding. In: Thirty-Second AAAI Conference on Artificial Intelligence (2018)

Anti-occluded Person Re-identification via Pose Restoration and Dual Channel Feature Distance Measurement

Bin Wu, Keyang Cheng(✉), Chunyun Meng, and Sai Liang

School of Computer Science and Communication Engineering, Jiangsu University, Zhenjiang 212013, China
kycheng@ujs.edu.cn

Abstract. In real scenes, persons are often blocked by obstacles. The purpose of occluded person re-identification is to identify the occluded persons in the non-shared view camera. In this paper, we propose a new framework, anti-occluded person re-identification model via pose restoration and dual channel feature extraction (PRAO). The network is divided into two modules: person pose repair module (PPR) and dual channel feature extraction module (DCFE). (1) In the person pose repair module, the instance segmentation network is used to detect the occlusion in the person image, and then the pre-trained edge smoothing GAN (e-GAN) is used to repair the person image. (2) In the dual channel feature extraction module, we change the original single channel person prediction structure into a dual channel person matching structure, which can accurately align the person features of the two channels, reduce the noise generated by image generation, and improve the identification accuracy of persons in the case of occlusion. Finally, a large number of experiments on occluded and non-occluded datasets show the performance of the method.

Keywords: Person re-identification · Feature expression · Similarity measure

1 Introduction

With the development of science and technology, person re-identification is more and more widely used, person re-identification is considered to be a sub-question of image retrieval. The purpose of person re-identification is to find persons with the same ID in camera without sharing vision. Recently, great progress has been made in person re-identification [1–4]. However, due to the challenges such as occlusion, person re-identification has remained in the academic field, and there is still a big gap from the practical application. As shown in Fig. 1, persons are easily blocked by obstacles, if the occluded features are also learned as person features in the model, it may lead to wrong retrieval results.

The first author is student.

© Springer Nature Switzerland AG 2021
H. Ma et al. (Eds.): PRCV 2021, LNCS 13022, pp. 399–410, 2021.
https://doi.org/10.1007/978-3-030-88013-2_33

Fig. 1. Persons were occluded by different things.

Recently, some works [5,7] have tried to solve the problem of person occlusion, but there are still some shortcomings in these works: (1) To ensure that the person image in the gallery is always the holistic person, but it does not conform to the real scene; (2) In the case of inconsistent occlusion areas, it is hard to align the person features that are not occluded; (3) It is difficult to detect the human semantic key-points, when person are occluded, the detection effect of human semantic key-points is still affected, for example, the prediction of confidence and position coordinates is not accurate enough, as shown in Fig. 2.

Fig. 2. Existing problem of person re-identification with occlusion.

In order to solve the existing problems. The proposed model is different from the traditional occlusion person re-identification model. In this model, the pose repair module (PPR) is used to reconstruct the occluded area in the occluded person image, and the holistic person pose is generated as far as possible to improve the performance of pose estimation. Then the dual channel feature extraction module (DCFE) is used to align the features. The contributions of our model are as follows:

(1) The person pose repair module is proposed to erase the occlusion in the person image and repair the overall person pose, so as to improve the performance of pose estimation and realize the overall person to overall matching.
(2) A dual channel feature extraction module is proposed, which uses feature distance measurement for feature matching to focus the network attention on the whole person area and reduce the noise outside the person area due to image generation.
(3) We have done a lot of experiments on occluded and whole Reid datasets, and the experimental results show that the modified model is better than the existing methods.

2 Related Works

2.1 Traditional ReID

As a specific person retrieval problem, person re-identification is widely studied on non-overlapping cameras. The early work of person re-identification is mainly to construct person features by hand [8] or metric learning methods [9,26]. With the rise of deep learning, person re-identification technology based on deep learning has achieved high accuracy [10–13]. However, there is still a big gap between the research-oriented scene and the actual scene in people's daily life. The key challenge is that a large amount of noise caused by different perspectives, pose, image texture and occlusion hinders the network learning. Traditional person re-identification methods mainly focus on the matching of the overall person image, but can not deal with the occluded image well, so it limits the application in the actual monitoring scene.

2.2 Occluded ReID

Occluded person re-identification methods aim to find a given occluded person image from the camera video surveillance which does not share the field of view [14]. This task is more challenging because the person image contains the noise information of occlusion or the occlusion area is inconsistent, which leads to the spatial alignment dislocation. Zhuo et al. [15] used occluded/non occluded binary classification loss to distinguish occluded images from the overall person image, there is no fundamental solution to the occlusion problem. Miao et al. [5] proposed a pose guided feature alignment method to match the occluded images in query and gallery, However, this does not take into account the negative effect of occlusion on pose estimation. On this basis, Wang et al. [7] proposed a method to distinguish features and robust alignment by learning high-order relations and topological information. Zhang et al. [6] proposed a mask guided de-occlusion method to deal with the problem of person occlusion. This solves the problem of person being blocked to some extent, but brings in new noise.

3 Proposed Method

This part mainly introduces the framework we proposed, including the person pose repair module (PPR) to remove the occlusion and repair the complete person pose, and the dual channel feature extraction module (DCFE) to extract the global and local features of person image. These two modules are trained in an end-to-end manner, and Fig. 3 shows our overall model.

3.1 Person Pose Repair

In this part, we propose a new person pose restoration method, which is used to remove the occlusion in the person image, repair the complete person pose, and

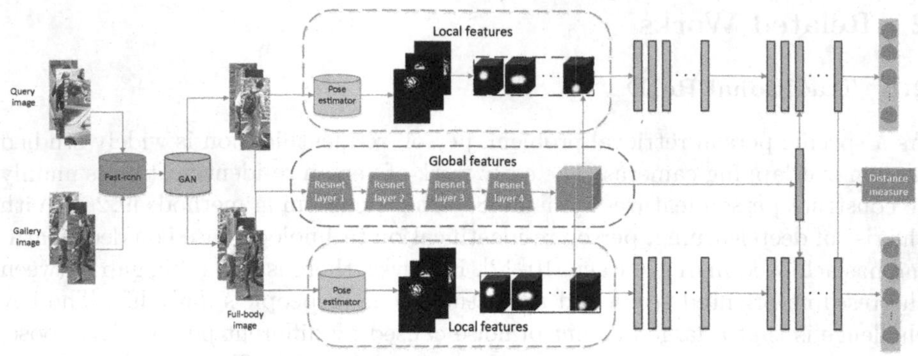

Fig. 3. An overview of the PRAO model.

realize the holistic image to the holistic image matching of the person image as far as possible. This part can be divided into two steps: the first step is to detect the occlusion and add mask to it; In the second step, the proposed e-GAN is used to generate the complete person pose. Through the experiment, it is found that the traditional GAN network does not have good smoothness for the mask edge when generating complete person pose. In order to solve this problem, we propose an edge smooth GAN (e-GAN). We hope that the e-GAN network will pay more attention to the features of the edge when it is generated.

The first step is to detect the occlusion. We assume that the target person is in the center of the image, while the main body including other persons is the occlusion, which is effective in most of the Reid public datasets. Firstly, the occluded person image is input into the instance segmentation model. Here, we retrain the instance segmentation model Fast-RCNN to detect occlusion. If the instance segmentation network detects other subjects except the central target person, we add mask to it.

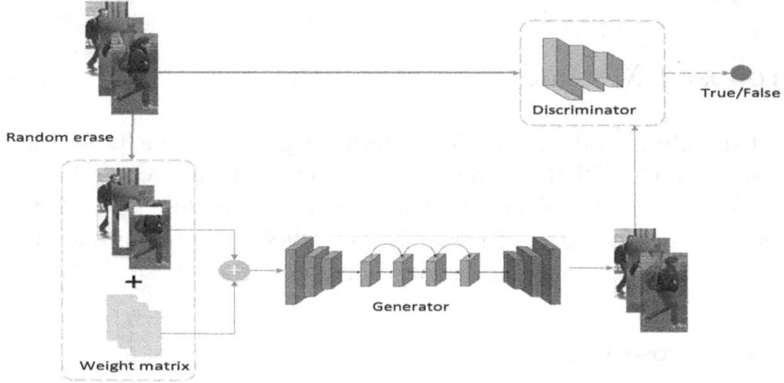

Fig. 4. The training process of e-GAN.

In the second step of training e-GAN network, we randomly add mask to the holistic person Reid dataset. Specifically, for a number of person images I randomly select a rectangular area I_m of size (w_m, h_m), and use blank pixel value to cover. Suppose that the area of the image I and the area I_m are $S = w \times h$ and $S_m = w_m \times h_m$, respectively. To determine a unique rectangular region, we initialize a point $P = (x_m, y_m)$ at random, if $x_m + w_m \leq w$, and $y_m + h_m \leq h$, We will select this rectangular area, otherwise we will repeat the above process until we find a suitable rectangular area. After the image is randomly added to the mask, the e-GAN network is pre-trained with the original image as the label. The specific training process is shown in Fig. 4 above.

In order to make the edge of person pose image smoother, we add random mask to person image and generate edge weight matrix W. The weight matrix at location (i, j) is defined as follows,

$$W_{(i,j)} = \begin{cases} 0.9^{\mu}; \mu = \min |i - w_m| + |j - h_m| \\ 0; \forall (i,j) \in S_m \end{cases} \tag{1}$$

The loss function of e-GAN network training is as follows:

$$\min_G \max_D V(D, G) = E_{x \sim P_{data}(x)}[\log(D(x))] + E_{m \sim P_m(m)}[\log(1 - D(G(m)))] \tag{2}$$

Among them, x is the real person image of the input network, m is the person mask image after random erasure, $P_{data}(x)$ is the real person data distribution, and $P_m(m)$ is the data distribution of the person mask image.

In the stage of repairing person pose image, we only keep the branches used to generate person image. Then the image with mask in the previous step is input into the pre-trained e-GAN network, which outputs an image with complete person pose image X. As shown in Fig. 5.

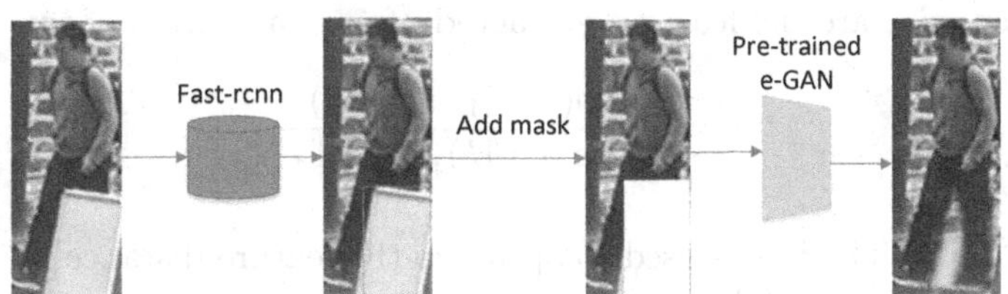

Fig. 5. Process of repairing complete person pose image.

3.2 Dual Channel Feature Extraction

The purpose of this module is to extract the features of human semantic keypoints. Because the person pose repair module can repair the complete person pose as much as possible, it is improved on the basis of the traditional occlusion person re-identification network. After a lot of experiments, we found that the performance of the dual channel matching structure is better than that of the single channel prediction structure.

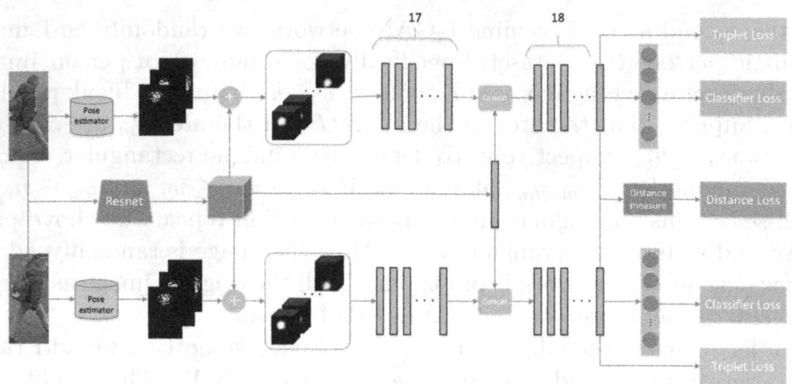

Fig. 6. An overview of dual channel feature extraction module.

The structure diagram of the module is shown in Fig. 6. First, the preprocessed person image X is given, we can get their feature F_g, and key-points heatmaps H, through ResNet-50 model and pose estimation model. The dimension of key-points heatmaps is $24 \times 8 \times 17$. Using matrix broadcast $B(\cdot)$ and global average pooling $g(\cdot)$, we can get human semantic local feature F_l guided by key points, in which the dimension of human semantic local feature is $24 \times 8 \times 17 \times 2048$.

$$F_l = g(B(G \otimes H)) \tag{3}$$

After extracting the local features of human pose F_l, in order to enhance the performance of the dual channel feature extraction module, we use feature distance measurement method d to determine whether the two images in the module are the same kind of person. Among them, f is the fully connected layer, F_{l1} and F_{l2} are the features extracted after convolution of two channels.

$$d = \frac{\exp(f\|F_{l1} - F_{l2}\|_1)}{1 + \exp(f\|F_{l1} - F_{l2}\|_1)} \tag{4}$$

Distance Loss. The loss is used to optimize the feature distance measurement d The loss is defined as follows.

$$L_d = \begin{cases} y \log d + (1-y)\log(1-d) \\ y = 1; if F_{l1} = F_{l2} \\ y = 0; otherwise \end{cases} \tag{5}$$

Loss Function. We use classification loss L_{cls}, triples loss L_{tri} and distance loss L_d as our optimization objectives. Among them, k is the number of human semantic key-points, C_i is the confidence level at the ith key-points, F_g is the global feature extracted by ResNet-50, F_{la}, F_{lp}, F_{ln} are the anchor feature, negative sample feature and positive sample feature of person image respectively, and α is the margin. y is used to judge whether the persons in two channels are the same person. If they are the same person, then $y = 1$, otherwise $y = 0$, λ is constants, which are used to balance the relationship between different loss functions.

$$L = \frac{1}{k}\sum_{i=1}^{k} C_i(L_{cls} + L_{tri}) + \lambda L_d \tag{6}$$

$$L_{cls} = -\log(F_g) \tag{7}$$

$$L_{tri} = \left[\alpha + \|F_{la} - F_{lp}\|_2^2 - \|F_{la} - F_{ln}\|_2^2\right]_+ \tag{8}$$

4 Experiment

4.1 Datasets and Evaluation Metrics

In order to prove the effectiveness of our method in person re-identification with occlusion and without occlusion, we evaluate it on occluded-DukeMTMC and two non- occluded person re-identification datasets Market1501 and DukeMTMC-ReID, respectively.

Occluded-DukeMTMC [5]**:** It is the largest occluded person re-identification dataset so far, and its training set contains 15618 images, covering a total of 702 identities. The test set contains 1110 identities, including 17661 gallery images and 2210 query images. The experimental results on the occluded Duke-MTMC data set show the superiority of our model in the case of person occlusion, and it does not need any manual clipping process as preprocessing.

Market1501 [16]**:** The dataset is collected in Tsinghua University campus, and the images come from 6 different cameras, one of which is low pixel. The training set contains 12936 images, and the test set contains 19732 images. There are 751 people in the training data and 750 people in the test set.

DukeMTMC-ReID [17,18]**:** The dataset was collected at Duke University with images from 8 different cameras. The training set contains 16522 images, the test set contains 17661 images and 2228 query images. There are 702 people in the training data, with an average of 23.5 training data for each class. It is the largest person re-identification dataset at present.

Evaluation Metrics: We use most of the standard indicators in the literature of person re-identification, namely cumulative matching characteristic (CMC) curves and mean average precision (mAP), to evaluate the quality of different person re-identification models.

4.2 Implementation Details

We use ResNet-50 [19] as our backbone network, and make a small modification to it: delete the average pooling layer and fully connected layer, the size of the input image is adjusted to 256 × 128, the batch size of training is set to 64, and the training epoch number is set to 60. Using Adam optimizer, the exponential decay rate of first-order moment estimation is 0.5, the exponential decay rate of second-order moment estimation is 0.999, and the initial learning rate is 0.1. In order to ensure the stability of training, a batch normalization layer is added after extracting the local features of person pose each time. The initial learning rate is 3.5e−4, and it decays to 0.1 when the epoch training reaches 30 to 60.

4.3 Comparative Experiments

In this subsection, we compare four methods, which are holistic person ReID methods, holistic ReID methods with key-points information, partial ReID methods and occluded ReID methods, in order to explore the better performance of our model in person occlusion, as show in Table 1. We have also conducted experiments on two common holistic ReID datasets Market-1501 and DukeMTMC-ReID, to explore our model has good generality, as show in Table 2.

Table 1. Performance comparison on Occluded-DukeMTMC.

Method	Rank-1 (%)	Rank-5 (%)	Rank-10 (%)	mAP (%)
HACNN [20]	34.4	51.9	59.4	26.0
PCB [21]	42.6	57.1	62.9	33.7
FD-GAN [22]	40.8	–	–	–
DSR [23]	40.8	58.2	65.2	30.4
SFR [24]	42.3	60.3	67.3	32.0
PGFA [5]	51.4	68.6	74.9	37.3
PARO (ours)	**53.9**	**65.4**	**75.6**	**40.9**

Table 2. Performance comparison on the holistic re-id datasets Market-1501 and DukeMTMC-ReID

Method	Market-1501		DukeMTMC-ReID	
	Rank-1 (%)	mAP (%)	Rank-1 (%)	mAP (%)
PAN [25]	82.8	63.4	71.7	51.5
DSR [23]	83.5	64.2	–	–
TripletLoss [26]	84.9	69.1	–	–
APR [27]	87.0	66.9	73.9	55.6
MutiScale [28]	88.9	73.1	79.2	60.6
PCB [21]	92.4	77.3	81.9	65.3
PGFA [5]	91.2	76.8	82.6	65.5
PRAO (ours)	**93.8**	**77.0**	**82.1**	**67.8**

Results on Occluded-DukeMTMC. As we can see, in the case of occlusion, there is no significant difference between the general overall Reid method and the partial Reid method, which indicates that it is not very good to deal with the occlusion problem by only focusing on the local features of the person visible area. However, it is not very obvious for the general overall Reid method to improve the performance of alignment of person features through pose guidance, because the occlusion areas are inconsistent and cannot be aligned. Our PRAO achieves 53.9% Rank-1 accuracy and 40.9% mAP accuracy. This is because we try our best to repair the person pose features through the pre-trained e-GAN network, which makes it easier for the person features to align, and adds the pose attention mechanism to suppress the noise information propagation generated by e-GAN.

Results on Market-1501 and DukeMTMC-ReID. As shown in Table 2, our method has achieved the same performance as the most advanced methods on both datasets, indicating that our method has good versatility.

4.4 Visualization

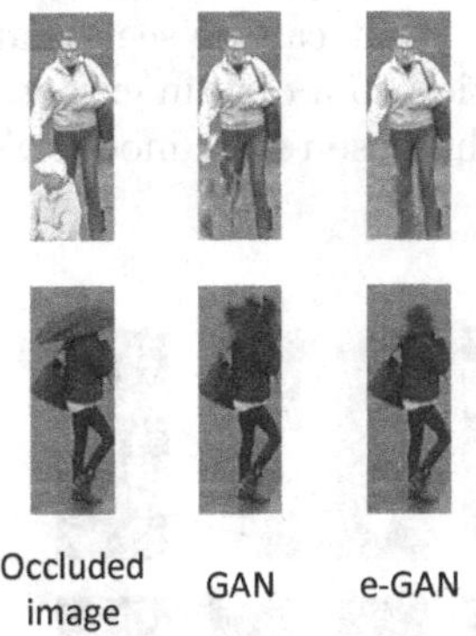

Fig. 7. Pose repair results.

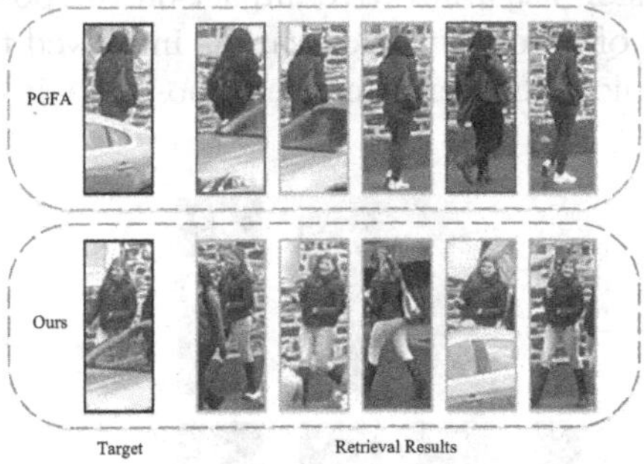

Fig. 8. Visual results of person retrieval.

Visualization of Pose Repair Module Results. The Fig. 7 shows the performance of the pose repair module in our method. It can be seen from the figure that when the person is occluded by other objects, the person pose repair module can remove the occlusion and repair the person pose as much as possible.

Visualization of Target Person Retrieval Results. Figure 8 shows the visual comparison between the new PRAO model and the PGFA model in person retrieval results. It can be seen from the figure that our new model has better performance in the case of inconsistent occlusion areas.

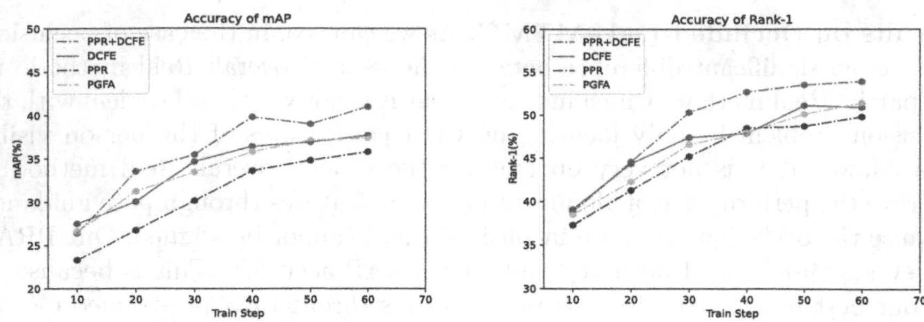

Fig. 9. Performance comparison of each module in different epochs.

4.5 Ablation Study

In this subsection, we use pose repair module (PPR) and dual channel feature extraction module (DCFE) for ablation experiments to explore the results of person re-identification under occlusion. Firstly, the PPR and DCFE are further analyzed under different training epoch, and each module is compared with the traditional occluded person re-identification to explore the effectiveness of the model, as shown in Fig. 9. Secondly, we visualize the pose estimation and attention heatmap in the network, as shown in Fig. 10. It can be seen that the occlusion has a negative impact on the pose estimation to a certain extent. The effect of pose estimation can be improved through the pose repair module, so as to explore the performance of pose repair.

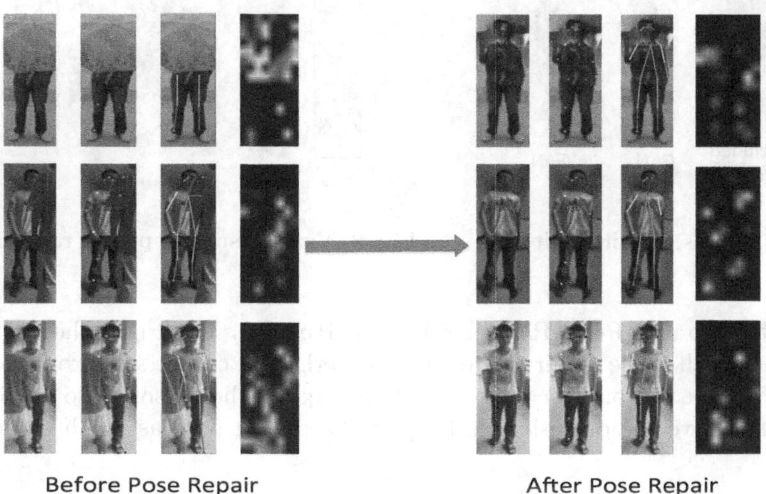

Fig. 10. After the person pose repair module, we can see that the performance of pose estimation has been improved.

5 Conclusion

In this paper, we propose a new framework to solve the problem of person occlusion. In order to realize the whole to whole matching of person image in the case of occlusion, a person pose repair module (PPR) is proposed to remove the occlusion. Finally, a dual channel feature extraction module (DCFE) is proposed to extract person features to further improve the performance of person re-identification. We have done a lot of experiments on occluded dataset and global dataset to prove the performance of the framework.

Acknowledgments. This research is supported by National Natural Science Foundation of China (61972183, 61672268) and National Engineering Laboratory Director Foundation of Big Data Application for Social Security Risk Perception and Prevention.

References

1. He, M.-X., Gao, J.-F., Li, G., Xin, Y.-Z.: Person re-identification by effective features and self-optimized pseudo-label. IEEE Access **9**, 42907–42918 (2021). https://doi.org/10.1109/ACCESS.2021.3062281
2. Li, Y., Chen, S., Qi, G., Zhu, Z., Haner, M., Cai, R.: A GAN-based self-training framework for unsupervised domain adaptive person re-identification. J. Imaging **7**, 62 (2021). https://doi.org/10.3390/jimaging7040062
3. Fu, Y., et al.: Horizontal pyramid matching for person re-identification. In: AAAI (2019)
4. Hu, M., Zeng, K., Wang, Y., Guo, Y.: Threshold-based hierarchical clustering for person re-identification. Entropy **23**, 522 (2021). https://doi.org/10.3390/e23050522
5. Miao, J., Wu, Y., Liu, P., Ding, Y., Yang, Y.: Pose-guided feature alignment for occluded person re-identification. In: 2019 IEEE/CVF International Conference on Computer Vision (ICCV), pp. 542–551 (2019). https://doi.org/10.1109/ICCV.2019.00063
6. Zhang, P., Lai, J., Zhang, Q., Xie, X.: MGD: mask guided de-occlusion framework for occluded person re-identification. In: Cui, Z., Pan, J., Zhang, S., Xiao, L., Yang, J. (eds.) IScIDE 2019. LNCS, vol. 11935, pp. 411–423. Springer, Cham (2019). https://doi.org/10.1007/978-3-030-36189-1_34
7. Wang, G., et al.: High-order information matters: learning relation and topology for occluded person re-identification. In: 2020 IEEE/CVF Conference on Computer Vision and Pattern Recognition (CVPR), pp. 6448–6457 (2020). https://doi.org/10.1109/CVPR42600.2020.00648
8. Ma, B., Su, Y., Jurie, F.: Covariance descriptor based on bio-inspired features for person re-identification and face verification. Image Vis. Comput. **32**(6–7), 379–390 (2014)
9. Chang, Y., et al.: Joint deep semantic embedding and metric learning for person re-identification. Pattern Recogn. Lett. **130**, 306–311 (2020)
10. Zhu, X., et al.: Heterogeneous distance learning based on kernel analysis-synthesis dictionary for semi-supervised image to video person re-identification. IEEE Access **8**, 169663–169675 (2020). https://doi.org/10.1109/ACCESS.2020.3024289
11. Wu, W., Tao, D., Li, H., Yang, Z., Cheng, J.: Deep features for person re-identification on metric learning. Pattern Recogn. **110**, 107424 (2021)

12. Vidhyalakshmi, M.K., Poovammal, E., Bhaskar, V., Sathyanarayanan, J.: Novel similarity metric learning using deep learning and root SIFT for person re-identification. Wirel. Pers. Commun. **117**(3), 1835–1851 (2020). https://doi.org/10.1007/s11277-020-07948-1
13. Zhang, S., Chen, C., Song, W., Gan, Z.: Deep feature learning with attributes for cross-modality person re-identification. J. Electron. Imaging **29**(03), 033017 (2020)
14. Wang, H., Haomin, D., Zhao, Y., Yan, J.: A comprehensive overview of person re-identification approaches. IEEE Access **8**, 45556–45583 (2020)
15. Zhuo, J., Chen, Z., Lai, J., Wang, G.: Occluded person re-identification. In: 2018 IEEE International Conference on Multimedia and Expo (ICME), pp. 1–6. IEEE (2018)
16. Zheng, L., Shen, L., Tian, L., Wang, S., Wang, J., Tian, Q.: Scalable person re-identification: a benchmark. In: ICCV (2015)
17. Ristani, E., Solera, F., Zou, R., Cucchiara, R., Tomasi, C.: Performance measures and a data set for multi-target, multi-camera tracking. In: Hua, G., Jégou, H. (eds.) ECCV 2016. LNCS, vol. 9914, pp. 17–35. Springer, Cham (2016). https://doi.org/10.1007/978-3-319-48881-3_2
18. Zheng, W.S., Li, X., Xiang, T., Liao, S., Lai, J., Gong, S.: Partial person re-identification. In: ICCV (2015)
19. He, K., Zhang, X., Ren, S., Sun, J.: Deep residual learning for image recognition. In: 2016 IEEE Conference on Computer Vision and Pattern Recognition (CVPR), pp. 770–778 (2016)
20. Li, W., Zhu, X., Gong, S.: Harmonious attention network for person re-identification. In: CVPR (2018)
21. Sun, Y., Zheng, L., Yang, Y., Tian, Q., Wang, S.: Beyond part models: person retrieval with refined part pooling (and a strong convolutional baseline). In: Ferrari, V., Hebert, M., Sminchisescu, C., Weiss, Y. (eds.) ECCV 2018. LNCS, vol. 11208, pp. 501–518. Springer, Cham (2018). https://doi.org/10.1007/978-3-030-01225-0_30
22. Ge, Y., Li, Z., Zhao, H., Yin, G., Yi, S., Wang, X., et al.: FD-GAN: pose-guided feature distilling GAN for robust person re-identification. In: NIPS (2018)
23. He, L., Liang, J., Li, H., Sun, Z.: Deep spatial feature reconstruction for partial person re-identification: alignment-free approach. In: CVPR (2018)
24. He, L., Sun, Z., Zhu, Y., Wang, Y.: Recognizing partial biometric patterns. arXiv preprint arXiv:1810.07399 (2018)
25. Zheng, Z., Zheng, L., Yang, Y.: Unlabeled samples generated by GAN improve the person re-identification baseline in vitro. In: ICCV (2017)
26. Hermans, A., Beyer, L., Leibe, B.: In defense of the triplet loss for person re-identification. arXiv preprint arXiv:1703.07737 (2017)
27. Lin, Y., et al.: Improving person re-identification by attribute and identity learning. Pattern Recogn. **95**, 151–161 (2019)
28. Chen, Y., Zhu, X., Gong, S.: Person re-identification by deep learning multi-scale representations. In: ICCVW (2017)

Dynamic Runtime Feature Map Pruning

Pei Zhang[1,2], Tailin Liang[1,2], John Glossner[1,2], Lei Wang[1], Shaobo Shi[1,2], and Xiaotong Zhang[1](✉)

[1] University of Science and Technology, Beijing 100083, China
{pei.zhang,tailin.liang}@xs.ustb.edu.cn,
{jglossner,wanglei,zxt}@ustb.edu.cn

[2] Hua Xia General Processor Technologies, Beijing 100080, China
sbshi@hxgpt.com

Abstract. High bandwidth requirements in edge devices can be a bottleneck for many systems - especially for accelerating both training and inference of deep neural networks. In this paper, we analyze feature map sparsity for several popular convolutional neural networks. When considering run-time behavior, we find a good probability of dynamically disabling many feature maps. By evaluating the number of 0-valued activations within feature maps, we find many feature maps that can be dynamically pruned. This is particularly effective when a ReLU activation function is used. To take advantage of inactive feature maps, we present a novel method to dynamically prune feature maps at runtime reducing bandwidth by up to 11.5% without loss of accuracy for image classification. We further apply this method on Non-ReLU activation functions by allowing the output of the activation function to be within an epsilon of 0. Additionally, we also studied how video streaming applications could benefit from bandwidth reduction.

Keywords: Dynamic pruning · Deep learning · Accelerating neural networks

1 Introduction

Deep Neural Networks (DNN) have been developed to identify relationships in high-dimensional data [1]. Recent neural network designs have shown superior performance over traditional methods in many domains including voice synthesis, object classification, and object detection. DNNs have many convolutional layers to extract features from the input data and map them to a latent space. These features maps then become the input to subsequent layers.

DNNs are required to be trained before inference can be performed. Training typically uses backward propagation and gradient computations to learn parameter values. The inference stage does not use backward propagation and therefore the computing requirements are significantly reduced. However, modern deep neural networks have become quite large with hundreds of hidden layers and upwards of a billion parameters [2]. With increasing size, it is no longer possible to maintain data and parameters in the processor's cache. Therefore data

© Springer Nature Switzerland AG 2021
H. Ma et al. (Eds.): PRCV 2021, LNCS 13022, pp. 411–422, 2021.
https://doi.org/10.1007/978-3-030-88013-2_34

must be stored in external memory, resulting in significantly increased bandwidth requirements. Many researchers have studied reducing DNN bandwidth usage and proposed methods of compressing networks. Results have shown the number of parameters can be significantly reduced with minimal or no loss of accuracy. Previous work includes parameter quantization [3], low-rank decomposition [4], and network pruning which we fully describe as follows.

Network pruning involves taking a designed neural network and removing neurons with the benefit of reducing computational complexity, power dissipation, and memory bandwidth. Neurons can often be removed without significant loss of accuracy. Network pruning generally falls into the categories of static pruning and dynamic pruning [5].

Static pruning chooses which neurons to remove before the network is deployed. Neurons with 0-values or that are not contributing to classification results are removed. Statically pruned networks may optionally be retrained [6]. Retraining may produce higher accuracy classifications [7], but requires significant computation time. A problem with static pruning is the resulting network structure is often irregular. Additionally, a fixed network is unable to take advantage of 0-valued input (image) data.

Dynamic pruning determines at runtime which parameters will not participate in the inference stage. It can overcome limitations of static pruning. When input data is changing, it can adjust the number of pruned parameters to reduce bandwidth usage and power dissipation. One implementation of dynamic runtime pruning considers any parameters that are trained as 0-values within a processing element (PE) in such a way that the PE is inhibited from participating in the computation [8].

A kernel is comprised of pre-trained coefficient matrices stored in external memory. The kernel (or a collection of kernels) is a filter that has the ability to identify features in the input data. Most dynamic runtime pruning approaches remove kernels of computation [6,9]. In this approach, bandwidth is reduced by suppressing the loading of coefficients often called weights.

Another approach to pruning CNNs is to dynamically remove feature maps. In this approach, inactive feature maps are removed at runtime. This type of pruning is the focus of this paper. Our approach proposes not to remove kernels but specific feature maps that do not contribute to the effectiveness of the network. This is done dynamically at runtime and may be combined with other static pruning techniques.

This paper is organized as follows. Section 2 discusses sparsity in several standard CNNs and presents our approach to dynamically pruning feature maps. Section 3 analyzes experimental results. In Sect. 4, we compare our method with related techniques. Finally, in Sect. 5, we describe our future research.

2 Runtime Feature Map Pruning

In this section we look at sparsity of feature maps and its affect on classification accuracy. We characterize bandwidth requirements for several CNNs. Then we present a method for dynamically marking unused feature maps and discuss the application of bandwidth reduction between image and video applications.

2.1 Dynamic Pruning

Even with memory performance improvements, bandwidth is still a limiting factor in many neural network designs [10]. Standard bus protocols such as PCIe limit the peak available bandwidth within a system. Static pruning can be applied when designing the network structure. However, for fixed network models that are already in deployment, dynamic runtime pruning can be applied to further reduce bandwidth. Our proposed approach reduces the number of feature maps being processed during inference. Unused feature maps do not need to be loaded into the processor thereby reducing bandwidth and decreasing inference latency.

Consider 5 kernels that produce 5 feature maps. Note that in this example we consider 1-dimensional (1D) feature maps without loss of generalization to higher dimensional feature maps. Consider the case where the kernels are applied to input data. The activation function (typically ReLU) is then applied to the output of each kernel producing the following 5 feature maps: $[1, 0, 0, 4], [0, 0, 0, 0], [0, 7, 2, 8], [0, 0, 0, 0], [9, 5, 3, 7]$. We define the *feature map element sparsity* as the number of 0-element values divided by the total number of elements. In this case there are 11 0-valued elements and 20 total elements. Therefore the feature map element sparsity is $11/20 = 0.55$. We define feature map sparsity as the number of feature maps with all 0-valued outputs. In this case $2/5 = 0.4$.

Because it is rare that every element in a feature map produces a 0-valued output, we introduce a heuristic criterion called *feature map element density*. Feature map element density is a metric used within a single feature map that measures the percent of 0-valued outputs divided by the total number of outputs. This is distinct from feature map element sparsity that considers all feature maps in the layer. We use a feature map element density of 99% meaning that 99% of outputs within a single feature map must have 0-valued outputs to be marked for removal.

In addition, not all feature maps output are exactly zero but many are close to zero. We define a threshold epsilon (ϵ) to be the distance from zero of the feature map element. It is applied after the activation function and is defined by Eq. 1. For any absolute value of x greater than ϵ, the function returns x. If the absolute value of x less than ϵ, it returns 0.

$$\text{activation}(x) = \begin{cases} x & |x| > \epsilon \\ 0 & |x| \leq \epsilon \end{cases} \tag{1}$$

We profiled both feature map element sparsity and feature map sparsity on convolutional layers for some common neural networks. We used the average of 1000 class images from the ImageNet2012 dataset [11]. Figure 1 shows feature map *element* sparsity. The leftmost bar of each network shows feature map

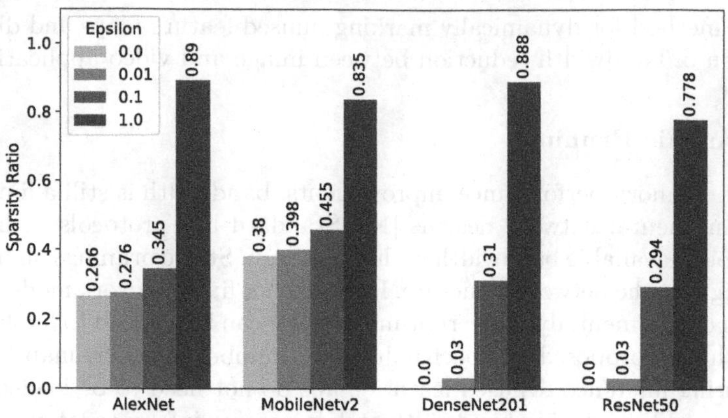

Fig. 1. Feature map element sparsity ratio of convolutional layers: the x-axis identifies some popular CNNs for a range of pruning thresholds (epsilon). The y-axis shows the element sparsity of feature maps for the network.

element sparsity for the case when each element is equal to 0 (epsilon = 0). For example, AlexNet has 27% 0-valued elements while ResNet50 don't have any.

Figure 2 shows feature map sparsity for a feature map element density of 99%. Although feature map sparsity is lower than feature map element sparsity, selecting which feature maps to mark for pruning is not resource intensive. Allowing values of epsilon to be 0.1 (meaning 99% of all feature map outputs are within 0.1 of zero) shows some networks can prune many more feature maps (e.g. ResNet50).

ReLU activation functions typically produce many 0-valued outputs. Leaky ReLU and some other activation functions which allow small negative values for gradient smoothing do not produce many 0-valued outputs [12]. ResNet50 and DenseNet201 use leaky ReLU and as shown in Fig. 1 have fewer 0-sparsity.

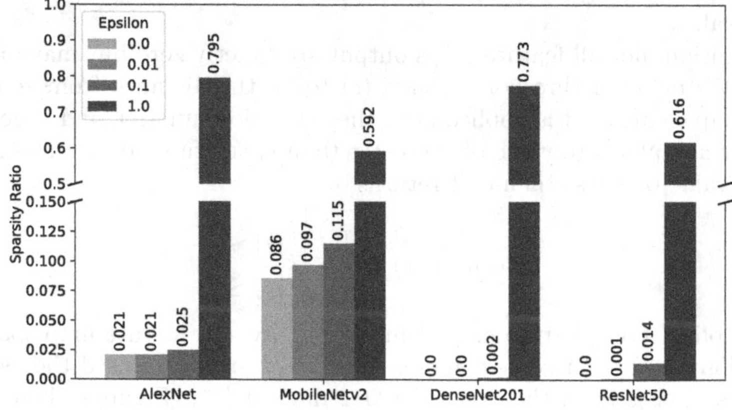

Fig. 2. Feature map sparsity on convolutional layers.

2.2 Dynamic Pruning Algorithm

Algorithm 1 describes a brute-force naive technique for dynamic feature map pruning. We profile a frame of video and apply the activation function of Eq. 1. We look at the element values in each feature map. If we determine that a feature map has 99% of elements less than a value of ϵ, we mark the feature map as inactive and subsequently do not process it. This feature map remains inactive until the next time a frame of video is profiled (called the recalibration time). Based on Darknet [13], an open-source neural network framework, we use a bitmap array to skip the marked feature maps using the GEMM algorithm. Our source code is available at GitHub[1].

Algorithm 1: Dynamic Feature Map Pruning

input : C - the number of feature maps, H - a feature map height, W - a feature map width

output: bitmap - the bit map marking whether a feature map can be pruned

```
feature_map_size = H × W;
for i = 0 to C do
    /* cnt - counting 0-value                                   */
    cnt = 0;
    for j = 0 to feature_map_size do
        cnt += !!abs(value[i × feature_map_size + j]);
    end
    /* set a 1% error rate                                      */
    bitmap[i] = (0.99 × feature_map_size) ≤ cnt;
end
```

2.3 Bandwidth Reduction in Video Streams

Video processing is particularly appropriate for our dynamic pruning approach since a series of video frames may often reuse feature maps to determine detection. In this section, we derive bandwidth saving based on criterion such as the image size, the number of feature maps, and the frame rate of the video stream. Figure 3 shows the cosine similarity of different frame intervals in three segments (beginning, middle, and end) of video from the YouTube-8M data-set [14].

Objects within 15 frames (which is typically half of a standard refresh rate) tend to be similar. Meanwhile, the objects' positions are relatively unchanged. In this case, the bounding box of the objects only moves slightly. Active feature maps tend to be reused and the feature maps marked for skipping remain marked and are not loaded. Depending upon the amount of motion in an arbitrary video, the length of time feature maps are reused may vary. Hence, we introduce a heuristic parameter called recalibration time that is the number of frames between reprofiling of unused feature maps.

[1] https://github.com/bit2erswe2t/darknet-pruning.

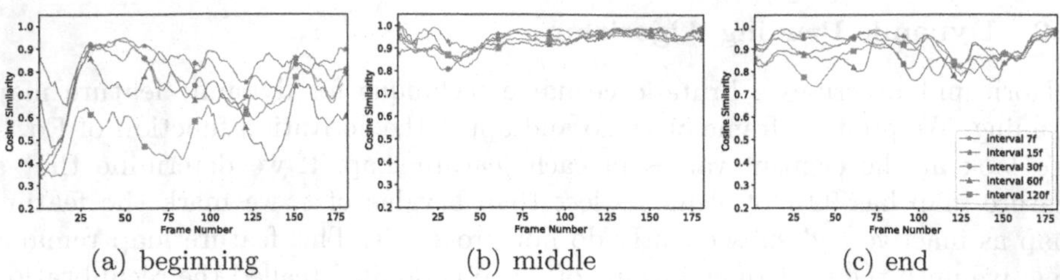

(a) beginning (b) middle (c) end

Fig. 3. The cosine similarity of different frame intervals in three segments of video.

To determine bandwidth reduction in the span of one second, consider an N layer network. If the input to the convolutional layer is $c_i \times n_i \times n_i$ size at a rate of f frame per second, where c_i is the number of feature maps, and n_i is the height and width of a feature map, we can use the same pruning mark at t frames in a recalibration stage and according to the pruning mark can skip feature maps in $t-1$ frames. Using M as recalibration stages, where k_{ij} feature maps can be pruned for the i layer in the j recalibration stage, the total bandwidth reduction R is determined by Eq. 2.

$$M = \frac{f}{t},\ R = \sum\nolimits_{i=1}^{N} \sum\nolimits_{j=1}^{M} ((t-1) \times k_{ij} \times n_i^2) \quad \text{subject to } k, t, f, n, f, M, N \in \mathbb{N}_+ \text{ and } t \leq f \tag{2}$$

Equation 2 shows greater bandwidth reduction for video streams that have a high frame rate and large numbers of features maps. However, if the object is fast-moving and the recalibration time is short, the bandwidth savings converges to the single-image classification rate.

3 Experiments

In this section, we characterize Top-1 and Top-5 classification accuracy using dynamic feature map pruning for the output of Eq. 1 within ϵ after the original activation function using a feature map element density of 99%. We further characterize the bandwidth savings for image and video workloads. We compute statistics by counting the number of feature maps loaded. We do not take into account in these results the effect of small processor caches that are unable to store an entire feature map.

To validate our technique we used the ILSVRC2012-1K image data-set containing 1000 classes [11]. Table 1 shows dynamic feature map pruning with a feature map element density of 99%. The results are characterized on all 1000 classes. ϵ, from Eq. 1, measures how far away from 0 the output is allowed to vary and still be marked for pruning. "Pruned" describes the percent of dynamically pruned feature maps. Top-1 and Top-5 show the base reference in the first columns and then the change in accuracy for subsequent columns for increasing values of ϵ.

Table 1. Feature map pruning accuracy vs. ϵ with element density = 99%

ϵ	/		0.0			0.01			0.1			1		
Network	Top-1	Top-5	Top-1	Top-5	Pruned	Top-1	Top-5	Pruned	Top-1	Top-5	Pruned	Top-1	Top-5	Pruned
AlexNet	56%	79%	56%	79%	2.1%	56%	79%	2.1%	56%	79%	2.5%	0%	1%	79.5%
MobileNetv2	71%	91%	71%	91%	8.6%	71%	91%	9.7%	71%	91%	11.5%	0%	1%	59.2%
DenseNet201	77%	93%	77%	93%	0%	77%	93%	0%	77%	93%	0.2%	0%	1%	77.3%
ResNet50	76%	93%	76%	93%	0%	76%	93%	0.1%	76%	93%	1.4%	0%	1%	61.6%

Our results show that with an $\epsilon = 0$ only ReLu activations in AlexNet and MobileNetv2 are pruned. Leaky ReLu used in DenseNet201 and ResNet50 do not contain many 0-valued activations in their feature maps and therefore are not pruned. Using an $\epsilon = 0.1$ for pruning has no significant loss in accuracy for the Top-1 and Top-5 while reducing feature map loading up to 11.5%. At $\epsilon = 1$, Top-1 and Top-5 accuracy drops to 0%.

Table 2. Top-1 classification accuracy of images w/o & w/0.1 pruning

Network	w/o pruning					$\epsilon = 0.1$ pruning					Reduced fmap loading
	Cat	Dog	Eagle	Giraffe	Horse	Cat	Dog	Eagle	Giraffe	Horse	Pruned/all
AlexNet	40.29%	19.03%	79.03%	36.44%	53.02%	40.24%	18.98%	78.91%	36.43%	52.97%	2.48% (10k/398k)
MobileNetv2	19.25%	39.04%	91.62%	29.62%	42.71%	23.95%	39.67%	91.31%	33.23%	42.32%	11.49% (1036k/9013k)
DenseNet201	43.47%	85.49%	71.41%	32.28%	22.86%	42.52%	85.33%	68.65%	32.46%	22.55%	0.15% (47k/30605k)
ResNet50	23.94%	95.11%	67.95%	76.72%	21.12%	23.91%	95.16%	67.99%	77.12%	21.00%	1.37% (162k/11831k)

Table 2 shows Top-1 image classification accuracy with and without dynamic feature map pruning for $\epsilon = 0.1$ for five classification categories. In some cases, the pruned network outperformed the unpruned (e.g., MobileNetv2 cat image). This is consistent with other researcher's findings [7,15]. The last column shows the number of feature maps pruned at $\epsilon = 0.1$. For example, MobileNetv2 reduced the number of feature maps loaded by 1036k, from 9013k to 7977k. This is approximately an 11.5% savings in the number of feature maps loaded.

Additional results for MobileNetv2 not shown in Table 2 reveals that MobileNetv2 particularly benefited from feature map pruning. With $\epsilon = 0$ pruning, MobileNetv2 reduced 36 out of 54 ReLU activated convolutional layers resulting in a feature map loading reduction of 8.6%. AlexNet reduced 3 out of 5 ReLU activated convolutional layers reducing feature map loading by 2.1%. Other networks using leaky ReLU, as anticipated, do not have reduced feature map loading with $\epsilon = 0$.

Figure 4 shows the feature map loading requirements for MobileNetv2 by convolutional layer. The y-axis displays the Mega-bytes of data required to be read. The x-axis displays the network layers. The stacked bars show the data

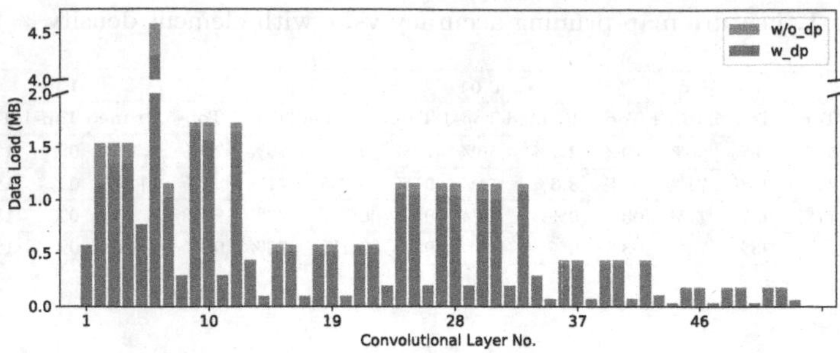

Fig. 4. Dynamic pruning performance on MobileNetv2 by convolutional layer.

requirements with and without dynamic pruning. $\epsilon = 0$ is used and shows that dynamic pruning can reduce the image data loading requirements by about 6.2% as averaged across all the convolutional layers. A few layers of MobileNetv2 use linear activation functions and therefore don't benefit from $\epsilon = 0$ pruning.

We also ran AlexNet experiments on Caffe[2] with[3] and without[4] static pruning. The results show a similar feature map sparsity on convolutional layers about 27%. The feature map pruning without static pruning is 0.79%. After static pruning is applied, the network still has 0.45% feature map loading could be pruned with dynamic runtime feature map pruning.

Using our simulator, we configured a processor capable of executing a single of convolution operations at one time. We ran experiments using MobileNetV2 at $\epsilon = 0.1$, element density = 99%, 224 × 224 resolution video stream, and a recalibration interval of 30 frames. The original network bandwidth usage is 34.35 MB per frame. The 29 frames between recalibration reduces 3.95 MB per frame. Our method reduces bandwidth requirements by 11.12%. As derived in Eq. 2, depending upon the number of layers and the input image size, we examine and mark which feature maps should be pruned once during the recalibration interval.

4 Related Work

Bandwidth reduction is accomplished by reducing the loading of parameters or the number of bits used by the parameters. This leads to further research on quantization, weight sharing and sparsity (pruning).

Bandwidth reduction using reduced precision values has been previously proposed. Historically most networks are trained using 32-bit single precision floating point numbers [16]. It has been shown that 32-bit single precision can be reduced to 8-bit integers for inference without significant loss of accuracy [17–19]. Even ternary and binary weights can be applied without significant loss of

[2] https://github.com/BVLC/caffe.
[3] https://github.com/songhan/Deep-Compression-AlexNet.
[4] http://dl.caffe.berkeleyvision.org/bvlc_alexnet.caffemodel.

accuracy on trivial datasets [20,21]. Our present work does not consider reduced precision parameters but may be incorporated into future research since it is complementary to our approach.

Compressing sparse parameter networks can save both computation and bandwidth. Chen [22] describes using a hash algorithm to decide which weights can be shared. Their work focused only on fully connected layers and used pre-trained weight binning rather than dynamically determining the bins during training. Han [6] describes weight sharing combined with Huffman coding. Weight sharing is accomplished by using a k-means clustering algorithm instead of a hash algorithm to identify neurons that may share weights. We don't currently share weights, but it is possible to combine our technique with weight sharing.

Network pruning is an important component for both memory size and bandwidth usage. It also reduces the number of computations. Early research used large-scale networks with static pruning to generate smaller networks to fit end-to-end applications without significant accuracy drop [23].

LeCun, as far back as 1990, proposed to prune non-essential weights using the second derivative of the loss function [24]. This static pruning technique reduced network parameters by a quarter. He also showed that the sparsity of DNNs could provide opportunities to accelerate network performance.

Guo [25] describes a method using pruning and splicing that compressed AlexNet by a factor of 7.7×. This significantly reduced the training iterations from 4800K to 700K. However, this type of pruning results in an asymmetric network complicating hardware implementation.

Most network pruning methods typically prune kernels rather than feature maps [6,25]. In addition to significant retraining times, it requires significant hyperparameter tuning. Parameters in fully connected layers often represent the majority of 0-values. AlexNet and VGG particularly have many parameters in fully connected layers. Our technique uses dynamic pruning of feature maps rather than kernels and requires no retraining. We reduce feature map loading to save up to 11.5% bandwidth without loss of accuracy.

Bolukbasi [26] has reported a system that can adaptively choose which layers to exit early. They format the inputs as a directed acyclic graph with various pre-trained network components. They evaluate this graph to determine leaf nodes where the layer can be exited early. Their work can be considered a type of dynamic layer pruning.

For instruction set processors, feature maps or the number of filters used to identify objects is a large portion of bandwidth usage [16] - especially for depth-wise or point-wise convolutions where feature map computations are a larger portion of the bandwidth [27]. Lin [8] used Runtime Neural Pruning (RNP) to train a network to predict which feature maps wouldn't be needed. This is a type of dynamic runtime pruning. They found 2.3× to 5.9× acceleration with top-5 accuracy loss from 2.32% to 4.89%. RNP, as a predictor, may need to be retrained for different classification tasks and may also increase the original network size.

Our technique only requires a single bit per feature map to determine if a feature map will be loaded.

Our technique prunes by feature map rather than elements. This benefits instruction set processors, particularly signal processors, because data can be easily loaded into the processor using sliding windows. Additionally, some pruning approaches only work with small datasets [28], such as MNIST and CIFAR-10. Our pruning technique works for both image and video data-sets.

5 Future Work

At present, our pruning algorithm uses comparison, counting and truncation to find feature maps that can be pruned. Our future research is focused on techniques to reduce the cost of marking feature maps for pruning. We also plan to investigate the effect of small processor caches that can only store part of a feature map. Finally, our experiments showed fluctuation in cosine similarity caused by the change of the frame interval of the video stream. We will study how to select the most suitable frame interval and how to dynamically adjust the recalibration time.

Acknowledgement. This work was supported by the National Natural Science Foundation of China, No. 61971031.

References

1. Lecun, Y., Bengio, Y., Hinton, G.: Deep learning. Nature **521**(7553), 436–444 (2015). https://doi.org/10.1038/nature14539
2. Iandola, F.N., Han, S., Moskewicz, M.W., Ashraf, K., Dally, W.J., Keutzer, K.: SqueezeNet: AlexNet-level accuracy with 50x fewer parameters and <0.5MB model size, February 2016. https://doi.org/10.1007/978-3-319-24553-9. https://arxiv.org/abs/1602.07360
3. Micikevicius, P., et al.: Mixed precision training. In: 6th International Conference on Learning Representations (ICLR 2018), October 2017. http://arxiv.org/abs/1710.03740
4. Denil, M., Shakibi, B., Dinh, L., Ranzato, M., de Freitas, N.: Predicting parameters in deep learning. In: Advances in Neural Information Processing Systems, pp. 2148–2156, June 2013. https://doi.org/10.1016/S0033-3506(78)80031-6. http://papers.nips.cc/paper/5025-predicting-parameters-in-deep-learning
5. Liang, T., Glossner, J., Wang, L., Shi, S., Zhang, X.: Pruning and quantization for deep neural network acceleration: a survey. Neurocomputing **461**, 370–403 (2021). https://doi.org/10.1016/j.neucom.2021.07.045, http://arxiv.org/abs/2101.09671
6. Han, S., Mao, H., Dally, W.J.: Deep compression: compressing deep neural networks with pruning, trained quantization and huffman coding. **45**(4), 199–203 (2015). arXiv preprint arXiv:1510.00149
7. Yu, R., et al.: NISP: pruning networks using neuron importance score propagation. In: 2018 IEEE/CVF Conference on Computer Vision and Pattern Recognition, pp. 9194–9203. IEEE, June 2018. https://doi.org/10.1109/CVPR.2018.00958. https://ieeexplore.ieee.org/document/8579056/

8. Lin, J., Rao, Y., Lu, J., Zhou, J.: Runtime neural pruning. In: 31st Conference on Neural Information Processing Systems (NIPS 2017), pp. 2178–2188 (2017). https://papers.nips.cc/paper/6813-runtime-neural-pruning.pdf
9. LeCun, Y., et al.: Backpropagation applied to handwritten zip code recognition. Neural Comput. **1**(4), 541–551 (1989). https://doi.org/10.1162/neco.1989.1.4.541. http://www.mitpressjournals.org/doi/10.1162/neco.1989.1.4.541
10. Rhu, M., O'Connor, M., Chatterjee, N., Pool, J., Kwon, Y., Keckler, S.W.: Compressing DMA engine: leveraging activation sparsity for training deep neural networks. In: 2018 IEEE International Symposium on High Performance Computer Architecture (HPCA), pp. 78–91. IEEE, February 2018. https://doi.org/10.1109/HPCA.2018.00017. http://ieeexplore.ieee.org/document/8327000/
11. Russakovsky, O., et al.: ImageNet large scale visual recognition challenge. Int. J. Comput. Vis. **115**(3), 211–252 (2015). https://doi.org/10.1007/s11263-015-0816-y. http://link.springer.com/10.1007/s11263-015-0816-y
12. Maas, A.L., Hannun, A.Y., Ng, A.Y.: Rectifier nonlinearities improve neural network acoustic models. In: ICML 2013, p. 3 (2013). https://doi.org/10.1016/0010-0277(84)90022-2
13. Redmon, J.: Darknet: Open Source Neural Networks in C (2016). http://pjreddie.com/darknet/
14. Abu-El-Haija, S., et al.: YouTube-8M: a large-scale video classification benchmark. arXiv preprint https://arxiv.org/abs/1609.08675, September 2016
15. Huang, Q., Zhou, K., You, S., Neumann, U.: Learning to prune filters in convolutional neural networks. In: Proceedings of the 2018 IEEE Winter Conference on Applications of Computer Vision, WACV 2018, pp. 709–718, January 2018. https://doi.org/10.1109/WACV.2018.00083. http://arxiv.org/abs/1801.07365
16. Sze, V., Chen, Y.H., Yang, T.J., Emer, J.S.: Efficient processing of deep neural networks: a tutorial and survey. Proc. IEEE **105**(12), 2295–2329 (2017). https://doi.org/10.1109/JPROC.2017.2761740. http://ieeexplore.ieee.org/document/8114708/
17. He, K., Zhang, X., Ren, S., Sun, J.: Deep residual learning for image recognition. In: 2016 IEEE Conference on Computer Vision and Pattern Recognition (CVPR), vol. 7, no. 3, pp. 171–180, December 2015. https://doi.org/10.3389/fpsyg.2013.00124. http://ieeexplore.ieee.org/document/7780459/
18. Ma, Y., Suda, N., Cao, Y., Seo, J.S., Vrudhula, S.: Scalable and modularized RTL compilation of convolutional neural networks onto FPGA. In: FPL 2016–26th International Conference on Field-Programmable Logic and Applications (2016). https://doi.org/10.1109/FPL.2016.7577356
19. Jacob, B., et al.: Quantization and training of neural networks for efficient integer-arithmetic-only inference. In: 2018 IEEE/CVF Conference on Computer Vision and Pattern Recognition, pp. 2704–2713. IEEE, June 2018. abs/1712.0. https://doi.org/10.1109/CVPR.2018.00286. https://ieeexplore.ieee.org/document/8578384/
20. Zhou, H., Alvarez, J.M., Porikli, F.: Less is more: towards compact CNNs. In: Leibe, B., Matas, J., Sebe, N., Welling, M. (eds.) ECCV 2016. LNCS, vol. 9908, pp. 662–677. Springer, Cham (2016). https://doi.org/10.1007/978-3-319-46493-0_40
21. Hubara, I., Courbariaux, M., Soudry, D., El-Yaniv, R., Bengio, Y.: Binarized neural networks. In: Advances in Neural Information Processing Systems, pp. 4114–4122 (2016). http://papers.nips.cc/paper/6573-binarized-neural-networks
22. Chen, W., Wilson, J., Tyree, S., Weinberger, K., Chen, Y.: Compressing neural networks with the hashing trick. In: International Conference on Machine Learning, pp. 2285–2294 (2015). http://arxiv.org/abs/1504.04788

23. Buciluă, C., Caruana, R., Niculescu-Mizil, A.: Model compression. In: Proceedings of the 12th ACM SIGKDD International Conference on Knowledge Discovery and Data Mining - KDD 2006, p. 535. ACM Press, New York (2006). https://doi.org/10.1145/1150402.1150464. http://portal.acm.org/citation.cfm?doid=1150402.1150464
24. Cun, Y.L., Denker, J.S., Solla, S.A.: Optimal brain damage. In: Advances in Neural Information Processing Systems, vol. 2, pp. 598–605 (1990). https://dl.acm.org/doi/10.5555/109230.109298
25. Guo, Y., Yao, A., Chen, Y.: Dynamic network surgery for efficient DNNs. In: Advances in Neural Information Processing Systems, vol. 29, pp. 1379–1387 (2016). http://papers.nips.cc/paper/6165-dynamic-network-surgery-for-efficient-dnns
26. Bolukbasi, T., Wang, J., Dekel, O., Saligrama, V.: Adaptive neural networks for efficient inference. In: Thirty-Fourth International Conference on Machine Learning, February 2017. https://arxiv.org/abs/1702.07811
27. Chollet, F., Google, C.: Xception: deep learning with depthwise separable convolutions. In: The IEEE Conference on Computer Vision and Pattern Recognition (CVPR), vol. 7, pp. 1251–1258. IEEE, July 2017. https://doi.org/10.1109/CVPR.2017.195. http://ieeexplore.ieee.org/document/8099678/
28. Anwar, S., Hwang, K., Sung, W.: Structured pruning of deep convolutional neural networks. ACM J. Emerg. Technol. Comput. Syst. (JETC) **13**(3), 32 (2015). https://doi.org/10.1145/3005348. https://dl.acm.org/citation.cfm?id=3005348

Special Session: New Advances in Visual Perception and Understanding

Multi-branch Graph Network for Learning Human-Object Interaction

Tongtong Wu, Xu Zhang, Fuqing Duan[(✉)], and Liang Chang

College of Artifical Intelligence, Beijing Normal University, 19 Xinjiekouwai Street, Haidian, Beijing 100875, People's Republic of China
fqduan@bnu.edu.cn

Abstract. In this work, we study the task of detecting human-object interactions (HOI) from images, which is defined as detecting triplets of (*human, predicate, object*). A common practice in the literatures is firstly localizing human and object instances and then inferring the triplets or predicates only as a classification task from the detected human-object pairs. A data sparsity issue arises when inferring the triplets because of the serious data imbalance among HOI classes, while a data variance issue arises when inferring predicates only since a predicate can carry different semantic meanings when being applied to different objects. To resolve the problem, we propose to decompose HOI classes with a same predicate into several semantic groups based on the appearance, semantic information and function of the objects. By doing this, semantic-related HOI classes are grouped together to compensate the data sparsity issue, while visually and functionally less related HOI classes are separated to relieve the data variance issue. We reveal multiple levels of decomposition in different granularities can provide richer auxiliary information to boost the performance. We implement this idea with a multi-branch graph network, while the multiple branches make classifications based on different levels of decompositions. We evaluate our method on popular HICO-Det dataset. Experimental results show that our method achieves state-of-the art performance.

Keywords: Human-object interaction · Graph · Multi-branch · Neural network · Deep learning

1 Introduction

Human-Object Interaction (HOI) Detection aims at localizing and inferring relationships between human and objects in an image, e.g., "ride bicycle", or "hold cup". A HOI Detection problem is in general defined as a triplet (*human, predicate, object*), where *human* and *object* are represented by bounding boxes, and *predicate* is the interaction between this (*human, object*) pair. Thanks to the success in object detection [18], many powerful off-the-shelf human and object detectors can be used to localize the human and object instances. Therefore, it

© Springer Nature Switzerland AG 2021
H. Ma et al. (Eds.): PRCV 2021, LNCS 13022, pp. 425–436, 2021.
https://doi.org/10.1007/978-3-030-88013-2_35

is a common practice to use these detectors to address human and object detection firstly and then infer the triplets or infer predicates only as a classification task from the detected human-object pairs. Because of the serious data imbalance among HOI classes, e.g., "kiss horse" is rare in available dataset but "ride horse" is common, a data sparsity issue arises when inferring the HOI triplets. On the other hand, since a predicate can carry different semantic meanings when being applied to different objects, e.g., "ride" applied to "bicycle" and "bus", a data variance issue arises when inferring predicates only. These issues lead to negative effects for feature and classifier learning, which greatly increases the difficulty of the task.

To resolve these issues, we propose decomposing the HOI classes with a same predicate into several groups, where each group represents a different semantics. By doing this, as Fig. 1 shows, semantic-related HOI classes (e.g., "ride bicycle" and "ride motorbike") are grouped together to compensate the data sparsity issue, while visually and functionally less related HOI classes (e.g., "ride bus" and "ride bicycle") are separated to relieve the data variance issue. For decomposition of HOI classes with a same predicate, we adopt external knowledge (appearance, semantic information and function of objects) to measure the similarity of objects, and HOI classes with same predicate and similar objects are considered semantic-related. We merge semantic-related HOI classes and treat them as one super class during training. Finally, we design a multi-branch network that for each input image we can get several super HOI classification results based on multi-level decompositions, and get the final HOI classification result by fusing the super HOI classification results. We build our proposed multi-branch network upon graph convolutional network [9]. Experiments on the main benchmark dataset demonstrate the effectiveness of our proposed method.

Our contributions are as follows: (1) To deal with the data sparsity issue and data variance issue in HOI learning, we propose to decompose HOI classes with a same predicate into several semantic groups. For the decomposition, we propose to learn feature embedding of object classes using multi-modal knowledge (appearance, semantic information and function of objects), adopt an unsupervised method to merge semantic-related HOI classes. (2) We propose a novel multi-branch graph network with each branch making HOI classification in a different level of decomposition and infer HOIs by fusing the multiple classication results. (3) Our method achieve state-of-the-art performance in HOI detection on the main HOI benchmark dataset.

2 Related Work

In recent years, benefiting from the huge success of deep learning [21] and the availability of large-scale datasets [2,3,10,26], many deep learning based HOI models are proposed. In early work [2], a large benchmark HOI dataset and a basic parallel network structure were proposed. Gkioxari *et al.* [6] adopted a Bayesian method that utilizes features of human to predict the distribution of object locations to enhance HOI learning. Attention mechanisms was applied for

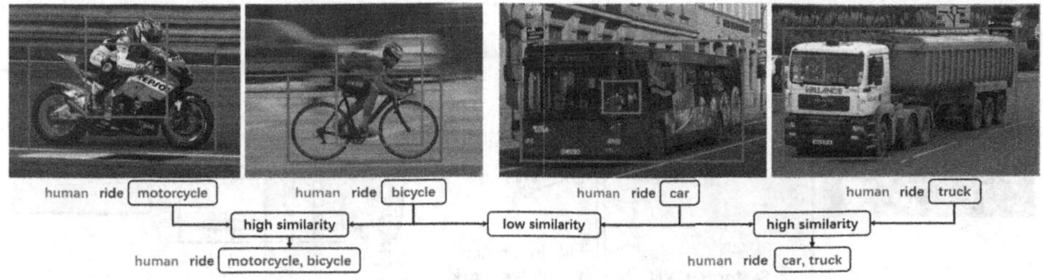

Fig. 1. HOI classes with the same predicates and similar objects are considered semantic-related and be merged as one super class during training.

catching useful clues from contextual information [5] and the synergy of human joints [4]. In [11], Li *et al.* used external datasets to transfer interactive knowledge to reduce negative interaction samples. In [1,15,19], several methods was proposed to implement zero-shot learning to detect unseen HOI relationships. These works are mainly based on convolutional neural network. In recent years, with the development of graph neural network [9] in visual relationships [24,25], some researchers have explored its application in HOI problem. In [23], a knowledge graph of human-object relationships was constructed and learned to enhance HOI learning. Qi *et al.* [16] incorporated structural knowledge and proposed a graph parsing neural network for HOI inference in images or videos.

Although considerable improvement were achieve by above approaches, there still exists a issue. All of them ignore the correlation of HOI classes. They simply infer the HOI triplets or infer predicates only as a classification task, which leads to a data sparsity issue or a data variance issue, and leads to negative effects for feature and classifier learning. Compared to these methods, our method focuses on improving the model by decomposing HOI classes with same predicate into several semantic groups to address the data sparsity issue and the data variance issue. HOI classes in same semantic group are merged and considered as one super class during training. This technique reduces the learning burden of the model and improves the classification performance. We design our network by using graph neural network to classify redefined super HOI classes. Also, we develop the graph network into multiple branches to adopt multiple levels of decomposition with different granularities. Experimental results show that our multi-branch network establishes new state-of-the-art performance.

3 Approach

3.1 Overview

Figure 2 shows the overview of our proposed approach. Our approach consists of two main stages, human/object detection and HOI classification. In the human/object detection stage, we adopt Faster R-CNN [18] as other HOI detection methods [5,11,19]. In the HOI classification stage, we conduct the decomposition via object embedding, which is realized by using external knowledge

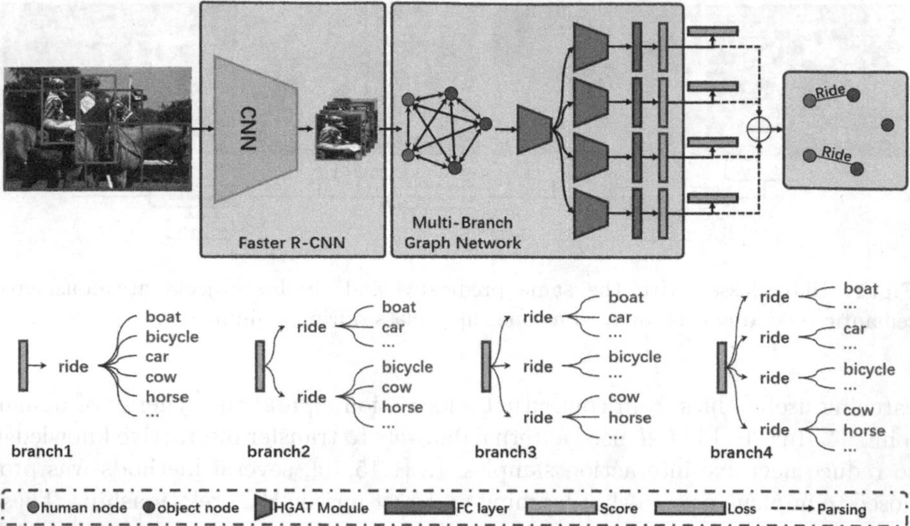

Fig. 2. Overview of our proposed approach. We first detect human/object instances in the input image using Faster R-CNN, then construct a graph with the detected instances and their feature maps. The graph is updated in HGAT (HOI graph attention) module, and fed to multi-branch network. In each branch of the network, the graph is updated again in HGAT module, and then fed to fully connected layers to predict scores for all human-object pairs. Different branches of the network are responsible to HOI classification tasks for different super HOI classes. During the inference stage, the scores of super HOI class are first parsed into HOI scores, and then we get the final HOI scores by averaging the HOI scores.

(appearance, semantic and function of objects). The HOI classes with same predicate and dissimilar objects is decomposed into different semantic groups, and the HOI classes with same predicate and similar objects are merged as one super HOI class (named "sHOI"). Finally, we design a multi-branch graph network for HOI classification, in which each branch network deals with different levels of decomposition.

3.2 Object Embedding

The object embedding aims to measure similarity of features of object classes. Since similar objects often have similar appearances, semantics and functions, we conduct the object embedding by utilizing visual appearance embedding, semantic word embedding and function-driven embedding of object classes. Denote $P = \{p_1, p_2, \ldots, p_m\}$ as the set of predicates and $O = \{o_1, o_2, \ldots, o_n\}$ as the set of object classes. Each HOI class can be represented by a triplet $(human, p_i, o_j), i \in \{1, \ldots, m\}, j \in \{1, \ldots, n\}$.

Visual Appearance Embedding. The inspiration of visual appearance embedding comes from object classification task. Object classification task is actually a correlation problem between visual features and general representation of object classes. An instance is considered as an object class if the feature vector of the instance is highly related to the object classifier parameters. Therefore, we can use parameters of the classifiers from external model as visual appearance embedding for object classes. Specifically, we choose a Faster R-CNN model, which is pre-trained on MS-COCO [13] dataset and contains classifiers for all object classes in O. We extract parameters from the output layer of the model. For each object class $o_i \in O$, the parameters from the corresponding classifier are used as the visual appearance embedding for the object class. We denote f_i^v as the visual appearance embedding of o_i.

Semantic Word Embedding. Word2vec [14] is a model for mapping words to vectors, which is widely used in natural language processing. Word vectors generated by the model have good semantics. In our work, we use the open source word2vec model [17] to generate embeddings for all object classes in O. We denote f_i^w as the semantic word embedding of o_i.

Function-Driven Embedding. Function-driven embedding aims to leverage the object similarity encoded in word vectors, and it uses predefined HOI classes in the public dataset. In our work, we choose the predefined HOI classes in the public HICO-Det dataset. For each $p_i \in P$ and $o_j \in O$, if $(human, p_i, o_j)$ is predefined, then we consider p_i as a function of o_j. The function-driven embedding for each object is a m dimensional multi-hot vector, where 1 represents the object has the function and 0 represents the opposite. We denote f_i^f as the function-driven embedding of o_i.

The object embedding is the combination of the three embeddings as follows:

$$f_i = (norm(f_i^v), norm(f_i^w), norm(f_i^f)) \tag{1}$$

where $norm$ indicates ℓ_2-normalization.

3.3 Multi-branch Network

After conducting object embedding, we use the object embeddings to measure the similarity of object classes to decompose HOI classes with a same predicate into different semantic groups and merge semantic-related HOI classes. We construct a multi-branch network, and apply multi-level sHOI classification tasks with multiple levels of decomposition with different granularities. In the following sections, we first introduce the multiple levels of sHOI, then introduce the branches of the network, and finally introduce the training and inference process.

Multiple Levels of sHOI. After obtaining the object embedding set $F = \{f_1, f_2, \ldots, f_n\}$, we cluster it into k clusters using Euclidean distance. Objects in the same cluster are considered highly similar, the same predicate applied to dissimilar objects is considered to have different semantics, and it is decomposed into different groups. The clustering has to be done only once before training. Considering that one decomposition strategy can lead to over-decomposing or under-decomposing for some predicates, we select multiple k values, and adopt multiply levels of decomposition with different granularities. We denote $K = \{k_1, k_2, \ldots, k_b\}$ as the set of cluster numbers, where b is the number of branches. For each $k \in K$, we construct a label transformation matrix $T_k \in \mathbb{R}^{c_k * c_O}$ where c_O is the number of HOI classes and c_k is the number of sHOI classification of k_{th} branch. The $t_{ij} \in T_k$ denotes the (i, j)-th entry of the matrix, and $t_{ij} = 1$ means that the i_{th} sHOI class contains the j_{th} HOI class while $t_{ij} = 0$ means opposite.

Branches of Network. Each branch network consists of a HGAT (HOI graph attention) module and two fully connected layers. The dimension of the first fully connected layer is 1024, while the dimension of the second fully connected layer is related to the number of sHOI classification in the branch. The branches are independent of each other, and the parameters of different branches are not shared. All branches share the same input. For each input image, we first construct a graph. The graph is updated once in the backbone, and then sent to branches and updated once again in the HGAT module of branches. The purpose is to generate multiple different graphs to fit different levels of sHOI classification tasks. The output of the HGAT module in each branch is a graph, which is parsed into human-object pairs for following inferring. For each human-object pair, we use a concatenation of the human node, the object node and the edge between them and feed it into the two fully connected layers to predict sHOI scores. The differences between different branches are reflected in the output of the branch. For each $k_i \in K$, the i_{th} branch outputs scores for c_i sHOI classes.

Training. During training, we use an average of sHOI losses for all branches and human-object pairs. We denote y_{ij} as the original HOI label for i_{th} human node and j_{th} object node, and $\widehat{y}_{ijk}$ as the output sHOI score of k_{th} branch. The total loss function is:

$$Loss = \frac{1}{n_h * n_o * n_k} \sum_{i=1}^{n_h} \sum_{j=1}^{n_o} \sum_{k=1}^{n_k} FL(T_k * y_{ij}, \widehat{y}_{ijk}) \tag{2}$$

where n_h, n_o and n_k is the number of human nodes, object nodes and branches, and FL is a sigmoid cross entropy function with focal loss [12].

Inference. During the inference stage, we first parse sHOI scores into HOI scores, and then average them as the final outputs for each human-object pair. Formally, the final HOI score is represented as:

$$S_{ij} = s_i^h * s_j^o * \frac{1}{n_k} \sum_{k=1}^{n_k} (T_k^{\mathrm{T}} * \widehat{y}_{ijk}) \tag{3}$$

where s_i^h and s_j^o are the detection confidence of the human and the object.

3.4 Graph Network

In the graph, we use nodes to represent instances and edges to represents spatial layouts. The information of instances comes from off-the-shelf detection model, and has been processed to fit the graph structure. In the graph update process, we refer to the graph attention mechanism [20] and make improvements. We call the updating method HGAT. We will first introduce the process of graph construction, then introduce the HGAT module.

Graph Construction. Given an image, we first detect all instances in it. Each instance is represented by a bounding box and a class annotation, and used to build a graph node. We use a Faster R-CNN with ResNet-50 [8] backbone, and use the output convolutional feature map of res4 block to build nodes. For each bounding box, we crop the region, pass it through a ROI-Pooling layer, a residual block, and an Average-Pooling layer. The residual block is the res5 block of ResNet-50. After these, each instance is embedded as a vector. Considering incorrect or incomplete detection results, we add an extra node which takes the entire feature map as content to ensure the integrity of the contextual information. For convenience, the extra node is considered the same as the other instance nodes. We add directed edges to any two nodes to form a fully connected graph. Each edge is a spatial embedding representing the spatial layout between the connected node pairs. We denote $B_i = (x_1^i, y_1^i, x_2^i, y_2^i)$ and $B_j = (x_1^j, y_1^j, x_2^j, y_2^j)$ as two bounding boxes of nodes, and $B_u = (x_1^u, y_1^u, x_2^u, y_2^u)$ as the smallest union bounding box containing the two bounding boxes. Here (x_1, y_1) is the top-left corner coordinate and (x_2, y_2) is the bottom-right corner coordinate. The spatial embedding of the node pair is:

$$f_{sp} = FC\left(\frac{x_1^i}{W^u}, \frac{y_1^i}{H^u}, \frac{x_2^i}{W^u}, \frac{y_2^i}{H^u}, \frac{x_1^j}{W^u}, \frac{y_1^j}{H^u}, \frac{x_2^j}{W^u}, \frac{y_2^j}{H^u}, \frac{A^i}{A^u}, \frac{A^j}{A^u}, \right.$$
$$\left. \frac{A^i}{A^I}, \frac{A^j}{A^I}, \frac{x_1^i - x_1^j}{x_2^j - x_1^j}, \frac{y_1^i - y_1^j}{y_2^j - y_1^j}, \log\frac{x_2^i - x_1^i}{x_2^j - x_1^j}, \log\frac{y_2^i - y_1^i}{y_2^j - y_1^j}\right) \tag{4}$$

where W^u, H^u are the width and height of union bounding box, A^i and A^j are the area of the two bounding boxes, A^u and A^I are the area of the union bounding box and the input image. The FC represents two fully connected layers with 256 and 512 dimensions.

HGAT Module. Denote $G = (V, E)$ as the graph. V is the set containing N nodes, and $v_i \in V, i \in \{1, 2, ..., N\}$ is the i_{th} node vector. E is the set of edges, and $e_{ij} \in E, i \in \{1, 2, ..., N\}, j \in \{1, 2, ..., N\}, i \neq j$ is the directed edge from v_i to v_j represented by the spatial embedding of the node pair. At each iteration k, we first compute the hidden state of nodes, then calculate an adjacency matrix, and finally use the adjacency matrix to update nodes. We denote d_v^k and d_e^k as the dimensions of nodes and edges in k_{th} iteration. The hidden state of node is as:

$$h_i^k = W_1^k * v_i^k \tag{5}$$

where $W_1 \in \mathbb{R}^{d_v^{k+1} * d_v^k}$ is learnable parameters achieved through a fully connected layer without bias. The calculation of the adjacency matrix A takes node pair features and edge features as input:

$$a_{ij} = leaky\_relu(W_2^k * (h_i^k, h_j^k, e_{ij}^k) + b_2^k) \tag{6}$$

$$A_{ij} = \frac{\exp(a_{ij})}{\sum_{d=1,d\neq i}^{N} \exp(a_{id})} \tag{7}$$

where $W_2 \in \mathbb{R}^{2d_v^{k+1}+d_e^k}$ and $b_2^k \in \mathbb{R}^1$ are learnable parameters achieved through a fully connected layer, and A_{ij} is the (i,j)-th entry of the adjacency matrix. Finally, the nodes are updated by:

$$v_i^{k+1} = relu(W_3^k * v_i^k + b_3^k) + \sum_{j=1,j\neq i}^{N} relu(A_{ij} * h_j^k + b_1^k) \tag{8}$$

where $b_1^k \in \mathbb{R}^{d_v^{k+1}}$ is a learnable bias, $W_3^k \in \mathbb{R}^{d_v^{k+1} * d_v^k}$ and $b_3^k \in \mathbb{R}^{d_v^{k+1}}$ are learnable parameters achieved through a fully connected layer.

4 Experiments

In order to verify the effectiveness of our proposed network, we evaluate it on the large-scale HICO-Det dataset. In this section, we introduce experimental details including dataset and evaluate metric, implement details, comparison with state-of-the-art methods and ablation study.

4.1 Dataset and Evaluate Metric

Dataset. HICO-Det is a dataset containing 80 object classes, 117 predicate classes and 600 HOI classes. Each HOI is annotated with a human bounding box, an object bounding box, and binary labels for HOI classes. It has the same 80 object classes as MS-COCO.

Evaluation Metrics. Following the standard settings in HICO-Det, we use mean average precision (mAP) as the evaluation metrics. A HOI detection is considered a true positive if both the human overlap IOU_h and object overlap IOU_o are greater than 0.5. In default HOI experiments, we reported performances for three different HOI sets: (a) all 600 classes (Full), (b) 138 classes with less than 10 training samples (Rare), and (c) the remaining 462 classes with more than 10 training samples (Non-Rare).

4.2 Implementation Details

Training Data Preparation. We use a Faster R-CNN which is pre-trained on MS-COCO dataset as the object detector. All instances with confidence over 0.8 are reserved. For each human-object pair, we match it with the HOI annotations in the dataset. If both the human overlap IOU_h and object overlap IOU_o are greater than 0.5 and the object classes are same, we apply the annotation to the pair. Mismatched pairs are considered to be negative samples for all HOI classes, and unmatched annotations are added to the training dataset as new pairs.

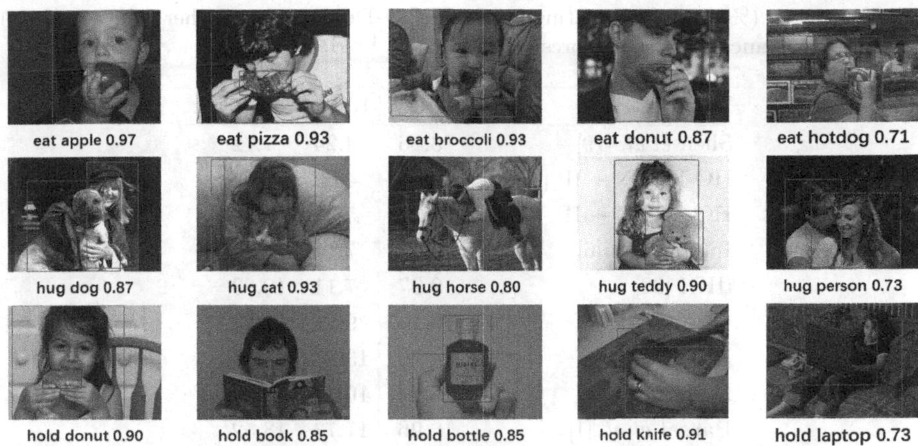

Fig. 3. HOI detection results on HICO-Det test images. Human and objects are shown in red and blue rectangles, respectively. (Color figure online)

Network. In the graph construction step, We fix the Res1-4 block during training. For each instance, we first crop the region from the outputs of Res4 block, then resize it to $14 * 14$ and pool to $7 * 7$. All feature maps of instances are sent to the following residual block, which is initialized with the parameters of the Res5 block. Nodes in the initial graph are of 2048 dimension, and 1024 dimension in following graph. All α and γ of focal loss are set to 0.8 and 2. In our experiments, we use a four branch network, and the corresponding cluster number is set as $K = \{4, 7, 10, 13\}$.

Training. We train the network for 800K iterations on the HICO-Det training set with a learning rate of 0.001, a batch size of 1, a weight decay of 0.0001 and a momentum of 0.9. All experiments are implemented on a single NVIDIA 1080Ti GPU.

4.3 Comparison with State-of-the-Art Methods

We compare our model with several state-of-the-art HOI detection approaches. As shown in Table 1, we achieve 20.45% for full classes, 16.78% for rare classes and 21.54% for non-rare classes, which outperforms all existing works. It shows that our proposed method has a good learning ability for learning human-object interaction. This is mainly because decomposing predicate into several semantic groups decrease the intra-class variance, and merging semantic-related HOI classes increases the available number of training samples of each class. This not only avoids the negative effects for feature and predicate classifier learning caused by the predicate ambiguity, but also turns ambiguity into useful information for enhancing model learning. Figure 3 shows some HOI detection results.

4.4 Ablation Study

In this section, we provide further analysis of our proposed method from the two aspects, merging semantic-related HOI classes and the number of branches. We

Table 1. mAP (%) in default setting for the HICO-Det dataset. Higher values indicate better performance. The best scores are marked in bold.

Methods	Full	Rare	Non-rare
Shen *et al.* [19]	6.46	4.24	7.12
HO-RCNN + IP [2]	7.30	4.68	8.08
HO-RCNN + IP + S [2]	7.81	5.37	8.54
InteractNet [6]	9.94	7.16	10.77
iHOI [22]	9.97	7.11	10.83
GPNN [16]	13.11	9.34	14.23
Xu *et al.* [23]	14.70	13.26	15.13
iCAN [5]	14.84	10.45	16.15
Bansal *et al.* [1]	16.96	11.73	18.52
Gupta *et al.* [7]	17.18	12.17	18.68
Interactiveness prior [11]	17.22	13.51	18.32
Peyre *et al.* [15]	19.40	15.40	20.75
Ours	**20.45**	**16.78**	**21.54**

Table 2. mAP (%) in the ablation study of our proposed method. A single branch network without HOI merging are used as baseline. The number in () represents cluster number, and (+) represents multi-branch.

Methods	Full	Rare	Non-rare
baseline	15.26	10.05	16.82
baseline+(4)	19.15	13.99	20.69
baseline+(4+7)	20.16	16.12	21.36
baseline+(4+7+10)	20.30	16.22	21.52
baseline+(4+7+10+13)	**20.45**	**16.78**	**21.54**

use a single branch network without HOI graph attention and HOI merging as baseline. Table 2 shows the details of results.

Effect of Merging Semantic-Related HOI Classes. We investigate the influence of merge semantic-related HOI classes on the model performance. From Table 2, we can see that this method improves 19.15% − 15.26% = 3.89%, 13.99% − 10.05% = 3.94% and 20.69% − 16.82% = 3.87% on the three HOI sets. It is a significant improvement. This shows that redefine the classification classes is a key to solve the HOI task.

Effect of Number of Branches. We investigate the influence of the number of branches. From the results in Table 2, we can see that multi-branch network have better performance than single-branch network. Using multi-branch network achieves 20.45%−19.15 = 1.30%, 16.78 −13.99% = 2.79% and 21.54%−20.69% =

0.85% improvement on the three HOI sets. The improvement are considerable, especially for the Rare classes. This confirms our idea that combining multiple levels of decomposition with different granularities can provide richer auxiliary information which leads to better performance.

5 Conclusion

In this paper, we propose a novel multi-branch graph network for learning human-object interaction. In order to resolve the data sparsity issue and data variance issue in HOI learning, we decompose HOI classes of a same predicate into several semantic groups and merge semantic-related HOI classes based on the appearance, semantic information and function of the objects. In the graph network, we adopt multiple levels of decompositions in different granularities, and each branch corresponds to one level decomposition. We evaluate this network on HICO-Det dataset, and achieve state-of-the-art performance. We hope that our work can provide reference for future research.

Acknowledgement. This work is supported by National Key Research and Development Project Grant, Grant/Award Number: 2018AAA0100802.

References

1. Bansal, A., Rambhatla, S.S., Shrivastava, A., Chellappa, R.: Detecting human-object interactions via functional generalization. arXiv preprint arXiv:1904.03181 (2019)
2. Chao, Y.W., Liu, Y., Liu, X., Zeng, H., Deng, J.: Learning to detect human-object interactions. In: 2018 IEEE Winter Conference on Applications of Computer Vision (WACV), pp. 381–389. IEEE (2018)
3. Chao, Y.W., Wang, Z., He, Y., Wang, J., Deng, J.: HICO: a benchmark for recognizing human-object interactions in images. In: Proceedings of the IEEE International Conference on Computer Vision, pp. 1017–1025 (2015)
4. Fang, H.S., Cao, J., Tai, Y.W., Lu, C.: Pairwise body-part attention for recognizing human-object interactions. In: Proceedings of the European Conference on Computer Vision (ECCV), pp. 51–67 (2018)
5. Gao, C., Zou, Y., Huang, J.B.: iCAN: instance-centric attention network for human-object interaction detection. arXiv preprint arXiv:1808.10437 (2018)
6. Gkioxari, G., Girshick, R., Dollár, P., He, K.: Detecting and recognizing human-object interactions. In: Proceedings of the IEEE Conference on Computer Vision and Pattern Recognition, pp. 8359–8367 (2018)
7. Gupta, T., Schwing, A., Hoiem, D.: No-frills human-object interaction detection: factorization, layout encodings, and training techniques. In: Proceedings of the IEEE International Conference on Computer Vision, pp. 9677–9685 (2019)
8. He, K., Zhang, X., Ren, S., Sun, J.: Deep residual learning for image recognition. In: Proceedings of the IEEE Conference on Computer Vision and Pattern Recognition, pp. 770–778 (2016)
9. Kipf, T.N., Welling, M.: Semi-supervised classification with graph convolutional networks. arXiv preprint arXiv:1609.02907 (2016)

10. Krishna, R., et al.: Visual genome: connecting language and vision using crowdsourced dense image annotations. Int. J. Comput. Vis. **123**(1), 32–73 (2017). https://doi.org/10.1007/s11263-016-0981-7
11. Li, Y.L., et al.: Transferable interactiveness knowledge for human-object interaction detection. In: Proceedings of the IEEE Conference on Computer Vision and Pattern Recognition, pp. 3585–3594 (2019)
12. Lin, T.Y., Goyal, P., Girshick, R., He, K., Dollár, P.: Focal loss for dense object detection. In: Proceedings of the IEEE International Conference on Computer Vision, pp. 2980–2988 (2017)
13. Lin, T.-Y., et al.: Microsoft COCO: common objects in context. In: Fleet, D., Pajdla, T., Schiele, B., Tuytelaars, T. (eds.) ECCV 2014. LNCS, vol. 8693, pp. 740–755. Springer, Cham (2014). https://doi.org/10.1007/978-3-319-10602-1_48
14. Mikolov, T., Sutskever, I., Chen, K., Corrado, G.S., Dean, J.: Distributed representations of words and phrases and their compositionality. In: Advances in Neural Information Processing Systems, pp. 3111–3119 (2013)
15. Peyre, J., Laptev, I., Schmid, C., Sivic, J.: Detecting unseen visual relations using analogies. arXiv preprint arXiv:1812.05736 (2018)
16. Qi, S., Wang, W., Jia, B., Shen, J., Zhu, S.C.: Learning human-object interactions by graph parsing neural networks. In: Proceedings of the European Conference on Computer Vision (ECCV), pp. 401–417 (2018)
17. Řehůřek, R., Sojka, P.: Software framework for topic modelling with large corpora. In: Proceedings of the LREC 2010 Workshop on New Challenges for NLP Frameworks, pp. 45–50. ELRA, Valletta, May 2010. http://is.muni.cz/publication/884893/en
18. Ren, S., He, K., Girshick, R., Sun, J.: Faster R-CNN: towards real-time object detection with region proposal networks. In: Advances in Neural Information Processing Systems, pp. 91–99 (2015)
19. Shen, L., Yeung, S., Hoffman, J., Mori, G., Fei-Fei, L.: Scaling human-object interaction recognition through zero-shot learning. In: 2018 IEEE Winter Conference on Applications of Computer Vision (WACV), pp. 1568–1576. IEEE (2018)
20. Veličković, P., Cucurull, G., Casanova, A., Romero, A., Lio, P., Bengio, Y.: Graph attention networks. arXiv preprint arXiv:1710.10903 (2017)
21. Wang, S., Cheng, Z., Deng, X., Chang, L., Duan, F., Lu, K.: Leveraging 3D blendshape for facial expression recognition using CNN. Sci. China Inf. Sci **63** (2020). Article number: 120114. https://doi.org/10.1007/s11432-019-2747-y
22. Xu, B., Li, J., Wong, Y., Zhao, Q., Kankanhalli, M.S.: Interact as you intend: Intention-driven human-object interaction detection. IEEE Trans. Multimed. **22**(6), 1423–1432 (2019)
23. Xu, B., Wong, Y., Li, J., Zhao, Q., Kankanhalli, M.S.: Learning to detect human-object interactions with knowledge. In: Proceedings of the IEEE Conference on Computer Vision and Pattern Recognition (2019)
24. Yang, J., Lu, J., Lee, S., Batra, D., Parikh, D.: Graph R-CNN for scene graph generation. In: Proceedings of the European Conference on Computer Vision (ECCV), pp. 670–685 (2018)
25. Yang, Z., Qin, Z., Yu, J., Hu, Y.: Scene graph reasoning with prior visual relationship for visual question answering. arXiv preprint arXiv:1812.09681 (2018)
26. Zhuang, B., Wu, Q., Shen, C., Reid, I., van den Hengel, A.: HCVRD: a benchmark for large-scale human-centered visual relationship detection. In: Thirty-Second AAAI Conference on Artificial Intelligence (2018)

FDEA: Face Dataset with Ethnicity Attribute

Jun Chen, Ting Liu, Fu-Zhao Ou, and Yuan-Gen Wang(✉)

School of Computer Science and Cyber Engineering, Guangzhou University, Guangzhou 510006, China
wangyg@gzhu.eud.cn

Abstract. Face attributes play an important role in face-related applications. However, existing face attributes (such as expression, age, and skin color) are subject to change. The ethnicity attribute is precious due to its invariance over time, but has not been developed well. This is partly because there is no large enough dataset and labeled accurately with ethnicity attribute. This paper proposes a new Face Dataset with Ethnicity Attribute (FDEA), intended for ethnicity recognition benchmark. For this purpose, we first collect an initial face dataset from CelebA and LFWA [10], MORPH [13], UTKFace [20], FairFace [8], and the web. The samples extracted from CelebA are not labeled with ethnicity attribute. To this end, we employ nine annotators to label these samples from CelebA, while cleaning the remaining samples manually. Finally, our FDEA contains 157,801 samples and is divided into three classes: Caucasian (54,438), Asian (61,522), and African (41,841). Moreover, we carry out a benchmark experiment by testing eight mainstream backbones on the proposed FDEA. The baseline results of the three-classification accuracy are all over 0.92. FDEA is publicly available at https://github.com/GZHU-DVL/FDEA.

Keywords: Face dataset · Deep convolution neural network · Ethnicity classification

1 Introduction

With the emergence of big data and the rapid development of hardware, deep learning has made tremendous progress. Deep learning algorithms have been successfully applied in various fields, such as video surveillance, object detection, and biometric recognition. In biometric recognition, more and more researchers have drawn their attention to face-related studies since face images contain salient and unique biometric information. These studies include face detection [4,19], face recognition on gender [1,3,5,12], face attribute classification [9,16], and so on. To enable these studies, a number of face datasets have been created, such as MegaFace [11] and IMDB-WIKI [14] for face recognition, and CelebA and LFWA [10], MORPH [13], UTKFace [20], FairFace [8], RFW [17] and WFLW

© Springer Nature Switzerland AG 2021
H. Ma et al. (Eds.): PRCV 2021, LNCS 13022, pp. 437–446, 2021.
https://doi.org/10.1007/978-3-030-88013-2_36

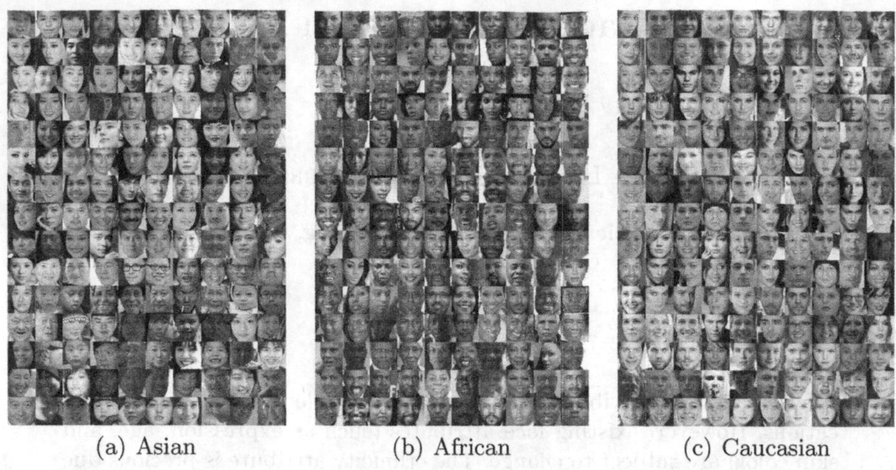

(a) Asian (b) African (c) Caucasian

Fig. 1. Illustration of random samples from our FDEA dataset.

[18] for face attribute classification. All of these datasets are labeled with various face attributes. These face attributes include age, gender, race, eyeglasses, pointy nose, wearing lipstick, beard, narrow eyes, blurry, big lips, smiling, and so on, which play a vital role in face-related applications. Among these attributes, the ethnicity attribute is critical due to its merit of invariance over time. Unfortunately, there is little focus on ethnic attribute to date.

For example, CelebA [10] is a large-scale dataset with 202,599 face images, each of which is labeled with 40 attributes, such as hair, oval face, pale skin, pointy nose, beard, and high cheekbones. However, it lacks the ethnicity label. Unlike CelebA, the LFWA dataset [10] is annotated with 73 face attributes, including a specific race attribute. The non-commercial release of MORPH [13] consists of 55,000 unique images of more than 13,000 subjects. This dataset records four ethnicity categories including African, European, Asian, and Hispanic. However, the distribution of the four categories is hugely unbalanced. UTKFace [20] consists of over 20,000 face images in the wild, and is labeled by age, gender, and race. Their race includes White, Black, Asian, Indian, and Others. We notice that this dataset contains 8,493 White and only 2,387 Asian. Hence, it is also an unbalanced dataset. FairFace [8] contains 108,501 images with an emphasis on balanced race composition. As far as we know, FairFace is the largest dataset with race annotation so far. However, the experimental results on the FairFace dataset show that the accuracy of race classification is somewhat low. This implies that the race annotation in FairFace might not be accurate. For the sake of comparison, the details of the above-reviewed datasets are illustrated in Table 1. It is essential for ethnicity classification tasks to create a large-scale dataset with balanced ethnicity categories and accurately annotated ethnicity attribute. It becomes a significant reason that motivates us to carry out this work.

Table 1. Statistics of race attribute datasets.

Dataset	Source	# of faces	White	Asian	Black	Balanced?
MORPH [13]	Public Data	55,000	Yes	Yes	Yes	No
IMDB-WIKI [14]	IMDB, WIKI	523,051	No	No	No	No
CelebA [10]	CelebFace, LFW	202,599	No	No	No	No
LFWA [10]	LFW (Newspapers)	13,143	Yes	Yes	Yes	No
UTKFace [20]	MORPH, CACD Web	23,708	Yes	Yes	Yes	No
FairFace [8]	Flicker, Twitter, Web	108,501	Yes	Yes	Yes	Yes

This paper proposes a new Face Dataset with Ethnicity Attribute (FDEA) emphasizing the amount, balance, and accurate annotation. FDEA contains 157,801 face images, which, to our best knowledge, is the largest scale face image dataset with ethnicity attributes. FDEA defines three ethnic groups: Caucasian (54,438), Asian (61,522), and African (41,841). The numbers of samples in the three ethnic groups are in good balance. As shown in Fig. 1, we can observe that these three ethnic groups have distinctive features. That is: 1) Asian is often characterized by yellowish buff skins, straight black hair, and high cheekbones. It mainly includes Southeast Asians in Southeast Asia, East Asians in the East, and Indians in the continent of North and South America. 2) Unlike Asians, dark skins, small curly black hair, thick and protruding lips are the significant African features. African is generally divided into two types: South Africa (sub-Saharan Africa) and North Africa. 3) The main feature with pale skins, blonde hair, blue eyes, and the Roman nose appears in Caucasians, who are initially distributed in Europe. After a long period of evolution and settlement, they spread to North Africa, West Asia, Central Asia, South Asia, whole Oceania, and North and South America. With this clear definition [2], our ethnicity annotation can be more accurately performed compared with the existing ethnicity annotations. Eight mainstream backbones are tested on FDEA and achieve over 0.92 classification accuracy.

The rest of this paper is organized as follows. In Sect. 2, we present the construction process of FDEA in detail. Section 3 provides several baseline experiments, followed by our conclusion in Sect. 4.

2 Proposed FDEA

2.1 Images Extracted from CelebA and Annotation

It is well known that CelebA has been widely used in face recognition. It contains many face attributes. Unfortunately, some valuable attributes are not yet annotated in CelebA, such as ethnicity and brown eyes. These attributes are generally very robust in an unconstrained environment. In this paper, we adopt the manual annotation to pick out three types of face images from the CelebA dataset according to the definition of ethnicity attribute. These three ethnic

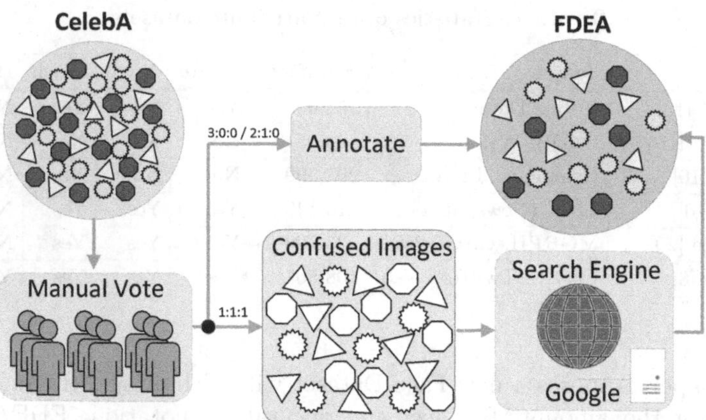

Fig. 2. Pipeline of extracting samples from CelebA. Here, the ratio represents the number of votes that a specific ethnicity obtains. For instance, 3:0:0 and 2:1:0 indicate that the image belongs to a particular class with a majority vote, while 1:1:1 indicates that the votes of three annotators are different from each other and thus the image is considered as a confusing image.

classes are Asian, African, and Caucasian. We employ nine annotators (students and staff from the university), who have been instructed with an hour tutorial of facial knowledge on ethnicity for face ethnicity annotation assignment, to classify the face images into the most apparent one of three classes. However, it is too labor-intensive and expensive for one person to annotate the overall dataset. Therefore, we divide this dataset into three parts. Each part contains the same number of images, namely 67,533 images. Then, each part is assigned to every three annotators. For each image, annotators need to take about five seconds to judge. If three or two annotators recognize an image as the same class, this image is annotated as an ethnicity ground truth. If three annotators do not agree on the class of an image, we use the online mapping engine to determine its class further. This kind of images is considered as confusing images in this paper. The detailed process is shown in Fig. 2.

For the above-mentioned confusing images (about two thousand images), we further use the online mapping engine to judge their class. We first upload the images with 1:1:1 vote onto the Google images engine[1] to grant the identities of the confusing images. Then we can further determine their ethnicity based on the information from Wikipedia[2]. Our strategy is based on the fact that humans are always subjective in the classification judgment task. In other words, there must be some biases towards the ethnic class of a face image. For example, a facial image with a Roman nose may be easily divided into Caucasian, and a man with dark skin is naturally considered as African. In fact, the Roman nose is also presented in some Asians. Therefore, the judgment of an ethnicity attribute

[1] https://www.google.com/imghp.

[2] https://www.wikipedia.org.

Fig. 3. Wrong annotated images in three categories. Here, noise images mean non-facial ones. We delete all of them during data cleaning. (a) Misclassified images in Asians. (b) Misclassified images in African. (c) Misclassified images in Caucasians. (d) Noise images.

should refer to multiple features. Besides, we think that it is not very meaningful if a mixed-race individual is deemed to be the fourth class (i.e. other class) except for our three main classes, as done in MORPH [13] and UTKFace [20]. This is because even if a mixed-race is classified to the fourth class, we still do not know which races are mixed. In other words, the fourth class does not provide helpful information for race recognition applications. Therefore, for a mixed-race face, we classify it into one of three main classes according to its salient race feature.

Finally, we converge the three parts as the first ingredient of our dataset with ethnicity ground truth. The first ingredient includes 30,152 images from CelebA, and the numbers of Caucasian, Asian, and African are 10,358, 9,852, and 9,924, respectively.

2.2 Image Collection from Annotated Datasets

Some DCNNs such as ResNet101 [7] and DenseNet161 are apt to result in overfitting problems when being trained on small-scale datasets. We notice that the number of samples extracted from CelebA is insufficient to train these deep and broad networks. To construct a larger scale dataset for deep learning, we focus on the annotated face datasets with race attribute. There have been some mainstream datasets such as LFWA [10], FairFace [8], UTKFace [20], and MORPH [13], which are all labeled with race attribute. Next, we extract face image samples from these four datasets.

First of all, we collect face images from LFWA [10]. The images labeled with White, Asian, or Black attribute are output to three categories, respectively. However, we find that the label file provided by the authors [10] contains many wrong labels. For instance, a face image is labeled with two different race attributes, and various samples of an identity are labeled with different race attributes. Thus, this is not a well-labeled dataset. We seek out the identities of the problematic annotations, and then all the samples of these identities are discarded. Finally, we get 6,785 face images from LFWA.

As done in LFWA, we then collect face images from the FairFace dataset [8]. Note that all the images in FairFace have no identifications. Hence, the abovementioned problem with LFWA will not appear in FairFace. We only need to collect the images with annotations of three categories according to the label file provided by the authors [8]. After collecting the samples from FairFace, we further collect images from UTKFace [20]. Interestingly, for UTKFace, the labels of each face image are written into its file name. So we can easily categorize images by their ethnicity labels. Nevertheless, some serious problems exist in UTKFace and FairFace, e.g. both the noise images (non-facial image) and misclassified images are also included. We show such bad examples in Fig. 3. Therefore, in order to obtain a high-quality dataset, we decide to delete all these samples manually. Then, we obtain 110,388 images from CelebA, LFWA, FairFace, and UTKFace. And the numbers of Caucasians, Asians, and Africans are 42,622, 38,648, and 28,967, respectively. By now, we notice that the number of the collected African faces is relatively tiny. Hence, we consider one more dataset called MORPH [13], which records subject ethnicity. The non-commercial release of MORPH dataset includes 55,000 unique images of more than 13,000 subjects. Since the MORPH dataset contains nearly four fifths of Africans, we collect more African images from MORPH. After that, we get 130,846 images from CelebA, LFWA, FairFace, UTKFace, and MORPH. And the numbers of Caucasians, Asians, and Africans are 50,206, 38,799, and 41,841, respectively. Note that all the datasets we used in this paper are publicly available for academic study.

2.3 Images Crawled from the Internet

To make the source of face image samples more diverse, we further use crawler technology to collect more face images that are publicly released on the Internet. Note that until now, the number of Asians is not large enough. This is because both the CelebA and LFWA datasets contain a relatively smaller number of Asians. Hence, in this stage, we mainly collect Asian star faces. The detailed strategy is described as follows. First, we get the names of famous stars by querying "star name" in Google search engine[3]. Then the names of Asian stars are manually selected as keywords. Next, we crawl star face images from Bing search engine[4] based on the keywords. Taking the balance of face image samples of each star into consideration, we choose no more than ten face images for each star in a random way. After that, we manually remove the misclassified, too blurred, or obscured face images. In the end, we obtain 26,955 face images from the Internet.

So far, our FDEA dataset consists of 157,801 face images. The details of the composition are shown in Table 2. Note that the sizes of our collected images are not the same, even different in width and height. This is inconvenient for deep learning backbones. To release a more helpful dataset, the size of each face image is aligned to 224 × 224, which is right the input standard of ResNet. To this end, we use the package of Dlib[5] to detect the faces in images with a square box, and then crop them. Finally, all the face images are cropped to 224 × 224 size.

[3] https://www.google.com.

[4] https://www.bing.com.

[5] dlib.net.

Table 2. The composition of our FDEA dataset.

Dataset	Caucasian	Asian	African	Grand total
LFWA	6,006	514	265	6,785
UTKFace	8,493	2,336	4,124	14,953
MORPH	7,584	151	12,874	20,609
CelebA	10,358	9,852	9,942	30,152
FairFace	17,765	25,946	14,636	58,347
Our FDEA	**54,438**	**61,522**	**41,841**	**157,801**

3 Experimental Results

This section shows the advantages of our dataset over the existing race face datasets from the following three aspects. The compared datasets include LFWA [10], MORPH [13], UTKFace [20], and FairFace [8]. First of all, we demonstrate the balance in the numbers of three ethnic categories. The bar chart of all the compared datasets is plotted in Fig. 4(b). We can see from Fig. 4(b) that our FDEA obtains a more balanced ratio of numbers of three ethnic categories than the other four datasets. It can also be observed that MORPH is heavily unbalanced in the three categories, and the ratio of Asians is too small to be present in the bar chart. Besides, we can see that LFWA is highly biased towards Caucasians. Next, we show a visualization result in quantity. The bar chart is shown in Fig. 4(a). It is clear that our FDEA has much more face samples than others. A larger dataset will significantly benefit the training of deeper and wider networks [6,15]. Finally, to provide a benchmark study, several typical networks including ResNet18, ResNet50, ResNet101, DenseNet161, AlexNet, VGG16, MobileNet, and GoogleNet are selected for training and testing. Hyperparameters setup of various DCNNs are listed in Table 3. Three classification accuracies of the four compared datasets are shown in Table 4 and the baseline results on the proposed dataset are shown in Table 5. In the experiment, stochastic gradient descent (SGD) optimization is adopted. Table 4 shows that our FDEA obtains the best balance in three classification accuracy among all the compared datasets. We can also see from Table 5 that most of the mainstream DCNNs on our FDEA can achieve 94% classification accuracy. This indicates that FDEA is suitable for the benchmark study of ethnicity classification based on deep learning.

Table 3. Hyperparameters setup of various DCNNs.

DCNNs	BatchSizes	Learning rate	Epochs
ResNet18	512	10e−3	30
ResNet50	128	10e−3	30
ResNet101	128	10e−3	30
DenseNet161	64	10e−3	30
AlexNet	1024	10e−3	30
VGG16	64	10e−3	30
MobileNet	512	10e−3	30
GoogleNet	256	10e−3	30

Table 4. Three categories accuracies of the compared datasets.

Dataset	Caucasian	Asian	African
LFWA	0.987	0.827	0.729
UTKFace	0.972	0.889	0.939
FairFace	0.939	0.917	0.877
FDEA	0.915	0.960	0.949

Table 5. Baseline results of the mainstream DCNNs on our FDEA.

Networks	ResNet18	ResNet50	ResNet101	DenseNet161	AlexNet	VGG16	MobileNet	GoogleNe
Size (MB)	44.8	94.3	170.6	107.0	228.1	228.1	9.1	22.5
Accuracy	0.943	0.946	0.945	0.950	0.930	0.943	0.923	0.944

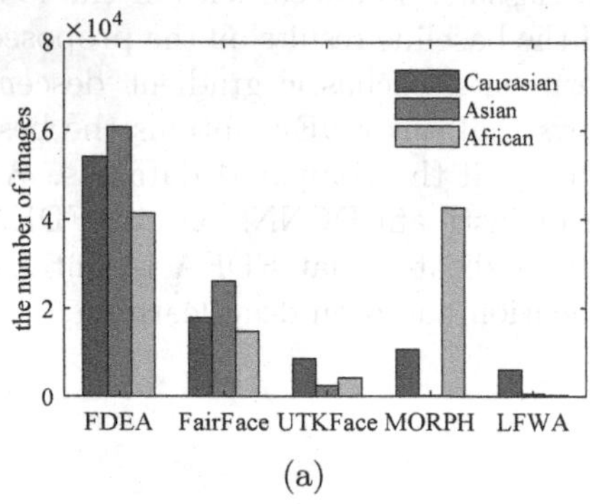

(a)

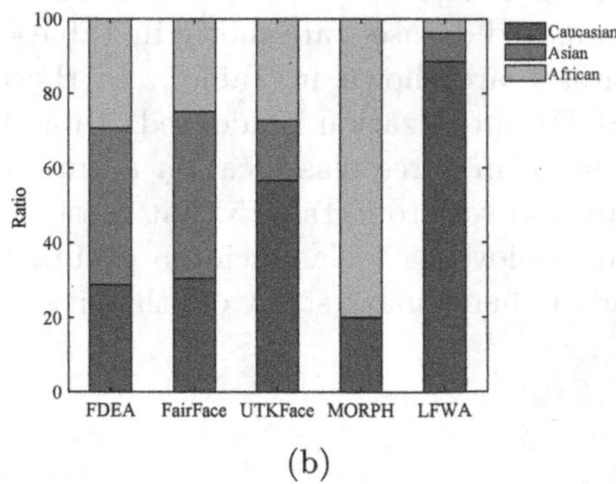

(b)

Fig. 4. (a) Illustration of the dataset scale. Here, the numbers of FDEA, FairFace, UTKFace, MORPH, and LFWA are 157,801, 58,347, 14,953, 20,609, and 6,785 respectively. (b) Illustration of Ratio of three categories in face datsets. Here, the bars from left to right are FDEA, FairFace, UTKFace, MORPH, and LFWA.

4 Conclusion

In this paper, we have created a new Face Dataset with Ethnicity Attributes (FDEA). FDEA contains 54,438 Caucasian images, 61,522 Asian images, and 41,841 African images, adding up to 157,801 face images. In addition, we test the performance of the mainstream DCNNs on FDEA for the benchmark establishment. We believe that the release of FDEA could promote the study of ethnicity classification tasks. The major contributions of the paper can be summarized as follows: 1) To our knowledge, FEDA has been the largest scale face image dataset with ethnicity attributes so far, which can help train the deeper and wider networks. 2) FDEA shows a good balance in the numbers of three categories. This facilitates the establishment of an unbiased model when being trained on the FDEA dataset. 3) FDEA is a high-quality dataset with sophisticated annotation. For this reason, most mainstream backbones tested on the FDEA dataset achieve competitive classification accuracy.

In addition, we notice that several more mixed-race classes would contribute to the identification of ethnic groups. However, identifying a mixed-race class is shown to be highly complex and controversial. For instance, Chinese mixed with Russian look like Caucasian with Chinese features. Which kind of mixed-race classes should it be identified? In this sense, considering a clear three-class is of great interest for an initial and at-a-glance race determination in many face-related applications. In the future, we plan to collect some mixed-race classes and conduct more comprehensive benchmarking experiments.

Acknowledgement. The authors would like to thank Peixin Tian for his help in using online mapping engine for the class judgment on confusing images. This paper is supported in part by the National Natural Science Foundation of China under Grant 61872099, in part by the Science and Technology Program of Guangzhou under Grant 201904010478, and in part by the Scientific Research Project of Guangzhou University under Grant YJ2021004.

References

1. Afifi, M., Abdelhamed, A.: AFIF4: deep gender classification based on AdaBoost-based fusion of isolated facial features and foggy faces. J. Vis. Commun. Image Represent. **62**, 77–86 (2019)
2. Banks, M.: Ethnicity: Anthropological Constructions. Routledge, New York (1996)
3. Boutellaa, E., Hadid, A., Bengherabi, M., Ait-Aoudia, S.: On the use of Kinect depth data for identity, gender and ethnicity classification from facial images. Pattern Recogn. Lett. **68**, 270–277 (2015)
4. Chaudhuri, B., Vesdapunt, N., Wang, B.: Joint face detection and facial motion retargeting for multiple faces. In: Proceedings of the IEEE Conference on Computer Vision and Pattern Recognition (CVPR), pp. 9719–9728 (2019)
5. Das, A., Dantcheva, A., Bremond, F.: Mitigating bias in gender, age and ethnicity classification: a multi-task convolution neural network approach. In: Proceedings of the European Conference on Computer Vision Workshops (ECCVW). pp. 1–13 (2018)

6. Donahue, J., Ji, Y., Vinyals, O., Hoffman, J., Zhang, N., Tzeng, E., Darrell, T.: DeCAF: a deep convolutional activation feature for generic visual recognition. In: Proceedings of the 31st International Conference on Machine Learning (ICML), pp. 647–655 (2013)
7. He, K., Zhang, X., Ren, S., Sun, J.: Deep residual learning for image recognition. In: Proceedings of the IEEE Conference on Computer Vision and Pattern Recognition (CVPR), pp. 770–778 (2016)
8. Karkkainen, K., Joo, J.: FairFace: face attribute dataset for balanced race, gender, and age. arXiv:1908.04913 (2019)
9. Li, S., Deng, W., Du, J.: Reliable crowdsourcing and deep locality-preserving learning for expression recognition in the wild. In: Proceedings of the IEEE Conference on Computer Vision and Pattern Recognition (CVPR), pp. 2852–2861 (2017)
10. Liu, Z., Luo, P., Wang, X., Tang, X.: Deep learning face attributes in the wild. In: Proceedings of the IEEE International Conference on Computer Vision (ICCV), pp. 3730–3738 (2015)
11. Miller, D., Brossard, E., Seitz, S., Kemelmacher-Shlizerman, I.: MegaFace: a million faces for recognition at scale. arXiv:1505.02108 (2019)
12. Narang, N., Bourlai, T.: Gender and ethnicity classification using deep learning in heterogeneous face recognition. In: Proceedings of the IEEE International Conference on Biometrics (ICB), pp. 1–8 (2016)
13. Ricanek, K., Tesafaye, T.: MORPH: a longitudinal image database of normal adult age-progression. In: Proceedings of the 7th International Conference on Automatic Face and Gesture Recognition (FG06), pp. 341–345 (2006)
14. Rothe, R., Timofte, R., Gool, L.V.: DEX: deep expectation of apparent age from a single image. In: Proceedings of the IEEE International Conference on Computer Vision (ICCV), pp. 10–15 (2015)
15. Rothe, R., Timofte, R., Gool, L.V.: Deep expectation of real and apparent age from a single image without facial landmarks. Int. J. Comput. Vis. **126**, 144–157 (2018)
16. Sun, Y., Yu, J.: General-to-specific learning for facial attribute classification in the wild. J. Vis. Commun. Image Represent. **56**, 83–91 (2018)
17. Wang, M., Deng, W., Hu, J., Tao, X., Huang, Y.: Racial faces in the wild: reducing racial bias by information maximization adaptation network. In: Proceedings of the IEEE International Conference on Computer Vision (ICCV), pp. 692–702 (2019)
18. Wu, W., Qian, C., Yang, S., Wang, Q., Cai, Y., Zhou, Q.: Look at boundary: a boundary-aware face alignment algorithm. In: Proceedings of the IEEE Conference on Computer Vision and Pattern Recognition (CVPR), pp. 2129–2138 (2018)
19. Zhang, S., Chi, C., Lei, Z., Li, S.Z.: RefineFace: refinement neural network for high performance face detection. arXiv:1909.04376 (2019)
20. Zhang, Z., Song, Y., Qi, H.: Age progression/regression by conditional adversarial autoencoder. In: Proceedings of the IEEE Conference on Computer Vision and Pattern Recognition (CVPR), pp. 5810–5818 (2017)

TMD-FS: Improving Few-Shot Object Detection with Transformer Multi-modal Directing

Ying Yuan[1,2,3], Lijuan Duan[1,2,3](✉), Wenjian Wang[1,2,3], and Qing En[1,2,3]

[1] Faculty of Information Technology, Beijing University of Technology, Beijing 100124, China
ljduan@bjut.edu.cn

[2] Beijing Key Laboratory of Trusted Computing, Beijing 100124, China

[3] National Engineering Laboratory for Critical Technologies of Information Security Classified Protection, Beijing 100124, China

Abstract. Few-shot object detection (FSOD) is a vital and challenging task in which the aim is to detect unseen object classes with a few annotated samples. However, the discriminative semantic information existing in the new category is not well represented in most existing approaches. To address this issue, we propose a new few-shot object detection model named TMD-FS with Transformer multi-model directing, where the lost discriminative information is mined by adapting multi-modal semantic alignment. Specifically, we transfer the multi-model information into a mixed sequence and map the visual and semantic information into the embedding space. Moreover, we propose a Semantic Visual Transformer (SVT) module to incorporate and align the visual and semantic embedding. Finally, the distance in terms of the visual and semantic embedding is minimized on the basis of the attention loss. Experimental results demonstrate that the performance of the model significantly with few samples. In addition, it achieves state-of-the-art performance when the amount of samples increases.

Keywords: Few shot object detection · Transformer · Multi-modal semantic fusion

1 Introduction

Object detection is one of the most fundamental research problems in the field of computer vision. By fully utilizing accurate box-level annotated training data, existing state-of-the-art approaches have the ability to predict satisfying bounding boxes. However, their performance drops significantly when facing less annotated unseen classes. Consequently, few-show object detection (FSOD) [6,8,9,14,24,26] methods are proposed in tackling the issue. Different from the fully supervised object detection methods, the objective of FSOD is to utilize one or a few annotated samples to detect new classes. Most

© Springer Nature Switzerland AG 2021
H. Ma et al. (Eds.): PRCV 2021, LNCS 13022, pp. 447–458, 2021.
https://doi.org/10.1007/978-3-030-88013-2_37

approaches [22,27] use a large number of labeled classes datasets for pre-training and add a few novel samples to fine tune the model. In this way, the generalization ability of the model can be obtained from only a few new labeled samples.

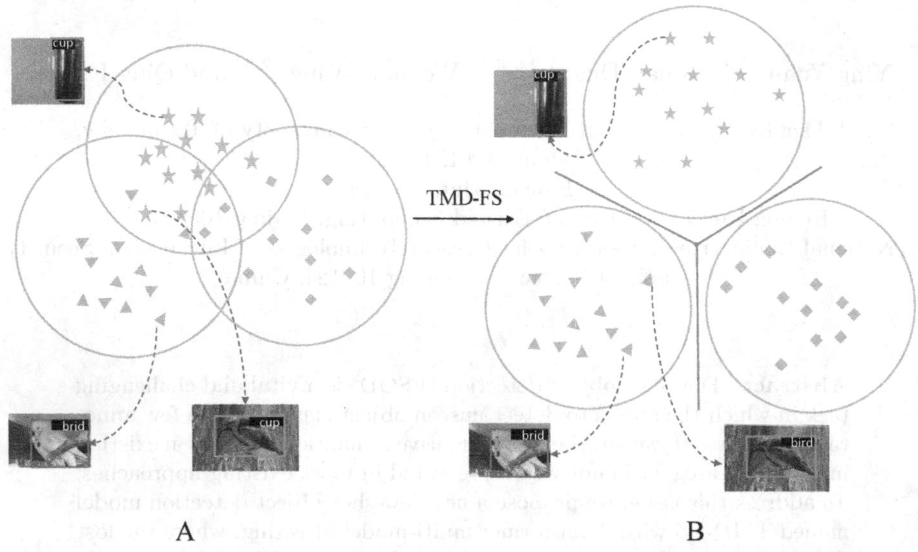

Fig. 1. The variation in object detection results before and after using our TMD-FS. A is the embedding spaces of different categories without the guidance of multi-modal information, and B is the embedding space using TMD-FS.

It is observed that the key reason for misclassification and missed detection in FSOD is that only a few samples of each category cannot cover all the attributes of this category. Most of the existing work [22,27] tends to learn the common attributes of categories on a large number of base class samples, and then transfer them to the novel class samples during the fine-tuning stage. In this way, unseen novel classes can be identified. However, due to the visual diversity of the novel class between test stage and fine-tuning stage, it is easy to cause class confusion. As shown in Fig. 1, when we only use TFA [22] to fine tune the model, the result in A shows that there is intersection between different classes in embedding space. To solve this issue, we introduce semantic information to supplement visual information. The experimental results show that this method can better distinguish different categories.

Inspired by [19,25], word embedding that learned from hundreds of textual datasets is applied as semantic information, which could measure the semantics of various categories effectively. We map visual features and semantic features into the same space by transferring them into the mixed sequence. In order to make better use of semantic information to make up for the lack of visual information, we introduced Transformer [21] to integrate multi-modal information.

The multi-modal information of the mixed sequence is aggregated into fusion block by SVT. Meanwhile, in order to make the word vector guide the visual information as desired, we add an attention loss to guide the learning of SVT.

The contributions of this paper are as follows:

- Proposing a novel few-shot object detection model named TMD-FS by adapting multi-modal semantic alignment for mining the discriminative information.
- Proposing a Semantic and Visual Alignment module (SVA) and a Semantic Visual Transformer module (SVT) to fuse and align the visual and semantic information. Proposing an attention loss to constrain the visual and semantic embedding.
- Gaining outstanding performance using the TMD-FS on two datasets: PASCAL VOC dataset [5] and Microsoft COCO dataset [11].

2 Related Work

At present, the previous few-shot object detection is mostly based on the traditional object detection models, such as SSD [12], YOLO series [1,15–17], Faster RCNN [18] and DETR [2,28] etc. FSOD are mostly based on meta learning method and fine-tuning method. Meta learning [20,23] mainly constructs support set and query set to form meta task when data is loaded. The model trained on a large number of meta tasks has generalization ability when facing the meta task composed of novel classes. Meta R-CNN [26] combines Faster RCNN [18] with meta learning [20] to locate and classify. Due to the large maneuverability of the fine-tuning method [22,24], great progress has been made at present. TFA [22] makes the fine-tuning approach for FSOD go beyond the meta learning method. [22] keeps the entire feature extractor of Faster RCNN [18] fixed during the fine-tuning stage, only fine-tuning the box classification and regression networks. It can be found that the method of fine-tuning by freezing parameters can achieve higher accuracy, and the operation is relatively simple. Therefore, we use the method of fine-tuning to train TMD-FS.

3 Methodology

In this section, we mainly introduce the proposed TMD-FS based on Transformer [21] with multi-modal information fusion. TMD-FS is built on Faster RCNN [18], as shown in Fig. 2. Firstly, in order to align the visual feature and the semantic feature, we design the Semantic and Visual Alignment (SVA) module. SVA maps the base feature obtained by backbone and the word embedding to the same space to obtain a mixed sequence. Then, Semantic Visual Transformer (SVT) is the fusion module that converges the multi-modal information of the mixed sequence into the fusion block. The RPN module processes the V-S feature generated by the fusion block to generate regional proposals, which generates the ROI feature through the ROI module. Finally, the ROI feature is classified and regressed by connecting two full connection layers.

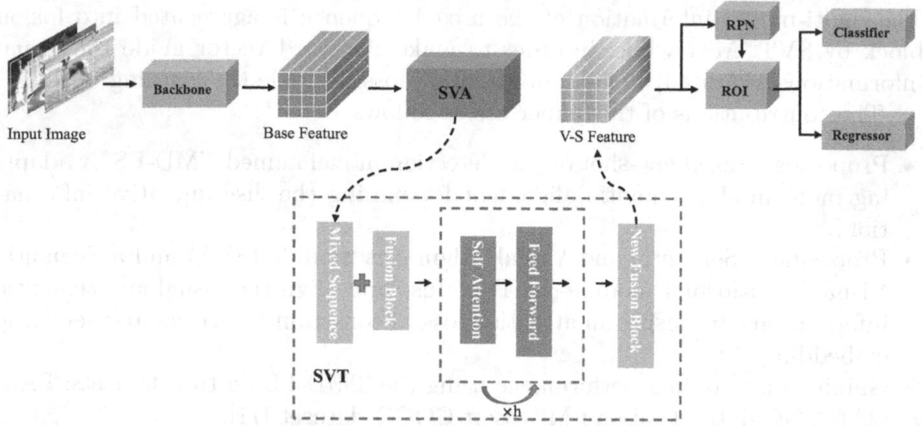

Fig. 2. The framework of TMD-FS

3.1 FSOD Fine-Tuning

Our TMD-FS is based on a fine-tuning method. We pre-train the network on an abundant labeled dataset D_{base}, which derives from the public dataset and contains only base classes. The pre-training stage is similar to the traditional object detection training. After that, the model initially has the ability to extract and classify detection boxes. Then the model is fine-tuned using a few-shot dataset D_{novel}, which contains not only the pre-trained base classes but also the unseened novel classes. Because the base class instances are far more than the novel class instances, we randomly sampled K instances from each base class and novel class respectively for K shot fine-tuning, K is 1, 2, 3, 5, 10. Inspired by [22], the backbone, RPN and ROI module parameters are class-generic. Hence, we frozen them during the fine-tuning stage and only fine tune the SVT and the last layers of the detection model (the box classification and regression networks).

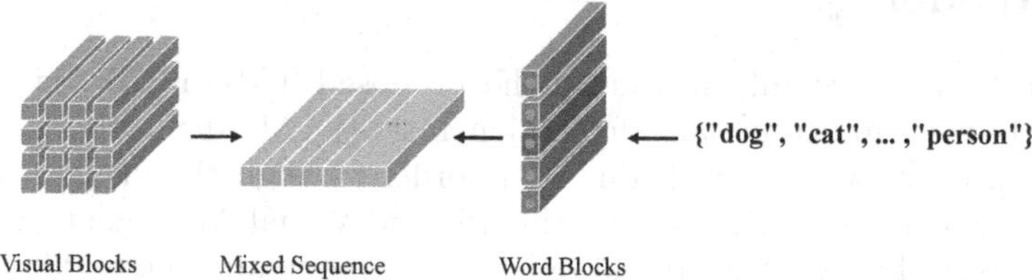

Fig. 3. SVA module

3.2 Semantic and Visual Alignment (SVA)

In order to align visual and semantic information effectively, we map them into the same space. The Semantic and Visual Alignment (SVA) module is shown in Fig. 3. Firstly, we get word embeddings $S \in R^{N \times C}$ from hundreds of text datasets by using GloVe [13], where N is the number of classes(including background to help distinguish objects from background), C is word embedding dimension. In order to acquire word blocks $W_S \in R^{N \times (1^2 \times D)}$, where 1×1 is the size of a word block and D is channel of base feature, we use the full connection layer to map C to D. Then, we take the base feature $V \in R^{D \times H \times W}$ obtained by backbone as the visual feature, where D, H and W represent channel, height and weight respectively. We can obtain visual blocks $V_S \in R^{P \times (1^2 \times D)}$ by rearranging V, $P = H \times W$ is the number of visual blocks. Finally, we concatenate W_S and V_S to get a mixed sequence $M \in R^{(P+N) \times D}$.

The mixed sequence obtained above is similar to the token embedding of VIT [4] network. The difference is that we do not process the 2D image directly but handle the base feature obtained through the backbone. Because the base feature already contains the location attribute, linear mapping or location information in VIT [4] network is not necessary. In this way, the mixed sequence is transferred to SVT (Semantic Visual Transformer) module for further attention fusion.

3.3 Semantic Visual Transformer (SVT)

In order to make word embedding more targeted to guide the visual feature, we propose a Semantic Visual Transformer (SVT) module for attention fusion. As shown in Fig. 4, we add an additional fusion block $F \in R^{1 \times (1^2 \times D)}$ to aggregate all the visual features and word embeddings information. Meanwhile, the mixed sequence M obtained by the SVA module combined with F is normalized and input into multi-head self-attention together. The number of heads of self-attention is adjusted according to the variable parameter h. Then, the self-attention module linearly transforms the mixed sequence and F into Q, K, V according to the variable parameter d. Q and K are used to generate the attention value A according to Eq. (1). Finally, A dot V for attention fusion.

$$A = softmax(QK^T \backslash \sqrt{d}) \tag{1}$$

The ultimate output of self attention is skip connected with the normalized mixed sequence and F. Then, it is transferred to the feedforward layer. The fully connected layer of Gelu activation function is used twice in the feedforward layer. Meanwhile, the output and input of feedforward layer adopt the same skip connection as before. The above operation is performed h times, we get the new mixed sequence $\hat{M}$ and the new $\hat{F}$ with multi-modal information. Finally, we separate $\hat{F}$ from the mixed sequence $\hat{M}$ and repeat it to the size of the base feature $R^{D \times H \times W}$, which is the V-S feature in Fig. 2.

SVT acquires the attention weight according to the advanced visual feature extracted from the image and the guidance information of word embeddings.

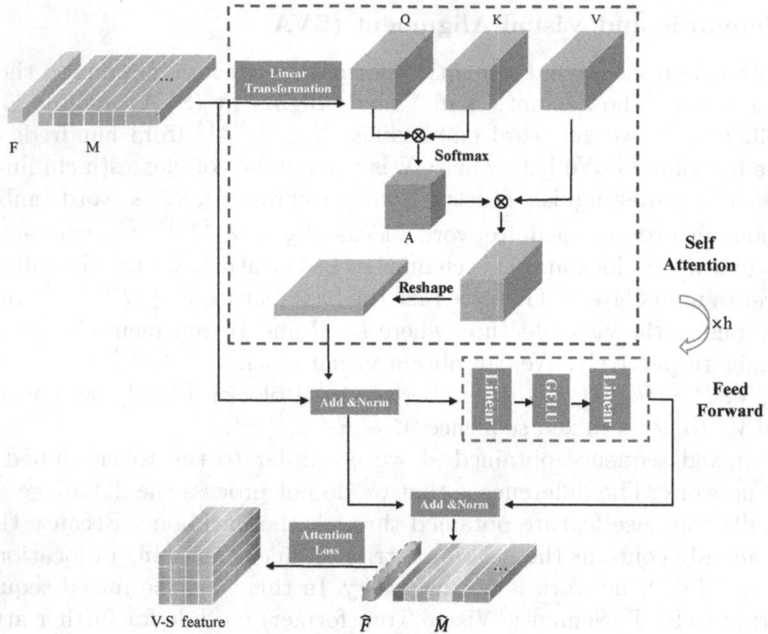

Fig. 4. SVT module

Then, it adjusts all the blocks in the mixed sequence and F adaptively. Finally, the multi-modal information in the mixed sequence is integrated into $\hat{F}$. The V-S feature obtained by $\hat{F}$ contains both advanced visual information and semantic guidance.

3.4 Loss

Although we introduce SVT to fuse visual and semantic information, it is difficult to control the learning direction of the model by simply integrating them. In order to make the word embedding guide the visual information according to the desired result, we propose the attention loss $L_{attention}$ of multi-modal fusion. Specifically, we map the fusion block $\hat{F}$ into a vector with dimension N (the number of classes), that is $\hat{F} = [f_1, f_2, ..., f_N]$. The label is $Y = [y_1, y_2, ..., y_N]$. Then, the cross entropy loss function is used to calculate attention loss seen as Eq. (2).

$$L_{attention} = -\sum_{n=1}^{N} y_n log(f_n) \tag{2}$$

The total loss function is shown in Eq. (3).

$$L = L_{rpn} + L_{cls} + L_{reg} + L_{attention} \tag{3}$$

The first three are RPN loss, classification loss and regression loss of Faster RCNN [18] respectively.

4 Experiments

In this section, we validate TMD-FS on PASCAL VOC [5] and COCO [11] datasets. By comparing with previous methods, our approach can reach the current high precision. Especially when the number of samples is rare, such as 1 shot and 2 shot, our method is more effective than most. Then we perform ablation experiments and visualization.

4.1 Implementation Details

Our model is based on Faster R-CNN [18], using ResNet-101 [7] and Feature Pyramid Network [10] as the backbone with SGD. In SVA, we choose F6 feature vector of FPN as visual feature and acquire the word embedding from abundant text datasets by using GloVe [13]. For self attention in SVT, we set the number of heads is 3, h is 1 and d is 256. In the pre-training phase, we follow the same training method as TFA [22]. In the few-shot fine-tuning phase, we add the SVT module and Attention Loss to train together. All the experiments are carried out using two GPUs with the batch size as 16, the learning rate as 0.008, the momentum as 0.9 and the weight decay as 0.0001.

4.2 Existing Benchmarks

Results on PASCAL VOC. For PASCAL VOC dataset, we use voc 2007 and 2012 train sets for training and 2007 test set for testing including twenty classes. Fifteen classes are divided into base classes, while the other five are novel classes. We divide the novel classes into three splits according to [22], and we conducted different k shot experiments on these three splits respectively and compared them with the previous work [3,8,9,22–24,26]. k could be selected from 1,2,3,5,10. The specific experimental results are shown in Table 1.

Table 1. FSOD performance (mAP50) on three splits of PASCAL VOC dataset

Method\shot	Novel split 1 (%)					Novel split 2 (%)					Novel split 3 (%)				
	1	2	3	5	10	1	2	3	5	10	1	2	3	5	10
FSRW [8]	14.8	15.5	26.7	33.9	47.2	15.7	15.3	22.7	30.1	40.5	21.3	25.6	28.4	42.8	45.9
MetaDet [23]	18.9	20.6	30.2	36.8	49.6	21.8	23.1	27.8	31.7	43.0	20.6	23.9	29.4	43.9	44.1
Meta R-CNN [26]	19.9	25.5	35.0	45.7	51.5	10.4	19.4	29.6	34.8	45.4	14.3	18.2	27.5	41.2	48.1
RepMet [9]	26.1	32.9	34.4	38.6	41.3	17.2	22.1	23.4	28.3	35.8	27.5	31.1	31.5	34.4	37.2
AttFDNet [3]	29.6	34.9	35.1	–	–	16.0	20.7	22.1	–	–	22.6	29.1	32.0	–	–
TFA [22]	39.8	36.1	44.7	55.7	56.0	23.5	26.9	34.1	35.1	39.1	30.8	34.8	42.8	**49.5**	49.8
MPSR [24]	41.7	–	**51.4**	55.2	**61.8**	24.4	–	**39.2**	**39.9**	**47.8**	35.6	–	42.3	48.0	49.7
Ours	**44.6**	**45.6**	43.9	**55.8**	56.3	**24.8**	**27.5**	34.7	35.6	39.3	**35.8**	**37.3**	**42.9**	**49.5**	**50.3**

As can be seen from Table 1, when the number of samples is fewer, our method can improve the detection performance significantly. It is 5–9% higher than the baseline [22] and has a greater advantage than other methods, which is consistent with our previous analysis. When samples are rare, the discriminative semantic information existing in the novel class is not well represented. We use multi-modal semantic information to supplement lost discriminative information, so as to distinguish the different categories. As the number of samples gradually increases (e.g., 10 shot), visual features are already representative to a certain extent. The network has preliminarily been able to identify this category by gathering the information of 10 images. Therefore, the improvement of detection performance with TMD-FS is more obvious in fewer samples.

We further verify whether the model forgets the representation of the base class after the transfer learning of the novel class. We find that the performance of the model on the base class did not decrease significantly after adding novel classes for fine-tuning. This shows that TMD-FS is stable.

Results on COCO. COCO dataset has 80 classes. We chose twenty classes that overlap with VOC as novel classes and the others as base classes. Meanwhile, we follow the same training strategy as [22], choosing k = 10, 30 for comparison, Table 2 shows that our method has been improved compared with previous work.

Table 2. FSOD performance on COCO dataset

Method	Novel AP (%)		Novel AP75 (%)	
	10 shot	30 shot	10 shot	30 shot
FSRW [8]	5.6	9.1	4.6	7.6
MetaDet [23]	7.1	11.3	6.1	8.1
Meta RCNN [26]	8.7	12.4	6.6	10.8
TFA [22]	10.0	13.7	9.3	13.4
MPSR [24]	9.8	14.1	**9.7**	**14.2**
Ours	**10.6**	**14.3**	9.5	13.9

Because the COCO dataset is relatively complex, it is more difficult to detect objects with only a small number of samples. However, as shown in Table 2, our method is still effective. This indicates that when faced with more complex scenes, the problem of insufficient class information can be alleviated by the assistance of multi-modal information.

4.3 Ablation Study

In this part, we examine the contribution of each module. Our experiment is based on 1 shot of novel split1 on Pascal VOC dataset. We use TFA [22] as baseline and add SVT with $L_{attention}$ progressively to compare the effects of each module. The results are shown in Table 3. Then, we compare the fusion strategy of word vectors and visual features with general attention and SVT, which are shown in Table 4.

Table 3. The ablation experiment compares the effects of each module

Method\module	SVT	$L_{attention}$	mAP50 (%)
Baseline (TFA) [22]	✗	✗	39.8
Ours	✓	✗	43.8
Ours	✓	✓	44.6

Results in Table 3 confirm that the two modules are valid. When we fuse the word vector and the visual feature through SVT module, the accuracy rate increased by 4%, which indicates that the multi-modal information fusion can improve the discrimination error of FSOD effectively. Besides, it could avoid the confusion of multiple classes, and make sure the supplement of word vector for few-shot information is correct. The performance of the model with $L_{attention}$ is further improved, which certificates that the addition of loss in the process of multimodal information fusion could constrain the learning direction of fusion features.

Table 4. The influence of different ways of attention fusion on experimental results

Attention method	Without attention	General attention	SVT
mAP50 (%)	39.8	41.9	44.6

In Table 4, the general attention method maps visual features to semantic space simply. Then, it generates attention weights with semantic features (word embedding) to further obtain fusion features for mapping them back to visual space. We contrast the general attention method with SVT, and find that SVT can get better results. Specifically, SVT carries out similarity search between visual blocks and word blocks. In this way, the multi-modal information is gathered into the fusion block. The similarity matching between blocks is more effective than the general attention fusion method to supplement the lost identification information.

4.4 Visualization

We visualize the 1 shot results of TMD-FS and baseline [22] on novel split 1 of Pascal VOC dataset, and compare them with ground truth. As shown in Fig. 5, section A and section B are visualizations of part of the image using baseline [22] and TMD-FS respectively. C shows the ground truth of images. In the first three groups of images, section A can not detect the novel object in the image but section B can. In the last two groups of images, section A mistakenly identifies the novel object into other categories. On the contrary, section B distinguishes the category correctly. This is because multi-modal information can pull apart images which are similar but belong to different categories, which makes up for the lack of visual information when there are few samples.

Fig. 5. Visualization of baseline, TMD-FS and ground truth.

5 Conclusion

In this paper, we propose a few-shot object detection model TMD-FS based on Transformer with multi-modal information fusion. The gaps of few-shot visual information are filled through multi-modal semantic information. We design SVA and SVT module to align and incorporate the visual and semantic embedding. Compared with others, our work is particularly effective on rare samples. We hope the proposed method could assist in this field.

Acknowledgement. The research is partially sponsored by The Beijing Municipal Education Commission Project (No. KZ201910005008), The National Natural Science Foundation of China (No.62176009).

References

1. Bochkovskiy, A., Wang, C.Y., Liao, H.Y.M.: YOLOv4: optimal speed and accuracy of object detection. arXiv preprint arXiv:2004.10934 (2020)
2. Carion, N., Massa, F., Synnaeve, G., Usunier, N., Kirillov, A., Zagoruyko, S.: End-to-end object detection with transformers. In: Vedaldi, A., Bischof, H., Brox, T., Frahm, J.-M. (eds.) ECCV 2020. LNCS, vol. 12346, pp. 213–229. Springer, Cham (2020). https://doi.org/10.1007/978-3-030-58452-8_13
3. Chen, X., Jiang, M., Zhao, Q.: Leveraging bottom-up and top-down attention for few-shot object detection. arXiv preprint arXiv:2007.12104 (2020)
4. Dosovitskiy, A., et al.: An image is worth 16 × 16 words: transformers for image recognition at scale. arXiv preprint arXiv:2010.11929 (2020)
5. Everingham, M., Van Gool, L., Williams, C.K., Winn, J., Zisserman, A.: The Pascal visual object classes (VOC) challenge. Int. J. Comput. Vis. **88**(2), 303–338 (2010). https://doi.org/10.1007/s11263-009-0275-4
6. Fan, Q., Zhuo, W., Tang, C.K., Tai, Y.W.: Few-shot object detection with attention-RPN and multi-relation detector. In: Proceedings of the IEEE/CVF Conference on Computer Vision and Pattern Recognition, pp. 4013–4022 (2020)
7. He, K., Zhang, X., Ren, S., Sun, J.: Deep residual learning for image recognition. In: Proceedings of the IEEE Conference on Computer Vision and Pattern Recognition, pp. 770–778 (2016)
8. Kang, B., Liu, Z., Wang, X., Yu, F., Feng, J., Darrell, T.: Few-shot object detection via feature reweighting. In: Proceedings of the IEEE/CVF International Conference on Computer Vision, pp. 8420–8429 (2019)
9. Karlinsky, L., et al.: RepMet: representative-based metric learning for classification and few-shot object detection. In: Proceedings of the IEEE/CVF Conference on Computer Vision and Pattern Recognition, pp. 5197–5206 (2019)
10. Lin, T.Y., Dollár, P., Girshick, R., He, K., Hariharan, B., Belongie, S.: Feature pyramid networks for object detection. In: Proceedings of the IEEE Conference on Computer Vision and Pattern Recognition, pp. 2117–2125 (2017)
11. Lin, T.-Y., et al.: Microsoft COCO: common objects in context. In: Fleet, D., Pajdla, T., Schiele, B., Tuytelaars, T. (eds.) ECCV 2014. LNCS, vol. 8693, pp. 740–755. Springer, Cham (2014). https://doi.org/10.1007/978-3-319-10602-1_48
12. Liu, W., et al.: SSD: single shot multibox detector. In: Leibe, B., Matas, J., Sebe, N., Welling, M. (eds.) ECCV 2016. LNCS, vol. 9905, pp. 21–37. Springer, Cham (2016). https://doi.org/10.1007/978-3-319-46448-0_2

13. Pennington, J., Socher, R., Manning, C.D.: GloVe: global vectors for word representation. In: Proceedings of the 2014 Conference on Empirical Methods in Natural Language Processing (EMNLP), pp. 1532–1543 (2014)
14. Perez-Rua, J.M., Zhu, X., Hospedales, T.M., Xiang, T.: Incremental few-shot object detection. In: Proceedings of the IEEE/CVF Conference on Computer Vision and Pattern Recognition, pp. 13846–13855 (2020)
15. Redmon, J., Divvala, S., Girshick, R., Farhadi, A.: You only look once: unified, real-time object detection. In: Proceedings of the IEEE Conference on Computer Vision and Pattern Recognition, pp. 779–788 (2016)
16. Redmon, J., Farhadi, A.: YOLO9000: better, faster, stronger. In: Proceedings of the IEEE Conference on Computer Vision and Pattern Recognition, pp. 7263–7271 (2017)
17. Redmon, J., Farhadi, A.: YOLOv3: an incremental improvement. arXiv preprint arXiv:1804.02767 (2018)
18. Ren, S., He, K., Girshick, R., Sun, J.: Faster R-CNN: towards real-time object detection with region proposal networks. In: Advances in Neural Information Processing Systems, vol. 28, pp. 91–99 (2015)
19. Schwartz, E., Karlinsky, L., Feris, R., Giryes, R., Bronstein, A.M.: Baby steps towards few-shot learning with multiple semantics. arXiv preprint arXiv:1906.01905 (2019)
20. Sun, Q., Liu, Y., Chua, T.S., Schiele, B.: Meta-transfer learning for few-shot learning. In: Proceedings of the IEEE/CVF Conference on Computer Vision and Pattern Recognition, pp. 403–412 (2019)
21. Vaswani, A., et al.: Attention is all you need. In: Advances in Neural Information Processing Systems, pp. 5998–6008 (2017)
22. Wang, X., Huang, T.E., Darrell, T., Gonzalez, J.E., Yu, F.: Frustratingly simple few-shot object detection. arXiv preprint arXiv:2003.06957 (2020)
23. Wang, Y.X., Ramanan, D., Hebert, M.: Meta-learning to detect rare objects. In: Proceedings of the IEEE/CVF International Conference on Computer Vision, pp. 9925–9934 (2019)
24. Wu, J., Liu, S., Huang, D., Wang, Y.: Multi-scale positive sample refinement for few-shot object detection. In: Vedaldi, A., Bischof, H., Brox, T., Frahm, J.-M. (eds.) ECCV 2020. LNCS, vol. 12361, pp. 456–472. Springer, Cham (2020). https://doi.org/10.1007/978-3-030-58517-4_27
25. Xing, C., Rostamzadeh, N., Oreshkin, B., Pinheiro, P.O.O.: Adaptive cross-modal few-shot learning. In: Advances in Neural Information Processing Systems, vol. 32, pp. 4847–4857 (2019)
26. Yan, X., Chen, Z., Xu, A., Wang, X., Liang, X., Lin, L.: Meta R-CNN: towards general solver for instance-level low-shot learning. In: Proceedings of the IEEE/CVF International Conference on Computer Vision, pp. 9577–9586 (2019)
27. Yang, Z., Wang, Y., Chen, X., Liu, J., Qiao, Y.: Context-transformer: tackling object confusion for few-shot detection. In: Proceedings of the AAAI Conference on Artificial Intelligence, vol. 34, pp. 12653–12660 (2020)
28. Zhu, X., Su, W., Lu, L., Li, B., Wang, X., Dai, J.: Deformable DETR: deformable transformers for end-to-end object detection. arXiv preprint arXiv:2010.04159 (2020)

Feature Matching Network for Weakly-Supervised Temporal Action Localization

Peng Dou, Wei Zhou, Zhongke Liao, and Haifeng Hu(✉)

School of Electronics and Information Technology, Sun Yat-sen University, Guangzhou 510006, Guangdong Province, China

{doup,zhouw75,liaozhk5}@mail2.sysu.edu.cn, huhaif@mail.sysu.edu.cn

Abstract. Weakly supervised temporal action localization needs to get the category of the action as well as the time period when the action of corresponding category occurs with only video level annotation during training. Currently, how to effectively localize the actions with weak discriminative information and distinguish background activities is the major challenge. To address these issues, we propose a feature matching network (FMNet) that can produce attention scores and perform different operations on them to represent different actions and background features. Moreover, we modify the cross-entropy loss to match different features. Experimental results on two standard datasets THUMOS14 and ActivityNet1.2 show the superiority of our methods.

Keywords: Weakly-supervised action localization · Feature matching mechanism · Attention

1 Introduction

In the case of using video classification label only, the weakly-supervised temporal action localization (WTAL) task not only needs to determine the category of the action instance in the videos, but also needs to localize the time when the corresponding action instance occurs. Since only classification labels are needed, the weakly-supervised methods greatly reduce the labeling cost compared to the fully-supervised methods.

The previous weakly-supervised temporal action localization methods utilize multiple instance learning (MIL) [11,17,22] to solve this problem. These methods first divide the video into segments, and then generate the segment-level class scores to obtain the class activation sequence (CAS). Finally, the top-k mechanism is used to combine the time series to get the video-level class scores. However, the methods based on multiple instance learning has a significant problem: when performing temporal action localization, the network can only locate the highly discriminative actions, while others with lower discriminativeness are ignored.

© Springer Nature Switzerland AG 2021

H. Ma et al. (Eds.): PRCV 2021, LNCS 13022, pp. 459–471, 2021.
https://doi.org/10.1007/978-3-030-88013-2_38

Fig. 1. Examples of challenges faced by the MIL framework. Both weak discriminative and strong discriminative actions needs to be captured. However, the MIL framework only has a good performance in capturing strong discriminative actions.

As shown in Fig. 1, the multiple instance learning methods can only capture the most discriminative parts of the action, making the temporal predicitions incomplete. Moreover, the existing methods commomly fail to model the background well, which makes the background segments more easy to be misclassified as actions.

To address the above limitations, we propose a feature matching network (FMNet) for weakly-supervised temporal action localization task. The network is divided into classification branch and attention branch. The attention branch predicts the attention value in the time dimension, and then performs four different strategies to obtain four types of attentions scores to represent different action or background features. In particular, these four attention scores modulate the CAS generated by the classification branch, and finally are aggregated in the time dimension to obtain the video-level class score. Since the four attention scores can represent four different features, we design different loss functions based on the cross-entropy loss, which can learn different features in a targeted manner.

In summary, the main contributions in this work are as follows: (i) We design a multi-attention branch to allow the network to focus on different parts of the action in the videos. (ii) We modify the cross-entropy loss so that the features of each branch of attention can be learned specifically. (iii) Extensive experiments on two benchmark datasets on the THUMOS14 [6] and ActivityNet [2] demonstrate the superiority of the FMNet model. Specifically, our FMNet model achieves 32.7% mAP when the IoU threshold on the THUMOS14 dataset is 0.5. When the IoU threshold on the ActivityNet1.2 data set is 0.75, 25.2% mAP is achieved.

2 Related Work

Fully-Supervised Temporal Action Localization. The fully-supervised action localization methods are mainly divided into two categories. The first category is proposal-based methods. In order to generate proposals, sliding window technology is mainly used [4,24,26,29,33]. The second category is frame-based methods, including [1,12–16,37], which directly predicts the frame-level action category and location. Recently, some graph structure methods [31,36] are proposed. Since the time nodes of the beginning and ending of each action instance need to be accurately labelled, the annotation cost of fully supervised methods are very expensive.

Weakly-Supervised Temporal Action Localization. Compared with the fully-supervised methods, the weakly-supervised methods only use video-level action category labels, which greatly reduce the cost of annotating. In particular, weakly-supervised temporal action localization methods are mainly divided into two categories. The first kind of methods [18,20,21,32,35] leverage foreground-background separation attention branches to construct video-level features, and then apply the action classifier to recognize the videos. The second kind of methods [11,17,22,34] treat the problem as a multi-instance learning task [39], that treat the untrimmed video as a bag containing positive and negative instances. They first obtain the class activation sequence (CAS), and then use the top-k mechanism to obtain the video-level classification score.

Currently, in order to make the performance of weakly-supervised methods close to that of fully-supervised methods, some works [10,13] attempt to model the action completeness. Moreover, HAMNet [7] proposes a hybrid attention mechanism, which separately processes the foreground, background, and discriminative action features. However, all branches of HAMNet are optimized with the loss function in the form of cross entropy, which is not conductive to learning each type of feature. To address these issues, we modify the cross-entropy loss to fit the characteristics of each type of feature. In the meanwhile, we design four attention branches to model more complete actions.

3 Network Structure

3.1 Problem Statement

For a training video V containing several action instances, each instance belongs to one of n_c action classes. Denote these action instances as $\mathbf{y} \in \{0, 1\}^{n_c}$, where $y_j = 1$ only if there is at least one instance of the jth action class in the video, and $y_j = 0$ if there is no instance of the jth action. Given such a training video, we need to predict which action appears in the video as well as the temporal localization of its instance, i.e., to output (t_s, t_e, ψ, c), where c is the action category, t_s, t_e, ψ are the start frame, end frame and prediction score corresponding to action c respectively.

3.2 Network Structure

The overall framework of our feature matching network (FMNet) is shown in Fig. 2. Following the two-stream strategy [3,5] for action recognition, we extract snippet-level features for both the RGB and flow streams. Specially, we divide each video into several non-overlapping snippets. These snippets are sent into a two-stream I3D extractor to obtain RGB features and flow features, both of which are 1048 dimensions. The two features are concatenated to a $2048 \times T_v$

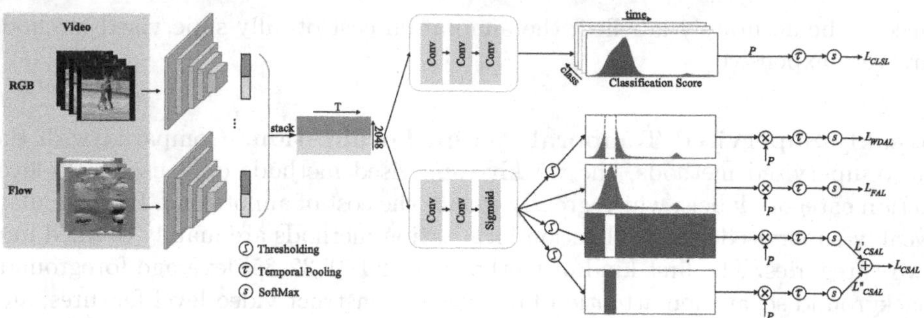

Fig. 2. Overall framework of our proposed FMNet architecture. RGB features and flow features are extracted by the I3D extractor, then concatenated together and sent to the classification branch and the attention branch. The attention branch calculates four attention scores and uses different loss functions for training.

dimensional feature, where T_v represents the number of segments in the video. The concatenated features are sent to the classification branch and the attention branch to localize the start and end time of the action.

Following the previous strategy, the output of the classification branch is the class activation sequence (CAS) [25]. The class activation sequence is a snippet-level representation, and each snippet has $c+1$ CAS. Formally, $c+1$ means c action categories and one background, and the CAS of the ith snippet is represented by $\mathbf{s}_i \in \mathbb{R}^{c+1}$. In order to integrate the snippet-level representation into the video-level scores, we adopt a top-k strategy for the CAS value of each category [22]:

$$v_j = \max_{\substack{l \subset 1,2,\ldots,T \\ |l|=k}} \frac{1}{k} \sum_{i \in l} s_i(j) \tag{1}$$

where $j = 1, 2, \ldots, c+1$. Then, we exploit the softmax to v_j along the category dimension to get the class score of the video level:

$$p_j = \frac{\exp(v_j)}{\sum_{j'=1}^{c+1} \exp(v_{j'})} \tag{2}$$

Finally, we calculate the cross-entropy loss between the real video-level class score $\mathbf{y}$ and the predicted score $\mathbf{p}$ to obtain the classification loss of the classification branch:

$$\mathcal{L}_{\mathrm{CLSL}} = -\sum_{j=1}^{c+1} y_j \log(p_j) \tag{3}$$

3.3 Attention Branch

Foreground Attention Score. We denote the score obtained through the attention branch as a_i. Since the a_i corresponding to the background snippets are low or even almost zero, we can use a_i to initially represent the foreground attention score. In order to establish a connection between a_i and category, we multiply the CAS $s_i(j)$ and a_i to obtain the foreground snippet-level class score $s_i^{fore}(j) = s_i(j) \otimes a_i$. Following Eqs. 1 and 2, we change the variable $s_i(j)$ to $s_i^{fore}(j)$. After the top-k strategy and softmax calculation, we get the substitute p_j^{fore} of p_j. Afterwards, following Eq. 3, we calculate the cross-entropy loss. Since we focus on the foreground, we only use the foreground label y_j^f when calculating the cross entropy, i.e., when $j = c+1$, $y_{c+1}^f = 0$. For video-level annotation, the number of background categories is much greater than that of action instance categories. After removing the background categories, the network can no longer learn background information, we re-weight the instance labels to reduce possibility of the network learning mistake information:

$$y_j^{f'} = (1-\epsilon)y_j^f + \epsilon/K \tag{4}$$

where $\epsilon = 0.005$, $k = 20$. Foreground attention loss is as follows:

$$\mathcal{L}_{\text{FAL}} = -\sum_{j=1}^{c+1} y_j^{f'} \log(p_j^{fore}) \tag{5}$$

Weak Discriminative Attention Score. The foreground attention score a_i includes the foreground with strong discrimination and the foreground with weak discrimination. By setting the threshold γ, we keep the foreground with relatively weak discrimination and screen out the foreground with strong discrimination:

$$a_i^{weak} = \begin{cases} a_i, & if\, a_i < \gamma \\ 0, & otherwise \end{cases} \tag{6}$$

where a_i^{weak} is the attention score with only weak discriminative foreground, and $\gamma \in [0,1]$. Since only the most discriminative parts of a_i is suppressed, while others stay consistent, the subsequent calculation process still exploits $y_j^{f'}$ as real label. Follow the calculation of foreground attention loss, the weak discriminative attention loss is as follows:

$$\mathcal{L}_{\text{WDAL}} = -\sum_{j=1}^{c+1} y_j^{f'} \log\left(p_j^{weak}\right) \tag{7}$$

Complementary Strong Attention Score. In order to maximize the contribution of different parts of the attention value, we follow Eq. 6 and set the value that meets the threshold condition to 1:

$$a_i' = \begin{cases} 1, & if\, a_i < \gamma \\ 0, & otherwise \end{cases} \qquad a_i'' = \begin{cases} 1, & if\, a_i > \gamma \\ 0, & otherwise \end{cases} \tag{8}$$

In the above formula, a_i' represents the strong attention score of the weak discriminative regions and the background, and a_i'' represents the strong attention score of the strong discriminative regions.

Following Eq. 1 and Eq. 2, we can get p_j' and p_j''. Inspired by focal loss, we do the following calculations for p_j' and p_j'' in order to solve the problem of sample imbalance after retaining only part of the attention regions.

$$\mathcal{L'}_{\text{CSAL}} = -\sum_{j=1}^{c+1} y_j (1 - p'_j)^{\gamma} \log(p'_j) \tag{9}$$

$$\mathcal{L''}_{\text{CSAL}} = -\sum_{j=1}^{c+1} y_j^{f'} (p''_j)^{\gamma} \log(1 - p''_j) \tag{10}$$

As discussed in the previous section, $\mathcal{L'}_{\text{CSAL}}$ pays attention to the background region, so the label $\mathbf{y}$ with background category is used, i.e., $y_{c+1} = 1$. $\mathcal{L''}_{\text{CSAL}}$ ignores the background area, so the label $y^{f'}$ of Eq. 4 is used. Then we get the complementary strong attention loss:

$$\mathcal{L}_{\text{CSAL}} = \mathcal{L'}_{\text{CSAL}} + \mathcal{L''}_{\text{CSAL}} \tag{11}$$

Loss Functions. After introducing the above loss function, we leverage the following joint loss function to train the FM-Net:

$$\mathcal{L} = \lambda_0 \mathcal{L}_{\text{CLSL}} + \lambda_1 \mathcal{L}_{\text{FAL}} + \lambda_2 \mathcal{L}_{\text{WDAL}} + \lambda_3 \mathcal{L}_{\text{CSAL}} + \alpha \mathcal{L}_{sparse} + \beta \mathcal{L}_{guide} \tag{12}$$

where λ_0, λ_1, λ_2, λ_3, α and β are hyper-parameters, and $\mathcal{L}_{\text{sparse}}$ means sparse loss, $\mathcal{L}_{\text{guide}}$ denotes guide loss respectively. According to [7], the sparsity loss and thc guide loss are valid which can be written as:

$$\mathcal{L}_{\text{sparse}} = \sum_{i=1}^{T} |a_i| \tag{13}$$

$$\mathcal{L}_{\text{guide}} = \sum_{i=1}^{T} |1 - a_i - \bar{s}_{c+1}| \tag{14}$$

where

$$\bar{s}_{c+1} = \frac{\exp(s_{c+1})}{\sum_{j=1}^{c} \exp(s_j)} \tag{15}$$

3.4 Temporal Action Localization

Firstly, we discard the classes whose video-level class scores are lower than the threshold 0.1. Then, in order to discard the background snippets, we threshold the foreground attention scores a_i of the remaining classes. Finally, we select the one-dimensional components of the remaining snippets to get classagnostic action proposals. As shown in Sect. 3.1, we represent the candidate action locations as $(t(s), t(e), \psi, c)$. Following the outer-inner score of AutoLoc [25], we calculate ψ, which is the classification score corresponding to class c. Notably, we should leverage foreground snippet-level class logits s_c^{fore} to calculate the score of a specific category:

$$\psi = \psi_{inner} - \psi_{outer} + \zeta p_c^{fore} \tag{16}$$

$$\psi_{inner} = \text{Avg}\left(s_c^{\text{fore}}(t_s : t_e)\right) \tag{17}$$

$$\psi_{\text{outer}} = \text{Avg}\left(s_c^{\text{fore}}(t_s - l_m : t_s) + s_c^{\text{fore}}(t_e : t_e + l_m)\right) \tag{18}$$

where ζ is a hyper-parameter, p_c^{fore} denotes the video-level score for class c, and $l_m = (t_e - t_s)/4$. For action proposals, we obtain them by applying different thresholds. In addition, we exploit non-maximum suppression to remove the overlapping segments.

4 Experiments

4.1 Datasets and Evaluation Metrics

To evaluate the effectiveness and superiority of our FMNet model, we conduct experiments on THUMOS14 [6] and ActivityNet1.2 [2]. THUMOS14 contains a total of 20 action categories, including 200 validation videos for task training, and it contains 213 testing videos for task testing. ActivityNet1.2 contains 200 action categories, a total of 4,819 videos for training and 2,382 videos for testing. We leverage ActivityNet official code [2] to calculate the evaluation metrics. We follow the standard evaluation and report that the mean Average Precision (mAP) at different intersection over union (IoU) threshold.

4.2 Implementation Details

We exploit the I3D network [3] pre-trained on the Kinetics dataset [8] to extract RGB and flow features. RGB and flow features should be divided into 16 frame chunks that do not overlap each other. The flow features are created by using the TV-L1 algorithm [28]. After extracting RGB and flow features, we concatenate them to obtain the snippet-level features with 2048 dimensions. When using the THUMOS14 dataset for training, we randomly sample 500 snippets for each video; when using the ActivityNet dataset for training, we randomly sample 80 snippets; and during testing, we take all the snippets for evaluation. The features are then sent to the classification branch and the attention branch. The classification branch is composed of two temporal convolution layers with kernel size 3. Each temporal convolution layer is followed by LeakyReLU activation. At the end of the layer, a linear fully-connected layer is used to predict the class logits. The attention branch is composed of two temporal convolutions with a kernel size 3, and finally followed by sigmoid activation, and an attention score between 0 and 1 is predicted.

We train 100 epochs for THUMOS14 and 20 epochs for ActivityNet. Hyper-parameters are determined by grid search, and we set $\lambda_0 = \lambda_1 = 0.8$, $\lambda_2 = \lambda_3 = 0.2$, $\alpha = \beta = 0.8$, $\gamma = 0.2$ on THUMOS14, and for top-k temporal pooling, k=50. In addition, we set $\lambda_0 = \lambda_1 = 0.4$, $\lambda_2 = \lambda_3 = 0.6$ and k=4 on ActivityNet, and apply additional average pooling to post-processing the final CAS. We use the Adam optimizer [9] with a learning rate of 0.00001. For action localization, we set the threshold from 0.1 to 0.9, the step size is 0.05, and perform non-maximum suppression to remove overlapping segments.

4.3 Ablation Studies

We conduct a set of ablation studies on the THUMOS14 dataset to analyze the contributions made by each of our branches. The experimental results are shown in Table 1. For Eq. 12, when $\mathcal{L}_{\text{FAL}}$, L_{WDAL}, $\mathcal{L}_{\text{CSAL}}$ are normal form of cross entropy (i.e., $\mathcal{L}_{\text{FAL}}, L_{\text{WDAL}}, \mathcal{L}'_{\text{CSAL}}$ and $\mathcal{L}''_{\text{CSAL}}$ use y_j^f, y_j^f, y_j and y_j^f to modulate $\log(p_j^{fore}), \log(p_j^{weak}), \log(p'_j)$ and $\log(p''_j)$, respectively), 29.6% mAP

Table 1. Comparison of different losses on Thumos14. "-" means the corresponding loss function is the normal form of cross-entropy, and "✓" means that the corresponding loss function is trained with the loss function proposed in this article.

Methods			mAP@IoUs							
$\mathcal{L}_{FAL}$	L_{WDAL}	$\mathcal{L}_{CSAL}$	0.1	0.2	0.3	0.4	0.5	0.6	0.7	AVG
-	-	-	64.6	58.3	50.7	40.0	29.6	20.0	10.5	39.1
✓	-	-	65.4	59.0	51.3	41.6	31.5	21.1	11.5	40.2
-	-	✓	65.6	59.0	51.2	41.5	30.8	21.0	11.2	40.0
✓	✓	-	65.2	59.0	51.1	41.6	31.3	21.0	11.7	40.1
✓	-	✓	65.8	59.5	51.6	**42.3**	32.7	22.1	11.9	40.8
-	✓	✓	65.9	59.1	51.3	41.5	30.9	21.1	11.1	40.1
✓	✓	✓	**66.1**	**59.5**	**51.6**	42.2	**32.7**	**22.1**	**12.0**	**40.9**

Table 2. Recent detection results on the ActivityNet1.2 dataset. The results includes both fully supervised methods and weakly supervised mothods. The results are evaluated on mAP at IoU threshold [0.5:0.05:0.95, AVG]. The AVE is the average mAP at IoU threshold [0.5:0.05:0.95].

Supervision	Method	IoU			
		0.5	0.75	0.95	AVG
Full	SSN [38]	41.3	27.0	6.1	26.6
Weak	UntrimmedNets [27]	7.4	3.2	0.7	3.6
	AutoLoc [25]	27.3	15.1	3.3	16.0
	W-TALC [22]	37.0	12.7	1.5	18.0
	TSM [32]	28.6	17.0	3.5	17.1
	3C-Net [19]	35.4	-	-	21.1
	BaSNet [11]	34.5	22.5	4.9	22.2
	DGAM [23]	41.0	23.5	5.3	24.4
	HAMNet [7]	41.0	24.8	5.3	25.1
	FM-Net (ours)	**41.0**	**25.0**	**5.3**	**25.2**

can be achieved when the IoU value is 0.5, and AVG mAP is 39.1%. Table 1 shows the performance when we change the cross entropy to the loss function proposed in this article. Compared with all branches using normal form of cross entropy loss for optimization, our method improves mAP by 3.1% when the IoU value is 0.5, and AVG mAP increases by 1.8%. Notably, when two or all of the improved loss functions are combined, mAP can be improved.

Table 3. Recent detection results on the Thumos14 dataset. The results includes both fully supervised methods and weakly supervised methods. The results are evaluated on mAP at IoU threshold [0.1:0.1:0.7].

Supervision	Method	Feature	IoU							
			0.1	0.2	0.3	0.4	0.5	0.6	0.7	AVG
Full	S-CNN [26]	–	47.7	43.5	36.3	28.7	19.0	10.3	5.3	–
	R-C3D [30]	–	54.5	51.5	44.8	35.6	28.9	–	–	–
	SSN [38]	–	66.0	59.4	51.9	41.0	29.8	–	–	–
	TAL-Net [4]	–	59.8	57.1	53.2	48.5	42.8	33.8	20.8	–
	BSN [15]	–	–	–	53.5	45.0	36.9	28.4	20.0	–
	G-TAD [31]	–	–	–	54.5	47.6	40.2	30.8	23.4	–
	P-GCN [36]	–	69.5	67.8	63.6	57.8	49.1	–	–	–
Weak	HaS [10]	–	36.4	27.8	19.5	12.7	6.8	–	–	–
	UntrimmedNets [27]	–	44.4	37.7	28.2	21.1	13.7	–	–	–
	AutoLoc [25]	UNT	–	–	35.8	29.0	21.2	13.4	5.8	–
	STPN [20]	I3D	52.0	44.7	35.5	25.8	16.9	9.9	4.3	26.4
	MAAN [34]	I3D	59.8	50.8	41.1	30.6	20.3	12.0	6.9	31.6
	W-TALC [22]	I3D	55.2	49.6	40.1	31.1	22.8	–	7.6	–
	3C-Net [19]	I3D	56.8	49.8	40.9	32.3	24.6	–	7.7	–
	Nguyen et al. [21]	I3D	60.4	56.0	46.6	37.5	26.8	17.6	9.0	36.3
	DGAM [23]	I3D	60.0	54.2	46.8	38.2	28.8	19.8	11.4	37.0
	HAM-Net [7]	I3D	65.4	59.0	50.3	41.1	31.0	20.7	11.1	39.8
	FMNet (ours)	I3D	**66.1**	**59.5**	**51.6**	**42.2**	**32.7**	**22.1**	**12.0**	**40.9**

Performance Comparison to State-of-the-Art. We summarise the comparison between our method and the state-of-the-art fully and weakly supervised TAL methods on the THUMOS14 in Table 3. Under weak supervision, the mAP corresponding to each IoU threshold has achieved excellent results, reaching 32.7% mAP when the IoU threshold is 0.5. With reference to the Table 2, we also evaluate our method on the ActivityNet1.2 dataset, and also achieved excellent results, verifying the effectiveness of our FMNet model.

Qualitative Performance. We show some representative examples in Fig. 3. For each video, the top row shows example frames, the next row represents ground-truth localization, "Ours" is our prediction, and "CE' means that $\mathcal{L}_{\mathrm{FAL}}$, $\mathcal{L}_{\mathrm{WDAL}}$, $\mathcal{L}_{\mathrm{CSAL}}$ are only optimized by cross entropy. Figure 3 shows that our method captures more action segments than "CE", and reduces the possibility of mistaking background for action.

Fig. 3. Visualization of the FMNet model. On the vertical axis, we plot the ground truth, the detection results with the loss function in the form of cross entropy, and the detection results with our loss function. The results show that our FMNet model has a more accurate localization effect.

5 Conclusion

For the task of weakly supervised temporal action localization, we propose a new framework called FM-Net. We construct four attention branches and design different loss functions for each branch to capture different features of the video, and then localize the complete time boundary of the action in the video. We conduct extensive experiments and analysis to prove the effectiveness of our method. Our method achieves excellent performance on THUMOS14 and ActivityNet1.2.

Acknowledgement. This work was supported in part by the National Natural Science Foundation of China (62076262, 61673402, 61273270, 60802069), the Natural Science Foundation of Guangdong Province (2017A030311029), the Science and Technology Program of Huizhou of China (2020SC0702002).

References

1. Buch, S., Escorcia, V., Ghanem, B., Fei-Fei, L., Niebles, J.C.: End-to-end, single-stream temporal action detection in untrimmed videos. In: Procedings of the British Machine Vision Conference 2017. British Machine Vision Association (2019)
2. Caba Heilbron, F., Escorcia, V., Ghanem, B., Carlos Niebles, J.: ActivityNet: a large-scale video benchmark for human activity understanding. In: Proceedings of the IEEE Conference on Computer Vision and Pattern Recognition, pp. 961–970 (2015)
3. Carreira, J., Zisserman, A.: Quo Vadis, action recognition? A new model and the kinetics dataset. In: Proceedings of the IEEE Conference on Computer Vision and Pattern Recognition, pp. 6299–6308 (2017)

4. Chao, Y.W., Vijayanarasimhan, S., Seybold, B., Ross, D.A., Deng, J., Sukthankar, R.: Rethinking the faster R-CNN architecture for temporal action localization. In: Proceedings of the IEEE Conference on Computer Vision and Pattern Recognition, pp. 1130–1139 (2018)
5. Feichtenhofer, C., Pinz, A., Zisserman, A.: Convolutional two-stream network fusion for video action recognition. In: Proceedings of the IEEE Conference on Computer Vision and Pattern Recognition, pp. 1933–1941 (2016)
6. Idrees, H., et al.: The THUMOS challenge on action recognition for videos "in the wild." Comput. Vis. Image Underst. **155**, 1–23 (2017)
7. Islam, A., Long, C., Radke, R.: A hybrid attention mechanism for weakly-supervised temporal action localization. arXiv preprint arXiv:2101.00545 (2021)
8. Kay, W., et al.: The kinetics human action video dataset. arXiv preprint arXiv:1705.06950 (2017)
9. Kingma, D.P., Ba, J.: Adam: a method for stochastic optimization. arXiv preprint arXiv:1412.6980 (2014)
10. Kumar Singh, K., Jae Lee, Y.: Hide-and-seek: forcing a network to be meticulous for weakly-supervised object and action localization. In: Proceedings of the IEEE International Conference on Computer Vision, pp. 3524–3533 (2017)
11. Lee, P., Uh, Y., Byun, H.: Background suppression network for weakly-supervised temporal action localization. In: Proceedings of the AAAI Conference on Artificial Intelligence, vol. 34, pp. 11320–11327 (2020)
12. Lin, C., et al.: Fast learning of temporal action proposal via dense boundary generator. In: Proceedings of the AAAI Conference on Artificial Intelligence, vol. 34, pp. 11499–11506 (2020)
13. Lin, T., Liu, X., Li, X., Ding, E., Wen, S.: BMN: boundary-matching network for temporal action proposal generation. In: Proceedings of the IEEE/CVF International Conference on Computer Vision, pp. 3889–3898 (2019)
14. Lin, T., Zhao, X., Shou, Z.: Single shot temporal action detection. In: Proceedings of the 25th ACM international conference on Multimedia, pp. 988–996 (2017)
15. Lin, T., Zhao, X., Su, H., Wang, C., Yang, M.: BSN: boundary sensitive network for temporal action proposal generation. In: Ferrari, V., Hebert, M., Sminchisescu, C., Weiss, Y. (eds.) ECCV 2018. LNCS, vol. 11208, pp. 3–21. Springer, Cham (2018). https://doi.org/10.1007/978-3-030-01225-0_1
16. Long, F., Yao, T., Qiu, Z., Tian, X., Luo, J., Mei, T.: Gaussian temporal awareness networks for action localization. In: Proceedings of the IEEE/CVF Conference on Computer Vision and Pattern Recognition, pp. 344–353 (2019)
17. Luo, Z., et al.: Weakly-supervised action localization with expectation-maximization multi-instance learning. In: Vedaldi, A., Bischof, H., Brox, T., Frahm, J.-M. (eds.) ECCV 2020. LNCS, vol. 12374, pp. 729–745. Springer, Cham (2020). https://doi.org/10.1007/978-3-030-58526-6_43
18. Min, K., Corso, J.J.: Adversarial background-aware loss for weakly-supervised temporal activity localization. In: Vedaldi, A., Bischof, H., Brox, T., Frahm, J.-M. (eds.) ECCV 2020. LNCS, vol. 12359, pp. 283–299. Springer, Cham (2020). https://doi.org/10.1007/978-3-030-58568-6_17
19. Narayan, S., Cholakkal, H., Khan, F.S., Shao, L.: 3C-Net: category count and center loss for weakly-supervised action localization. In: Proceedings of the IEEE/CVF International Conference on Computer Vision, pp. 8679–8687 (2019)
20. Nguyen, P., Liu, T., Prasad, G., Han, B.: Weakly supervised action localization by sparse temporal pooling network. In: Proceedings of the IEEE Conference on Computer Vision and Pattern Recognition, pp. 6752–6761 (2018)

21. Nguyen, P.X., Ramanan, D., Fowlkes, C.C.: Weakly-supervised action localization with background modeling. In: Proceedings of the IEEE/CVF International Conference on Computer Vision, pp. 5502–5511 (2019)
22. Paul, S., Roy, S., Roy-Chowdhury, A.K.: W-TALC: weakly-supervised temporal activity localization and classification. In: Ferrari, V., Hebert, M., Sminchisescu, C., Weiss, Y. (eds.) ECCV 2018. LNCS, vol. 11208, pp. 588–607. Springer, Cham (2018). https://doi.org/10.1007/978-3-030-01225-0_35
23. Shi, B., Dai, Q., Mu, Y., Wang, J.: Weakly-supervised action localization by generative attention modeling. In: Proceedings of the IEEE/CVF Conference on Computer Vision and Pattern Recognition, pp. 1009–1019 (2020)
24. Shou, Z., Chan, J., Zareian, A., Miyazawa, K., Chang, S.F.: CDC: convolutional-de-convolutional networks for precise temporal action localization in untrimmed videos. In: Proceedings of the IEEE Conference on Computer Vision and Pattern Recognition, pp. 5734–5743 (2017)
25. Shou, Z., Gao, H., Zhang, L., Miyazawa, K., Chang, S.-F.: AutoLoc: weakly-supervised temporal action localization in untrimmed videos. In: Ferrari, V., Hebert, M., Sminchisescu, C., Weiss, Y. (eds.) ECCV 2018. LNCS, vol. 11220, pp. 162–179. Springer, Cham (2018). https://doi.org/10.1007/978-3-030-01270-0_10
26. Shou, Z., Wang, D., Chang, S.F.: Temporal action localization in untrimmed videos via multi-stage CNNs. In: Proceedings of the IEEE Conference on Computer Vision and Pattern Recognition, pp. 1049–1058 (2016)
27. Wang, L., Xiong, Y., Lin, D., Van Gool, L.: Untrimmednets for weakly supervised action recognition and detection. In: Proceedings of the IEEE Conference on Computer Vision and Pattern Recognition, pp. 4325–4334 (2017)
28. Wedel, A., Pock, T., Zach, C., Bischof, H., Cremers, D.: An improved algorithm for TV-L^1 optical flow. In: Cremers, D., Rosenhahn, B., Yuille, A.L., Schmidt, F.R. (eds.) Statistical and Geometrical Approaches to Visual Motion Analysis. LNCS, vol. 5604, pp. 23–45. Springer, Heidelberg (2009). https://doi.org/10.1007/978-3-642-03061-1_2
29. Xiong, Y., Zhao, Y., Wang, L., Lin, D., Tang, X.: A pursuit of temporal accuracy in general activity detection. arXiv preprint arXiv:1703.02716 (2017)
30. Xu, H., Das, A., Saenko, K.: R-C3D: region convolutional 3D network for temporal activity detection. In: Proceedings of the IEEE International Conference on Computer Vision, pp. 5783–5792 (2017)
31. Xu, M., Zhao, C., Rojas, D.S., Thabet, A., Ghanem, B.: G-TAD: sub-graph localization for temporal action detection. In: Proceedings of the IEEE/CVF Conference on Computer Vision and Pattern Recognition, pp. 10156–10165 (2020)
32. Yu, T., Ren, Z., Li, Y., Yan, E., Xu, N., Yuan, J.: Temporal structure mining for weakly supervised action detection. In: Proceedings of the IEEE/CVF International Conference on Computer Vision, pp. 5522–5531 (2019)
33. Yuan, J., Ni, B., Yang, X., Kassim, A.A.: Temporal action localization with pyramid of score distribution features. In: Proceedings of the IEEE Conference on Computer Vision and Pattern Recognition, pp. 3093–3102 (2016)
34. Yuan, Y., Lyu, Y., Shen, X., Tsang, I.W., Yeung, D.Y.: Marginalized average attentional network for weakly-supervised learning. arXiv preprint arXiv:1905.08586 (2019)
35. Zeng, R., Gan, C., Chen, P., Huang, W., Wu, Q., Tan, M.: Breaking winner-takes-all: iterative-winners-out networks for weakly supervised temporal action localization. IEEE Trans. Image Process. **28**(12), 5797–5808 (2019)

36. Zeng, R., et al.: Graph convolutional networks for temporal action localization. In: Proceedings of the IEEE/CVF International Conference on Computer Vision, pp. 7094–7103 (2019)
37. Zhao, P., Xie, L., Ju, C., Zhang, Y., Wang, Y., Tian, Q.: Bottom-up temporal action localization with mutual regularization. In: Vedaldi, A., Bischof, H., Brox, T., Frahm, J.-M. (eds.) ECCV 2020. LNCS, vol. 12353, pp. 539–555. Springer, Cham (2020). https://doi.org/10.1007/978-3-030-58598-3_32
38. Zhao, Y., Xiong, Y., Wang, L., Wu, Z., Tang, X., Lin, D.: Temporal action detection with structured segment networks. In: Proceedings of the IEEE International Conference on Computer Vision, pp. 2914–2923 (2017)
39. Zhou, Z.H.: Multi-instance learning: a survey. Technical report, Department of Computer Science & Technology, Nanjing University, 2 (2004)

LiDAR-Based Symmetrical Guidance for 3D Object Detection

Huazhen Chu, Huimin Ma[(✉)], Haizhuang Liu, and Rongquan Wang

School of Computer and Communication Engineering, University of Science and Technology Beijing, 100083 Beijing, China
mhmpub@ustb.edu.cn

Abstract. Object detection from 3D point clouds is an essential task for autonomous driving. Current approaches usually focus on the characteristics of the point cloud while ignoring the structural characteristics of the object itself. This paper designs a new symmetric structure enhancement network SS-PV-RCNN according to the symmetry of car structure, inspired by the human symmetry visual cognition system. Using the symmetrically strengthened point cloud to help the network learn the features of the symmetric structure, improve the robustness of the network in the occlusion area, and then improve the accuracy of 3D object detection. This method is verified on the KITTI dataset, and it has a particular improvement compared to the baseline method.

Keywords: 3D object detection · Point cloud · Symmetrical structure

1 Introduction

3D object detection has been receiving increasing attention from both industry and academia thanks to its wide applications in various fields such as autonomous driving and robotics. LiDAR sensors are widely adopted in autonomous driving vehicles and robots for capturing 3D scene information as sparse and irregular point clouds, which provide vital cues for 3D scene perception and understanding. This paper proposes a new method for 3D object detection on point clouds to achieve high performance by designing a novel symmetrical strengthening PV-RCNN (SS-PV-RCNN) network.

Although the point cloud can not be affected by the weather and light, the point cloud has very serious sparsity. There are still problems of missed detection, false detection, and inaccurate positioning for the objects with occlusion. Therefore, we study the human visual system and find the symmetry visual perception in the human visual system. As a result, we apply the symmetry visual perception to the point cloud-based detection task.

The human visual system is susceptible to the processing of bilateral symmetry of visual input stimuli. Many studies [1–3] show that the perceptual organization of visual input is directly involved in symmetry processing. For example, symmetry influences the figure-background separation process, one of the critical

© Springer Nature Switzerland AG 2021
H. Ma et al. (Eds.): PRCV 2021, LNCS 13022, pp. 472–483, 2021.
https://doi.org/10.1007/978-3-030-88013-2_39

steps in object perception formation. Driver et al. [1] found that when ambiguous shapes were used as visual stimuli, subjects tended to regard perceived symmetrical shapes as graphics and asymmetric shapes as backgrounds.

From a geometric point of view, the concept of symmetry involves isometric isomorphisms, mirror symmetry (also known as mirror symmetry or bilateral symmetry), rotational symmetry, translational symmetry (also known as repetition), and their composite forms. Although the human visual system is sensitive to all of these forms of symmetry, bilateral symmetry is probably the single most significant, most frequently mentioned, and most relevant to humans. From a phenomenological point of view, the outstanding feature of symmetry is its ability to highlight the object's structure when the observer inspects it.

Inspired by the human visual cognitive system, we use bilateral symmetry as the starting point of our research and propose a new symmetric-enhanced network. The symmetric branch of the network is trained with the symmetrically reinforced data. Then the original branch is constrained to learn the content as close as possible to the symmetric branch to promote the branch to learn the structural information about the symmetry. In this way, the original network can learn symmetric structure information from the original point cloud to improve its performance of 3D detection.

We make the following three contributions in this work:

i Based on human symmetry visual perception, we propose a symmetric structure enhancement network to help the network learn the structural information about symmetry. Moreover, we verify the validity of the symmetric structure by using the existing algorithm on KITTI dataset.
ii According to the symmetry of car structure, we propose a method to generate symmetrically enhanced car point cloud data. Furthermore, use the symmetrically enhanced point cloud data to help the network learn the symmetric structure information.
iii We innovatively proposed feature consistency loss to constrain the network at the feature level to learn symmetric information.

2 Related Work

3D object detection aims to predict three-dimensional rotated bounding boxes. There are three main methods in this field:

Multi-modal 3D Object Detection. MV3D [4] converts the point cloud to the birdview and front view, integrates the information from multiple perspectives accordingly, and inferences the 3D information of objects. AVOD [5] takes RGB image and point cloud birdview as the network's input uses FPN network to extract features and re-projects a small amount of 3D physical similarity regions onto the feature maps of different modes accurate 2D candidate region features. Finally, accurate 3D object detection is achieved through secondary fusion. Pixor [6] and Contfuse [7] take point cloud projection map as input and improve the detection framework and fusion strategy, thus improving the detection performance.

Single-Stage 3D Object Detection. VoxelNet [8] first discretized the three-dimensional space and divided the three-dimensional space into multiple voxel units of the same size. Then, such normalized point clouds were successively sent into 3D CNN and 3D RPN to output the three-dimensional detection results. In order to solve the problem of high time cost, Second [9] took advantage of the sparsity of the point cloud and proposed the method of sparse 3D convolution to accelerate 3DCNN. The high efficiency of sparse convolution improves researchers' confidence in the use of 3DCNN. 3DSSD [10] improves the distance calculation method of FPS by taking advantage of the difference between the foreground and the background points of outdoor scenes and improves the recall rate of foreground object instance level, thus further improving the network efficiency. SA-SSD [11] used 3DCNN to extract the backbone network features, and the secondary network features were transformed to the BEV plane and then sent to the detection head. By constructing additional tasks, the constraints of the network were enhanced. CIA-SSD [12] proposed the spatial-Semantic Feature Aggregation (SSFA) module for more robust feature extraction in 3D convolution and introduced classification fraction and location fraction to represent the confidence degree of the frame jointly, thus improving NMS. SE-SSD [13] proposes a self-integrated single-stage object detector, which is optimized by soft target consistency constraint.

Two-Stage 3D Object Detection. PointNet [14] and PointNet++ [15] are classical feature extraction methods in 3D detection. In recent years, many 3D target detection algorithms based on PointNet have also emerged. F-PointNet [16] uses 2D detection box and cone geometry to input the point cloud inside the cone into the PointNet to segment the point cloud instances, and obtains the semantic category of each point cloud, and then uses a PointNet to predict the 3D detection box. PointRCNN [17] uses PointNet++ to segment the foreground point of the point cloud and puts forward global and local coordinate systems to form a more stable feature expression. VoteNet [18] adopted Pointnet++ as the backbone network of point cloud and added a voting mechanism in the aggregation stage of point cloud features to stabilize the network and extract features. PV-RCNN [19] is a combination of point cloud and voxelization method, which combines features at all levels after voxelization to improve the network's learning ability.

3 Method

Compared with the original point cloud, the symmetrically completed point cloud has complete structural information. The original point cloud has an incomplete structure due to occluding, distance, and other factors. If the symmetrically strengthened point cloud is sent into the network, the network can learn the symmetric structure information. In contrast, if the missing point cloud is directly sent into the network, the network will correspondingly lose the symmetric structure information. This section describes in detail how the network learns symmetric structure information from the original point cloud.

3.1 Generation of Symmetric Annotations

In the driving scene, the incomplete point cloud is mainly caused by occlusion. In this paper, we use the symmetry of the object structure to supplement the invisible part of the point cloud to generate complete point cloud information. A car is a rigid object, and its structure is symmetrical about the central axis of the driving direction. Therefore, by using the symmetry of the car and the annotation of the data set itself, a complete annotation of the car can be generated to supplement the point cloud information of the occluded part.

First, according to the label of the detection box, the symmetric point cloud in the three-dimensional box is calculated according to its symmetry axis. The symmetrical point cloud is added to the original point cloud data, and a relatively complete symmetrical point cloud can be obtained.

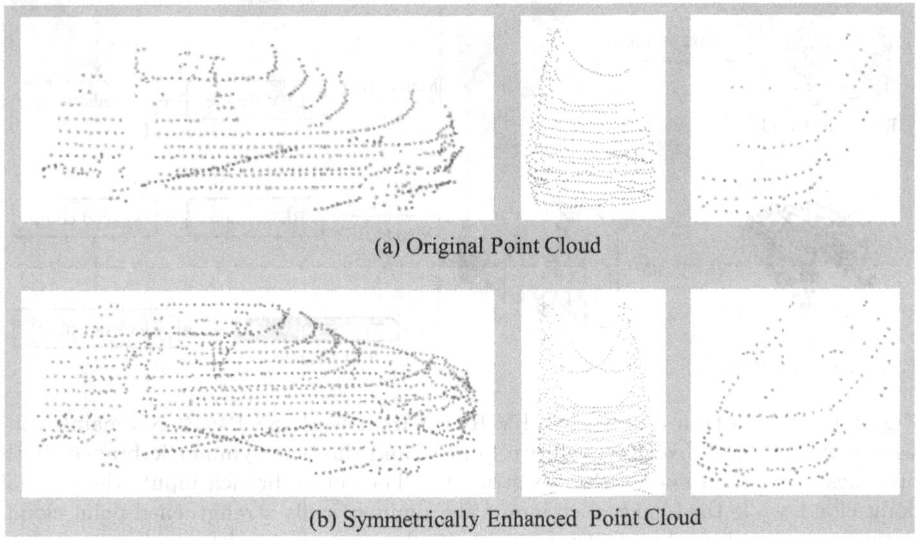

Fig. 1. Visualization of the (a) original point cloud and (b) symmetrically enhanced point cloud.

As shown in Fig. 1, the top is the original point cloud, and the bottom is the point cloud strengthened by symmetry. After symmetry enhancement, the structural features of cars at different positions will be more obvious. In addition, part of the point cloud will be completed in the shaded places according to their symmetrical structures. Therefore, the analysis of the shaded part is no longer blank. Point cloud strengthened by symmetry retains more surface information of the car, and the occlusion part is clearer so that the car's position can be located more accurately. Validity verification experiment of symmetrically enhance is introduced in detail in Sect. 4.1.

3.2 SS-PV-RCNN

Figure 2 shows the framework of SS-PV-RCNN, which consists of the original branch (top) and the symmetric branch (bottom), both of which use the same PV-RCNN [19] network. The input point cloud is voxelized and sent to the four-layer sparse convolution to extract voxel-based features. Then, the last layer of the convolution feature is projected onto the top view to get 2D features, and 2D detection is carried out. In addition, the original point cloud extracts the key points, then aggregates and splices the key points in the features of different convolutional layers and the top view, and sends them into the detection head to output the three-dimensional detection results.

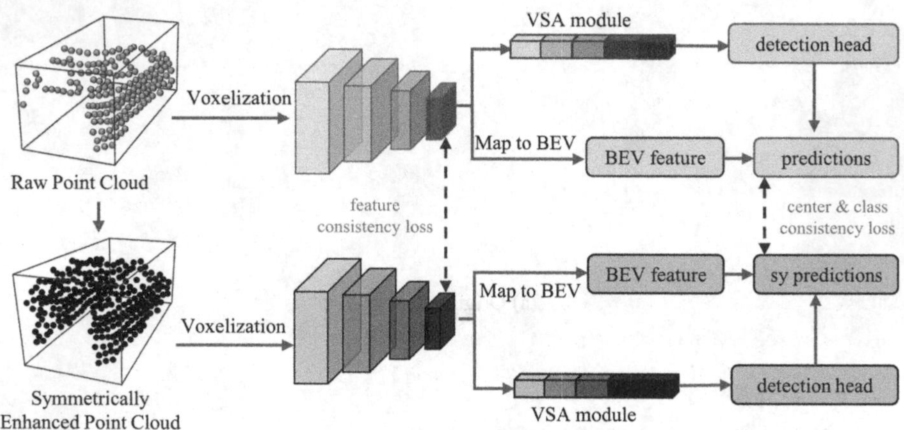

Fig. 2. Overview of our proposed SS-PV-RCNN framework. SS-PV-RCNN mainly consists of two parts, the yellow primitive branch, and the blue symmetric branch. Both branches adopt the same PV-RCNN structure. The yellow branch inputs the original point cloud, while the blue branch inputs the symmetrically strengthened point cloud. Between the two branches, feature consistency loss, center consistency loss, and class consistency loss help the original branch learn the symmetric structure information from the symmetric branch. (Color figure online)

In training, we first trained the symmetric branch, fixed its parameters, and trained the original branch. When training the original branch, we add feature consistency loss, center consistency loss, and class consistency loss to constraining the original branch to learn symmetry-related information from the symmetric branch. Symmetry awareness of the original branch is developed by enforcing the consistency of the output of the original branch and the symmetric branch.

3.3 Consistency Loss

Symmetry enhancement is generated according to ground truth, but the object to be detected does not have a position label. To this end, we propose three different consistency losses to help the network learn symmetrical structure information from the original point cloud.

We adopt a structure similar to knowledge distillation to make the network learn information about symmetry independently. Teacher networks and student networks share the same network structure. As shown in Fig. 2, in our design, the symmetrically strengthened yellow branch is the teacher network, while the unstrengthened blue branch is the student branch. Since the input of the point cloud is strengthened by symmetry, the teacher branch can learn information about symmetry that cannot be learned by the student branch in the process of feature learning. In order to make the student network learn symmetrical information in the process of training, the feature consistency loss is added into the last layer of the feature, which constrains the feature output of the student network and the teacher network to be as similar as possible. The calculation of the consistency loss is shown in Formula 1:

$$\mathcal{L}_{feature} = \tfrac{1}{N} \times \textstyle\sum_{i=1}^{N} \mathcal{L}_{fi}^{c}$$
$$and \qquad \mathcal{L}_{fi}^{c} = \begin{cases} 0.5 * (f_{si} - f_{ri})^2, & if\, |f_{si} - f_{ri}| < 1 \\ |f_{si} - f_{ri}| - 0.5, & otherwise \end{cases} \tag{1}$$

Where f_{si} represents the feature of the symmetric branch, f_{ri} represents the feature of the original branch, and N represents the number of features. The prototype for consistency loss is Smooth L1 [20] Loss.

In addition, the results of the symmetrical branching test are more accurate and have a high recall rate. Therefore, in the output results, we constrained the category of output results to be consistent with the center point of the box. For this reason, we added the category consistency and center point consistency constraints to encourage the student network to learn more accurately center and category.

Inspired by SESS [21], $C_r = \{c_r\}$ is used to represent the predicted 3D bounding boxes by student network, and $C_s = \{c_s\}$ is used to represent the 3D bounding boxes of symmetric teacher network prediction. For each $c_s \in C_s$, we do the alignment by searching for the its nearest neighbor in C_r based on the minimum Euclidean distance between the centers of the bounding boxes. We further use C_r' to denote the elements from C_r that are aligned with each element in C_s.

$$C_r' = \{\cdots, c_{r_i}', \cdots\}$$
$$and \qquad c_{r_i}' = \arg\min_{c_r} \|c_r - c_{s_i}\|_2, \forall c_r \in C_r \tag{2}$$

We define center consistency as:

$$\mathcal{L}_{\text{center}} = \frac{2 * \sum_{c_s} \|c_s - c_r'\|_2}{|C_r| + |C_s|} \tag{3}$$

In addition, we use Kullback-Leibler (KL) divergence to calculate category consistency, and the prediction category of symmetric branches is the learning objective of the original branch prediction category. P_s and P_r are used to represent the category probability of the predicted target of the symmetric branch and the original branch, respectively.

$$\mathcal{L}_{\text{class}} = \frac{1}{|P_s|} \sum D_{KL} (p_r \| p_s) \tag{4}$$

Finally, the total consistency loss is a weighted sum of all the three consistency terms described earlier:

$$\mathcal{L}_{\text{consistency}} = \lambda_1 \mathcal{L}_{\text{feature}} + \lambda_2 \mathcal{L}_{\text{center}} + \lambda_3 \mathcal{L}_{\text{class}} \tag{5}$$

where λ_1, λ_2, and λ_3 are the weights to control the importance of the corresponding consistency term.

4 Experiments

We evaluate our SS-PV-RCNN method on challenging KITTI [22] object detection benchmark. The KITTI dataset provides 7481 training samples and 7518 test samples, where the training samples are generally divided into the train split (3712 samples) and the val split (3769 samples). We compare SS-PV-RCNN with state-of-the-art methods on val split.

4.1 Symmetry Enhances Data Analysis

In order to prove the effectiveness of symmetry for point cloud detection, we took the truth values of all cars in 7481 training samples and strengthened the symmetry of all internal point clouds of cars according to their central axis planes to form a new data set after symmetry. Then, PV-RCNN was trained and verified on the data sets before and after symmetric reinforcement, respectively. The division of training and verification sets was consistent with that of KITTI, and the setting of the PV-RCNN network's hyperparameter was also consistent. The experimental results are shown in Table 1. When trained on the original KITTI data and verified on the symmetrically enhanced verification set, the accuracy increased by 5.78 on Hard, 2.91 on Moderate, and 0.45 on Easy. After symmetric enhancement of training data, the accuracy rate increased by 9.92 on Hard, 5.37 on Moderate, and 1.07 on Easy. This result fully shows that the enhancement of symmetry significantly affects the improvement of detection accuracy under challenging samples.

We use the symmetrically strengthened point cloud to train the symmetric branch model. The trained model has fixed parameters. As our symmetric teacher branch, both teacher and student branches are a complete PV-RCNN network structure. The original point cloud and the symmetrically strengthened point cloud are sent to the original student PV-RCNN branch and the symmetric teacher PV-RCNN branch. In order to make the student network learn more information about symmetry in the training process, the feature consistency loss, the significant consistency loss of the final result, and the category consistency loss are added. In the training process, only the weights of students' branches are updated, but not the weights of teachers' branches. In the prediction process, only the parameters of students' branches are used for prediction.

Table 1. Comparison of validation results of PV-RCNN method in KITTI and symmetrically enhanced KITTI datasets. RT and RV respectively represent the train set and val set of the original KITTI dataset. In contrast, ST and SV represent the train set and val set of the symmetrically strengthened KITTI dataset.

Method	Train	Val	Car-3D detection			Car-BEV detection		
			Easy	Mod	Hard	Easy	Mod	Hard
PV-RCNN	RT	RV	89.43	83.26	78.76	90.03	87.88	87.43
	RT	SV	89.88	86.17	84.54	90.26	88.81	88.31
			↑0.45	↑2.91	↑5.78	↑0.23	↑0.93	↑0.88
	ST	SV	90.50	88.99	88.68	90.67	89.97	89.81
			↑1.07	↑5.37	↑9.92	↑0.64	↑2.09	↑2.41

Table 2. Comparison with PV-RCNN detectors on KITTI val split for car detection, in which "R40" means 40 sampling recall points for AP.

Method	Metric	Car-3D detection			Car-BEV detection		
		Easy	Mod	Hard	Easy	Mod	Hard
PV-RCNN	AP	89.43	83.26	78.76	90.03	87.88	87.43
	AP_R40	91.43	84.47	82.22	92.97	90.56	88.41
SS-PV-RCNN	AP	89.62	84.25	79.13	90.44	88.49	87.94
	AP_R40	92.36	85.10	82.82	94.98	91.26	88.91

4.2 Comparison with State-of-the-Arts

As shown in Fig. 2, we used PV-RCNN [19] as the baseline, the yellow branch is a separate PV-RCNN network, and the blue branch as well. The setting of its

Table 3. Performance comparison on the moderate level car class of KITTI val split with mAP calculated by 11 recall positions.

Method	Reference	Modality	3D mAP
MV3D [4]	CVPR 2017	RGB + LiDAR	62.68
ConFuse [7]	ECCV 2018	RGB + LiDAR	73.25
AVOD-FPN [5]	IROS 2018	RGB + LiDAR	74.44
F-PointNet [16]	CVPR 2018	RGB + LiDAR	70.92
VoxelNet [8]	CVPR 2018	LiDAR only	65.46
SECOND [9]	Sensors 2018	LiDAR only	76.48
PointRCNN [17]	CVPR 2019	LiDAR only	78.63
Fast Point R-CNN [23]	ICCV 2019	LiDAR only	79.00
STD [24]	ICCV 2019	LiDAR only	79.80
PV-RCNN [19]	CVPR2020	LiDAR only	83.90
SS-PV-RCNN (ours)	-	LiDAR only	**84.28**

Fig. 3. Visualization of our results on the KITTI val split set. The ground-truth 3D boxes and the predicted 3D boxes of the baseline method and our method are drawn in green, blue, and purple, respectively, in the LiDAR phase. The first row shows RGB images, and the second shows the LiDAR pattern. (Color figure online)

Table 4. Recall of different proposal generation networks on the car class at moderate difficulty level of the KITTI val split set.

Method	PointRCNN [17]	STD [24]	PVRCNN [19]	SS-PV-RCNN
Recall (IoU = 0.7)	74.8	76.8	75.2	85.4

super parameters and the detailed implementation of the network was based on PV-RCNN. We empirically set hyperparameters $\lambda_1 = 1$, $\lambda_2 = 0.6$, and $\lambda_3 = 0.6$.

Metric. All results are evaluated by the mean average precision and recall with IoU threshold of 0.7 for cars. The mean average precisions on the test set are calculated with 40 recall positions on the official KITTI test server. The results on the val set in Table 2 are calculated with 11 recall positions to compare with the results of the previous works.

Our PV-RCNN framework is trained from scratch in an end-to-end manner with the ADAM optimizer. For the KITTI dataset, we train the entire network with the batch size 2, learning rate 0.01 for 80 epochs on 4 TITAN Xp GPUs, which takes around 23 h. In order to make a more unbiased experimental comparison, we trained PV-RCNN several times on our equipment and selected the best results as the baseline. All PV-RCNN results presented in this paper are our reproduction results.

As shown in Table 2, we compared the detection results of SS-PV-RCNN and PV-RCNN on the KITTI val split for car detection. Compared to baseline, our method has nearly 1 point improvement on the mod of 3D Detection and also has some improvement on other levels. Table 3, we compared our method with the prior works on the KITTI val split. Although there is still a particular gap between our method and the latest method, there is still a certain improvement in detection accuracy compared with the baseline method.

Figure 3 shows the comparison between our method and PV-RCNN in the detection results. In the LIDAR diagram, green represents groundtruth, blue represents the detection results of PV-RCNN, and purple represents the detection results of our method. In order to show it more clearly, only the groundtruth (green) and the detection results of our method (purple) are shown in the RGB figure. In the two figures in the first row, although SS-PV-RCNN detected some boxes without labeling, these boxes were all actual cars in the distance, which were not labeled due to the distance when labeling. It can be seen that our method is still robust to small distant targets. In the two figures in the second row, some error boxes detected by PV-RCNN are not found in our method, and our method is also more accurate in orientation prediction.

Since some small targets without labeling can also be detected by our method, the accuracy of our method will be relatively low. In order to further verify the effectiveness of our method, we compared the recall rate of SS-PV-RCNN and some typical methods on the val split when IOU = 0.7. As shown in Table 4, compared with PV-RCNN, the recall rate of our method has been improved by nearly 10 points, indicating that our method can detect more truth boxes.

4.3 Ablation Study

As can be seen from Table 1, the symmetry of the point cloud plays a significant role in 3D object detection based on point cloud. However, compare Table 1 and Table 2, it can be seen that the symmetrical information in the SS-PV-RCNN network we designed does not have such a prominent effect as that in Table 1. In future research work, we will further improve the design of network structure, hoping to make more effective use of symmetric structure to help improve the performance of 3D object detection. At the same time, we also hope that more researchers can pay attention to the critical role of symmetrical structure and work with us to introduce symmetry into 3D object detection better.

5 Conclusion

Inspired by the human symmetric visual cognitive system, we propose a symmetrically enhanced network SS-PV-RCNN, which can learn about symmetric structures from the point cloud by using symmetrically enhanced point clouds. Furthermore, we verify that symmetrical structure plays a significant role in the 3D detection of point clouds. SS-PV-RCNN can improve the accuracy of 3D object detection by using the learned symmetric structure information. Experimental results on the KITTI benchmark dataset demonstrate the effectiveness and robustness of our SS-PV-RCNN. In the future, we will try to introduce symmetric structure information into the single-stage model to further improve the accuracy of 3D object detection.

Acknowledgments. This work was supported by the National Natural Science Foundation of China (No.U20B2062), the fellowship of China Postdoctoral Science Foundation (No.2021M690354), the Beijing Municipal Science & Technology Project (No.Z191100007419001).

References

1. Driver, J., Baylis, G., Rafal, R.: Preserved figure-ground segregation and symmetry perception in visual neglect. Nature **360**, 73–75 (1992)
2. Machilsen, B., Pauwels, M., Wagemans, J.: The role of vertical mirror symmetry in visual shape detection. J. Vis. **9**(12), 11 (2009)
3. Helm, P.A., Treder, M.: Detection of (anti)symmetry and (anti)repetition: perceptual mechanisms versus cognitive strategies. Vis. Res. **49**, 2754–2763 (2009)
4. Chen, X., Ma, H., Wan, J., Li, B., Xia, T.: Multi-view 3D object detection network for autonomous driving. In: Proceedings of the IEEE Conference on Computer Vision and Pattern Recognition, pp. 1907–1915 (2017)
5. Ku, J., Mozifian, M., Lee, J., Harakeh, A., Waslander, S.L.: Joint 3D proposal generation and object detection from view aggregation. In: 2018 IEEE/RSJ International Conference on Intelligent Robots and Systems (IROS), pp. 1–8. IEEE (2018)
6. Yang, B., Luo, W., Urtasun, R.: PIXOR: real-time 3D object detection from point clouds. In: 2018 IEEE/CVF Conference on Computer Vision and Pattern Recognition, pp. 7652–7660 (2018)

7. Liang, M., Yang, B., Wang, S., Urtasun, R.: Deep continuous fusion for multi-sensor 3D object detection. In: Ferrari, V., Hebert, M., Sminchisescu, C., Weiss, Y. (eds.) ECCV 2018. LNCS, vol. 11220, pp. 663–678. Springer, Cham (2018). https://doi.org/10.1007/978-3-030-01270-0_39
8. Zhou, Y., Tuzel, O.: VoxelNet: end-to-end learning for point cloud based 3D object detection. In: Proceedings of the IEEE Conference on Computer Vision and Pattern Recognition, pp. 4490–4499 (2018)
9. Yan, Y., Mao, Y., Li, B.: SECOND: sparsely embedded convolutional detection. Sensors **18**(10), 3337 (2018)
10. Yang, Z., Sun, Y., Liu, S., Jia, J.: 3DSSD: point-based 3d single stage object detector. In: 2020 IEEE/CVF Conference on Computer Vision and Pattern Recognition (CVPR), pp. 11037–11045 (2020)
11. He, C., Zeng, H., Huang, J., Hua, X., Zhang, L.: Structure aware single-stage 3D object detection from point cloud. In: 2020 IEEE/CVF Conference on Computer Vision and Pattern Recognition (CVPR), pp. 11870–11879 (2020)
12. Zheng, W., Tang, W., Chen, S., Jiang, L., Fu, C.-W.: CIA-SSD: confident IoU-aware single-stage object detector from point cloud. In: AAAI (2021)
13. Zheng, W., et al.: SE-SSD: Self-Ensembling Single-Stage Object Detector From Point Cloud. In: Proceedings of the IEEE/CVF Conference on Computer Vision and Pattern Recognition(CVPR), pp. 14494–14503 (2021)
14. Qi, C., Su, H., Mo, K., Guibas, L.: PointNet: deep learning on point sets for 3d classification and segmentation. In: 2017 IEEE Conference on Computer Vision and Pattern Recognition (CVPR), pp. 77–85 (2017)
15. Qi, C., Yi, L., Su, H., Guibas, L.: PointNet++: deep hierarchical feature learning on point sets in a metric space. In: NIPS (2017)
16. Qi, C.R., Liu, W., Wu, C., Su, H., Guibas, L.J.: Frustum PointNets for 3D object detection from RGB-D data. In: Proceedings of the IEEE Conference on Computer Vision and Pattern Recognition, pp. 918–927 (2018)
17. Shi, S., Wang, X., Li, H.: PointRCNN: 3D object proposal generation and detection from point cloud. In: Proceedings of the IEEE/CVF Conference on Computer Vision and Pattern Recognition, pp. 770–779 (2019)
18. Ding, Z., Han, X., Niethammer, M.: VoteNet: a deep learning label fusion method for multi-atlas segmentation. In: Shen, D., et al. (eds.) MICCAI 2019. LNCS, vol. 11766, pp. 202–210. Springer, Cham (2019). https://doi.org/10.1007/978-3-030-32248-9_23
19. Shi, S., et al.: PV-RCNN: point-voxel feature set abstraction for 3D object detection. In: Proceedings of the IEEE/CVF Conference on Computer Vision and Pattern Recognition, pp. 10529–10538 (2020)
20. Liu, W., et al.: SSD: single shot MultiBox detector. In: Leibe, B., Matas, J., Sebe, N., Welling, M. (eds.) ECCV 2016. LNCS, vol. 9905, pp. 21–37. Springer, Cham (2016). https://doi.org/10.1007/978-3-319-46448-0_2
21. Zhao, N., Chua, T.S., Lee, G.H.: SESS: self-ensembling semi-supervised 3D object detection. In: Proceedings of the IEEE/CVF Conference on Computer Vision and Pattern Recognition, pp. 11079–11087 (2020)
22. Geiger, A., Lenz, P., Stiller, C., Urtasun, R.: Vision meets robotics: the KITTI dataset. Int. J. Robot. Res. **32**(11), 1231–1237 (2013)
23. Chen, Y., Liu, S., Shen, X., Jia, J.: Fast point R-CNN. In: Proceedings of the IEEE/CVF International Conference on Computer Vision, pp. 9775–9784 (2019)
24. Yang, Z., Sun, Y., Liu, S., Shen, X., Jia, J.: STD: sparse-to-dense 3D object detector for point cloud. In: Proceedings of the IEEE/CVF International Conference on Computer Vision, pp. 1951–1960 (2019)

Few-Shot Segmentation via Complementary Prototype Learning and Cascaded Refinement

Hanxiao Luo, Hui Li, Qingbo Wu(✉), Hongliang Li, King Ngi Ngan, Fanman Meng, and Linfeng Xu

University of Electronic Science and Technology of China, Chengdu, 611731, China
{lhx,huili}@std.uestc.edu.cn, {qbwu,hlli,knngan,fmmeng,lfxu}@uestc.edu.cn

Abstract. Prototype learning has been widely explored for few-shot segmentation. Existing methods typically learn the prototype from the foreground features of all support images, which rarely consider the background similarities between the query images and the support images. This unbalanced prototype learning strategy limits its capability to mutually correct the segmentation errors between the foreground and background. In this paper, we propose a Complementary Prototype Learning and Cascaded Refinement (CPLCR) network for few-shot segmentation. Firstly, both the foreground and background features of the support images are used to learn our complementary prototypes. Then, the foreground and background similarity maps are jointly derived between the query image feature and our complementary prototypes, which capture more comprehensive prior information. Finally, we fuse the query image feature, foreground prototype and the foreground/background similarity maps together, and feed them to a cascaded refinement module, which recursively reuses the output of previous iteration to refine the segmentation result. Extensive experimental results show that the proposed CPLCR model outperforms many state-of-the-art methods for 1-shot and 5-shot segmentation.

Keywords: Few-shot segmentation · Semantic segmentation · Prototype learning

1 Introduction

Deep learning methods based on convolutional neural networks have achieved progressive success in most visual tasks, which depends on a large amount of labeled data to supervise the training process [1]. However, the cost of pixel-level annotation is very expensive especially for the dense prediction tasks such as semantic segmentation tasks [8,18,24]. Under the situation that the labeled data is not enough or the model is adapted to unseen categories, the segmentation performance will decreases sharply. Though additional data available can help for training, the fine-tune process still consumes training time and computing

© Springer Nature Switzerland AG 2021
H. Ma et al. (Eds.): PRCV 2021, LNCS 13022, pp. 484–495, 2021.
https://doi.org/10.1007/978-3-030-88013-2_40

resources. Few-shot segmentation methods [9,16,19,20] are proposed to alleviate expensive annotation cost and improve the model generalizability for unseen classes, which can only leverage a small amount of labeled samples to deal with new classes.

Most of the current few-shot segmentation methods usually adopt shared feature extractor to perform feature extraction on support images and query images, and leverage average pooling strategy to generate the prototype vector for each category. Then, segmentation of query images is achieved by analysing the relationship between the query feature and the prototype vector, such as calculating the cosine similarity matrix, generating cascaded feature maps, or feature fusion. For example, Shaban et al. proposed a parallel two-branch network OSLSM [5], which solves the few-shot segmentation problem by learning different classifier weights for different categories. Co-FCN [12] directly cascaded the feature of support set and query set to achieve segmentation. In order to extract the foreground and background information in support set effectively, SG-One [11] used masked average pooling to obtain the guidance features, and calculated the cosine similarity between the guidance features and the query features. PANet [13] optimized prototype representations by adopting prototype alignment regularization for support branch and query branch, and fully mined the information of support images. FWB [15] used the difference between foreground and background of support images to generate a more discriminative prototype vector, and obtained a similarity mask by calculating the cosine similarity between the query feature and the prototype vector.

For a training episode in few-shot segmentation, the areas annotated at pixel-wise is seen as the foreground of support images and the other areas is seen as the background. Existing prototypical feature based few-shot segmentation methods [3,15,22,23] typically learn the prototype from the foreground features of all support images, which rarely consider the background similarities between the query feature and the support feature. However, due to the diversity of visual content, the background segmentation may be easier than the foreground segmentation and vice versa, which provides important complementary information for mutual correction.

In this paper, we propose a Complementary Prototype Learning and Cascaded Refinement (CPLCR) network for few-shot segmentation. Adopting complementary prototypes and leveraging the background similarities between query features and support features, CPLCR can effectively correct the segmentation errors between the foreground and background, so that it adapt to unseen categories well and achieve better segmentation performance. Firstly, the complementary prototypes including foreground prototype and background prototype are extracted from support features. Then, the foreground and background similarity maps are jointly derived between the query feature and our complementary prototypes, which capture more comprehensive prior information. Finally, the query image feature, foreground prototype and the foreground/background similarity maps are fused together, and we feed the fusion feature to a cascaded refinement module to refine the segmentation result.

To summarize, this paper has following contributions:

1. We propose a Complementary Prototype Learning and Cascaded Refinement (CPLCR) network for few-shot segmentation, which can mutually correct the segmentation errors between the foreground and background by generating complementary prototypes and exploiting the background similarities between query features and support features.
2. In CPLCR, we design a Prototype Relationship Module (PRM) to predict the foreground and background similarity maps which can better represent the similarities between support prototypes and query features. Besides, we adopt a cascaded refinement module, which recursively reuses the output of previous iteration to refine the segmentation result.
3. Extensive experimental results show that our CPLCR outperforms many state-of-the-art methods for 1-shot and 5-shot segmentation by effectively capturing the background similarities between support images and query images.

2 Method

2.1 Method Overview

The overall structure of our CPLCR is shown in Fig. 1. Depending on the support pixel-wise annotation mask, we generate complementary prototypes including the foreground prototype and the background prototype from support features by the Prototype Generation Module (PGM). Then the foreground and background similarity maps are jointly derived between the query feature and our complementary prototypes by the Prototype Relationship Module (PRM). The next feature fusion module fuses query feature, support foreground prototype and foreground/background similarity maps to generate segmentation features. Lastly, the cascaded refinement module is designed to generate segmentation masks for query images and refine the segmentation result.

2.2 Complementary Prototype Learning and Cascaded Refinement

Feature Extraction Network. Features in shallow layers usually contain low-level characteristic, such as texture, edge and color. In contrast, deep features imply high-level semantic information such as object categories. In order to enhance extracted features, we elaborate the feature extraction network which performs feature fusion on the shallow feature and the deep feature to contain low-level image characteristic and high-level semantic information.

Firstly, the input support image or query image I is transformed to feature F_I whose size is a quarter of the input image by sequentially passing the convolutional layer, the batch normalization layer, the ReLU activation layer and the max pooling layer. More specifically, the convolutional layer has a kernel size of 7×7, a padding size of 2 and a step size of 1. Then, F_I is sent to $Block1$ and $Block2$ to obtain the low-level features F_{low}. The next $Block3$ convert F_{low} to

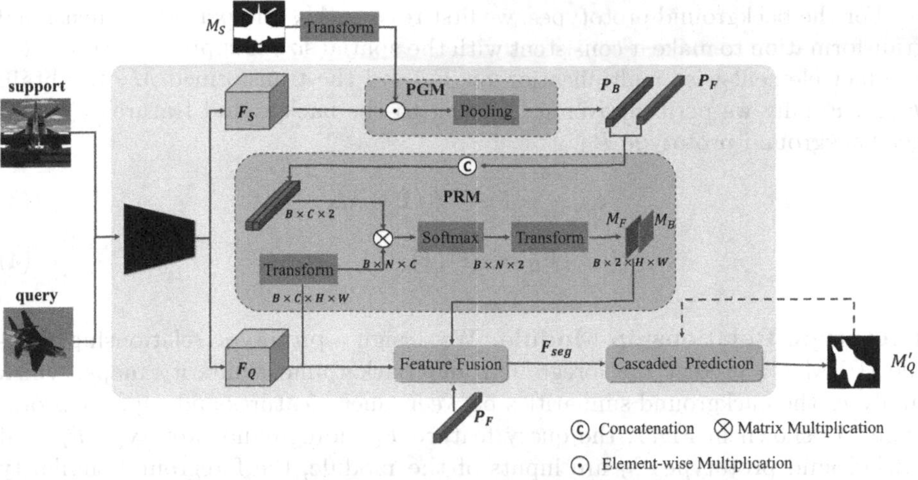

Fig. 1. The schematic illustration of the Complementary Prototype Learning and Cascaded Refinement (CPLCR) network.

F_{high}. Note that the $Block1-3$ have a similar structure with the feature extraction part of ResNet, but the first convolutional layer of $Block3$ has a kernel size of 3×3, a step size of 1, a padding of 2, and a void rate of 2.

To make the feature contains low-level characteristic and high-level semantic information, we cascade F_{low} and F_{high} along channel dimension to acquire the fused feature F_{fusion}. Finally, a convolutional layer with a kernal size of 3×3, a step size of 1, a padding of 2, and a void rate of 2 is used to reduce the dimension of F_{fusion}, and the final output feature F is obtained through another ReLU activation function and Dropout layer.

Prototype Generation Module. In this section, we explain the generation of complementary prototypes. The inputs of prototype generation module are support pixel-wise annotation mask M_S and support feature F_S. The corresponding outputs is the complementary prototypes including the support foreground prototype P_F and the background prototype P_B. For the foreground prototypes, we first perform dimensional transformation for M_S to make it consistent with the spatial size of support feature. Then F_S and the transformed M_S conduct element-wise multiplication to obtain F_{fore}, which presents the foreground categories of support images. Finally we conduct average pooling on the foreground features F_{fore} to get the foreground prototype P_F. Note that, T and AP in the following descriptions indicate dimensional transformation and average pooling respectively.

$$F_{fore} = F_S \odot T(M_S) \tag{1}$$

$$P_F = AP(F_{fore}) \tag{2}$$

For the background prototypes, we first reverse M_S and perform dimensional transformation to make it consistent with the spatial size of support feature, then conduct element-wise multiplication on F_S and the transformed M_S to obtain F_{back}. Finally we perform average pooling to the background features F_{back} to get background prototype P_B.

$$F_{back} = F_S \odot T\left(1 - M_S\right) \tag{3}$$

$$P_B = AP\left(F_{back}\right) \tag{4}$$

Prototype Relationship Module. We design a prototype relationship module (PRM) to predict the foreground and background similarity maps, which analyses the background similarities between query features and support prototype. As shown in Fig. 1, the query feature F_Q, foreground prototype P_F and background prototype P_B are inputs of the module, the foreground similarity map M_F and the background similarity map M_B are corresponding outputs. We first transfer the query feature $F_Q \in R^{B\times C\times H\times W}$ to $F_Q' \in R^{B\times N\times C}$, then concatenate P_F and P_B along the channel dimension. Next we multiply the concatenation result with $F_Q' \in R^{B\times N\times C}$ to obtain F_Q'', the batch matrix multiplication is denoted as BM in the following equations. After a Softmax layer and another dimension transformation, the prototype relationship module generates foreground similarity map M_F and background similarity map M_B which have the same size as query features.

$$F_Q'' = BM\left(F_Q', [P_F, P_B]\right) \tag{5}$$

$$Prob_F = Softmax\left(F_Q''\right) \tag{6}$$

$$M_F, M_B = T\left(Prob_F\right) \tag{7}$$

Feature Fusion Module. The feature fusion module aims to perform feature fusion on query features, foreground prototypes, and foreground/background similarity maps, which can promote the network to effectively leverage the similarities between support prototypes and query features. We first upsample P_F to get P_F', then concatenate P_F', F_Q, M_F and M_B to obtain new feature F'. Next, perform feature transformation and channel reduction on F' by the convolutional layer with a kernel size of 3×3, a step size of 1, a padding of 2, and a void rate of 2. The final segmentation feature F_{seg} are generated after a ReLU activation function and a Dropout layer.

$$F_{seg} = Dropout\left(ReLU\left(Conv\left(F'\right)\right)\right) \tag{8}$$

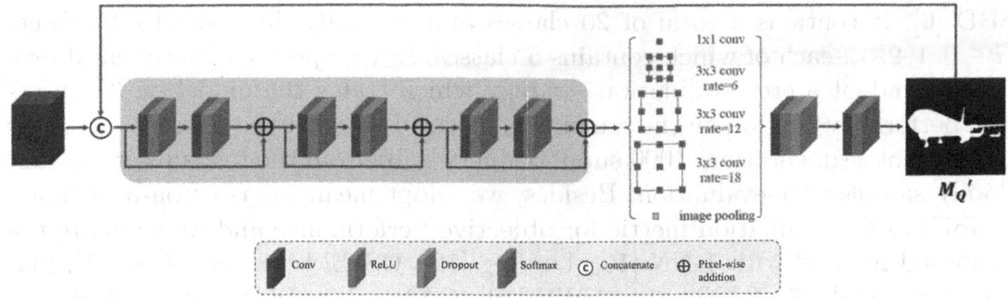

Fig. 2. Illustration of the cascaded refinement module.

Cascaded Refinement Module. In order to acquire more refined predictions for query images, the segmentation prediction module adopts a cascaded structure, which recursively reuses the output of previous iteration to refine the segmentation result. The schematic diagram is shown in Fig. 2. The segmentation feature F_{seg} is concatenated with prediction mask M_Q', and the concatenation result is sent into three cascaded residual blocks to obtain F_{seg}''. Each of the block is consist of two 3×3 convolution layers and a ReLU activation function layer. Then F_{seg}'' are sent into a Atrous Spatial Pyramid Pooling module (ASPP) proposed in [2] to capture multi-scale contextual information. The output F_{seg}''' of pyramid pooling module passes a 1×1 convolution layer whose channel amount is the number of classes. In the end, the final prediction mask M_Q' are generated after dimension transform and Softmax operation. Note that the initial segmentation probability mask M_Q' is initialized to 0.

2.3 Loss Function

In the proposed Complementary Prototype Learning and Cascaded Refinement (CPLCR) network, we adopt cross-entropy loss function to measure the difference between the predicted segmentation spectrum M_Q' and the groundtruth M_Q of the query image.

$$loss_{seg} = L_{CrossEntropy}\left(M_Q', M_Q\right) \tag{9}$$

3 Experiments

To evaluate the performance of our proposed method, we conduct extensive experiments on the Pascal-5^i dataset [12]. More specifically, we not only evaluate the segmentation performance of the proposed method quantitatively and qualitatively, but also analyze the complexity of the model.

3.1 Datasets and Evaluation Metric

In this paper, we choose Pascal-5^i to evaluate the proposed method. Pascal-5^i is consists of images from PASCAL VOC 2012 [4] and extra annotations from

SBD [6]. It contains a total of 20 classes and is evenly divided into 4 subsets ($i \in 0, 1, 2, 3$), each of which contains 5 classes. In the specific experimental process, we adopt a cross-validation strategy which trains the model on 3 subsets and perform evaluation on the remaining subset. Following the inference strategy of few-shot segmentation, 1000 support-query pairs from the test subset are randomly sampled for evaluation. Besides, we adopt mean intersection-over-union (mIoU) as the evaluation metric for objective performance and we compare the proposed method with 1-NN [12], LogReg [12], OSLSM [12], co-FCN [11], SG-One [23], AMP [7], PANet [14], FWB [10], CANet [22], PGNet [21], PPNet [7] and RPMMs [17].

3.2 Implementation Details

The proposed method is implemented on the framework of Pytorch and all the experiments run on a workstation with a single NVIDIA Titan Xp GPU. During the training process, input images are firstly transformed with horizontal flip and random scale from [1 − 1.5], all the images are normalized with a mean value of 0.456 and 0.406 and a variance of 0.229, 0.224 and 0.225, finally the images are cropped to 321 × 321 as training samples. For the testing process, we do not adopt any additional data augmentation and crop the test images to 321 × 321 directly. SGD optimizer with a momentum of 0.9 and a weight decay of 0.0005 is adopted to optimize the model. The learning rate is set to 0.00025 and the batch size is 4. The model is trained for a total of 200 epochs. When verifying the 5-shot segmentation performance, for a query image of class c, we randomly sample 5 support images and corresponding annotation masks with the same class, and concatenate them for model input.

3.3 Comparison to State-of-the-Art

At first, we quantitatively compare the 1-shot performance of our model with the state-of-the-art methods. From Table 1, it's obvious that our method has the best overall performance, which has an average mIoU of 57.61 on 4 subsets and achieves an increase of 1.27 compared with the best-performing RPMMs. The mIoU on Pascal-5^0 and Pascal-5^3 are 56.26 and 53.73, which are 1.11 and 3.05 higher than RPMMs respectively, and the performance on Pascal-5^1 is only 0.29 lower than RPMMs. Although the mIoU on Pascal-5^2 is lower than that of PPNet, the performance of our method on the other three subsets is much higher than PPNet, more specifically, the average mIoU is 4.77 higher than PPNet.

In Tabel 2, we compare our model with the state-of-the-art methods in 5-shot experiment setting. Due to the increase of supporting samples, the average mIoU on 4 subsets increased by 1.45, which is better than that of 1-shot. Besides, performance of the proposed method is still the best, with an average mIoU of 59.06, which gets an increase of 0.56 compared to the best-performing PGNet in the compared methods.

To intuitively present the effectiveness of our method, we also visualizes the prediction results of 1-shot segmentation. The segmentation results of birds,

Table 1. Comparison of 1-shot performance with the state-of-the-art on Pascal-5^i.

Method	Pascal-5^0	Pascal-5^1	Pascal-5^2	Pascal-5^3	Mean
1-NN [12]	25.30	44.90	41.70	18.40	32.60
LogReg [12]	26.90	42.90	37.10	18.40	31.40
OSLSM [12]	33.60	55.30	40.90	33.50	40.80
co-FCN [11]	36.70	50.60	44.90	32.40	41.10
SG-One [23]	40.20	58.40	48.40	38.40	46.30
AMP [7]	41.90	50.20	46.70	34.70	43.40
PANet [14]	42.30	58.00	51.10	41.20	48.10
FWB [10]	47.04	59.64	52.51	48.27	51.90
CANet [22]	52.50	65.90	51.30	51.90	55.40
PGNet [21]	56.00	66.90	50.60	50.40	56.00
PPNet [7]	48.58	60.58	**55.71**	46.47	52.84
RPMMs [17]	55.15	**66.91**	52.61	50.68	56.34
Ours	**56.26**	66.62	53.83	**53.73**	**57.61**

Table 2. Comparison of 5-shot performance with the state-of-the-art on Pascal-5^i.

Method	Pascal-5^0	Pascal-5^1	Pascal-5^2	Pascal-5^3	Mean
1-NN [12]	34.50	53.00	46.90	25.60	40.00
LogReg [12]	35.90	51.60	44.50	25.60	39.30
OSLSM [12]	35.90	58.10	42.70	39.10	43.95
Co-FCN [11]	37.50	50.00	44.10	33.90	41.40
SG-One [23]	41.90	58.60	48.60	39.40	47.10
AMP [7]	41.80	55.50	50.30	39.90	46.90
PANet [14]	51.80	64.60	59.80	46.05	55.70
FWB [10]	50.87	62.86	**56.48**	50.09	55.08
CANet [22]	55.50	67.80	51.90	53.20	57.10
PGNet [21]	57.70	**68.70**	52.90	54.60	58.50
RPMMs [17]	56.28	67.34	54.52	51.00	57.30
Ours	**58.64**	67.46	54.28	**55.85**	**59.06**

trains, cats, airplanes, cars, dogs, boats, bottles, and sheep are respectively shown in Fig. 3. For better presentation of segmentation results, the pixel-wise annotation masks and the predicted mask for query images are marked with red foreground. When the objects in query images have different sizes (birds in the first row, cats in the third row, and boats in the seventh row), our method can effectively segment the foreground objects. When the query image has multiple instances (such as the sheep in the fourth, fifth and sixth columns of the ninth row), our method can also segment all the foreground objects without missing detection.

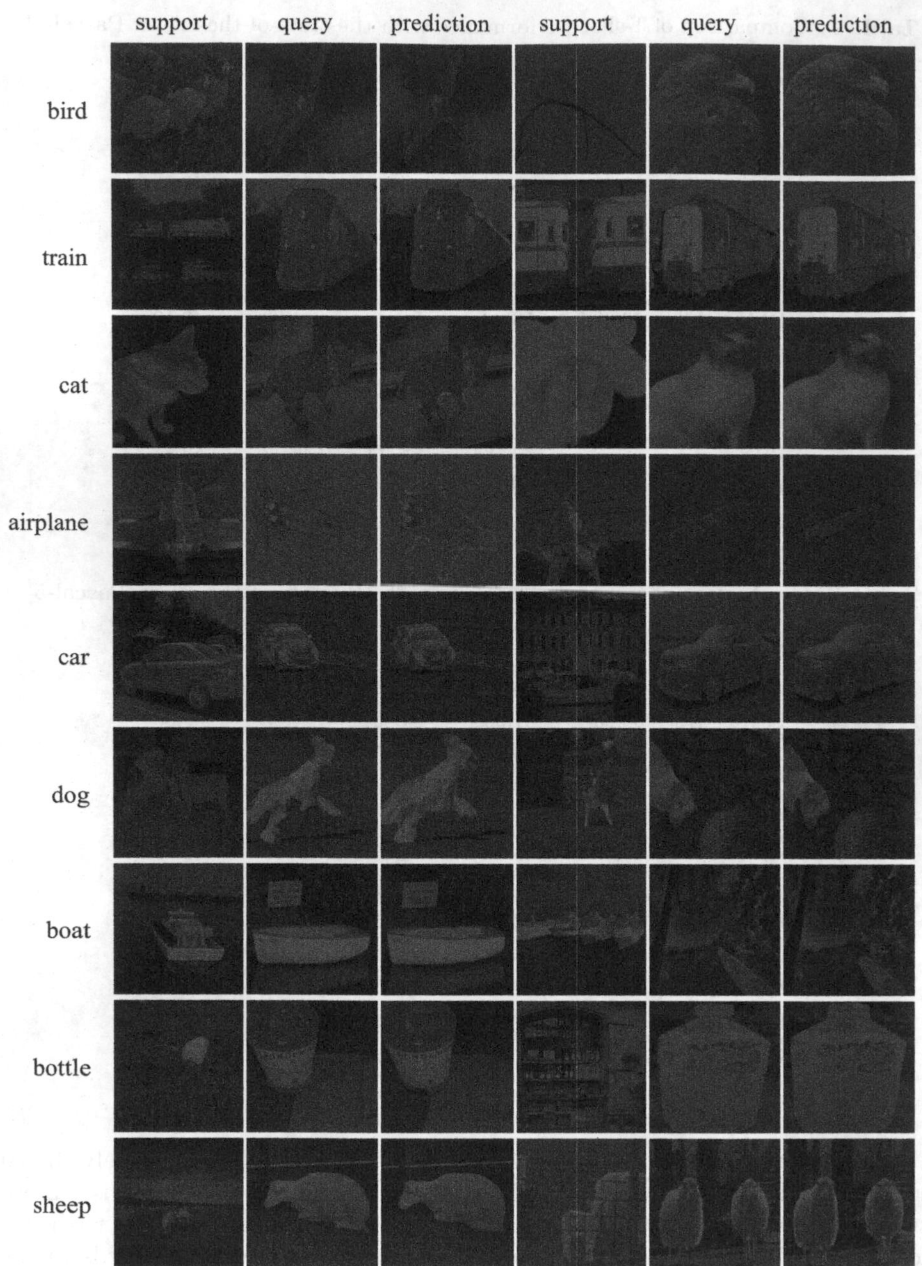

Fig. 3. Visualizations of the 1-shot predicted segmentation results.

3.4 Ablation Study

We conduct ablation experiments on Pascal-5^i to exploit the influence of different cascaded layers on the segmentation performance. The comparison results are shown in Table 3 and Table 4. Concretely, in Table 3, when the number of cascaded layers increases from 1 to 4, the average mIoU of 1-shot segmentation on 4 subsets gradually increases from 55.21 to 57.61. When the number of cascaded layers is 5, the mIoU on Pascal-5^0 and Pascal-5^2 subsets are 55.18 and 53.81, and the performance decreases by 1.08 and 0.02 respectively, which leads to the average mIoU performance decreasing by 0.05.

Table 3. 1-shot segmentation performance for different cascading layers on Pascal-5^i.

Cascaded layers	Pascal-5^0	Pascal-5^1	Pascal-5^2	Pascal-5^3	Mean
1	53.49	66.16	51.15	50.02	55.21
2	54.66	66.35	52.77	52.53	56.58
3	55.43	66.64	53.16	53.51	57.19
4	**56.26**	66.62	**53.83**	53.73	**57.61**
5	55.18	**66.97**	53.81	**54.29**	57.56

For 5-shot setting, the results present similar changes with 1-shot performance in Table 3. In Table 4, when the number of cascaded layers increases from 1 to 4, the average mIoU of 5-shot segmentation on 4 subsets gradually increases from 56.76 to 59.06, and the performance improves by 2.3. However, when the number of cascaded layers is 5, the mIoU on Pascal-5^1 and Pascal-5^3 subsets are 67.02 and 55.58, and the performance decreases by 0.44 and 0.27 respectively, which leads to the average mIoU performance decreasing by 0.08. As the number of cascaded layers increases, the training time and resource consumption will gradually increase. Considering the trade-off between segmentation performance and resource consumption, the number of cascaded layers in our experiments is set to 4.

Table 4. 5-shot segmentation performance for different cascading layers on Pascal-5^i.

Cascaded layers	Pascal-5^0	Pascal-5^1	Pascal-5^2	Pascal-5^3	Mean
1	56.37	66.11	51.82	52.75	56.76
2	57.99	66.79	53.50	53.96	58.06
3	57.96	66.68	54.23	54.83	58.43
4	58.64	**67.46**	54.28	**55.85**	**59.06**
5	**58.86**	67.02	**54.41**	55.58	58.98

In addition, we also make comparison on the number of training parameters. In Table 5, OSLSM [12] has a total of 276.7M parameters, with the largest network complexity and calculation amount, followed by AMP [7], co-FCN [11], PPNet [7] and RPMMs [17]. On the contrary, the proposed method has a parameter amount of 19.0M, which is equivalent to the parameter amount of SG-One [23] and CANet [22], and rank only second only to PANet [14].

Table 5. Comparison of different methods on the number of parameters.

Method	OSLSM	co-FCN	SG-One	AMP	PANet	CANet	PPNet	RPMMs	**Ours**
Params(M)	276.7	34.2	19.0	34.7	14.7	19.0	23.5	19.6	19.0

4 Conclusion

In this paper, we propose a Complementary Prototype Learning and Cascaded Refinement (CPLCR) network for few-shot segmentation. By leveraging the complementary prototypes and the foreground/background similarity maps, the model can effectively exploit the background similarities between the query images and the support images to promote generalization ability for unseen classes. Extensive experiments and ablation studies on 1-shot and 5-shot segmentation have demonstrated the superiority of our proposed method.

Acknowledgement. This work was partially supported by National Natural Science Foundation of China (No. 61971095, 61871078, 61831005, and 61871087).

References

1. Badrinarayanan, V., Kendall, A., Cipolla, R.: SegNet: a deep convolutional encoder-decoder architecture for image segmentation. IEEE Trans. Pattern Anal. Mach. Intell. **39**(12), 2481–2495 (2017)
2. Chen, L.C., Papandreou, G., Schroff, F., Adam, H.: Rethinking atrous convolution for semantic image segmentation. arXiv preprint arXiv:1706.05587 (2017)
3. Dong, N., Xing, E.P.: Few-shot semantic segmentation with prototype learning. In: BMVC, vol. 3 (2018)
4. Everingham, M., Gool, L., Williams, C.K.I., Winn, J., Zisserman, A.: The pascal visual object classes (VOC) challenge. Int. J. Comput. Vis. **88**, 303–338 (2009)
5. Everingham, M., Van Gool, L., Williams, C.K., Winn, J., Zisserman, A.: The pascal visual object classes (VOC) challenge. Int. J. Comput. Vis. **88**(2), 303–338 (2010)
6. Hariharan, B., Arbeláez, P., Bourdev, L.D., Maji, S., Malik, J.: Semantic contours from inverse detectors. In: 2011 International Conference on Computer Vision, pp. 991–998 (2011)
7. Liu, Y., Zhang, X., Zhang, S., He, X.: Part-aware prototype network for few-shot semantic segmentation. ArXiv abs/2007.06309 (2020)
8. Long, J., Shelhamer, E., Darrell, T.: Fully convolutional networks for semantic segmentation. In: Proceedings of the IEEE Conference on Computer Vision and Pattern Recognition, pp. 3431–3440 (2015)

9. Luo, K., Meng, F., Wu, Q., Li, H.: Weakly supervised semantic segmentation by multiple group cosegmentation. In: 2018 IEEE Visual Communications and Image Processing (VCIP), pp. 1–4 (2018)
10. Nguyen, K.D.M., Todorovic, S.: Feature weighting and boosting for few-shot segmentation. In: 2019 IEEE/CVF International Conference on Computer Vision (ICCV), pp. 622–631 (2019)
11. Rakelly, K., Shelhamer, E., Darrell, T., Efros, A.A., Levine, S.: Conditional networks for few-shot semantic segmentation. In: ICLR (2018)
12. Shaban, A., Bansal, S., Liu, Z., Essa, I., Boots, B.: One-shot learning for semantic segmentation. ArXiv abs/1709.03410 (2017). arXiv:1709.03410
13. Siam, M., Oreshkin, B.N., Jagersand, M.: AMP: adaptive masked proxies for few-shot segmentation. In: Proceedings of the IEEE/CVF International Conference on Computer Vision, pp. 5249–5258 (2019)
14. Wang, K., Liew, J., Zou, Y., Zhou, D., Feng, J.: PANet: few-shot image semantic segmentation with prototype alignment. In: 2019 IEEE/CVF International Conference on Computer Vision (ICCV), pp. 9196–9205 (2019)
15. Wang, K., Liew, J.H., Zou, Y., Zhou, D., Feng, J.: PANet: few-shot image semantic segmentation with prototype alignment. In: Proceedings of the IEEE/CVF International Conference on Computer Vision, pp. 9197–9206 (2019)
16. Xu, X., Meng, F., liang Li, H., Wu, Q., Ngan, K.N., Chen, S.: A new bounding box based pseudo annotation generation method for semantic segmentation. In: 2020 IEEE International Conference on Visual Communications and Image Processing (VCIP), pp. 100–103 (2020)
17. Yang, B., Liu, C., Li, B., Jiao, J., Ye, Q.: Prototype mixture models for few-shot semantic segmentation. ArXiv abs/2008.03898 (2020)
18. Yang, M., Yu, K., Zhang, C., Li, Z., Yang, K.: DenseASPP for semantic segmentation in street scenes. In: Proceedings of the IEEE Conference on Computer Vision and Pattern Recognition, pp. 3684–3692 (2018)
19. Yang, Y., Meng, F., Li, H., Ngan, K., Wu, Q.: A new few-shot segmentation network based on class representation. In: 2019 IEEE Visual Communications and Image Processing (VCIP), pp. 1–4 (2019)
20. Yang, Y., Meng, F., Li, H., Wu, Q., Xu, X., Chen, S.: A new local transformation module for few-shot segmentation. ArXiv abs/1910.05886 (2020)
21. Zhang, C., Lin, G., Liu, F., Guo, J., Wu, Q., Yao, R.: Pyramid graph networks with connection attentions for region-based one-shot semantic segmentation. 2019 IEEE/CVF International Conference on Computer Vision (ICCV), pp. 9586–9594 (2019)
22. Zhang, C., Lin, G., Liu, F., Yao, R., Shen, C.: CANet: class-agnostic segmentation networks with iterative refinement and attentive few-shot learning. In: Proceedings of the IEEE/CVF Conference on Computer Vision and Pattern Recognition, pp. 5217–5226 (2019)
23. Zhang, X., Wei, Y., Yang, Y., Huang, T.: SG-One: similarity guidance network for one-shot semantic segmentation. IEEE Trans. Cybern. **50**(9), 3855–3865 (2020)
24. Zhao, H., Shi, J., Qi, X., Wang, X., Jia, J.: Pyramid scene parsing network. In: Proceedings of the IEEE Conference on Computer Vision and Pattern Recognition, pp. 2881–2890 (2017)

Couple Double-Stage FPNs with Single Pipe-Line for Solar Speckle Images Deblurring

Fuhai Li[1], Murong Jiang[1(✉)], and Lei Yang[2]

[1] School of Information Science and Engineering, Yunnan University, Kunming, China
jiangmr@ynu.edu.com

[2] Yunnan Observatories, Chinese Academy of Sciences, Kunming, China

Abstract. Solar speckle images acquired by ground-based optical telescope usually are blurred or degraded seriously with more noise and fuzzy local details. Most of the deep learning deblurring methods are suitable for the natural images which have sufficient contextualized and gradient information, but for solar speckle images may cause some problems such as over-smoothing, high-frequency loss, and artifacts generated. In this paper, we propose a deblurring method based on coupling double-stage feature pyramid networks (FPN) with a single pipe-line (DSFSP) to reconstruct high-resolution solar speckle images. In stage1, one FPN is used to recover structure features; In stage2, another FPN is used to enhance the structural contextualized, and the single pipe-line coupled with this FPN is used to extract gradient information. After fusing these to generate a reconstructed image, discriminators are used to make it closer to the reference. Experiments show that DSFSP has a strong ability to strengthen the gradient spatial and contextualized information, improve image clarity, restore high-frequency details and drop artifacts.

Keywords: Double-stage · FPN · Single pipe-line · Gradient spatial · Contextualized information · Solar speckle image

1 Introduction

Due to the influence of atmospheric turbulence and atmospheric disturbance, the solar activity observation image by ground-based optical telescope would be seriously blurred or degraded, which needs image restoration method for reconstruction. As deep learning is widely used in computer vision and image processing, how to use deep learning methods to reconstruct solar speckle images has become one of the research hotspots in astronomical image processing. In recent years, two blind deblurring methods based on deep learning have been widely used. These two methods are the kernel estimation method and the image-to-image regression method.

For the method of kernel estimation, there has been lots of work with great results [1–4]. This kind of method is often used in super-resolution and deblurring tasks. Since GT kernels are usually needed in training, it is generally active on synthetic datasets. However, the degradation process of blurred images taken naturally is unknown, which greatly increases the difficulty of deblurring.

© Springer Nature Switzerland AG 2021
H. Ma et al. (Eds.): PRCV 2021, LNCS 13022, pp. 496–507, 2021.
https://doi.org/10.1007/978-3-030-88013-2_41

For the method of image-to-image regression, some work [5, 6] has found that skipping the step of blur kernel estimation would omit the connection of prior hypothesis, and get a more natural deblurred image. As discovered by Ledig et al. [7], a generative adversarial network (GAN) can reconstruct sharp edges effectively. However, improper handling of the adversarial process may distort the local detail in the generated image. To solve this problem, Ma et al. [8] use a gradient-guided approach to help the generator pay more attention to local detail. Kupyn et al. [9] introduce a multi-scale generator based on a feature pyramid network (FPN) [10] to obtain features at different scales. And they constructed a two-scale discriminator, focusing on local and global features respectively. The structure allows them to obtain brilliant results on the public datasets. Some reconstruction works on the astronomical image also use a deep learning network. Ren et al. [11] apply Cycle-GAN [12] to the restoration of solar images. Based on the original network structure, they improve the content loss and add a perceptual loss to make the deblurred image more realistic. Correspondingly, Jia et al. [13] also use Cycle-GAN for the reconstruction of solar images. But the difference is that they use a frame selection algorithm to select multiple parts with large information content from a large number of blurred images and use them as the training set of the neural network. This approach allows the network to have a strong generalization ability and can restore images with great visual effects.

The above-mentioned work has made great progress in reconstruction, but it is not suitable for the reconstruction task of solar speckle images. The main reason is that solar speckle images usually contain single structural features, low contrast and fuzzy local details.

In order to strengthen gradient spatial and contextualized features, a deblurring method based on coupling double-stage FPNs with a single pipe-line (DSFSP) is proposed. The paper content is arranged as follows: In Sect. 2, three parts including design ideas, generator and discriminator, and loss function are introduced in detail; In Sect. 3, experiments and analysis prove the effectiveness of DSFSP; In Sect. 4, advantages and disadvantages of this method are summarized.

2 Method Description

2.1 Main Idea

In order to make the results obtained by DSFSP closer to the reconstruction effect of the Level1+ method [14] used by the Yunnan Observatory, part of reconstruction results of the Level1+ method are used as the supervised image (GT Sharp), and the paired blurred image be the input image (Blur). The main framework of our method DSFSP is shown in Fig. 1. The Sharps (Stage1 Sharp, Stage2 Sharp) are the reconstruction results of stage1 and stage2, and the Gradient is the gradient information captured by the stage2. The GT Gradient is the gradient image of GT Sharp.

DSFSP has two contributions for solar speckle images reconstruction:

1) Redesign the gradient structure which is proposed by Ma et al. [8] to better extract the spatial information. It uses a single pipe-line method to obtain features from the

decoder of FPN2 step by step. This design is quite different from theirs and greatly reduce the dependence on the gradient information of original input images.

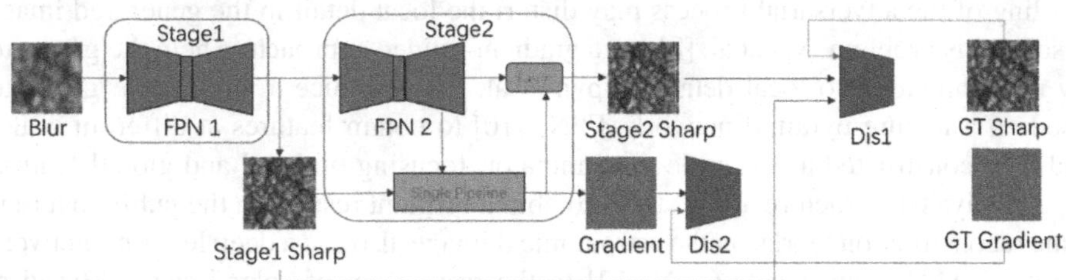

Fig. 1. The main framework of our method (DSFSP).

2) Design a double-stage generator structure based on FPN. With the help of FPN's powerful multi-scale capabilities, it can easily extract the contextualized information. This double-stage structure can split complex deblurring problem into multiple sub-problems. After the first stage processed, the gradient structure of the second stage can capture more accurate gradient information. Therefore, this double-stage structure can be more effective than a single-stage.

Above two contributions can enhance the model's ability to acquire contextualized and spatial information at the same time. But this requires that gradient information must be sufficiently accurate, so the gradient information as a gradient image would be output separately, a discriminator used to optimize it. Therefore, DSFSP should have two discriminators, one for discriminating generated images (Dis1) and another for discriminating gradient images (Dis2).

2.2 Description of the Generator

Double-Stages FPNs and Single-Pipe Gradient Structure. To prevent the generator from acquiring noisy gradient information, we construct a double-stage FPNs structure. And this structure inevitably increases the difficulty of model training, so we introduce the supervised attention module (SAM) proposed by Zamir et al. [15] to help the model enable progressive learning. More precisely, we use SAM to connect two FPN networks that can reconstruct the image step by step. Then we output features of different scales from the decoder of the second FPN network, and import them into a single-pipe structure to capture gradient information. This single-pile design without down sampling can greatly retain the spatial information of the image. And we fuse outputs of single-pipe and FPN to get the final reconstruction result. In addition, to reduce the artifacts caused by the generator after feature stacking, we adopt the Residual in Residual Dense Block (RRDB) module proposed by Wang et al. [16], which can improve its stability during generator training and produce fewer artifacts. The generator structure of our method is shown in Fig. 2.

Gradient Spatial and Contextualized Information. With gradients, powerful spatial information can be captured. Unlike public datasets, the gradient information of solar speckle images is very difficult to obtain. Therefore, our method gradually captures the gradient information from the reconstruction process. The gradient information acquisition can refer to Fig. 3.

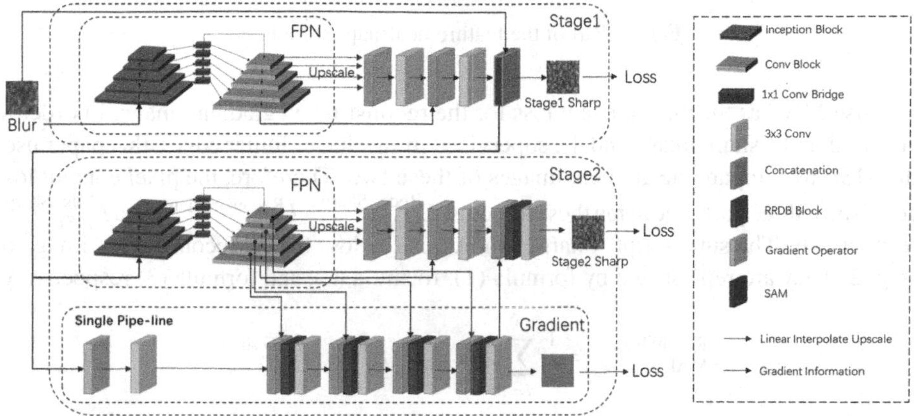

Fig. 2. The structure of generator.

Fig. 3. The gradient information.

Inspired by Kupyn et al. [9], we also use the FPN as an encoder-decoder for blurred images. The powerful multi-scale design of FPN can focus on image features of different scales and positions, so as to obtain rich contextualized information. Different from the rich contextualized information of natural images, the contextualized information of solar speckle images is mainly reflected in the rice grain's shape of the speckle and the gap between the rice grains. It can be seen from the feature heatmaps (Fig. 4) that FPN can effectively pay attention to these, so as to extract the contextualized information of solar speckle images.

Loss Function of the Generator. Since the loss functions used in the generated sharp images of stage1 and stage2 are the same, we take the loss of stage2 as an example. For the convenience of naming, we call the "Stage1 Sharp" as "Sharp1" and the "Stage2 Sharp" as "Sharp2".

Pixel Content Loss. We use the mean absolute error (MAE) as the pixel content loss for the reconstructed sharp image. Consistent with the consideration of the sharp image, we

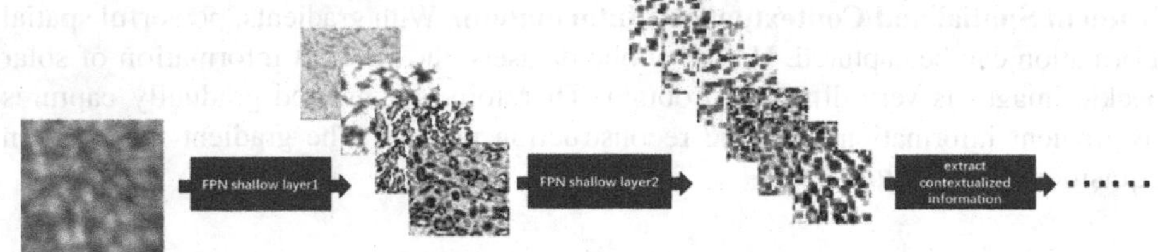

Fig. 4. Part of the feature heatmaps from FPN.

also use MAE as the pixel content loss for the reconstructed gradient image. In order to ensure that the sharp image and the supervised image have similar edges, this paper uses the MSE to compare the gradient images of these two. Therefore, the pixel content loss consists of three parts, we name these losses as $L_{\text{MAE}}^{\text{ReconSharp2}}$, $L_{\text{MAE}}^{\text{ReconGradient}}$, and $L_{\text{MSE}}^{\text{EdgeSharp2}}$ respectively. The superscript "Sharp2" indicates the loss for the reconstructed image of stage2. They are represented by formula (1), formula (2), and formula (3) respectively.

$$L_{\text{MAE}}^{\text{ReconSharp2}} = \frac{1}{N}\sum_{i=1}^{N} ||G_{\text{sharp2}}(I_i^{\text{Blur}}) - I_i^{\text{GTsharp}}||_1 \tag{1}$$

$$L_{\text{MAE}}^{\text{ReconGradient}} = \frac{1}{N}\sum_{i=1}^{N} ||G_{\text{gradient}}(I_i^{\text{Blur}}) - M(I_i^{\text{GTsharp}})||_1 \tag{2}$$

$$L_{\text{MSE}}^{\text{EdgeSharp2}} = \frac{1}{N}\sum_{i=1}^{N} ||M(G_{\text{sharp2}}(I_i^{\text{Blur}})) - M(I_i^{\text{GTsharp}})||_2^2 \tag{3}$$

The I_i^{Blur} and I_i^{GTsharp} indicate the i-th blurry input images and the i-th paired supervised images reconstructed by the Level1 + method respectively. The $G_{\text{sharp2}}(I_i^{\text{Blur}})$ and $G_{\text{gradient}}(I_i^{\text{Blur}})$ respectively represent the sharp image reconstructed in stage2 of the generator and the gradient image reconstructed by the generator. The $M(\bullet)$ represents the gradient operator of the image [8].

Perceptual Loss. To make better perceptual effect, we introduce perceptual loss [17]. The calculation formula of the perceptual loss is shown in formula (4). The $\Phi(\bullet)$ represents the VGG19 network [18] for capturing perceptual features.

$$L_{\text{Perceptual}}^{\text{Sharp2}} = \frac{1}{N}\sum_{i=1}^{N} ||\Phi(G_{\text{sharp2}}(I_i^{\text{Blur}})) - \Phi(I_i^{\text{GTsharp}})||_1 \tag{4}$$

Adversarial Loss. In order to obtain more high-quality reconstructed images and more efficient gradient images, we use relativistic average least squares GAN loss (RaLsGAN) [19] as our adversarial loss. It can acquire higher-quality perception effects and realistic high-frequency information. The calculation formula of its generator part is shown in formula (5).

$$L_{\text{G}}^{\text{RaLsGAN}} = \text{E}_{z\sim p_z(z)}[(D(G(z)) - \text{E}_{x\sim p_{\text{data}}(x)}D(x) - 1)^2] + \text{E}_{x\sim p_{\text{data}}(x)}[(D(x) - \text{E}_{z\sim p_z(z)}D(G(z)) + 1)^2] \tag{5}$$

The $p_{data}(x)$ represents the target (real) distribution, and the $p_z(z)$ represents the generated (fake) distribution. In this relative adversarial loss, the purpose of the discriminator D is to identify the probability that one sample is more real than another. Therefore, as the number of training iterations increases, the discriminator $D(G(z))$ would increase, while the discriminator $D(x)$ would decrease, and eventually, the two would reach a balance.

Total Loss of the Generator. Finally, adding the above loss functions can get the total loss of the generator. It is worth mentioning that the same loss except the generated gradient loss (formula (2)) must be used in the stage1 of the generated image (Sharp1). The calculation formula of the total loss function of the generator is shown in formula (6).

$$L_G = \min_G(\alpha(L_{MAE}^{ReconSharp1} + L_{MAE}^{ReconSharp2}) + \beta(L_{MAE}^{ReconGradient}) + \chi(L_{MSE}^{EdgeSharp1} + L_{MSE}^{EdgeSharp2}) + \delta(L_{Perceptual}^{Sharp1} + L_{Perceptual}^{Sharp2}) + \varepsilon(L_{G_{Sharp1}}^{RaLsGAN} + L_{G_{Sharp2}}^{RaLsGAN}) + \phi(L_{G_{Gradient}}^{RaLsGAN})) \quad (6)$$

The $L_{G_{Sharp1}}^{RaLsGAN}$, $L_{G_{Sharp2}}^{RaLsGAN}$, and the $L_{G_{Gradient}}^{RaLsGAN}$ respectively represents the adversarial loss for the Sharp1, the adversarial loss for the Sharp2, and the adversarial loss for the gradient image generated by the generator. It is worth mentioning that the Sharp1 and the Sharp2 use one discriminator, and the gradient image uses another different discriminator. The value of the α, β, χ, δ, ε, ϕ are set to 0.01, 0.5, 0.01, 0.05, 0.05, 0.05.

2.3 Discriminators

To obtain a more realistic generated image, we introduce a multi-scale discriminator designed by Chen et al. [20], which can obtain different features at three scales for identification. And we use two discriminators of the same structure to respectively discriminate the generated images including Sharp1 and Sharp2, and the generated gradient image. Since stacking convolutional layers would obtain a larger receptive field, this stacking method of three different scales can identify areas of different sizes in the image. Then combining the losses of the three scales as a comprehensive decision helps to more accurately identify the reality.

Corresponding to the generator's adversarial loss, the RaLsGAN calculation formula used by the discriminator is shown in formula (7).

$$L_D^{RaLsGAN} = E_{x\sim p_{data}(x)}[(D(x) - E_{z\sim p_z(z)}D(G(z)) - 1)^2] + E_{z\sim p_z(z)}[(D(G(z)) - E_{x\sim p_{data}(x)}D(x) + 1)^2] \quad (7)$$

Therefore, the loss functions of the two discriminators used in this paper are shown in formula (8) and formula (9) respectively.

$$L_{D_{Sharp}} = \min_{D_{Sharp}}(L_{D_{Sharp1}}^{RaLsGAN} + L_{D_{Sharp2}}^{RaLsGAN}) \quad (8)$$

$$L_{D_{Gradient}} = \min_{D_{Gradient}} L_{D_{Gradient}}^{RaLsGAN} \quad (9)$$

The D_{Sharp} represents the discriminator for generated sharp images including the Sharp1 and the Sharp2. And the $D_{Gradient}$ represents the discriminator for the generated gradient image.

3 Experiments and Analysis

3.1 Solar Speckle Datasets

In this paper, we use the continuous solar speckle images taken by the 1m New Vacuum Sun Telescope (NVST) from Fuxian Lake as the datasets. Although the amount of observation data is huge, not all captured images are suitable for reconstruction work. Thanks to the work of Jia et al. [13], they find that the deep learning network can complete the model training only by using the same wavelength images and a small number of high-definition reference images. And it can recover most of the captured images at this wavelength. Following their work of datasets, we select the blurred images (Blur) and then crop them together with the paired supervised images (GT Sharp) reconstructed by Level1+. Finally, we obtained more than 50000 patches with the size of 256 × 256 as our training datasets.

3.2 Implementation Details

To reduce the memory usage and back propagation problems, we separate the training of stage1 and stage2. Specifically, stage1 trains separately and froze the stage2 parameters. During stage2 training, the parameters of stage1 should be frozen. All experiments in this paper are trained and tested on a single Nvidia 1080ti GPU.

3.3 Experimental Evaluation

We compare our method with several current mainstream methods [3, 8, 9] on public datasets and astronomical methods [11, 13]. Since the method proposed by Kupyn et al. [9] contains two methods, for the convenience of naming, we call his mobile method as mobile and call his inception method as inception. In addition, our method is named DSFSP in the evaluation results.

Quantitative Comparison. In order to ensure the fairness of the comparison, this paper adopts the evaluation indicators that have appeared in the above research: Peak Signal-to-Noise Ratio (PSNR) and Structural SIMilarity (SSIM). The quantitative comparison results are shown in Table 1. It can be seen that the method proposed in this paper has achieved good results on both PSNR and SSIM.

Qualitative Comparison. From a more intuitive point of view, DSFSP can effectively approach the supervised image (GT Sharp). And it can be found from Fig. 5 that the double-stage FPNs and single pipe-line gradient structure method can clearly restore the overall edges of the image. In addition, it can also show that DSFSP effectively reduces the generated artifacts and restores the realistic local high-frequency information.

Table 1. PSNR and SSIM comparison on the Solar Speckle Datasets

Method	PSNR/dB	SSIM
Guo et al. [3]	24.2742	0.6524
Ma et al. [8]	22.9655	0.6383
Kupyn et al. [9]-mobile	24.4764	0.6526
Kupyn et al. [9]-inception	24.0640	0.6741
Ren et al. [11]	25.1237	0.7442
Jia et al. [13]	23.6201	0.6947
DSFSP	**27.8010**	**0.8510**

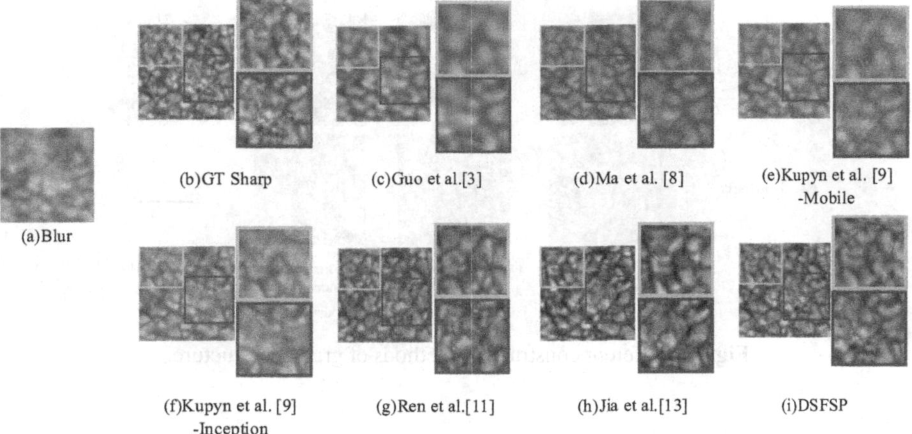

Fig. 5. Comparison of different methods.

3.4 Ablation Experiment

Gradient Information. It is worth mentioning that we also use the gradient structure to enhance the spatial information like Ma et al. [8], but our design is quite different from theirs. Due to the different task, their gradient information is obtained by the encoder of the generator. Such a design heavily depends on the edge features of the input image. It can be found from (b) in Fig. 6 that we get less information if we obtain the gradient directly from the input image. Therefore, depending on the original gradient information are not suitable for solar speckle images. To avoid this problem, our generator captures the gradient information from the decoder which is after the feature bridge of the second FPN. Through the purpose of this design, more effective spatial features can be obtained from the decoder, rather than the blurry features extracted from the encoder. For the fair comparison with Ma et al. [8], our structure retains only the second stage. That means the blurred image directly inputs to stage2 and this structure is named single-stage. It can be seen from (c) and (d) in Fig. 6 that after we redesign the gradient structure, the final gradient image information is significantly greater than the result of Ma et al. [8]. And to prove that this different is not caused by FPN, we modify the gradient structure on our method. The specific results can refer to Fig. 7. In addition, we design a double-stage FPNs, which can further improve the utilization rate of the gradient structure. It can be seen from the comparison between (d) and (e) in Fig. 6.

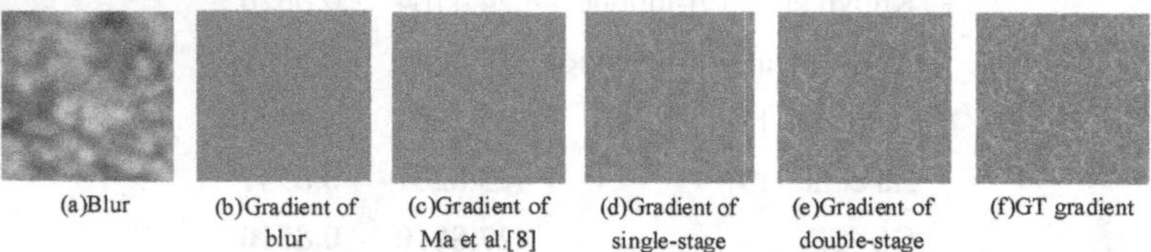

Fig. 6. Ablation experiment of gradient information.

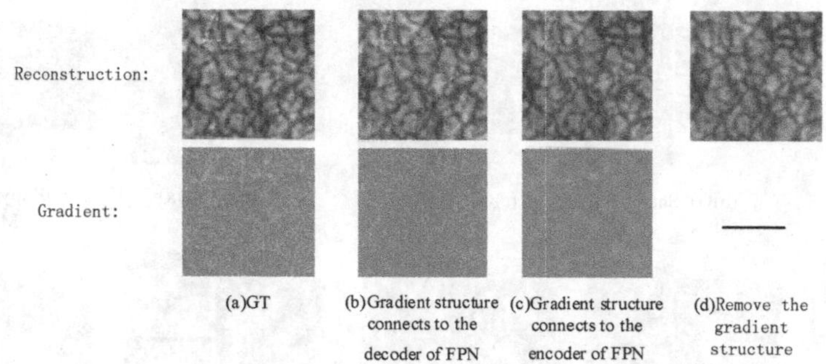

Fig. 7. Different construction methods of gradient structure.

Moreover, the gradient acquisition is related to the clarity of the input image. If the input image has obvious gradient information, the gradient structure is not even needed anymore. And it can get a good effect without a double-stage structure, which we will prove in the experiment of public datasets later.

Multi-stage Structure. Multi-Stage can significantly improve the acquisition of gradient information, which means that model can acquire more spatial information. But it is not that the more stages, the better effects. When the number of FPNs increases to 3, the reconstruction effect decreases instead. This is because as the number of stages increases, the parameters of the model are rising rapidly. More parameters mean that the model is more difficult to train and overfitting is more serious.

Therefore, we use 2 stages of FPNs to construct the generator. This design can improve the effectiveness of the single-pipe gradient, thereby helping us to obtain more spatial information. The comparison of the number of stages can refer to Fig. 8.

3.5 Comparison Results on Public Datasets

To verify whether the proposed method is applicable to general blurry, this paper also compares the public datasets. The public datasets we choose include DVD datasets [21]

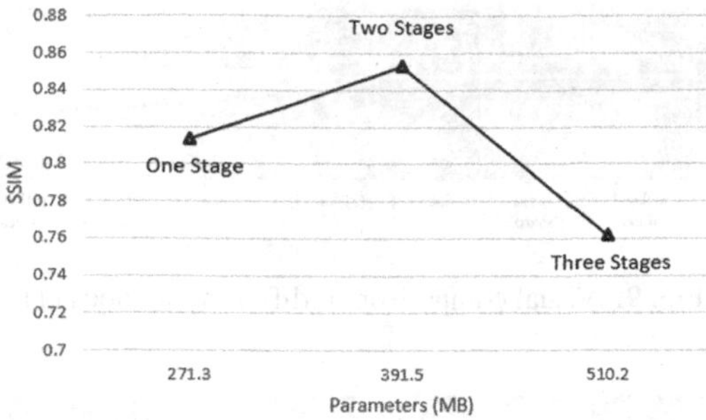

Fig. 8. Comparison with different number of stages.

and GoPro datasets [5]. The quantitative evaluation results are shown in Table 2 and Table 3, and the qualitative evaluation results are shown in Fig. 9 and Fig. 10. Since public datasets usually have obvious gradient and contextualized information, we try to extract the second stage separately for experimentation.

Table 2. PSNR and SSIM comparison on the DVD datasets.

Method	PSNR/dB	SSIM
Kupyn et al. [9]-mobile	28.54	0.9294
Kupyn et al. [9]-inception	28.85	**0.9327**
DSFSP (only second stage)	28.69	0.9312
DSFSP	**28.94**	0.9306

Table 3. PSNR and SSIM comparison on the GoPro datasets.

Method	PSNR/dB	SSIM
Solar et al. [1]	24.64	0.8419
Nah et al. [5]	29.08	0.9135
Tao et al. [6]	**30.26**	0.9342
Kupyn et al. [9]-mobile	28.17	0.9254
Kupyn et al. [9]-inception	29.55	**0.9344**
DSFSP (only second stage)	28.85	0.9232
DSFSP	28.92	0.9212

It can be seen from the results above that the method proposed in this paper is also competitive in the public datasets and can effectively restore the local details of the image. However, it can also be seen from the evaluation results that the double-stage and gradient structure has not significantly improved in terms of indicators. This is because

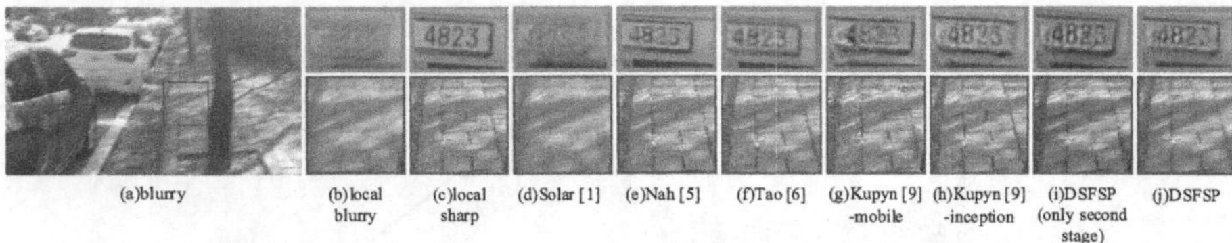

Fig. 9. Visual comparison of different methods (1)

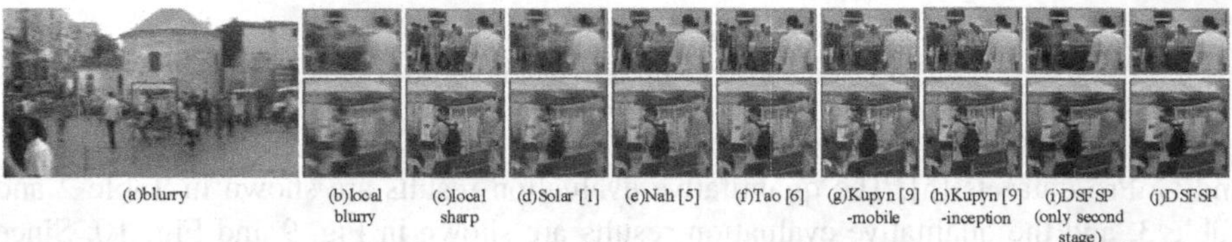

Fig. 10. Visual comparison of different methods (2)

the blurry images in the public datasets generally have clear spatial and contextualized features, so some multi-scale networks are sufficient to capture spatial and contextualized information. This is different from our solar speckle datasets, which do not have obvious information like that. Our method is more focused on solving this complicated situation.

4 Conclusion

Because of solar speckle images having single structural features, low contrast and fuzzy local details, we use FPNs to enhance the structural contextualized, use the single pipe-line coupled with FPN to extract gradient information, and finally reconstruct high-resolution images. Experimental results show that our method has a strong ability in the reconstruction of solar speckle images, and its visual quality and evaluation indicators are significantly better than other existing mainstream deep learning methods.

Although DSFSP can be very close to the GT images reconstructed by the Level1+ method, it would also learn some noise and artifacts in GT, and its time efficiency needs to be further improved. In future work, we will try to introduce an unsupervised method to reconstruct the solar speckle images and reduce the dependence on GT.

Acknowledgments. This work is supported by National Nature Science Foundation under Grant 11773073, the Supported by program for Innovative Research Team in University of Yunnan Province (IRTSTYN).

References

1. Solar, J., Cao, W., Xu, Z., et al.: Learning a convolutional neural network for non-uniform motion blur removal. In: IEEE Conference on Computer Vision and Pattern Recognition, pp. 769–777 (2015)

2. Gu, J., Lu, H., Zuo, W., et al.: Blind super-resolution with iterative kernel correction. In: Conference on Computer Vision and Pattern Recognition, pp. 1604–1613 (2019)
3. Guo, Y., Chen, J., Wang, J., et al.: Closed-loop matters: dual regression networks for single image super-resolution. In: IEEE Conference on Computer Vision and Pattern Recognition, pp. 5406–5415 (2020)
4. Kaufman, A., Fattal, R.: Deblurring using analysis synthesis networks pair. In: IEEE Conference on Computer Vision and Pattern Recognition, pp. 5810–5819 (2020)
5. Nah, S., Kim, T., Lee, K.: Deep multi-scale convolutional neural network for dynamic scene deblurring. In: IEEE Conference on Computer Vision and Pattern Recognition, pp. 257–265 (2017)
6. Tao, X., Gao, H., Shen, X., et al.: Scale-recurrent network for deep image deblurring. In: IEEE Conference on Computer Vision and Pattern Recognition, pp. 8174–8182 (2018)
7. Ledig, C., Theis, L., Huszar, F., et al.: Photo-realistic single image super-resolution using a generative adversarial network. In: IEEE Conference on Computer Vision and Pattern Recognition, pp. 4681–4690 (2017)
8. Ma, C., Rao, Y., Cheng, Y., et al.: Structure-preserving super resolution with gradient guidance. In: IEEE Conference on Computer Vision and Pattern Recognition, pp. 7766–7775 (2020)
9. Kupyn, O., Martyniuk, T., Wu, J., et al.: DeblurGAN-v2: deblurring (orders-of-magnitude) faster and better. In: IEEE International Conference on Computer Vision and Pattern Recognition, pp. 8877–8886 (2019)
10. Lin, T., Dollar, P., Girshick, R., et al.: Feature pyramid networks for object detection. In: IEEE Conference on Computer Vision and Pattern Recognition, pp. 936–944 (2017)
11. Ren, Y., Jiang, M., Yang, L., et al.: Reconstruction of single-frame solar speckle image with cycle consistency loss and perceptual loss. In: IEEE 6th International Conference on Information Science and Control Engineering, pp. 439–443 (2019)
12. Zhu, J., Park, T., Isola, P., et al.: Unpaired image-to-image translation using cycle-consistent adversarial networks. In: IEEE International Conference on Computer Vision, pp. 2242–2251 (2017)
13. Jia, P., Huang, Y., Cai, B., et al.: Solar image restoration with the CycleGAN based on multi-fractal properties of texture features. Astrophys. J. Lett. **881**(2), L30 (2019)
14. Xiang, Y.: Research on high-resolution and high-speed solar reconstruction algorithm dissertation. University of Chinese Academy of Sciences, Beijing, pp. 19–22 (2016)
15. Zamir, S., Arora, A., Khan, S., et al.: Multi-stage progressive image restoration. In: CVPR (2021)
16. Wang, X., et al.: ESRGAN: enhanced super-resolution generative adversarial networks. In: Leal-Taixé, L., Roth, S. (eds.) ECCV 2018. LNCS, vol. 11133, pp. 63–79. Springer, Cham (2019). https://doi.org/10.1007/978-3-030-11021-5_5
17. Johnson, J., Alahi, A., Li, F.: Perceptual losses for real-time style transfer and super-resolution. arXiv preprint arXiv:1603.08155 (2016)
18. Simonyan, K., Zisserman, A.: A very deep convolutional networks for large-scale image recognition. arXiv preprint arXiv:1409.1556 (2014)
19. Jolicoeur-Martineau, A.: The relativistic discriminator: a key element missing from standard GAN. arXiv preprint arXiv:1807.00734 (2018)
20. Chen, R., Huang, W., Huang, B., et al.: Reusing discriminators for encoding: towards unsupervised image-to-image translation. In: IEEE International Conference on Computer Vision and Pattern Recognition, pp. 8165–8174 (2020)
21. Su, S., Delbracio, M., Wang, J., et al.: Deep video deblurring for hand-held cameras. In: IEEE International Conference on Computer Vision and Pattern Recognition, pp. 237–246 (2017)

Multi-scale Image Partitioning and Saliency Detection for Single Image Blind Deblurring

Jiaqian Yan[1,2,3], Yu Shi[1,2,3](✉), Xia Hua[1,2,3], Zhigao Huang[1,2,3], and Ruzhou Li[1,2,3]

[1] School of Electrical and Information Engineering, Wuhan Institute of Technology, Wuhan 430205, China

[2] Hubei Key Laboratory of Optical Information and Pattern Recognition, Wuhan 430205, China

[3] Laboratory of Hubei Province Video Image and HD Projection Engineering Technology Research Center, Wuhan 430205, China

Abstract. Solving the problem of the blurred image degraded by natural environment or human induced camera exposure has always been a challenge. The researches on blind deblurring are generally to use the statistical prior of the image as the regularization term, which can extract the critical information from the image itself. However, such methods are unable to achieve desired results because the blur kernel will be non-uniform in practice, so the inconsistencies of kernels in different image regions should be considered. Many patch-wise deblurring algorithms have certain limitations, such as the unreasonableness of partition. In this paper, we propose an adaptive multi-scale image partitioning method from coarse to fine, which provides a more accurate partition for kernel estimation locally, and uses the structural similarity value of the kernel as the criterion of partitioning. Then, we introduce the image saliency detection to obtain more edge details from the image, which can contribute to the better kernel estimation. In addition, a weighted window function is applied to the joint of image patches with different sizes to obtain the final restored image. Extensive experiments on space-invariant and space-variant blurred images demonstrate that the proposed method achieves better performance against many classical methods.

Keywords: Image blind deblurring · Non-uniform · Multi-scale partitioning · Saliency detection

1 Introduction

Single image deblurring is one of the fundamental issues in image processing, which is caused by several reasons, such as the physical limitations of the camera system, the relative motion between the camera and the scene during exposure, atmospheric turbulence and so on. Image deblurring can be divided into space-invariant deblurring and space-variant deblurring, and the ultimate aim of both is to recover the latent image from the input blurred image. For the space-invariant image deblurring problem, given a space-invariant blurred image, the process of image degradation can be defined as

$$y = k * x + n \tag{1}$$

© Springer Nature Switzerland AG 2021
H. Ma et al. (Eds.): PRCV 2021, LNCS 13022, pp. 508–523, 2021.
https://doi.org/10.1007/978-3-030-88013-2_42

where $*$ is the convolution operator, k is the blur kernel, x is the desired latent image, and n is the noise. In practice, such a problem is generally the blind deblurring with unknown blur kernel. It requires to estimate the latent image and the blur kernel together from the given blurred image, which is a highly ill-posed problem because the number of unknowns to be solved is more than the number of known ones.

2 Related Work

In recent years, the image blind deblurring method has received increasing attention, many researchers use the image statistical prior as regularization term, such as image gradient, image edge information, total variation and so on. Cho et al. [1] introduce the bilateral filtering function to estimate the strong edges in image, which can improve the robustness of the kernel estimation and the convergence speed. Xu et al. [2] consider to select the image edges that can be more beneficial to kernel estimation, and use the total variation to obtain the optimal restoration. Pan et al. [3] use both image gradient prior and intensity prior to remove the blur effectively. Then, Pan et al. [4] introduce a L_0 regularization term to enhance the sparsity of the dark channel in the image, which can effectively perform blind image deblurring. In reference [5], the local maximum gradient is used as a prior to establish a new framework, which has a good effect.

Different with the space-invariant deblurring, the image degradation of the space-variant deblurring is non-uniform due to the camera shake or the random interference of atmospheric turbulence dynamic environment [6, 7]. The space-variant degraded problem has a seriously impact on the target recognition, detection and positioning in practical application. Because of the non-uniformity of the blur kernel, estimating the kernel accurately becomes more difficult, which can't be solved as the same as the solution in the space-invariant deblurring.

Therefore, the researches on space-variant image restoration have attracted wide attention. There are many methods based on global deblurring, the SVD is applied to decompose the kernel, and TV regularization is used to solve the deblurring problem in [8]. Gupta et al. [9] model the blur kernel from three degrees in the camera motion as a motion density function, including the horizontal and vertical rotation and translation. Cho et al. [10] use a set of plane perspective projections to describe the process of 3D non-uniform blur. However, these methods require a large amount of computation and memory. In the previous work, the efficient filter flow (EFF) method proposed in [11] divides the blurred image into patches according to the set numbers of partitioning. The method considers that the patches are space-invariant, and uses the blind deblurring method to restore the image, but it will result in the problems such as expensive computation and inaccurate kernel estimation. Harmeling et al. [12] use global constraints to ensure the similarity between blur kernels in kernel estimation after image partitioning, but such global constraints lead to the problem that kernels cannot be solved in closed form. Inspired by the same patch-wise method, in [13], the blurred image is divided into overlapping patches, and then a pixel level blur matrix is constructed to restore the image. In [14], the similarity of adjacent kernel is considered and the kernel mapping regularization is used to improve the kernel estimation accuracy. Barnsley et al. [15] apply the phase diversity method to the kernel estimation of each patch, thus the image can be restored globally. In [16], after the image is divided into patches, the kernel of each patch is estimated by prior knowledge combined with dictionary to solve the non-uniform deblurring problem in real life. From the above methods, it can be seen that applying the appropriate method to image partitioning is important for accurate kernel estimation.

In this paper, to achieve this goal, we propose an image blind deblurring method based on multi-scale image adaptive partitioning, which consists of three parts: first, we can achieve the adaptive image partitioning without predetermined image patches, and using the structural similarity of the kernel as the criterion to decide whether to divide or merge image patches. Second, a saliency detection is introduced as a prior to estimate the kernel more accurately and preserve more details. Third, the adjacent deblurred patches of different sizes can be jointed with the weighted window function to obtain the final restored image. The experimental results verify that, compared with several existing classical deblurring methods, the proposed method performs well on space-invariant and space-variant blurred images.

3 Multi-scale Adaptive Image Partition and Merging

This section introduces the overall steps of adaptive image partition and merging, and we use the structural similarity evaluation (SSIM) as the criterion to measure the similarity of two estimated kernels.

We know that the visual effect of human eyes is a gradual blurring process generally when observing an object at close and long distances, and the scale of the observed image is decreasing, specially, different scales can reflect the different details in image. Here, if the scale of the input image is not lower than a preset value (set as $C = 128$ in this paper), we make the scale variation on the image. We adopt a multi-scale adaptive image partitioning and merging method from coarse to fine, as shown in Fig. 1.

(1) First, assuming that the size of input blurred image I_0 is $I_h \times I_v (I_h, I_v > C)$, and reducing the scale of image in half proportion until the image size is just close to C. Reduced scale can get images of different scales $I_1, I_2, \ldots, I_n$, n is the counter of reduced scale;
(2) The image with the smallest size is divided into average patches to estimate the blur kernel of each patch. Calculating the SSIM of the blur kernels between the adjacent image patches to decide whether to partition or not. The structures of kernels are more similar if the value is closer to 1.
(3) When the value cannot satisfy the threshold (we set 0.91), it means that the image needs to be partitioned at the maximum scale n. Then returning to the image I_{n-1} of the previous scale and carrying out the partitioning once, next according to step (1), judging whether each patch requires to continue to partition at current scale. If the criterion satisfies the threshold or the image has returned to the original size at a certain scale, it is judged that the image is no longer divided and the result of image partitioning can be obtained.

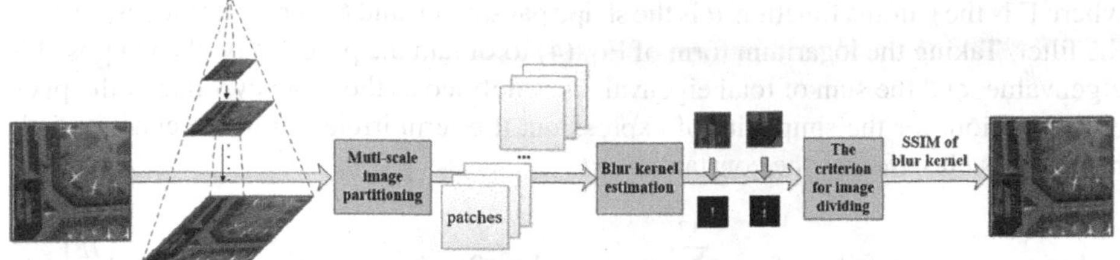

Fig. 1. The process flow of the image adaptive partition.

4 Blind Deblurring Based on Saliency Detection

Whatever it is to judge the SSIM of the kernels in the image partition, and to restore the obtained image patches, it is necessary to accurately estimate the kernels of image patches. This section discusses the blind deblurring based on saliency detection.

4.1 Saliency Detection Based on SUN

As the significant areas of the image contain a large amount of image information and edge details, we desire a method that can pay more attention to obtain these areas. In order to achieve this goal, we introduce a saliency detection [17] based on the Bayesian probability framework to define the bottom-up saliency which can be naturally expressed as the self-information of visual features, and the overall saliency can be obtained by combining it with the top-down information. First, the saliency of each pixel in the image can be defined using the logarithmic form of probability

$$\log s_z = -\log p(F = f_z) \tag{2}$$

where z represents the pixel in the image, F is the observed image feature, f_z is the eigenvalues at pixel z. It shows that the rarer a feature is, the more attention it can get.

Secondly, the response of the linear filter is used to calculate the pixels' features in the image, and f_z can be further understood as the response of the filter at the pixel z. Therefore, we use the Gaussian differential filter (DOG), which is defined as

$$DOG(a, b) = \frac{1}{\sigma^2} \exp\left(-\frac{a^2 + b^2}{\sigma^2}\right) - \frac{1}{(1.6\sigma)^2} \exp\left(-\frac{a^2 + b^2}{(1.6\sigma)^2}\right) \tag{3}$$

where (a, b) is the location. We perform the convoluting operation on the color channels of the image with four different filters (supposing that they are all independent) so as to generate D responses (D means twelve if color channels are three). Using the exponential power distribution to get the estimated distribution of each response

$$p(f; \sigma, \theta) = \frac{\theta}{2\sigma\Gamma\left(\frac{1}{\theta}\right)} \exp\left(-\left|\frac{f}{\sigma}\right|^{\theta}\right) \tag{4}$$

where Γ is the gamma function, θ is the shape parameter, and f represents the response of the filter. Taking the logarithm form of Eq. (4) to obtain the probability of each possible eigenvalue, and the sum of total eigenvalues is defined as the saliency value at the pixel z. In addition, for the simplicity of expression, the term irrelevant to the characteristic response is classified as the constant *const*.

$$\log s_z = -\log p(F = f_z) = \sum_{i=1}^{12} \log \theta_i - \log 2 - \log \sigma_i - \log \Gamma\left(\frac{1}{\theta_i}\right) - \left|\frac{f_i}{\sigma_i}\right|^{\theta_i}$$

$$= \sum_{i=1}^{12} \left|\frac{f_i}{\sigma_i}\right|^{\theta_i} + const \quad (5)$$

4.2 Blind Deblurring Model and Solution

After saliency detection, we can obtain the saliency map of the input image and denote it as $P \cdot x$. Because of the sparsity of saliency value, $\|P \cdot x\|_0$ can be used as a constraint term to extract the saliency structure in the image. Besides, the gradient constraint of the image $\|\nabla x\|_0$ and the intensity constraint of the image $\|x\|_0$ are introduced for better deblurring, the overall model can be established as

$$\min_{x,k} \|x \otimes k - y\|_2^2 + \alpha\|P \cdot x\|_0 + \beta\|\nabla x\|_0 + \gamma\|x\|_0 + \lambda\|k\|_2^2 \quad (6)$$

where x, y and k denote the latent image, blurred image and kernel, respectively, $\|k\|_2^2$ is the L_2 norm about k, $\nabla = (\nabla_h, \nabla_v)^T$ is the image gradient operator, $\otimes$ is the convolution operator, $\cdot$ is the point multiplication operation between matrix elements, and α, β, γ and λ are the positive weight parameters.

In Eq. (6), it is necessary to estimate two unknowns x and k, so Eq. (6) can be divided into two steps by alternating iteration scheme

$$\min_{k} \|x \otimes k - y\|_2^2 + \lambda\|k\|_2^2 \quad (7)$$

$$\min_{x} \|x \otimes k - y\|_2^2 + \alpha\|P \cdot x\|_0 + \beta\|\nabla x\|_0 + \gamma\|x\|_0 \quad (8)$$

Solving k with given x

For sub-problem (7), the latent image is fixed to solve the blur kernel. In addition, to ensure the accuracy of the kernel estimation, L_2 norm is used to estimate the kernel in the gradient space

$$\min_{k} \|\nabla x \otimes k - \nabla y\|_2^2 + \lambda\|k\|_2^2 \quad (9)$$

After derivation, FFT transform is used to solve the problem in frequency domain

$$k = F^{-1}\left(\frac{\overline{F(\nabla x)}F(\nabla y)}{\overline{F(\nabla x)}F(\nabla x) + \lambda}\right) \tag{10}$$

Solving x with given k

For sub-problem (8), the latent image is estimated with fixed blur kernel. According to the basic idea of split-Bregman algorithm, three auxiliary variables d_1, d_2 and d_3 are introduced and corresponded to $P \cdot x$, ∇x, and x, respectively. Thus, by applying Bregman iteration to strictly execute constraints, Eq. (8) can be converted into unconstrained minimization form

$$\min_{x,d_1,d_2,d_3} \|x \otimes k - y\|_2^2 + \alpha\|d_1\|_0 + \beta\|d_2\|_0 + \gamma\|d_3\|_0 + \frac{\mu_1}{2}\|d_1 - P \cdot x - q_1\|_2^2 + \frac{\mu_2}{2}\|d_2 - \nabla x - q_2\|_2^2 + \frac{\mu_3}{2}\|d_3 - x - q_3\|_2^2 \tag{11}$$

where μ_1, μ_2 and μ_3 are the penalty parameters, q_1, q_2 and q_3 are the Bregman variables, and Eq. (11) can be divided into three simpler sub-problems.

- Sub-problem related to x:

$$\min_x \left\|x \otimes k^l - y\right\|_2^2 + \frac{\mu_1}{2}\left\|d_1^l - P \cdot x - q_1^l\right\|_2^2 + \frac{\mu_2}{2}\left\|d_2^l - \nabla x - q_2^l\right\|_2^2 + \frac{\mu_3}{2}\left\|d_3^l - x - q_3^l\right\|_2^2 \tag{12}$$

which is the least squares problem, and can be solved as

$$x^{l+1} = \frac{2\left(k^l\right)^T y + \mu_1 P \cdot \left(d_1^l - q_1^l\right) + \mu_2 \nabla^T\left(d_2^l - q_2^l\right) + \mu_3\left(d_3^l - q_3^l\right)}{2\left(k^l\right)^T k^l + \mu_1 P^2 + \mu_2 \nabla^T \nabla + \mu_3} \tag{13}$$

For the Eq. (13), it can be solved effectively in frequency domain by FFT.

- Sub-problem related to d_1, d_2 and d_3:

$$\min_{d_1} \alpha\|d_1\|_0 + \frac{\mu_1}{2}\left\|d_1 - P \cdot x^{l+1} - q_1^l\right\|_2^2 \tag{14}$$

The problem of (14) can be solved by shrinking operator as follows

$$d_1^{l+1} = shrink\left(P \cdot x^{l+1} + q_1^l, \frac{\alpha}{\mu_1}\right) \tag{15}$$

where the shrink operator can be expressed as

$$shrink(e, \xi) = \frac{e}{|e|} * \max(e - \xi, 0) \tag{16}$$

When x^{l+1} is estimated, we can also obtain the values of d_2 and d_3, which can be expressed as

$$\begin{cases} d_2^{l+1} = shrink\left(\nabla x^{l+1} + q_2^l, \frac{\beta}{\mu_2}\right) \\ d_3^{l+1} = shrink\left(x^{l+1} + q_3^l, \frac{\gamma}{\mu_3}\right) \end{cases} \tag{17}$$

Finally, we can update the variables q_1, q_2 and q_3 by following formula

$$\begin{cases} q_1^{l+1} = q_1^l + \left(P \cdot x^{l+1} - d_1^{l+1}\right) \\ q_2^{l+1} = q_2^l + \left(\nabla x^{l+1} - d_2^{l+1}\right) \\ q_3^{l+1} = q_3^l + \left(x^{l+1} - d_3^{l+1}\right) \end{cases} \tag{18}$$

5 Weighted Window Function for Image Patches Joint with Different Sizes

Suppose that we can obtain m restored patches. In the image patches joint, firstly, the sizes of two patches are supposed to be $r_1 \times v_1$ and $r_2 \times v_2$, in which $v_1 > v_2$, and their expanded patches R_1 and R_2 can be obtained. Here, we only consider the horizontal joint, and the sizes of the expanded patches are $(r_1 + c_1) \times v_1$ and $(r_2 + c_2) \times v_2$, c_1 and c_2 are the padding values in the horizontal direction. In practice, because of $v_1 > v_2$, we only consider the actual joint part in R_1, whose size is $(r_1 + c_1) \times v_2$. For each image patch R_t $(1 \le t \le m)$, assuming that its size is $u_t \times z_t$, then establishing a two-dimensional weighted window function, which can be expressed as

$$w_t(i, j) = w(i, u_t)\, w(j, z_t)^T \tag{19}$$

where i, j represent the row and col in the w_t, and $w(\cdot)$ can be defined as

$$w(n, N) = \begin{cases} 0.42 - 0.5\cos\left(\frac{2\pi n}{N-1}\right) + 0.08\cos\left(\frac{4\pi n}{N-1}\right), & 0 \le n \le N-1 \\ 0, & otherwise \end{cases} \tag{20}$$

where N corresponds to the image patch size u_t or z_t, and n represents a discrete variable specified by the location of the element in w_t. And w_t is only non-zero in the region of the actual partitioning image, and is set to 0 otherwise. Finally, the window function is multiplied by the current expanded image patch to achieve the mitigated boundary, which can be described as $w_t(i, j). * R_t(i, j)$. Figure 2 shows the joint method in the horizontal direction, and the joint in the vertical direction can be understood similarly.

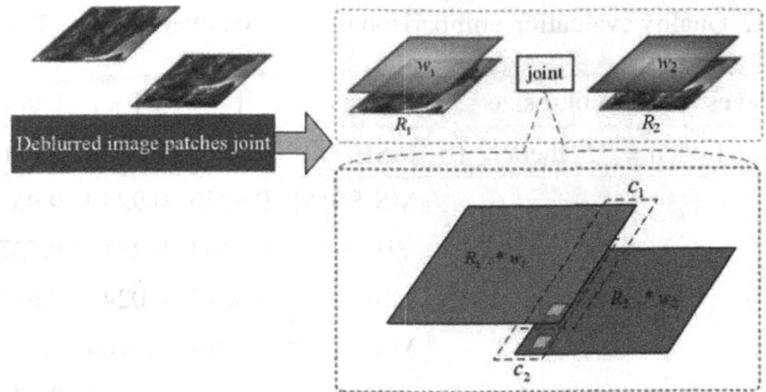

Fig. 2. The joint process of image patches in horizontal direction

6 Experiments and Results

All the experiments in this paper are implemented in MATLAB 2018a, and the computer is configured with 2.90 Ghz CPU and 8GB RAM. The parameters setting involved are: $\alpha \in [2e^{-4}, 4e^{-3}]$, $\beta \in [2e^{-4}, 2e^{-3}]$, $\gamma \in [2e^{-4}2e^{-3}]$, $\lambda = 2$, and the maximum values of μ_1, μ_2 and μ_3 are 2^4, $1e^3$ and $1e^4$, respectively. The parameters of the compared algorithms are set according to the way suggested in their papers.

6.1 The Comparisons with the State-of-the-Art Methods on the Space-Invariant Blurred Image

In order to prove the effectiveness of our method, we select four natural test images for simulation, as shown in Fig. 3. In our experiment, we set two different degrees of motion blur and convolute them with the clear images to generate four space-invariant blurred images for simulation. And their motion angles *theta* and motion pixels *len* are (theta = 10, len = 15) and (theta = 15, len = 20), respectively.

We compare the performance of our method on the test images with methods [2, 3]. To evaluate the quality of results correctly, the mean square error (MSE), multi-scale structure similarity index (MS-SSIM) and visual information fidelity (VIF) are used as the reference. Note that the lower value of MSE indicates the better effect of image restoration, the higher value of MS-SSIM shows the better structural similarity between the restored image and the original image, and the higher value of VIF shows the higher visual fidelity of the image. The quality evaluation data of the compared methods and the proposed method are shown in Table 1.

(a) street1 (b) street2 (c) tree (d) floor

Fig. 3. Original images. (a)–(d) are four natural test images.

Table 1. Quality evaluation comparison of restored images with [2] and [3].

Images	Motion blur size	Indices	[2]	[3]	Ours
street1	len = 15, theta = 10	MSE	0.0213	0.0279	**0.0103**
		MS-SSIM	0.9256	0.9240	**0.9842**
		VIF	0.2467	0.2715	**0.5270**
	len = 20, theta = 15	MSE	0.0218	0.0240	**0.0129**
		MS-SSIM	0.9019	0.9168	**0.9717**
		VIF	0.2107	0.2424	**0.4277**
street2	len = 15, theta = 10	MSE	0.0343	0.0408	**0.0224**
		MS-SSIM	0.8782	0.8863	**0.9466**
		VIF	0.1801	0.2170	**0.3132**
	len = 20, theta = 15	MSE	0.0337	0.0361	**0.0211**
		MS-SSIM	0.8365	0.8892	**0.9526**
		VIF	0.1573	0.2221	**0.3441**
tree	len = 15, theta = 10	MSE	0.0424	0.0514	**0.0304**
		MS-SSIM	0.7778	0.8384	**0.9128**
		VIF	0.1079	0.1656	**0.2299**
	len = 20, theta = 15	MSE	0.0453	0.0452	**0.0325**
		MS-SSIM	0.7212	0.8520	**0.8867**
		VIF	0.0870	0.1594	**0.2047**
floor	len = 15, theta = 10	MSE	0.0251	0.0194	**0.0140**
		MS-SSIM	0.8959	0.9512	**0.9698**
		VIF	0.2725	0.3783	**0.4557**
	len = 20, theta = 15	MSE	0.0297	0.0270	**0.0181**
		MS-SSIM	0.8269	0.9137	**0.9519**
		VIF	0.1972	0.2863	**0.3937**

It can be observed in Table 1 that proposed method outperforms the other two algorithms on MSE, MS-SSIM and VIF value. We show the deblurred results on the simulated blurred image of Fig. 3 (a). In this group of experiment, the blurred image shown in Fig. 4 (b) is generated by the second blur, the deblurred results demonstrate that the proposed method achieves a competitive performance, as shown in Fig. 4 (f), the proposed method obtains relatively clearer result in detail, which appear more similar to the original clear image.

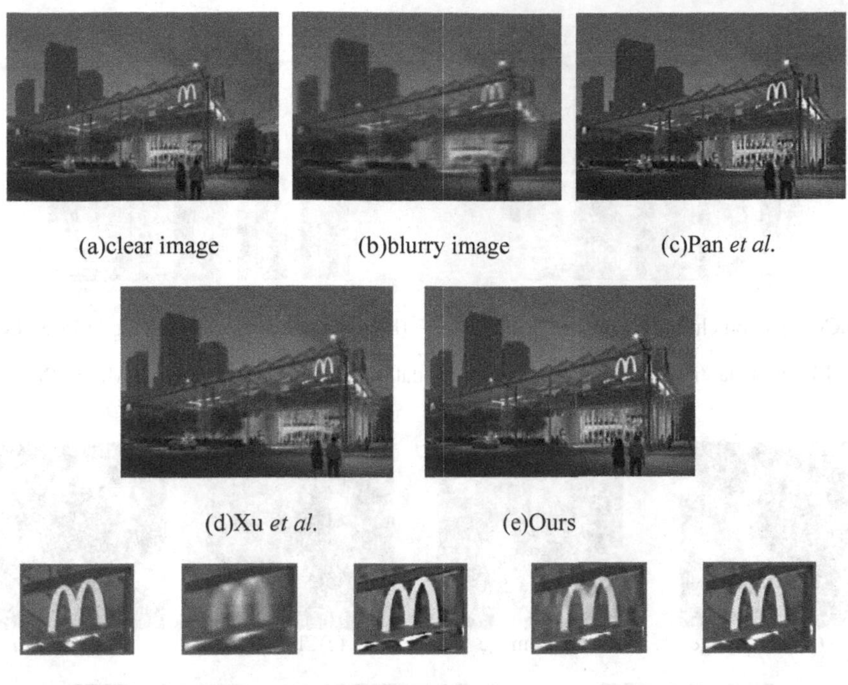

(a)clear image (b)blurry image (c)Pan *et al.*

(d)Xu *et al.* (e)Ours

(f)

Fig. 4. Restored results of street1 image. (a), (b) are clear image and blurry image, (c)–(e) are restorations of [2, 3] and the proposed method respectively, (f) are the close-up views of (a)–(e) image regions extracted from this example.

6.2 Quantitative Evaluations

Furthermore, in order to verify the effectiveness of the saliency prior used in this method, we compare the results from the methods in [1, 2, 4] and [19] with the proposed method on Levin's dataset [18]. The dataset totally consists of 32 images, which are synthesized by four clear images and eight kinds of kernels. We calculate the average PSNR and MS-SSIM values of eight different blurred images corresponding to each clear image, and the average PSNR and MS-SSIM values of all images in the whole dataset. The results are shown in Fig. 5, it can be seen that the proposed method boost the performance in all compared methods. Figure 6 shows the restoration of one of the degraded images, we can also observe that compared with other methods, the proposed method achieves clearer restoration and better visual effect to a certain extent.

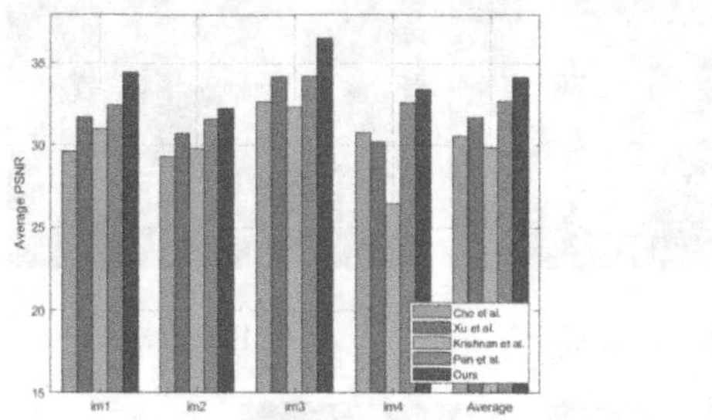

(a)Comparison chart of average PSNR

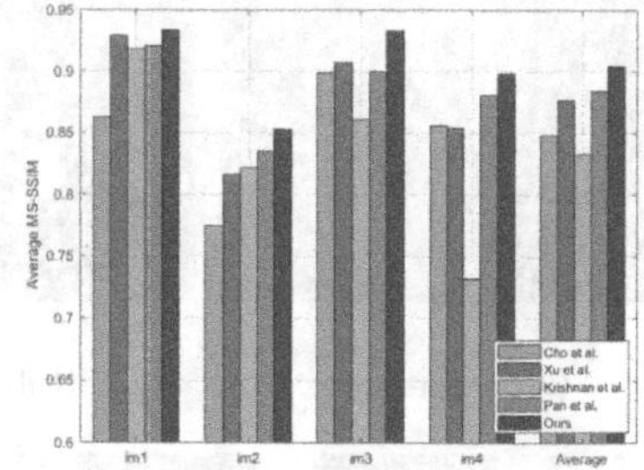

(b)Comparison chart of average MS-SSIM

Fig. 5. Quantitative evaluation on Levin's dataset, in terms of PSNR and MS-SSIM.

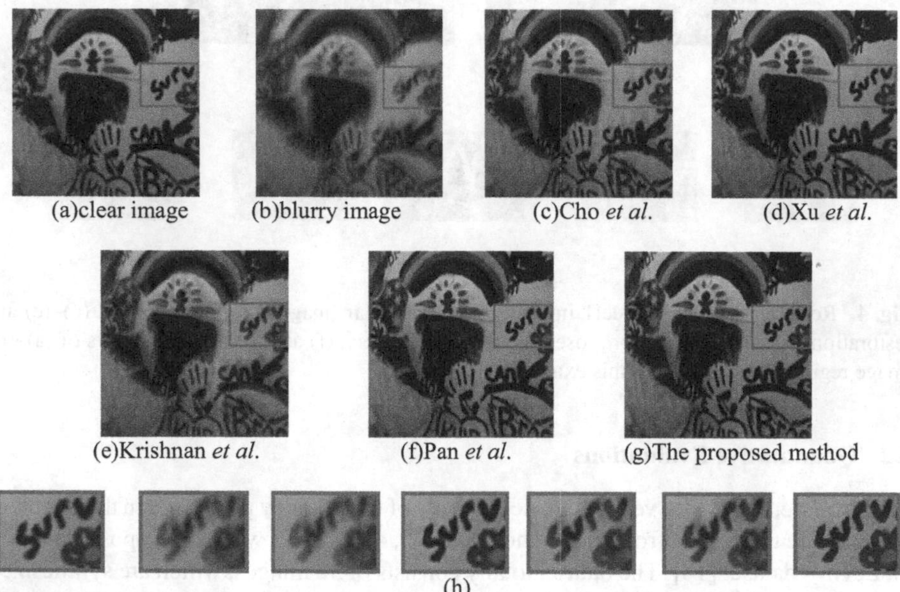

(a)clear image (b)blurry image (c)Cho *et al.* (d)Xu *et al.*

(e)Krishnan *et al.* (f)Pan *et al.* (g)The proposed method

(h)

Fig. 6. Visual comparison of image restoration. (a) and (b) are the clear image and the blurry image in [18]. (c)–(g) are the restored images obtained by the four methods used for comparison and the proposed method. (h) are the close-up views in (a)–(g).

6.3 Comparison with the State-of-the-Art Methods on the Space-Variant Blurred Image

In this section, we demonstrate that the proposed method is applicable and effective for the space-variant blurred images. We perform the proposed method compared with several algorithms on the space-variant blurred image, and these images and comparison results are provided in [23]. Figure 7 shows several restored results of papers [20–22] and the proposed method. From the experimental results, we can observe that the proposed

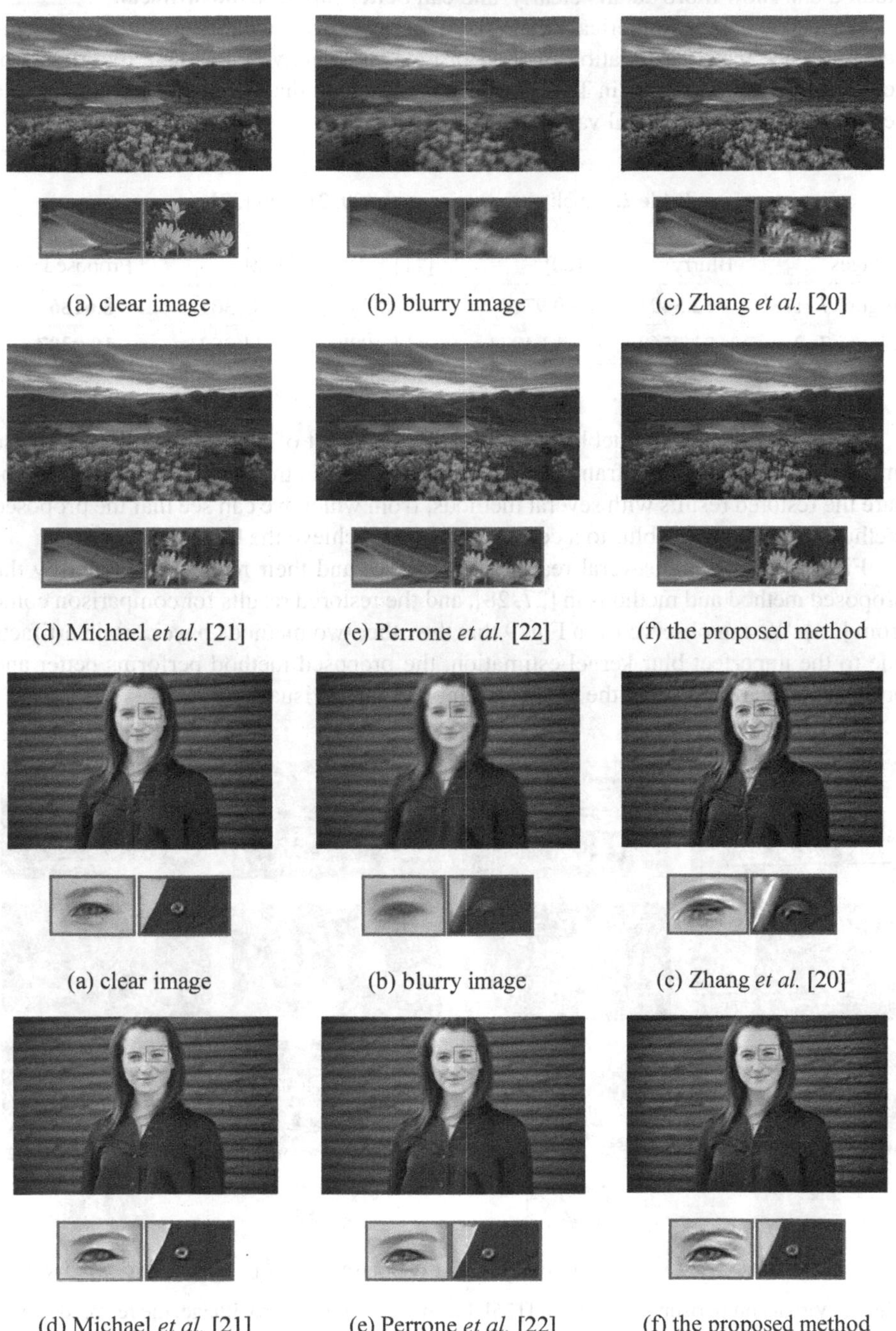

(a) clear image (b) blurry image (c) Zhang *et al.* [20]

(d) Michael *et al.* [21] (e) Perrone *et al.* [22] (f) the proposed method

(a) clear image (b) blurry image (c) Zhang *et al.* [20]

(d) Michael *et al.* [21] (e) Perrone *et al.* [22] (f) the proposed method

Fig. 7. The visual comparison on the synthetic images. (a) and (b) are clear image and blurry image respectively, (c)–(f) are comparisons of restored results respectively.

method is capable of removing the blur better. And from the close-up views, the proposed method can show more details clearly, and can better suppress the artifacts.

We also make the numerical comparison on the experimental results, and apply the non-reference metric evaluation method in [24] to objectively evaluate the effects of deblurred results, as shown in Table 2. It can be observed that the proposed method also performs better in numerical value.

Table 2. Quality evaluation with [20, 21] and [22].

Images	Blurry	[20]	[21]	[22]	Proposed
Figure 7 (1)	−12.5491	−9.9714	−9.4379	−8.7361	**−8.6186**
Figure 7 (2)	−21.5568	−13.4973	−11.1008	−11.9871	**−10.9307**

In Fig. 8, we show the deblurred comparison on a set of blurred images. And these images are from one of the frames of the blurred images in the dynamic scene. We compare the restored results with several methods, from which we can see that the proposed method can remove the blur to a certain extent and achieve the better performance.

Figure 9 shows the several real blurred images and their results generated by the proposed method and methods in [27, 28], and the restored results for comparison come from [13]. We can observe from Fig. 9 that the other two methods have certain artifacts due to the imperfect blur kernel estimation, the proposed method performs better and produces less artifacts, and the results are more natural visually.

(a) blurry image (b) Tao *et al.* [25] (c) Kupyn *et al.* [26] (d) the proposed method

Fig. 8. Visual comparison with [25] and [26]. From left to right: blurry image, the restored results by [25, 26] and the proposed method.

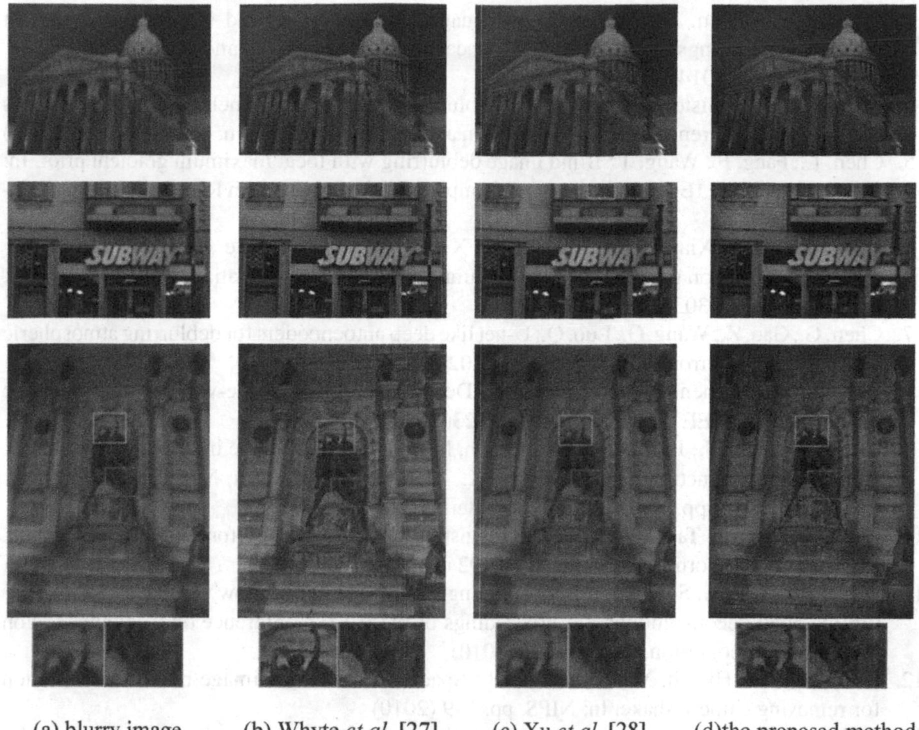

(a) blurry image (b) Whyte *et al.* [27] (c) Xu *et al.* [28] (d)the proposed method

Fig. 9. Comparison on the real blurred images. From left to right: blurry image, the restored images by [27, 28] and the proposed method, respectively.

7 Conclusion

In this work, we propose an effective approach for adaptive multi-scale image partitioning by viewing the structural similarity as the criterion, so that the image can be divided adaptively from coarse to fine. In addition, the saliency detection is introduced as the prior to obtain better performance of image restoration. And the image patches with different sizes can be joined with the weighted window function. The experiments show that the proposed approach can be applied to both the space-invariant blurred image and the space-variant blurred image and get an improvement of image deblurring.

Acknowledgement. This work was supported by a project of the National Science Foundation of China (61701353, 61801337).

References

1. Cho, S., Lee, S.: Fast motion deblurring. ACM Trans. Graph. **28**(5), 89–97 (2009)
2. Xu, L., Jia, J.: Two-phase kernel estimation for robust motion deblurring. In: Daniilidis, K., Maragos, P., Paragios, N. (eds.) ECCV 2010. LNCS, vol. 6311, pp. 157–170. Springer, Heidelberg (2010). https://doi.org/10.1007/978-3-642-15549-9_12

3. Pan, J., Hu, Z., Su, Z.: Deblurring text images via L0-regularized intensity and gradient prior. In: Proceedings of the IEEE Conference on Computer Vision and Pattern Recognition, pp. 2901–2908 (2014)
4. Pan, J., Sun, D., Pfister, H.: Blind image deblurring using dark channel prior. In: Proceedings of the IEEE Conference on Computer Vision and Pattern Recognition, pp. 1628–1636 (2016)
5. Chen, L., Fang, F., Wang, T.: Blind image deblurring with local maximum gradient prior. In: Proceedings of the IEEE Conference on Computer Vision and Pattern Recognition, pp. 1742–1750 (2019)
6. Yan, J., Bai, X., Xiao, Y., Zhang, Y., Lv, X.: No-reference remote sensing image quality assessment based on gradient-weighted natural scene statistics in spatial domain. J. Electron. Imaging **28**(1), 013033 (2019)
7. Chen, G., Gao, Z., Wang, Q., Luo, Q.: U-net like deep autoencoders for deblurring atmospheric turbulence. J. Electron. Imaging **28**(5), 053024 (2019)
8. Sroubek, F., Kamenicky, J., Lu, Y.-M.: Decomposition of space-variant blur in image deconvolution. IEEE Signal Process. Lett. **23**(3), 346–350 (2016)
9. Gupta, A., Josh, N., Lawrence, Z.C., Cohen, M., Curless, B.: Single image deblurring using motion density functions. In: Daniilidis, K., Maragos, P., Paragios, N. (eds.) ECCV 2010. LNCS, vol. 6311, pp. 171–184. Springer, Berlin (2010)
10. Cho, S., Cho, H., Tai, Y.-W., Lee, S.: Registration based non-uniform motion deblurring. Comput. Graph. Forum **31**(7–2), 2183–2192 (2012)
11. Hirsch, M., Sra, S., Scholkopf, B., Harmeling, S.: Efficient filter flow for space-variant multiframe blind deconvolutions. In: Proceedings of the IEEE Conference on Computer Vision and Pattern Recognition, pp. 607–614 (2010)
12. Harmeling, S., Hirsch, M., Scholkopf, B.: Space-variant single-image blind deconvolution for removing camera shake. In: NIPS, pp. 1–9 (2010)
13. Ji, H., Wang, K.: A two-stage approach to blind spatially-varying motion deblurring. In: Proceedings of the IEEE Conference on Computer Vision and Pattern Recognition, pp. 73–80 (2012)
14. Shen, Z., Xu, T., Pan, J.: Non-uniform motion deblurring with Kernel grid regularization. Signal Process. Image Commun. **62**, 1–15 (2018)
15. Bardsley, J., Jefferies, S., Nagy, J., Plemmons, R.: A computational method for the restoration of images with an unknown, spatially-varying blur. Opt. Express **14**(5), 1767–1782 (2006)
16. Cao, X., Ren, W., Zuo, W., Guo, X., Hassan, F.: Scene text deblurring using text-specific multiscale dictionaries. IEEE Trans. Image Process **24**(4), 1302–1314 (2015)
17. Zhang, L., Tong, M., Marks, T., Shan, H., Cottrell, G.: SUN: a bayesian framework for saliency using natural statistics. J. Vis. **8**(32), 1–20 (2008)
18. Levin, A., Weiss, Y., Durand, F., Freeman, W.T.: Understanding and evaluating blind deconvolution algorithms. In: Proceedings of the IEEE Conference on Computer Vision and Pattern Recognition, pp. 1964–1971 (2009)
19. Krishnan, D., Tay, T., Fergus, R.: Blind deconvolution using a normalized sparsity measure. In: Proceedings of the IEEE Conference on Computer Vision and Pattern Recognition, pp. 233–240 (2011)
20. Zhang, H., Wipf, D., Zhang, Y.: Multi-image blind deblurring using a coupled adaptive sparse prior. In: Proceedings of the IEEE Conference on Computer Vision and Pattern Recognition, pp. 1051–1058 (2013)
21. Michaeli, T., Irani, M.: Blind deblurring using internal patch recurrence. In: Fleet, D., Pajdla, T., Schiele, B., Tuytelaars, T. (eds.) ECCV 2014. LNCS, vol. 8691, pp. 783–798. Springer, Cham (2014). https://doi.org/10.1007/978-3-319-10578-9_51
22. Perrone, D., Favaro, P.: Total variation blind deconvolution: the devil is in the details. In: Proceedings of the IEEE Conference on Computer Vision and Pattern Recognition, pp. 2909–2916 (2014)

23. Lai, W.-S., Huang, J.-B., Yang, M.-H.: A comparative study for single image blind deblurring. In: Proceedings of the IEEE Conference on Computer Vision and Pattern Recognition, pp. 64–72 (2016)
24. Liu, Y., Wang, J., Cho, S., Finkelstein, A., Rusinkiewicz, S.: A no-reference metric for evaluating the quality of motion deblurring. ACM SIGGRAPH Asia **32**(175), 1–12 (2013)
25. Tao, X., Gao, H., Wang, Y., Shen, X., Wang, J., Jia, J.: Scale-recurrent network for deep image deblurring. In: Proceedings of the IEEE Conference on Computer Vision and Pattern Recognition, pp. 8147–8182 (2018)
26. Kupyn, O., Budzan, V., Mykhailych, M., Mishkin, D., Matas, J.: Deblurgan: blind motion deblurring using conditional adversarial networks. In: Proceedings of the IEEE Conference on Computer Vision and Pattern Recognition, pp. 8183–8192 (2018)
27. Whyte, O., Sivic, J., Zisserman, A., Ponce, J.: Non-uniform deblurring for shaken images. Int. J. Comput. Vis. **98**, 168–186 (2012)
28. Xu, L., Zheng, S., Jia, J.: Unnatural L_0 sparse representation for natural image deblurring. In: Proceedings of the IEEE Conference on Computer Vision and Pattern Recognition, pp. 1–8 (2013)

CETransformer: Casual Effect Estimation via Transformer Based Representation Learning

Zhenyu Guo[1,2], Shuai Zheng[1,2], Zhizhe Liu[1,2], Kun Yan[1,2], and Zhenfeng Zhu[1,2(✉)]

[1] Beijing Jiaotong University, Beijing, China
{zhyguo,zs1997,zhzliu,kunyan,zhfzhu}@bjtu.edu.cn
[2] Beijing Key Laboratory of Advanced Information Science and Network Technology, Beijing, China

Abstract. Treatment effect estimation, which refers to the estimation of causal effects and aims to measure the strength of the causal relationship, is of great importance in many fields but is a challenging problem in practice. As present, data-driven causal effect estimation faces two main challenges, i.e., selection bias and the missing of counterfactual. To address these two issues, most of the existing approaches tend to reduce the selection bias by learning a balanced representation, and then to estimate the counterfactual through the representation. However, they heavily rely on the finely hand-crafted metric functions when learning balanced representations, which generally doesn't work well for the situations where the original distribution is complicated. In this paper, we propose a CETransformer model for casual effect estimation via transformer based representation learning. To learn the representation of covariates (features) robustly, a self-supervised transformer is proposed, by which the correlation between covariates can be well exploited through self-attention mechanism. In addition, an adversarial network is adopted to balance the distribution of the treated and control groups in the representation space. Experimental results on three real-world datasets demonstrate the advantages of the proposed CETransformer, compared with the state-of-the-art treatment effect estimation methods.

Keywords: Transformer · Casual effect estimation · Adversarial learning

1 Introduction

Causal effect estimation is an crucial task that can benefit many domains including health care [2,10], machine learning [14,28], business [24] and sociology science [9]. For example, in medicine, if two pharmaceutical companies have both developed anti-hyperlipidemic drugs, which one is more effective for a given patient? Suppose we consider different anti-hyperlipidemic drugs as different

© Springer Nature Switzerland AG 2021
H. Ma et al. (Eds.): PRCV 2021, LNCS 13022, pp. 524–535, 2021.
https://doi.org/10.1007/978-3-030-88013-2_43

treatments, the therapeutic effects of the drugs can be obtained by estimating causal effects. As described above, the causal effect is used to measure the difference in outcomes under different interventions.

In practice, we often obtain drug treatment effects by means of randomized controlled trials(RCT), and similar methods such as A/B tests are used to obtain average effects of a new feature in recommendation systems [27]. However, for individual causal effects, we cannot collect them by means of RCT because we lack counterfactual outcomes. Since counterfactuals are not directly available, causal effect estimation through massive data has become an important task in the era of big data and has been widely adopted [19,25,26]. Nevertheless, data-driven causal effect estimation approaches face two main challenges, i.e., **treatment selection bias** and **missing counterfactuals outcomes**.

Firstly, in contrast to RCT, treatments in observational data are usually not randomly assigned. In the healthcare setting, physicians consider a range of factors when selecting treatment options, such as patient feedback on treatment, medical history, and patient health status. Due to the presence of selection bias, the treated population may differ significantly from the controlled population. Secondly, in real life, we only observe the factual outcome and never all the potential outcomes that could have occurred if we had chosen a different treatment option. However, the estimation of treatment effects requires to compare the results of a person under different treatments. These two issues make it challenging to obtain an assessment of the treatment effect from the observed data.

To address both of these challenges, existing approaches [13,19] project the observed data into a balanced representation space where different treatment groups are close to each other, and then train an outcome prediction model to estimate the counterfactual. To the best of our knowledge, existing methods use finely hand-crafted metric functions to approximate the distribution of different treatment groups, and the network structures are the simplest fully connected neural networks. In [25], the authors considered propensity scores as the relative position of individuals in the covariate space and performed the construction of triplet pairs. They adopted a hand-crafted metric function between the midpoint from different treatment groups to balance the distribution. By adopting an integral probability metric (IPM) [26], the similarity between two distributions is measured. The network architecture used in all of the above approaches is the most primitive fully connected network. To reduce the difference between different distributions, using manually designed similarity metric functions alone is not well adapted to the situation where the original distribution is complicated. Meanwhile, more attention should be paid to the correlation between covariates to generate a more discriminative representation, while the fully connected network is shown to exploit only the relationship between individuals [7].

Aiming at solving the above problems, we propose an casual effect estimation model via transformer based representation learning (CETransformer). The key contributions of this work are as follows:

- The recently popular Transfomer network is adopted as a converter for mapping individuals into a latent representation space. Hence, the correlation between different covariates can be effectively exploited through self-attention mechanism to benefit the representation learning.
- To make the transformer trainable in the situation of limited number of individuals, we take a form of self-supervision via auto-encoder to realize the augmentation of training data.
- Rather than simply using a metric function, the adversarial learning is utilized to balance the distribution between the different treatment groups.

We organize the rest of our paper as follows. Technical background including the basic notations, definitions, and assumptions are introduced in Sect. 2. Our proposed framework is presented in Sect. 3. In Sect. 4, experiments on three public datasets are provided to demonstrate the effectiveness of our method. Finally, Sect. 5 draws our conclusions on this work.

2 Preliminary and Background

Suppose that the observational data $X = \{X_i \in \mathbb{R}^d\}_{i=1}^n$ contain n units (individual-s/samples) with each containing d feature variables, and that each individual received one of two treatments. Let T_i denote the binary treatment assignment on unit X_i, i.e., $T_i = 0$ or 1. For the unit X_i in the treated group, $T_i = 1$, and it will belong to the control group if $T_i = 0$. Before the treatment assignment, any outcome Y_1^i(treated) or Y_0^i(control), is taken as a *potential outcome*. After the intervention, the outcome $Y_{T_i}^i$ will be the *observed outcome* or *factual outcome*, and the other treatment's outcome $Y_{1-T_i}^i$ is the *counterfactual outcome*.

Throughout this paper, we follow the potential outcome framework for estimating treatment effects [17,21]. Specifically, the individual treatment effect (ITE) for unit x_i is defined as the difference between the potential treated and control outcomes:

$$ITE_i = Y_1^i - Y_0^i, (i = 1, \cdots, n). \tag{1}$$

Meanwhile, the average treatment effect (ATE) is the difference between the potential treated and control outcomes, which is defined as:

$$ATE = \frac{1}{n}\sum_{i=1}^{n}(Y_1^i - Y_0^i), (i = 1, \cdots, n). \tag{2}$$

Under the potential outcome framework, the common assumptions to ensure the identification of ITE include: *Stable Unit Treatment Value Assumption (SUTVA)*, *Consistency*, *Ignorability* and *Positivity* [8,16,17]. With these four assumptions satisfied, we can successfully estimate the counterfactual outcome required by ITE.

3 Methodology

3.1 Overview of the Proposed CETransformer Model

In [1], it has been shown that the bound for the error in the estimation of individual causal effects mainly consists of the difference between the treated and control groups and the loss of outcome prediction. Out of consideration of reducing the difference between treated and control groups for robust estimation of counterfactual, we propose a CETransformer model for casual effect estimation via transformer based representation learning. As shown in Fig. 1, the proposed framework of CETransformer contains three modules: 1) Self-supervised Transformer for representation learning which learns the balanced representation; 2) Discriminator network for adversarial learning to progressively shrink the difference between treated and control groups in the representation space; 3) Outcome prediction that uses the learned representations to estimate all potential outcome representations. For the details about each module, they will be presented in the following sections.

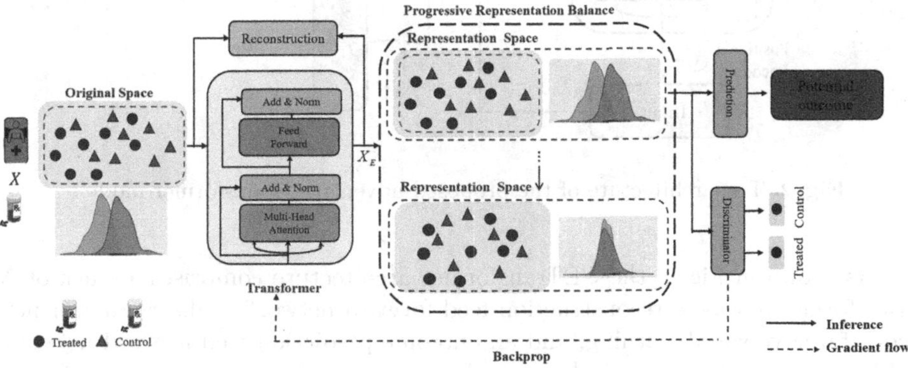

Fig. 1. Illustration of the proposed CETransformer model for casual effect estimation via transformer based representation learning.

3.2 Self-supervised Transformer

Existing works, such as [25,26], learn representations of individuals through fully connected neural networks, and their core spirit is to balance the distribution between different treatment groups by means of carefully designed metric functions. Meanwhile, more attention should be paid to the correlation both between covariates and between individuals to generate more discriminative representation. However, according to the theoretical analysis in [7], simple fully connected networks only approximate learning the similarity function between samples. Based on the above observations, we propose a CETransformer model that is built upon transformers [22] to learn robust and balanced feature-contextual representation of individual features. Specifically, CETransformer models the corresponding correlations between different individuals features and obtains a robust representation of the individual by means of self-attention mechanism.

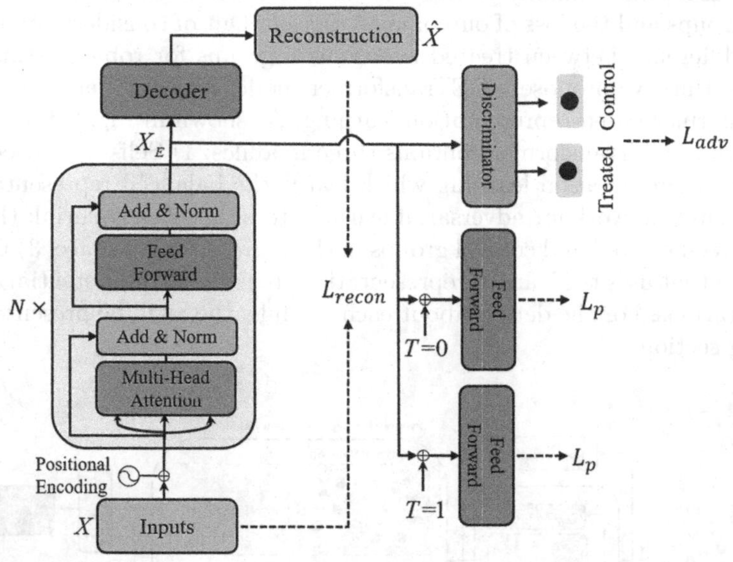

Fig. 2. The architecture of the proposed adversarial transformer model.

As shown in Fig. 2, the CETransformer architecture comprises a stack of N transformer blocks, a reconstruction feed-forward network, a discriminator network for adversarial learning, and an outcome prediction feed-forward network. CETransformer first learns the embedding representation via the transformer $X_E = f_{trans}(X; \Theta_{trans})$, where X_E denotes the embedding representation, and $f_{trans}(\cdot; \Theta_{trans})$ denotes the transformer with Θ_{trans} as its parameters. For a transformer, its core capability is to capture arbitrary distance dependencies through a self-attention mechanism:

$$Attention(Q, K, V) = softmax(\frac{Q \cdot K^T}{\sqrt{d_k}})V \tag{3}$$

where Q, K, and V represent Query, Key, Value, respectively, and d_k stands for the dimension of Key. For Q, K, and V, all of them are obtained from the input X through three different mapping networks.

Since the training of transformer requires a large amount of data, to learn a robust representation for the transformer in the case of limited number of individuals is very difficult and even untrainable. In view of this situation, the way of self-supervision is explored in the transformer framework to overcome this limitation to some extent. In particular, we adopt a simple fully connected network $f_{recon}(\cdot;\Theta_{dec})$ as a decoder to obtain a reconstructed representation $\hat{X} = f_{recon}(X_E;\Theta_{dec})$, where Θ_{dec} is the network parameters. Here, MSE is used as the loss function to measure the reconstruction error:

$$L_{reco} = \left\| X - \hat{X} \right\|_F^2 \tag{4}$$

Compared with existing fully connected network-based approaches, our proposed CETransformer has the following advantages: 1) with the help of the self-attentive mechanism in Transformer, the correlations among different covariates are well exploited; 2) by the way of self-supervised learning via auto-encoder to realize the augmentation of training data, the transformer can be trainable in the situation of limited number of individuals.

3.3 Adversarial Learning for Distribution Balancing

In order to satisfy the theoretical analysis mentioned in [1] that the distribution of treated and control groups should overlap, the learned representations of the two groups should be balanced. Briefly, if it is not, there is a problem of covariates shift, which will lead to inaccurate estimation of potential outcomes. To the best of our knowledge, all existing works on causal effect estimation adopt a hand-crafted metric function to balance the distribution between the two groups. However, these approaches heavily rely on a carefully designed metrics. Therefore, it is not a trivial task to deal with the complicated original distribution.

Unlike the previous methods, we take adversarial learning to balance the distribution between the control and treated groups. Generative adversarial networks (GAN) is generally used to approximate the output distribution from the generator to the distribution of the real data. However, as far as causal reasoning is concerned, there is no such thing as real and generated data. To solve this problem, a straightforward way is to take the representation of the treated group as real data and the representation of the control group as generated data.

For this case, to train a generative adversarial network, let $D(X_E^i)$ denote the discriminator network that maps the embedding representations of treated and control groups to the corresponding treatment assignment variables T_i. The discriminator network consists of a fully connected network, and the generator $G(\cdot)$ is the aforementioned transformer model. Due to the contradictory problems of the objective function in original GAN, which can lead to training instability and mode collapse. Many works [3,11,18] tries to solve these problems and in this paper we adopt WGAN [3] as our framework. Technically, WGAN minimizes a reasonable and efficient approximation of the Earth Mover (EM) distance, which is benefit for the stability of training. The loss function adopted by WGAN:

$$L_{adv} = \min_G \max_D \mathbb{E}_{X_E \sim \mathbb{P}_t}[D(X_E)] - \mathbb{E}_{\tilde{X}_E \sim \mathbb{P}_c}[D(\tilde{X_E})] \tag{5}$$

where $\mathbb{P}_t$ and $\mathbb{P}_c$ represent the distributions of the treated and control groups, respectively.

3.4 Outcome Prediction

After obtaining the balanced representation, we employed a two-branch network to predict the potential output Y_i after a given T_i based on the representation X_E^i of the input X_i. Each branch is implemented by fully connected layers and one output regression layer. Let $\tilde{Y}_i = h(X_E^i, T_i)$ denote the corresponding output prediction network. We aim to minimize the mean squared error in predicting factual outcomes:

$$L_p = \frac{1}{n}\sum_{i=1}^{n}(\tilde{Y}_i - Y_i)^2 \tag{6}$$

Ultimately, our total objective function can be expressed in the following form:

$$L = \alpha L_{reco} + \beta L_{adv} + \gamma L_p \tag{7}$$

where the hyper-parameter α, β, γ controls the trade-off between the three function.

4 Experiments

4.1 Datasets and Metric

In this section, we conduct experiments on three public datasets which is same as [29], including the IHDP, Jobs, and Twins. On IHDP and Twins datasets, we average over 10 realizations with 61/27/10 ratio of train/validation/test splits. And on Jobs dataset, because of the extremely low treated/control ratio, we conduct the experiment on 10 train/validation/test splits with 56/24/20 split ratio, as suggested in [20].

The expected Precision in Estimation of Heterogeneous Effect (PEHE) [12] is adopted on IHDP and Twins dataset. The lower the ε_{PEHE} is, the better the method is. On Jobs dataset, only the observed outcomes are available and the ground truth of ITE is unavailable. We adopt the policy risk [20] to measure the expected loss when taking the treatment as the ITE estimator suggests. Policy risk reflects how good the ITE estimation can guide the decision. The lower the policy risk is, the better the ITE estimation model can support the decision making.

4.2 Competing Algorithms

We compare CETransformer with a total of 12 algorithms. First we evaluate least squares regression using treatment as an additional input feature (OLS/LR_1), we consider separate least squares regressions for each treatment (OLS/LR_2), we evaluate balancing linear regression (BLR) [13], k-nearest neighbor (k-NN) [6], Bayesian additive regression trees (BART) [5], random forests (R-Forest) [4], causal forests (C-Forest) [23], treatment-agnostic representation network (TARNET), counterfactual regression with Wasserstein distance (CARW ASS) [20], local similarity preserved individual treatment effect (SITE) [25], adaptively similarity-preserved representation learning method for Causal Effect estimation (ACE) [26], deep kernel learning for individualized treatment effects (DKLITE) [29].

Table 1. Mean performance (lower better) of individualized treatment effect estimation and standard deviation.

	IHDP($\sqrt{\epsilon_{PEHE}}$)		Twins($\sqrt{\epsilon_{PEHE}}$)		Jobs($\mathcal{R}_{pol}(\pi_f)$)	
	In-sample	Out-sample	In-sample	Out-sample	In-sample	Out-sample
OLS/LR$_1$	5.8 ± .3	5.8 ± .3	.319 ± .001	.318 ± .007	.22 ± .00	.23 ± .02
OLS/LR$_2$	2.4 ± .1	2.5 ± .1	.320 ± .002	.320 ± .003	.21 ± .00	.24 ± .01
BLR	5.8 ± .3	5.8 ± .3	.312 ± .003	.323 ± .018	.22 ± .01	.26 ± .02
K-NN	2.1 ± .1	4.1 ± .2	.333 ± .001	.345 ± .007	.22 ± .00	.26 ± .02
BART	2.1 ± .1	2.3 ± .1	.347 ± .009	.338 ± .016	.23 ± .00	.25 ± .02
R-FOREST	4.2 ± .2	6.6 ± .3	.366 ± .002	.321 ± .005	.23 ± .01	.28 ± .02
C-FOREST	3.8 ± .2	3.8 ± .2	.366 ± .003	.316 ± .011	.19 ± .00	.20 ± .02
TARNET	.88 ± .02	.95 ± .02	.317 ± .002	.315 ± .003	.17 ± .01	.21 ± .01
CAR$_{WASS}$	.72 ± .02	.76 ± .02	.315 ± .007	.313 ± .008	.17 ± .01	.21 ± .01
SITE	.60 ± .09	.65 ± .10	.309 ± .002	.311 ± .004	.22 ± .00	.22 ± .00
ACE	.49 ± .04	.54 ± .06	.306 ± .000	.301 ± .002	.21 ± .00	.21 ± .00
DKLITE	.52 ± .02	.65 ± .03	.288 ± .001	.293 ± .003	.13 ± .01	.14 ± .01
CETransformer (ours)	**.46 ± .02**	**.51 ± .03**	**.287 ± .001**	**.289 ± .002**	**.12 ± .01**	**.13 ± .00**

4.3 Prediction Performance Results

With the same settings as [29], we report in-sample and out-of-sample performance in Table 1. CETransformer adopts the transformer network as a backbone and learns balanced representations via adversarial learning. With this approach, we outperform all competing algorithms on each benchmark dataset. Probably the most relevant of these comparisons are the three works [25,26,29], which generate overlapping representations of the treatment and control groups by means of neural networks and hand-designed inter-distributional similarity metric functions. Compared to them, the improvement in performance better highlights the predictive power of our representation. In addition to performance, we are also interested in whether the learned representations are balanced. Figure 3 shows the visualization of the learned representations in the three datasets through t-SNE [15]. Stars and circles represent the two-dimensional representations of the treated and control groups respectively, and we can find that the distance between the two distributions is well approximated by the adversarial learning of CETransformer, which indicates that no covariate shift occurs.

Table 2. Ablation on CETransformer: performance comparison on three datasets.

Dataset		CETransformer	Without transformer	Without discriminator
IHDP	In-sample	.46 ± .02	.50 ± .03	2.8 ± .13
	Out-sample	.51 ± .03	.56 ± .03	2.9 ± .22
Twins	In-sample	.287 ± .001	.292 ± .001	.335 ± .003
	Out-sample	.289 ± .002	.295 ± .002	.317 ± .012
Jobs	In-sample	.12 ± .01	.13 ± .01	.18 ± .00
	Out-sample	.13 ± .00	.15 ± .01	.20 ± .02

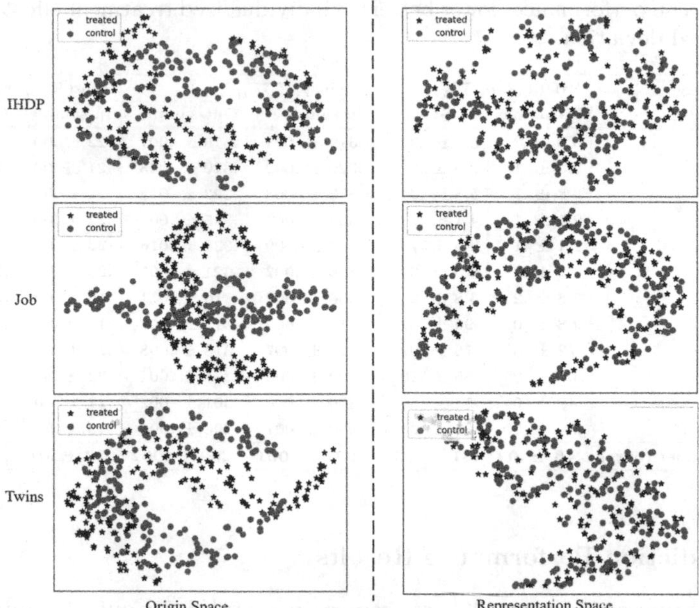

Fig. 3. Visualization of the learned representations in the three datasets through t-SNE. By sampling the dataset and performing dimensionality reduction using t-SNE, we can find that the representations learned by CEtransformer for different treatment groups are highly overlapping, which is in accordance with our expectation.

Meanwhile, quantitative metric, i.e., K-L divergence, of the different treatment groups is given in Fig. 4. We can find that the difference between the treated and control groups in the representation space decreases rapidly with the number of training iterations. As we inferred from the t-SNE visualization results, the differences in the distributions between the different treatment groups are wiped out under the constraints of the adversarial network.

4.4 Ablation Study

Experimental results on three datasets show that CETransformer is able to estimate causal effects more accurately compared to existing representation-based learning methods. In this section, we further explore the extent to which the changes made in CETransformer: Transformer backbone and adversarial learning affect the results. We compare CETransformer with CETransformer without Transformer and CETransformer without adversarial learning. Table 2 shows the results.

Our motivation for replacing the fully connected network with Transformer is that Transformer's self-attention can better capture the correlation between different features, and that correlation is expected to yield a more predictive representation. The results confirm our conjecture, and we find that replacing

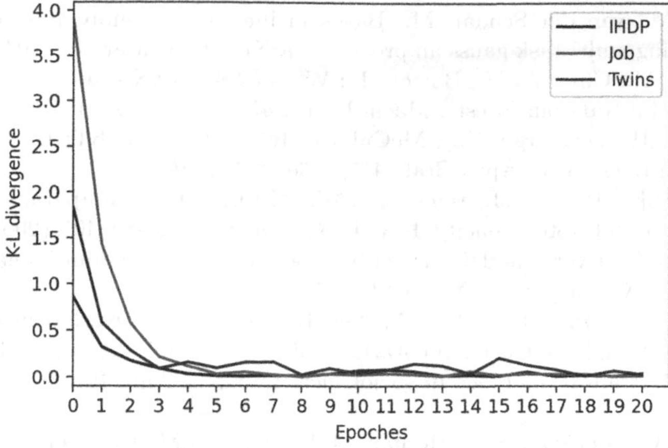

Fig. 4. KL divergence between control and treated groups in representation space.

the transformer with a fully connected network will cause a different degree of performance degradation. Then, the distribution of the two groups is balanced using an adversarial learning rather than a hand-crafted metric function. When the adversarial learning part is removed, the distribution imbalance should exist in the representation space as shown by the theoretical analysis in [1]. The experimental results also confirm our conjecture, and it can be found that after removing the adversarial learning part, the performance of CETransfoermer is similar to that of using traditional supervised learning methods alone.

5 Conclusion

In many domains, understanding the effect of different treatments on the individual level is crucial, but predicting their potential outcome in real-life is challenging. In this paper, we propose a novel balanced representation distribution learning model based on Transformer for the estimation of individual causal effects. We fully exploit the correlation information among the input features by the Transformer structure and automatically balance the distribution between the treated and control groups by the adversarial learning. Extensive experiments on three benchmark datasets show that CETransformer outperforms the state-of-the-art methods, which demonstrates the competitive level of CETransformer in estimating causal effects. We further demonstrate the effectiveness of components in CEtransformer through ablation study.

References

1. Alaa, A., Schaar, M.: Limits of estimating heterogeneous treatment effects: guidelines for practical algorithm design. In: International Conference on Machine Learning, pp. 129–138. PMLR (2018)

2. Alaa, A.M., van der Schaar, M.: Bayesian inference of individualized treatment effects using multi-task gaussian processes. arXiv preprint arXiv:1704.02801 (2017)
3. Arjovsky, M., Chintala, S., Bottou, L.: Wasserstein GAN (2017)
4. Breiman, L.: Random forests. Mach. Learn. **45**(1), 5–32 (2001)
5. Chipman, H.A., George, E.I., McCulloch, R.E., et al.: BART: Bayesian additive regression trees. Ann. Appl. Stat. **4**(1), 266–298 (2010)
6. Crump, R.K., Hotz, V.J., Imbens, G.W., Mitnik, O.A.: Nonparametric tests for treatment effect heterogeneity. Rev. Econ. Stat. **90**(3), 389–405 (2008)
7. Domingos, P.: Every model learned by gradient descent is approximately a kernel machine. arXiv preprint arXiv:2012.00152 (2020)
8. D'Amour, A., Ding, P., Feller, A., Lei, L., Sekhon, J.: Overlap in observational studies with high-dimensional covariates. J. Econometrics **221**(2), 644–654 (2021)
9. Gangl, M.: Causal inference in sociological research. Ann. Rev. Sociol. **36**, 21–47 (2010)
10. Glass, T.A., Goodman, S.N., Hernán, M.A., Samet, J.M.: Causal inference in public health. Annu. Rev. Public Health **34**, 61–75 (2013)
11. Gulrajani, I., Ahmed, F., Arjovsky, M., Dumoulin, V., Courville, A.: Improved training of Wasserstein GANs. arXiv preprint arXiv:1704.00028 (2017)
12. Hill, J.L.: Bayesian nonparametric modeling for causal inference. J. Comput. Graph. Stat. **20**(1), 217–240 (2011)
13. Johansson, F., Shalit, U., Sontag, D.: Learning representations for counterfactual inference. In: International Conference on Machine Learning, pp. 3020–3029. PMLR (2016)
14. Kuang, K., Cui, P., Li, B., Jiang, M., Yang, S.: Estimating treatment effect in the wild via differentiated confounder balancing. In: Proceedings of the 23rd ACM SIGKDD International Conference on Knowledge Discovery and Data Mining, pp. 265–274 (2017)
15. Van der Maaten, L., Hinton, G.: Visualizing data using t-SNE. J. Mach. Learn. Res. **9**(11) (2008)
16. Pearl, J., et al.: Causal inference in statistics: an overview. Stat. Surv. **3**, 96–146 (2009)
17. Rubin, D.B.: Estimating causal effects of treatments in randomized and nonrandomized studies. J. Educ. Psychol. **66**(5), 688 (1974)
18. Salimans, T., Goodfellow, I., Zaremba, W., Cheung, V., Radford, A., Chen, X.: Improved techniques for training GANs. arXiv preprint arXiv:1606.03498 (2016)
19. Schwab, P., Linhardt, L., Bauer, S., Buhmann, J.M., Karlen, W.: Learning counterfactual representations for estimating individual dose-response curves. In: Proceedings of the AAAI Conference on Artificial Intelligence, vol. 34, pp. 5612–5619 (2020)
20. Shalit, U., Johansson, F.D., Sontag, D.: Estimating individual treatment effect: generalization bounds and algorithms. In: International Conference on Machine Learning, pp. 3076–3085. PMLR (2017)
21. Splawa-Neyman, J., Dabrowska, D.M., Speed, T.: On the application of probability theory to agricultural experiments. essay on principles. Section 9. Stat. Sci. 465–472 (1990)
22. Vaswani, A., et al.: Attention is all you need. arXiv preprint arXiv:1706.03762 (2017)
23. Wager, S., Athey, S.: Estimation and inference of heterogeneous treatment effects using random forests. J. Am. Stat. Assoc. **113**(523), 1228–1242 (2018)

24. Wang, P., Sun, W., Yin, D., Yang, J., Chang, Y.: Robust tree-based causal inference for complex ad effectiveness analysis. In: Proceedings of the Eighth ACM International Conference on Web Search and Data Mining, pp. 67–76 (2015)
25. Yao, L., Li, S., Li, Y., Huai, M., Gao, J., Zhang, A.: Representation learning for treatment effect estimation from observational data. In: Advances in Neural Information Processing Systems, vol. 31 (2018)
26. Yao, L., Li, S., Li, Y., Huai, M., Gao, J., Zhang, A.: Ace: Adaptively similarity-preserved representation learning for individual treatment effect estimation. In: 2019 IEEE International Conference on Data Mining (ICDM), pp. 1432–1437. IEEE (2019)
27. Yin, X., Hong, L.: The identification and estimation of direct and indirect effects in a/b tests through causal mediation analysis. In: Proceedings of the 25th ACM SIGKDD International Conference on Knowledge Discovery & Data Mining, pp. 2989–2999 (2019)
28. Zhang, K., Gong, M., Schölkopf, B.: Multi-source domain adaptation: a causal view. In: Proceedings of the AAAI Conference on Artificial Intelligence, vol. 29 (2015)
29. Zhang, Y., Bellot, A., Schaar, M.: Learning overlapping representations for the estimation of individualized treatment effects. In: International Conference on Artificial Intelligence and Statistics, pp. 1005–1014. PMLR (2020)

An Efficient Polyp Detection Framework with Suspicious Targets Assisted Training

Zhipeng Zhang[1,2], Li Xiao[1,2,3(✉)], Fuzhen Zhuang[4,5(✉)], Ling Ma[1(✉)], Yuan Chang[6(✉)], Yuanyuan Wang[1], Huiqin Jiang[1], and Qing He[1,2]

[1] Henan Institute of Advanced Technology, Zhengzhou University, Zhengzhou, China
{xiaoli,heqing}@ict.ac.cn, {ielma,iehqjiang}@zzu.edu.cn
[2] Key Lab of Intelligent Information Processing of Chinese Academy of Sciences (CAS), Institute of Computing Technology, CAS, Beijing, China
[3] Ningbo Huamei Hospital, University of the Chinese Academy of Sciences, Ningbo, China
[4] Institute of Artificial Intelligence, Beihang University, Beijing 100191, China
zhuangfuzhen@buaa.edu.cn
[5] Xiamen Institute of Data Intelligence, Xiamen, China
[6] The First Affiliated Hospital of Zhengzhou University, Zhengzhou, China

Abstract. Automatic polyp detection during colonoscopy is beneficial for reducing the risk of colorectal cancer. However, due to the various shapes and sizes of polyps and the complex structures in the intestinal cavity, some normal tissues may display features similar to actual polyps. As a result, traditional object detection models are easily confused by such suspected target regions and lead to false-positive detection. In this work, we propose a multi-branch spatial attention mechanism based on the one-stage object detection framework, YOLOv4. Our model is further jointly optimized with a top likelihood and similarity to reduce false positives caused by suspected target regions. A similarity loss is further added to identify the suspected targets from real ones. We then introduce a Cross Stage Partial Connection mechanism to reduce the parameters. Our model is evaluated on the private colonic polyp dataset and the public MICCAI 2015 grand challenge dataset including the CVC-Clinic 2015 and Etis-Larib, both of the results show our model improves performance by a large margin and with less computational cost.

Keywords: Polyp detection · Suspected target · Semi-supervised learning

1 Introduction

Colorectal cancer is one of the most common malignancies of the digestive system in the world. Most colorectal cancers originate from adenomatous polyp, and colonoscopy is an important way to screen for colorectal cancer [1]. Colonoscopy-based polyp detection is a key task in medical image computing. In recent years, Deep learning detection models are widely used in polyp detection [2–4,8,16].

© Springer Nature Switzerland AG 2021
H. Ma et al. (Eds.): PRCV 2021, LNCS 13022, pp. 536–547, 2021.
https://doi.org/10.1007/978-3-030-88013-2_44

However, influenced by the complex environment of the intestinal tract, bubbles, lens reflection, residues, and shadows may display polyp-like features. Those features can form the suspected target and confuse the model. See Fig. 1 below.

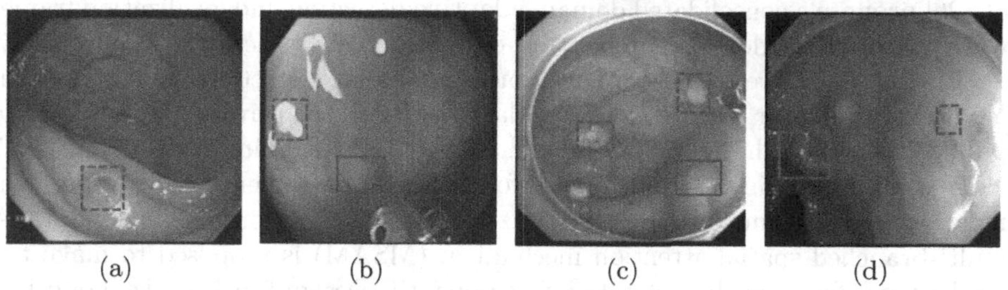

Fig. 1. (a) Bubbles; (b) Lens reflection; (c) Residues; (d) Virtual shadow

Currently two-stage [2–4,6] and one-stage [5,8,16,23] models are the most widely used models in object detection. Faster R-CNN [6] as the most widely used two-stage object detection model, has been adopted in various polyp detection tasks. Mo et al. [2] provide the first evaluation for polyp detection using Faster R-CNN framework, which provides a good trade-off between efficiency and accuracy. Shin et al. [4] propose FP learning. They first trained a network with polyp images and generated FP samples with additional normal videos. Then retrained the network by adding back the generated FP samples. Sornapudi et al. [3] propose a modified region-based convolutional neural network (R-CNN) by generating masks around polyp detected from still frames. One stage model such as You only look once (YOLO) [5] is also widely used for lesion detection with the advantage of its efficiency. Wang et al. [8] propose a new anchor free polyp detector, which can achieve real-time performance. Liu et al. [23] investigated the potential of the single shot detector (SSD) [18] framework for detecting polyps in colonoscopy videos. Three different feature extractors, including ResNet50, VGG16, and InceptionV3 are assessed. Tian et al. [16] propose a one-stage detection and classification approach for a new 5-class polyp classification problem.

To deal with the suspected target regions, some mechanisms such as attention mechanism (CBAM) [7] propose to make the model more focused on true target regions. Recently, Xiao et al. [10] propose a new sampling method based on the Faster R-CNN model to automatically learn features from the suspected target regions directly and effectively reduce false positives. Guo et al. [24] propose a method based on active learning to tackle false positives detected by the CADe system. But both [24] and [4] methods add the FP samples to the training set after finding the false-positive region to retrain the network, this process is more complicated. We design a semi-supervised method to automatically learn suspicious targets to solve this problem.

In addition, there are other methods to detect polyps. Tajbakhsh et al. [22] is based on a hybrid context-shape approach, which utilizes context information to remove non-polyp structures and shape information to reliably localize polyps. Tian et al. [25] integrate few-shot anomaly detection methods designed to perform the detection of frames containing polyps from colonoscopy videos with a method that rejects frames containing blurry images, feces and water jet sprays. Liu et al. [26] propose a consolidated domain adaptive detection and localization framework to bridge the domain gap between different colonosopic datasets effectively.

In this paper, we propose a novel one-stage polyp detection model based on YOLOv4. Moreover, Our model is validated on both the private dataset and the public dataset of the MICCAI 2015 challenge [11] including CVC-Clinic 2015 and Etis-Larib, brings significant performance improvements and outperform most cutting-edge models. To summarize, our main contributions include: (i) A multi-branched spatial attention mechanism (MSAM) is proposed to make the model more focus on the polyp lesion regions. (ii) Design the Top likelihood loss (Tloss) with a multi-scale sampling strategy to reduce false positives by learning from suspected regions from the background. (iii) Further propose Cosine similarity loss (Csimloss) to improve the discrimination ability between positive and negative images. (iv) A cross stage partial connection mechanism is further introduced to make the model more efficient. (v) Finally, from the large amount of experiments using the private and public datasets, we demonstrate that our detection model shows improved detection performance compared with other recent studies in the colonoscopy image datasets.

2 Methods

Our detailed model is shown in Fig. 2. The proposed framework consists of three parts: (1) A multi-branch spatial attention mechanism (MSAM) is proposed to make the model pay more attention to the polyp lesion regions (Sect. 2.1); (2) Top likelihood loss and cosine similarity loss are designed to the one-stage model for false-positive reduction (Sect. 2.2); (3) Cross Stage Partial Connection is introduced to reduce model parameters through feature fusion (Sect. 2.3). During training, the proposed model jointly optimizes positive and negative images. The positive images are trained by the original loss function, the negative images are trained with the top likelihood loss added. The pairs of positive and negative images are further optimized by the cosine similarity loss.

2.1 Multi-branch Spatial Attention Mechanism

In order to make the model pay more attention to the polyp lesion regions and eliminate the effect of background contents, inspired by the idea of spatial attention mechanism (SAM) [7] which locates the most important information on the feature map, we propose a multi-branch spatial attention mechanism (MSAM). We put them in the three output positions of feature fusion, as shown in C-M-Block in Fig. 2, MSAM is a concrete structure. There are three different scales of feature maps for feature fusion, the receptive fields of the three scales are targeted to different sizes of objects.

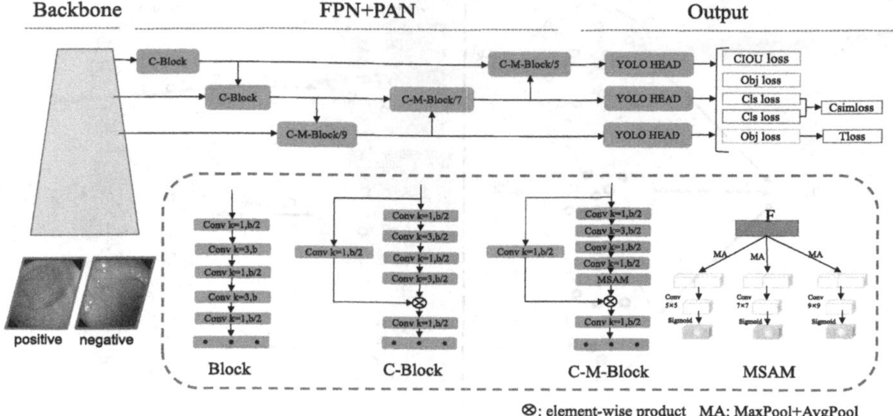

Fig. 2. The architecture of the model. C-Block is the structure after adding cross stage partial connection, and C-M-Block is the structure after adding cross stage partial connection and multi-branch spatial attention mechanism (MSAM), the number represent the convolution kernel size, setting $\mathrm{k}' \in \{5, 7, 9\}$ in our model, They correspond to the three scales in the model.

Given an input F, we compute the MSAM map $A_s = \sigma\left(\sum_{\mathrm{k}'} f^{\mathrm{k}'\times \mathrm{k}'}(F)\right)$. Where, $f^{\mathrm{k}'\times\mathrm{k}'}$ represents the convolution operation with the kernel size of $\mathrm{k}' \times \mathrm{k}'$, and σ represents the sigmoid activation function. Setting $\mathrm{k}' \in \{5, 7, 9\}$ in our model, They correspond to the three scales in the model. The 9×9 convolution kernel corresponds to the smaller receptive field, the 7×7 convolution kernel corresponds to the middle scale receptive field, and the 5×5 convolution kernel corresponds to the larger receptive field.

2.2 Top Likelihood and Similarity Loss

We design the top likelihood loss and cosine similarity loss to reduce false positives. The implementation details of the loss can be summarized in Fig. 3.

Top Likelihood Loss. When optimizing negative samples, since those images do not have any annotation information, this means that all areas will be randomly sampled with equal chance. As a result, the suspected target regions will have a small chance to get trained since it usually only occupies a small portion of the image. The prediction result may bias towards normal features, leading to some false positive detection. To solve this problem, we design top likelihood loss with multi-scale sampling strategy in a one-stage model. When dealing with negative images, we use top likelihood loss and select the proposals with top confidence scores.

Different from two-stage models, YOLOv4 directly generates object confidence score, category probability, and border regression. When training negative

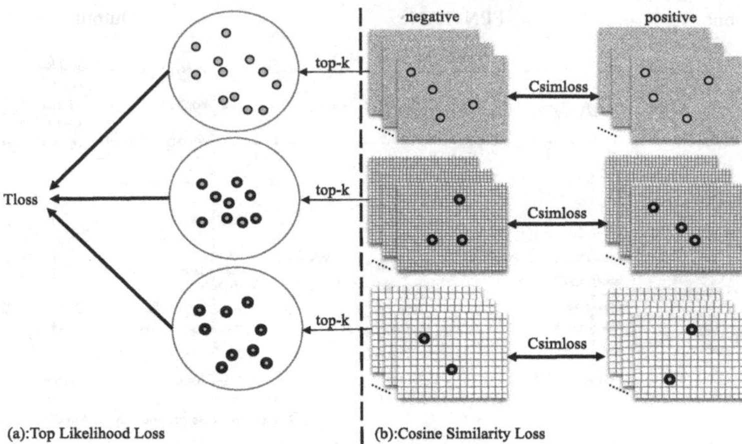

Fig. 3. The illustration of the multi-scale top likelihood loss and cosine similarity loss where the solid point represents the selected sample: (a) show top likelihood loss with multi-scale sampling strategy, the K of each scale is set to 50. (b) In the same batch, positive and negative samples of the same scale calculate cosine similarity loss.

images, we compute the confidence scores and select the top 50 anchor boxes score negative anchor boxes on each scale (150 in total) to calculate the loss. The boxes with high scores will be more likely to represent the suspected target region, and as long as the boxes with high scores are minimized, all the boxes would be optimized to be negative regions. This top likelihood loss is defined as:

$$\mathrm{L_{tloss}} = \frac{1}{\mathrm{obj}} \sum_{i \in \text{ tops}} L_{\mathrm{obj}} \left(p_i, p_i^* = 0\right) \tag{1}$$

Here, i represents the index of anchor in a batch, and p_i represents the predicted score of the i-th anchors. L_{obj} is the cross-entropy loss.

Cosine Similarity Loss. We further propose the cosine similarity loss to improve the discrimination ability between positive and negative images. To make our model trained sufficiently, we make use all of the pairs of positive and negative images for computing the cosine similarity loss. Specifically, in each batch, positive images and negative images are random. In order to fully learn the characteristics between positive and negative images, we design a program to let the positive and negative images in the same batch size calculate the similarity loss between each other, and finally take the average. When the network processes the positive images, we take the positive samples with top K scores. Then, when the network processes negative images, we select the highest predicted K classification scores and pair them with positive ones. Assume A positive images and B negative images within one batch, there are $A \times B$ positive-negative pairs. The similarity loss is obtained by computing the cosine similarity of K paired eigen-vectors and summing over the $A \times B$ pairs.

$$L_{\text{csimloss}}\left(X_1, X_2\right)=\frac{1}{A \times B} \sum_j^{\text{AxB}}\left[\frac{1}{K} \sum_{i=1}^K \operatorname{csim}\left(X_1^i, X_2^i\right)\right] \tag{2}$$

Where X_1^i, X_2^i are the feature vectors from positive and negative images, *csim* is cosine similarity loss, $\operatorname{csim}\left(X_1^i, X_2^i\right)=\frac{X_1^i \cdot X_2^i}{\left\|X_1^i\right\|\left\|_2^i\right\|}=\frac{\sum_{i=1}^n X_1^i \times X_2^i}{\sqrt{\sum_{i=1}^n\left(X_1^i\right)^2} \times \sqrt{\sum_{i=1}^n\left(X_2^i\right)^2}}$.

2.3 Cross Stage Partial Connection

We further introduce the Cross Stage Partial Network (CSPNet) [13] in our model. By dividing the gradient flow, CSPNet can make the gradient flow propagate through different network paths, which can improve the reasoning speed. As shown in Fig. 2, the feature fusion part includes five modules: three up-sampling and two down-sampling. As shown in C-Block and C-M-Block in the bottom right of Fig. 2, the Block represents the original connection, C-Block and C-M-Block represents the connection after adding CSP. through the split and merge strategy, the number of gradient paths can be doubled. Because of the cross-stage strategy, which can alleviate the disadvantages caused by using explicit feature map copy for concatenation. As shown in Table 1, the number of parameters significantly decrease by adding such an operation.

3 Experiment

3.1 Datasets

In order to verify the effectiveness of the proposed method, we conduct experiments on two datasets, the private colonic polyp dataset and the public dataset including CVC-Clinic 2015 and Etis-Larib.

Private Polyp Dataset. A dataset of private colonic polyp dataset is collected and labeled from the Colorectal and Anorectal Surgery Department of a local hospital, which contains 175 patients with 1720 colon polyp images. The 1720 images are randomly divided into training and testing set with a ratio of 4:1. We simulate the actual application scenes of colonoscopy and expand the dataset accordingly, including the expansion of blur, brightness, deformation and so on, finally expanding to 3582 images. The colon polyp images are combined with 1000 normal images without annotation information to build the training set. The original image size is varied from 612 × 524 to 1280 × 720. And we resize all the images to 512 × 512.

MICCAI 2015 Colonoscopy Polyp Automatic Detection Classification Challenge. The challenge contains two datasets, the model is trained on CVC-Clinic 2015 and evaluated on Etis-Larib. The CVC-Clinic 2015 dataset contains 612 standard well-defined images extracted from 29 different sequences. Each sequence consists of 6 to 26 frames and contains at least one polyp in a variety of viewing angles, distances and views. Each polyp is manually annotated by a mask that accurately states its boundaries. The resolution is 384×288. The Etis-Larib dataset contains 196 high-resolution images with a resolution of 1225×966, including 44 distinct polyps obtained from 34 sequences.

3.2 Evaluation and Results

Evaluation Criteria. We use the same evaluation metrics presented in the MICCAI 2015 challenge to perform the fair evaluation of our polyp detector performance.

Since the number of false negative in this particular medical application is more harmful, we also calculate the F1 and F2 scores as follows. The evaluation criteria are as follows:

$$\begin{aligned} Precision &= \frac{TP}{TP+FP} \qquad & Recall &= \frac{TP}{TP+FN} \\ F1 &= \frac{2*Precision*Recall}{Precision+Recall} \qquad & F2 &= \frac{5*Precision*Recall}{4*Precision+Recall} \end{aligned} \tag{3}$$

where TP and FN denote the true positive and false negative patient cases. FP represents the false positive patient cases.

Implementation Details. Our model uses the Pytorch framework and runs on NVIDIA GeForce RTX 2080Ti GPU servers. We set the batch size to 8. During training, we use the SGD optimization method, we also perform random angle rotation and image scaling data for data augmentation. The training contains 2000 epochs with 574 iterations for each epoch, Normally the training process starts with a high learning rate and then decreases every certain as the training goes on. However, a large learning rate applies on a randomly initialized network may cause instability for training. To solve this problem, we apply a smooth cosine learning rate learner [12]. The learning rate α_t is computed as $\alpha_t = \frac{1}{2}\left(1+\cos\left(\frac{t\pi}{T}\right)\right)\alpha$, where t represents the current epoch, T represents the epoch and α represents initial learning rate.

Ablation Experiments on Private Dataset. In order to study the effect of MSAM and the new loss function, we conduct ablation experiments on our private dataset. As shown in Table 1, Compared to the YOLOv4 baseline, our proposed MSAM increases the Recall by 4.5%, resulting in a score increase of F1 and F2 by 2.2% and 4.0%, respectively. Adding the top likelihood loss only increases the Precision by 4.4%, and combining top likelihood loss together increases both Precision and Recall, leading to an increase of Precision by 2.9% and Recall by 3.1%. Finally, the model achieves the performance boosting over all the metrics when combining MSAM, Top likelihood and similarity loss, CSP module together, leading to increases of Precision by 4.4%, Recall by 3.7%, F1 by 4.0%,

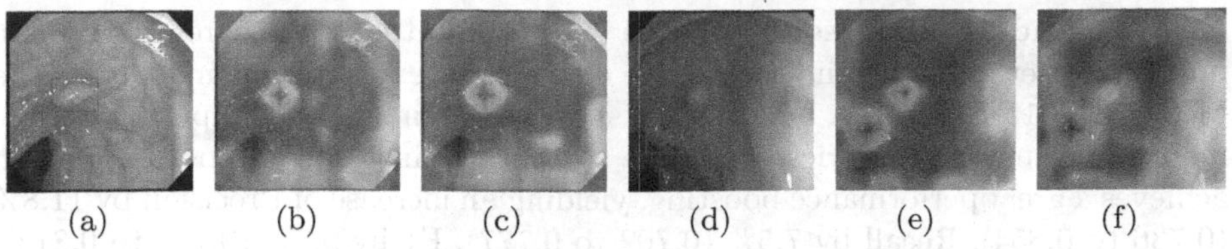

Fig. 4. (a) Origin image with ground truth label (solid line box); (b) Heatmap generated by the original YOLOv4; (c) Heatmap generated by YOLOv4+MSAM; (d) Origin image with ground truth label (solid line box) and suspected target regions (dashed line box); (e) Heatmap generated by YOLOv4+MSAM; (f) Heatmap generated by YOLOv4+MSAM+Tloss (top likelihood loss);

and F2 by 3.8%. It is also worth noting that CSP makes the model more efficient and leads decreases of FLOPs by 10.74% (8.66 to 7.73), and Parameters by 15.7% (63.94 to 53.9).

We also show some visualization results of the heatmap (last feature map of YOLOv4) for ablation comparison (shown in Fig. 4). The results demonstrate that MSAM makes the model more focus on the ground truth areas, and the top likelihood loss let the model better identify the suspected target regions and pay less attention to such areas.

Table 1. The results on the private polyp datasets.

	SAM	MSAM	Tloss	Csimloss	CSP	Precision	Recall	F1	F2
YOLOv4						0.876	0.851	0.863	0.856
	✓					0.864	0.897	0.88	0.89
		✓				0.874	0.896	0.885	0.896
			✓			0.92	0.845	0.881	0.859
				✓		0.878	0.888	0.883	0.886
					✓	0.869	0.851	0.86	0.854
		✓	✓			0.905	0.882	0.894	0.887
			✓	✓		0.914	0.885	0.899	0.891
			✓	✓	✓	0.907	0.898	0.902	0.9
		✓	✓	✓	✓	0.92	0.888	0.903	0.894
Model parameters						FLOPs (GMac)		Params (M)	
						8.66		63.94	
		✓	✓	✓		8.82		65.32	
		✓	✓	✓	✓	7.73		53.9	

Results and Comparisons on the Public Dataset. The results on the public dataset are shown in Table 2, we also test several previous models for the MICCAI 2015 challenges. The results show that our method improves performance on almost all metrics. Compare to the baseline, our proposed approach achieves a great performance boosting, yielding an increase of Precision by 11.8% (0.736 to 0.854), Recall by 7.5% (0.702 to 0.777), F1 by 9.5% (0.719 to 0.814), F2 by 8.2% (0.709 to 0.791). It is worth noting that the depth of CSPDarknet53 backbone for YOLOv4 is almost the same as Resnet50. However, our proposed approach even significantly outperforms the state-of-the-art model Sornapudi et al. [3] with a backbone of Resnet101 and Liu et al. [23] with a backbone of Inceptionv3. Comparison with Liu et al. [23], although it slightly decreases the Recall by 2.6% (0.803 to 0.777), it increases Precision by 11.5% (0.739 to 0.854), F1 by 4.6% (0.768 to 0.814), and F2 by 0.2% (0.789 to 0.791). We presented the Frame Per Second (FPS) for each model. It shows that our one-stage model is much faster than other models. It is 5.3 times faster than the Faster R-CNN (37.2 vs 7), 11.6 times faster than Sornapudi et al. [3] (37.2 vs 3.2) and 1.2 times faster than Liu et al. [23] (37.2 vs 32). Furthermore, The PR curve is plotted in Fig. 5. Comparison with baseline, our proposed approach increases the AP by 5.1% (0.728 to 0.779).

Table 2. Results of the different modes on MICCAI 2015 challenge dataset.

	Backbone	Precision	Recall	F1	F2	FPS
OUS	–	0.697	0.63	0.661	0.642	0.2
CUMED	–	0.723	0.692	0.707	0.698	5
Faster RCNN [6]	Resnet101	0.617	0.644	0.63	0.638	7
Zheng et al. [19]	–	0.76	0.668	0.711	0.685	–
YOLOv3 [17]	Darknet53	0.764	0.577	0.658	0.607	**37**
Qadir et al. [21]	Resnet50	0.8	0.726	0.761	0.74	–
Sornapudi et al. [3]	Resnet50	0.632	0.769	0.694	0.737	–
Sornapudi et al. [3]	Resnet101	0.729	0.803	0.764	0.787	3.2
Jia et al. [20]	Resnet50	0.639	**0.817**	0.717	0.774	–
Xu et al. [27]	Darknet53	0.832	0.716	0.77	0.736	35
Liu et al. [23]	Inceptionv3	0.739	0.803	0.768	0.789	32
Tian et al. [25]	Resnet50	0.736	0.644	0.687	0.661	–
YOLOv4	CSPDarknet53	0.736	0.702	0.719	0.709	36.9
Proposed approach	CSPDarknet53	**0.854**	0.777	**0.814**	**0.791**	**37.2**

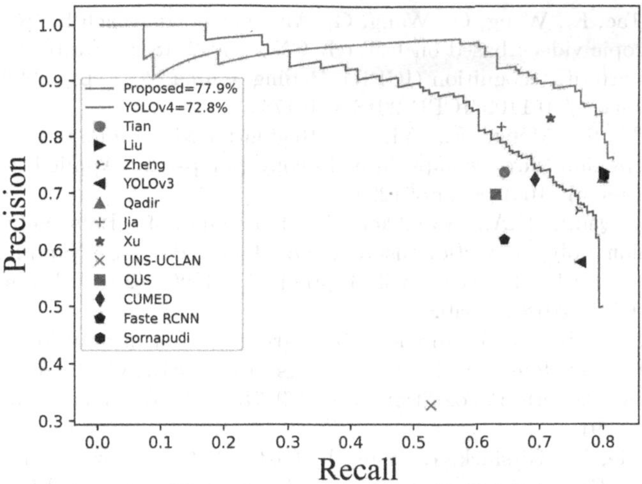

Fig. 5. Precision-Recall curves for all the methods. The performance of Proposed approach is much better than the teams that attended the MICCAI challenge

4 Conclusions

In this paper, we propose an efficient and accurate object detection method to detect colonoscopic polyps. We design a MSAM mechanism to make the model pay more attention to the polyp lesion regions and eliminate the effect of background content. To make our network more efficient, we develop our method based on a one-stage object detection model. Our model is further jointly optimized with a top likelihood and similarity loss to reduce false positives caused by suspected target regions. A Cross Stage Partial Connection mechanism is further introduced to reduce the parameters. Our approach brings performance boosting compare to the state-of-the-art methods, on both a private polyp detection dataset and public MICCAI 2015 challenge dataset. In the future, we plan to extend our model on more complex scenes, such as gastric polyp detection, lung nodule detection, achieving accurate and real-time lesion detection.

Acknowledgments. The research work supported by the National Key Research and Development Program of China under Grant No. 2018YFB1004300, the National Natural Science Foundation of China under Grant No. U1836206, U1811461, 61773361 and Zhengzhou collaborative innovation major special project (20XTZX11020).

References

1. Zhang, P., Sun, X., Wang, D., Wang, X., Cao, Y., Liu, B.: An efficient spatial-temporal polyp detection framework for colonoscopy video. In: 2019 IEEE 31st International Conference on Tools with Artificial Intelligence, pp. 1252–1259. IEEE, Portland (2019). https://doi.org/10.1109/ICTAI.2019.00-93

2. Mo, X., Tao, K., Wang, Q., Wang, G.: An efficient approach for polyps detection in endoscopic videos based on faster R-CNN. In: 2018 24th International Conference on Pattern Recognition (ICPR), Beijing, China, 2018, pp. 3929–3934 (2018). https://doi.org/10.1109/ICPR.2018.8545174
3. Sornapudi, S., Meng, F., Yi, S.: Region-based automated localization of colonoscopy and wireless capsule endoscopy polyps. In: Applied Sciences (2019) . https://doi.org/10.3390/app9122404
4. Shin, Y., Qadir, H.A., Aabakken, L., Bergsland, J., Balasingham, I.: Automatic colon polyp detection using region based deep CNN and post learning approaches. In: IEEE Access, vol. 6, pp. 40950–40962 (2018). https://doi.org/10.1109/ACCESS.2018.2856402
5. Redmon, J., Divvala, S., Girshick, R., Farhadi, A.: You only look once: unified, real-time object detection. In: Proceedings of the IEEE Conference on Computer Vision and Pattern Recognition, pp. 779–788 (2016). https://doi.org/10.1109/CVPR.2016.91
6. Ren, S., He, K., Girshick, R., Sun, J.: Faster R-CNN: towards real-time object detection with region proposal networks. In: Advances in Neural Information Processing Systems, pp. 91–99 (2015)
7. Woo, S., Park, J., Lee, J.-Y., Kweon, I.S.: CBAM: convolutional block attention module. In: Ferrari, V., Hebert, M., Sminchisescu, C., Weiss, Y. (eds.) ECCV 2018. LNCS, vol. 11211, pp. 3–19. Springer, Cham (2018). https://doi.org/10.1007/978-3-030-01234-2_1
8. Wang, D., et al.: AFP-Net: realtime anchor-free polyp detection in colonoscopy. In: 2019 IEEE 31st International Conference on Tools with Artificial Intelligence (ICTAI), Portland, OR, USA, pp. 636–643 (2019). https://doi.org/10.1109/ICTAI.2019.00094
9. Bochkovskiy, A., Wang, C.Y., Liao, H.Y.M.: YOLOv4: optimal speed and accuracy of object detection. In: arXiv:2004.10934 (2020)
10. Xiao, L., Zhu, C., Liu, J., Luo, C., Liu, P., Zhao, Y.: Learning from suspected target: bootstrapping performance for breast cancer detection in mammography. In: Shen, D., et al. (eds.) MICCAI 2019. LNCS, vol. 11769, pp. 468–476. Springer, Cham (2019). https://doi.org/10.1007/978-3-030-32226-7_52
11. Bernal, J., Sanchez, F.J., Fernandez-Esparrach, G., Gil, D., Rodrguez, C., Vilarino, F.: WM-DOVA maps for accurate polyp highlighting in colonoscopy: validation vs. saliency maps from physicians. In: Computerized Medical Imaging and Graphics, vol. 43, pp. 99–111 (2015)
12. Loshchilov, I., Hutter, F.: SGDR: stochastic gradient descent with warm restarts. In: arXiv preprint arXiv:1608.03983 (2016)
13. Wang, C.Y., Liao, H.Y.M., Wu, Y.H., et al.: CSPNet: a new backbone that can enhance learning capability of CNN. In: 2020 IEEE/CVF Conference on Computer Vision and Pattern Recognition Workshops (2020)
14. Yuan, Z., IzadyYazdanabadi, M., Mokkapati, D., et al.: Automatic polyp detection in colonoscopy videos. In: Medical Imaging 2017: Image Processing, Orlando, Florida, USA, vol. 2017 (2017)
15. Tajbakhsh, S., Gurudu, R., Liang, J.: Automatic polyp detection in colonoscopy videos using an ensemble of convolutional neural networks. In: 2015 IEEE 12th International Symposium on Biomedical Imaging (ISBI), Brooklyn, NY, USA, pp. 79–83 (2015). https://doi.org/10.1109/ISBI.2015.7163821

16. Tian, Y., Pu, L.Z.C.T., Singh, R., Burt, A.D., Carneiro, G.: One-stage five-class polyp detection and classification. In: 2019 IEEE 16th International Symposium on Biomedical Imaging (ISBI 2019), Venice, Italy, pp. 70–73 (2019). https://doi.org/10.1109/ISBI.2019.8759521
17. Redmon, J., Farhadi, A.: YOLOv3: an incremental improvement. arXiv preprint arXiv:1804.02767 (2018)
18. Liu, W., et al.: SSD: single shot multibox detector. In: Leibe, B., Matas, J., Sebe, N., Welling, M. (eds.) ECCV 2016. LNCS, vol. 9905, pp. 21–37. Springer, Cham (2016). https://doi.org/10.1007/978-3-319-46448-0_2
19. Zheng, Y., et al.: Localisation of colorectal polyps by convolutional neural network features learnt from white light and narrow band endoscopic images of multiple databases. In: EMBS, pp. 4142–4145 (2018)
20. Jia, X., et al.: Automatic polyp recognition in colonoscopy images using deep learning and two-stage pyramidal feature prediction. IEEE Trans. Autom. Sci. Eng. **17**, 1570–1584 (2020). https://doi.org/10.1109/TASE.2020.2964827
21. Qadir, H.A., Shin, Y., Solhusvik, J., Bergsland, J., Aabakken, L., Balasingham, I.: Polyp detection and segmentation using mask R-CNN: does a deeper feature extractor CNN always perform better? In: 2019 13th International Symposium on Medical Information and Communication Technology (ISMICT), pp. 1–6. IEEE (2019)
22. Tajbakhsh, S., Gurudu, R., Liang, J.: Automated polyp detection in colonoscopy videos using shape and context information. IEEE Trans. Med. Imag. **35**(2), 630–644 (2016). https://doi.org/10.1109/TMI.2015.2487997
23. Liu, M., Jiang, J., Wang, Z.: Colonic polyp detection in endoscopic videos with single shot detection based deep convolutional neural network. IEEE Access **7**, 75058–75066 (2019). https://doi.org/10.1109/ACCESS.2019.2921027
24. Guo, Z., et al.: Reduce false-positive rate by active learning for automatic polyp detection in colonoscopy videos. In: 2020 IEEE 17th International Symposium on Biomedical Imaging (ISBI), pp. 1655–1658 (2020). https://doi.org/10.1109/ISBI45749.2020.9098500
25. Tian, Y., Pu, L., Liu, Y., et al.: Detecting, localising and classifying polyps from colonoscopy videos using deep learning. arXiv preprint arXiv:2101.03285v1 (2021)
26. Liu, X., Guo, X., Liu, Y., et al.: Consolidated domain adaptive detection and localization framework for cross-device colonoscopic images. Med. Image Anal. (2021). https://doi.org/10.1016/j.media.2021.102052
27. Xu, J., Zhao, R., Yu, Y., et al.: Real-time automatic polyp detection in colonoscopy using feature enhancement module and spatiotemporal similarity correlation unit. In: Biomedical Signal Processing and Control, vol. 66 (2021). https://doi.org/10.1016/j.bspc.2021.102503. ISSN 1746–8094

Invertible Image Compressive Sensing

Bingfeng Sun and Jian Zhang(✉)

Peking University Shenzhen Graduate School, Shenzhen, China
zhangjian.sz@pku.edu.cn

Abstract. Invertible neural networks (INNs) have been widely used to design generative models and solve inverse problems. However, there is little research on applying invertible models to compressive sensing (CS) tasks. To address this challenge, in this paper, a novel and memory-efficient invertible image compressive sensing framework, dubbed InvICS, is proposed, which conducts a practical integration of optimization-based CS methods and INNs. In particular, InvICS is composed of three subnets: sampling subnet, initialization subnet, and invertible recovery subnet, and all the parameters in it are learned end-to-end, rather than hand-crafted. Through building effective modules in each phase of the invertible recovery subnet, the activations for most layers need not be stored in memory during backpropagation, which easily allows training our model with 100+ phases (1000+ layers) even on a single Nvidia 2070 GPU. Moreover, extensive experiments on several common benchmark datasets demonstrate that the proposed InvICS outperforms most state-of-the-art methods by a large margin.

Keywords: Compressive sensing · Invertible neural networks · Image reconstruction · Deep network

1 Introduction

Compressive Sensing (CS) has been applied in a series of imaging applications, such as single-pixel camera [4], magnetic resonance imaging (MRI) [15], wireless tele-monitoring [48], cognitive radio communication [33] and snapshot compressive imaging [39], *etc.* Mathematically, given the measurement $\mathbf{y} = \mathbf{\Phi x} + \mathbf{w}$, where $\mathbf{x} \in \mathbb{R}^N$ is the signal, $\mathbf{\Phi} \in \mathbb{R}^{M \times N}$ is called the measurement matrix, and $\mathbf{w} \in \mathbb{R}^M$ is the measurement noise, reconstructing $\mathbf{x}$ from $\mathbf{y}$ when $M \ll N$ is typically ill-posed. However, CS theory [6,7,11] states that the signal $\mathbf{x}$ can be recovered perfectly even from a small number of $M = \mathcal{O}(s \log(\frac{N}{s}))$ random linear measurements provided that the signal is s-sparse in some sparsifying domain.

Over the past decade, several reconstruction methods have been proposed. Model-based methods [13,23,46,47,50–54] usually assume that natural images can be sparsely represented by a dictionary, and thus learn the sampling matrix

This work was supported in part by National Natural Science Foundation of China (61902009).

© Springer Nature Switzerland AG 2021
H. Ma et al. (Eds.): PRCV 2021, LNCS 13022, pp. 548–560, 2021.
https://doi.org/10.1007/978-3-030-88013-2_45

and sparse dictionary simultaneously through solving a sparsity regularized optimization problem. However, their iterative nature renders the algorithms computationally expensive. Deep network-based algorithms [8,17,29–31,35,37,38] propose to learn the non-linear reconstruction operator through neural networks. Benefiting from the powerful learning ability of neural networks, these methods achieve a good balance between the reconstruction performance and time complexity. In the earlier periods, network-based models are trained like a black-box and have low interpretability. Researchers [41–45] combine these two kinds of methods, and their proposed methods enjoy the advantages of fast and accurate reconstruction with well-defined interpretability. However, as networks grow wider and deeper, storing the activations will cause an increasing memory burden [14], which may possibly limit their performances.

To address this problem, we propose a new image compressive sensing framework, dubbed InvICS (see Fig. 1). It's inspired by the traditional Iterative Shrinkage-Thresholding Algorithm (ISTA). In contrast to optimization-based networks, we don't rely upon sparse assumptions, and use deep invertible layers to obtain the optimal estimation in an iterative manner. The proposed InvICS algorithm is proved effective and efficient.

Contributions. The main contributions of this paper are summarized as follows:

- Our proposed InvICS, is an effective integration of optimization-based methods and invertible networks. It easily allows training with 1000+ layers even on a single Nvidia 2070 GPU without a memory bottleneck.
- We use an order-preserving multi-channel fusion mechanism in the invertible recovery subnet, which is proved as an efficient method to boost performance.
- Extensive experiments on natural image CS reconstruction clearly show that InvICS significantly outperforms the state-of-the-art.

The paper is organized as follows. Section 2 introduces some related works. Section 3 describes InvICS in detail. Section 4 is the experimental results. And in Sect. 5, we conclude this paper and discuss the future works.

2 Related Work

2.1 Compressive Sensing

Existing learning-based CS methods can be generally grouped into two categories.

Black Box End-to-End. The first category is to learn the inverse transformation from measurement vector $\mathbf{y}$ to original signal $\mathbf{x}$ using a deep convolutional network. A representative method is ReconNet [21] which employs a convolutional neural network for reconstruction in a block-wise manner. Similar schemes are SDA based methods [31], DeepInverse [29], *etc.* The main feature of this kind is that they are non-iterative, which can dramatically reduce time complexity. However, their lack of structural diversity, leading to low interpretability, is the bottleneck for further performance improvement.

Optimization-Inspired Networks. The second category blends data-driven networks with sparse-signal-recovery algorithms. Methods, such as [28,44,45,49], are of this kind. Among them, OPINE-Net$^+$ [45] is a notable one. It can be viewed as a perfect fusion between optimization-based methods and network-based methods. Simply put, it casts Iterative Shrinkage-Thresholding Algorithm (ISTA) into deep network form. Instead of using a fixed sampling matrix, it adopts a learnable one, and jointly optimizes it and the non-linear recovery operator. What's more, it utilizes pixel shuffle operation, which can exploit the inter-block relationship and thus eliminate block artifacts.

2.2 Invertible Neural Network

Invertible network [9,10] is born to perform inverse problems since it can map a prior distribution to the desired one easily. It acts in an unsupervised manner and relies on bijectivity to ensure the mappings validity. Given a latent variable $\mathbf{z}$ from a simple distribution $p_{\mathbf{z}}(\mathbf{z})$, *e.g.*, isotropic Gaussian, it can generate an image with more complex distribution. Due to such flexibility, INNs have attracted much more attention in recent years, and have been applied successfully in applications, *e.g.*, classification [3,26], generation [2,10,20], and rescaling [40].

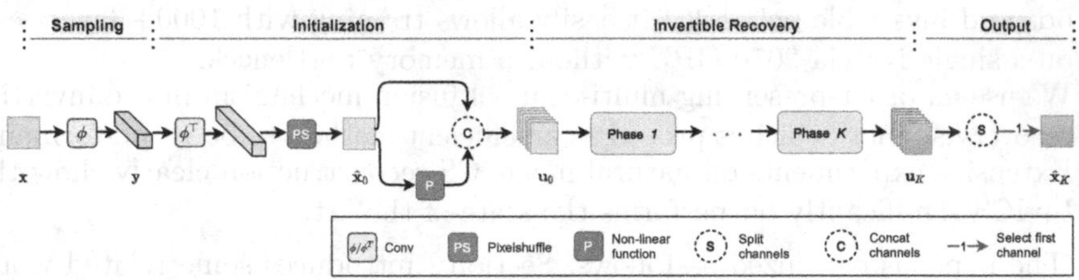

Fig. 1. The illustration of our proposed InvICS framework. It consists of three subnets, *i.e.*, sampling, initialization, and invertible recovery subnet, while the invertible recovery subnet is composed of K invertible phases. InvICS can extend to 100+ phases, which enables us to achieve better recovery accuracy.

3 Proposed InvICS

Gaining insight from OPINE-Net$^+$ [45], we make a bright new attempt to integrate with the invertible networks. And with the help of memory-saving technologies based on INNs, we can design deeper networks to fully tap the potential.

3.1 Sampling Subnet

As inspired by other popular designs [36,45], we adopt a sampling matrix with network. For an image block of shape $\sqrt{N} \times \sqrt{N}$, we utilize a convolutional layer with M filters of size $\sqrt{N} \times \sqrt{N}$ and stride $[\sqrt{N}, \sqrt{N}]$ to mimic the sampling process with ratio $\frac{M}{N}$, and we term it as $\phi(\cdot)$. Thus, it plays the same role as the traditional sampling matrix $\mathbf{\Phi} \in \mathbb{R}^{M \times N}$. Note that in our implementation, we use $N = 1089$. Benefiting from this design, InvICS can adapt to input with any size, not fixed to $\sqrt{N} \times \sqrt{N}$. For larger image, by means of this manner, we can exploit the inter-block information, and then eliminate the block artifacts to achieve better recovery accuracy. For simplicity, we limit the image to with single channel, therefore, the measurement $\mathbf{y}$ will be of size $M \times 1 \times 1$.

3.2 Initialization Subnet

Some existing deep networks [1,12,36] introduce extra $N \times M$ parameters for initialization, which causes exploding parameters and then increases the training time. We use the similar scheme proposed in OPINE-Net$^+$. It's composed of two consecutive models: a 1×1 convolutional layer, termed $\phi^\top(\cdot)$, and a pixel shuffle layer [34]. The convolutional layer shares the same parameter space as the sampling subnet and its weights can be obtained through a transpose operation. It enriches the measurements with more feature maps, while the pixelshuffle block rearranges these features to an image, leading to our initial estimation $\hat{\mathbf{x}}_0$.

The initial estimation $\hat{\mathbf{x}}_0$ is of a single channel. To give full play to the role of the INNs, we first use a non-linear block which is composed of a combination of two linear convolutional operators (without bias terms) separated by a rectified linear unit (ReLU), termed *P Block* as demonstrated in Fig. 1, to extend it to expected z channels. It will later be concatenated with the initial $\hat{\mathbf{x}}_0$ to form $\mathbf{u}_0$:

$$\mathbf{u}_0 = \text{Concat}(\hat{\mathbf{x}}_0, P(\hat{\mathbf{x}}_0)), \tag{1}$$

where $\mathbf{u}_0$ is of shape $z \times \sqrt{N} \times \sqrt{N}$, while $\hat{\mathbf{x}}_0$ is of $1 \times \sqrt{N} \times \sqrt{N}$.

3.3 Invertible Recovery Subnet

The invertible recovery subnet is composed of K invertible phases, and each phase consists of two consecutive modules. The kth phase transforms $\mathbf{u}_{k-1}$ to $\mathbf{u}_k$ in a deep multi-channel fusion manner. The final optimal estimation $\hat{\mathbf{x}}_K$ is obtained through extracting the first channel from $\mathbf{u}_K$.

Gradient-Descent Module. Gaining insights from the ISTA algorithm, we design a gradient-descent block, termed GD, which forms the main part of the gradient-descent module (GDM). The GD block finds the local optimal estimation $\mathbf{r}_k$ through the negative gradient direction:

$$\mathbf{r}_k = \hat{\mathbf{x}}_{k-1} - \rho_k \phi^\top(\phi(\hat{\mathbf{x}}_{k-1}) - \mathbf{y}), \tag{2}$$

where $\hat{\mathbf{x}}_{k-1} = \mathbf{u}_{k-1}[0:1]$, and ρ_k stands for the learnable step size for each phase. Later, $\mathbf{r}_k$ will be concatenated again to form the input to the second step:

$$\text{GDM}_k(\mathbf{u}_{k-1}) = \hat{\mathbf{u}}_k = \text{Concat}(\mathbf{r}_k, \mathbf{u}_{k-1}[1:z]). \tag{3}$$

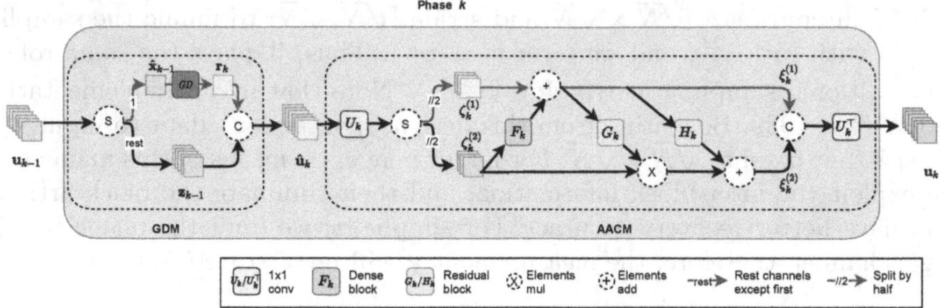

Fig. 2. The design of each phase, which contains two consecutive modules: a Gradient-Descent Module (GDM) and an Additive & Affine Coupling Module (AACM). GDM tries to get a new optimal estimation through the gradient-descent method, and then forward to AACM to make it more accurate in a multi-channel fusion manner.

The GD block is invertible if $\rho_k \neq 1$, and this can be ensured through employing an extra sigmoid operation with normalized range (1.0, 2.0) to the original learned ρ_k^*, *i.e.*, $\rho_k = \sigma(\rho_k^*) + 1.0$. Thus, the reverse formula of $\text{GDM}_k(\cdot)$ are:

$$\hat{\mathbf{x}}_{k-1} = (\mathbf{I} - \rho_k \mathbf{\Phi}^\top \mathbf{\Phi})^{-1}(\hat{\mathbf{u}}_k[0:1] - \rho_k \phi^\top(\mathbf{y})), \tag{4}$$

$$\text{GDM}_k^{-1}(\hat{\mathbf{u}}_k) = \mathbf{u}_{k-1} = \text{Concat}(\hat{\mathbf{x}}_{k-1}, \hat{\mathbf{u}}_k[1:z]), \tag{5}$$

where the $\mathbf{\Phi}$ is obtained from the weights of convolutional layer ϕ.

Additive and Affine Coupling Module. As inspired by [24,40], the proposed AACM combines an additive coupling layer [45] and an affine coupling layer [10] together. Moreover, we adopt the same permutation layer used in [32] to improve the representation capability, and meanwhile, fix the optimal recovery result in the first channel.

Mathematically, as demonstrated in Fig. 2, given the input $\hat{\mathbf{u}}_k$, the AACM firstly utilizes one orthogonal convolutional layer $U_k(\cdot)$ to rearrange the channel order, and then split it to equivalent two halves along channel dimension:

$$\zeta_k^{(1)} = U_k(\hat{\mathbf{u}}_k)[0:\frac{z}{2}], \zeta_k^{(2)} = U_k(\hat{\mathbf{u}}_k)[\frac{z}{2}:z]. \tag{6}$$

Afterward, the combination of coupling layers processes on each half of ζ_k in an alternative manner. We denote this transform as $Q_k(\cdot) : \zeta_k \rightarrow \xi_k$,

$$\xi_k^{(1)} = \zeta_k^{(1)} + F_k(\zeta_k^{(2)}), \xi_k^{(2)} = g(G_k(\xi_k^{(1)})) \odot \zeta_k^{(2)} + H_k(\xi_k^{(1)}), \tag{7}$$

where $F_k(\cdot)$ stands for a density block, while $G_k(\cdot)$ and $H_k(\cdot)$ represent two residual blocks, and $\odot$ is the element-wise product. Based on the insights of [5], we adopt sigmoid function as the scaling function $g(\cdot)$, and the output of it is normalized to range $(0.5, 1)$ to enhance stability.

By the way, the inverse of the above operation can be obtained easily as follows, and we denote it as $Q_k^{-1}(\cdot) : \xi_k \to \zeta_k$,

$$\zeta_k^{(2)} = (\xi_k^{(2)} - H_k(\xi_k^{(1)})) \oslash g(G_k(\xi_k^{(1)})), \zeta_k^{(1)} = \xi_k^{(1)} - F_k(\zeta_k^{(2)}), \tag{8}$$

where $\oslash$ is the element-wise divide operation.

Finally, $(\xi_k^{(1)}, \xi_k^{(2)})$ are concatenated along the channel dimension to ξ_k. The other orthogonal convolutional layer, termed as $U_k^\top(\cdot)$, is adopted to recover ξ_k:

$$\xi_k = \text{Concat}(\xi_k^{(1)}, \xi_k^{(2)}), \mathbf{u}_k = U_k^\top(\xi_k), \tag{9}$$

where weights of $U_k^\top(\cdot)$ can be obtained through the exact transpose of $U_k(\cdot)$.

To sum up, since $U_k(\cdot)$, $U_k^\top(\cdot)$ and $Q_k(\cdot)$ are all invertible, the entire AACM_k is also invertible, and the bidirectional operation can be formulated as follows. Furthermore, the entire k^{th} recovery phase is invertible as well.

$$\text{AACM}_k(\hat{\mathbf{u}}_k) = \mathbf{u}_k = U_k^\top(Q_k(U_k(\hat{\mathbf{u}}_k))), \tag{10}$$

$$\text{AACM}_k^{-1}(\mathbf{u}_k) = \hat{\mathbf{u}}_k = U_k^\top(Q_k^{-1}(U_k(\mathbf{u}_k))). \tag{11}$$

Memory-Saving Skills. Many methods [14,18,22] have been proposed regarding how to reduce GPU memory consumption. We adopt the framework proposed by van de Leemput *et al.*, termed MemCNN [22]. In our implementation, we wrap each phase through the MemCNN framework. By means of it, the input activation $\mathbf{u}_{0:K-1}$, plus the intermediate gradient graph during deep recovery, will not be stored. Because each phase contains at least 10 convolutional layers, taking 100 phases for example, almost 1000+ layers' activations will be freed, which will reduce the total GPU memory consumption to a large extent.

3.4 Network Parameters and Loss Function

The learnable parameter set in InvICS, denoted by $\mathbf{\Theta}$, consists of the equivalent sampling matrix $\mathbf{\Phi}$ (the weights of the sampling module actually), the parameters $\text{P}(\cdot)$ of the *P Block*, and the parameters in each recovery phase, *i.e.*, $\text{GDM}_k(\cdot)$, $\text{AACM}_k(\cdot)$. Thus, $\mathbf{\Theta} = \{\mathbf{\Phi}, \text{P}(\cdot), \text{GDM}_k(\cdot), \text{AACM}_k(\cdot)\}$. Given the training dataset $\{\mathbf{x}^i\}_{i=1}^{N_b}$, InvICS tries to train the sampling matrix and the recovery module synchronously, and then gets the final estimation $\hat{\mathbf{x}}_K^i$. It aims to reduce the discrepancy between $\mathbf{x}^i$ and $\hat{\mathbf{x}}_K^i$, and maintain the orthogonality of the sampling matrix. Therefore, the loss function designed looks like follows:

$$L_{total}(\mathbf{\Theta}) = L_{disc} + \gamma \times L_{orth}, \tag{12}$$

where $L_{disc} = \frac{1}{N_b N}\sum_{i=1}^{N_b} \| \mathbf{x}^i - \hat{\mathbf{x}}_K^i \|_2^2$, $L_{orth} = \frac{1}{M} \| \mathbf{\Phi}\mathbf{\Phi}^\top - \mathbf{I} \|_2^2$, and the regularization parameter γ is fixed to 0.01 by default.

4 Analysis and Experiments

The training data are obtained through randomly extracting specified size of image blocks based on the Train400 dataset, while for testing, we utilize three widely used benchmark datasets: Set11 [21], BSD68 [27] and Urban100 [16]. In general, We adopt a 2-step training strategy: a) at first train with 33×33 block with learning rate $1e^{-4}$ to 100 epochs; b) then fine-tune it with extra 10 epochs with larger image block size, *i.e.*, 99×99, and lower learning rate $1e^{-5}$. By this mean, we can train with faster speed, and meanwhile, take the advantage of inter-block training to eliminate block artifacts. We use the Adam [19] optimization method to train. All the experiments are performed on a workstation with Intel Core i3-9100 CPU and RTX2070 GPU unless otherwise stated. In our implementation, we set $z = 32$ by default, while K is set to 30. Note that the recovered results are evaluated with Peak Signal-to-Noise Ratio (PSNR) and Structural Similarity Index (SSIM).

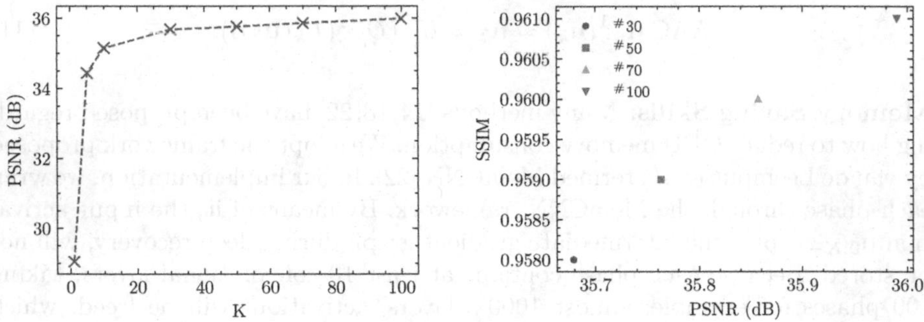

Fig. 3. Illustration of PSNR improvement as phase number K increases on Set11 dataset at CR = 25%. Utilizing more phases than existing methods, InvICS can obtain huge improvement on PSNR.

4.1 Study of Phase Number

As stated in OPINE-Net$^+$ that recovery PSNR is almost stable when phase number K is larger than 9, therefore OPINE-Net$^+$ sets $K = 9$ by default. Our architecture, by contrast, can get obvious improvement with larger K. As demonstrated in Fig. 3, through extending K from 9 to 30, we can obtain near 0.5 dB gain. What's more, as phase number K increases from 30 to 100, we can still obtain 0.3 dB improvements. However, considering the trade-off between computational complexity and recovery performance, we choose $K = 30$ by default.

4.2 Comparison with State-of-the-Art

We compare InvICS with four other representative network-based methods, *i.e.*, BCS [1], AdapReconNet [25], ISTA-Net$^+$ [44], and OPINE-Net$^+$ [45]. As shown in Table 1, InvICS achieves the best quality on all the test datasets and at all CRs. And we find that InvICS performs especially better at high CRs, *e.g.*, it obtains up to 1.5 dB gain over OPINE-Net$^+$ at CR = 50%. Visual comparison results are provided in Fig. 4, and we find that InvICS can obtain more structural details than other methods.

Table 1. Quantitative results (PSNR/SSIM) on common benchmark datasets. Our framework outperforms most methods, especially at high CRs, in which cases InvICS can obtain a significant >1.0 dB gain.

Dataset	CS ratio	ISTA-Net$^+$ [44]	BCS [1]	AdapReconNet [25]	OPINE-Net$^+$ [45]	InvICS
Set11	1%	17.42/0.403	19.15/0.441	19.63/0.485	20.15/0.534	**20.40/0.550**
	4%	21.32/0.604	23.19/0.663	23.87/0.728	25.69/0.792	**26.08/0.803**
	10%	26.64/0.809	26.04/0.797	27.39/0.852	29.81/0.888	**30.34/0.899**
	25%	32.59/0.925	29.98/0.893	31.75/0.926	34.86/0.951	**35.68/0.958**
	50%	38.11/0.971	34.61/0.944	35.87/0.963	40.17/0.980	**41.24/0.983**
Set68	1%	19.14/0.416	21.24/0.462	21.50/0.483	22.11/0.514	**22.18/0.525**
	4%	22.17/0.549	23.94/0.619	24.30/0.649	25.20/0.683	**25.48/0.697**
	10%	25.32/0.702	26.07/0.754	26.72/0.782	27.82/0.805	**28.21/0.818**
	25%	29.36/0.853	29.18/0.873	30.10/0.890	31.51/0.906	**32.21/0.918**
	50%	34.04/0.942	33.18/0.940	33.60/0.948	36.35/0.966	**37.45/0.973**
Urban100	1%	16.90/0.385	18.97/0.436	19.14/0.451	19.82/0.501	**19.88/0.515**
	4%	19.83/0.538	21.55/0.599	21.92/0.639	23.36/0.711	**23.93/0.736**
	10%	24.04/0.738	23.58/0.723	24.55/0.780	26.93/0.840	**27.86/0.863**
	25%	29.78/0.895	26.75/0.841	28.21/0.884	31.86/0.931	**33.32/0.947**
	50%	35.24/0.961	30.65/0.913	31.88/0.943	37.23/0.974	**38.76/0.981**

4.3 Ablation Studies

Order-Preserving Multi-channel Fusion. As shown in Fig. 5, we can observe that with larger z the recovery accuracy increases significantly during each iteration. By this means, we can obtain huge representational power for recovery tasks, which forms a main contribution of our framework.

Dense Block vs. Residual Block. In this section, we provide a comparison between different F block designs in each phase. The architecture with dense block achieves higher recovery accuracy than a residual block (see Fig. 6), which fully meets our expectations, since the dense block can ensure maximum information flow and feature map fusion.

Memory-Saving. After utilizing memory-saving skills, the GPU memory consumption drops dramatically. To get more intuitive impressions, we experiment on Nvidia 1080Ti GPU (see Fig. 6). We observe that our model can run with $K = 60$ almost if no memory-saving skill is involved, in which case it consumes up to 10.0 GB GPU memories. But after we enable the memory-saving, the total GPU memory consumption drops to 2.43 GB, which incredibly saves up to three quarters compared with disabling the memory-saving option.

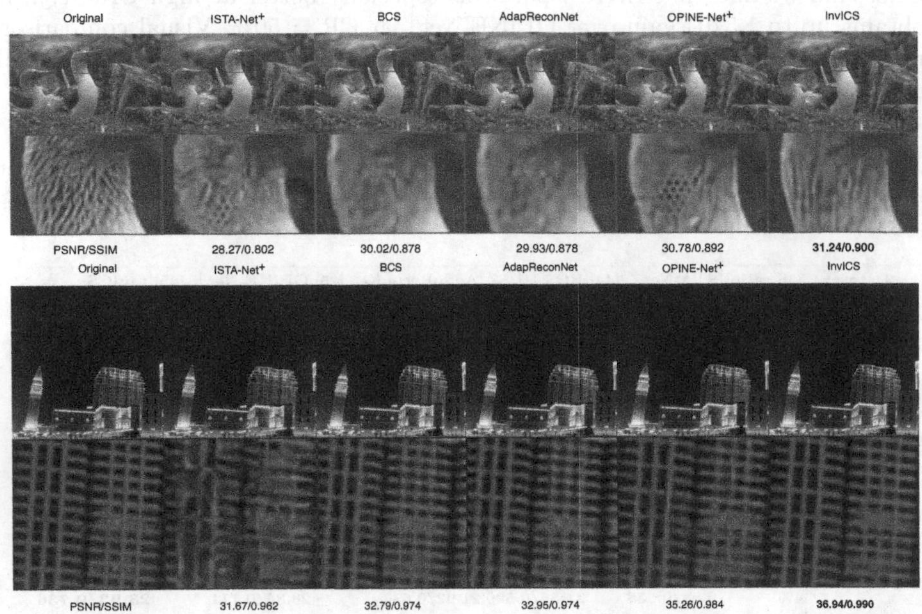

Fig. 4. The visual comparison with four other competing methods on two images, one from Set68 at CR = 10%, while the another from Urban100 dataset at CR = 25% respectively. We observe that InvICS can obtain more structural details than other methods.

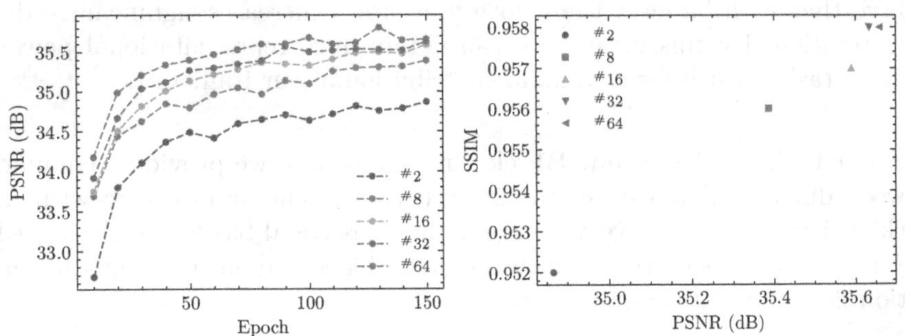

Fig. 5. Illustration of the effect of order-preserving multi-channel fusion method on Set11 dataset. We observe that the PSNR increases a lot as z increases. We choose $z = 32$ by default, through which we can achieve a perfect balance between performance and the model size. This special design is one big difference from other CS methods, and it provides another source of gain to InvICS.

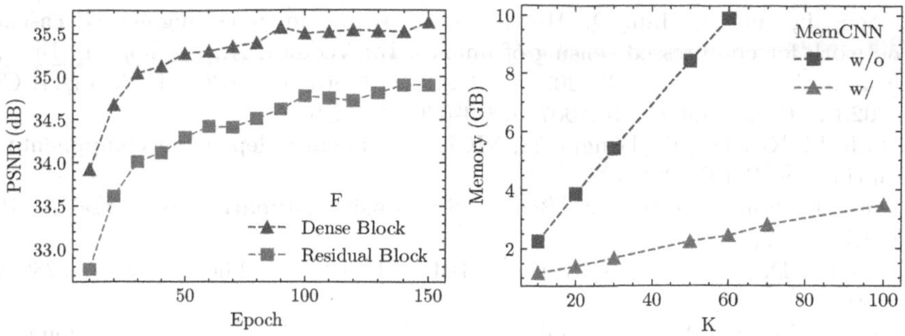

Fig. 6. (Left) indicates the improvement when using dense block; (Right) shows the efficient memory-saving result.

5 Conclusion and Future Work

In this paper, we propose a novel and memory-efficient invertible image compressive sensing framework, dubbed InvICS. By introducing invertible networks to the deep recovery subnet, the activations for most layers need not be stored in memory during backpropagation, which easily allows training InvICS with 100+ phases (1000+ layers) even on a single Nvidia 2070 GPU. What's more, we adopt an order-preserving multi-channel fusion approach, which can make full use of the multiple feature maps. Extensive experiments demonstrate that InvICS significantly improves both quantitative and qualitative performance. Since we only utilize the invertible layers in the deep recovery subnet, InvICS is partially invertible. Thus, Our future work will be focused on how to extend it to a fully invertible one, and we believe it will bring further improvements.

References

1. Adler, A., Boublil, D., Elad, M., Zibulevsky, M.: Block-based compressed sensing of images via deep learning. In: MMSP (2017)
2. Ardizzone, L., Lüth, C., Kruse, J., Rother, C., Köthe, U.: Guided image generation with conditional invertible neural networks. In: ICLR (2020)
3. Ardizzone, L., Mackowiak, R., Rother, C., Köthe, U.: Training normalizing flows with the information bottleneck for competitive generative classification. In: NeurIPS (2020)
4. Baraniuk, R.G., et al.: Single-pixel imaging via compressive sampling. IEEE Signal Process. Mag. **25**, 83–91 (2008)
5. Behrmann, J., Vicol, P., Wang, K.C., Grosse, R., Jacobsen, J.H.: Understanding and mitigating exploding inverses in invertible neural networks. In: AISTATS (2021)
6. Candès, E.J., Romberg, J., Tao, T.: Robust uncertainty principles: exact signal reconstruction from highly incomplete frequency information. IEEE Trans. Inf. Theory **52**(2), 489–509 (2006)
7. Candes, E.J., Tao, T.: Near-optimal signal recovery from random projections: universal encoding strategies. IEEE Trans. Inf. Theory **52**(12), 5406–5425 (2006)

8. Chen, J., Sun, Y., Liu, Q., Huang, R.: Learning memory augmented cascading network for compressed sensing of images. In: Vedaldi, A., Bischof, H., Brox, T., Frahm, J.-M. (eds.) ECCV 2020. LNCS, vol. 12367, pp. 513–529. Springer, Cham (2020). https://doi.org/10.1007/978-3-030-58542-6_31
9. Dinh, L., Krueger, D., Bengio, Y.: NICE: non-linear independent components estimation. In: ICLR (2015)
10. Dinh, L., Sohl-Dickstein, J., Bengio, S.: Density estimation using real NVP. In: ICLR (2017)
11. Donoho, D.L.: Compressed sensing. IEEE Trans. Inf. Theory **52**(4), 1289–1306 (2006)
12. Du, J., Xie, X., Wang, C., Shi, G., Xu, X., Wang, Y.: Fully convolutional measurement network for compressive sensing image reconstruction. Neurocomputing **328**, 105–112 (2019)
13. Gao, X., Zhang, J., Che, W., Fan, X., Zhao, D.: Block-based compressive sensing coding of natural images by local structural measurement matrix. In: DCC (2015)
14. Gomez, A.N., Ren, M., Urtasun, R., Grosse, R.B.: The reversible residual network: backpropagation without storing activations. In: NeurIPS (2017)
15. Hot, E., Sekulić, P.: Compressed sensing MRI using masked DCT and DFT measurements. In: MECO (2015)
16. Huang, J.B., Singh, A., Ahuja, N.: Single image super-resolution from transformed self-exemplars. In: CVPR (2015)
17. Iliadis, M., Spinoulas, L., Katsaggelos, A.K.: Deep fully-connected networks for video compressive sensing. Digit. Signal Process. **72**, 9–18 (2018)
18. Jacobsen, J.H., Smeulders, A., Oyallon, E.: I-REVNet: deep invertible networks. In: ICLR (2018)
19. Kingma, D.P., Ba, J.: Adam: a method for stochastic optimization. In: ICLR (2014)
20. Kingma, D.P., Dhariwal, P.: Glow: generative flow with invertible 1x1 convolutions. In: NeurIPS (2018)
21. Kulkarni, K., Lohit, S., Turaga, P., Kerviche, R., Ashok, A.: ReconNet: non-iterative reconstruction of images from compressively sensed measurements. In: CVPR (2016)
22. van de Leemput, S.C., Teuwen, J., Manniesing, R.: MemCNN: a framework for developing memory efficient deep invertible networks. In: ICLR (2018)
23. Li, C., Yin, W., Jiang, H., Zhang, Y.: An efficient augmented Lagrangian method with applications to total variation minimization. Comput. Opt. Appl. **56**(3), 507–530 (2013)
24. Liu, Y., et al.: Invertible denoising network: a light solution for real noise removal. In: CVPR (2021)
25. Lohit, S., Kulkarni, K., Kerviche, R., Turaga, P., Ashok, A.: Convolutional neural networks for noniterative reconstruction of compressively sensed images. IEEE Trans. Comput. Imaging **4**(3), 326–340 (2018)
26. Mackowiak, R., Ardizzone, L., Köthe, U., Rother, C.: Generative classifiers as a basis for trustworthy computer vision. In: CVPR (2021)
27. Martin, D., Fowlkes, C., Tal, D., Malik, J.: A database of human segmented natural images and its application to evaluating segmentation algorithms and measuring ecological statistics. In: ICCV (2001)
28. Metzler, C.A., Mousavi, A., Baraniuk, R.G.: Learned D-AMP: principled neural network based compressive image recovery. In: NeurIPS (2017)
29. Mousavi, A., Baraniuk, R.G.: Learning to invert: signal recovery via deep convolutional networks. In: ICASSP (2017)

30. Mousavi, A., Dasarathy, G., Baraniuk, R.G.: DeepCodec: adaptive sensing and recovery via deep convolutional neural networks. In: Annual Allerton Conference on Communication, Control, and Computing (Allerton) (2017)
31. Mousavi, A., Patel, A.B., Baraniuk, R.G.: A deep learning approach to structured signal recovery. In: Annual Allerton Conference on Communication, Control, and Computing (Allerton) (2015)
32. Putzky, P., Welling, M.: Invert to learn to invert. In: NeurIPS (2019)
33. Sharma, S.K., Lagunas, E., Chatzinotas, S., Ottersten, B.: Application of compressive sensing in cognitive radio communications: a survey. IEEE Commun. Surv. Tutor. **18**(3), 1838–1860 (2016)
34. Shi, W., et al.: Real-time single image and video super-resolution using an efficient sub-pixel convolutional neural network. In: CVPR (2016)
35. Shi, W., Jiang, F., Liu, S., Zhao, D.: Image compressed sensing using convolutional neural network. TIP **29**, 375–388 (2019)
36. Shi, W., Jiang, F., Liu, S., Zhao, D.: Scalable convolutional neural network for image compressed sensing. In: CVPR (2019)
37. Shi, W., Jiang, F., Zhang, S., Zhao, D.: Deep networks for compressed image sensing. In: ICME (2017)
38. Sun, Y., Chen, J., Liu, Q., Liu, B., Guo, G.: Dual-path attention network for compressed sensing image reconstruction. IEEE Trans. Image Process. **29**, 9482–9495 (2020)
39. Wu, Z., Zhang, Z., Song, J., Zhang, J.: Spatial-temporal synergic prior driven unfolding network for snapshot compressive imaging. In: ICME (2021)
40. Xiao, M., et al.: Invertible image rescaling. In: Vedaldi, A., Bischof, H., Brox, T., Frahm, J.-M. (eds.) ECCV 2020. LNCS, vol. 12346, pp. 126–144. Springer, Cham (2020). https://doi.org/10.1007/978-3-030-58452-8_8
41. Yang, Y., Sun, J., Li, H., Xu, Z.: Deep ADMM-Net for compressive sensing MRI. In: NeurIPS (2016)
42. You, D., Xie, J., Zhang, J.: ISTA-Net++: flexible deep unfolding network for compressive sensing. In: ICME (2021)
43. You, D., Zhang, J., Xie, J., Chen, B., Ma, S.: COAST: COntrollable arbitrary-sampling NeTwork for compressive sensing. IEEE Trans. Image Process. **30**, 6066–6080 (2021)
44. Zhang, J., Ghanem, B.: ISTA-Net: interpretable optimization-inspired deep network for image compressive sensing. In: CVPR (2018)
45. Zhang, J., Zhao, C., Gao, W.: Optimization-inspired compact deep compressive sensing. IEEE J. Sel. Top. Signal Process. **14**(4), 765–774 (2020)
46. Zhang, J., Zhao, C., Zhao, D., Gao, W.: Image compressive sensing recovery using adaptively learned sparsifying basis via L0 minimization. Signal Process. **103**, 114–126 (2014)
47. Zhang, J., Zhao, D., Gao, W.: Group-based sparse representation for image restoration. IEEE Trans. Image Process. **23**(8), 3336–3351 (2014)
48. Zhang, Z., Jung, T.P., Makeig, S., Rao, B.D.: Compressed sensing for energy-efficient wireless telemonitoring of noninvasive fetal ECG via block sparse Bayesian learning. IEEE Trans. Biomed. Eng. **60**(2), 300–309 (2012)
49. Zhang, Z., Liu, Y., Liu, J., Wen, F., Zhu, C.: AMP-Net: denoising-based deep unfolding for compressive image sensing. IEEE Trans. Image Process. **30**, 1487–1500 (2020)
50. Zhao, C., Ma, S., Gao, W.: Image compressive-sensing recovery using structured Laplacian sparsity in DCT domain and multi-hypothesis prediction. In: ICME (2014)

51. Zhao, C., Ma, S., Zhang, J., Xiong, R., Gao, W.: Video compressive sensing reconstruction via reweighted residual sparsity. IEEE Trans. Circ. Syst. Video Technol. **27**(6), 1182–1195 (2016)
52. Zhao, C., Zhang, J., Ma, S., Gao, W.: Compressive-sensed image coding via stripe-based DPCM. In: DCC (2016)
53. Zhao, C., Zhang, J., Ma, S., Gao, W.: Nonconvex LP nuclear norm based ADMM framework for compressed sensing. In: DCC (2016)
54. Zhao, C., Zhang, J., Wang, R., Gao, W.: CREAM: CNN-regularized ADMM framework for compressive-sensed image reconstruction. IEEE Access **6**, 76838–76853 (2018)

Gradient-Free Neural Network Training Based on Deep Dictionary Learning with the Log Regularizer

Ying Xie[1], Zhenni Li[1(✉)], and Haoli Zhao[2]

[1] School of Automation, Guangdong University of Technology, Guangzhou 510006, China
lizhenni@gdut.edu.cn

[2] School of Computer Science and Engineering, Sun Yat-sen University, Guangzhou 510006, China

Abstract. Gradient-free neural network training is attracting increasing attentions, which efficiently to avoid the gradient vanishing issue in traditional neural network training with gradient-based methods. The state-of-the-art gradient-free methods introduce a quadratic penalty or use an equivalent approximation of the activation function to achieve the training process without gradients, but they are hardly to mine effective signal features since the activation function is a limited nonlinear transformation. In this paper, we first propose to construct the neural network training as a deep dictionary learning model for achieving the gradient-free training of the network. To further enhance the ability of feature extraction in network training based on gradient-free method, we introduce the logarithm function as a sparsity regularizer which introduces accurate sparse activations on the hidden layer except for the last layer. Then, we employ a proximal block coordinate descent method to forward update the variables of each layer and apply the *log*-thresholding operator to achieve the optimization of the non-convex and non-smooth subproblems. Finally, numerical experiments conducted on several publicly available datasets prove the sparse representation of inputs is effective for gradient-free neural network training.

Keywords: Deep dictionary learning · *log* regularizer · Block coordinate descent · Sparse proximal operator · Gradient-free network

1 Introduction

Deep neural networks (DNN) have achieved great success in many applications, such as image recognition [1] and speech recognition [2]. Backpropagation based on Stochastic Gradient Descent (SGD) [3] is widely used for training neural networks due to its efficiency. However, SGD suffers from a variety of problems such as the gradient vanishing problem, which makes the training difficult or unstable. To solve this problem, some methods introduce rectified linear units (ReLU) [4],

© Springer Nature Switzerland AG 2021
H. Ma et al. (Eds.): PRCV 2021, LNCS 13022, pp. 561–574, 2021.
https://doi.org/10.1007/978-3-030-88013-2_46

batch normalization (BN) [5], or residual convolutional neural network (ResNet) [6]. However, they still have drawbacks such as difficulty in tuning and parallelization [7]. Other works [8–12] have been proposed gradient-free methods for the neural network training, which do not suffer from gradient vanishing issue due to the avoidance of using classical backpropagation. The work [10] proposed the method of auxiliary coordinates (MAC) which introduced a quadratic penalty to the objective function to relax the equality constraints and trained the network by alternating optimization over the parameters and the auxiliary coordinates. The works [8,9] used the augmented Lagrangian method to relax network constraints by introducing penalty in the objective function and optimized it by the alternating direction method of multipliers (ADMM). The works [11,12] also adopted the introduction of a quadratic penalty in the objective function to relax the network constraints, but proposed the proximal block coordinate descent (BCD) method to solve the minimization optimization to train networks. The works [7,13] employed the equivalent representation of the activation function to solve the nonlinear constraint problems in the optimization problems and the network was trained by BCD method. However, the activation functions used in the training of gradient-free networks in these works are very limited non-linear transformations, which hardly mine effective signal features.

Deep dictionary learning (DDL) aims to learn latent representations of data by learning multi-level dictionaries, which can be considered as the gradient-free neural network training model. The work [14] showed that the output of the neural network using dictionary learning is more discriminative and class specific than the traditional fully connected layer. The work [15] took the advantage of the convolutional neural network for convolution feature extraction, by learning dictionary for sparse representation to achieve scene recognition. DDL normally introduces sparsity constraint to restrict the learning procedure from the overcomplete underdetermined system. The work [16] showed that compared to shallow dictionary learning, DDL learned sparse representation by applying l_1-norm on the features and using the linear classifier for classification can achieve better classification accuracy.

In this paper, we propose a new gradient-free network training model based on DDL with the *log* sparsity regularizer, which trains the network by learning the multi-layer dictionaries and then obtains sparse activations in network by learning sparse representation of inputs. In details, firstly, we formulate the neural network training model as a DDL model by regarding the weight matrix in the neural network as a dictionary, the activations of the hidden layer correspond to the coefficients of DDL. Secondly, in order to obtain a accurate sparse representation of inputs, we employ the *log* sparsity regularizer on the hidden layer neurons of network except for the last hidden layer, which could enforce strong sparsity and obtain accurate estimation. The reason why not impose the sparsity constraint on the last hidden layer is as follows, we regard the function of the last two layers as a classifier, where a two-layer structure can perform better feature classification than a single-layer structure. Thirdly, we propose to use the proximal BCD method to optimize a block variable by fixing other block variables. Due to the nonconvexity of the *log* regularizer, we employ the *log*-thresholding operator to solve the corresponding optimization problem with respect to the activations. Finally, numerical experiments verify that the proposed gradient-free training model based on DDL is effective and superior to others training methods.

The main contributions are summarized as follows:

1) To overcome the gradient vanishing issue, a DDL-based gradient-free neural network training model is proposed, where the dictionary and the sparse coefficient correspond to the weight matrix and activation respectively.
2) To obtain accurate and sparse representation of inputs on proposed gradient-free network training model, we propose to employ the nonconvex logarithm-based function as sparsity regularizer which can enforce strong sparsity and obtain accurate representation. The model takes advantage of sparse representation for feature extraction to improve the performance of the gradient-free training model.
3) We apply the proximal block coordinate descent method to train the gradient-free network and update the variables of each layer in a forward update manner, and employ the proximal operator to solve the non-convex *log* regularized subproblems, which developed our proposed LOG-PBCD algorithm.

The rest of this paper is organized as follows. Section 2 describes some current gradient-free neural network training methods and the connection between DDL and DNN. Section 3 shows how to apply the *log* regularizer to achieve the purpose of sparse activations, and solve the objective function containing *log* regularizer through proximal BCD optimization with *log*-thresholding operator. Section 4, we verify the effectiveness of proposed model through experiments. We conclude this paper in Sect. 5.

2 Related Work

2.1 Notation

We briefly summarize notations in this paper. A boldface uppercase letter such as $\boldsymbol{A}_l$ denotes a matrix. A lowercase element such as a_{cj} denotes the entry in the c-th row and the j-th column of $\boldsymbol{A}$. A lowercase Greek letter φ denotes an activation function that acts column-wise on a matrix, $\boldsymbol{I}$ denotes the identity operator. Let d_l be the number of neurons in l_{th} layer. Define a neural network with l layers, where $l = 0, 1, 2, ..., L$. The first layer ($l = 0$) is the input layer, the input signals are composed of M training samples. The last layer ($l = L$) is the output layer with K categories, namely K neurons. Let $\boldsymbol{A}_0 \in \mathbb{R}^{d_0 \times M}$ be the input training data, $\boldsymbol{A}_l \in \mathbb{R}^{d_l \times M}, l = 1, 2, ..., L-1$ be the activations of hidden layer, $\boldsymbol{W}_l \in \mathbb{R}^{d_l \times d_{l-1}}, l = 1, 2, ..., L$ be the weight matrix between the l_{th} and $(l-1)_{th}$ layers, $\boldsymbol{Y} \in \mathbb{R}^{d_L \times K}$ be the one-hot matrix of labels, $\boldsymbol{B}_l \in \mathbb{R}^{d_l \times M}, l = 1, 2, ..., L$ be the bias matrix of hidden layer and every column of it is same. $k = 1, 2, ..., N$ means iteration.

2.2 Neural Network Training and Deep Dictionary Learning

Neural network produces predictive output $\hat{\boldsymbol{Y}}$ through feed-forward recursion $\hat{\boldsymbol{Y}} = \boldsymbol{W}_L\boldsymbol{A}_{L-1} + \boldsymbol{B}_L$ given below,

$$\boldsymbol{A}_l = \varphi(\boldsymbol{W}_l\boldsymbol{A}_{l-1} + \boldsymbol{B}_l), l = 1, 2, 3..., L-1 \quad (1)$$

where φ is the activation function such as sigmoid function or ReLU function that acts column-wise on a matrix. Without loss of generality, we can remove $\boldsymbol{B}_l$ by adding an extra column to $\boldsymbol{W}_l$ and a row of ones to $\boldsymbol{A}_{l-1}$. Then Eq. (1) simplifies to

$$\boldsymbol{A}_l = \varphi(\boldsymbol{W}_l\boldsymbol{A}_{l-1}), l = 1, 2, 3..., L-1 \quad (2)$$

Define an auxiliary variable $\boldsymbol{Z}_l = \boldsymbol{W}_l\boldsymbol{A}_{l-1}$. Then, $\boldsymbol{A}_l = \varphi(\boldsymbol{Z}_l), l = 1, 2, 3..., L-1$, gradient-free network training problem can be formulated as the minimization problem,

$$\boldsymbol{A}_l, \boldsymbol{W}_l, \boldsymbol{Z}_l \leftarrow \underset{\boldsymbol{A}_l, \boldsymbol{W}_l, \boldsymbol{Z}_l}{argmin}\ \mathcal{L}(\boldsymbol{Z}_L, \boldsymbol{Y}) \quad (3)$$

subject to $\boldsymbol{Z}_l = \boldsymbol{W}_l\boldsymbol{A}_{l-1}$, for $l = 1, 2, ..., L$. $\boldsymbol{A}_l = \varphi(\boldsymbol{Z}_l)$, for $l = 1, 2, ..., L-1$. Following the method of auxiliary coordinates (MAC) method [10], instead of directly solving the Eq. (3), the constrained problem may be solved with quadratic-penalty methods using alternating optimization over the parameters and the auxiliary coordinates. Inspired by ADMM algorithm, the work [8] also try to optimize above Eq. (3), they impose Lagrangian constraints on the output layer. Unlike MAC method, the output layer adopts the linear activation function rather than non-linear activation function. The proximal BCD proposed by [12] is another method to solve Eq. (3) in gradient-free network training problem, which they call it three-splitting formulation. Compared with the two-splitting formulation, the advantage of adopting the three-splitting formulation is that almost all updates use simple proximal updates or just least-squares problems, but the disadvantage is that more storage memory is required. Recent works accelerate gradient-free training based on the BCD method [17] and use the equivalent representation of the activation function to solve the nonlinear constraint problem in the optimization problem [7,13], they improve and accelerate the training process but hardly employ sparse to learn the deep representation of the inputs.

DDL can be seen as a special form of the gradient-free neural network since their structure and optimization methods are similar, that is, regarding the weight matrix as a dictionary and the activation of a certain layer of neurons as sparse coefficients. In addition, both use the same activation function. For example, the activation function employed in multi-layer dictionary learning assures that the L levels of dictionaries are not collapsible into one, so that deep dictionary learning can learn deeper features. But unlike a neural network which is directed from the input to the representation, the dictionary learning kind of network points in the other direction, from representation to the input [16].

In this paper, DDL for sparse representation and its similarity to DNN inspires us to learn the sparse representation of the inputs, which will lead to the sparse activations in DNN. We propose a gradient-free network training model based on DDL and employ the proximal block coordinate descent method to train all variables. The proximal operator and the *log*-thresholding operator are employed to update the activations. An overview of our algorithm is shown in Fig. 1.

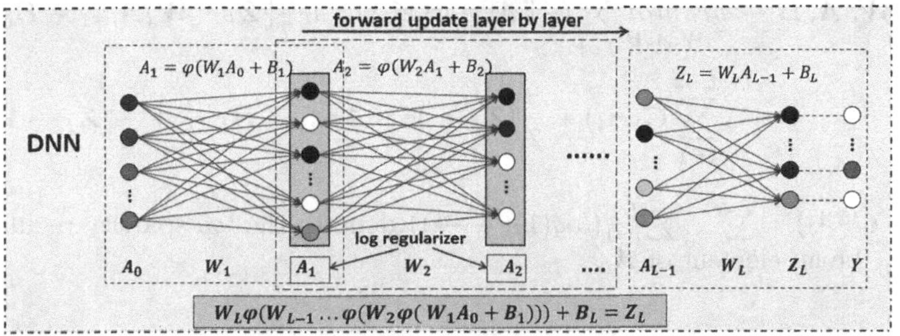

Fig. 1. An overview of the structure of DNN. The $\boldsymbol{Y}$ denotes labels. We apply *log* regularizer to the activation of hidden layer neurons of DNN from $\boldsymbol{A}_1$ to $\boldsymbol{A}_{L-2}$ except the last hidden layer $\boldsymbol{A}_{L-1}$. The update of parameters adopts forward updating: $\boldsymbol{W}_l \rightarrow \boldsymbol{B}_l \rightarrow \boldsymbol{Z}_l \rightarrow \boldsymbol{A}_l$, $l = 1, 2, ..., L$.

3 Gradient-Free Neural Network Training Based on Deep Dictionary Learning with the *Log* Regularizer

In this section, we first formulate our gradient-free network training problem where the *log* sparsity regularizer is employed for accurate and sparse representation of inputs and simultaneously get sparse activations. Second, we employ the proximal block coordinate descent method and the *log*-thresholding operator to solve the non-convex problems. For the problem of updating variables with *log* sparse constraints, we employ the proximal gradient descent method and *log*-thresholding operator to update, and through proximal step update variables without sparse constraints. In the third part, we summarize the proposed algorithm in Algorithm 1.

3.1 Problem Formulation

In order to achieve gradient-free neural network training based on DDL. we regard the weight matrix of the gradient-free neural network as a dictionary and the activations of hidden layer as coefficients, retain the bias of the neural network and select ReLU function as the activation function. Unlike [12], we maintain the usual structure of the neural network which the final output is the activations without the nonlinear transformation. Unlike DDL, we introduce the *log* sparse constraint on the activations $\boldsymbol{A}_l$, $l = 1, 2, ..., L-2$ of the remaining layers, except for the activations $\boldsymbol{A}_{L-1}$ of the last hidden layer, where we expect to keep the structure of the last two layers of the neural network and regard last two layers as a classifier. Our problem of gradient-free network training based DDL can be formulated as follows,

$$\begin{aligned}\boldsymbol{Z}, \boldsymbol{W}, \boldsymbol{A}, \boldsymbol{B} \leftarrow \underset{\boldsymbol{Z},\boldsymbol{W},\boldsymbol{A},\boldsymbol{B}}{argmin} \sum_{l=1}^{L-1}(\frac{\gamma}{2}\|\boldsymbol{A}_l - \varphi(\boldsymbol{Z}_l)\|_F^2 + \frac{\rho}{2}\|\boldsymbol{Z}_l - \boldsymbol{W}_l\boldsymbol{A}_{l-1} - \boldsymbol{B}_l\|_F^2) \\ + \lambda\sum_{l=1}^{L-2}\boldsymbol{G}(\boldsymbol{A}_l) + \frac{\beta}{2}\|\boldsymbol{Z}_L - \boldsymbol{W}_L\boldsymbol{A}_{L-1} - \boldsymbol{B}_L\|_F^2 + \frac{\alpha}{2}\|\boldsymbol{Z}_L - \boldsymbol{Y}\|_F^2\end{aligned} \tag{4}$$

where $\boldsymbol{G}(\boldsymbol{A}_l) = \sum_{c=1}^{C}\sum_{j=1}^{J}(log(1 + \frac{|a_{cj}|}{\epsilon}))$ denotes the *log* sparsity regularizer. Let a_{cj} be an element of $\boldsymbol{A}_l$.

3.2 Proposed Algorithm

In order to solve the above non-convex and non-smooth optimization problem Eq. (4), we employ the proximal block coordinate descent method to update $\boldsymbol{A}_l$ or $\boldsymbol{W}_l$ by fixing all other blocks of variables and employ the *log*-thresholding operator to solve the subproblems regarding to *log* regularizer. We retain the network bias and specific steps are as follows,

Updating $\boldsymbol{W}_l$,$\boldsymbol{B}_l$,$l = 1, 2, ..., L$. The proximal BCD algorithm fixes other block variables and perform a proximal step to update $\boldsymbol{W}_l$,$\boldsymbol{B}_l$ via as follows,

$$\boldsymbol{W}_l^{k+1} \leftarrow \underset{\boldsymbol{W}_l^k}{argmin}\, \frac{\rho}{2}\|\boldsymbol{Z}_l^k - \boldsymbol{W}_l^k\boldsymbol{A}_{l-1}^{k+1} - \boldsymbol{B}_l^k\|_F^2 + \frac{\delta}{2}\|\boldsymbol{W}_l^k - \boldsymbol{W}_l^{k-1}\|_F^2 \tag{5}$$

$$\boldsymbol{B}_l^{k+1} \leftarrow \underset{\boldsymbol{B}_l^k}{argmin}\, \frac{\rho}{2}\|\boldsymbol{Z}_l^k - \boldsymbol{W}_l^k\boldsymbol{A}_{l-1}^{k+1} - \boldsymbol{B}_l^k\|_F^2 + \frac{\delta}{2}\|\boldsymbol{B}_l^k - \boldsymbol{B}_l^{k-1}\|_F^2 \tag{6}$$

The Eq. (5) and Eq. (6) have closed-form solutions. Then, the update rule of Eq. (5) and Eq. (6) can be rewritten as,

$$\boldsymbol{W}_l^{k+1} = (\delta\boldsymbol{W}_l^k + \rho(\boldsymbol{Z}_l^k - \boldsymbol{B}_l^k)\boldsymbol{A}_{l-1}^k)(\delta\boldsymbol{I} + \rho(\boldsymbol{A}_{l-1}^k(\boldsymbol{A}_{l-1}^{k+1})^T))^{-1} \tag{7}$$

$$\boldsymbol{B}_l^{k+1} = (\delta\boldsymbol{B}_l^k + \rho(\boldsymbol{Z}_l^k - \boldsymbol{W}_l^k\boldsymbol{A}_{l-1}^{k+1}))/(\rho + \delta) \tag{8}$$

Updating $\boldsymbol{Z}_l$,$l = 1, 2, ..., L-1$. The variables $\boldsymbol{Z}_l$ are updated as follows,

$$\boldsymbol{Z}_l^{k+1} \leftarrow \underset{\boldsymbol{Z}_l^k}{argmin}\, \frac{\gamma}{2}\|\boldsymbol{A}_l^k - \varphi(\boldsymbol{Z}_l^k)\|_F^2 + \frac{\rho}{2}\|\boldsymbol{Z}_l^k - \boldsymbol{W}_l^{k+1}\boldsymbol{A}_{l-1}^{k+1} - \boldsymbol{B}_l^{k+1}\|_F^2 + \frac{\delta}{2}\|\boldsymbol{Z}_l^k - \boldsymbol{Z}_l^{k-1}\|_F^2 \tag{9}$$

Since Eq. (9) contains the ReLU activation function, we obtain the solutions by the Lemma 13 in the appendix of [12]. Then Eq. (9) can be written as,

$$\boldsymbol{Z}_l^{k+1} \leftarrow \underset{\boldsymbol{Z}_l^k}{argmin} \frac{1}{2}\|\boldsymbol{A}_l^k - \varphi(\boldsymbol{Z}_l^k)\|_F^2 + \frac{\rho+\delta}{2\gamma}\|\boldsymbol{Z}_l^k - \frac{\delta \boldsymbol{Z}_l^{k-1} + \rho(\boldsymbol{W}_l^{k+1}\boldsymbol{A}_{l-1}^{k+1} + \boldsymbol{B}_l^{k+1})}{\rho+\delta}\|_F^2 \tag{10}$$

Where $\eta = \frac{\rho+\delta}{\gamma}$, $\boldsymbol{S}_l^k = \frac{\delta \boldsymbol{Z}_l^{k-1} + \rho(\boldsymbol{W}_l^{k+1}\boldsymbol{A}_{l-1}^{k+1} + \boldsymbol{B}_l^{k+1})}{\rho+\delta}$. Then Eq. (10) is equivalent to the following form:

$$\boldsymbol{Z}_l^{k+1} \leftarrow \underset{\boldsymbol{Z}_l^k}{argmin} \frac{1}{2}\|\boldsymbol{A}_l^k - \varphi(\boldsymbol{Z}_l^k)\|_F^2 + \frac{\eta}{2}\|\boldsymbol{Z}_l^k - \boldsymbol{S}_l^k\|_F^2 \tag{11}$$

Then Eq. (11) reduces to the following one-dimensional minimization problem. The $z_{cj}^k, a_{cj}^k, s_{cj}^k$ is an element of $\boldsymbol{Z}_l^k, \boldsymbol{A}_l^k, \boldsymbol{S}_l^k$

$$z_{cj}^{k+1} \leftarrow \underset{z_{cj}^k}{argmin} \frac{1}{2}(a_{cj}^k - \varphi(z_{cj}^k))^2 + \frac{\eta}{2}(z_{cj}^k - s_{cj}^k)^2 \tag{12}$$

The iteration of z_{cj} can be obtained as,

$$z_{cj}^{k+1} = prox_{\frac{1}{2\eta}(a_{cj}^k - \varphi(z_{cj}^k))^2}(s_{cj}^k) = \begin{cases} \frac{a_{cj}^k + \eta s_{cj}^k}{1+\eta}, & \text{if } a_{cj}^k + \eta s_{cj}^k \geq 0, s_{cj}^k \geq 0 \\ \frac{a_{cj}^k + \eta s_{cj}^k}{1+\eta}, & \text{if } -(\sqrt{\eta(\eta+1)} - \eta)a_{cj}^k \leq \eta s_{cj}^k < 0 \\ s_{cj}^k, & \text{if } -a_{cj}^k \leq \eta s_{cj}^k \leq -(\sqrt{\eta(\eta+1)} - \eta)a_{cj}^k \\ \min(s_{cj}^k, 0), & \text{if } a_{cj}^k + \eta s_{cj}^k < 0 \end{cases} \tag{13}$$

Updating $\boldsymbol{A}_l$,$\boldsymbol{l = 1, 2, ..., L-2}$. Due to the introduction of the *log* regularizer, the update of $\boldsymbol{A}_l$ is as follows,

$$\boldsymbol{A}_l^{k+1} \leftarrow \underset{\boldsymbol{A}_l^k}{argmin} \frac{\gamma}{2}\|\boldsymbol{A}_l^k - \varphi(\boldsymbol{Z}_l^{k+1})\|_F^2 + \frac{\rho}{2}\|\boldsymbol{Z}_l^{k+1} - \boldsymbol{W}_l^{k+1}\boldsymbol{A}_{l-1}^{k+1} - \boldsymbol{B}_l^{k+1}\|_F^2 + \frac{\delta}{2}\|\boldsymbol{A}_l^k - \boldsymbol{A}_l^{k-1}\|_F^2 + \lambda G(\boldsymbol{A}_l^k) \tag{14}$$

where $\boldsymbol{G}(\boldsymbol{A}_l^k)$ is the *log* sparsity regularizer. The iterations Eq. (14) can be rewritten by using the proximal operator [18]. Then, the update rule of Eq. (14) can be rewritten as,

$$\boldsymbol{A}_l^{k+1} \leftarrow \underset{\boldsymbol{A}_l^k}{argmin} \frac{\delta}{2}\|\boldsymbol{A}_l^k - \boldsymbol{X}_l^k\|_F^2 + \lambda \boldsymbol{G}(\boldsymbol{A}_l^k) \tag{15}$$

where $\boldsymbol{X}_l^k = \boldsymbol{A}_l^k - \frac{1}{\delta}\Big((\rho(\boldsymbol{W}_{l+1}^{k+1})^T\boldsymbol{W}_{l+1}^{k+1} + \gamma I)\boldsymbol{A}_l^k - \rho(\boldsymbol{W}_{l+1}^{k+1})^T(\boldsymbol{Z}_{l+1}^{k+1} - \boldsymbol{B}_{l+1}^{k+1}) - \gamma\varphi(\boldsymbol{Z}_l^{k+1})\Big)$.

Then, employing the *log*-thresholding operator [18] to update $\boldsymbol{A}_l$, where $\boldsymbol{G}(\boldsymbol{A}_l^k) = \sum_{c=1}^{C}\sum_{j=1}^{J}(log(1 + \frac{|\boldsymbol{a}_{cj}|}{\epsilon}))$. The variable $\boldsymbol{A}_l$ is updated via as follows,

$$\boldsymbol{A}_l^{k+1} \leftarrow \underset{\boldsymbol{A}_l^k}{argmin} \frac{\delta}{2}\|\boldsymbol{A}_l^k - \boldsymbol{X}_l^k\|_F^2 + \lambda\sum_{k=1}^{K}\sum_{j=1}^{J}(log(1 + \frac{|\boldsymbol{a}_{cj}|}{\epsilon})) \tag{16}$$

The update of $\boldsymbol{A}_l$ can be obtained by the *log*-thresholding operator to Eq. (17),

$$a_{cj}^{c+1} = [prox_{log,\lambda/\delta}(\boldsymbol{X}_l^k)]_{cj} = \begin{cases} \frac{1}{2}((x_{cj}^k - \epsilon) + \sqrt{(x_{cj}^k + \epsilon)^2 - \frac{4\lambda}{\delta}}) & \text{, if } x_{cj}^k > x_0 \\ \frac{1}{2}((x_{cj}^k + \epsilon) - \sqrt{(x_{cj}^k - \epsilon)^2 - \frac{4\lambda}{\delta}}) & \text{, if } x_{cj}^k < -x_0 \\ 0 & \text{, otherwise} \end{cases} \tag{17}$$

where $x_0 = \sqrt{\frac{4\lambda}{\delta}} - \epsilon$, x_{cj} is an element of $\boldsymbol{X}_l$, The symbol $prox_{log,\lambda/\delta}$ is the proximal operator for the *log* regularizer.

Updating $\boldsymbol{A}_{L-1}$. Without introducing a sparsity constraint on the last hidden layer, the iteration of $\boldsymbol{A}_{L-1}$ is given as,

$$\boldsymbol{A}_{L-1}^{k+1} \leftarrow \underset{\boldsymbol{A}_{L-1}^k}{argmin} \frac{\gamma}{2}\|\boldsymbol{A}_{L-1}^k - \varphi(\boldsymbol{Z}_{L-1}^{k+1})\|_F^2 + \frac{\rho}{2}\|\boldsymbol{Z}_L^k - \boldsymbol{W}_L^k\boldsymbol{A}_{L-1}^{k+1} - \boldsymbol{B}_L^k\|_F^2 + \frac{\delta}{2}\|\boldsymbol{A}_{L-1}^k - \boldsymbol{A}_{L-1}^{k-1}\|_F^2 \tag{18}$$

The Eq. (18) has closed-form solution. Then, the update rule of Eq. (18) can be rewritten as,

$$\boldsymbol{A}_{L-1}^{k+1} = \left(\rho(\boldsymbol{W}_L^k)^T)\boldsymbol{W}_L^k + (\rho+\delta)\boldsymbol{I}\right)^{-1}\left(\delta\boldsymbol{A}_{L-1}^k + \rho((\boldsymbol{W}_L^k)^T(\boldsymbol{Z}_L^k - \boldsymbol{B}_L^k)) + \gamma\varphi(\boldsymbol{Z}_{L-1}^k)\right) \tag{19}$$

Updating $\boldsymbol{Z}_L$. Due to without activation function in output layer, the optimization problem of variable $\boldsymbol{Z}_L$ in the output layer is different from other layers. We update $\boldsymbol{Z}_L$ by using a simple proximal update via as follows,

$$\boldsymbol{Z}_L^{k+1} \leftarrow \underset{\boldsymbol{Z}_L^k}{argmin} \frac{\beta}{2}\|\boldsymbol{Z}_L^k - \boldsymbol{W}_L^{k+1}\boldsymbol{A}_{L-1}^{k+1} - \boldsymbol{B}_L^{k+1}\|_F^2 + \frac{\alpha}{2}\|\boldsymbol{Z}_L^k - \boldsymbol{Y}\|_F^2 + \frac{\delta}{2}\|\boldsymbol{Z}_L^k - \boldsymbol{Z}_L^{k-1}\|_F^2 \tag{20}$$

Eq. (20) is a convex problem and has a closed-form solution,

$$\boldsymbol{Z}_L^{k+1} = (\beta\boldsymbol{W}_L^{k+1}\boldsymbol{A}_{L-1}^{k+1} + \boldsymbol{B}_L^{k+1} + \alpha\boldsymbol{Y} + \delta\boldsymbol{Z}_L^k)/(\alpha+\beta+\delta) \tag{21}$$

3.3 The Overall Algorithm

The algorithm updates each layer sequentially, starting from the first layer, and its parameters are updated according to $\boldsymbol{W}_l \rightarrow \boldsymbol{B}_l \rightarrow \boldsymbol{Z}_l \rightarrow \boldsymbol{A}_l$. Only update $\boldsymbol{W}_L \rightarrow \boldsymbol{B}_L \rightarrow \boldsymbol{Z}_L$ in the output layer. The structure of the proposed algorithm is outlined in Algorithm 1.

4 Numerical Experiments

In this section, we conducted numerical experiments to evaluate the performance of the proposed algorithm. The first experiment was to find the proper hyperparameters of the proposed algorithm on the MNIST dataset, the hyperparameters

Algorithm 1. Proximal BCD algorithm with *log* sparsity regularizer (LOG-PBCD)

Input: $\boldsymbol{A}_0$ denotes training samples, the $\lambda,\gamma,\epsilon,\rho,\alpha,\beta$ are hyperparameters, $\boldsymbol{Y}$ denotes labels
Output: $\boldsymbol{W}_l, \boldsymbol{Z}_l, \boldsymbol{B}_l, l = 1, 2, \ldots, L. \boldsymbol{A}_l, l = 1, 2, \ldots, L-1$

Solving the probelm:
$\boldsymbol{Z}, \boldsymbol{W}, \boldsymbol{A}, \boldsymbol{B} \leftarrow \min_{\boldsymbol{Z},\boldsymbol{W},\boldsymbol{A},\boldsymbol{B}} \sum_{l=1}^{L-1}(\frac{\gamma}{2}\|\boldsymbol{A}_l - \varphi(\boldsymbol{Z}_l)\|_F^2 + \frac{\rho}{2}\|\boldsymbol{Z}_l - \boldsymbol{W}_l\boldsymbol{A}_{l-1} - \boldsymbol{B}_l\|_F^2 + \lambda G(\boldsymbol{A}_l) + \frac{\beta}{2}\|\boldsymbol{Z}_L - \boldsymbol{W}_L\boldsymbol{A}_{L-1} - \boldsymbol{B}_L\|_F^2 + \frac{\alpha}{2}\|\boldsymbol{Z}_L - \boldsymbol{Y}\|_F^2$, where $G(\boldsymbol{A}_l) = \sum_{c=1}^{C}\sum_{j=1}^{J}(log(1+\frac{|a_{cj}|}{\epsilon}))$, $a_{cj} \in \boldsymbol{A}_l$
Update all parameters until convergence.
for $k = 1, 2, \ldots, N$ **do**
  update the network parameters
  for $l = 1, 2, \ldots, L-1$ **do**
    $\boldsymbol{W}_l^{k+1} = (\delta\boldsymbol{W}_l^k + \rho(\boldsymbol{Z}_l^k - \boldsymbol{B}_l^k)\boldsymbol{A}_{l-1}^k)(\delta\boldsymbol{I} + \rho(\boldsymbol{A}_{l-1}^k(\boldsymbol{A}_{l-1}^k)^T))^{-1}$
    $\boldsymbol{B}_l^{k+1} = (\delta\boldsymbol{B}_l^k + \rho(\boldsymbol{Z}_l^k - \boldsymbol{W}_l^k\boldsymbol{A}_{l-1}^k))/(\rho+\delta)$
    $\boldsymbol{Z}_l^{k+1} = \left[prox_{\frac{1}{2\eta}(a_l^k - \varphi(z_l^k))^2}(\boldsymbol{S}_l^k)\right]_{cj}$, where $\boldsymbol{S}_l{}^k = \frac{\delta(\hat{\boldsymbol{Z}}_l)^k + \rho(\boldsymbol{W}_l^{k+1}\boldsymbol{A}_{l-1}^k + \boldsymbol{B}_l^{k+1})}{\rho+\delta}$, $\eta = \frac{\rho+\delta}{\gamma}$
    if update $\boldsymbol{A}_l^{k+1}, l = 1, 2, ..L-2$ **then**
      $\boldsymbol{A}_l^{k+1} = \left[prox_{log,\lambda/\delta}(\boldsymbol{X}_l^k)\right]_{cj}$, where $\boldsymbol{X}_l^k = \boldsymbol{A}_l^k - ((\rho(\boldsymbol{W}_{l+1}^{k+1})^T\boldsymbol{W}_{l+1}^{k+1} + \gamma\boldsymbol{I})\boldsymbol{A}_l^k - \rho(\boldsymbol{W}_{l+1}^{k+1})^T)(\boldsymbol{Z}_{l+1}^{k+1} - \boldsymbol{B}_{l+1}^{k+1}) - \gamma\varphi(\boldsymbol{Z}_l^{k+1}))/\delta$
    end if
    if update $\boldsymbol{A}_l^{k+1}, l = L-1$ **then**
      $\boldsymbol{A}_{L-1}^{k+1} = \left(\rho(\boldsymbol{W}_L^k)^T)\boldsymbol{W}_L^k + (\rho+\delta)\boldsymbol{I}\right)^{-1}\left(\delta\boldsymbol{A}_{L-1}^k + \rho((\boldsymbol{W}_L^k)^T(\boldsymbol{Z}_L^k - \boldsymbol{B}_L^k)) + \gamma\varphi(\boldsymbol{Z}_{L-1}^{k+1})\right)$
    end if
  end for
  for $l = L$ **do**
    $\boldsymbol{W}_L^{k+1} = (\delta\boldsymbol{W}_L^k + \rho(\boldsymbol{Z}_L^k - \boldsymbol{B}_L^k)\boldsymbol{A}_{L-1}^{k+1})(\delta\boldsymbol{I} + \rho(\boldsymbol{A}_{L-1}^{k+1}(\boldsymbol{A}_{L-1}^{k+1})^T))^{-1}$
    $\boldsymbol{B}_L^{k+1} = (\delta\boldsymbol{B}_L^k + \rho(\boldsymbol{Z}_L^k - \boldsymbol{W}_L^k\boldsymbol{A}_{L-1}^{k+1}))/(\rho+\delta)$
    $\boldsymbol{Z}_L^{k+1} = \beta(\boldsymbol{W}_L^k\boldsymbol{A}_{L-1}^{k+1} + \boldsymbol{B}_L^{k+1} + \alpha\boldsymbol{Y} + \delta\boldsymbol{Z}_L^k)/(\alpha+\beta+\delta)$
  end for
end for

of the third experiment would be adjusted based on this series of hyperparameters. The second experiment showed that proposed algorithm was effective compared to other training algorithms, and had better classification accuracy and sparse activations. The third experiment verified that proposed algorithm was still effective on different datasets. All experiments were conducted on pytorch 1.5.1, Intel(R) Core(TM)i5-10400F CPU and GTX1080Ti GPU.

4.1 Parameter Setting

In order to determine the proper choice of hyperparameters, we compared the experimental results with different hyperparameters in Algorithm 1 to find the most proper value of λ or ρ by fixing the remaining hyperparameters. From the Eq. (17), the $x_0 = \sqrt{\frac{4\lambda}{\delta}} - \epsilon$ is jointly determined by δ, ϵ and λ. So we determined the remaining two parameters based on the λ in the *log*-thresholding operator. After the numerical experiments (See in Fig. 2), we obtained an optimal set of hyperparameters, namely $\lambda = 3e{-}6$, $\epsilon = 0.001, \rho = 1.7, \delta = 1$.

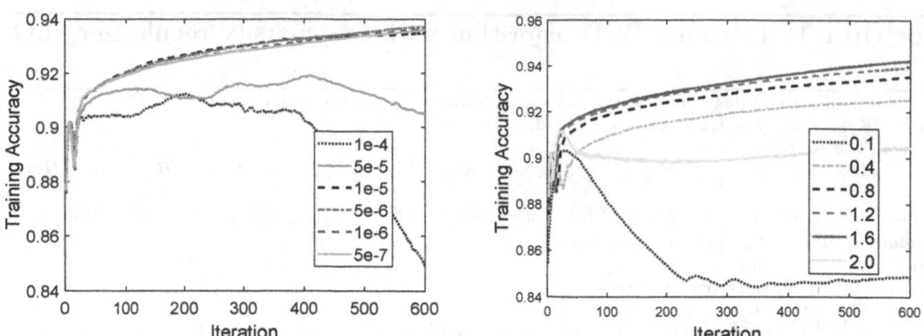

(a) Training accuracy with different λ values (b) Training accuracy with different ρ values

Fig. 2. Training accuracy under different hyperparameters. The value of training accuracy was obtained when other hyperparameters are fixed and only one hyperparameter is changed. When $\lambda = 5e - 6$, $\rho = 1.6$, the highest accuracy can be achieved.

4.2 Classification Experiments on MNIST

We compared the proposed training algorithms with other gradient-free training algorithms: proximal BCD [11], ADMM [8] and the traditional gradient-based training algorithm: SGD. Proximal BCD method performs a proximal step for each parameter except the auxiliary variables in a Gauss-Seidel fashion. ADMM uses alternating direction methods and Bregman iterations to train networks without gradient descent steps. SGD is a common traditional gradient-based neural network training method. In order to prove the effectiveness of sparse representation of inputs, we employed the *log* sparsity regularizer in other gradient-free training methods. Just like LOG-PBCD algorithm, the LOG-ADMM algorithm is a training method that applies the combination of *log* sparsity regularizer and ADMM algorithm [8] rather than BCD algorithm. Our network adopted a structure of 784-500-500-10, where the numbers represented the number of neurons in each layer. The learning rate of SGD algorithm was 0.1. We maintained the initialization parameters of the proposed LOG-PBCD algorithm and the proximal BCD algorithm consistent, and selected the proper hyperparameters obtained in the parameter setting experiment. ADMM did the same. All algorithms used the same training batch size of 60,000 samples and testing batch size of 10,000 samples in work [11].

Figure 3(a) and (b) shows the experimental results of different training algorithms, but SGD converges the slowest. Although the classification accuracy of SGD can be improved, the best result is less than the proposed LOG-PBCD algorithm. Figure 3(a) and (b) shows LOG-PBCD algorithm can exceed the highest accuracy of other algorithms in a few iterations and has always maintained the highest accuracy, which benefits from sparse activations. See in Table 1, The proposed LOG-PBCD algorithm achieves superior to other algorithms and has the highest training and testing accuracy. The proposed LOG-ADMM algorithm improves the training and testing accuracy with ADMM algorithm, which shows that sparse representation of inputs is effective in other training algorithms. It is

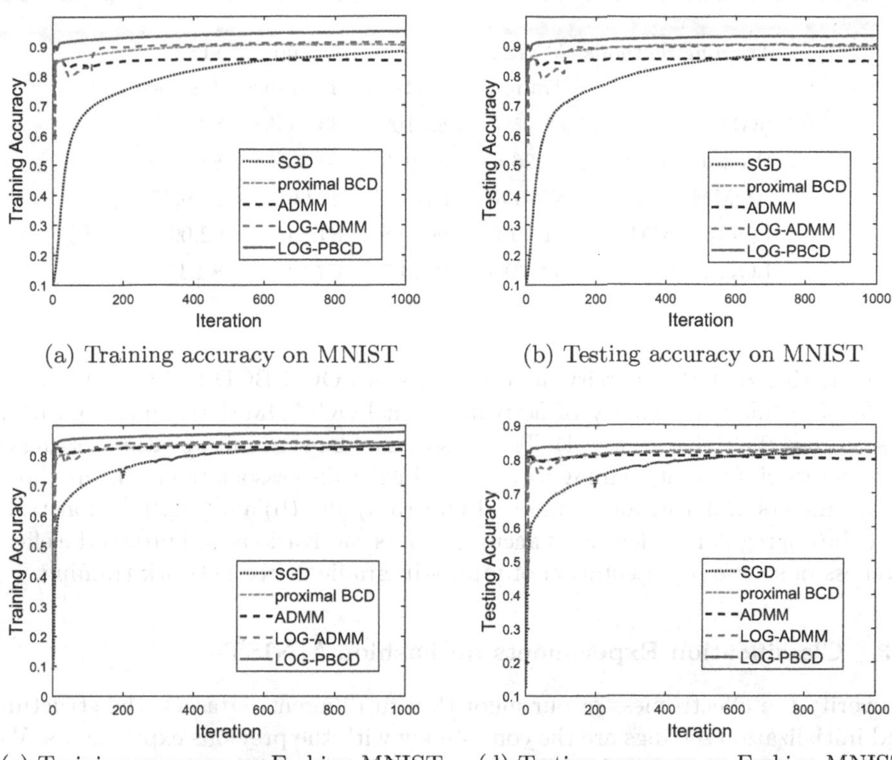

(a) Training accuracy on MNIST (b) Testing accuracy on MNIST

(c) Training accuracy on Fashion MNIST (d) Testing accuracy on Fashion MNIST

Fig. 3. Classification accuracy with different training algorithms on different datasets. (a) and (b) respectively are training and testing accuracy with proposed algorithm and other algorithms on MNIST. (c) and (d) respectively are training and testing accuracy with proposed algorithm and other algorithms on Fashion MNIST. The proposed LOG-PBCD achieves superior to other algorithms.

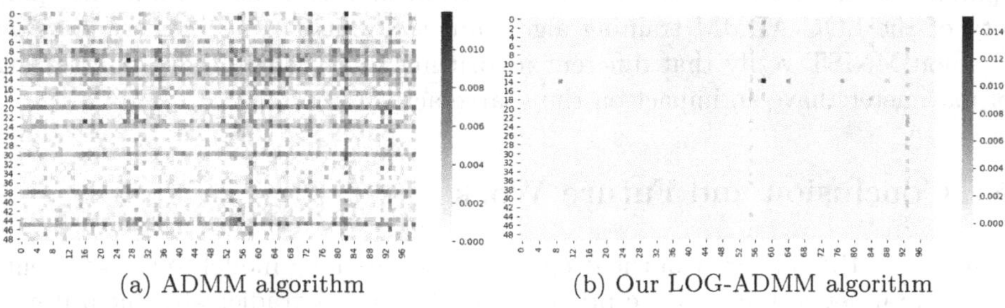

(a) ADMM algorithm (b) Our LOG-ADMM algorithm

Fig. 4. The partial activations in some samples. (a) The activations after training by ADMM algorithm. (b) The activations after training by proposed LOG-ADMM algorithm.

Table 1. Classification accuracy with different training algorithm on different datasets.

Training methods	MNIST		Fashion MNIST	
	Train-acc	Test-acc	Train-acc	Test-acc
SGD	88.05%	89.10%	83.61%	82.53%
Proximal BCD	90.26%	89.91%	84.33%	82.44%
ADMM	84.91%	84.82%	82.06%	79.93%
LOG-ADMM	91.10%	90.55%	84.64%	82.09%
LOG-PBCD	**94.79%**	**93.47%**	**87.89%**	**84.15%**

worth noting that the sparsity of activations in LOG-PBCD training algorithm is 23.4%, while the sparsity of activations in LOG-ADMM training algorithm has reached 95.21% (See Fig. 4). The reason may be that initialization setting of parameters of different training methods, which is also associated to the methods of parameters updating and training. Figure 3(a) and (b) and Fig. 4 demonstrate that the *log* regularizer learns an accurate sparse activations and proves the effectiveness of sparse representation of inputs in gradient-free network training.

4.3 Classification Experiments on Fashion MNIST

To verify the effectiveness of our algorithm in different datasets, the structure and initialization settings are the consistency with the previous experiments. We implemented the proposed LOG-PBCD and LOG-ADMM algorithms on the Fashion MNIST dataset. The experimental hyperparameter settings of LOG-PBCD here is $\rho = 1, \epsilon = 0.0001, \lambda = 1e\text{–}7$. The learning rate of SGD is 0.3 and the hyperparameters of other methods remain unchanged. Figure 3(c) and (d) shows that SGD still maintains a very slow convergence rate, but its training and test accuracy will surpass proximal BCD and ADMM methods with enough iterations. See in Table 1 and Fig. 3(c) and (d), the proposed LOG-PBCD algorithm still achieves superior to other training algorithms in classification accuracy. The sparsity of the LOG-PBCD training algorithm here is 21.69%, while the sparsity of the LOG-ADMM training algorithm is about 94.15%. Experiments on Fashion MNIST verify that different algorithms and their initialization setting of parameters have an impact on the sparse activations.

5 Conclusion and Future Work

Inspired by the similarity of the deep dictionary learning model to the gradient-free neural network model, we proposed a DDL-based gradient-free neural network training model, which regards the weight matrix in the neural network as a dictionary and the activations of hidden layer corresponds to the coefficients of DDL. To obtain accurate and sparse representation, we employ the nonconvex log function as sparsity regularizer which can enforce sparsity and accurate estimation. In order to solve the non-convex non-smooth optimization problems involved in the training, we use the proximal BCD algorithm and the *log*-thresholding operator to optimize the objective function, achieving forward propagation training method without gradient. Numerical experiments show that the proposed LOG-PBCD algorithm performs superior to other algorithms on public datasets, which proves that sparse representation of inputs is effective in the application of gradient-free networks. Future work includes accelerating our algorithm while decreasing the memory consumption and considering additional datasets to verify the effectiveness of proposed model.

References

1. Brock, A., De, S., Smith, S.L., Simonyan, K.: High-performance large-scale image recognition without normalization. arXiv preprint arXiv:2102.06171 (2021)
2. Wu, Z., Zhao, D., Liang, Q., Yu, J., Gulati, A., Pang, R.: Dynamic sparsity neural networks for automatic speech recognition. In: ICASSP 2021–2021 IEEE International Conference on Acoustics, Speech and Signal Processing (ICASSP), pp. 6014–6018. IEEE (2021)
3. Woodworth, B., et al.: Is local SGD better than minibatch SGD? In: International Conference on Machine Learning, pp. 10334–10343. PMLR (2020)
4. Kristiadi, A., Hein, M., Hennig, P.: Being Bayesian, even just a bit, fixes overconfidence in ReLU networks. In: International Conference on Machine Learning, pp. 5436–5446. PMLR (2020)
5. Yao, Z., Cao, Y., Zheng, S., Huang, G., Lin, S.: Cross-iteration batch normalization. In: Proceedings of the IEEE/CVF Conference on Computer Vision and Pattern Recognition, pp. 12331–12340 (2021)
6. Peng, S., Huang, H., Chen, W., Zhang, L., Fang, W.: More trainable inception-ResNet for face recognition. Neurocomputing **411**, 9–19 (2020)
7. Li, J., Xiao, M., Fang, C., Dai, Y., Xu, C., Lin, Z.: Training neural networks by lifted proximal operator machines. IEEE Trans. Pattern Anal. Mach. Intell. (2020)
8. Taylor, G., Burmeister, R., Xu, Z., Singh, B., Patel, A., Goldstein, T.: Training neural networks without gradients: a scalable ADMM approach. In: International Conference on Machine Learning, pp. 2722–2731. PMLR (2016)
9. Wang, J., Yu, F., Chen, X., Zhao, L.: ADMM for efficient deep learning with global convergence. In: Proceedings of the 25th ACM SIGKDD International Conference on Knowledge Discovery & Data Mining, pp. 111–119 (2019)
10. Carreira-Perpinan, M., Wang, W.: Distributed optimization of deeply nested systems. In: Artificial Intelligence and Statistics, pp. 10–19. PMLR (2014)
11. Lau, T.T.K., Zeng, J., Wu, B., Yao, Y.: A proximal block coordinate descent algorithm for deep neural network training. arXiv preprint arXiv:1803.09082 (2018)
12. Zeng, J., Lau, T.T.K., Lin, S., Yao, Y.: Global convergence of block coordinate descent in deep learning. In: International Conference on Machine Learning, pp. 7313–7323. PMLR (2019)
13. Gu, F., Askari, A., El Ghaoui, L.: Fenchel lifted networks: a lagrange relaxation of neural network training. In: International Conference on Artificial Intelligence and Statistics, pp. 3362–3371. PMLR (2020)
14. Chen, Y., Su, J.: Dict layer: a structured dictionary layer. In: Proceedings of the IEEE Conference on Computer Vision and Pattern Recognition Workshops, pp. 422–431 (2018)

15. Liu, Y., Chen, Q., Chen, W., Wassell, I.: Dictionary learning inspired deep network for scene recognition. In: Proceedings of the AAAI Conference on Artificial Intelligence, vol. 32 (2018)
16. Singhal, V., Aggarwal, H.K., Tariyal, S., Majumdar, A.: Discriminative robust deep dictionary learning for hyperspectral image classification. IEEE Trans. Geosci. Remote Sens. **55**(9), 5274–5283 (2017)
17. Qiao, L., Sun, T., Pan, H., Li, D.: Inertial proximal deep learning alternating minimization for efficient neutral network training. In: ICASSP 2021–2021 IEEE International Conference on Acoustics, Speech and Signal Processing (ICASSP), pp. 3895–3899. IEEE (2021)
18. Li, Z., Zhao, H., Guo, Y., Yang, Z., Xie, S.: Accelerated log-regularized convolutional transform learning and its convergence guarantee. IEEE Trans. Cybern. (2021)

Author Index

by Baker & Taylor Publisher Services

Printed in the United States
by Baker & Taylor Publisher Services